This Was America

THIS WAS

America

TRUE ACCOUNTS OF PEOPLE AND PLACES · MANNERS
AND CUSTOMS · AS RECORDED BY EUROPEAN TRAV-
ELERS TO THE WESTERN SHORE IN THE EIGHTEENTH ·
NINETEENTH · AND TWENTIETH CENTURIES ·

HARVARD UNIVERSITY PRESS · CAMBRIDGE

OSCAR HANDLIN, Editor

TO FREDERICK MERK

Preface to the Reissue

~~~~~~

THE FIRST EDITION OF THIS VOLUME APPEARED TWENTY YEARS AGO. AT that time, questions about the national character of the people of the United States already occupied the thoughts of critics in every part of the world. The image of the American was, however, far different from what it has become since. In 1949, strains among the wartime allies had already appeared, but they had not overshadowed the memory of the services of the United States in saving the world from Fascist domination. In Europe and Asia, where wartime damage was still visible, America was not only the source of past liberation from oppression but also the sole hope of early reconstruction. The earliest phases of the cold war had just begun to raise the cry, "Yankee Go Home"; but anti-Americanism was not yet widely fashionable.

A great deal has changed in the intervening years, particularly among intellectuals both within the United States and outside it. Recollections of the Second World War have faded; and to the extent that Europeans have ceased to fear a threat from the east, they have tended to forget the part the United States played in establishing their security. Moreover, the tremendous success of American society has infuriated the intellectuals who predicted its imminent collapse. The ability of the economy to grow and the revolution that impelled society toward equality flew in the face of all anticipations. Experience thus contradicted passionately held dogmas. The rage at being wrong left many intellectuals in an unforgiving mood and decisively altered the image of the United States, although it is by no means clear that the change reflects a widespread popular attitude.

The shifting views of the past two decades are an indication of the variability of the opinions about the United States. Even before this country was large and powerful, it aroused the concern of Europeans who saw in it the development of forces they either disliked or cherished. Their accounts as travelers through the nation reflected their prejudices.

Yet, there was always something of value even in the distorted accounts. One could not expect that the observers would shed their prejudices or be able themselves to compensate for the peculiarities of their points of view. But the sensitive reader who was aware of those prejudices could find much of value in the observations that went with them.

One other circumstance is now somewhat clearer than it was in 1949. With the great war just a few years behind, Americans at that time were still dedicated to the ideal of one world. They therefore tended to underestimate the significance of national differences and believed in the similarities under the skin of men of all backgrounds. It is now clear that the writers whose comments are collected in this book represent a single tradition. They were French and Russian, Italian and Norwegian, and they lived in the eighteenth, nineteenth, and twentieth centuries. Still, they brought to their observations the presumptions and values of a common culture. In some ways, that was as significant in the observations they made as were the divisive elements of class, religion, or social affiliation.

The collection has served a whole generation of general readers as well as of students, who found this material useful in supplementing conventional accounts of American social and cultural history. It appears in its present form in the hope that this reissue will be equally valuable.

Oscar Handlin

Cambridge, Massachusetts
March 1, 1969

Contents

Part Three
URBAN AMERICA   293

This Was America

Introduction

FROM THE VERY MOMENT OF ITS DISCOVERY, THE NEW WORLD WAS THE subject of excited descriptions for the benefit of the Old. The letters of Columbus to Spain were first in a long series in which other voyagers sent homeward accounts of their finds—Spaniards and Portuguese, Frenchmen and Englishmen, Hollanders and Swedes, more numerous with time as successive colonies dotted the long Atlantic Coast.

There was a sense of wonder and expectation about the New World: wonder because it was new, because it had at once widened immensely the universe of western man; expectation because it offered an incalculable challenge, promised unpredictable rewards. Visions so long fixed within the narrow Eurasian peninsula suddenly overleaped the old Mediterranean and Atlantic limits to rest upon breath-taking vistas reaching out to far and unknown horizons. In an era grown impatient of old restraints, counting its old forms outmoded, these Elysian spaces held out a refreshing opportunity for new beginnings. The hemisphere of the West was the New World, and in that simple designation were summed up the anticipations, in which wish and fear commingled, that the new would differ from the old.

Midway through the eighteenth century, the observers of America became conscious that its newness, particularly in the English colonies, pervaded not only the physical foundation and social structure, but the core of its human population. Before the century was over the first glimmering had lighted up into brilliant certainty. On the new land, and in a new way, were living new men, Americans. A mighty, popular convulsion had thrown off the last surviving transatlantic ties in a large part of the continent, and creative statesmanship had brought a republic prosperously, safely through a difficult period of beginnings.

Thereafter, the very existence of the United States was a challenge and a threat to the peoples and governments of the Old World. For more than a half century the anxious regard of Europe was fixed upon the experiment in free and popular institutions. Developments in political structure, in family life, in artistic and intellectual activity were brought to testify on whether the new forms, or, what seemed to many the absence of any forms, resulted in a liberal upsurge or in a licentious dissipation of energies. When, later, the peaceful binding-up of the wounds of civil war reaffirmed the strength and vitality of popular government, the skeptical and fearful uncovered different grounds for questioning in the problems arising from the growth of cities and the burgeoning of industry. Without the cushioning protection of rigid social institutions, the pursuit of wealth seemed to draw the Americans headlong into an alien materialistic civilization, devoid of old values. To the old anxieties the twentieth century added the uncomfortable conviction that power, and with it control over western civilization, would increasingly be concentrated in the United States.

Concern with America and the Americans has, in this manner, reflected the dominant uneasinesses in the minds of Europeans. Across the Atlantic lay the unescapable contrast, a constant invitation to comparison. The eighteenth-century readers of the *New Heloise* identified the noble savage with the citizens who walked the lanes of Philadelphia and Nantucket. The participants in three decades of intermittent revolution after 1820 counted the advantages and disadvantages of democracy in the ballots cast in Massachusetts and South Carolina. Those who lived in the shadow of the consequences thrown over Europe by the factory and the railroad attempted to judge the results of social equality on the basis of the life of New York and Chicago under the impact of similar innovations. And the survivors of two world wars looked to the fastness of Missouri for an omen of what security meant.

America, in a sense, took its place with Parthia, Persia, Icaria, and Erewhon, the imaginary realms into which Europeans projected their hopes and fears. Like the projections in other forms, Europe's visions of America offer valuable clues to the temper and mind of the Old World.

The same visions are enlightening in the study of the New World. The continual quest for contrasts forced the authors of these accounts to search out that which was distinctive and unique. The comparison, whether implicitly or explicitly, was always in terms of a differentiation between that which was familiar, inherited, European, and that which was strange, original, American. Particularly was this true in the case of voyagers who were not English and who were therefore not blinded by the assumption of common descent. Men of Continental cultures, unlike most visitors from Great Britain, often perceived that surface similarities concealed fundamental differences.

Few among the travelers were professional literary people. Some were businessmen, land speculators, merchants; others were government officials or exiles, naturalists and big game hunters, artists and students, priests and working people. Usually their publications were incidental by-products of visits undertaken for other reasons. They went where their business took them. They could not possibly see everything. They sometimes kept to the main traveled roads, and tended to spend more time in town than in country, in the Atlantic ports than in the interior. Such circumstances introduced a bias to these writings; there was always the tendency to generalize on a partial and incomplete basis. But that bias was self-compensating, open and visible enough so that allowance could be made for it. And the same circumstance relieved these works of the ideological and linguistic self-consciousness of the social scientist, gave them a directness of perception and of expression exceedingly valuable to those who seek light on the American social past.

The variety of interests that led these tourists to the United States matched the variety of subjects on which they chose to write. Some found most noteworthy the country itself, the physical beauty of its scenery and its spaciousness; Niagara thundered endlessly through their pages. Others found social and governmental institutions impressive. Those who were unfailingly taken to see Perkins Institute, as relentlessly described it. Those who took the trouble to unravel the complexities of American federalism or of municipal government rarely were willing to forego the opportunity to commit their discoveries to paper. But more important than these matters, on which, after all, there is an abundance of other material, were the observations on the new men, the Americans themselves, and on their "domestic manners," their way of life and mode of adaptation to a new continent, a new society.

The most significant pages in the long array of travelers' accounts were those which either speculated upon or offered data to explain the American national character. Here the capacity of foreigners to make comparisons with familiar conditions elsewhere was particularly valuable. Here the absence of alternative evidence from direct observation is most burdensome to the student.

No thinking man today can fail to take account of national character, for today more than ever before people of strange nationalities rub against each other and become aware of the differences among themselves, as well as of the need for by-passing or surmounting those differences. To look backward into the pages of earlier comparisons may throw light on the development of such traits. Are such characteristics national or merely agglomerative, for instance? In either case, what is their relationship to class, to section, to ethnic origin? From the start, these were problems interesting and exciting to the voyagers to America. Their evidence may be not without relevance now.

The compiler of such a volume as this soon comes face-to-face with the temptation to accept the judgments of the past and to lean heavily on the well-known authors who were successful at once and whose reputation has snowballed steadily since the publication of their works. That these familiar accounts are already available in English translation certainly multiplies the force of the temptation. Yet many an obscure visitor, by his very obscurity, penetrated to places and to situations that brought him exceptional visions of the quality of American life. The well-connected, on the other hand, often discovered that their stay in America was "a daily warfare against kindness, and politeness, and curiosity" which left them "weary and worn out." I have tried not to slight the travelers whose names leap immediately to the mind. But I have not been guided by reputation alone, for immediate success is not necessarily an index of accuracy of observation or pertinence of judgment. Above all, I have attempted to put aside the scissors and paste pot in the interests of a selection that would, out of the wealth of available material, present an orderly and connected picture of the people of the American past.

The translations are free. For the purpose at hand, I have not felt it necessary to preserve archaic inelegancies or awkwardness of style. I have also taken considerable liberty in editing, transposing whole sections to eliminate repetition and to add coherence. But I trust I have been faithful to the meaning of the original. I have used older translations when available, but in such cases have checked against the original and made changes as I found them necessary.

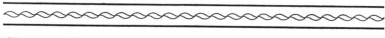

Part One

SOURCES OF AMERICAN NATIONALITY

Sources of American Nationality

~~~~~~

THE ENGLISH COLONIES HAD SCARCELY COMPLETED THEIR FIRST CENTURY of settlement when subtle changes in the composition of the population began to bring forth rich, significant consequences. Steadily the percentage of residents born in Great Britain dropped; an ever-larger proportion of those who lived between the District of Maine and the Province of Georgia were American-born, many the sons of fathers themselves American-born. And among the newcomers who continued to arrive were large contingents from the continent of Europe, Germans and Frenchmen, and a host of others. Among all these groups there was no direct connection with England; for them "mother country" became increasingly an empty figure of speech, devoid of concrete meaning.

The absence of a primary English experience, of close contact with British ways and manners, gave free play to indigenous influences, whether these sprang from the life of the new and expanding cities, from the trials of American agriculture on plantation and farm, or from encounters with the ever-present frontier and with the ever-receding aborigines who lived along it. Meanwhile the growth of the population, the filling in of empty space, and the development of a continuous line of settlement gave the colonial community a mounting sense of integration.

The Revolution climaxed a process already well under way. Independence gave formal recognition to the fact of American nationality, but the manner of its attainment involved even more. The struggle against the British Empire evoked pride in the measure of the accomplishment and also determination that the new country must aggressively push its interests, justify the Revolution by success. Furthermore, the course of the struggle had built up a fund of theory about the nature of the government and of men's relations to it, that served, in the first instance, as a source of arguments against the Crown. But the fund, once accumulated, remained to furnish nourishment for the democratic ideas of a whole generation. Finally, the internal revolution, the liquidation of large segments of the old ruling class, the creation of new fortunes on the ruins of the old, and the instability of class and of social status set in motion a chain of dynamic changes.

The four decades after independence were, on many levels, occupied with the problem of completing American independence, internally and externally. Politically, that involved the establishment of constitutional federal and state governments, and the conduct of foreign affairs with a regard to American interests in the succession of wars arising from the French Revolution. Economically, it involved the reëstablishment of trade, the readjustment of the southern plantation, the continued extension of cultivation into frontier areas, and the creation of a stable organization of production that would no longer be dependent upon integration into the British commercial system. Socially, it called for the attainment of a new equilibrium among the various classes upset by removal of the topmost levels. And intellectually, completion of American independence hinged upon the strengthening of internal sources of culture to reduce the reliance upon importations from abroad.

The remarkable vitality of efforts in all these directions elicited comments from the long succession of visitors who wrote about this section of North America in the seventy years between 1750 and 1820. Whatever their condition and background, naturalists, adventurers, political exiles, were impressed by the struggles of a nation coming into being, and noted, whether favorably or not, that powerful forces from within, from the mass of the people, were at work fashioning a national character.

1.

A HOLLANDER AMONG THE INDIANS

Of this author we know only the initials and what he himself reveals in his book, that he was a native of Rotterdam who lived for more than two decades among the Indians in North America. He was evidently familiar with that of which he wrote and was unusually interested in the commonplaces of the redmen's lives. His "Accurate Description of North America" (1780) has a simple and authentic charm.

Now I must portray for my readers the manners of the savages, their dispositions, their marriages, their work, their dances, hunting, and how they governed themselves, all of which, together with their mode of life, I myself investigated in the twenty-two or twenty-three years since I came to this land. They have altered their customs but slightly, need little more than kettles, axes, knives, and iron for their arrows, since few among them have firearms.

Their food was fish and meat, roasted and boiled. To roast the meat, they slice it into strips and split a stick, from which they suspend it before the fire. Each has his own stick. As soon as a slice is done on one side they begin eating, cutting the pieces off with a bone sharpened on a rock, which serves them in place of a knife of iron or steel. When they have eaten everything that was ready they again toast the raw meat before the fire, take another piece, and dispose of it in the same manner. When they have finished a whole side of meat they immediately drag another in its place. And so it goes, through the whole day.

Fish, they roast on a split board which serves as gridiron, or even directly on the coals. But it must be well done before they will eat it. All the children roast away in the same manner as the others, with split sticks, and over the coals.

All this roasting is only, so to speak, the first course; it functions to awaken the appetite. Meanwhile, a kettle stands boiling on another side. This kettle is made of wood shaped like a great trough. They make it of the stump of some thick tree that happens to be around. Having hardly any tools for that purpose, they cannot shape it very well. Their regular method of working it out is to use a stone axe, well sharpened, and tied securely between two pieces of wood. They hack at the tree little by little, far down enough from the top to give them a kettle of the size they wish. This cut, they turn it bottom up and burn out the inside of the tree to a depth of about four fingers, then scrape out the burnt part with sharp stones and big pointed bones. They repeat this process of burning and scraping until the kettle is the proper size for them.

The kettle is then ready to be used. They fill it with water and put in what they wish to cook. But since the water cannot be heated from below, they must go to work in the following manner. Great pieces of stone are put in the fire until they are red hot, when the Indians take them out with sticks and throw them into the kettle in which the water begins to boil. Meanwhile, other stones are heated to replace the first as those lose warmth. This procedure continues until all the meat is ready.

In case there were among them any women or girls in their period, they were compelled to stand to one side while others fed them their share. During this time they were not supposed to eat alone. They did nothing and dared not touch anything, especially food, but were compelled to remain apart.

In all these rejoicings, in the feasting and banqueting, the Indians array themselves in their finest clothing. In the summer the men wear coats of well-cured elkskin, decorated from top to bottom with a sort of lace, two fingers wide. Some wear ornaments in layers or rows, or strewn with the figures of animals, according to the fancy of the maker. They contrive all these figures in red, purple, or blue, applying these colors with certain bones which they dip into the pigment while quite hot and in such a manner that, once put on, it will not be washed out by water.

To prepare the skins, they clean them and spread them out in the sun, allowing them to heat up on the leather side from which they wish to pull the hair. Then they fasten it somewhere and with bones made expressly for that purpose, scratch the hair off. As soon as there is none left they anoint the skin with birds' livers and a few drops of fish-oil. After having thoroughly rubbed it between their hands, they put it on top of a smooth board shaped like a donkey's back (in the same way as we stretch skins over iron to make gloves) and massage it until it becomes pliant and easily managed. Then they wash it and wring it out with a piece of wood until the water comes out clean, and then they spread it again to dry.

All the clothes, whether for men or for women, are made in the form of a blanket. The women drape their garments about them in the manner of the Gypsies, with the opening on the side. The men hang them around their shoulders and tie the two ends with leather strings under their chins; the rest remains open. Their bodies are naked except for the private parts, which are covered with a soft and thin skin, wrapped around in the form of a girdle.

As far as marriage is concerned, a young man desirous of a girl was bound to serve her father for several years. The service consisted of aid in the chase and the demonstration that he was a good hunter, competent to maintain his wife in a proper household, skilled in making bows, arrows, and even a canoe, all of which are man's work. Whatever he produced was for the benefit of the girl's father, but in case of need he had the use of them. His sweetheart meanwhile made his clothes and shoes to show her skill in that work. The father, mother, daughter, and the young man all slept in the same hut, the girl next to her mother and the boy on the other side. The other women and children also slept there, but there were never any irregularities, for the girls were chaste and always were covered with a wide elkskin hanging to below the knees. And the modesty of these girls was such that they would rather hold their water for twenty-four hours than be seen in the deed by a young man.

When the proper time had passed, it became necessary to speak of the wedding ceremony. The parents of the youth came to inquire of those of the girl whether they were satisfied. If the maiden's father was willing, the wishes of the two parties were consulted. If either was dissatisfied the marriage was canceled; there was no compulsion. If all went well, however, they fixed upon a day to celebrate the nuptials. Meanwhile the young man went out hunting, trying his very best to accumulate enough food to regale the whole assemblage of guests with all manner of meats.

On the appointed day, with all the kin gathered and everything prepared, they all go into the hut, the old people sitting on the higher end near the elders (the higher end being on the left hand as one enters) and going around to the right-hand side. No women come in there except the mother of the groom. Each having taken his place (they squat

on their haunches like apes), the bridegroom brings in the food in a
great bark platter. He divides it into as many portions as there are
people, filling each dish with practically enough to feed twelve, and all
fall to eating. The bridegroom also has a large vessel of meat juice
from which he first drinks as much as he can and, having quenched his
thirst, passes it to his neighbor who does the same. When it is emptied,
it is at once refilled. When everyone has eaten and drunk to capacity,
there is a pause during which one of the elders delivers a discourse in
praise of the bridegroom and recounts his whole genealogical register,
pointing to his descent from a line of ten or twelve generations of
famous men. He lists all their notable deeds, their prowess in battle and
in the chase, their wisdom in council, and all their memorable achievements, beginning with the oldest and coming down from generation to
generation to the father of the bridegroom, after which he admonishes
the young man not to allow himself to be outdone in bravery by his ancestors. This speech being finished, the whole assembly lets out two or
three yells, *hau, hau, hau*. Then the groom thanks them and the guests
let out the same yells. Then the bridegroom begins to dance, singing a
war song that works up his courage, telling of the toll of animals he
killed and of the feats he intends to perform. While dancing, he seizes
a bow and arrow, together with a long spear tipped with a pointed elk
bone, with which the Indians hunt in the winter when the ground is
covered with snow. These things he takes up in his hands from time to
time, accompanying his motions with an appropriate song. Then he acts
the part of a madman. When he puts an end to this act, the whole company once more begin their cries, *hau, hau, hau,* as a sign of their mirth
and approval. At this point they again begin to eat and drink until they
are satisfied. Then they call in their women and children, who come at
once and who, in their turn, fall to eating from the vessels that are
handed over.

They maintain certain degrees of kinship amongst themselves that
would prevent a marriage. Thus a marriage never takes place between
a brother and sister, nor between cousins in the second generation. In
case a young woman in the space of two or three years bears her man
no children, he may put her aside and send her off in order to take
another. He is not held to service as for the first wife, merely gives
gifts of clothes, hides, or pottery and must furnish a feast for the father
of the bride, although not so ceremoniously as in the first case. Thus it

happens that if a woman becomes pregnant they prepare a great banquet in her honor. If she does not, they get rid of her.

When a man's wife becomes pregnant he ceases to see her. It is for this reason that they may take as many wives as they wish, provided they are not lazy and are good enough hunters to induce the girls to accept them. Thus you see savages who have two or three pregnant wives at one time, and they rejoice in the prospect of having a great many children. Yet if a woman feels herself pregnant while she is suckling one child, she often commits an abortion upon herself with the aid of some midwife, but keeps the matter a secret. They say the reason is that suckling two children at once would dry up the breasts, at which they keep the children for two or three years.

The women bathe their children in cold water as soon as they are delivered, no matter how cold it is. The mothers immediately swaddle the babies in marten or beaver skins and tie them to a plank. If it was a little boy, they would let his penis hang through a hole, so that the urine might run off; if it was a girl they made a little drain for the same purpose of a piece of bark between the legs. Under the buttocks, in either case, they put some dry, moldy, putrid wood, to take care of other filthiness, so they would not have to unbind the children through the day. Since the babies' most sensitive parts were exposed to the air even during a frost, many froze and died, especially the boys, who were more naked in that respect than the girls. A strap was tied to either side of the plank and was passed across the forehead of the mother so that the plank could hang down her back. Consequently, the mother's arms were not encumbered, but remained free while she worked or went through the forest, although on the march the child might be injured by the branches.

After the savages have lived for some time in a place, and have plucked the neighborhood of the hut clean, they move away some twenty miles or so. The women and the girls take up the hut and all their possessions, lock, stock, and barrel, and move on while the men and boys carry nothing.

Having reached their new place of residence, they must, that is the women and girls must, set up the hut. Some go to drag in firs from the forest, others break off boughs from the trees, while the little girls bring them in. The mistress or foremost wife, that is, the one who first brings a son into the world, does not go into the forest; she remains in the clearing to which the others bring everything. She arranges the boughs in correct order, and spreads the firs to make their carpet and bed. As soon as the home is ready they proceed to set up two hearth-stones in a circle, covered with canvas against the rains.

In the hunt, the sons help the father to feed the family. The daughters work to aid the mother, going into the forest to fetch water or to bring the killed animals to the hut. There is always an old woman near the girls to direct them and to show them the proper ways.

The children are not very naughty, since the Indians give them all that they wish, without ever allowing them to cry. The older ones take care of the younger and the father and mother would give the last morsels from their mouths if the child desired it. They love their children very much and spare nothing to satisfy them, for these are their riches.

Yet there were once many more savages than now. The hunting was better then. They lived without cares, and ate neither salted nor spiced meats. They drank only the richest broth, which accounted for their long lives. They were vigorous and prolific and would have propagated themselves even more, did not the women subject their infants to rigorous treatment.

2.

PETER KALM, SCIENTIST FROM SWEDEN

Pehr Kalm was a northern product of the Enlightenment. Born in 1716 in Åugermanland, Sweden, he was educated as a naturalist under Carl von Linné. With his teacher, the young scientist made a tour of Russia in 1744, an experience which proved valuable four years later when he embarked upon a long voyage through North America. By then professor at the University of Åbo and member of the Swedish Academy of Science which sponsored his trip, Kalm was primarily interested in observation of flora and fauna. But he was a man of broad sympathies and of cosmopolitan understanding who was also interested in the human beings he met. His account, En Resa til Norra America *(1753–61), proved immediately popular and was translated within a few years into German, English, and Dutch. Kalm himself became a priest after his return, but remained in Åbo, where he died in 1779.*

It is remarkable that the inhabitants of this country commonly acquire understanding sooner, but also grow old sooner than the people in Europe. It is not uncommon to see little children giving sprightly and ready answers to questions that are proposed to them, so that they seem to have as much understanding as old men. But they do not attain to such an age as the Europeans, and it is almost unheard of that a person born in this country lives to be eighty or ninety years of age. I speak only of the Europeans that settle here; for the savages, or first inhabitants, frequently attain a great age, though not so much at present because of the great use of brandy which the Indians learned from the Europeans.

Furthermore, those who are born in Europe attain a greater age than those who are born here of European parents. In the last war it plainly appeared that the new Americans were by far less hardy than the Europeans in expeditions, sieges, and long sea voyages, and died in large numbers. It is very difficult for them to accustom themselves to a climate different from their own. The women cease bearing children after they are forty or forty-five years old, and some leave off in their thirties. I inquired into the cause of this, but none could give me a good answer. Some said it was owing to the affluence in which people live here. Some ascribed it to the inconstancy and changeableness of the weather, and believed that there was hardly a country on earth in which the weather changed so often in a day as it does here. For if it were ever so hot, one could not be certain that in twenty-four hours there would not be a piercing cold. Indeed, sometimes the weather changes four, five, or six times a day.

It has also been observed that the Europeans in North America, whether they were born in Sweden, England, Germany, Holland, or in North America of European parents, always lost their teeth much sooner than usual. The women especially were subject to this disagreeable fate. Girls not above twenty years old frequently had lost half of their teeth, without any hopes of getting new ones. I have attempted to determine the cause of this early loss, but I know not whether I have hit upon the true one. Many people are of the opinion that the air of this country hurts the teeth. Others ascribe it to the great quantities of fruit and sweetmeats which are here eaten. But I have known many people who never eat any fruit, and still have hardly a tooth left.

I began to suspect the tea, which is drunk here in the morning and afternoon, especially by women, and is so common at present that there is hardly a farmer's wife or a poor woman who does not drink tea in the morning. I was confirmed in this opinion when I took a journey through some parts of the country which were still inhabited by Indians. Major General Johnson told me at that time, that several of the Indians who lived close to the European settlements had learned to drink tea; and it has been observed that such Indian women as had accustomed themselves too much to this beverage lost their teeth prematurely, in the same manner as the Europeans, while those who had not used tea preserved their teeth strong and sound to a great age.

I found afterwards that the use of tea could not entirely cause this condition. Several young women who lived in this country, but were born in Europe, complained that they had lost most of their teeth after they had come to America. I asked whether they did not think that it arose from the frequent use of tea. But they answered that they had lost their teeth before they had begun to drink tea. Continuing my inquiries, I found at last a sufficient cause for it. Each of these women admitted that they were accustomed to eat everything hot, and nothing was good in their opinion unless they could eat it as soon as it had come from the fire. This was likewise the case with the women in the country, who lost their teeth much sooner and more generally than the men. They drank tea in greater quantity and much oftener, in the morning, and even at noon, when employment would not allow the men to sit at the tea table. Besides that, the Englishmen then cared very little for tea; a bowl of punch was much more agreeable to them. When the English women drank tea, they never poured it out of the cup into the saucer to cool it, but drank it hot as it came from the teapot. The Indian women, in imitation of them, swallowed their tea in the same manner. On the other hand, those Indians whose teeth were sound never ate anything hot, but took their meat either cold or only just lukewarm.

No disease is more common here than intermittent or recurrent malaria, which the English call "fever and ague." It often happens that a person who has had chills and fever, after being free from them for a week or two, has them again every other second or third day. The fever often attacks the people at the end of August or beginning of September, and commonly continues during autumn and winter till toward spring, when it ceases entirely. It generally begins with a headache followed by chills and fever. Often the chill is so great that the patient, the bed upon which he lies, and everything else, shakes violently. During the fever, and also between the intervals of it, the afflicted one has a severe headache and occasionally, during the fever, a pain under his heart.

Strangers who arrive here are commonly attacked by this sickness the first or second year after their arrival, and it acts more violently upon them than upon the natives, so that they sometimes die of it. But if they escape the first time, they have the advantage of not being visited again the next year, or perhaps ever. It is commonly said here that strangers get the fever to accustom them to the climate. In some parts of the country the natives of European ancestry have annual fits of this ague. The Indians also suffer from it, but not so violently as the Europeans. No age is safe against it. In those places where it rages annually you see old men and women attacked by it, and even children in the cradle sometimes not over three weeks old. It is a pity to see these poor children tormented when a chill comes upon them and to hear how they cry and suffer. It is the same with them as with the older people.

People who are afflicted with the illness look as pale as death and are greatly weakened, but in general are not prevented from doing their work in the intervals. It is remarkable that every year there are great parts of the country where this fever rages, and others where scarcely a single person has been taken ill. It is likewise worthy of notice that there are places where the people cannot remember having heard of its ravages, though at present it begins to grow more common. Yet there is no visible difference between the various locations.

All the old Swedes, Englishmen, and Germans unanimously asserted that the fever had never been so violent or of such continuance when they were boys as it is at present. They were also of the opinion that about the year 1680 there were not so many people afflicted with it as at this time. However, others, equally old, were of the opinion that the fever was proportionately as common formerly as it is at present, but that it could not at that time be so easily perceived because of the scarcity of inhabitants and the great distance of settlements from each other. It is therefore probable that the effects of the fever have at all times been the same.

It is difficult to determine the true causes of this disease; they seem to be numerous, and not always alike. Sometimes, and I believe often, several unite. I have taken all possible care to find the opinions of physicians on that subject, and I here offer them to the reader.

Some think that the peculiar qualities of the air of this country cause this fever; but most assert that it is generated by the standing and putrid water, a theory which seems confirmed by experience. For it has been observed that such people as live in the neighborhood of morasses or swamps, or in places where stagnant, stinking water is found, are commonly infected with the fever and ague every year, and get it more readily than others. This chiefly happens at a time of the year when those stagnant waters are most evaporated by the heat of the sun, and the air is filled with the most noxious vapors. The fever likewise is very violent in all places which have a low location, and where salt water comes up with the tide twice in twenty-four hours and unites with the stagnant, fresh water in the country. On traveling in summer over such low places, where fresh and salt water unite, the nauseous stench arising often forces the traveler to hold his nose. On that account most of the inhabitants of Penn's Neck and Salem in New Jersey are annually infected with the fever to a much greater degree than inhabitants of the higher part of the country. If a settler moves into the lower regions, he may be well assured that the fever will attack him at the usual time, and that he will get it again every year. However, this cannot be the sole cause of the fever, as I have been in several parts of the country two or three degrees further north which had a low elevation and stagnant waters near them, where the people declared they seldom suffered from this sickness.

Others were of the opinion that diet had much to do with it, and chiefly laid the blame upon the inconsiderate and intemperate consumption of fruit. This is particularly the case with the Europeans who come to America and are not used to its climate and its fruit, for those who are born here can bear more, yet are not entirely free from the bad effects of eating too much. I have heard many speak from their own experience on this point. They were certain that after eating a watermelon once or twice before breakfast they would have the fever and the ague in a few days. Yet it is remarkable that the French in Canada told me the fevers were less common in that country, though they consumed as many watermelons as the English colonies, and it had never been observed that this indulgence occasioned a fever. But on coming in the hot season to the Illinois, an Indian nation which lives in nearly the same latitude as Delaware, they could not eat a watermelon without feeling the shaking fits of an ague and the Indians therefore warned them not to eat of so dangerous a fruit.

Does not this lead us to believe that the greater heat in Pennsylvania and the territory of the Illinois, which are both five or six degrees more southerly than Canada, makes fruit in some measure more dangerous? In the English North American colonies every countryman plants watermelons which are eaten while the people make hay or during the harvest when they have nothing upon their stomachs, in order to cool them during the great heat, as that juicy fruit seems very suitable for refreshment. In the same manner, melons, cucumbers, pumpkins, squashes, mulberries, apples, peaches, cherries, and such fruit are eaten here in summer, and altogether contribute to the attacks of the ague.

But that the manner of living contributes greatly toward it may be concluded from the unanimous accounts of old people concerning the times of their childhood, according to which the inhabitants of these parts were at that time not subject to so many diseases as they are at present, and people were seldom sick. But those who first settled in America lived very frugally; they were poor, and could not buy rum, brandy, or other strong liquors, which they seldom distilled themselves, although they sometimes had a good strong beer. They did not understand the art of making cider, which is now so common in the country. Tea, coffee, chocolate, which at present constitute even the country people's daily breakfast, were wholly unknown to them. Most of them had never tasted sugar or punch.

Lastly, some people pretended that the loss of many odoriferous plants, with which the woods were filled at the arrival of the Europeans, but which the cattle have now destroyed, might be a cause of the greater progress of the fever at present. The number of those strong plants occasioned a pleasant scent to rise in the woods every morning and evening. It is therefore not unreasonable to imagine that the noxiousness of the effluvia from decaying substances was then prevented, so that they were not so dangerous to the inhabitants.

In spite of such diseases the people multiply faster here than in Europe. It does not seem difficult to find the reasons why. As soon as a person is old enough he may marry without any fear of poverty. There is such an amount of good land yet uncultivated that a newly married man can, without difficulty, get a spot of ground where he may comfortably subsist with his wife and children. The taxes are very low, and he need not be under any concern on their account. The liberties he enjoys are so great that he considers himself a prince in his possessions.

Everyone who acknowledges God to be the Creator, Preserver, and Ruler of all things, and teaches or undertakes nothing against the state or against the common peace, is at liberty to settle, stay, and carry on his trade here, be his religious principles ever so strange. No one is here molested because of misleading doctrines which he may follow, if he does not exceed the above-mentioned bounds. And he is so well secured by the laws, both as to person and property, and enjoys such liberties that a citizen here may, in a manner, be said to live in his house like a king. It would be difficult to find anyone who could wish for and obtain greater freedom.

On careful consideration of what I have already said, it will be easy to conceive why a city like Philadelphia should rise so suddenly from nothing into grandeur and perfection, without any powerful monarch contributing to it either by punishing the wicked or by giving great supplies of money. And yet its fine appearance, good regulations, agreeable location, natural advantages, trade, riches, and power are by no means inferior to those of any, even of the most ancient towns in Europe. It has not been necessary to force people to come and settle here; on the contrary, foreigners of different languages have left their country, houses, property, and relations and have ventured over wide and stormy seas in order to come hither. Other countries, which have been peopled for a long time, complain of the small number of their inhabitants. But Pennsylvania, which was no better than a wilderness in the year 1681 and contained hardly 1,500 people, now vies in population with several kingdoms in Europe. It has received hosts of people which other countries, to their infinite loss, have either neglected, belittled, or expelled.

Philadelphia reflects this prosperity. All the streets, except two which are nearest the river, run in a straight line and make right angles at the intersections. Most of the streets have a pavement of flags a fathom or more broad, laid before the houses, and four-foot posts put on the outside three or four fathoms apart. Those who walk on foot use the flagstones, but riders and teams use the middle of the street. The above-mentioned posts prevent horses and wagons from injuring the pedestrians inside the posts, who are there secure from careless teamsters and from the dirt thrown up by horses and carts. Under the roofs are gutters which are carefully connected with pipes, and by this means those who walk under them when it rains or when the snow melts need not fear being wet by the water from the roofs.

The houses make a good appearance, are frequently several stories high, built either of bricks or of stone. The former are more commonly used, since they are made near the town and are of good quality. The stone employed in building houses is a mixture of a loose and quite small-grained limestone and of a black or grey glimmer running in undulating veins. This stone is now obtained in great quantities in the country, is easily cut, and has the good quality of not attracting moisture in a wet season. Very good lime is burned everywhere hereabouts for masonry.

The houses are covered with cedar shingles. The wood is very light, rots less than any other, and for that reason is exceedingly good for roofs, for it is not too heavy for the walls and will last forty or fifty years. But many people already begin to fear that these roofs will in time be regarded as very detrimental to the city. Since cedar is so light, most people who built their houses of stone or brick were led to make their walls extremely thin. At present this kind of wood is almost entirely gone. Whenever, therefore, in process of time these roofs decay, the people will be obliged to resort to heavier materials, tiles or the like, which the walls will not be strong enough to bear. The roof will therefore require more support or the people will be obliged to pull down the walls and build new ones, or to take other steps for securing them. Several people have already in late years begun to make roofs of tiles.

The town has two great fairs every year, one on May 16 and the other on November 16. But besides these fairs there are every week two market days, Wednesday and Saturday. On those days the country people in Pennsylvania and New Jersey bring to town a quantity of food and other products of the country, and this is a great advantage to the town. You are sure to find on market days every produce of the season which the country affords. But on other days they are sought for in vain.

Provisions are always to be got fresh here, and for that reason most of the inhabitants never buy more at a time than what will be sufficient till the next market day. In summer there is a market almost every day, for the victuals do not keep well in the great heat. There are two places in town where these markets are held. The principal one near the court-house begins about four or five o'clock in the morning and ends about nine in the forenoon.

New York comes after Boston and Philadelphia in size, but with regard to fine buildings, opulence, and extensive commerce, vies with them for supremacy. At present, it is about half as large again as Göte-borg in Sweden.

The streets do not run so straight as those of Philadelphia; however, they are very spacious and well-built, and most of them are paved, except in high places where it has been found useless. Trees are planted in the chief streets, which in summer give them a fine appearance and during the excessive heat afford a cooling shade. I found it ex-tremely pleasant to walk in the town, for it seemed like a garden. The trees are chiefly the water beech, which is very plentiful and gives an agreeable shade in summer by its great and numerous leaves, and the locust.

There is no good water in the town itself, but at a little distance away there is a large spring which the inhabitants use for their tea and for other kitchen purposes. Those people, however, who are less particular in this matter, use the water from the wells in town, though it be very bad. The want of good water is hard on the horses of stran-gers that come to the place, for the beasts do not like to drink the well water.

Both towns are extensive seaports. Philadelphia carries on a great trade both with the inhabitants of the country and with other parts of the world, especially the West Indies, South America, and the Antilles, England, Ireland, Portugal, and the various English colonies in North America. Yet none but English ships are allowed to come into this port.

Philadelphia reaps the greatest profits from its trade with the West Indies. For thither the inhabitants ship almost every day flour, butter, meat, and other victuals, timber, planks, and the like. In return they receive either sugar, molasses, rum, indigo, mahogany, and other goods, or ready money. The true mahogany which grows in Jamaica is at present almost all cut down. Philadelphians send both West India goods and their own productions to England; the latter include all sorts of woods, especially black walnut and oak planks for ships, ships ready-built, iron, hides, and tar. The last-named product is bought in New Jersey, the forests of which province are consequently more ruined than elsewhere. Ready money is likewise sent over to England, from whence in return they get all sorts of manufactured goods, fine and coarse cloth, linen, iron ware and other wrought metals, and East India goods. For it is to be observed that England supplies Philadelphia with almost all stuffs and articles which are wanted here.

A great quantity of linseed goes annually to Ireland, together with many of the ships which are built here. Portugal gets wheat, corn, flour, and grain which is not ground. Spain sometimes takes some grain. But all the money which is gotten in these countries must immediately be sent to England in payment for goods from thence, and yet those sums are not sufficient to pay all the debts.

New York probably carries on a more extensive commerce than any town in the English North American provinces. The trade of New York extends to many places, and it is said they send more ships to London than do the Philadelphians. They export to that capital the various skins which they buy of the Indians, sugar, logwood, and other dyeing woods, rum, mahogany, and many other goods which are the produce of the West Indies, together with all the specie which they get in the course of trade. Every year several ships are built here which are sent to London and there sold; and of late years a quantity of iron has been shipped to England. In return, cloth is imported from London, and so is every article of English growth or manufacture, together with all sorts of foreign goods. England, and especially London, profits immensely by its trade with the American colonies; for not only New York, but also all the other English towns on the continent import so many articles from England that all their specie, together with the goods which they get in other countries, must go to England to pay their accounts there, and still are insufficient.

New York sends many ships to the West Indies with flour, grain, biscuit, timber, casks, boards, beef and pork, butter, and other provisions, together with some of the few fruits that grow here. Many ships go to Boston in New England with grain and flour, and take in exchange meat, butter, timber, different sorts of fish, and other articles, which they carry further to the West Indies. They now and then carry rum from Boston, which is distilled there in great quantities, and sell it here at a considerable advantage. Sometimes the merchants send vessels with goods from New York to Philadelphia, and at other times from Philadelphia to New York, which is only done, as appears from the gazettes, because certain articles are cheaper at one place than at the other. They send ships to Ireland every year, laden with all kinds of West India goods, but especially with linseed which is collected in this country. The people of Ireland, in order to have better flax, make use of the plant before the seed is ripe, and therefore are obliged to send for foreign seed. It thus becomes one of the chief articles of trade. At this time a bushel of linseed is sold for eight shillings of New York currency.

Payment for the goods sold in the West Indies is either in ready money or in West India goods, which are brought to New York or sent immediately to England or Holland. If a ship does not choose to take West India goods on its return to New York, or if nobody will freight it, it often goes to Newcastle in England to take on coal for ballast, which when brought home sells for a pretty good price. In many parts of New York coal is used both for kitchen fires and in other rooms because it is considered cheaper than wood, which at present costs thirty shillings of New York money per fathom. New York also has some trade with South Carolina, to which it sends grain, flour, sugar, rum, and other goods, and takes rice in return, which is almost the only commodity exported from South Carolina.

The goods in which the province of New York trades are not numerous. It exports chiefly the skins of animals, which are bought of the Indians about Oswego; great quantities of boards, coming for the most part from Albany; timber and casks from that part of the country which lies about the Hudson River; and lastly, wheat, flour, barley, oats, and other kinds of grain, which are brought from New Jersey and the cultivated parts of this province. I have seen vessels from New Brunswick laden with wheat which lay loose on board, with flour packed up in barrels, and also with great quantities of linseed. New York also ships out pork and other meat from its own province, but not in any great amount; nor is the quantity of peas which the people about Albany bring for export very large. Iron, however, may be had more plentifully, as it is found in several parts of this province and is of considerable value; but all other products of this country are of little account.

There are also numerous smaller towns in America. Six miles from Philadelphia, for instance, lies Germantown. This settlement has only one street but is nearly two English miles long. It is for the greatest part inhabited by Germans, who come from their country to North America and settle here because they enjoy such privileges as they possess nowhere else. Most of the inhabitants are tradesmen, and make almost everything in such quantity and perfection that in a short time this province will want very little from England. Most of the houses are built of stone mixed with glimmer, which is found everywhere around Philadelphia but is scarcer further on. Several houses, however, are made of brick. They are commonly two stories high and sometimes higher. The roofs consist of shingles of white cedar wood. Their shape resembles that of the roofs in Sweden, but the angles they form at the top may be either obtuse, right-angled, or acute, according as the slopes are steep or gentle.

Beyond the towns live the great body of agriculturists. Again and again as we traveled through the forests of Pennsylvania we saw at moderate distances little fields which had been cleared of wood. Each of these was a farm. These farms were commonly very pretty, and a walk of trees frequently led from them to the highroad. The houses were all built of brick or of the stone which is found here everywhere. Every countryman, even the poorest, had an orchard with apples, peaches, chestnuts, walnuts, cherries, quinces, and such fruits, and sometimes we saw vines climbing in them. The valleys were frequently blessed with little brooks of crystal-clear water. The fields by the sides of the road were almost all mown, and of grain crops only corn and buckwheat were still standing. Corn was to be met with near each farm, in greater or lesser quantities; it grew very well and to a great length, the stalks being from six to ten feet high and covered with fine green leaves. Buckwheat likewise was quite common, and in some places the people were beginning to reap it.

The rye grows very poorly in most of the fields, chiefly because of careless agricultural practices and the poor soil, which is seldom or never manured. After the inhabitants have converted into a tillable field a tract of land which was a forest for many centuries, and which consequently had a very fine soil, they use it as long as it will bear any crops. When it ceases to bear any they turn it into pastures for the cattle, and take new grain fields in another place, where a rich black soil can be found that has never been used. This kind of agriculture will do for a time; but it will afterwards have bad consequences. A few of the inhabitants, however, treat their fields a little better.

The English in general have carried agriculture to a higher degree of perfection than any other nation. But the depth and richness of the soil found here by the settlers on land covered with woods from times immemorial misled them, and made them careless husbandmen. The Indians lived in this country for several centuries before the Europeans came, chiefly by hunting and fishing, and had hardly any agriculture. They planted corn and some species of beans and pumpkins; but a plot of such vegetables as serve an Indian family during one year takes up no more ground than a farmer in our country takes to plant cabbage for his family. Commonly, the little villages of Indians were about twelve or eighteen miles distant from each other. Hence one may judge how little ground was formerly employed for planting; the rest was overgrown with large, tall trees. And though they cleared new ground as soon as the old had lost its fertility, such little pieces as they used were very inconsiderable when compared to the vast forest which remained.

Thus the upper fertile soil increased considerably for centuries; and the Europeans coming to America found a rich, fine soil before them, lying as loose between the trees as the best bed in a garden. They had nothing to do but to cut down the wood, put it up in heaps, and clear the dead leaves away. They could then immediately proceed to plowing, which in such loose ground is very easy; and having sown their grain, they got a most plentiful harvest. This easy method of getting a rich crop has spoiled the settlers, and induced them to adopt the same method of agriculture as the Indians; that is, to sow uncultivated grounds as long as they will produce a crop without manuring, but to turn them into pastures as soon as they can bear no more, and to take on new spots of ground, covered since ancient times with woods, which have been spared by the fire or the hatchet since the Creation.

This is also the reason why agriculture and its science is so imperfect here that one can travel several days and learn almost nothing about the land, neither from the English, nor from the Swedes, Germans, Dutch, and French, except that from their gross mistakes and heedlessness of the future, one finds opportunities every day of making all sorts of observations, and of growing wise by their errors. In a word, the grain fields, the meadows, the forests, and the cattle, are treated with equal carelessness; and the characteristics of the English nation, so well-skilled in these branches of husbandry, are scarcely recognizable here. We can hardly be more hostile toward our woods in Sweden and Finland than they are here; their eyes are fixed upon the present gain, and they are blind to the future. Their cattle grow poorer daily in quality and size because of hunger. On my travels I observed several wild plants which the horses and cows preferred to all others, and which grew well on the driest and poorest ground where no others would thrive. But the inhabitants did not know how to turn this to their advantage, owing to the slight respect for natural history, that science being here, as in other parts of the world, looked upon as a mere trifle and the pastime of fools. I am certain, and my certainty is founded upon experience, that by means of these plants, in the space of a few years, I should be able to turn the poorest ground, which would hardly afford food for a cow, into the richest and most fertile meadow where great flocks of cattle would find superabundant food and grow fat. I was astonished when I heard the country people complaining of the badness of the pastures: but I also perceived their negligence, and often saw excellent plants growing on their own grounds, which only required a little more attention and assistance from their inexperienced owners. I found everywhere the wisdom and goodness of the Creator; but too seldom saw any inclination among men to make use of them.

The resources of the rivers, by contrast, were better esteemed. We saw many boats in which fishermen were busy catching oysters, using for that purpose a kind of rake with long iron teeth bent inwards. These they used either singly or two tied together in such manner that the teeth were turned toward each other. About New York they find innumerable quantities of excellent oysters, and there are few places which have oysters of such an exquisite taste and of so great a size. They are pickled and sent to the West Indies and other places, which is done in the following manner. As soon as the oysters are caught their shells are opened and the fish washed clean; some water is then poured into a pot, the oysters are put into it, and they are boiled for a while; the pot is then taken off the fire again and the oysters taken out and put upon a dish till they are almost dry. Then some nutmeg, allspice, and black pepper are added, and as much vinegar as is thought sufficient to give a sourish taste. All this is mixed with half the liquor in which the oysters are boiled, and put to boil again with great care to skim off the thick scum. At last the whole pickling liquid is poured into a glass or earthen vessel, the oysters are put into it, and the vessel is well stopped to keep out the air. In this manner oysters will keep for years, and may be sent to the most distant parts of the world.

Oysters are here reckoned very wholesome, and some people assured us that they had not felt the least inconvenience after eating a considerable quantity of them. It is also a common rule here that oysters are best in those months which have an "r" in their names such as September and October, but that they are not so good in other months. However, there are poor people who live all year long upon nothing but oysters and a little bread.

Among the numerous shellfish found on the seashore are some which by the English are called clams and which bear some resemblance to the human ear. They have considerable thickness and are chiefly white, excepting the pointed end which both without and within is of a bluish color, between purple and violet. They are found in vast numbers on the seashore of New York, Long Island, and other places. The shells contain a large amount of meat, which is eaten both by Indians and Europeans.

A considerable commerce is carried on in this fish product with such Indians as live further up the country. When these people inhabited the coast they were able to dig their own clams, which at that time constituted the great part of their food; but at present this is the business of the Dutch and English, who live on Long Island and the other maritime provinces. As soon as the clams are dug the soft part is taken out of the shells, drawn upon a wire, and hung in the open air to dry by the heat of the sun. The fish is then packed and carried to Albany upon the Hudson; there the Indians buy them, and reckon them one of their best dishes. In addition, many Indians come annually down to the seashore to get clams, proceeding with them afterwards in the manner I have just described. They are ordinarily prepared like oysters. Sometimes they are baked in their shells, sometimes stewed in butter. They are also boiled and placed in soups. They are often served on a platter with steaks or other meat. No matter how prepared they make a palatable food. I have often eaten them during my travels, but they seemed a little hard for the stomach to digest.

The servants employed in the English-American colonies are either free persons or slaves, and the former again are of two different classes. Some are entirely free and serve by the year. They are not only allowed to leave their service at the expiration of their year, but may leave it any time when they do not agree with their masters. However, in that case they are in danger of losing their wages, which are very considerable. A manservant who has some ability gets between sixteen and twenty pounds in Pennsylvania currency, but those in the country do not get so much. A maidservant gets eight or ten pounds a year. These servants have their food besides their wages, but they must buy their own clothes or depend on their master's generosity for whatever they may get as gifts.

The second kind of free servants consists of such persons as annually come from Germany, Ireland, England, and other countries, in order to settle here. These newcomers are very numerous every year; there are old and young of both sexes. Some have fled from oppression. Others have been driven from their country by religious persecution. But most of them are poor and have not money enough to pay their passage, which is between six and eight pounds sterling for each person. Therefore, they agree with the captain that they will suffer themselves to be sold for a few years on their arrival. In that case the person who buys them pays the cost of transportation. Frequently, very old people come over who cannot pay their passage. They therefore sell their children for several years, who serve both for themselves and for their parents. There are also some who pay part of their passage, and are sold only for a short time. From these circumstances it appears that the price on the poor foreigners who come over to North America varies considerably, and that some of them have to serve longer than others. When their time has expired they get a new suit of clothes from their master and some other things. He is obliged to feed and clothe them during the years of their servitude. Many of the Germans who come hither bring money enough with them to pay their passage, but prefer to be sold, hoping that during their servitude they may get a knowledge of the language and character of the country and its life, that they may the better be able to consider what they shall do when they have gotten their liberty.

Indentured servants are preferable to all others, because they are not so expensive. To buy a Negro or black slave requires too much money at one time; and men or maids who get yearly wages are likewise too costly. But this kind of servant may be gotten for half the money, and even less; for they commonly pay fourteen pounds, Pennsylvania currency, for a person who is to serve four years. Their wages, therefore, are not above three pounds Pennsylvania currency per annum.

When a person has bought such a servant for a certain number of years, and has an intention to sell him again, he is at liberty to do so, but is obliged, at the expiration of the term of servitude, to provide the usual suit of clothes for the servant, unless he has made that a part of the bargain with the purchaser. The English and the Irish commonly sell themselves for four years, but the Germans frequently agree with the captain before they set out to pay him a certain sum of money for a certain number of persons. As soon as they arrive in America they go about and try to get a man who will pay the passage for them. In return they give, according to their circumstances, one or several of their children to serve a certain number of years, and make their bargain with the highest bidder.

The Negroes, or blacks, constitute the third kind of servants. They are in a manner slaves; for when a Negro is once bought he is the purchaser's servant as long as he lives. However, it is not in the power of the master to kill his Negro for a fault, but he must leave it to the magistrates to proceed according to the laws. A man who kills his Negro is, legally, punishable by death, but there is no instance here of a white man ever having been executed for this crime. A few years ago it happened that a master killed his slave. His friends and even the magistrates secretly advised him to make his escape, as otherwise they could not avoid taking him prisoner, and then he would be condemned to die according to the laws of the country without any hopes of being saved. This leniency was granted toward him, that the Negroes might not have the satisfaction of seeing a master executed for killing his slave. Such an execution might lead them to all sorts of dangerous designs against their masters, and to value themselves too much.

Formerly the Negroes were brought over from Africa, and bought by almost everyone who could afford it, the Quakers alone excepted. But the latter are no longer so particular and now they have as many Negroes as other people. However, many people cannot conquer the idea that it is contrary to the laws of Christianity to keep slaves. There are several free Negroes in town who were lucky enough to get a very zealous Quaker for their master, from whom they secured their liberty after faithfully serving him for a time.

At present Negroes are seldom brought to the English colonies, for those already there have multiplied rapidly. In regard to marriage they proceed as follows: in case you have not only male but likewise female Negroes, they may intermarry, and then the children are all your slaves. But if you possess a male only and he has an inclination to marry a female belonging to a different master, you do not hinder your Negro in so delicate a point; but it is of no advantage to you, for the children belong to the master of the female. Therefore it is in practice advantageous to have Negro women.

The price of Negroes varies with their age, health, and ability. A full-grown Negro costs from 40 to 100 pounds, Pennsylvania currency. A Negro boy or girl of two or three years old can hardly be gotten for less than 8 or 14 pounds in Pennsylvania money.

Not only the Quakers but also several Christians of other denominations sometimes set their Negroes at liberty. When a gentleman has a faithful Negro who has done him great services, he sometimes declares him independent at his own death. This is, however, very expensive; for the masters are obliged to make a provision for the Negro thus set at liberty, to afford him subsistence when he is grown old, that he may not be driven by necessity to wicked actions or fall a charge to anybody, for these free Negroes become very lazy and indolent afterwards. But the children which the free Negro has begot during his servitude are all slaves, though their father be free. On the other hand, those children born after the parent was freed are free.

The Negroes in the North American colonies are treated more mildly and fed better than those in the West Indies. They have as good food as the rest of the servants, and they possess equal advantages in all things, except that they are bound to serve their whole lifetime and get no other wages than what their master's goodness allows them. They are likewise clad at their master's expense. On the contrary, in the West Indies, and especially in the Spanish Islands, they are treated very cruelly; therefore no threat makes more impression upon a Negro here than that of sending him over to the West Indies in case he will not reform.

To prevent any disagreeable mixtures of the white people and Negroes, and to hinder the latter from forming too great opinions of themselves, to the disadvantage of their masters, I am told there was a law passed prohibiting the whites of both sexes to marry Negroes, under pain of capital punishment, with deprivation of privileges and other severer penalties for the clergyman who married them. But that the whites and blacks sometimes copulated appears in children of a mixed complexion who are sometimes born.

It is greatly to be pitied that the masters of these Negroes take little care of their spiritual welfare, and let them live on in their pagan darkness. There are even some who would be very ill-pleased and would in every way hinder their Negroes from being instructed in the doctrines of Christianity. To this they are led partly by the conceit of its being shameful to have a spiritual brother or sister among so despicable a people; partly by thinking that they would not be able to keep their Negroes so subjected afterwards; and partly through fear of the Negroes growing too proud on seeing themselves upon a level with their masters in religious matters.

The freedom of the country enables many people of different language and religion to live peacefully together. Besides the different sects of Christians, many Jews have settled in New York. They possess great privileges, have a synagogue, own their dwelling houses, own large countryseats, and are allowed to keep shops in town. They also have several ships, which they load and send out with their own goods. In short, they enjoy all the privileges common to the other inhabitants of this town and province.

During my residence in New York, both at this time and for the next two years, I was frequently in company with Jews. I was informed, among other things, that these people never boiled any meal for themselves on Saturday, but that they always did it the day before, and that in winter they kept a fire during the whole Saturday. They commonly eat no pork; yet I have been told by several trustworthy men that many of them (especially the young Jews) when traveling did not hesitate the least about eating this or any other meat that was put before them, even though they were in company with Christians. I was in their synagogue last evening for the first time, and today at noon I visited it again; each time I was put in a special seat which was set apart for strangers or Christians. A young rabbi read the divine service, which was partly in Hebrew and partly in the rabbinical dialect. Both men and women were dressed entirely in the English fashion; the former had their hats on, and did not once take them off during the service. The galleries, I observed, were reserved for the ladies, while the men sat below. During prayers the men spread a white cloth over their heads, which perhaps is to represent sackcloth. But I observed that the wealthier sort of people had a much richer cloth than the poorer ones. Many men had Hebrew books, from which they sang and read alternately. The rabbi stood in the middle of the synagogue and read with his face turned toward the east; he spoke, however, so fast as to make it almost impossible for anyone to understand what he said.

In Albany the inhabitants are almost all Dutchmen. They speak Dutch, have Dutch preachers, and the divine service is performed in that language. Their manners are likewise quite Dutch, although their dress is like that of the English. The avarice, selfishness, and immeasurable love of money of the inhabitants of Albany are very well-known throughout all North America. If a real Jew, who understands the art of getting forward perfectly well, should settle amongst them, they would not fail to ruin him. For this reason nobody comes to this place without the most pressing necessity. I found that the judgment which other people formed of the Dutch was not without foundation. For though they seldom see any strangers (except those who go from the British colonies to Canada and back again) and one might therefore expect to find victuals and accommodation for travelers cheaper than in places where they always resort, yet I experienced the contrary. I was obliged to pay for everything twice, thrice, and four times as much as in any part of North America through which I have passed. If I wanted their assistance I was obliged to pay them very well for it, and when I wanted to purchase anything or be helped in some case or other I could at once see what kind of blood ran in their veins, for they either fixed exorbitant prices for their services or were very reluctant to assist me.

The behavior of the inhabitants of Albany during the war between England and France, which ended with the peace of Aix la Chapelle, has, among several other causes, contributed to make them the object of hatred in all the British colonies, but more especially in New England. For at the beginning of that war, when the Indians of both parties had received orders to commence hostilities, the French engaged theirs

to attack the inhabitants of New England, which they faithfully executed, killing everybody they met with and carrying off whatever they
found. During this time the people of Albany remained neutral, and
carried on a great trade with the very Indians who murdered the inhabitants of New England. In the present war it will sufficiently appear
how backward the other British provinces in America are in assisting Albany, and the neighboring places, in case of an attack from
the French or Indians. The hatred which the English bear against the
people at Albany is very great, but that which the latter return the
English is carried to a degree ten times higher. This hatred has existed
ever since the time when the English conquered this section, and is
not yet extinguished, though they could never have gotten larger advantages under the Dutch government than they have obtained under that
of the English. For, in a manner, their privileges are greater than those
of Englishmen themselves.

In their homes the inhabitants of Albany are much more sparing
than the English and are stingier with their food. Generally, what they
serve is just enough for the meal and sometimes hardly that. The punch
bowl is much more rarely seen than among the English. The women
are perfectly well-acquainted with economy; they rise early, go to sleep
very late, and are almost superstitiously clean in regard to the floor,
which is frequently scoured several times in the week. Inside the homes
the women are neatly but not lavishly dressed. The children are taught
both English and Dutch.

Each English colony in North America is independent of the other,
each has its own laws and coinage and may be looked upon in several
lights as a state by itself. Hence it happens that in time of war things
go on very slowly and irregularly here. Not only is the opinion of one
province sometimes directly opposite to that of another, but frequently
the views of the governor and those of the assembly of the same province are quite different. It is easy to see, therefore, that while the people
are quarreling about the best and cheapest manner of carrying on the
war, an enemy has it in his power to take one place after another. It
has usually happened that while some provinces have been suffering
from their enemies, the neighboring ones have been quiet and inactive,
as if it did not in the least concern them. They have frequently taken
up two or three years in considering whether or not they should give

assistance to an oppressed sister colony, and sometimes they have expressly declared themselves against it. There are instances of provinces which were not only neutral in such circumstances, but which even carried on a great trade with the power which at that very time was attacking and laying waste some other provinces.

The French in Canada, who are but an unimportant body in comparison with the English in America, have by this position of affairs been able to obtain great advantages in times of war. For if we judge from the number and power of the English, it would seem very easy for them to get the better of the French in America.

It is, however, of great advantage to the crown of England that the North American colonies are near a country like Canada under the government of the French. There is reason to believe that the king never was in earnest in his attempts to expel the French from their possessions there, though it might have been done with little difficulty. The English colonies in this part of the world have increased so much in their number of inhabitants, and in their riches, that they almost vie with Old England. Now, in order to keep up the authority and trade of their mother country and to answer several other purposes, they are forbidden to establish new manufactures which would turn to the disadvantage of the British commerce. They are not allowed to dig for any gold or silver, unless they send it to England immediately. With few exceptions, they have not the liberty of trading with any areas that do not belong to the British dominion, nor are foreigners allowed to trade with them. These and other restrictions cause the inhabitants of the English colonies to grow less tender for their mother country, and this coldness is kept up by the foreigners, German, Dutch, and French, who have no particular attachment to Old England. Add to this also that many people can never be contented with their possessions, no matter how large. They will always be desirous of getting more, and of enjoying the pleasure which arises from a change. Their extraordinary liberty and their luxury often lead them to unrestrained acts of a selfish and arbitrary nature.

I have been told by Englishmen, and not only by such as were born in America but also by those who came from Europe, that the English colonies in North America, in the space of thirty, forty, or fifty years, would be able to form a state by themselves, entirely independent of Old England. But as the whole country which lies along the seashore is unguarded, and on the land side is harassed by the French, these dangerous neighbors in times of war are sufficient to prevent the connection of the colonies with their mother country from being quite broken off. The English government has therefore sufficient reason to consider means of keeping the colonies in due submission.

3.

THE AMERICAN FARMER—GALLIC STYLE

The "American Farmer" was Hector St. Jean de Crèvecœur, a Frenchman, born in Caen in 1735, who settled in Canada at the age of nineteen. In 1765, after the close of the French and Indian War, he migrated across the border to the English colonies, and lived until the Revolution in Orange County, New York. Crèvecœur had some difficulties in the course of the struggle for independence, and finally left for France in 1780. He spent seven years more in this country as French consul between 1783 and 1790, but then returned to the land of his birth, where he died in 1813.

His Letters from an American Farmer *(1782) were written in English in Orange County between 1770 and 1775. Their impassioned rhetoric clothes a beautiful vision of the potentialities of American life. By no means blind to the darker aspects of what he saw, Crèvecœur was nevertheless a hopeful man, writing in a hopeful era, and his vision was substantially accurate.*

I wish I could be acquainted with the feelings and thoughts which must agitate the heart and present themselves to the mind of an enlightened Englishman when he first lands on this continent. He must greatly rejoice that he lived at a time to see this fair country discovered and settled. He must necessarily feel a share of national pride when he views the chain of settlements which embellishes these extended shores. When he says to himself, this is the work of my countrymen who, when convulsed by factions, afflicted by a variety of miseries and wants, restless and impatient, took refuge here. They brought along with them their national genius, to which they principally owe what liberty they enjoy and what substance they possess. Here he sees the industry of his native country displayed in a new manner, and traces, in their works, the embryos of all the arts, sciences, and ingenuity which flourish in Europe. Here he beholds fair cities, substantial villages, extensive fields, an immense country filled with decent houses, good roads, orchards, meadows, and bridges, where a hundred years ago all was wild, woody, and uncultivated! What a train of pleasing ideas this fair spectacle must suggest! It is a prospect which must inspire a good citizen with the most heartfelt pleasure!

The difficulty consists in the manner of viewing so extensive a scene. He is arrived on a new continent; a modern society offers itself to his contemplation, different from what he had hitherto seen. It is not composed, as in Europe, of great lords who possess everything, and of a herd of people who have nothing. Here are no aristocratic families, no courts, no kings, no bishops, no ecclesiastical dominion, no invisible power giving to a few a very visible one, no great manufacturers employing thousands, no great refinements of luxury. The rich and the poor are not so far removed from each other as they are in Europe. Some few towns excepted, we are all tillers of the earth, from Nova Scotia to West Florida. We are a people of cultivators, scattered over an immense territory, communicating with each other by means of good roads and navigable rivers, united by the silken bands of mild government, all respecting the laws, without dreading their power, because they are equitable. We are all animated with the spirit of an industry which is unfettered and unrestrained, because each person works for himself.

If he travels through our rural districts, the stranger views not the hostile castle and the haughty mansion contrasted with the clay-built hut and miserable cabin, where cattle and men help to keep each other warm, and dwell in meanness, smoke, and indigence. A pleasing uniformity of decent competence appears throughout our habitations. The meanest of our log houses is a dry and comfortable habitation. Lawyer or merchant are the fairest titles our towns afford; that of a farmer is the only appellation of the rural inhabitants of our country. It must take some time ere he can reconcile himself to our dictionary, which is but short in words of dignity and names of honor. There, on a Sunday, he sees a congregation of respectable farmers and their wives, all clad in neat homespun, well-mounted, or riding in their own humble wagons. There is not among them an esquire, saving the unlettered magistrate. There he sees a parson as simple as his flock, a farmer who does not riot on the labor of others. We have no princes, for whom we toil, starve, and bleed. We are the most perfect society now existing in the world. Here man is free as he ought to be.

The next wish of this traveler will be to know whence came all these people? They are a mixture of English, Scotch, Irish, French, Dutch, Germans, and Swedes. From this promiscuous breed, that race, now called Americans, have arisen. In this great American asylum the poor of Europe have by some means met together, and in consequence of various causes. To what purpose should they ask one another what countrymen they are? Alas, two-thirds of them had no country. Can a wretch, who wanders about, who works and starves, whose life is a continual scene of sore affliction or pinching penury; can that man call England or any other kingdom his country, a country that had no bread for him, whose fields produced him no harvest; who met with nothing but the frowns of the rich, the severity of the laws, with jails and punishments; who owned not a single foot of the extensive surface of this planet? No! Urged by a variety of motives, here they came. Everything has tended to regenerate them: new laws, a new mode of living, a new social system. Here they are become men. In Europe they were so many useless plants, wanting vegetative mold and refreshing showers. They withered; and were mowed down by want, hunger, and war. But now, by the power of transplantation, like all other plants, they have taken root and flourished! Formerly they were not numbered in any civil lists of their country, except in those of the poor; here they rank as citizens.

By what invisible power has this surprising metamorphosis been performed? By that of the laws and that of the people's industry. The laws, the indulgent laws, protect them as they arrive, stamping on them the symbol of adoption. They receive ample rewards for their labors; these accumulated rewards procure them lands; those lands confer on them the title of freemen; and to that title every benefit is affixed which men can possibly require. This is the great operation daily performed by our laws. Whence proceed these laws? From our government. Whence that government? It is derived from the original genius and the strong desire of the people ratified and confirmed by the crown.

What attachment can a poor European emigrant have for a country where he had nothing? The knowledge of the language, the love of a few kindred as poor as himself, were the only cords that tied him. His country is now that which gives him land, bread, protection, and consequence. "Ubi panis ibi patria" is the motto of all emigrants. He is either a European, or the descendant of a European; hence that strange mixture of blood which you will find in no other country. I could point out to you a man whose grandfather was an Englishman, whose wife was Dutch, whose son married a French woman, and whose present four sons have now four wives of different nations. *He* is an American, who, leaving behind him all his ancient prejudices and manners, receives new ones from the new mode of life he has embraced, the new government he obeys, and the new rank he holds. He becomes an American by being received in the broad lap of our great alma mater. Here individuals of all nations are melted into a new race of men, whose labors and posterity will one day cause great changes in the world. Americans are the western pilgrims who are carrying along with them that great mass of arts, sciences, vigor, and industry which began long since in the east. They will finish the great circle.

The Americans were once scattered all over Europe. Here they are incorporated into one of the finest systems of population which has ever appeared, and which will hereafter become distinct by the power of the different climates they inhabit. The American is a new man, who acts upon new principles; he must therefore entertain new ideas and form new opinions. From involuntary idleness, servile dependence, penury, and useless labor, he has passed to toils of a very different nature, rewarded by ample subsistence— This is an American.

British America is divided into many provinces, forming a large association, scattered along a coast of 1500 miles extent and about 200 wide. This society I would fain examine, at least such as it appears in the middle provinces; if it does not afford that variety of tinges and gradations which may be observed in Europe, we have colors peculiar to ourselves. For instance, it is natural to conceive that those who live near the sea must be very different from those who live in the woods; the intermediate space will afford a separate and distinct class.

Those who live near the sea feed more on fish than on flesh. They often encounter the sea, that boisterous element. This renders them more bold and enterprising; this leads them to neglect the confined occupations of the land. They see and converse with a variety of peo-

ple. Their intercourse with mankind becomes extensive. The sea inspires them with a love of traffic, a desire of transporting produce from
one place to another; and leads them to a variety of resources, which
supply the place of labor.

Those who inhabit the middle settlements, by far the most numerous, must be very different. The simple cultivation of the earth purifies
them; but the indulgences of the government, the soft remonstrances
of religion, the rank of independent freeholders, must necessarily inspire them with sentiments very little known in Europe among a people
of the same class. What do I say? Europe has no such class of men.
The early knowledge they acquire, the early bargains they make, give
them a great degree of sagacity. As freemen they will be litigious. Pride
and obstinacy are often the cause of law-suits; the nature of our laws
and governments may be another. As citizens, it is easy to imagine that
they will carefully read the newspapers, enter into every political dis-
quisition, freely blame or censure governors and others. As farmers,
they will be careful and anxious to get as much as they can, because
what they get is their own. As northern men, they will love the cheerful
cup. As Christians, religion curbs them not in their opinions; the general indulgence leaves every one to think for himself in spiritual matters. The law inspects our actions; our thoughts are left to God.
Industry, good living, selfishness, litigiousness, country politics, the
pride of freemen, religious indifference, are their characteristics. If you
recede still farther from the sea, you will come into more modern settlements; they exhibit the same strong lineaments in a ruder appearance.
Religion seems to have still less influence, and manners are still less
improved.

Now we arrive near the great woods, near the last inhabited districts. There men seem to be placed still farther beyond the reach of
government, which, in some measure, leaves them to themselves. How
can it pervade every corner, as they were driven there by misfortunes,
necessity of beginnings, desire of acquiring large tracts of land, idleness, frequent want of economy, ancient debts. The reunion of such
people does not afford a very pleasing spectacle. When discord, want
of unity and friendship, when either drunkenness or idleness, prevail
in such remote districts, contention, inactivity, and wretchedness must
ensue. There are not the same remedies to these evils as in a long-

established community. The few magistrates they have are, in general, little better than the rest. They are often in a perfect state of war: that of man against man, sometimes decided by blows, sometimes by means of the law; that of man against every wild inhabitant of these venerable woods, of which they are come to dispossess them. There men appear to be no better than carnivorous animals, of a superior rank, living on the flesh of wild animals when they can catch them, and when they are not able, subsisting on grain.

He who would wish to see America in its proper light, and have a true idea of its feeble beginnings and barbarous rudiments, must visit our extended line of frontiers, where the last settlers dwell, and where he may see the first labors of settlement, the mode of clearing the earth, in all their different appearances. There, remote from the power of example and check of shame, many families exhibit the most hideous parts of our society. They are a kind of forlorn hope, preceding, by ten or twelve years, the most respectable army of veterans which come after them. In that space, prosperity will polish some, vice and law will drive off the rest, who, uniting again with others like themselves, will recede still farther, making room for more industrious people, who will finish their improvements, convert the log house into a convenient habitation, and, rejoicing that the first heavy labors are finished, will change, in a few years, that hitherto-barbarous country into a fine, fertile, well-regulated, district. Such is our progress, such is the march of the Europeans toward the interior parts of this continent.

It is with men as it is with the plants and animals that grow and live in the forests. They are entirely different from those that live in the plains. By living in or near the woods, their actions are regulated by the wildness of the neighborhood. The deer often come to eat their grain, the wolves to destroy their sheep, the bears to kill their hogs, the foxes to catch their poultry. This surrounding hostility immediately puts the gun into their hands. They watch these animals; they kill some; and thus, by defending their property, they soon become professed hunters. This is the progress. Once hunters, farewell to the plough. The chase renders them ferocious, gloomy, and unsocial. A hunter wants no neighbors; he rather hates them, because he dreads the competition. In a little time their success in the woods makes them neglect their tillage. They trust to the natural fecundity of the earth, and therefore do little.

Carelessness in fencing often exposes what little they sow to destruction. They are not at home to watch. In order, therefore, to make up the deficiency, they go oftener to the woods.

That new mode of life brings along with it a new set of manners, which I cannot easily describe. These new manners, being grafted on the old stock, produce a strange sort of lawless profligacy, the impressions of which are indelible. The manners of the Indian natives are respectable compared with this European medley. Wives and children live in sloth and inactivity, and, having no proper pursuits, you may judge what education the latter receive. Their tender minds have nothing else to contemplate but the example of their parents; like them they grow up a mongrel breed, half-civilized, half-savage, except nature stamps on them some constitutional propensities.

To all these reasons you must add their lonely situation, and you cannot imagine what an effect on manners the great distances they live from each other has! Consider one of the last settlements in its first view. Of what is it composed? Europeans, who have not that sufficient share of knowledge they ought to have in order to prosper; people who have suddenly passed from oppression, dread of government, and fear of laws, into the unlimited freedom of the woods. This sudden change must have a very great effect on most men, and on that class particularly. Eating of wild meat, whatever you may think, tends to alter their temper, though all the proof I can adduce is that I have seen it; and, having no place of worship to resort to, what little society this might afford is denied them. Is it then surprising to see men, thus situated, immersed in great and heavy labors, degenerate a little? It is rather a wonder the effect is not more diffusive.

The Moravians and the Quakers are the only instances in exception to what I have advanced. The first never settle singly; it is a colony of the society which emigrates. They carry with them their forms, worship, rules, and decency. The others never begin so hard; they are always able to buy improvements, in which there is a great advantage, for by that time the country is recovered from its first barbarity. Thus, our bad people are those who are half cultivators and half hunters; and the worst of them are those who have degenerated altogether into the hunting state. As old ploughmen and new men of the woods, as Europeans and new-made Indians, they contract the vices of both. They adopt the moroseness and ferocity of a native, without his mildness or even his industry at home. Hunting is but a licentious idle life, and, if it does not always pervert good disposition, yet, when it is united with bad luck, it leads to want. Want stimulates that propensity to rapacity and injustice, too natural to needy men, which is the fatal gradation. After this explanation of the effects which follow by living in the woods, shall we yet vainly flatter ourselves with the hope of converting the Indians? We should rather begin with converting our back settlers.

Europe contains hardly any other distinctions but lords and tenants; this fair country alone is settled by freeholders, the possessors of the soil they cultivate, members of the government they obey, and the framers of their own laws, by means of their representatives. Our distance from Europe, far from diminishing, rather adds to our usefulness and consequence as men and subjects. Had our forefathers remained there, they would only have crowded it, and perhaps prolonged those convulsions which had shaken it for so long. Every industrious European, who transports himself here, may be compared to a sprout growing at the foot of a great tree; it enjoys and draws but a little portion of sap; wrench it from the parent roots, transplant it, and it will become a tree bearing fruit also. It is here, then, that the idle may be employed, the useless become useful, and the poor become rich. But by riches I do not mean gold and silver; we have but little of those metals. I mean a better sort of wealth: cleared lands, cattle, good houses, good clothes, and an increase of people to enjoy them.

There is no wonder that this country has so many charms, and presents to Europeans so many temptations to remain in it. A traveler in Europe becomes a stranger as soon as he quits his own kingdom; but it is otherwise here. We know, properly speaking, no strangers. This is every person's country; the variety of our soils, situations, climates, governments, and produce, has something which must please everybody. No sooner does a European arrive, no matter of what condition, than his eyes are opened upon the fair prospect. When in England, he was a mere Englishman; here he stands on a larger portion of the globe. He does not find, as in Europe, a crowded society, where every place is overstocked; he does not feel that perpetual collision of parties, that difficulty of beginning, that contention which oversets so many. There is room for everybody in America. Has he any particular talent or industry, he exerts it in order to procure a livelihood, and it succeeds.

I do not mean that everyone who comes will grow rich in a little time; no, but he may procure an easy, decent maintenance by his industry. Instead of starving he will be fed, instead of being idle he will have employment; and these are riches enough for such men as come over here. The rich stay in Europe; it is only the middling and poor that emigrate. It is no wonder that the European, who has lived here a few years, is desirous to remain; Europe, with all its pomp, is not to be compared with this continent for men of middle stations or laborers.

A European, when he first arrives, seems limited in his intentions as well as in his views; but he very suddenly alters his scale; two hundred miles formerly appeared a very great distance, it is now but a trifle; he no sooner breathes our air than he forms schemes, and embarks in designs he never would have thought of in his own country. There the plenitude of society confines many useful ideas, and often extinguishes the most laudable schemes which here ripen into maturity. Thus Europeans become Americans.

But how is this accomplished in that crowd of low indigent people who flock here every year from all parts of Europe? I will tell you: they no sooner arrive than they immediately feel the good effects of that plenty of provisions we possess; they fare on our best food, and are kindly entertained; their talents, character, and peculiar industry are immediately inquired into; they find countrymen everywhere disseminated, let them come from whatever part of Europe. Let me select one as an epitome of the rest. He is hired, he goes to work, and works moderately; instead of being employed by a haughty person he finds himself with his equal, placed at the substantial table of the farmer, or else at an inferior one as good; his wages are high, his bed is not like that bed of sorrow on which he used to lie. If he behaves with propriety, and is faithful, he is caressed, and becomes as it were a member of the family. He begins to feel the effects of a sort of resurrection; hitherto he had not lived, but simply vegetated; he now feels himself a man, because he is treated as such. Judge what an alteration there must arise in the mind and the thoughts of this man; he begins to forget his former servitude and dependence. His heart involuntarily swells and glows; this first swell inspires him with those new thoughts which constitute an American.

He looks around and sees many a prosperous person, who, but a few years before, was as poor as himself. This encourages him much; he begins to form some little scheme, the first, alas, he ever formed in his life. If he is wise, he thus spends two or three years, in which time he acquires knowledge, the use of tools, the modes of working the lands, felling trees, and so on. This prepares the foundation of a good name, the most useful acquisition he can make. He is encouraged, he has gained friends; he is advised and directed, he feels bold, he purchases some land; he gives all the money he has brought over, as well as what he has earned, and trusts to the God of harvests for the discharge of the rest. His good name procures him credit; he is now possessed of the deed, conveying to him and his posterity the fee simple and absolute property of two-hundred acres of land, situated on such a river. What an epoch in this man's life! He is become a freeholder, from perhaps a German boor; he is now an American, a Pennsylvanian, an English subject. He is naturalized, his name is enrolled with those of the other citizens of the province. Instead of being a vagrant, he has a place of residence; he is called the inhabitant of such a county, or of such a district, and for the first time in his life counts for something; for hitherto he had been a cipher.

How much wiser, in general, the honest Germans are than almost all other Europeans; they hire themselves to some of their wealthy landsmen, and, in that apprenticeship, learn everything that is necessary. They attentively consider the prosperous industry of others, which imprints in their minds a strong desire of possessing the same advantages. This forcible idea never quits them. They launch forth, and, by dint of sobriety, rigid parsimony, and the most persevering industry, they commonly succeed. Their astonishment at their first arrival from Germany is very great; the contrast must be very powerful indeed. They observe their countrymen flourishing every place. They travel through whole counties where not a word of English is spoken; and, in the names and the language of the people, they retrace Germany. They have been a useful acquisition to this continent, and to Pennsylvania in particular. To them it owes some share of its prosperity; to their mechanical knowledge and patience it owes the finest mills in all America, the best teams of horses, and many other advantages.

The Scotch and the Irish might have lived in their own country perhaps as poor; but, enjoying more civil advantages, the effects of their new situation do not strike them so forcibly, nor has it so lasting an effect. Whence the difference arises I know not; but, out of twelve families of emigrants of each country, generally seven Scotch will succeed, nine German, and four Irish. The Scotch are frugal and laborious, but their wives cannot work so hard as German women, who vie with their husbands and often share with them the most severe toils of the field. The Irish do not prosper so well; they love to drink and to quarrel; they are litigious, and soon take to the gun, which is the ruin of everything; they seem, besides, to labor under a greater degree of ignorance in husbandry than the others; perhaps it is that their industry had less scope, and was less exercised at home.

There is no tracing observations of this kind without making at the same time very great allowances, as there are everywhere to be found a great many exceptions. The Irish themselves, from different parts of that kingdom, are very different. It is difficult to account for this surprising localization. One would think, on so small an island, an Irishman must be an Irishman; yet it is not so; they are different in their aptitude to, and in their love of, labor.

The Scotch, on the contrary, are all industrious and saving; they want nothing more than a field to exert themselves in, and they are commonly sure of succeeding. The only difficulty they labor under is that technical American knowledge requires some time to obtain; it is not easy for those who seldom saw a tree, to conceive how it is to be felled, cut up, and split into rails and posts.

Nantucket has nothing deserving of notice but its inhabitants; here you meet with neither ancient monuments, spacious halls, solemn temples, nor elegant dwellings; not a citadel or any kind of fortification; not even a battery to rend the air with its loud peals on any solemn occasion. As for their rural improvements, they are many, but all of the most simple and useful kind.

Sherborn is the only town on the island, which consists of about 530 houses, that have been framed on the mainland; they are lathed and plastered within, handsomely painted and boarded without; each has a cellar underneath, built with stones fetched also from the main. They are all of a similar construction and appearance; plain and entirely devoid of exterior or interior ornament. I observed but one which was built of bricks, but like the rest it is unadorned.

Their streets are not paved, but this is attended with little inconvenience, as it is never crowded with country carriages; and those they have in the town are seldom made use of but in the time of the coming in and before the sailing of their fleets. At my first landing I was much surprised at the disagreeable smell which struck me in many parts of the town; it is caused by the whaleoil, and is unavoidable; the neatness peculiar to these people can neither remove nor prevent it.

There are near the wharves a great many storehouses, where their staple commodity is deposited, as well as the innumerable materials which are always wanted to repair and fit out so many whalemen. They have three docks, each 300 feet long, and extremely convenient; at the head of which there are ten feet of water. Between these docks and the town there is room sufficient for the landing of goods and for the passage of numerous carts; for almost every man here has one. The wharves to the north and south of the docks are built of the same materials, and give a stranger, at his first landing, a high idea of the prosperity of these people; and there is room around these three docks for 300 sail of vessels. When their fleets have been successful the bustle and hurry of business on this spot, for some days after their arrival, would make you imagine that Sherborn is the capital of a very opulent and large province.

There are but few gardens and arable fields in the neighborhood of the town, for nothing can be more sterile and sandy than this part of the island; they have, however, with unwearied perseverance, by bringing a variety of manure, and by cow-penning, enriched several spots where they raise Indian corn, potatoes, pumpkins, turnips, and so on. On the highest part of this sandy eminence four windmills grind the grain they raise or import; and contiguous to them a rope walk is to be seen, where full half of their cordage is manufactured. Between the shores of the harbor, the docks, and the town, there is a most excellent piece of meadow, enclosed and manured with such cost and pains as show how necessary and precious grass is at Nantucket. Toward the Point of Shemah the island is more level and the soil better; and there they have considerable lots well fenced and richly manured, where they diligently raise their yearly crops. There are but very few farms on this island, because there are but very few spots that will admit of cultivation without the assistance of dung and other manure which is very expensive to fetch from the main.

Not far from Shemah Point they have a considerable tract of even ground, being the least sandy and the best on the island. It is divided into seven fields, one of which is planted by that part of the community which is entitled to it. This is called the common plantation, a simple but useful expedient; for were each holder of this tract to fence his property, it would require a prodigious quantity of posts and rails, which you must remember are to be purchased and fetched from the main. Instead of those private subdivisions, each man's allotment of land is thrown into the general field, which is fenced at the expense of the parties; within it everyone does with his own portion of the ground whatever he pleases. This apparent community saves a very material expense, a great deal of labor, and perhaps raises a sort of emulation among them, which urges everyone to fertilize his share with the greatest care and attention. Thus, every seven years, the whole of this tract is under cultivation, and, enriched by manure and ploughing, yields afterwards excellent pasture to which the town cows, amounting to 500, are daily led by the town shepherd, and as regularly driven back in the evening.

Not every person on the island is either a landholder or concerned in rural operations. The greater part are at sea, busily employed in their different fisheries; others are mere strangers, who come to settle as mechanics. And, even among the natives, few are possessed of determinate shares of land; for, engaged in sea affairs or trade, they are satisfied with possessing a few sheep pastures, by means of which they may have perhaps one or two cows. Many have but one; for the great number of children they have has caused such subdivisions of the original proprietorship as is sometimes puzzling to trace; and several of the most fortunate at sea have purchased and realized a great number of these original pasture titles.

Nantucket has yearly the benefit of a court of common pleas, and their appeal lies to the supreme court at Boston. The Friends compose two-thirds of the magistracy of this island. Thus they are the proprietors of its territory, and the principal rulers of its inhabitants. But, with all this apparatus of law, its coercive powers are seldom wanted or required. Seldom is it that any individual is amerced or punished; their jail conveys no terror; no man has lost his life here judicially since the foundation of this town, which is upwards of a hundred years. Solemn tribunals, public executions, humiliating punishments, are altogether unknown.

But how is a society composed of 5,000 individuals preserved in the bonds of peace and tranquillity? How are the weak protected from the strong? I will tell you. Idleness and poverty, the causes of so many crimes, are unknown here; each seeks, in the prosecution of his lawful business, that honest gain which supports them; every period of their time is full, either on shore or at sea. A probable expectation of reasonable profits, or of kindly assistance, if they fail of success, renders them strangers to licentious expedients. The simplicity of their manners shortens the catalogue of their wants; the law at a distance is ever ready to exert itself in the protection of those who stand in need of its assistance. The greatest part of them are always at sea, pursuing the whale, or raising the cod from the surface of the banks; some cultivate their little farms with the utmost diligence; some are employed in exercising various trades; others again in providing every necessary resource in order to refit their vessels or repair what misfortunes may happen, looking out for future markets, and so on. Such is the rotation of those different scenes of business which fill the measure of their days, of that part of their lives, at least, which is enlivened by health, spirits, and vigor. It is but seldom that vice grows on a barren sand like this, which produces nothing without extreme labor.

The easiest way of becoming acquainted with the modes of thinking, the rules of conduct, and the prevailing manners of any people, is to examine what sort of education they give their children; how they treat them at home, and what they are taught in their places of public worship. At home their tender minds must be early struck with the gravity, the serious though cheerful deportment, of their parents. They are inured to a principle of subordination, arising neither from sudden passions nor inconsiderate pleasure. They are gently held by a uniform silk cord, which unites softness and strength. They are corrected with tenderness, nursed with the most affectionate care, clad with that decent plainness, from which they observe their parents never to depart. In short, by the force of example, which is superior even to the strongest instinct of nature, more than by precepts, they learn to follow the steps of their parents, to despise ostentatiousness as being sinful.

Frugal, sober, orderly parents cannot fail of training up children to the same uniformity of life and manners. If they are left with fortunes, they are taught how to save them, and how to enjoy them with moderation and decency; if they have none they know how to venture, how to work and toil, as their fathers have done before them. If they fail of success, there are always in this island established resources, founded on the most benevolent principles.

At their meetings, they are taught the few, the simple, tenets of their sect; tenets, as fit to render men sober, industrious, just, and merciful, as those delivered in the most magnificent churches and cathedrals. They are instructed in the most essential duties of Christianity, so as not to offend the Divinity by the commission of evil deeds, to dread His wrath, and the punishments He has denounced. They are taught at the same time to have a proper confidence in His mercy, while they deprecate His justice. As every sect, from their different modes of worship and their different interpretations of some parts of the Scriptures, necessarily have various opinions and prejudices, which contribute something in forming their characteristics in society, so those of the Friends are well-known: obedience to the laws, even to nonresistance, justice, good-will to all, benevolence at home, sobriety, meekness, neatness, love of order, fondness and appetite for commerce.

At school they learn to read, and write a good hand, until they are twelve years old. They are then in general put apprentices to the cooper's trade, which is the second essential branch of business followed here. At fourteen they are sent to sea, where in their leisure hours their companions teach them the art of navigation, which they have an opportunity of practicing on the spot. They learn the great and useful art of working a ship in all the different situations which the sea and wind so often require; and surely there cannot be a better or a more useful school of that kind in the world. They then go gradually through every station of rowers, steersmen, and harpooners. Thus they learn to attack, to pursue, to overtake, to cut, to dress, their huge game; and after having performed several such voyages, and perfected themselves in this business, they are fit either for the countinghouse or the chase.

The first proprietors of this island, or rather the first founders of this town, began their career of industry with a single whaleboat, with which they went to fish for cod. The small distance from their shores at which they caught the cod enabled them soon to increase their business, and those early successes first led them to conceive that they might likewise catch the whales, which hitherto sported undisturbed on their banks. After many trials, and several miscarriages, they succeeded. Thus they proceeded, step by step; the profits of one successful enterprise helped them to purchase and prepare better materials for a more extensive one: as these were attended with little costs, their profits grew greater. The south sides of the island, from east to west, were divided into four equal parts, and each part was assigned to a company of six, which, though thus separated, still carried on their business in common.

Thus they went on, until the profits they made enabled them to purchase larger vessels, and to pursue the whales farther, when they quitted the coast. Those who failed in their enterprises returned to the cod fisheries, which had been their first school and their first resource. They even began to visit the banks of Cape Breton, the Isle of Sable, and all the other fishing places with which this coast of America abounds. By degrees they went whaling to Newfoundland, to the Gulf of St. Lawrence, to the Straits of Belle Isle, the coast of Labrador, Davis's Straits, even to Cape Desolation, in 70° of latitude, where the Danes carry on some fisheries in spite of the perpetual severities of that inhospitable climate. In process of time they visited the western islands, the latitude of 34°, famous for that fish, the Brazils, the coast of Guinea. Would you believe that they have already gone to the Falkland Islands, and that I have heard several of them talk of going to the South Seas? Their confidence is so great, and their knowledge of this branch of business so superior to that of any other people, that they have acquired a monopoly of this commodity.

Their catches are sometimes disposed of in the towns of the continent, where they are exchanged for such commodities as are wanted; but they are most commonly sent to England, where they always sell for cash. When this is intended, a vessel larger than the rest is fitted out to be filled with oil on the spot where it is found and made, and thence she sails immediately for London. This expedient saves time, freight, and expense; and from that capital they bring back whatever they want. They employ also several vessels in transporting lumber to the West Indian Islands, from whence they procure in return the various productions of the country, which they afterwards exchange wherever they can hear of an advantageous market. Being extremely acute, they well know how to improve all the advantages which the combination of so many branches of business constantly affords; the spirit of commerce, which is the simple art of a reciprocal supply of wants, is well understood here by everybody. They are well-acquainted with the cheapest method of procuring lumber from Kennebeck River, Penobscot, and so on; pitch and tar from North Carolina; flour and biscuit from Philadelphia; beef and pork from Connecticut. They know how to exchange their codfish and West Indian produce for those articles which they are continually either bringing to their island or sending off to other places where they are wanted. By means of all these commercial negotiations they have greatly cheapened the fitting out of their whaling fleets, and therefore much improved their fisheries. They are indebted for all these advantages, not only to their national genius but to the poverty of their soil.

The vessels most proper for whale fishing are brigs of about 150 tons burden, particularly when they are intended for distant latitudes. They always man them with thirteen hands, in order that they may row two whaleboats, the crews of which must necessarily consist of six, four at the oars, one standing on the bows with the harpoon, and the other at the helm. It is also necessary that there should be two of these boats, that, if one should be destroyed in attacking the whale, the other, which is never engaged at the same time, may be ready to save the hands. Five of the thirteen are always Indians. The last of the complement remains on board to steer the vessel during the action. They have no wages; each draws a certain established share in partnership with the proprietor of the vessel, by which economy they are all proportionably concerned in the success of the enterprise and all equally alert and vigilant.

As soon as they arrive in those latitudes where they expect to meet with whales, a man is sent up to the masthead; if he sees one, he immediately cries out "AWAITE PAWANA, here is a whale"; they all remain still and silent until he repeats "PAWANA, a whale," when in less than six minutes the two boats are launched, filled with every implement necessary for the attack.

When these boats are arrived at a reasonable distance, one of them rests on its oars and stands off, as a witness of the approaching engagement; near the bows of the other the harpooner stands up, and on him principally depends the success of the enterprise. He wears a jacket closely buttoned, and round his head a handkerchief tightly bound. In his hands he holds the dreadful weapon—made of the best steel, marked sometimes with the name of their town, and sometimes with that of their vessel—to the shaft of which the end of a cord of due strength, coiled up with the utmost care in the middle of the boat, is firmly tied. The other end is fastened to the bottom of the boat. Thus prepared, they row in profound silence, leaving the whole conduct of the enterprise to the harpooner and to the steersman, attentively following their directions. When the former judges himself to be near enough to the whale, that is, at the distance of about fifteen feet, he bids them stop.

He balances high the harpoon, trying in this important moment to collect all the energy of which he is capable. He launches it forth—she is struck! From her first movement they judge of her temper as well as of their future success. Sometimes, in the immediate impulse of rage, she will attack the boat, and demolish it with one stroke of her tail. Were the whale armed with the jaws of the shark, and as voracious, they never would return home to amuse their listening wives with the interesting tale of the adventure. At other times she will dive and disappear from human sight; and everything must then give way to her velocity, or else all is lost. Sometimes she will swim away as if untouched, and draw the cord with such swiftness that it will set the edge of the boat on fire by the friction. If she rises before she has run out the whole length, she is looked upon as a sure prey. The blood she has lost in her flight weakens her so much, that, if she sinks again, it is but for a short time. The boat follows her course with an almost equal speed. She soon reappears; tired at last with convulsing the element, which she tinges with her blood, she dies, and floats on the surface.

The next operation is to cut, with axes and spades, every part of her body which yields oil; the kettles are set boiling, they fill their barrels as fast as it is made; but, as this operation is much slower than that of cutting-up, they fill the hold of their ship with those fragments, lest a storm should arise and oblige them to abandon their prize.

That long abstemiousness to which these men are exposed, the breathing of saline air, the frequent repetitions of danger, the boldness acquired in surmounting them, the very impulse of the winds to which they are exposed, all these, one would imagine, must lead them when on shore to no small desire of inebriation, and a more eager pursuit of those pleasures of which they have been so long deprived and which they must soon forego. Yet, notwithstanding the powerful effects of all these causes, I observe here, at the return of their fleets, no material irregularities. All was peace here, and a general decency prevailed throughout.

The reason, I believe, is that almost everybody here is married, for they get wives very young; and the pleasure of returning to their families absorbs every other desire. The motives that lead them to the sea are very different from those of most other seafaring men. It is neither idleness nor profligacy that sends them to that element; it is a settled plan of life, a well-founded hope of earning a livelihood; it is because their soil is bad that they are early initiated to this profession. The sea therefore becomes to them a kind of patrimony; they go to whaling with as much pleasure and tranquil indifference, with as strong an expectation of success, as a landman undertakes to clear a piece of swamp.

As I observed, every man takes a wife as soon as he chooses, and that is generally very early. No portion is required, none is expected. No marriage articles are drawn up by skillful lawyers to puzzle and lead posterity to the bar, or to satisfy the pride of the parties. Americans give nothing with their daughters; education, health, and the customary outset, are all that the fathers of numerous families can afford. As the wife's fortune consists principally in her future economy, modesty, and skillful management, so the husband's is founded on his abilities to labor, on his health, and the knowledge of some trade or business. Their mutual endeavors after a few years of constant application seldom fail of success, and of bringing them the means to rear and support the new race which accompanies the nuptial bed.

But you may perhaps be solicitous to ask, what becomes of that exuberancy of population which must arise from so much temperance, from healthiness of climate, and from early marriage. You may justly conclude that their native island and town can contain but a limited number. Emigration is both natural and easy to a maritime people, and that is the very reason why they are always populous. They yearly go to different parts of this continent constantly engaged in sea affairs; as our internal riches increase, so does our external trade, which consequently requires more ships and more men. Sometimes they have emigrated like bees, in regular and connected swarms. Some of the Friends, fond of a contemplative life, yearly visit the several congregations which this society has formed throughout the continent. By their means a sort of correspondence is kept up among them all. By thus traveling, they unavoidably gather the most necessary observations concerning the various situations of particular districts, their soils, their produce, their distance from navigable rivers, the price of the land, and so on.

Thus, though this fruitful hive constantly sends out swarms as industrious as themselves, yet it always remains full without having any useless drones; on the contrary, it exhibits constant scenes of business and new schemes; the richer an individual grows, the more extensive his field of action becomes; he that is near ending his career drudges on as well as he who has just begun it; nobody stands still.

Yet there are not at Nantucket so many wealthy people as one would imagine, after having considered their great successes, their industry, and their knowledge. Many die poor, though hardly able to reproach fortune with a frown; others leave not behind them that affluence which the circle of their business and of their prosperity naturally promised. The reason of this is, I believe, the peculiar expense necessarily attending their tables; for, as their island supplies the town with little or nothing, everyone must procure what they want from the main. A vast number of little vessels from the main and from the Vineyard are constantly resorting here, as to a market. Sherborn is extremely well supplied with everything, but this very constancy of supply necessarily drains off a great deal of money.

There are but two congregations in this town. They assemble every Sunday in meetinghouses, as simple as the dwelling of the people; and there is but one priest on the whole island. This lonely clergyman is a Presbyterian minister, who has a very large and respectable congregation. The other congregation is composed of Quakers, who, you know, admit of no particular person who in consequence of being ordained becomes exclusively entitled to preach, to catechize, and to receive certain salaries for his trouble. Among them, everyone may expound the Scriptures who thinks he is called so to do; beside, as they admit of neither sacrament, baptism, nor any other outward forms whatever, a priest would be useless. Most of these people are continually at sea, and have often the most urgent reasons to worship the Parent of Nature in the midst of the storms which they encounter. These two sects live in perfect peace and harmony with each other; those ancient times of religious discords are now gone (I hope never to return) when each thought it meritorious not only to damn the other, which would have been nothing, but to persecute and murder one another for the glory of that Being who requires no more of us than that we should love one another and live!

Singular as it may appear to you, there are but two medical professors on the island; for of what service can physic be in a primitive society, where the excesses of inebriation are so rare? What need of Galenical medicines, where fevers, and stomachs loaded by the loss of the digestive powers, are so few? Temperance, the calm of passions, frugality, and continual exercise, keep them healthy and preserve unimpaired that constitution which they have received from parents as healthy as themselves, who, in the unpolluted embraces of the earliest and chastest love, conveyed to them the soundest bodily frame which nature could give.

But, as no habitable part of this globe is exempt from some diseases, proceeding either from climate or modes of living, here they are sometimes subject to consumptions and to fevers. Since the foundation of that town no epidemical distempers have appeared which, at times, cause such depopulations in other countries. Many of the people here are extremely well-acquainted with the Indian methods of curing simple diseases, and practice them with success. You will hardly find, anywhere, a community composed of the same number of individuals possessing such uninterrupted health; and this is indeed one of the principal blessings of the island, which richly compensates their want of the richer soils of the South.

One single lawyer has, of late years, found means to live here, but his best fortune proceeds more from having married one of the wealthiest heiresses of the island than from the emoluments of his practice. However, he is sometimes employed in recovering money lent on the main, or in preventing those accidents to which the contentious propensity of its inhabitants may sometimes expose them. He is seldom employed as the means of self-defense, and much seldomer as the channel of attack, to which they are strangers, except the fraud is manifest and the danger imminent.

Here, happily, unoppressed with any civil bondage, this society of fishermen and merchants live, without any military establishments, without governors, or any masters but the laws; and their civil code is so light that it is never felt. A man may pass through the various scenes of a long life, may struggle against a variety of adverse fortune, peaceably enjoy the good when it comes, and never, in that long interval, apply to the law either for redress or assistance. The principal benefit it confers is the general protection of individuals, and this protection is purchased by the most moderate taxes, which are cheerfully paid, and by the trifling duties incident in the course of their lawful trade. Nothing can be more simple than their municipal regulations, though similar to those of the other counties of the same province, because they are more detached from the rest, more distinct in their manners, as well as in the nature of the business they pursue, and more unconnected with the populous province to which they belong. The same simplicity attends the worship they pay to the Divinity; their elders are the only teachers of their congregations, the instructors of their youth, and often the example of their flock. They visit and comfort the sick; after death, the society bury them with their fathers, without pomp, prayers, or ceremonies—not a stone or monument is erected, to tell where any person was buried; their memory is preserved by tradition. The only essential memorial that is left of them is their former industry, their kindness, their charity, or else their most conspicuous faults.

The Presbyterians live in great charity with the Friends, and with one another; their minister, as a true pastor of the gospel, inculcates to them the doctrines it contains, the rewards it promises, the punishments it holds out to those who shall commit injustice. Nothing can be more disencumbered likewise from useless ceremonies and trifling forms than their mode of worship; it might with great propriety have been called a truly primitive one, had that of the Quakers never appeared.

Let me not forget another peculiar characteristic of this community: there is not a slave, I believe, on the whole island, at least among the Friends; whilst slavery prevails all around them, this society alone, lamenting that shocking insult offered to humanity, has given the world a singular example of moderation, disinterestedness, and Christian charity, in emancipating their Negroes.

The manners of "The Friends" are entirely founded on that simplicity which is their boast, and their most distinguished characteristic; and those manners have acquired the authority of laws. Here they are strongly attached to plainness of dress as well as to that of language. They are so tenacious of their ancient habits of industry and frugality that, if any of them were to be seen with a long coat, made of English cloth, on any other than the First Day (Sunday), he would be greatly

ridiculed and censured; he would be looked upon as a careless spend-
thrift whom it would be unsafe to trust and in vain to relieve. A few
years ago two single-horse chairs were imported from Boston, to the
great offence of these prudent citizens; nothing appeared to them more
culpable than the use of such gaudy painted vehicles, in contempt of
the more useful and more simple single-horse carts of their fathers.
One of the possessors of these profane chairs, filled with repentance,
wisely sent it back to the continent; the other, more obstinate and perverse, in defiance of all remonstrances, persisted in the use of this chair
until by degrees they became more reconciled to it, though I observed
that the wealthiest and the most respectable people still go to meeting
or to their farms in a single-horse cart, with a decent awning fixed
over it.

Idleness is the most heinous sin that can be committed in Nantucket. This principle is so thoroughly well understood, and is become
so universal, so prevailing a prejudice, that, literally speaking, they are
never idle. Even if they go to the market place, which is, if I may be
allowed the expression, the coffeehouse of the town, either to transact
business or to converse with their friends, they always have a piece of
cedar in their hands, and, while they are talking, they will instinctively
employ themselves in converting it into something useful. I must confess that I have never seen more ingenuity in the use of the knife; thus
the most idle moments of their lives become usefully employed. In the
many hours of leisure, which their long cruises afford them, they cut
and carve a variety of boxes and pretty toys in wood, adapted to different uses, which they bring home as testimonies of remembrance to
their wives or sweethearts. Therefore, almost every man in this island
has always two knives in his pocket, one much larger than the other,
and, though they hold everything that is called fashion in the utmost
contempt, yet they are as difficult to please, and as extravagant in the
choice and price of their knives as any young buck in Boston would be
about his hat, buckles, or coat.

As the sea excursions are often very long, their wives, in their absence, are necessarily obliged to transact business, to settle accounts,
and, in short, to rule and provide for their families. These circumstances
being often repeated give women the abilities as well as a taste for that
kind of superintendency, to which, by their prudence and good management, they seem to be in general very equal. This employment

ripens their judgment, and justly entitles them to a rank superior to that of other wives; and this is the principle reason why those of Nantucket are so fond of society, so affable, and so conversant with the affairs of the world. The men at their return, weary with the fatigues of the sea, full of confidence and love, cheerfully give their consent to every transaction that has happened during their absence, and all is joy and peace. "Wife, thee hast done well" is the general approbation they receive for their application and industry.

To this dexterity, in managing the husband's business whilst he is absent, the Nantucket wives unite a great deal of industry. They spin or cause to be spun, in their houses, abundance of wool and flax, and would be forever disgraced and looked upon as idlers if all the family were not clad in good, neat, and sufficient homespun cloth. Only on First Days is it lawful for both sexes to exhibit some garments of English manufacture; even these are of the most moderate price, and of the gravest colors. There is no kind of difference in their dress, they are all clad alike, and resemble in that respect the members of one family.

4.

MORAVIAN TRAVELS IN THE INTERIOR

This graphic account of travel in the Revolutionary era records the journey of Bishop John Frederick Reichel of the Moravian Church to a frontier outpost in North Carolina. The Bishop had been commissioned by a Synod in Saxony in 1775 to inspect the Moravian communities in America and to make sure they were organized in accordance with the rules of the Church. He arrived in Pennsylvania in 1779 and, in the next year, set out for Salem in the company of his wife, three other couples, one single Brother, and one single Sister, together with four teamsters who managed the equipment. The diary, "Reise-Diarium der Geschw. Reichels" (1780), from which this extract was drawn, was kept by one of the group en route.

May 22, 1780. Journeying from Lititz in Pennsylvania to Salem in the Wachau (North Carolina), we reached Anderson's Ferry, where the Susquehannah is one and one-quarter miles wide. On the side from

which we approached there is a high sandy bank, and the wheels of
Conrad's wagon sank to the axle in the sand, and were freed only after
one and a half hours of work with levers and extra horses. On the other
side is a high stony ridge. We were so fortunate as to get our two
wagons and three riding horses across within two hours, by means of
two Flats, which are too small for a river of such considerable size; but
frequently travelers are detained here for an entire day. Each crossing
takes only ten minutes, and the ferrymen race with each other. But they
had to cross over and back three times, and the loading and unloading
takes as much time as the crossing. Here they charge $56 (Continental)
for taking over a six-horse wagon, and $8 for a horse and rider; at
Wright's Ferry, where the Susquehannah is two miles wide, the charge
is $90 for a six-horse wagon, and $12 for a horse and rider. Some two
miles from the Susquehannah, on a creek called Susquehannah Creek,
we made our first outdoor night camp, in a pretty open space surrounded by tall trees.

The 23. After strengthening ourselves with coffee at breakfast we
traveled to the top of the Susquehannah ridge, from whence a beautiful
view of plantations, houses, fields, orchards and meadows, hills and
valleys, extended all the way to York, which we reached about eleven
o'clock. We made 17 miles today, and camped for the night on a green
hill close by a house. Here for the first time we were all in tents, and
rested very well.

The 24. It was so cold a morning that we could scarcely keep warm
at breakfast. We broke camp at six o'clock. This morning in a rough
piece of woodland, Conrad's wagon, in going down a hill, ran into a
tree and crushed the left front wheel. We thanked the Saviour that
the wagon and horses were not thrown to the ground, for it looked as
if that might easily have happened. This accident detained us an hour
until the wagon could be repaired. At one-thirty we reached Hanover
where we had a beautiful midday rest in a barn. We refreshed ourselves on the good beer to be obtained here. Toward evening we passed
through Petersburg and camped for the night two miles farther on, on
the Maryland line.

The 25. The morning again was cool. It was after six o'clock when
we broke camp. Taneytown is a little village with one solitary street,
lying seven miles from our camp at a point where the forests are
sprinkled with pines. The road thither was full of people today, as it

was the Catholic festival of Corpus Christi and they were going to the Catholic Church in Taneytown. On the way we passed the home of Adam Loesch, and spoke with him. He was planning to sell his house and move to Holston River in Virginia, four hundred miles from there. Beyond Taneytown, which we had reached at nine-thirty, Hauser's wagon almost upset. Br. Reichel had alighted when to our pleasure we were met by Br. Schweisshaupt, and the two Brethren Weller and Kampf from Monocacy, the road from the latter place here coming out into the main road to Frederick, Maryland. They showed us the way to a pretty midday resting place on Pine Creek, over which there is a bridge now impassable.

Br. Schweisshaupt and the two Brn. from Monocacy, who were able to supply us with fresh provision, accompanied us for two miles to the place where the road from Baltimore to Monocacy crosses the road to Carolina at right angles, then took friendly leave of us, commending us to the good guidance of our God. From there it is nine miles to Monocacy, and about fifty to Baltimore. Today we made twenty miles, and camped about seventy-five miles from Lititz and eight from Frederick, in a beautiful green spot.

The 26. At seven-thirty we crossed the Monocacy, and at nine-thirty reached Frederick, where we stopped at the inn of Mr. Grosh, where we had a good meal. He has a pleasant English wife, who waited on us in a kind and courteous manner; she has many lively, attractive children, who speak only English. The old father is still bright and well.

Frederick has a pleasant location, a stream runs through it, and it contains good houses. Congress money still has good value here—40 to 1—many say 30 to 1; indeed there is little silver in the town. It was necessary for us to exchange silver for Congress money, as we were going into Virginia where for the most part there is little money and silver is little used, and Br. Blum found a man who gave us 55 for 1. Then we resumed our journey, and made camp near Mr. Th. Noland's house, close to the road which turns to the right from the Foart Road towards Noland's Ferry, which crosses the Potomac two miles from here.

So far our journey had been very pleasant. Now, however, the Virginia air brought storms. Here and there in the woods we saw Virginia cabins, built of unhewn logs and without windows. Kitchen, living room, bedroom, and hall are all in one room into which one enters when the house door opens. The chimney is built at the gable end, of unhewn logs looking like trees, or it is omitted altogether. Everywhere we saw the Negroes moving about; one came in the evening to our tent, probably to see what was worth stealing. Neither we nor the teamsters liked the place, which was not convenient for a camp; but no one knew of a better place or had the courage to seek one, for the sun had set when we reached there. Yet all had a presentiment of impending trouble.

The 27. The next morning, rising early, we found that Br. Reichel's chest, containing all his books and papers, the Deed to the Wachau, letters, and his and his wife's clothing, had been stolen from the wagon, together with a flask of rum, some food, and Hauser's sickles and clothing, which filled us with consternation! This delayed our further journey until about eight o'clock. Br. Aust rode back two miles to tell Leonh. Heil, who keeps an inn. He returned with him at once, and Heil suggested writing out a description of the stolen articles, which could be put into an advertisement and posted up everywhere, and this was at once done. He promised to do his best to find the stolen goods. Meanwhile Mr. Th. Noland had risen, and was informed of the occurrence. He seemed much embarrassed and perplexed, and said he feared the theft had been committed by some of his Negroes, and promised to try and find the guilty party. He rode two miles into the woods saying they had probably hidden the things there, but soon returned saying he believed the thieves had fled across the Potomac. On this supposition Leonh. Heil went with us to the Potomac, and promised the ferrymen, who are also Negroes, that they should have a large fee if they would find the stolen property.

Mr. Th. Noland and his father and father-in-law have two hundred Negroes in this neighborhood, on both sides of the Potomac, and this neighborhood is far-famed for robbery and theft. Travelers should take care here. The road on to the Potomac was bad. Going down a steep hill to a bridge Hauser's wagon almost upset, which excited much alarm. About nine o'clock we reached the Potomac, and as there was only one small ferry boat it was eleven-thirty before we and the wagons and horses were all across.

It was very hot today, and there was a storm in the afternoon. Sr. Reichel was not quite well these two days. Our journey today was short, and we made our night camp two miles from Leesburg.

This evening the two Carolina riding horses ran away again two miles into the woods. It took Br. Blum until eleven o'clock to find and bring them back, and meanwhile his traveling coat, which he had hung on a stump between the tents, was stolen, as were also two bells, two towels, and the feed sacks. We now keep watch all night, but the watchman could not prevent this theft, for the night was very dark and the Negroes, who had a free evening, were roaming everywhere. We have learned by sad experience that Virginia is full of thieves.

The 28. We made our noonday camp on the great Goose Creek, eight miles beyond Leesburg, and as it was Sunday we rested until four o'clock. The way here, and beyond, was very hilly and stony. We cooked with rice the hens we had bought in Leesburg, but the pot tipped over and we had to cook a second time. In the afternoon we made five miles more, and stopped for the night in an open place by a run.

The 29. In the morning we found that the two Carolina horses had run off through the woods towards home, and they fed themselves bountifully in a fine field of clover. The worst of it was that we suspected they had been stolen, which might easily happen to us in Virginia where there is much horse stealing, and we thought this the more because a man, whom we later learned to be only simple, had hung about eyeing our every movement as intently as though he were watching someone or were planning some roguery. As we thought that the quickest way to recover the horses would be to promise a reward to the rogue, we did so, but the horses did not appear. Having spent till eight o'clock on the matter we then continued our journey, leaving Br. Blum to seek the horses; and with the help of three men, to whom he had to give over a hundred dollars Continental currency for their trouble, he found them about midday in the aforesaid clover field, and brought them to us after we had camped for the night. At noon we had halted in the woods, one and a half miles from Red House. Red House is 25 miles from Leesburg, and 130 from Lititz, that is, 195 from Bethlehem. We camped for the night eight miles beyond Red House. The ticks, whose acquaintance we had already made at the Susquehannah, now began to be very troublesome.

The 30. We soon reached Nevill's Tavern, which is ten miles from Red House, and six miles further passed through Germantown—when one is in the town one asks where the town is. Today we made only fourteen miles, partly on account of the hilly, rough, and marshy road, partly because Hauser's wagon broke several times and got stuck in a deep hole, and it took four extra horses (that is, ten in all) to pull and twist it out. Since we left the Potomac it has thundered every day and especially this entire afternoon, and in the evening it began to rain and rained all night, so that tents and beds and clothes were all soaked.

The 31. It was very muddy and wet, but we made fair progress. About eight-thirty we forded the Rappahannock, where there is neither bridge nor ferry. After a heavy rainstorm we halted for our midday lunch. Then we went on through thunder and rain till we reached a new house, whose owner, Mr. Shelton, had gone on a trip to North Carolina. His wife, who had two sick children, gave friendly answer to our request and showed us into a room where there were four beautiful double beds. We were glad to be under a roof, and to sleep in the dry. As a matter of precaution Br. and Sr. Blum stayed with the wagons, which drove a little farther into the woods.

June 2. We started at 5:30 A.M. and crossed the Rapidan safely. The water only came up to the wagon beds today. Here the teamsters bought a good supply of feed for the horses, for we were approaching the section where the English prisoners were and knew we would be able to get little, as the commissary had bought it up for them. After crossing the Rapidan one follows the bank of the river for about four miles, and all kinds of beautiful trees are mingled together. If a town were laid out here and the land brought into a better state of cultivation this would be an unusually pretty section. In spite of the hills we made twenty miles today, which is much for us.

The 3. We started out at five o'clock and made twenty-three miles, which was our longest day's journey. It was very hot and oppressive, and in the afternoon we had a severe thunderstorm and heavy rain. About five o'clock, as Conrad was trying in vain to force his horses to pull the wagon over a particularly steep place, there was a flash of lightning and crack of thunder, and instantly the horses had the wagon over the bad place. Hauser's wagon was standing by a mudhole, and his horses shied, almost upsetting the wagon. We camped half a mile from Bird's Ordinary. (Ordinary is the Virginia name for an inn.)

The 4. We wished to make an early start, but Conrad's horses strayed off, and that detained us two hours. It would have been longer had not Br. Stoehr found them and brought them to our camp. We shortened our midday rest because eight continental wagons camped near us. Already on the 28th and 29th of May we had met a number of wagons, belonging with these, which had been to South Carolina with arms and ammunition and were now returning. We made about eighteen miles today, and camped for the night half a mile from Payne's Tavern in a large uncultivated field in which a schoolhouse stood.

The 5. We had seven miles to go to reach the James River, which we crossed by means of a small ferry, getting over about eleven o'clock. To reach the ferry we had to drive down such a steep and badly washed hill that it was a wonder that the wagon did not turn over. On the other side of the river we lunched on a beautiful green height. In the afternoon we refreshed ourselves on the first ripe cherries. From two gentlemen, who came through Salem, we received certain information that Charleston had been forced to surrender to the British, the report being confirmed by the stories of both sides. This made a great stir in Virginia. From there on we saw many people fleeing from South and North Carolina, and the Virginians thought us queer creatures to be going to North Carolina. While we were camped six miles from Cumberland Courthouse a hundred militiamen rode by, who had been drafted at Cumberland Courthouse. A drunken fellow kept us a whole hour that evening telling us the circumstances of the capture of Charleston. We were thankful when he finally departed without talking all night.

The 6. We set out at five o'clock, and passed Cumberland Courthouse. In the afternoon we went five or six miles out of our way, for the Appomattox ford was impassable and the teamsters thought a side track to the right would lead to a bridge across the creek. It thundered and rained and grew to be dark night before we found a place where there was water and where we could camp. We were now in a section where there are few springs, and the soil is mostly sand, glittering with isinglass.

The 7. Starting about six o'clock we found the right way to the bridge over the Appomattox, which we crossed about eight-thirty. It is a small but deep stream, with steep banks which make fording impossible. From then till noon we traveled a miserable road over hills and valleys, and through a creek with steep banks, and saw large orchards along the way. In the afternoon, after we had passed the Academy, which had many broken windowpanes, our track turned again into the

main road. In the evening after we had set up our tents there came
a thunder and rain storm. We were twenty-eight miles from Roanoke
River.

The 8. During the morning we met Mr. Shelton, in whose house we
spent the night of May 31. We gave him news of his family, and he expressed pleasure that we had lodged there. We crossed a bridge over
the little Roanoke, a small but very deep stream, and passed Charlotte
Courthouse. We had rain until nearly noon, when it cleared somewhat.
But as we finished lunch there came a thunderstorm with strong wind
and pouring rain. We crept into and under the wagons and so protected
ourselves from the rain. In the afternoon it was clear, and we crossed
marshy ground on a corduroy road half a mile long, to drive over which
would certainly be good medicine for a hypochondriac. We spent the
night in a pretty open green spot, where we ate the first journeycakes
with a good appetite. It was a very cool night.

The 9. In the morning we crossed a bridge all full of holes, and were
grateful to the Saviour for our safety as we considered the very apparent danger. We also passed safely through the deep bottom as we
neared Roanoke River and across its ford whose steep approaches gave
the teamsters much trouble. It took eight horses to pull Conrad's wagon
out, and that with difficulty. On the farther bank we stopped at noon,
and nine miles beyond made our night's camp.

The 10. The roads were very bad. Steep hills washed by the heavy
rains alternated with deep bottoms and swampy places. Everything
fell out of the wagons. Our night camp was half a mile from Old Halifax, one hundred miles from Salem.

The 11. When we were in Old Halifax we asked about this famous
town and received the information, "You are in the very city." There
are only a couple of houses here. Sr. Reichel had a headache today, but
it was better in the afternoon. At noon as she lay on a bed in the shade
a hog jumped over her because the dog was after it, and that cured her.
(This creature is far too familiar in Virginia, and must be forcibly
driven away.) The heat was great, and we had storms every day. We
made nineteen miles today, and camped at Lynch's Tavern.

The 13. A miserable road, ruts filled with sand by the rain, stony,
hilly, and full of holes. Hauser nearly had a bad accident with his
horses and wagon, for as they were going down a steep hill the breast
chain broke and the near horse was thrown under the wheel; but the

driver saw it in time and the horse escaped serious injury, being only scratched on the crupper and one foot. The hand of the Lord protected us so that we did not have a terrible misfortune. This morning we crossed the Carolina line, and our noon rest was for the first time on Carolina soil.

The 14. In the morning we came to within a short mile of the Mayo River. As we rested by a beautiful spring we were joined by a Presbyterian minister, who came hither from Virginia last spring, and who asked us all sorts of questions concerning our position on political matters, and after an earnest but discreet conversation bade us a friendly farewell. There is an outdoor pulpit here where he probably preaches. The semblance of a pulpit is built of logs and boards fastened between two trees; the benches are of logs, resting on blocks.

The 15. We rose early and took up our journey with joy, crossing the Dan River safely, and reaching the Brethren in Salem at about six in the evening, thankful to the Saviour who had guided and led us like children, and had given us to feel His peace and presence throughout the entire way. We were welcomed with trombones, which played "Euren Eingang segen Gott."

June 16. The wagons, which were left behind yesterday, arrived safely this morning. And so we are in Salem, in this town of the Lord's peace—may He bless us and be with us in all we shall do for Him. Amen!

5.

A REVOLUTIONARY IN THE MAKING

Jean Pierre Brissot, the son of an innkeeper, was born in Chartres in 1754. He studied law but broke with his father over religion and, at the age of twenty, set off for Paris to pursue a literary career. Swept away by the spirit of the Enlightenment, he became interested in reform, specializing, after the manner of the times, in chemistry and in criminal law. He traveled in England and in Switzerland, but early came to regard the United States as the model for a new society. By 1788 he had already expressed that view in books attacking Chastellux for unfavorable comments, and defending Crèvecœur, for favorable ones. In that year, with Crèvecœur and others, Brissot organized a Gallo-American society to develop commerce between the two nations, and set off for the New World as agent for a syndicate that wished to speculate in American debts and American lands.

Brissot returned to become deeply involved in revolutionary politics. A leader of the Girondins, he was executed in 1793 when the radical Jacobins seized power. Meanwhile his work, Nouveau Voyage dans les États-Unis de l'Amérique septentrionale *(1791), had proved immensely popular; within the decade, it would be published in translation in Germany, England, America, and Sweden.*

Boston is just rising from the devastations of war, and its commerce is flourishing; its manufactures, productions, arts, and sciences, suggest a number of curious and interesting observations.

The manners of the people are not exactly the same as described by M. de Crèvecœur. You no longer meet here that Puritan austerity which interdicted all pleasures, even that of walking; which forbade traveling on Sunday; which induced men to persecute those whose opinions were different from their own. The Bostonians now unite simplicity of customs with that French politeness and delicacy of manners which render virtue more amiable. They are hospitable to strangers and obliging to friends; they are tender husbands, fond and almost idolatrous parents, and kind masters. Music, which their teachers formerly proscribed as a diabolic art, begins to form part of their education. In some houses you hear the pianoforte. This art, it is true, is still in its infancy; but the young novices who exercise it are so gentle, so complaisant, and so modest, that the proud perfection of art gives no pleasure equal to what they afford.

The young women here enjoy the liberty they do in England, that they did in Geneva when morals were there and the republic existed; and they do not abuse it. Their frank and tender hearts have nothing to fear from the perfidy of men. Examples of this perfidy are rare; the vows of love are believed; and love always respects them, or shame forever follows the guilty.

The Bostonian mothers are reserved; their air is however frank, good, and communicative. Entirely devoted to their families, they are occupied in rendering their husbands happy, and in training their children. The law which imposes heavy penalties such as the pillory and imprisonment for adultery has scarcely ever been called into execution, because families are happy; and they are pure, because they are happy.

Neatness without luxury is a characteristic feature of this purity of manners; and this neatness is seen everywhere in Boston—in dress, in houses, and in churches. Nothing is more charming than a church on Sunday. The good cloth coat covers the men, while calicoes and chintzes serve the women and children, unspoiled by those gewgaws which whim and caprice have added among our women. Powder and pomade never sully the heads of infants and children. I see them with pain, however, on the heads of men who invoke the art of the hairdresser; for, unhappily, this art has already crossed the seas.

I shall never call to mind, without emotion, the pleasure I had one day in hearing a sermon by Mr. Clarke, successor to the learned Doctor Cooper, to whom every good Frenchman, and every friend of liberty, owes a tribute of gratitude for the love he bore the French and the zeal with which he defended and preached American independence. I remarked in his audience the exterior ease and contentment of which I have spoken; that collected calmness resulting from the habit of gravity and the conscious presence of the Almighty; that religious decency which is equally distant from groveling idolatry and from the light and wanton airs of those Europeans who go to a church as to a theater. But to crown my happiness, I saw none of those livid wretches covered with rags, who in Europe, soliciting our compassion at the foot of the altar, seem to bear testimony against Providence, our humanity, and the disorder of society. The discourse, the prayer, the worship, everything had the same simplicity. The sermon breathed the best morality and was heard with attention.

The excellence of this morality characterizes almost all the sermons of all the sects throughout the Continent. Universal tolerance, the product of American independence, has banished the preaching of dogmas, which always leads to discussion and quarrels. All the sects admit nothing but morality, which is the same in all, and the only preaching proper for a great society of brothers. Everyone at present worships God in his own way. Anabaptists, Methodists, Quakers, and even Catholics, profess openly their opinions. The ministers of different sects live in such harmony that they supply each other's places when any one is detained from his pulpit.

Before this opinion was so general among them, they had established another: the necessity of reducing divine worship to the greatest
simplicity, to disconnect it from all the superstitious ceremonies which
gave it the appearance of idolatry; and particularly, not to give their
priests enormous salaries to enable them to live in luxury and idleness—
in a word, to restore evangelical simplicity. They have succeeded. In
the country the church has a glebe; in town the ministers live on collections made each Sunday in the church and on the rent of pews. It is
an excellent practice to induce the ministers to be diligent in their
studies and faithful in their duty. For the preference is given to him
whose discourses please the most, and his salary is the most considerable, while among us the ignorant and the learned, the debauchee and
the man of virtue, are always sure of their livings.

Since the ancient Puritan austerity has disappeared, you are no
longer surprised to see a game of cards introduced among these good
Congregationalists. When the mind is tranquil, in the enjoyment of
competence and peace, it is natural to occupy it in this way, especially
in a country where there is no theater, where men do not make a business of paying court to the women, where they read few books, and
cultivate still less the sciences. This taste for cards is certainly unhappy
in a republican state; the habit contracts the mind. Happily it is not
very considerable in Boston. You see here no fathers of families risking
their whole fortunes in it.

There are many clubs in Boston. I went several times to a private
club that convened once a week, and was much pleased with their
politeness to strangers and the knowledge displayed in their conversation. There is no true café in Boston, New York, or Philadelphia. One
house in each town, that they call a coffeehouse, serves as a merchants'
exchange.

One of the principal pleasures of the inhabitants of these towns
consists in little parties in the country among families and friends. The
principal expense, especially after dinner, is tea. In this, as in their
whole manner of living, the Americans in general resemble the English. Punch, warm and cold, before dinner, excellent beef and mutton,
always solidly and abundantly served, and Spanish, Madeira, and Bordeaux wines cover their tables. Spruce beer, excellent cider, and Philadelphia porter precede the wines. This porter is equal to the English;
its manufacture saves a vast tribute formerly paid to the English indus-

try. The same may soon be said with respect to cheese. I have often found American cheese equal to the best Cheshire of England, or the Roquefort of France. This may with truth be said of that made on Governor Bowdoin's farm in Weymouth.

After forcing the English to give up their domination, the Americans determined to rival them in everything. This spirit of emulation has opened to the Bostonians many channels of commerce which lead them to all parts of the globe. No danger, no distance, no obstacle impedes them. What have they to fear? All mankind are their brethren; they wish peace with all.

The same spirit of emulation shows itself everywhere. It has erected at Boston an extensive glass manufactory, belonging to Mr. Breck and others. It has brought to perfection so many manufactories of cordage in this town and has erected filatures for hemp and flax, proper to occupy young people without crowding them together in such numbers as to ruin their health and their morals; proper likewise, to occupy that class of women whom the long voyages of seafaring husbands and other contingencies reduce to inactivity. To the same spirit are also due the salt, nail, paper, and paper-hanging factories which have multiplied in this state. The rum distilleries are on the decline since the suppression of the slave trade, in which this liquor was employed, and since the diminution of the use of strong spirits by the country people. This is fortunate for the human race; and American industry will soon repair the small loss it sustains from the decline of this fabrication of poisons.

Boston has the glory of having given in 1636 the first college or university to the New World. It is located on an extensive plain, four miles from Boston, at a place called Cambridge. The imagination could not fix on a place that could better unite all the conditions essential to a seat of education, sufficiently near to Boston to enjoy all the advantages of communication with Europe and the rest of the world, and yet sufficiently distant not to expose the students to the contagion of licentious manners common in commercial towns.

The air of Cambridge is pure, and the environs charming, offering a vast space for the exercise of the youth. The buildings are large, numerous, and well distributed. But, as the number of students increases every day, it will be necessary soon to add to the buildings. The library, and the cabinet of natural philosophy, do honor to the institution. The former contains 13,000 volumes. The heart of a Frenchman

palpitates on finding the works of Racine, of Montesquieu, and the
Encyclopedia, where one hundred and fifty years ago arose the smoke
of the savage calumet.

The regulation of the course of studies here is nearly the same as
that at the University of Oxford. But the late revolution must inevitably
introduce a great reform. Free men ought to strip themselves of their
prejudices, to perceive that, above all, it is necessary to be a man and
a citizen, and that the study of the dead languages, of a fastidious
philosophy and theology, ought to occupy few moments of a life which
might be usefully employed in studies more advantageous to the human
race. Such a change in studies is the more probable, as an academy
has been formed in Boston, composed of respectable men who cultivate all the sciences and who, disengaged from religious prejudices,
will doubtless soon contrive a course of education, more directly and
more certainly calculated to form good citizens and philosophers.

Mr. Bowdoin, president of this academy, is a man of universal talents. He combines with profound erudition the virtues of a magistrate
and the principles of a republican politician. His conduct has never
disappointed the confidence of his fellow citizens, though his son-in-
law, Mr. Temple, incurred their universal detestation for his activity
during the war and his open attachment to the British since the peace,
for all of which the English have given him the post of consulate-
general in America.

But to return to the university of Cambridge, superintended by
President Willard. Among the associates in the conduct of the studies,
Dr. Wigglesworth and Dr. Dexter are distinguished. The latter is professor of natural philosophy, chemistry, and medicine, a man of extensive knowledge and great modesty. He told me, to my great satisfaction,
that he gave lectures on the experiments of our school of chemistry.
The excellent work of my respectable master, Dr. Fourcroy, was in his
hands; from it he learned of the rapid strides that this science has lately
made in Europe.

In a free country everything ought to bear the stamp of patriotism.
This patriotism, so happily displayed in the foundation, endowment,
and encouragement of this university, is demonstrated every year in
a solemn feast celebrated at Cambridge in honor of the sciences. This
feast, which takes place once a year in all the colleges of America, is

called commencement and resembles the exercises and distribution of prizes in our colleges. It is a day of joy for Boston; almost all its inhabitants assemble in Cambridge. The most distinguished students display their talents in the presence of the public; and these exercises, which are generally on patriotic subjects, are terminated by an open-air feast, where the freest gaiety and the most cordial fraternity reign.

The sciences are not carried on to any high degree in countries chiefly devoted to commerce. This remark applies to Boston. The university certainly contains men of worth and learning; but science is not diffused among the inhabitants of the town. Commerce occupies all their ideas, turns all their heads, and absorbs all their speculations. Thus you come across few worth-while works, and few authors. The costs of the first volume of the memoirs of the academy of this town has not yet been covered, although it is two years since it appeared. Some time ago a very well written *History of the Late Troubles in Massachusetts* was published. The author found it difficult to indemnify himself for the expense of printing it. For want of encouragement, the valuable history of Massachusetts by Winthrop has never appeared as a whole.

Poets, for the same reason, must be even rarer than other writers. An original but lazy poet, by the name of Allen, has some reputation; his verses are said to be full of warmth and force. His manuscript poem on the famous battle of Bunker Hill is particularly mentioned; but he will not print it. He is as careless as La Fontaine of his fame and his money.

They publish one magazine here, but the number of newspapers is very considerable. The multiplicity of gazettes reflects the activity of commerce, and the taste for politics and news; the merits and variety of literary and political magazines are signs of the culture of the sciences.

You may judge from these details that the arts, except those that respect navigation, do not receive much encouragement here. The history of Mr. Pope's planetarium is a proof of it. Mr. Pope is a very ingenious clockmaker. The machine which he constructed to explain the movement of the heavenly bodies is astonishing, especially in view of the fact that he received no help from Europe and very little from books. He owes the whole to himself; he is, like the painter Trumbull, the child of nature and of meditation. After ten years of his life were occupied in perfecting this planetarium, he opened a subscription to pay for his trouble; but the subscription was never completed.

This discouraged artist told me one day that he would go to Europe to sell this machine and to construct others. "This country," said he, "is too poor to encourage the arts." These words, "This country is too poor," struck me. I reflected that if they were pronounced in Europe they might lead to wrong ideas of America; for the idea of poverty carries with it that of rags, of hunger, and no country is more distant from that sad condition. Riches centered in a few hands accumulate in great surpluses which may be applied to pleasures and to the agreeable and frivolous arts. But riches equally divided in society leave little in the way of surplus and consequently few means of encouraging the arts. Yet which of these societies is rich, and which poor? According to the European ideas, and in the sense of Mr. Pope, the first is rich; but to the eye of reason it is not. For the other is the happiest. Therefore, the ability to encourage the agreeable arts is a symptom of national calamity.

Let us not blame the Bostonians; they think of the useful before the beautiful. They have no brilliant monuments, but they have neat and commodious churches, they have good houses, they have superb bridges, and excellent ships. Their streets are well illuminated at night, while many ancient cities of Europe containing proud monuments of art have never yet thought of preventing the fatal effects of nocturnal darkness.

Besides the societies for the encouragement of agriculture and manufactures, they have another, known as the Humane Society, the object of which is to recover drowned persons. It is formed after the model of the one at London, as that is copied from the one at Paris. They follow the same methods as in Europe, and have made important rescues. The Medical Society is as useful. It corresponds with all the country towns to learn the symptoms of local diseases, proposes the proper remedies, and gives instruction to all the citizens.

Another worthy establishment is the almshouse, set up for the poor, who by age and infirmity are unable to gain their living. It contains at present about one hundred and fifty persons. Still another, called the workhouse, or house of correction, is not so much peopled as you might imagine. In a rising country, in an active port, where provisions are

cheap, good morals predominate and the number of thieves and vaga-
bonds is small. These are vermin attached to misery, and there is no
misery here.

The profession of the law is unhappily one of the most lucrative
employments in the state. The expensive forms of the English practice,
which good sense and the love of order ought to suppress, are still
preserved here and render advocates necessary. These have likewise
borrowed from their fathers, the English, the habit of demanding exorbitant fees. But notwithstanding the abuses of legal proceedings,
there are few complaints against the lawyers. Men like Sumner, Wendell, Lowell, and Sullivan, with whom I have been acquainted, appear
to enjoy a great reputation for integrity. They did themselves honor
in the affair of the Tender Act, by working against its enactment, and
afterwards, by struggling, as much as possible, against its unjust effects.
The law of March 1788, which condemns to heavy penalties all persons
who import or export slaves or who are concerned in this infamous
traffic, is also attributed in part to their enlightened philanthropy.
Finally, they took a prominent part in the Revolution, by their writings,
by their discourses, and by participation in the affairs of Congress and
in foreign negotiations.

To recall this memorable period brings to mind one of the greatest
ornaments of the American bar, the celebrated John Adams, who, from
the humble station of schoolmaster raised himself to the highest dig-
nities; whose name is as much respected in Europe as in his own country, for the difficult missions with which he was charged. He has finally
returned to his retreat with the applause of his fellow-citizens, and is
occupied in the cultivation of his farm, forgetting what he was when
he trampled on the pride of his king, who had once put a price upon
his head, and who was then forced to receive him as the ambassador
of a free country.

Mr. Adams is not the only man distinguished in this great Revolution who has retired to the obscure labors of a country life. General
Heath is another worthy imitator of the Roman Cincinnatus, for he
likes not the American Cincinnati: their eagle appears to him a gew-
gaw, proper only for children. With what joy did this respectable man
show me all parts of his farm! What happiness he enjoys on it! He is a
true farmer. A glass of cider which he presented to me with frankness
and good humor appeared to me superior to the most exquisite wines.

With this simplicity men are worthy of liberty, and they are sure of enjoying it for a long time.

This simplicity characterizes almost all the men of this state who have acted distinguished parts in the Revolution: such, among others, as Samuel Adams and Mr. Hancock, the present governor. If ever a man was sincerely an idolater of republicanism, it is Samuel Adams; and never a man united more virtues to give respect to his opinions: untainted probity, simplicity, modesty, and above all, firmness. He will have no mediation with abuses; he fears as much the despotism of virtue and talents as the despotism of vice. Cherishing the greatest love and respect for Washington, he voted to take from him the command at the end of a certain term; he recollected that Caesar only succeeded in overturning the republic by prolonging his command of the army. Events have proved the analogy false; but it was by a miracle, and the safety of a country should not be risked on faith in a miracle.

Samuel Adams is the best supporter of Governor Hancock's party. You know the great sacrifices which the latter made in the Revolution and the boldness with which he declared himself at the beginning of the insurrection. The same spirit of patriotism animates him still. Great generosity combined with vast ambition dominate his character. He has the virtues and the manner of popularism; that is to say, that, without effort, he shows himself the equal and the friend of all. I supped at his house with a hatter who appeared to be intimately familiar with him. Mr. Hancock is amiable and polite when he wishes to be; but they say he does not always choose it. He has a marvelous gout, which excuses him from all obligations and forbids access to his house. Mr. Hancock has not the learning of his rival, Mr. Bowdoin; he seems even to disdain the sciences. The latter is more esteemed by enlightened men; the former more beloved by the people.

The distance between Boston and New York is about 260 miles. Many persons have united in establishing a kind of diligence, or public stage, which passes regularly for the convenience of travelers. In the summer season the journey is performed in four days.

We set out from Boston at four o'clock in the morning, and passed through the handsome town of Cambridge. The country appears well cultivated as far as Weston, where we breakfasted; thence we passed to Worcester to dinner, 48 miles from Boston. This town is elegant and well peopled; the printer Isaiah Thomas has rendered it famous through all the continent. He prints most of the works which appear; and it must be granted his editions are correct. The tavern, where we had a good American dinner, is a charming house of wood, well ornamented; it is kept by Mr. Pease, one of the proprietors of the Boston stage. He deserves much credit for his activity and industry; but it is to be hoped that he will change the present plan so far as it respects his horses. These are overworked with the length and difficulty of the courses, which ruins them in a short time besides very much delaying the journey.

We slept the first night at Spenser, a new village in the midst of the woods. The tavern was but half built; but the finished part had an air of cleanliness which pleases because it bespoke a degree of competence and moral and delicate habits never seen in our French villages. The chambers were neat, the beds good, the sheets clean, supper passable, cider, tea, punch, and all for fourteen pence a head.

We left Spenser at four o'clock in the morning, new carriage, new proprietor. This was a kind of wagon without springs. A Frenchman who was with me began, at the first jolt, to curse the carriage, the driver, and the country. "Let us wait a little," said I, "before we form a judgment; every custom has its cause. There is doubtless some reason why this kind of carriage is preferred to one hung with springs." Indeed, by the time we had run thirty miles among the rocks we were persuaded that a carriage with springs would very soon have turned over and crashed.

The traveler is well rewarded for the fatigue of this route by the variety of romantic situations, by the beauty of the prospects which it offers at each step, by the perpetual contrast of savage nature and the efforts of art. Country houses may be seen through all the forests of Massachusetts. Neatness characterizes them all. They have frequently but one story and a garret; their walls are papered; tea and coffee appear on their tables; their daughters, clothed in calicoes, display the traits of civility, frankness, and decency, virtues which always follow contentment and ease. Almost all these houses are inhabited by men who are both cultivators and artisans; one is a tanner, another a shoemaker, still another sells goods; but all are farmers. The country stores are well assorted; you find in the same shop hats, nails, liquors. This order of things is necessary in a new settlement. It is to be hoped it will continue, for this general retailing diverts fewer hands from the great object of agriculture.

Not one-third of the land of Massachusetts is under cultivation and it is difficult to say when it will all be, considering the advantages of the western country and the Province of Maine. But the uncleared lands are all allocated, and the proprietors have inclosed them with fences of different sorts. These several kinds of fences are composed of different materials, which reflect the different degrees of culture in the country. Some are composed of the light branches of trees; others of the trunks of trees laid one upon the other; a third sort is made of long pieces of wood, supporting each other by making angles at the end; a fourth kind is made of long pieces of hewn timber supported at the ends by passing into holes made in an upright post; a fifth is like the garden fences in England; the last kind is made of stones thrown together to the height of a few feet. This last is most durable and is common in Massachusetts.

From Spenser the road is good as far as the town of Brookfield. The term, town, in the interior of America refers to an area of eight or ten miles, where are scattered a hundred or two hundred houses. This division into towns is necessary for assembling the inhabitants for elections and other purposes. Without this division the inhabitants might go sometimes to one meeting and sometimes to another, which would lead to confusion. Besides, it would render it impossible to know the population of any particular county.

While breakfast was being prepared at Brookfield, I read the gazettes and journals distributed through the country. Our breakfast consisted of coffee, tea, boiled and roasted meat; the whole for tenpence, New England currency, for each traveler. The road is covered with rock, and bordered with woods from this place to Wilbraham. There we found a new proprietor. A small carriage, well suspended and drawn by two horses, took the place of our heavy wagon. We could not conceive how five of us could fit in this little Parisian chariot and demanded another. The conductor said he had no other, that there were so few travelers in this part of the road that he could not afford to run with more than two horses, since most of the traffic from New York ended in Connecticut and most of that from Boston in Worcester. We were obliged to submit. We started like lightning and arrived in an hour and a quarter at Springfield, ten miles away.

The conductor was one of the most lively and industrious and, at the same time, most patient men I ever met. In two journeys through this place I heard many travelers treat him with very harsh language. He either remained silent or answered by giving good reasons. Most of the men of this profession in this country observe the same conduct in such cases; while the least such injury in Europe would precipitate bloody quarrels. This fact proves to me that in a free country reason extends her empire over all classes of men.

Springfield, where we dined, resembles a European town; that is, the houses are placed close together. On a hill overlooking the town is an armory belonging to the state of Massachusetts, which the rebel Shays endeavored to take, but which was so happily defended by General Shepard. After dinner we set out from Springfield for Hartford.

Hartford is a substantial rural town; the greater part of the inhabitants live by agriculture, so that ease and abundance universally reign in it. It is considered as one of the most agreeable in Connecticut, on account of its society, and is the residence of one of the most respectable men in the United States, Colonel Wadsworth. He enjoys a considerable fortune, which he owes entirely to his own labor and industry. Perfectly versed in agriculture and commerce, universally known for the service he rendered to the American and French armies during the war, generally esteemed and beloved for his great virtues, he crowns all his qualities by an amiable and singular modesty. His address is frank, his countenance open, and his discourse simple.

The environs of Hartford display a charming cultivated country; neat, elegant houses, vast meadows covered with herds of enormous cattle, destined for the market of New York and even Philadelphia. There are sheep resembling ours, but not like ours watched by shepherds and tormented by dogs; there are prodigious hogs, surrounded with numerous families of pigs, wearing on the neck a triangular piece of wood invented to hinder them from passing the barriers which inclose the cultivated fields; and geese and turkeys in abundance. Potatoes and all other vegetables are excellent and cheap. The fruits, however, are less attended to. Apples serve for making cider, and great quantities of them are likewise exported.

To describe the neighborhood of Hartford is to describe Connecticut. Nature and art have here displayed all their treasures; it is really the paradise of the United States. The state owes all its advantages to its situation. It is a fertile plain, enclosed between two mountains which render difficult its communications by land with the other states. It is watered by the superb Connecticut River, safe and easy to navigate, which flows into the sea. The riches of this state are here more equally divided, since they are based upon agriculture. There is here more equality, less misery, more simplicity, more virtue, more of everything which constitutes republicanism.

Connecticut appears like one continuous town. On quitting Hartford you enter Wethersfield, no less elegant. Wethersfield is remarkable for its vast fields, uniformly covered with onions, great quantities of which are exported to the West Indies. It is likewise remarkable for its stately meetinghouse or church. On Sunday it is said to offer an enchanting spectacle, by the number of young handsome persons who assemble there and by the agreeable music with which they intermingle the divine service.

New Haven yields not to Wethersfield for the beauty of the fair sex. At balls during the winter it is not rare to see a hundred charming girls dressed in graceful simplicity and adorned with those brilliant complexions seldom met with in journeying to the South. You will not go into a tavern without meeting with neatness, decency, and decorum. The tables are served by a young girl, respectable and pretty, by an amiable mother, whose age has not effaced the agreeableness of her features, or by men who have that air of dignity which the idea of equality inspires and who are not ignoble and base like most of our own tavern keepers. On the road you often come upon those fair Connecticut girls driving a carriage or galloping boldly alone on horseback and wearing fine hats, white aprons, and calico gowns. Such encounters prove the early cultivation of their intellect, since they are trusted so young by themselves. They also reflect the safety of the roads and the general innocence of manners. You will see maidens hazarding themselves alone without protectors in the public stagecoaches. I am wrong to say hazarding. Who can offend them? They are here under the protection of public morals, and of their own innocence, consciousness of which renders them so complaisant and so good; for a stranger takes them by the hand and laughs with them, and they are not offended at it.

Other proofs of the prosperity of Connecticut are the number of new houses and of rural manufactories arising on every side. But even in this state many lands are for sale because of the taste for emigration to the western country. The desire for improvement embitters the contentment even of the inhabitants of Connecticut. Perhaps this desire arises from the hope of escaping taxes, which appear very heavy though small, and almost nothing in comparison with those of Europe. In a country like the United States everything favors new settlement. The newcomers are sure everywhere of finding friends and brothers who speak their own language and admire their courage. Provisions are cheap the whole way. There is nothing to fear from the search of customhouse clerks on entering from one province to another. There are no river tolls, no imposts, no vexations; man is free as the air he breathes. The impulse toward emigration is daily strengthened by the accounts in the public papers of the arrival of different families. Man everywhere is like a sheep; he says, "Such a one has succeeded, why shall not I succeed! I am nothing here; I shall be something on the Ohio. I work hard here; I shall not work so hard there."

Before arriving at Middletown, where we were to breakfast, we stopped on the hill which overlooks that town and the immense valley on which it is built. It is one of the finest and richest prospects that I have seen in America. Middletown is built like Hartford, broad streets, trees on the sides, and handsome houses. We changed horses and carriages at Durham; and after admiring a number of picturesque situations on the road, arrived at New Haven, where we dined. We were obliged to quit this charming town to arrive in the evening at Fairfield. We passed the inconvenient ferry at Stratford; afterwards, assailed by a violent storm, we were well enough protected by a double curtain of leather which covered the carriage. The driver, though saturated with the rain, continued his route through the obscurity of a very dark night. Heaven preserved us from accident, at which I was most astonished. We passed the night at Fairfield, a town unhappily celebrated in the last war; it suffered all the rage of the English, who burned it. The vestiges of this infernal fury still persist. Most of the houses are rebuilt; but the air of ease, and even of opulence, that distinguished it before the war has not yet returned.

The agreeable part of our journey ended at Fairfield. From there to Rye, 33 miles, we had to struggle against rocks and precipices. I knew not which to admire most in the driver, his intrepidity or dexterity. I cannot conceive how he avoided twenty times dashing the carriage in pieces, and how his horses could retain themselves in descending the steep rocks. One of these is called Horseneck; a chain of rocks so precipitous, that if a horse should slip the carriage must fall two or three hundred feet into a valley.

It is 31 miles from Rye to New York. The road is good, even, and gravelly. We stopped at one of the best taverns I have seen in America, kept by Mrs. Haviland. We had an excellent and cheap dinner. The air of the mistress was infinitely graceful and obliging; and she had a charming daughter, genteel and well educated, who played the piano very well. Before arriving at New York, we passed by those places which the English had so well fortified while they were masters of them, and which attest to the folly of this fratricidal war.

On November 15, 1788, I set out from Philadelphia for Wilmington, a distance of 28 miles, by a tolerably good road. Wilmington stands on a creek near the Delaware. The basis of its commerce is the export of flour. One mile above Wilmington is the town of Brandywine, the name of which calls to mind a famous battle won by the English over the Americans eight miles from this town, on a river of the same name. This town is famous for its fine mills, the most substantial of which is a paper mill belonging to Mr. Gilpin and Myers Fisher. Their process of making paper, especially in pounding the rags, is much more simple than ours. I have seen specimens both for writing and printing equal to the finest made in France.

The road to Baltimore is frightful, built over clay soil, full of deep ruts, always in the midst of forests, and frequently obstructed by trees uprooted by the wind, which obliged us to seek a new passage among the woods. I cannot conceive why the stage does not often meet with disaster. Both the drivers and their horses develop great skill and dexterity, being accustomed to these roads. But why are they not repaired? Overseers of the roads are indeed appointed, and fines are sometimes pronounced on delinquencies of this kind; but they are ill collected. Everything is here degraded; it is one of the effects of slavery. The slave works as little as possible; and the master, eager for vile enjoyments, has other concerns than sending his Negroes to repair the roads.

Vast fields of Indian corn badly cultivated, pale faces worn by the fever and ague, naked Negroes, and miserable huts are the most striking images to meet the eye of the traveler in Maryland.

Baltimore contains almost 2,000 houses and 14,000 inhabitants. It is irregularly built on land but little elevated above the surface of Patapsco Bay, on the north of which it forms a crescent. The bay is not sufficiently deep to receive the largest ships, which anchor near Fell's Point two miles from the center of the town. There are still stagnant waters in the town, few of the streets are paved, and the great quantities of mud after rain indicate that the air must be unhealthy. But the inhabitants deny this. One may say here, like the Swiss in the heat of a battle, "If you believe these people, nobody can die here!"

Baltimore was but a village before the war; but during that period a considerable portion of the commerce of Philadelphia moved to this place. The greatest ships come as far as here; but can go no farther. Vast quantities of provisions descend the Susquehannah and when that river becomes navigable Baltimore will be a very sizable port. The quarrel about federalism divided the town at the time I was in it; and the two parties almost came to blows on the election of their representatives.

We left Baltimore for Alexandria at four in the morning, distance about 60 miles, bad roads, a rough wagon, excellent horses, skillful conductors, poor cultivation, wretched huts, and miserable Negroes. We dined at Bladenburg, 16 miles from Alexandria. We could find nothing there to drink but brandy or rum mixed with water. In countries cultivated by slaves there is no industry or domestic economy. The people know neither the advantages nor the method of making beer or cider on their farms.

Georgetown, the last point in the state of Maryland, overlooks the Potomac, has an agreeable location, and a considerable commerce. Regulations and imposts inconsiderately laid on commerce by the state of Virginia have banished to Georgetown a substantial part of the trade of Alexandria.

The latter place is eight miles below Georgetown on the opposite side of the Potomac. Alexandria has grown from nothing to its present size within these forty years. It is not so large as Baltimore, which it ought to surpass, and is almost as irregular and as destitute of pavement. You see here a greater parade of luxury; but it is a contemptible luxury, servants with silk stockings in boots, women elegantly dressed and their heads adorned with feathers.

The inhabitants at the close of the war imagined that every natural circumstance united to render this a great commercial town—the healthfulness of the air, the depth of the river which allowed the largest ships to anchor near the quay, an immense extent of back country, fertile and abounding in provisions. They therefore built on every side commodious storehouses and fine wharves; but commerce still languishes on account of the restraints mentioned above.

I hastened to get to Mount Vernon, the seat of General Washington, ten miles below Alexandria on the same river. This route traverses a considerable wood, and after having passed over two hills, leads to a country house of elegant and majestic simplicity. Before it lie grass lawns. On one side of the avenue are the stables; on the other, a greenhouse and houses for a number of Negro mechanics. In a spacious back yard are turkeys, geese, and other poultry. The house itself overlooks the Potomac, enjoys an extensive view, has a vast and elevated portico on the river side, and a convenient distribution of rooms within.

The General came home in the evening fatigued from a journey to lay out a new road in some part of his plantations. He has often been compared to Cincinnatus; the comparison is doubtless just. This celebrated general is nothing more at present than a good farmer, constantly occupied in the care of his estate and the improvement of cultivation. He has lately built a barn, 100 feet in length and considerably more in breadth, destined to receive the productions of his farm and to shelter his cattle, horses, asses, and mules. It follows a plan sent him by the famous English farmer, Arthur Young, but much improved by the General. This brick building cost but 300 pounds; I am sure in France it would have cost 3,000. He planted this year 700 bushels of potatoes. All this is new in Virginia, where they know not the use of barns, and where they lay up no provisions for their cattle. His 300 Negroes are distributed in log houses in different parts of his plantation, which in this neighborhood consists of 10,000 acres. Colonel Humphreys assured me that the General possesses in different parts of the country more than 200,000 acres.

Everything has an air of simplicity in his house. His table is good, but not ostentatious; and no deviation is seen from regularity and domestic economy. Mrs. Washington superintends the whole, and adds to the qualities of an excellent housewife that simple dignity which ought to characterize a woman whose husband has acted the greatest part on the theater of human affairs. She also possesses that amenity, and manifests that attention to strangers, which render hospitality so charming. The same virtues are conspicuous in her attractive niece, who, however, unhappily appears not to enjoy good health.

Chesapeake Bay divides Maryland into two nearly equal parts. The western division is the most peopled. Numerous bays and navigable rivers render this state singularly fit for commerce, and it would soon thrive if slavery were banished from it, if a more advantageous culture were substituted for that of tobacco, and if the spirit of the Catholic religion had not adulterated the taste for order, regularity, and severity of manners which characterize the other sects and which have so great an influence in civil and political economy.

Cotton is raised in Maryland, as in Virginia; but little care is taken to perfect either its culture or its manufacture. There are excellent lands in these two states, but very few good meadows, though the latter might be made in abundance. For want of attention and labor, the inhabitants gather little hay; and what they have is not good. They likewise neglect the cultivation for their cattle of potatoes, carrots, and turnips, of which their neighbors of the North make great use. Their beasts are left without shelter in winter, and nourished with the tops of Indian corn. Many consequently die of cold and hunger; and those that survive the winter are miserably meager.

In this country they have so perfected the English method of inoculation for smallpox that the practice is hardly dangerous. General Washington assured me that he makes it a custom to have all his Negroes inoculated, and that he never lost one in the operation. Whoever inoculates in Virginia is obliged by law to inform his neighbors within a radius of two miles.

The horses of Virginia are, without exception, the finest in the country; but they command double the price of those in the northern states. The practice of racing, borrowed from the English by the Virginians, is falling into disuse. The places well known for this business are all abandoned, and it is not a misfortune; they were centers of gambling, drunkenness, and quarrels.

The General informed me that he could perceive a great reformation in his countrymen in this respect, that they are less given to intoxication. It is no longer fashionable for a man to force his guests to drink and to make it an honor to send them home drunk. You no longer hear the taverns resounding with the noisy parties once so common.

The sessions of the courts of justice are no longer the theaters of gambling, inebriation, and bloodshed.

The towns in Virginia are but small; this is true even of Richmond with its capitol. This capitol turns the heads of the Virginians; they imagine that from it they shall, like the old Romans, one day give law to the whole earth. There is a glass factory 40 miles from Alexandria which exported last year glass worth £10,000; and notwithstanding the general character of indolence in this state, the famous Potomac canal is being built with rapidity. Crimes are more frequent in Virginia than in the northern states, a result of the unequal division of property and of slavery.

Wherever luxury is common, and especially a degraded luxury, there provisions, even of the prime necessity, will be dear. I found this in Virginia. At a tavern there I paid a dollar for a supper which in Pennsylvania would have cost me two shillings, in Connecticut, one. Porter, wine, and every other article bears an excessive price here.

Tobacco requires a strong fertile soil, and an uninterrupted care in transplanting, weeding, defense against insects, cutting, curing, rolling, and packing. Nothing but a great crop, and the total abnegation of every comfort, to which the Negroes are condemned, can compensate for the cost of raising this product and getting it to market. Thus, in proportion as the good lands are exhausted, and less hard labor is required of the slaves by the spread of humane principles, this culture must decline.

Already in Virginia many areas are fenced in, and meadows and wheat fields begin to take the place of tobacco. This is the procedure of the proprietors who best understand their interest, among whom I place General Washington, who has lately renounced the culture of that plant. If the Virginians knew our wants, and understood what articles would be most profitable to themselves, they would pay more attention to the culture of cotton, the consumption of which mounts so prodigiously in Europe.

I will not enlarge further on the subject of tobacco, which many authors have explained; but I will give some description of that kind of paper currency called tobacco money, the use of which proves that nations need not have so much concern as they usually do about the absence of specie. In a free and fertile country the constant produce of the land may give a fixed value to any kind of representation of property.

The state has public warehouses, where the tobacco is deposited. Inspectors in charge test the quality of the tobacco which, if merchantable, is accepted, and the proprietor is given a note for the quantity deposited. The note circulates freely in the state, varying in value with the known price of tobacco. The price is different according to the place of inspection. The tobacco travels to one place or the other, according to its quality, and if it is refused at all places it is exported to the islands or consumed in the country. There are two cuttings a year of this crop, of which the first only is presented for inspection; the second is consumed in the country or smuggled to the islands.

As Virginia produces about 80,000 hogsheads, there circulates in the state about £800,000 in these notes; this is the reason why the Virginians do not need a great quantity of specie or of copper coin. The rapid circulation of this tobacco money takes their place.

The scarcity of small money, however, subjects the people to great inconveniences, and gives rise to the pernicious practice of cutting pieces of silver coin into halves and quarters, a source of many little knaveries. Someone cuts a dollar into three pieces, keeps the middle piece, and passes the other two for half dollars. The person who receives these without weighing loses the difference, and the one who takes them by weight makes a fraudulent profit by passing the pieces again at their pretended value; and so the cheat goes round. But notwithstanding this pitiful recourse of cutting the silver, there is still a shortage of small change and society suffers thereby. It is calculated that in the towns the small expenses of a family are doubled on account of this difficulty. This circumstance reflects a striking want of order in the government and increases the misery of the poor.

Though tobacco exhausts the land to a prodigious degree, the proprietors take no pains to restore its vigor; they take what the soil will give, and abandon it when it yields no longer. They prefer to clear new lands than to regenerate the old. Yet the abandoned lands would still be fertile if they were properly manured and cultivated. The Virginians take no tobacco in substance, either in the nose or mouth; some of them smoke, but this practice is not so general among them as in the Carolinas.

6.

THE BITTER THOUGHTS OF PRESIDENT MOREAU

*Méderic Louis Élie Moreau de Saint-Méry was born in Marti-
nique in 1750. Educated in Paris, he became a judge in Santo Domingo
and compiled a great treatise on the laws of the French West Indies.
In Paris as a member of the colonial administration when the Revolution broke out, he participated as a móderate, holding office for a time
as president of the Paris commune. But Robespierre's accession to
power drove Moreau, like other moderates, into exile.*

*From 1794 to 1798 Moreau lived in Norfolk, New York, and Phila-
delphia, working first as a shipping clerk and then as printer and proprietor of a bookshop that became a center for the French émigrés in
Philadelphia. In 1798 the return of the conservatives to power brought
him back to France where he held a succession of offices and died in
1819.*

*The journal from which Moreau hoped to compile a book was not
published in his lifetime, and remained in manuscript until 1913 when
it was rescued by Stewart L. Mims, who edited it under the title* Voyage
aux États-Unis de l'Amérique, 1793–1798.

Norfolk in Virginia has anchorage for some 300 ships. The principal place of debarkation is on the wharves which lie along a hollow
at the foot of a square. From the water each can be reached by a kind
of ladder or inclined plane made of joists, which hangs down from the
wharf to the point of low tide.

The square is really a long rectangle. Shops and taverns line its
sides, and at its upper end a market is held until nine in the morning
every day but Sunday. No street in the town is paved, as a result of
which the passer-by is covered either with mud or with dust, depend-
ing on the season. One also finds little sewers which are crossed by
narrow rude plank bridges.

Norfolk has about 500 houses, quite close to each other except at
the upper part of the town. Formerly there were fewer, and those were
built of brick. But during the war for independence, Lord Dunmore,
then governor of Virginia for the King of England, had them burned

by fire from the warship *Liverpool* on January 1, 1776. The blackened ruins in many places still speak eloquently of that destruction and seem destined to impress it for a long time on the memories of Americans.

Now most of the houses are made of wood, generally of one story, although some have two or even three. Their number grows daily, mostly in the direction of Elizabeth River which is being encroached on by new wharves. As everywhere in America, these wharves are erected solely for the profit of the proprietors, without a general plan, without foresight for the future, and without worrying as to the effect on the appearance of the city. On these wharves are built shops, supported by logs or large pieces of round wood, resting in turn on a brick foundation, while the remainder is of planks. Some of these shops are three stories high. The common opinion in Norfolk is that houses built of pine will not last more than ten years, a conviction that induces the owners to avoid repairs during the short life span.

Norfolk has three churches; one Anglican, one Presbyterian, and a third, Methodist. The last named has the largest body of communicants. Most of the Methodists are Negroes, whose grimaces, sighs, and inarticulate noises attract the curious on those Sundays when a minister, dressed in his lay best, speaks to them. His words are sometimes gentle, but more often he thunders about the suffering in the other world to spread terror in these superstitious souls. Although the minister teaches the equality of eternal punishments, everything else in the wooden church reflects the power of human distinctions. The women are on the right, the men on the left, and there is a barrier between the slaves and the free colored people.

I cannot refrain from comparing the religious life of American Negroes and that of our colonies. In the latter, religion is administered by missionaries of the various orders, particularly the Capuchins, for the monks generally lead a more rigorous and less worldly life than the seculars. Their simplicity is more appropriate to the habits and opinions of the blacks. When the slaves complain of their miserable condition, the Capuchins tell them: "You may think your lot due to your color, but we who are white like your masters also live poorly. In the other world, however, if you have been good there will be no difference between you and your owners and you will have a share in the eternal blessings. Console yourselves, therefore; the evils you now suffer will help you earn heaven." The words of the monks are soothing. But when a Methodist preacher tells a Negro slave, "Unhappy man, you are condemned to suffer in this world and you will be forever tormented in the next," how can such doctrines which give birth to despair relieve the unfortunate slaves?

There is also a place consecrated to the practice of Roman Catholicism. Such is the description applied to a very disorderly room ever since a zealous ruddy Irishman came to teach the unfortunate refugees from Santo Domingo the necessity of humility and of submission to the orders from on high. This minister holds his powers from Mr. Carroll, a native of Maryland and consecrated a Catholic bishop in London.

Norfolk has two printing presses and two newspapers. The presses have scarcely any business but that of putting out the papers in which one finds announcements of Negroes for sale or for rent, of fugitive slaves, and also notices of departures. The city also has a library.

The taste for luxury is common in this neighborhood; it is so often the concomitant of slavery. In a population of 3,000, which is considerable for the city's size, one often sees a surprising number of men wasting their time. Frequently ten or twelve people can be found chatting on the corners.

The furniture is simple; there are no mirrors or tapestries. Tables, buffets, and chests are of mahogany, always in the English style. And as the ultimate demonstration of cleanliness, the floors are scrupulously scrubbed.

The heat of the place has influenced home architecture and led to the introduction of a kind of corridor called a hall, in which the family gathers as soon as the cold season is over. Open doors at both ends serve to draw in a breeze which offers some relief from the suffocating warmth, especially on the days when the air is laden with thunderstorms.

Heat gives Norfolk a murderous climate. Bilious and intermittent fevers which stretch out through several years are common. Other illnesses may perhaps be attributed to an excess of quinine, which is taken here without any precautions and often without system. Sicknesses arising from vermin are also well known. The farmers who have lived for a long time in Virginia purge themselves regularly in August as a precaution, and the residents of Norfolk are so fearful of their city that all those who can afford it take a trip during the summer, even if

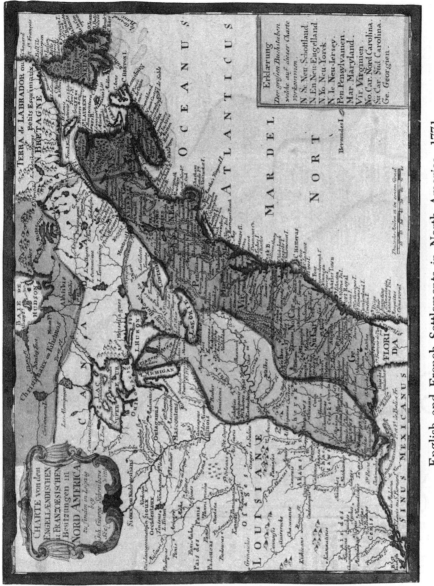

English and French Settlements in North America, 1771

Indian Households

it be only to sea. It is true that the whole neighboring district is marshy and less healthy than the city itself. In the environs are many pools of standing water from which arise emanations that poison the air and breed swarms of insects which are a heavy trial even in the daytime. The widespread fear of the disease called Yellow Fever was so augmented in Norfolk in 1794 because of the epidemic in Philadelphia, that a young woman resident of Santo Domingo was refused admission to a boardinghouse after having debarked from a boat from Le Havre. She had had a hard crossing of 119 days, and died eight days later in a house which only reluctantly took her in.

A great many people therefore die during the summer in Norfolk. Burials there are more elaborate than anywhere else on the continent. The corpse is shaved and dressed, and vanity calls for a beautiful coffin. The minister comes to preach at the home of the deceased, after which there is a procession to the cemetery, with this peculiarity, that the doctor escorts the clergyman. Important persons are brought to the church before being buried. In the cemeteries, flat stones are erected vertically with the name of the person and there are frequently large marble slabs on brick bases on which are inscribed the unread eulogies of the dead.

Second marriages are frequent in Norfolk, and since the climate is harsher on men than on women it is common to see a mother whose offspring bear different names. Nevertheless, the children in Virginia are treated with unparalleled tenderness. Their every fancy is satisfied. The marriages are very gay. A good friend of the bride prepares for the occasion all sorts of pastries and acts the hostess at the party which follows the ceremony performed by the minister in the home. At this feast, as at all others in America, the women are seated first, but always leave the table as soon as the men manifest a preference for Bacchus over Venus.

In the summer, Norfolk enjoys the performances, in a brick theater, of players who winter in Richmond. In the spring of 1794 Rickett and Macdonald came to display their horsemanship and attracted great crowds who paid seventy-five cents to a dollar according to place. There was a separate section for the colored people. In general, however, the manner of life is rather monotonous; the crowd of young ladies who came to hear my niece, a young Parisian, pluck upon the

harp gave proof that that instrument was absolutely new to them. The
men are rather attracted to free masonry; at least so one would suppose, since there are several lodges in the city.

The New York streets are narrow, as are the sidewalks where such
exist. Furthermore, the entrances to cellars which open onto the sidewalks cut off much of their width. The cellars are very bad and very
damp and, in rainy spells and floods, fill with water. The custom of
building kitchens in the cellar is, however, less widespread than in
Philadelphia. The streets are not very even and one can see all sorts of
animals wandering about, particularly cows and pigs. On Saturdays the
sidewalks and windows are cleaned. But no one thinks of removing
the dead dogs, cats, and rats from the streets. In front of almost every
door are two white seats facing each other at right angles to the house.
There, in the summer, people enjoy the fresh air.

People commonly drink excellent water, coming from a spring and
called tea water because it makes fine tea. It is carried to all the houses
by 24 horse-drawn carts and costs a little more than one cent a bucket.
The owner of the spring rents his wells and his pump, operated by two
horses and a boy, for $1,000. The carters in turn buy the water for
1/16 of a dollar a cask.

About 200 orphans are now lodged in the poorhouse and raised at
the expense of the city. They wear no special uniform, since the magistrates wish to spare them the humiliation of clothing that would mark
their condition. In that respect they differ from the children of both
sexes whom one sees dressed in blue every Sunday in Trinity (Epis-
copal) Church. The latter belong to the less fortunate families of that
communion and receive an education and clothing from the corporation. The municipal government, however, has no sympathy with this
English practice and, on the contrary, seeks to avoid any symbol that
would disrupt civic unity.

In the Bridewell, or house of correction, are lodged convicts and
slaves, punished by various tasks for the profit of the city. There is
also a hospital on the left side of Broadway. This institution does not
belong to the city, but was built by private subscription, and the subscribers, among whom are many Quakers, select the directors. The two-
story building generally holds 50 to 60 invalids. Each has a wooden
bed, a mattress, and sheets. The two sexes are separated and the Ne-

groes are in a different room. There are besides four cells for the insane, one of which is now occupied. There is a surgeon attached to the hospital which altogether has 24 employees, and 4 doctors who serve without pay. The annual expenses are $2,000 to $3,000, toward which invalids of means pay $2.00 a week.

There is no uniformity to the character of the Americans in the United States, a country that fills a whole continent. Nevertheless, there are some traits that may be considered general. Notwithstanding an ostensible hatred for them, they really love and fear the English. Despite their pride, the Americans have a vague feeling that they are somehow inferior to the Britons. Their tastes, customs, and, most of all, their habits, make true Englishmen of them. If the former mother country were to exploit this tendency by sending here as ambassador a famous man, titled and rich, his parties and flattery would assure a popular conquest. Instead, the London government has not ceased, since the peace of 1783, to show by its conduct a marked disdain for the United States. It gave evidence of that sentiment in the choice of its first representative, Temple, whose behavior in America before the Revolution, whose debts and immoderate conduct, had left a feeling of dislike. Mr. Hammond, new to diplomacy, was also a poor choice; his distaste for Americans and his temper prevented him from keeping quiet about anything, and sometimes gave a critical character to incidents he should not have noticed at all. Mr. Bond, the consul general, was born in America but hates the country intensely. He has no striking qualities except a strong influence over Mr. Hammond, which however is no sign of talent.

Despite everything, one is astonished at the rapidity with which Americans have formed settlements in the interior. Their manner of life seems well-adapted to such undertakings, and when the mercantile and grasping spirit makes room for the virtues proper to a great nation, this country will probably enjoy perfect peace, although the inhabitants of the eastern states scorn the southerners, the Virginians, Carolinians, and Georgians.

It is said that the American is the perfect mean between the European and the Indian. But it is evident that he is departing steadily from the latter and approaching the former. Indifferent to almost everything, he sometimes takes an energetic stand, and then follows it with a nonchalance which indicates that he is not capable of feeling real enthusiasm. That indifference sometimes seems basic to American character, and the embellishments of friendship and philanthropy foreign to it. Doctor Ross, a Scot established in Philadelphia, told me in 1795, "I've lived in Philadelphia more than ten years and belong to several societies in which my position as a physician has brought me many contacts, but there are nevertheless not even two American homes to which I could go for dinner without being invited."

There was an attempt in Philadelphia to assemble a purse for the American prisoners in Algeria, but it hardly raised 1,200 francs. The comedians of the city gave a performance for the benefit of the prisoners which yielded almost 6,000 francs, but without much public enthusiasm. Thus it was the very needy English players who showed most sensitivity for the unfortunate seamen who had traveled far from home in the interests of their country and had left their women and children behind in misery.

In the winter of 1793, in skating on the Delaware River near Philadelphia, a young man disappeared beneath the breaking ice. There were loud cries of distress, but after a few moments he reappeared and was drawn out, after which people began skating again. Fifteen minutes later another disappeared and was drowned, but the skating continued without any display of emotion.

The frontiersman offers complete proof of the American indifference in love and in friendship and of failure to form attachments to anything. In the course of a lifetime he may begin as many as four clearings. He abandons, without reluctance, the place where he first drew breath, the church in which he first perceived the idea of a supreme being, the tombs of his ancestors, the friends of his infancy, the companions of his youth, and all the pleasures of his society. He emigrates, especially if he be a northerner, to go South or West, to the backwoods of the United States on the Ohio, disposing of his property, selling the house, the wagon, the horse, the dog, anything that will fetch a price.

The American has no dignity when it comes to money. A rich Philadelphia merchant met me at my door in 1795 and, as if by chance, said, "Don't refuse me, I need six hundred dollars until tomorrow morning." But I didn't have the sum he wished. The next day he met me on South Fourth Street near his house and said, "You have no money, well, in a little while I'll have a lot." Note that this merchant had only spoken to me once before in buying on credit.

As far as generosity is concerned, there is much disparity in the American character, which includes some traits close to stinginess. A senator, asked to buy a very beautiful harp for one of his daughters, said, "I'd buy it all right, but the expense of the strings is too high." A widow in Philadelphia took in a Frenchman to teach the language to her daughter. This rich woman, realizing that her daughter could not take her lesson one Saturday, demanded a proportionate reduction from the monthly price. Another scholar, a very distinguished gentleman, having been absent a week, was paid for two months in Portuguese money hard to discount.

Love of gold often goes so far as to overwhelm delicacy. A well-known Democrat learned that a London trading house in January 1796 was using the services of a rival American firm in the attempt, in behalf of the English government, to forestall the market in flour. He said to Talleyrand, "That's too bad of them; I let that London company make more money than the one they picked." As a result, this Democrat was instrumental in having the people reject the Anglo-American commercial treaty of 1795.

There is no security in business. A borrower must be dunned a hundred times before a loan is repaid. One of my friends, a merchant in Guadaloupe, sent $15,000 with an order to buy bank stock. He received an answer which read, "I have received and executed the orders of your letter of —." Three years later the Guadaloupian arrives and asks for his shares, which have risen in value. They tell him that they have resold them, but will reimburse him with interest. He refuses. But the lawyers advise him to settle because a trial would take four years and cost 6,000 francs. In the end he gets back only his $15,000. In the South the clerks have a poor reputation for trustworthiness. If they are alone they regularly sell above the price and pocket the difference.

It is almost impossible to get an American to undertake a job he never did or never saw done. It took remarkable exertions on my part to get a man to make me boxes of different dimensions to hold seals.

One of the factors that makes American character hard to understand is the circumstance that they originated in different nations and have kept some of the marks of that original influence. Among the white residents of Philadelphia, for instance, are Englishmen, Scots, Irishmen, and Europeans of all nations, to say nothing of native Americans born in the various states of the United States who also have a diversified European ancestry. Thus the Americans descended from Dutchmen unite to a high degree the indolence of the first people and the avarice of the second, which augments the avidity for profit characteristic of both countries. It is impossible to push stinginess any further. They hardly feed themselves and treat their slaves badly.

In the United States the manner of living is always the same. They breakfast at nine on ham or salt fish such as shad, accompanied by coffee or tea and slices of toasted bread and butter. Dinner at two o'clock contains no real soup, but sometimes broth. The main dish is an English roast with potatoes. Then come peas boiled in water on which they put butter which melts in the heat, or else a spicy sauce. Then there are eggs, boiled or fried; fish, boiled or fried; a salad which sometimes contains cabbage cut into very thin slices which each one seasons to taste in his own dish; pastries; and sweets of which they are very fond. For dessert, there is a little fruit, cheese, or pudding. The whole meal is accompanied by cider, by weak or strong beer, and by claret. During the dinner and while they eat they follow the English custom of exposing on a buffet in the dining room all the silver of the household.

At the entremets, they bring in Bordeaux or Madeira wine which lasts through dessert, at the end of which the ladies retire to their own devices, leaving the men free to drink as much as they please, for they continue to pass the bottle around the table, each one helping himself in his turn. They give toasts, smoke cigars, and run to the corner of the room seeking in the vessel on the bedside stand the means of making room for more liquor. Finally, bored, exhausted, or drunk they leave the dinner table, having thus worked themselves well into the night.

At about seven or eight o'clock of the evenings when there are no formal dinners they have tea as in the morning, but with no meat. At tea the whole family is reunited and friends, acquaintances, and even strangers are invited. These are the three meals of the day, for there is no supper. Tea in the evening is accompanied by a boring and dull etiquette. The mistress of the house serves, and passes the cups around. Until you turn over the cup and put the spoon on top they will keep bringing you fresh cups. There are a thousand stories, true or false, of Frenchmen, ignorant of this customary signal, who were drowned with that beverage.

A letter of recommendation to an American, if it is not concerned only with business, is ordinarily good for a dinner. When one enters an American home to dine, one leaves stick, hat, and coat in the entrance hall. Then, if the host already has one or more guests, he takes the newcomer, who now seems to live in the house, by the hand and presents him in order to each person, giving his name and the name of the individual to whom he is being introduced. This wise custom would be worth introducing in France, for among the French one occasionally makes insulting remarks about people who are present but whom one does not know.

All Americans are smokers. They also chew and sometimes they indulge in both activities in the manner dear to sailors. But the American of either sex who takes snuff is a rare phenomenon. The women do not deform their noses and do not soil themselves in this exercise which, despite all the excuses invented by those Europeans who have the habit, is more contrary to propriety than useful to health.

Americans have a great love for oysters, which they eat at all hours, even in the streets. They are sold in open baskets, by the dozen or the hundred, and are hawked through the streets with horrible noises until ten at night. There is also immoderate use of hot liquids. Tea is drunk boiling hot, but in the summer the water is cold or iced. They like liquors—rum, brandy, whisky—and they mix brandy with what they call grog.

Fresh fruit is in good demand. They eat seven or eight times as much meat as bread and they sleep too long in feather beds. Although the painting in their houses is renewed almost every year at the beginning of the autumn, the Americans continue to live in their homes without interruption.

For hard work and solid character, the natives do not compare with the German-born who form a large part of the population. The Pennsylvania Germans are less often drunkards, and their families are larger, contain as many as 12 and 14 children, while in 27 American families I found only one of 13 and one of 12. The Quakers grow weaker in numbers because many of their children leave the sect.

There are few centenarians in the United States, and the stones of the Philadelphia cemetery reveal only one nonagenarian. Ordinarily the group within which deaths are most common is that between the ages of 35 and 45.

American men are in general well-built, but seem to lack vigor. They are tall and thin, especially the Quakers. They are negligent in dress, those in the cities more so than the others. Both sexes lack color, are brave, but often irresolute.

As far as white women in general are concerned, we may begin with a remark very flattering and appropriate for them: no woman in the United States, whatever be the rank at which she was born (unless it be the result of some accident) has one of those figures, very common in Europe, even in France, among the lower classes, that repulse by their sheer ugliness; eyes, bloodshot or bleary; misformed in features. If one meets such a figure, one may be sure that she was recently imported from elsewhere and not the product of a soil well-favored in this respect.

American girls are pretty, and their eyes are alive with expression; but their complexions are wan, bad teeth spoil the appearance of their mouths, and there is also something disagreeable about the length of their legs. In general, however, they are of good height, are graceful, and, in enumerating their charms, one must not forget the shapeliness of their breasts.

Philadelphia has thousands of beauties between fourteen and eighteen. To offer but a single proof: on the north side of Market Street, between Third and Fifth Street, on a single winter's day I saw four hundred young maidens promenading, each one of whom would surely have been followed in Paris, a seductive tribute that could be offered by perhaps no other city in the world.

But these girls soon become pale, and an indisposition which is reckoned among the most unfavorable for the maintenance of the freshness of youth is very common among them. They have thin hair and bad teeth, and are given to nervous illnesses. The elements which embellish beauty, or rather which compose and order it, are not often bestowed by the graces. Finally, they are charming, adorable at fifteen, dried up at twenty-three, old at thirty-five, decrepit at forty or fifty. It is no accident that the usual age of marriageableness is fourteen.

The period at which the power of reproduction ceases is generally between forty and forty-five, and that revolution so dangerous in our climates is there passed without accident.

Girls do not appear in society until puberty. But one is constantly astonished to see young and pretty maidens in the streets going back and forth to school. Their hair hangs long and they wear petticoats closed by a seam. But at the marriageable age their hair is raised by a comb. From that time on they show themselves to society, they become their own mistresses, may walk alone, and take a lover.

The choice of a lover is unexceptional, it is public, and the parents hardly take notice because such are the customs of the country. The chosen man comes into the house whenever he pleases. He takes the object of his affections for a walk wherever he likes. He often comes for her on Sunday in a cabriolet and brings her back in the evening without being questioned as to their doings.

Girls generally hold on to their lovers, at least unless urgent causes force him to leave. In that case, they will choose a second. Similar causes can lead to several shifts in affection. But if the lover remains in the same place, he is always bound by the same chains, unless, having exhausted the expectations of pleasure, he escapes by a criminal inconstancy, and lets loose a flood of tears from the sweetheart he betrayed.

But universal indignation and the marks of infamy will catch up with one who is known as a villainous seducer, the betrayer of a married woman, for instance, no matter to what point he might flee, so long as that point is in the United States. Never, no never, in this vast country will he be able to obtain any kind of a post, even that of a watchman.

It is true that one must know how to be virtuous by system and by disposition. A maiden trusts herself to the restraint of her lover and charges him with the preservation of a respect that she herself cannot always command. Each day they are left alone. Since it is the daughter in many homes who awaits the return of the servants whom nothing can hold in after evening, and who often do not return until midnight, her lover is her only protection. The father, mother, and the whole family go to sleep. The lover and his girl remain alone, and sometimes on returning, the servants find them fallen asleep and the candle gone out—so cold is love in this country!!

When a girl notes some coolness in the man of her choice, she publicly overwhelms him with the most bitter reproaches, and will make known her prior rights in no uncertain terms if another woman, either through accident or design, attempts to supplant her. Nevertheless, these American young ladies are cold and passionless. They give always the impression of calculation. Without emotion enough to alter the expression they will engage for hours in that which ought not be tolerated except in the grip of an irresistible ecstasy.

In view of the unlimited freedom of the unmarried woman, it is astonishing to discover the eagerness of all to be married, for marriage brings about an absolute change in the life of the girl. She ceases to be the young, scatterbrained irresponsible, knowing no laws but caprice and the good humor of a lover. She becomes a woman who exists only for her husband and for the care of her household. She is little more than a nursemaid; often, indeed, the first and only servant. But that very eagerness is a consequence of selfish calculation, because it is commonly believed that failure to find a husband is a reflection of some fault which repels lovers.

I am about to say something almost incredible. These women without the capacity for true love or passion give themselves over at an early age to a sensual enjoyment of themselves. Nor are they strangers to the taste for the pleasures of a misguided imagination in a person of the same sex. Among the common people, say in the home of an innkeeper or shopkeeper, the daughters and servant girls sleep together. In the space of eight or ten years a girl may share her bed with fifty or sixty different creatures, of whom no more may be known than their names, who may be dirty, unhealthy, infected with communicable diseases, and with habits fatal to a young person.

The Philadelphia women are luxuriously supplied with shoes, with ribbons, and with lingerie, although they still lack gauze, laces, and artificial flowers. They have a habit, which they think in good taste, of letting the men pay for what they buy in the shops and forgetting to reimburse them. They have a decided taste for finery and a great desire to show themselves off, which is at once the consequence of, and contributes to, the love of finery. They are not, however, as well turned out as Frenchwomen.

Although in general one notices a great deal of modesty in the Philadelphia girls, their manners are not altogether pure, and the carelessness of some parents as to the way in which their daughters may have acquired trinkets which they did not give them must favor some indiscretions. These, however, will not spring from love, for Americans are not very sentimental. But the women do have certain ridiculous scruples about being unwilling to hear certain words pronounced. And the extent to which that scruple is observed discloses rather an excess of knowledge than of ignorance.

American women also have a false modesty that makes them unwilling to discuss, even with their husbands, bodily ailments that may become serious. That is the source of so many bad teeth, of stomach troubles, and of poor skins. Americans divide the whole body into two parts: from the top to the waist is the stomach; from there to the bottom, the limbs. Imagine then the difficulties of a doctor who must guess from these rudimentary indications the nature and the seat of an illness. The slightest contact is forbidden and the ill woman will, even at the risk of death, not make the vagueness more specific.

Here is an example. A young woman, having borne her first child, found one of her breasts cracked. She suffered terribly but would only tell the doctor that her stomach hurt. The illness got worse. A feminine neighbor to whom she spoke of the condition, but who was unable to convince her to be frank with the doctor, revealed the matter to me. I resolved to speak to this woman, using all the arts that her stubborn prejudices demanded. I referred to the risks she ran, the possibility of death, and its effect on the little boy she loved so much. I charged her with failure in a duty toward nature and religion, and warned her that her obstinacy was a form of suicide.

I spoke with such eloquence, that I convinced the patient, who made her difficulties clear to the doctor. She regained her health after a long treatment. But the upshot was that this young mother thereafter refused to speak to me or even to greet me despite her awareness that I was responsible for saving her life.

In the eyes of the Yankee ladies, French women are not quite proper because there are points at which their chemise shows. I am sorry to say, that precisely because the American girls have so much shame when it comes to anything that concerns that garment that they own few of them and consequently change them infrequently, the result being that these are not quite clean and often become depositories for marks of a need to which nature has subjected all animals.

The character of children is strongly conditioned by their upbringing and the examples they see about them. They are raised at home and generally are free and mischievous. They often exercise their mischievousness by annoying the little Negroes. They throw snowballs at passers-by, and I myself have not been exempt from experiences which testify to their poor upbringing. The very youngest children whose mothers work are kept in cradles which are rocked mercilessly from morning to night by the mother's foot, with such force that the infant must be in a constant state of dizziness. If there are other women or children in the household, that task is relegated to them.

When the children are a little older they are sent to schools where they learn reading, writing, and arithmetic. As far as writing is concerned, these schools have a great advantage in uniformity of system. They all teach English and a legible hand. Consequently, a child taught writing in any part of the continent is sure to find the same practice and the same characters wherever he may go.

In almost every city on the continent, especially in the North, there are officials who warn the parents that they must send their children to school when they are seven years old. If the parents do not heed the advice they are warned again with a time limit, at the expiration of which the officials take the children to school.

The result of this minute care is that a man who knows how to read and write doubles the value of his intelligence, in a manner of speaking, over people who lack those two skills. All Americans of both sexes have those abilities. I remember while working in the admiralty in Martinique where it was my duty to receive declarations, I could always extend the pen to American sailors, while most Frenchmen were ignorant, a fact very offensive to my national pride.

When the children are still older they are sent to boarding schools, if the parents can afford the expense. There they are taught languages, Latin and Greek, for in North America the latter language is taught like Latin. But lazy and insubordinate children behave badly in these institutions, for the masters and instructors are only concerned with keeping them and give way to their whims with a most unhappy complaisance.

Americans are quarrelsome, and many quarrels lead to pugilism, an indication of their English origin. Boxing has its own rules and regulations. The two athletes choose their field of combat. They strip to the waist, keeping on only their undershirts, which they roll up to the elbows. At a given signal they run toward each other, striking at the stomach and face with blows whose force can only be appreciated by those who have participated in such events.

After each charge they step back, then take up the attack again. If one falls his adversary must not touch him as long as he is on the ground. But at the slightest movement to get up he has the right to knock him down again. No one steps in to separate the two contestants. A ring forms around the struggling men, and partisans urge their champions on. Until one is willing to quit, the other continues to beat him with his fists. Once having conceded defeat, the loser picks himself up, dresses, is free and can retire until a new challenge leads him back to the field of battle.

At the end of a fight one or both of the contestants is thoroughly beaten up, disfigured, covered with blood which pours from mouth and nose. Teeth are broken, eyes blackened and sometimes closed entirely. Most fights take place at night by moonlight, except when drunkenness precipitates the issue in open daylight and before the eyes of curious onlookers.

The Americans also follow the English mode when they use boxing matches as the occasion for exercising their passion for betting. But cockfights are the chief recourse of gamblers. These take place every day. Men spend all their time and energy preparing cocks for battle. They miss no opportunity to train their animals and excite them to fight, regulating their diet and using hard liquor to that end. The cocks are armed with iron spurs and their crests are shaven to give less grip to the enemy. They are urged on by cries and ringed in to prevent flight. In the midst of a crowd, which might be entirely composed of Englishmen, but really is so only by inheritance, the fight goes on and pitiful birds, torn and dying, settle wagers, the profits of which are consumed in nearby taverns by the atrocious winners. I will only say of dueling with pistols that this English custom daily gains favor in the United States.

7.

A MERCHANT OF HAMBURG

The anonymous author of this account, Reise von Hamburg nach Philadelphia *(1800), appears to have been a German merchant, resident in Hamburg, who seems to have spent a year in the United States, chiefly in Baltimore and Philadelphia. He was well-acquainted with the mercantile community, both native and German; and his description throws light on life in the thriving American seaports.*

In no circle of society did I notice a decided addiction to cards; these people seem to have better ways of spending their time. They leave this pleasure almost entirely to Englishmen, who appear uncomfortable in a gathering where there is no gaming, and who often risk their fortunes in friendly play.

In the summer, as soon as the weather permits, the Americans are fond of excursions on the water. Many have their own boats, some of which are tastefully built and not outdone in splendor by Venetian gondolas. It is not unusual to see a large number of such vessels riding about. In the evening they often return to the accompaniment of music. Bedecked as they are with lanterns, they make a splendid sight from a distance. In Philadelphia and in other large cities people commonly sail about thus in the late evening when it is not too cool. Several groups get together; there are hundreds of little vessels; everywhere are fiddlers. The crowd is colorful and the music is not disrupted by loud noises; only the beat of the oars is heard.

The American seems well-disposed toward the theater; there is a very good playhouse in Philadelphia. Everywhere else marriage is the central concern of the drama; the plot develops up to that point and is generally resolved thereby. But such a content will be sought in vain in the pieces brought to the stages of the United States. Liberty is the central theme of these. Everything turns about that. At the heart of the play is always some republican idea and the development is marked by the warmest patriotism.

A German is always pleasantly surprised at the beautiful highways of England. But in America the roads are even better than in England.

Much more is spent in maintaining them, and nowhere can one travel more comfortably or more swiftly. The stagecoaches in the United States are very light; they hold eight or nine people comfortably; and not more than that are carried. I traveled in such a vehicle from Philadelphia to Baltimore in one day. The distance was twenty-five German miles. Yet only four horses were needed. The speed of these animals amazed me; I could hardly get a good look at the country through which we sped.

Baltimore does not approach Philadelphia in external splendor or in beauty of appearance. It is nevertheless a very nice town, with a population of about 30,000, and growing monthly. At the time of the War of Independence it was not a fourth so large. Commerce and freedom are the sources that nourish this growth. The houses are substantially built, the streets are broad enough to permit three wagons to pass each other easily, and on either side are stone walks for pedestrians, wide enough so that six people may walk abreast.

There is no better perspective from which to make judgments about a nation's character than from the observation of the manner in which it celebrates its national holidays. In the summer of 1796, in Baltimore, I observed a festive occasion, the third [sic] of July, anniversary of American independence. Several thousand militia soldiers, arrayed in fine uniforms, assembled in an open place and swore to fight to the death every enemy of freedom and of the republic.

Every republican spectator felt and thought as they did. Each man found pleasure in the thought that he was a citizen of so fortunate a country. The governor thanked them in the name of the state for these patriotic sentiments and loudly called out, "Long live the Republic!" A thousand voices responded. No one felt deceived. Tears dimmed the eyes of no man at the thought that his heart, if it could, would speak otherwise than his tongue.

After this festive scene the people returned to the city and gave themselves over to expressions of joy. Every ship in the harbor put out its banners, and the American flag waved even over many homes. In the evening the whole city was lighted up.

A few more words about Baltimore. Trade and shipping are not the only occupations of its inhabitants; there are also important mills and factories here. More than 300 French exiles, having requested an asylum, were invited by the government to take residence in a section of the suburbs. There they settled. Since these people were not accustomed to idleness in their former lives, they gave the government no cause to regret its benevolence. They show a praiseworthy industry. The diligence with which they apply themselves in the factories built since their arrival earns every sort of commendation. In another suburb on the other side of the city is a glass factory that grows ever more important. A few merchants in Baltimore and one in Bremen invested in this enterprise, and the profits they draw from it are said to be very large.

The environs of Baltimore are also exceedingly pleasant. Wherever the eye wanders it meets a pleasant scene. About four English miles from the city is an inn which is very popular in summer. It is built on a beautiful site on the Chesapeake, and has gardens in the English manner. Often a merchant who comes here to spend an afternoon with his family will be delighted by observing the arrival of one of the ships he believes still far off. Many gatherings naturally assemble here. Those who come by water instead of by land, rowing out to the place in boats, have a pleasant trip, with interesting scenery all the way.

The German in America is not a great favorite; superior women are not well-disposed toward him. In Baltimore, however, this situation is not so prevalent. Here the number of Germans is large. But newcomers discover that their countrymen in America are not what they were in the Fatherland. American manners of thinking often influence their conduct. They try to ape the Americans, and lose their sense of discipline. Perhaps the attempt to be like the Americans, nowhere so prominent as in Baltimore, accounts for the friendliness of the maidens to the Germans. Many young German merchants have married into well-connected families and thereby cut their last ties with the homeland. Alas, there are also some fine young men who came to Baltimore innocent in heart and were duped by attractive women. These men must pay dearly for their errors, losing peace and good name. A substantial young man fell into the clutches of one of these worthless females who emptied his pockets and led him into the most shameful dealings. Having already abandoned several men, she wished to complete her ruinous work by marrying him and he was too much enraptured with her to deny her anything. But his countrymen took a hand in the matter. Although he had, out of shame, avoided them and not confided in them they felt obliged to rescue him. Against his will, they took him to a ship, sails set, which brought him back to his homeland.

The German women who marry in Baltimore do not live in the pleasantest circumstances. There are only a few here, and these are, on the whole, obliged to stay by themselves. The American women do not seek their company and let them know, in no uncertain terms, that they are reluctant to become acquainted. One of these Germans is a very clever person and contrives to keep herself well-occupied. She seems capable of circumventing very easily the whims of the Americans. I only wish that fate had blessed this good women with a more suitable man than her husband. Money alone does not always lead to happiness, nor travel to understanding. This man, who has enjoyed both advantages, still does not know how to provide for the happiness of himself or of his family.

In Baltimore, as in other cities, the merchants occupy the highest social position; the ship captains are just below. Many captains manage to accumulate large fortunes, profiting from their dauntlessness and their willingness to risk their lives wherever there is a prospect of making money. Their skill supports them in their dangerous journeys; they never despair where others, in their place, would give up hope. The seamen of this place have an extraordinary knowledge of navigation, it is true. That is why they are so highly esteemed here. No other captains, no Germans, for instance, are so highly valued. Only those who come often to Baltimore may earn a respect above that accorded their countrymen, by real knowledge and by the absence of that avarice which makes them unbearable to Americans.

The fearful yellow fever took its toll in Baltimore in the autumn of 1797. All manner of regulations were vainly imposed to cut off communications with Philadelphia where the epidemic raged in full fury. Fate brought to Baltimore the same disaster that devastated the northern cities. Many people were snatched away in the prime of life; not a few Europeans were halted in the midst of their travels, as the fever put a swift end to their lives. A promising young German, despite every warning, could not forbear to visit a friend afflicted with the illness. He paid dearly for his friendship, was also stricken, and died. His father received the sad news at the same time that another letter, no less tragic, brought information of the death of his oldest son who, after a hard trip from Europe, found a grave in the waters of the Chesapeake.

Baltimore did not suffer from as complete a stoppage in business affairs as a result of the epidemic as did Philadelphia; but still there was a marked departure from normal. Many distinguished people moved out of the city, some shops were closed, ships fled from the harbor half-loaded, for they could not escape too swiftly. Considerable profits were thereby lost to the consignees; but even more damage was done to many houses by the fact that European goods were held back. Many vessels in German harbors were ready to sail for the United States when it became known that yellow fever had broken out in America. Some seamen fled from their vessels; others made difficulties about getting under way. This situation lasted long enough so that the best time for the disposal of European wares was past before it was settled.

The young Americans of Baltimore dress somewhat like those of Philadelphia. They wear very expensive garments; fine linens, coats of the best materials must call for not a little funds. They are, however, not overly concerned with the niceties of the toilet. One finds it not at all shocking to see a young man appear for a walk in shining white linens but in dressing gown and bedroom slippers.

It is a sign of a certain solidity in the character of Americans that they are not at all inconsistent in following the fashions. One will seek in vain the signs of foreign clothing even on young men returned from Europe. In Baltimore, as in Philadelphia, feminine hairdressing is always simple, not built up elaborately as in many German cities. The hair alone, which is worn short and curled, is the ladies' only adornment; they rarely wear hats. They seldom appear in the open outside of their own social circles. In the summer, unless one has been introduced into a family, one must entirely renounce their company; in the autumn they are not so parsimonious with their presence, since they enjoy the fresh air now and then.

The charge commonly made against American women that their manner of living is too free, that they appear everywhere without propriety, is altogether untrue. They certainly do not show themselves as often as do Parisian beauties on the boulevards and in the Tuilleries. They have more breeding than to appear, even with escorts, in the public places where the *dames entretenues* and other abandoned creatures are found.

Although Baltimore is the largest, wealthiest, most important city in Maryland, although it must soon catch up to Philadelphia, it is not the capital of the state. That dignity is held by Annapolis, a small town inhabited by some 10,000 people, which lies thirty-four miles from Baltimore, but which can be reached in about four hours by Americans who like to speed along the roads. There is no trade in Annapolis, but many rich merchants who made their fortunes in Baltimore come here to enjoy their money in peace. They settle on a convenient spot, spend large sums in building, and thereby beautify the place.

8.

A BOTANIST'S GLEANINGS

The son of a botanist and traveler, François André Michaux followed in the footsteps of his father. After a thorough education in forestry and medicine, he embarked upon an exploratory expedition to the western states in 1802 at the age of thirty-two. His journal, Voyage à l'ouest des monts alléghanys, dans les états de l'Ohio, du Kentucky, et du Tennessée . . . *(1804), was popular, translated into English and German. Perhaps not as popular, but far more important scientifically, was his great treatise on North American trees published in 1810 and repeatedly reprinted in many languages. For the latter work he was rewarded by the French Academy of Science. In middle life he retired to an estate in Vauxréal, where he lived tranquilly until 1855.*

Pittsburgh is situated at the junction of the Monongahela and Allegheny rivers, which together form the Ohio. The city is built on 40 or 50 acres shaped like a triangle, the three sides of which are enclosed either by the bed of the two rivers or by high hills. The houses, principally of brick, number about 400, and are clustered along the Monongahela, the most commercial part of the town.

The air is very salubrious at Pittsburgh and its environs; intermittent fevers are unknown there, although so common in the southern states, nor is the district tormented in the summer with mosquitoes. A person may subsist there for one-third of what he pays at Philadelphia. Two printing offices have been long established, and, for the amusement of the curious, each publishes a bi-weekly newspaper.

Pittsburgh was long considered by the Americans the key to the western country. The town has now lost its importance as a military post, but it has acquired a still greater one in respect to commerce. It serves as an entrepôt for the merchandise that Philadelphia and Baltimore send, in the beginning of the spring and autumn, to supply the states of Ohio, Kentucky, and the settlement of Natchez.

Goods are carried from Philadelphia to Pittsburgh in large covered wagons, drawn by four horses two abreast. The cost of transportation varies according to the season; but in general it does not exceed six piastres the quintal. It is about 300 miles from Philadelphia to Pittsburgh, and the carriers generally make the journey in from 20 to 24 days. The price of conveyance would not be so high as it is, were it not that the wagons frequently return empty, although they sometimes bring back fur skins from Illinois, and ginseng, which is very common in western Pennsylvania.

Pittsburgh is, in addition, the market place for the numerous settlements on the Monongahela and Allegheny. The produce of that part of the country finds an easy and advantageous outlet through the Ohio and Mississippi. Corn, hams, and smoked pork are the principal articles sent to New Orleans, from which they are reëxported to the Caribbean Islands. They also export, for the consumption of Louisiana, bar iron, coarse linen, bottles manufactured at Pittsburgh, whiskey, and salt butter. A great part of these provisions come from Redstone, a small commercial town on the Monongahela, about 55 miles beyond Pittsburgh. Together, these advantages of location have, within the last ten years, increased tenfold the population and price of articles in Pittsburgh and have contributed to the daily improvement of the town.

The major part of the merchants settled at Pittsburgh are partners or factors of Philadelphia firms. Their brokers at New Orleans sell, as much as they can, for ready money; or even better, take in exchange cottons, indigo, raw sugar, the produce of lower Louisiana, which they send off by sea to the houses at Philadelphia and Baltimore, and thus cover their first advances. The bargemen return by sea to Philadelphia or Baltimore, whence they go by land to Pittsburgh where most of them live. They prefer this 20 or 30 day passage from New Orleans to one of these two ports and the 300 mile journey by land. This way is not so difficult as the route by land alone, a matter of 1,400 or 1,500 miles from New Orleans to Pittsburgh. However, when the barges go only to Limestone, Kentucky, or Cincinnati, Ohio, the bargemen come back by land, a trip of 400 or 500 miles.

The navigation of the Ohio and Mississippi is so much improved of late that they can tell almost to a certainty the distance from Pittsburgh to New Orleans, which they compute to be 2,100 miles. The barges in the spring season usually take 40 or 50 days for a passage, which two or three persons in a *pirogue* (an Indian boat) make in 25.

Many Europeans are perhaps unaware that they build large vessels at Pittsburgh. The timber they use, oak, cherrywood, and pine, all being near at hand, the expense of building is not so great as in the Atlantic ports. The cordage is manufactured at Redstone and Lexington, where there are extensive ropewalks, which also supply rigging to ships built at Marietta and Louisville.

The three new western states have grown rapidly in population. Those states, where 30 years ago there were scarcely 3,000 inhabitants, now contain upwards of 400,000. Although the farms on the road are scarcely four miles distant from each other, it is very rare to find one, even the most flourishing, where one cannot with confidence ask the owner from whence he has emigrated, or, according to the light manner of the Americans, "What part of the world do you come from?" as if these immense and fertile regions were to be the asylum common to all the inhabitants of the globe. Now if we consider these astonishing and rapid improvements, what ideas must we not form of the height of prosperity to which the western country is rising, and of the recent expansion that the commerce, population, and culture of the country is undergoing since the addition of Louisiana to the American territory.

The region watered by the Monongahela River is extremely fertile; and the settlements formed upon the banks are not very far apart. Of all the little towns built upon the Monongahela, New Geneva and Redstone have the most active commerce. The former has a glasshouse, the produce of which is exported chiefly into the western country; the latter has shoe and paper manufactories, several flour mills, and contains about 500 inhabitants. At this town a great number of those who emigrate from the eastern states embark to go to the West. It is also famous for building large boats, called Kentucky Boats, used in the Kentucky trade.

I agreed to go to Kentucky by the Ohio, preferring that way, although longer by 140 miles, to the land route which is more expensive. However, as the waters were low at that season we were advised to embark at Wheeling, a small town 80 miles lower down the stream, to gain time and to avoid a considerable winding in the river.

On July 14, in the evening, we set out on foot and crossed the Monongahela at John's Ferry. After having skirted the borders of the Ohio about a mile and a half, we entered the wood, and went to sleep at an indifferent inn at Charter Creek, where there was but one bed for wayfarers. Whenever several come together, the last arrivals sleep on the floor wrapped in the rug which is always carried when traveling into the remote parts of the United States.

The following day we made upwards of twenty miles, and went to lodge with one Patterson. On this route the clearings are two or three miles distant from each other, and more numerous than in the interior of the country. The inhabitants of this part of Pennsylvania are precise in their behavior and very religious. We saw, in some places, churches isolated in the woods, and in others, pulpits placed beneath large oaks. Patterson holds an extensive farm and a corn mill built upon a small river. He sends his corn to New Orleans. The rivers and creeks are rather scarce in this part of Virginia, as a result of which they are obliged to have recourse to mills turned by horses. The flour they produce is consumed in the district, and does not enter into trade. No one has yet thought of constructing windmills, although there are favorable situations sufficiently cleared on the tops of several hills.

On July 16 we arrived at Wheeling very much fatigued. We were on foot and the heat was extreme. Our journey was rendered more difficult from the nature of the country, which is covered with hills, on some of which it took almost half an hour before we could reach the summit. Farms are numerous in the environs and the soil is extremely fertile. The produce of the land varies; it yields from 15 to 20 bushels of corn an acre, when entirely cleared, and only 12 to 15 when there are many stumps left, for in clearing they begin by cutting the trees within two feet of the ground and after that dig up the stumps. It is proper to observe that the inhabitants give only one tillage, use no manure, and never let the soil lie fallow. The value of this land varies with its quality. The best, with 20 to 25 acres cleared out of a plot of 200 or 300, is not worth more than three or four piastres an acre. The taxes are a penny or two an acre. Hands being very scarce, labor is dear, and by no means in proportion to the price of produce. The result ,is, that in all the middle and southern states, within 50 miles of the sea, each proprietor clears very little more than what he can cultivate with his own family, or with the mutual aid of his neighbors. This is even more true in the western country, where every individual may easily procure land and is excited to labor by its incomparable fertility.

On our way we passed through a narrow valley about four miles long, the borders of which contained beds of coal from five to six feet thick. This mineral is extremely common in all that part of Pennsylvania and Virginia, but as the country is nothing but one continuous forest and the population is scarce, these mines are of no account. Were they situated in the eastern states, where the great towns burn coal imported from England, their value would be great.

Wheeling has not been in existence more than twelve years. It consists of about seventy houses, built of wood, which, as in all the new American towns, are separated by an interval of several fathoms. This little town is bounded by a long hill, nearly two-hundred fathoms high, the base of which is not more than two-hundred fathoms from the river. In this space the houses are built, forming but one street, in the middle of which is the main road, which follows the windings of the river for a distance of more than two-hundred miles. From fifteen to twenty large shops, well stocked, supply the inhabitants twenty miles round with provisions. Wheeling also shares with Pittsburgh in the export trade carried on with the western country. Some Philadelphia merchants prefer to send their goods here, although the journey is a day longer. That trifling inconvenience is well compensated for by the advantage gained in avoiding the long winding of the Ohio beyond Pittsburgh.

We passed the night with Captain Reymer who keeps the Sign of the Wagon and takes in boarders at the rate of two piastres a week. The accommodation, on the whole, is very comfortable, provisions in that part of the country being remarkably cheap. A dozen fowls could be bought for one piastre and a hundred-weight of flour was then only worth a piastre and a half.

Until the years 1796 and 1797 the banks of the Ohio were so little populated that they scarcely contained 30 families in 400 miles. But since that epoch a great number of immigrants have come from the mountainous parts of Pennsylvania and Virginia and settled there. In consequence, the settlements are now so increased that they are not farther than two or three miles distant from each other. When on the river we always had a view of some of them.

The inhabitants along the Ohio employ the greatest part of their time in deer and bear hunting, for the sake of the skins which they sell. The taste for this kind of life is prejudicial to the cultivation of their lands. They have scarcely any time to improve their new possessions, and clear no more than eight or ten of their two or three hundred acres. Nevertheless, the produce that they derive from that area, with the milk of their cows, is sufficient for themselves and for their very numerous families. The houses that they inhabit are built upon the borders of the river, generally in a pleasant location from which they enjoy the most delightful views.

Still, their mode of building does not correspond with the beauties of the spot. They have nothing but miserable log huts, without windows, and so small that two beds take up the greatest part of them. In less than three days two men can erect and finish one of these habitations, which by their diminutive size and sorry appearance seem rather to belong to a country where timber is very scarce than to a place that abounds with forests.

The inhabitants on the borders of the Ohio do not hesitate to receive travelers who claim their hospitality. They give them a lodging, that is to say, they permit them to sleep upon the floor wrapped up in their rugs. They are accommodated with bread, Indian corn, smoked ham, milk, and butter, but seldom anything else, although the price of provisions is very moderate in this part of the United States, and all through the western country.

No attention is paid by the inhabitants to anything but the culture of Indian corn; and although it is brought to no great perfection, the soil being so full of roots, the stems are from ten to twelve feet high, and produce from twenty-five to thirty hundred weight of corn per acre. The Americans in the interior cultivate other grains only for speculation, to send the flour to the seaports. For their own consumption, ninetenths of them eat no other bread but that made from Indian corn. They make eight to ten-pound loaves of it, baked in ovens, or else small cakes baked on a board before the fire. This bread is generally eaten hot, and is not very palatable to those not used to it.

Those who have been settled for no more than eight or nine years on the two banks of the Ohio, properly speaking, or on the borders of the rivers that run into it, share but very meagerly in the commerce that is carried on through the Mississippi. Their trade consists at present of hams and salt pork, brandies distilled from corn and peaches, butter, hemp, skins, and various sorts of flour. They also send cattle to the Atlantic States. Peddlers from Pittsburgh and Wheeling go up and down the river in canoes and bring them haberdashery goods, and more especially tea and coffee, in return for some of their produce.

More than half of those who inhabit the borders of the Ohio are the first settlers, a kind of men who cannot remain upon the soil that they have cleared and who, under pretense of finding better land, more wholesome country, or a greater abundance of game, push forward, incline perpetually toward the most distant fringes of American settlement, and plant themselves in the neighborhood of the savage nations. Their ungenerous mode of treating the Indians stirs up frequent broils that bring on bloody wars, in which they generally fall victim rather on account of fewness of numbers than through deficiency of courage.

Prior to our arrival at Marietta we met one of these settlers, an inhabitant of the environs of Wheeling, who accompanied us down the Ohio, and with whom we traveled for two days. Alone in a canoe, eighteen to twenty feet long and twelve to fifteen inches broad, he was going to survey the Missouri River a hundred and fifty miles beyond its mouth. The excellent quality of the land, reputed to be more fertile there than on the shores of the Ohio, which the Spanish government at that time distributed freely, and the quantity of beavers, elks, and bisons, were the attractions that induced him to emigrate to this remote part of the country. After having determined on a suitable spot to settle with his family, he would return to fetch them from the borders of the Ohio, a journey of fourteen or fifteen hundred miles. His costume, like that of all the American hunters, consisted of a waistcoat with sleeves, a pair of pantaloons, and a large red and yellow worsted sash. A carabine, a tomahawk or little axe, which the Indians use to cut wood and to terminate the existence of their enemies, two beaver traps, and a large knife suspended at his side constituted his hunting equipment. A rug comprised the whole of his luggage. Every evening he camped on the banks of the river, where, after having made a fire, he passed the night. Whenever he found the place favorable for the chase, he remained in the woods for several days. From the produce of his sport he gained the means of subsistence, and with the skins of the animals that he had killed, new ammunition.

Such were the first inhabitants of Kentucky and Tennessee, of whom but very few now remain. It was they who began to clear those fertile tracts and wrested them from the savages who ferociously disputed their right; it was they, in short, who made themselves masters of the territory, after five or six years of bloody war. But the habits of a wandering and idle life have prevented them from enjoying the fruit of their labors, or from profiting by the price to which these lands have risen in so short a time. They have emigrated to more remote parts of the country, and formed new settlements.

It will be the same with most of those who live along the Ohio. The same inclination that led them there will induce them to emigrate. They will be succeeded by fresh emigrants from the Atlantic states, who abandon their possessions to go in quest of a milder climate and a more fertile soil. The money the latter get for their old properties will suffice to pay for their new acquisitions, the peaceful enjoyment of which is assured by a numerous population. The last comers will put wooden houses in place of the log cabins that satisfy the present inhabitants; they will clear a greater quantity of the land, and be as industrious and persevering in the improvement of their new possessions as the former were indolent in everything but hunting. To the culture of Indian corn they will add that of other grain, hemp, and tobacco. Rich pasturages will nourish innumerable flocks, and an advantageous sale of all the country's produce will be assured them through the channel of the Ohio.

For some time past the inhabitants of Kentucky have taken to rearing and training horses; and by this lucrative branch of trade they derive considerable profit on account of the superfluous quantity of Indian corn, oats, and other forage. Most of these animals were brought by emigrants from Virginia, which is said to have the finest coach and saddle horses. The number of horses, now very considerable, increases daily. Almost all the inhabitants employ themselves in training and improving the breed of these beasts; and so great a degree of importance is attached to breeding that the owners of fine stallions charge fifteen or twenty dollars for covering a mare. These stallions come from Virginia, and, I have been told, some were at different times imported from England. The horses that descend from them are elegantly formed, have slim legs and a well-proportioned head.

With draft horses it is quite different. The inhabitants pay no attention to improving this breed which, as a result, is small, wretched in appearance, and similar to those made use of by the peasantry in France. They appeared to me still worse in Georgia and upper Carolina. In short, I must say that throughout the United States there is not a single draft horse that can be in any wise compared with the poorest that I have seen in Picardy.

Many individuals profess to treat sick horses, but none of them has any regular notions of the veterinary art, an art which is so necessary in a breeding country, and which has recently acquired so high a degree of perfection in England and France.

The southern states, and in particular South Carolina, are the principal markets for Kentucky horses. They are taken there in droves of fifteen, twenty, and thirty at a time, in the early part of winter when most business is transacted in Carolina and when the drivers are in no fear of the yellow fever, of which the inhabitants of the interior have the greatest apprehension. It usually takes 18 or 20 days to go from Lexington to Charleston. This distance, about 700 miles, makes a difference of 25 or 30 per cent in the price of horses. A fine saddle horse in Kentucky costs $130 to $140.

The number of horned cattle is very considerable in Kentucky; those who deal in them purchase them lean and drive them in herds of from 200 to 300 along the Potomac to Virginia, where they sell them to graziers who fatten them for the markets of Baltimore and Philadelphia. The price of a good milch cow in Kentucky is $10 to $12. The milk in a great measure comprises the chief sustenance of the inhabitants. The butter that is not consumed in the country is put into barrels, and exported by the river to the West Indies.

Hogs are the most numerous of the domestic animals; they are kept by all the inhabitants. These animals never leave the woods, where they always find sufficient food, especially in autumn and winter. They grow extremely wild and generally go in herds. They are of a bulky shape, middling size, and straight eared. Every inhabitant recognizes his own by the particular manner in which the ears are cut. The pigs stray sometimes into the forests and do not make their appearance again for several months. Their owners accustom them, however, to return every now and then to the plantation, by throwing them Indian corn once or twice a week. It is surprising that in so vast a country, covered with forests, so thinly populated, and with so few destructive animals, pigs have not increased more.

In all the western states, and eastward to within two-hundred miles of the seacoast, everyone is obliged to give salt to the cattle. Otherwise no food would make these beasts look well; in fact they are so fond of it that they go of their own accord to implore it at the doors of the houses every week or ten days, and spend hours together in licking the trough into which a bit was scattered for them. This desire manifests itself most among the horses; but it may be because they have it given them more frequently.

Salt provisions form another important article of the Kentucky trade. The quantity exported in the first six months of the year 1802 was 72,000 barrels of smoked and 2,485 of salt pork.

The inhabitants of Kentucky, as we have before stated, are nearly all natives of Virginia, and particularly of the remotest parts of that state. Apart from the gentlemen of the law, physicians, and a small number of citizens who have received an education suitable to their professions in the Atlantic states, the Kentuckians have preserved the manners of the Virginians. They carry the passion for gaming and for spirituous liquors to an excess, which frequently leads to quarrels degrading to human nature. The public houses are always crowded, especially so during the sittings of the courts of justice. Horses and lawsuits comprise the usual topics of conversation. If a traveler happens to pass by, his horse is appraised. If he stops, he is presented with a glass of whiskey, and then asked a thousand questions, such as: Where do you come from? Where are you going? What is your name? Where do you live? What is your profession? Were there any fevers in the different parts of the country through which you came? These questions, which are frequently repeated in the course of a journey, become tedious, but it is easy to check these inquiries by a little tact, their only object being the gratification of that curiosity so natural to people who live isolated in the woods and seldom see a stranger. The questioning is never dictated by mistrust; for from whatever part of the globe a person comes, he may visit all the ports and principal towns of the United

States, stay there as long as he pleases, and travel in any part of the country without ever being interrogated by a public officer.

The residents of Kentucky eagerly recommend their state to strangers as the best part of the United States. There the soil is most fertile, the climate most salubrious, and all the inhabitants are there because they were attracted by the love of liberty and independence! The interiors of their houses are generally very neat. This induced me, whenever opportunity offered, to lodge with a private family rather than at a public house, where the accommodation is inferior although the charges are considerably higher.

The women seldom assist in the labors of the field. But they are very attentive to their domestic concerns, including the spinning of hemp or cotton, which they convert into linen for the use of their family. This employment alone is truly laborious, as few houses contain less than four or five children.

The Methodists and Baptists are the most numerous of the various sects that exist in Kentucky. The spirit of religion has acquired fresh strength among the country people within the past seven or eight years. Sundays are scrupulously observed, and they also assemble, during the summer, in the course of the week, to hear sermons. These meetings, which frequently consist of two or three thousand persons who come from all parts of the country within fifteen or twenty miles, take place in the woods, and continue for several days. Each person brings his provisions and spends the night round a fire. The clergymen are very vehement in their discourses. Often in the midst of the sermons heads are lifted up, imaginations exalted, and the inspired fall backwards, exclaiming, "Glory! glory!" This species of infatuation strikes chiefly the women, who are carried out of the crowd and put under a tree, where they lie a long time, heaving the most lamentable sighs.

There have been instances of two or three hundred in a congregation thus affected during the performance of divine service; so that one-third of the hearers were engaged in reviving the rest. I was present at one of these meetings in Lexington. The better-informed people do not share the opinion of the multitude with regard to this state of ecstasy, and are therefore branded with the appellation of bad folks. Except during the continuance of this preaching, religion is very seldom the topic of conversation. Although divided into several sects, the people live in the greatest harmony. Religious difference is never considered an obstacle to an alliance between families; the husband and wife pursue whatever worship they like best, and the children, when they grow up, do just the same, without the interference of parents.

Throughout the western country the children are kept punctiliously at school, where they learn reading, writing, and the elements of arithmetic. The schools are supported at the expense of the inhabitants, who send for masters as soon as population and circumstances permit. It is consequently very rare to find an American who does not know how to read and write. Upon the Ohio and in the Barrens, where the settlements are farther apart, the inhabitants have not yet been able to procure this advantage which is the anxious desire of every family.

The two Carolinas and Georgia are divided by nature into an upper and a lower section, the former being the greater. Just at the point where the tidewater ends, the soil begins to rise gradually till it reaches the Allegheny Mountains. This up-country is, on the whole, rather irregular than mountainous, and is interspersed with little hills as far as the mountains. The most fertile lands are situated upon the borders of little creeks that rise in the Alleghenies. The intermediate areas are much less fertile, and are not much cultivated. Those who own these lands are obliged to be perpetually clearing them in order to obtain more abundant harvests. As a result, a great number emigrate to the western country. They are attracted by the extreme fertility of the soil and low price of land; that of the first class may be purchased for the same money as that of the second in the upper Carolinas, and the latter is scarcely to be compared to that which in Kentucky and the Cumberland Valley is ranked in the third.

Everywhere the soil is well adapted for the growth of wheat, rye, and Indian corn. An acre of good land produces more than twenty bushels of Indian corn, commonly worth about half a dollar a bushel. This grain is generally consumed by the inhabitants, since few other than those of German origin use wheaten bread. Not much wheat is raised and the small quantity of flour that is exported to Charleston and Savannah is sold 15 per cent cheaper than that imported from Philadelphia.

The low price to which tobacco has fallen in Europe has ended its culture in these states. Green-seed cotton has taken its place to the great advantage of the inhabitants, many of whom have made their fortunes by it. The separation of the seed from the pod that envelops it is a tedious process which required many hands but is now simplified by a machine for which the inventor obtained a patent from the federal government. Three years ago the legislature of South Carolina paid him $50,000 so that every inhabitant of the state might have the privilege of erecting one. This machine, very simple and not above $60 in cost, is put in motion by a horse or by a current of water. It separates 300 or 400 pounds of cotton from the seed in a day, while a man by the usual method was not able to separate above 30 pounds. This machine, it is true, has the inconvenience of shortening the fiber by haggling it; the cotton on that account is rather inferior in point of quality, but this drawback is well compensated for by the saving of time and labor.

The commercial intercourse of the upper Carolinas and Georgia is carried on in a great measure with Charleston, which is not much further than Wilmington and Savannah. The inhabitants prefer to trade in Charleston because commerce is more active and sales easier there. They carry to market cotton, tobacco, hams, salt butter, wax, stag and bear skins, and cattle, and take in return coarse ironware, tea, coffee, powder, sugar, coarse cloths, and fine linen. They also bring salt from the seaports, since there are no salt pits. But they need no bar iron; the upper country abounds in mines of that metal, and those which are worked are sufficient for the wants of the inhabitants. They carry the goods in large four-wheeled wagons, drawn by four or six horses, travel twenty-four miles a day, and camp every evening in the woods. The cost of transportation is about three shillings and fourpence per hundredweight for every hundred miles.

Eight-tenths of the inhabitants of the upper Carolinas are in the same situation as those of Tennessee and Kentucky. They reside like the latter in log houses isolated in the woods and left open in the night as well as the day. They live in the same manner with regard to their domestic affairs, and follow the same plans of agriculture. Their moral characters are, however, probably not so unspotted as those of the westerners. They associate too much with the Scotch and Irish who come every year in great numbers to settle in the country, and who teach them the vices and defects that spring up among a great population. Most of these new immigrants go into the upper country, where they engage to serve for a year or two those persons who paid the captain of the ship for their passage.

The low country of the two Carolinas extends inward from the sea for 120 or 150 miles, widening toward the south. It contains an even and regular soil formed by a blackish sand, rather deep in parts, in which there are neither stones nor flints; in consequence of which they seldom shoe their horses in that section.

The best rice plantations are established in the great swamps, where water is plentiful. The harvests are abundant there, and the rice is larger, more transparent, and commands a higher price than that grown in a drier soil, where there are not the means and facility for irrigation. The culture of rice in the southern states has fallen off within the past few years; it has been in a great measure replaced by that of cotton, which affords greater profit to the planters. The result is that many rice fields have been turned over to cotton.

The soil most adapted to the culture of cotton is in the isles off the coast. Those which belong to Georgia produce the best, known in the French trade as Georgia cotton, fine staple, and in England as Sea Island Cotton. The seed of this kind of cotton is deep black, and the fiber fine and very long. The cotton planters particularly dread the frosts that set in very early and that frequently do great damage to the crops by freezing one-half of the stalks so that the cotton has no opportunity to ripen.

In all the plantations they cultivate Indian corn. They plant it, as well as the cotton, about two and a half feet apart in parallel furrows from fifteen to eighteen inches high. The seed of this corn is round and very white. When boiled it is preferable to that cultivated in the middle and western states. The chief part of what they grow is destined to support the Negroes nine months in the year. The allowance is about two pounds a day. The slaves boil it in water after pounding it a little. The other three months they are fed upon yams. Meat they never receive. In other parts of the United States the blacks are better treated, and live nearly upon the same as their masters without having any set allowance.

Through the whole of the low country the agricultural labors are performed by Negroes. The planters even use them to drag the plough; they think the land is thus better cultivated and calculate besides that in the course of a year a horse, for food and care, costs more than a slave whose annual expense does not exceed fifteen dollars.

A View of the Boats and Manner of Navigating on the Mohawk River, 1810

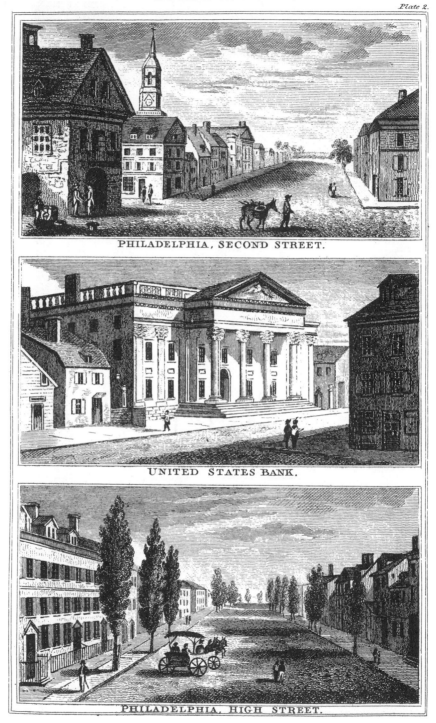

PHILADELPHIA, SECOND STREET.

UNITED STATES BANK.

PHILADELPHIA, HIGH STREET.

Street Scenes, 1820

9.

A BOURBON WHO REFUSED TO FORGET

The author of this bitter account—taken from his book, Voyage fait dans les années 1816 et 1817, de New-Yorck à la Nouvelle-Orléans et de l'Orénoque au Mississipi . . . (1818)—*was the descendant of the ancient family of de Pardiac, also called de Montlezun, from its chateau in Gascony. He had had a trying time in the revolutionary years and was not disposed to remain in Paris in 1815 when Napoleon returned from Elba. Even the restoration brought no relief to this malcontent. An ultra-royalist, who felt that Louis XVIII had disgraced the Bourbon tradition by conceding the meager constitution of 1816, de Montlezun traveled through the West Indies and through the United States, rubbing salt into his own wounds by contact with the democracy from which so many evils flowed.*

From Washington to Acquia Creek by steamboat is 40 miles. It is 18 more to Fredericksburg by a stagecoach on a road that runs along a creek subject to overflowing in the rainy season when travel simply ceases. Passage on the boat and a seat in the stage together come to $6.25, and includes a supper. It is true I had an additional expense from some bad paper money that I could not avoid taking in exchange for my own good currency. This new form of imposition is extremely burdensome. It would be very desirable to reëstablish the national bank, the notes of which circulated freely throughout the United States. Such a project, it seems, is contemplated but will not be put into effect until next year. They are still busy collecting the capital of some $25,000,000. When they were recently short by some $3,338,000 in completing the subscriptions, Stephen Girard, the Croesus of Philadelphia, said to the committee, "Gentlemen, I will take the rest." The most expeditious, and, I believe, the cheapest procedure, is to do as I did, that is, to pay a 15 per cent premium for good paper which will circulate anywhere. That 15 per cent can be a great economy in dealings with people who would not scruple to cause you a loss of 15 per cent in the exchange.

I must repeat again and again that the American stagecoaches are untrustworthy, and often an insult to common sense. It is impossible to

conceive the frightful inconvenience of these vehicles. You are fully
exposed to inclement weather and soaked as if you were out of doors.
You are crushed, shaken, thrown about, bumped in a manner that cannot adequately be described. Every mile there is a new accident and
you must get out into the mud while the damage is repaired. It is not
unusual to see the coaches shattered, the passengers crippled, and the
horses drowned. Yesterday a stage turned over near Washington and
broke the arm of a traveler. The roads are truly breakneck, likely at
any moment to upset you. If you comment at all on these conditions
you are stared at without comprehension. To pass from a steamboat to
a stage, especially in bad weather, is to descend from paradise to hell.

Fredericksburg is pleasantly situated. The principal street runs
parallel to the Rappahannock some hundred yards away. The ground
slopes gradually upward to the west to a beautiful plateau on which the
streets are laid out. The houses are set off by themselves and handsome,
although built of wood. There are gardens, but the charm of the place
is spoiled by a scowling sky, a hostile climate, and humid lands, to say
nothing of the somber solitude, of the bad manners and gross customs,
of the religious fanaticism, of the unbearable democracy of the great
mass of white inhabitants, of the comic pride of the wealthy classes, of
the lack of good tone and good taste, of the urbanity of an advanced
society. *Savoir-faire* is one of the charms of good birth; the absolute
lack of all these qualities and the too real presence of their antithesis
strongly repel the European in the United States and remind him always of the land of his ancestors.

Traveling from Fredericksburg, I arrived at Montpellier at the home
of President Madison. His residence is not at all elegant and hardly
comports with the dignity of its proprietor. It scarcely peeps through
the trees with which it is surrounded, but its interior is agreeably laid
out and conveniently furnished. The grounds are set out in the form
of an English garden, the lawn reaching up to the edge of the house
itself.

When I arrived I had the honor of meeting Mr. Madison, to whom
I presented my letters of recommendation, by virtue of which I was
well received and invited to remain for several days. The President
spoke French with difficulty, so I was forced to use his language. His
son who had recently returned from a profitable tour of Europe spoke
French well and seemed well educated. I also had the honor of being

presented to Mrs. Madison who arrived a little later. She is a handsome woman, although past her prime. Her features are noble, her manner gracious, and her speech pleasant. I was obliged to speak in English with Mrs. Madison too. The President, although rather cold and reserved, was extremely polite and affable; he is still vigorous and enjoys perfect health. After some conversation I was led to a room which gave out upon a view of the plain surrounded by blue mountains.

The evening passed with conversation and with music. Mistress Dade and her sister, Mistress Mason, sang, accompanying each other on the piano. We had tea and coffee and retired at an early hour. The next day I went to see a machine for beating wheat on one of the President's farms. This "strashing machine" is made up of two parts, one of which receives the sheaves fed to it by Negroes who strip them, while the other, made up of great toothed gears, set in motion by four horses, turns a wooden cylinder which acts upon the first machine. In one day this machine yields two hundred bushels. On the same farm, there are large flocks of merinos and of long-tailed rams from the cape of Good Hope, and of their half-breeds, the wool of which is well esteemed and sold at a high profit.

Sunday was rainy and displayed its customary gloom. The chill and dampness that descend even at the end of the very warm days made the little fire in the salon very comfortable. Reading, dining, some conversation, and chess (despite the sanctity of the day and the pressure of habits) kept us from boredom and led painlessly to bedtime.

In my private conversation with Mr. Madison, each day, I uncovered unexpected wisdom and a very wide knowledge. Exceedingly modest, he has a judicious and decisive spirit, is sagacious, and maintains an excellent tone in discussion. Never sharp, he always seems to grant that the one with whom he talks is his superior in mind and training. He is very well informed as to the politics of all the powers, and keeps abreast of events everywhere. Work seems easy for him. He reads and writes almost every day and often into the night. In joining a social group he relaxes, his face lights up. He takes pleasure in a well-turned phrase. He speaks gaily and with a simplicity that does him honor and that is particularly notable in the high places to which his talents have led him.

I also stayed with Mr. Jefferson at Monticello. His house is an irregular octagon with porticoes in the west and east, and peristyles in the north and south. In size it is about 110 by 90 feet. The Doric exterior is surmounted by balustrades. The interior is decorated in different orders of architecture: the vestibule, Ionic; the dining room, Doric; the drawing room, Corinthian; and the dome, Attic. The various rooms, eleven on the ground floor, six on the first, and four on the top, are decorated to conform with the style of their architecture, in their true proportions, after Palladio. From north to south at the level of the cellars is a passageway of 300 feet, leading to two wings each of which ends in a two-story pavilion. The upper story forms a gallery and is decorated with a balustrade in the Chinese fashion, rather low, not to obstruct the view. Further off are the kitchens, the servants' quarters, and other outbuildings.

Mr. Jefferson possesses an extensive library, a large collection of mathematical and optical instruments, and several curious Indian relics. In the vestibule also are a painting of a battle between the Panis and the Osages and a map of the Missouri River, both executed by Indians upon buffalo skin. There are bows, arrows, poisoned spears, peace pipes, moccasins, and other utensils of the Mandans and other tribes. The same place also contains a colossal bust of Mr. Jefferson, perched on a column whose pedestal is ornamented with symbols of the twelve tribes of Israel and the twelve signs of the zodiac; a statue of Cleopatra reclining and surrendering to the bite of the asp; busts of Voltaire and of Turgot in plaster; and a model of the great pyramid of Egypt.

Monticello has some 11,000 acres, of which about 1,500 are under cultivation. In addition, Mr. Jefferson owns land in Bedford County from which he draws large amounts of tobacco and grain to supply the population of his plantations. He also has merinos, Cape rams, a cotton and wool factory, and a nail works.

In this part of the country I often imagine myself back in one of our colonies. The labor on the land and the service in the homes are in the hands of colored people as in the Antilles. These are treated well in Maryland and Virginia, but not in the two Carolinas, in Georgia, and, above all, in Louisiana, where fear of insurrections leads to constant oversight and harsh treatment of the unfortunate blacks. Even in Virginia, in Richmond, the Negroes rebelled a little time ago, but the uprising failed and order was quickly reëstablished.

The number of slaves is very large. I saw Negresses with more than twenty children. The planters of the Carolinas and Georgia come here to buy their hands who are very expensive, ranging from $700 to $800. Mr. Madison has more than 300 and there are even more in Mr. Jefferson's Monticello.

The upcountry of Virginia is healthy and much superior to the lowland. Except in the cities and on the shores of navigable rivers the low country is almost entirely deserted and given over to forests. Meanwhile, population grows in the higher parts where there is purer air, more fertile soil, pleasanter scenery, and plenty of water.

Yesterday I attended the opening performance of the Baltimore theater. The newly decorated hall contained two rows of boxes in a semicircle decorated with Corinthian columns, an upper gallery, and a pit on the ground floor. It holds five hundred persons. The mechanical arts of the theater are backward here; at each change of scene one can see the men moving the sets about. Before the curtain went up the orchestra played a hodgepodge of musical pieces which made noise but no sense at all.

The main offering was an English drama, *She Stoops to Conquer*. The cast, as everywhere, even in Paris, was made up of the good, the mediocre, and the bad. A man named Jefferson was the most natural actor, the truest and the most facile that I saw; the rest are not worth mentioning. The women were uniformly bad. The play itself was tedious. It would be too tiresome to go into detail about the writing, which had no merit and bored with its length.

Before the second item on the program a dancer performed a few steps that would have drawn peals of laughter in any French city, but it disturbed the gravity of the Americans not for a moment. Between the acts the ladies, generally dressed in *mousseline*, sat in the front of their boxes with their backs to the audience, apparently so that one would be able to judge their figures from every point of view.

The second offering was a melodrama so annoying that I could hardly force myself to stay through to the end. It was a hash of robbers, caves, and kidnapings, stripped of any charm. After five hours of sitting, the spectacle was finally finished to my great satisfaction, and I returned to my hotel where neither the master nor the servants were on duty to attend to the needs of travelers, although almost a hundred people were lodged there.

The first night I passed in Philadelphia, thirteen months ago, I was

awakened by cries of fire; and so it was again the first night of my
return. But this time, by reason of the frequency of such incidents and
the prevailing apathy toward these noises, I was hardly more disturbed
than by the cries of the watchman who called out the time and the
weather. Philadelphia is no more gay than last year. It seemed to me
there were fewer strangers and less trade. As in the other American
cities, most of the women wore black, no doubt so as not to vary the
endless monotony of the country.

The women spend their days shopping; that is their favorite occupation. The men who are not now fully occupied with business hardly
know what to do with their time. Almost all the Frenchmen one meets
here, merchants, traders, and travelers are infected with revolutionary
poison. The natives, with a few exceptions among those who have seen
European society, are strongly democratic.

Their zealotry, although in appearance everywhere, is however
genuine only in the lower classes; everyone agrees that there is great
hypocrisy in the upper. Men in the United States are, so to speak, compelled to adopt a certain outward humility, from the fear of being suspected of a deficiency in republican principles. Any man may be
compelled to prove in a disagreeable manner that the lowest individual
in the lowest class has the same rights as he. The result is that the highest social classes, whether by rank or fortune, act with a certain air of
restraint, nature being the same everywhere and the same causes producing the same effects, particularly when it comes to such natural
human sentiments as pride and pomp.

The further result is that the women are deprived of the possibility
of satisfying their immense vanity by the disdainful countenances and
the superior air of their husbands and of the people with whom they
appear in public. Not being able to stifle that passion they trample
under foot their modesty, that irresistible charm with which nature endowed them, and assume a masculine, severe, haughty air. Their natural graces disappear beneath the severity of their appearance and the
affectation of male manners, as ridiculous as disgusting. This is to say
nothing of the fact that they are generally thin and ugly, with enormous
feet, an attribute of the lower classes which wealth cannot alter in one
or two generations and which often gives away the low birth of respectable persons.

People of good birth (an advantage praised by Homer, and before

Homer, and destined to be praised to the end of the world) have larger fortunes than the traders, have dignity and knowledge unattainable by those who spend all their time in the pursuit of profits and the calculation of interests. In addition, the wellborn are generally physically superior, more urbane, more polished, and have a better tone. Yet they seem so often simple and unpretentious as to stand out by that alone.

The cause is simple. The esteem they enjoy has deep roots, nourished through centuries. It is so well established and so undisputed that it gives birth to a modesty that causes those who witness it to be lavish in devotion with which they would have been miserly had it been demanded of them.

By contrast, when money alone raises us above the common herd, into which we may relapse at the slightest accident and from which fortune may raise the most obscure to our own level, the result is a ridiculous arrogance by which we accord to ourselves that which no one else will accord to us. And in this case, the obstacles, multiplied and increased, offend those who encounter them, harden their hearts and make of them the most detestable individuals that society can possibly be infested with.

In New York in the middle of October winter descends upon us. My eyes, accustomed to the blueness of southern skies, can hardly adjust themselves to the clouds that roll in from the sea. While the wise man devotes himself to his studies under his solitary roof, society gathers itself, coteries form, the idle are themselves again. Boxes fill up, Cupid unlooses his arrows, passions clash, the public places are full, the crowd sounds its bells, and stupidity tricked out in triangles and squares, in ribbons and in gravely ridiculous toys, draws a prolific breath, and, blindfolded, aspires to the honor of producing light; a miserable opaque mass surrounded by the blackest shadows!

In this country, where the word liberty never is omitted in conversation, there is the greatest tyranny of opinion; that is, of political opinion, for that is the only kind that seems important. You are pursued by such talk for twenty-seven years, you flee from Europe to escape it, and you fall here into a veritable whirlpool of it. You try hard to call off the hounds, speak vaguely, and turn away the conversation, but it always comes back. Good taste, bad taste, they must absolutely know if you are for the Federalists or for the Democrats. Are you convinced the American sailors will whip the English? Does your heart bleed for the independence of the Latin American colonies or do you think it unjust to interfere in that quarrel? Can you doubt that the United States in twenty-five years will have a population of forty million, and be the first country in the world? At the slightest deviation from the line of the fanatics, you are a marked man. You will be met coldly, the rules of politeness will be suspended in your case, and you will encounter unexpected reverses in your business, the origin of which only the inexperienced would find it difficult to guess.

Ease here is only superficial, but misery shows itself in all reality in its most hideous form. Yesterday, a white woman, nude on one side to the waist, sat on the sidewalk near Broadway exposing her sores to the view of the public and begging for alms. This country is hard and difficult, as much from a disgraceful climate, from its sandy soil, as from the disposition of almost all its inhabitants. One finds here some people distinguished by education, culture, politeness, and knowledge of how to live; but the number is infinitely small.

A certain disgust has overwhelmed me in the last few days and made writing repugnant. A pall seems to hang over New York, which certainly has not the amusements of the great capitals. Properly to describe this country one must speak eternally of the same things, the churches, the sects, the sermons, religious zeal and political fanaticism, revolution, patriots, insurrections, the great achievements of the Americans, their superiority over the English, the French, the whole world in the arts of peace and war, on land and sea, in shipbuilding, in the competence of their officers, in the incomparable courage of their leaders, their soldiers, their commodores, their sailors.

I, who have eyes and experience, who have some acquaintance with men and things, I have my own manner of looking at things, independently of the judgments of others, particularly when ignorance and blind presumption mold their opinions. Since it is not pleasant to tell people that which will offend them, I hide my ideas as much as possible. But they will find you out simply from the failure to go the full length they desire in exaggerated praise. In any case, nature has not made me capable of calling a frog a bull, no matter how it blows itself up.

The dominant character of Americans is arrogance carried to an extreme by various causes. In the case of most, lack of education is the root. Others know the political impotence of their country and moreover know the opinion that Europeans have of them because of their recent origin. These people can have no illusions about themselves. Their self-love is thus deeply wounded, and since nothing can wipe out this recollection or remedy this illness, this arrogance, born of desperation, is easily imitated by the people and inoculated among them by a crass ignorance. To arrogance is joined a great deal of superstition and fanaticism, of grandiloquent words about the rights of man and of the people, although slavery flourishes in most of their country; and declamations without end against tyrants and nobles, although there are none as bad as among them and although the aristocracy of riches, acquired God knows how, affects the most ridiculous pretensions. Joined to that is also a pronounced intolerance, a propensity for masonic stupidities and foolishness, a continual turgidity, a vanity born of the idea of their own merit and of the pretended superiority of a clownish population made up of odds and ends, of blacks, of yellows, and of whites, of European adventurers and their obscure descendants, scattered over a wretched land stolen from the peaceful Indian peoples. And all that is supported by an army of ten thousand raw troops, a navy of eight or ten frigates, three ships of the line, and some brigs of war, no forts, provinces open to attack from every side. Yet the end-result is an insatiable greed that satisfies itself at no matter what cost, a ridiculous presumption, a self-love that is more than comic. There you have a picture of the Americans and of their country.

Yesterday I had tea with some Americans. One of them spoke of the War of Independence, and when the subject of the capture of the Comte de Grasse came up, said to me with an imbecilic air, perfectly suited to him, "The French were flogged that day, weren't they?"

A deep silence accompanied my response. "I believe," I said, "that it is always better to use the proper word, the one you employed does not fit. The French were beaten on April 12 but they were victorious three days earlier. They had won near your shores when your masters, the English, attempted to punish you as rebels; these same Frenchmen gave you powerful aid in gaining your independence, and without them, there is no doubt that the British would have triumphed. Then it would have been said in Europe, 'the Americans have been flogged and forced to obey!'"

Above the room in which I write is a lodge of those who call themselves masons. I hear them sing, and I shrug my shoulders. I hear them

knock, and I blush. If these antics had existed at the time when that
ancient sought a man, lantern in hand, he would have turned aside at
the sight of them. It took no less than all the modern poverty of spirit,
united with a suffocating pride, to give birth to this mass of childish
absurdities. The United States is singularly good soil in which these
sprout. The students have indeed surpassed the teachers.

My window looks out upon Saint John's Hall, a masonic lodge.
Above the sign is a figure of the sun. Only half the golden ball shows,
apparently to indicate that the new hemisphere alone is blessed with
its light while the old is still buried in darkness.

At four in the afternoon, in spite of the sanctity of the Sabbath,
so rigorously respected in other respects, I saw the most bizarre spectacle I ever witnessed in my life. Many people gathered in the street
to watch. Five or six companies of masons, with about fifty men in
each, came out, led by an archmason, sword in hand, apron spread,
a red sash tied around. Behind the leaders, two brothers held a kind
of taper, lighted and crossed; after these, two others carried a little
box (apparently Pandora's); and finally, the host of followers decked
out in the costumes of the lodges, aprons, bouquets, belts, sashes, com-
pass, and all the knickknacks of the *illuminati*. One could only blush
to see them. And these same people mock the processions of the Roman
Catholics, consider themselves the most enlightened of mortals. One
might understand it if this were a gathering of workers and artisans;
but among them were men of education, who should have had sense.
It is impossible to account for all this.

How stupid human beings are! How steeped in insoluble darkness
and encrusted with errors! Why did not whistles, sardonic laughter, and
signs of contempt do justice to this burlesque mummery, this shameful
parade, this social degradation? The reason is simple. The whole mass
of people here is gangrened and the few individuals enlightened
enough to laugh and mock are too far dominated.

And what was the function of this parade of three-hundred bourgeois, marching to the sound of music, their trousers half hidden by a
scrap of cloth?—It was a funeral.—Whose? A member of the government?—No.—A general?—No.—A distinguished citizen?—No.—Well,
then whose?—Why simply one of the brethren who knew how to recognize certain signs and pronounce certain magic words, to knock three
times on a table, to drink and howl, to deck himself out in rags and

believe himself initiated into the superhuman sciences, to such important secrets, that by their discovery the human spirit is raised to its highest possible level. What poor devils there are in this world!

On disembarking at New Orleans it is immediately apparent that one is in a French city. The place contains 28,000 to 30,000 souls, of which three-quarters are Negroes or have colored blood. It is heart-rending to see in the streets white people whose misery contrasts with the insolent luxury of some colored women. The French inhabitants are mad Bonapartists; there are scarcely a dozen royalists among them.

Here we are at the end of the world; these are, so to speak, the modern pillars of Hercules. The local newspapers print old news, and gather all the revolutionary muck to quench the public's thirst for the intoxicating light of the century. At this very moment a treacherous war is being levied against Spain, without any formal declaration. Last week pirates brought into this port a prize loaded with about 200,000 piastres in specie and merchandise of great value. Today it is learned that a vessel armed in New Orleans, from which it sallied out a few days ago, met four Spanish ships in the gulf on their way from Vera Cruz to the Mississippi, captured them and took them to Matagorda to be declared prizes. Every honest man shudders at these shameful depredations against a brave, loyal, generous nation, and one that is religiously scrupulous in keeping its treaties.

Trade is now stagnant in Louisiana, as in the other parts of the United States. Goods sell at a very low price and the back country will offer no exports until the season for collecting the sugar and cotton.

Louisiana sugar is not first rate. There are few refineries, and not more than fifty or sixty Negro slaves are employed there. The Negroes generally cost about a thousand piastres. The cold weather causes many illnesses among them and often the amputation of an arm or a leg. Many are thus lost. Others fall prey to crimps who assist them to escape. Cotton culture is subject to heavy losses. Cold weather, caterpillars, and other insects make war on this plant which needs a warm and consistent climate.

At every step, in the streets, and in the markets, one meets groups of Indians, men, women, and children. These people are gentle and peaceful. Their features are ignoble but the rest of their body seems cast in a mold, and the beauty of their arms and legs is particularly

admirable. The women are hideous. They all walk about clothed only
in a little cloth blanket, which they pass across the shoulders and wrap
around themselves down to the thighs.

The children of Louisiana, like those of every other part of America,
are absolute masters of their fates. The authority of the parents is no
restraint at all. Two passions which develop in them from the earliest
age add to the force of habit, to the uncontrolled manners, to the weakness of the heads of the family, to the difficulties of teaching and of
giving a proper education. The young boys hardly reach the age of ten
when they give over whole days to hunting; others, even younger,
manage to follow this pursuit in the precious times that should be devoted to primary studies. The taste for the chase, once inculcated, becomes all absorbing. The girls from the age of seven on think only of
the ball. The wisdom of parents and their wishes must yield to this
unstoppable force. Indeed, nothing can check it, for it always emerges
triumphant, despite the very grave consequences.

In the course of the past year New Orleans was visited by two
plagues, by a fire which consumed the exhibition hall and the surrounding quarter, and by a flood which forced half the inhabitants to desert
their homes and seek refuge on the roofs of those not yet reached by
the water. But no sentiment of compassion arose in the hearts of neighbors, who eagerly profited from the situation by doubling the price of
lodging, certain that necessity would submit to any conditions.

The morose habits of the sad American have not won out here.
Sunday is a day of pleasures as in France. The balls are attended with
an inconceivable avidity. The passion for dancing is at its height. The
carnival is about to begin. It is a time for dressing up, for games, for
love. The comedy is only a medium for relaxation, for more immediate
and more piquant pleasures. The ladies who live in the country come
into the city to take part in the gaiety and to contest the prize for
beauty, for elegance, and for grace.

The legislature of the state of Louisiana is now in session. I listened
to the House of Representatives yesterday in a little room, bad in
appearance, where a dozen or so champions of liberty, equality, and
fraternity sat. A French lawyer had the floor when I entered. He advo-
cated at length new obstacles to the enfranchisement of slaves when
they were the securities for the loans of the masters. The speech was
summarily translated by an interpreter; and the preachers of liberty,

agreeing with the orator, sanctioned for their own territory the most abject slavery. At the very same time they tolerated, in time of peace, the equipment of an insurrection against a friendly country under the ridiculous pretext that the sweet liberty was not enjoyed there of injuring the sovereigns, the office holders, and property, and that it was forbidden to parade in the street carrying on the front of one's trousers a piece of rag embellished with a trowel, or a sash, or a wooden taper symbolizing the high light of the honorable brother masons, carpenters, shoemakers, joiners, artists, lawyers, merchants, shopkeepers, clerks, innkeepers, laborers, all sorts of working people and others enlightened by the Grand Orient and called to regenerate the world and shed upon it the light that shines from these gentlemen.

It is with such benevolent objectives that the levelers of this country have laid hold of Matagorda, a port on the coast of Mexico, after having excited a rebellion of which they were the firmest supporters. To this coast, vessels loaded with arms, powder, and munitions are daily sent from New Orleans. That was the occupation of the *Firebrand* when Lieutenant Cunningham who commanded it was compelled to lower his flag and surrender to the Spaniards who took him for a pirate.

The Americans let no opportunity go by to take root in Louisiana. With the aid of money or jobs, they insinuate themselves into the old homes, and already several have established matrimonial alliances with French families. The latter, full of confidence, know neither the character nor habits of the newcomers, and ignore the very startling differences in manners. But the Yankees will never triumph, because of the inexpressible repugnance felt here for their somberly morose character and their archfanatical disposition.

The Americans have a special fondness for the upper part of the city, near the Faubourg Sainte Marie. There they have built some miserable red houses, according to their custom, with windows like guillotines, and they have also erected a little octagonal edifice where a pedant, as proud as he is ignorant, delivers harangues on sin before an audience of hypocrites.

The money of Louisiana is that of Spain, the piastre and the doubloon; the latter is worth sixteen dollars, the piastre is worth eight escalins or four gourdes; the smallest piece is the demi-escalin or picayune, worth six French sous.

Since their arrival, the Americans have formed banks which emit their paper at will. Confidence having failed recently, the public presented its bank notes for payment in specie, but payment could not be made for more than twenty-four hours. The banks were closed and all sorts of ruses employed to reëstablish tranquillity and to restore the circulation of the paper.

The place is now flooded with paper notes so dirty and so disgusting that one can hardly bear to touch them. The notes for one, two, or four escalins hardly show their printing; and their decrepitude makes it necessary to stitch them together out of three or four scraps. Often it seems like a poor joke to be offered these miserable rags for a piece of money.

Yesterday I attended the ball of the white ladies; they thus distinguish this affair from that of the ladies of color. It took place in a very large and beautiful hall, square and long, where the lodges ordinarily meet. Two-hundred candles supplied light without offending the sight, as do those abominable Argand lamps, that a barbarous fad has lately adopted in France.

Sixty young maidens were the ornaments of the ball. They were dressed in white gowns, elegantly made, although simple. Almost all wore white roses in their hair, which was artistically curled, plaited with taste, and draped with grace in elastic and floating curls on virginal foreheads, and about snow-white necks and rose-colored cheeks.

Here, as in other warm climates, love of the dance is the dominant passion of the young girls. The women conserve the taste for it until an advanced age. And young mothers, finishing a waltz, go off to suckle their new babies, which the freedom of their costume makes possible with slight effort.

The ball began at eight and lasted until three in the morning. The ladies went home on foot, in all the modesty of a primitive epoch. Before the sidewalks which now embellish the city were built, the ladies were forced to come to the ballroom barefooted while their slaves brought along the finery in which they would ultimately bedeck themselves. In returning they had to take off their inconvenient footwear, and, in the manner of the first ages, those delicate feet were planted in the mud which was never lacking in New Orleans in the season when the carnival took place, for the streets were not paved, since the region contained no stones.

Despite the efforts of the Americans to unite Louisiana with the other states, to amalgamate its population with theirs, and to reshape its laws and customs in the intolerant form of their own hateful mold, nature, stronger, laughs at their vain attempt. French gaiety remains unperturbable. The American is still the stranger in the land; the general spirit still contrasts sharply with his own, and I do not think that he can reasonably flatter himself with the hope that Louisiana will ever be truly American.

10.

THE JESUIT SCHOLAR

Giovanni Antonio Grassi, one of the first novices in the reconstituted Society of Jesus, was born near Parma in 1775. Educated by the Order in Russia, he became rector of its nobles' college in Polotsk in 1804. Thereafter he spent several years in Portugal and in England, and, in 1810, came to the United States. His book, Notizie varie sullo stato presente della repubblica degli Stati Uniti dell' America . . . *(1819), was the result of that visit. For five years, after 1812, he served as president of Georgetown College, then returned to Rome to do administrative work for the Order. Later, he became rector in Turin and confessor to King Charles Felix of Sardinia. Father Grassi died in 1849.*

Approximately one-seventh of the total population of the republic are Negroes, who are held in servitude in apparent contradiction to one of the first articles of the constitution which proclaims liberty an inalienable right inherent in man. It is undeniable, on the other hand, that there are good reasons for not according freedom all at once to the mass of slaves. But let no one believe that the shores of the American republic are today the scenes of the inhuman spectacle of ships landing cargoes of these unfortunate victims of human avarice. The Negroes who are found in the United States are the descendants of those Africans who in former times were transported to the colonies of the New World. The importation of slaves from abroad is now severely prohibited. But the internal trade in these miserable beings still continues; men are sold to men, and the sad clang of servile chains may yet often be heard beneath the sun of liberty.

In many states the Negroes are well treated and even better fed than European peasants; but in many others they are left in a total ignorance of religion. There is no oversight of their manners, they are not baptized nor, in due time, are they united in the sacred bonds of matrimony. The avaricious master counts it enough that they labor; for the rest, they are allowed to follow like animals the dark impulses of their passions, to practice witchcraft and superstitions which surpass belief. This takes place chiefly in the southern states; in the North slavery is abolished, and that example will little by little be imitated everywhere.

Many Europeans imagine that a large proportion of the inhabitants of America are civilized aboriginal Indians. But this is an error, since the population is almost entirely made up of Europeans—English, Irish, German, French, and others. And it is worthy of remark that these people generally came into possession of their land in a much different way from that by which the Spaniards became masters of South America and the English of a large part of the East Indies. The Americans came into possession not through violent invasion, sword in hand, but peacefully through friendly treaties with the Indians themselves, who ceded or sold their lands and retired up the rivers ever further into the interior.

It will not be inopportune to mention how the land is sold and what plan the government adopts to put every industrious person in a position to become a freeholder and to prevent monopolies, while at the same time obtaining an income for the republic. The plan is as follows. Before the land ceded by the Indians to the government is exposed to sale it is surveyed by order of the public authorities, divided into townships and subdivided into sections. Each township is six miles square and is divided into thirty-six sections. Each section contains 640 acres and each is distinguished by numbers from 1 to 36. Number 16, approximately in the center, is reserved for the support of a school and the three adjacent sections are set aside for the government, to be sold in the future if Congress should see fit. In Washington, seat of the supreme government of the United States, there is a general office for land sales and in each district there are subordinate offices to make sales. The smallest quantity the government will sell is 160 acres at $2 each, one-quarter payable at once, and the rest over four years. Whoever can purchase for cash can buy at $1.64 an acre.

This is the plan; now let us see the effects. Every industrious person capable of paying the small sum of $80 can become a free owner of land; and although he has not a dollar more, he always succeeds in paying the balance before the end of the four years, with the proceeds from the timber that he cuts to prepare the land for cultivation. He finds it necessary, of course, to think of the long voyage, to provide himself with several animals, agricultural utensils, and the means of maintenance until he is able to make a harvest from his land. But he then becomes a peaceful landowner, with no further impositions to pay except a tiny tax on his holdings, and can live on happily. This is one of the principle reasons why the population of the United States grows without limits. The father of a numerous family gives a small capital to his adult sons, who go into the interior, buy there, and work on the land. They put themselves in a position to support themselves, a wife, and children well. Someone else, who can barely make a living where he is, sells his few possessions, goes into the interior, and with the price received from the sale of his old possessions acquires a holding ten times as large and one that is, furthermore, capable of meeting the needs of his family.

It will readily be understood how different the situation of the colonists established in new lands will be from those of the inhabitants of cities and of areas already well populated. The new settlers live at first in houses formed of logs with the spaces between stopped up with stones and mud which scarcely suffice to keep out the wind. When they become more settled they build a frame house, which can be kept much neater and cleaner. The servants' quarters, the kitchen, the coach house, the stable, barn, and a shed for keeping meat, are generally separate from the building in which the master lives. Those settlers who become rich build themselves houses entirely of bricks, and thus approach the style of the towns.

The American cities have the rare advantage of being built according to well-designed and uniform plans. The streets are wide and straight, with poplars now and then along the way. Along the sides are convenient walks which spare the pedestrians the inconveniences they meet in most European cities from wagons, carriages, and horses.

Except for some government buildings, and a few banks, the architecture is simple and monotonous. The façades of the houses are of red bricks, with little intervals of white. In the rooms there are few pictures, statues, or decorated furniture; instead they prefer mahogany furniture and fine carpets on the floors. If these lack the Italian magnificence, they have, in general, an air of ease, of simplicity, and of cleanliness.

In the cities the window glass, the floors, and the thresholds of the doors are washed at least once a week. The buildings seem rather weak and always are built with a very large amount of wood, which accounts for the frequency of fires. But the safeguards for extinguishing them are effective, since each quarter has its night watchmen, and there are also men appointed to appear at first sound of the alarm, bringing pumps, ladders, pails, axes, and other instruments that may be needed.

Palaces like the Italian are altogether unknown. The houses are made in such a manner that each is used exclusively by one family; the rooms each occupies may be one above another and not all on the same floor. It would seem very strange to an American to learn that in Europe one family lives on the first floor of a house, another on the second, and still another on the third. And it would seem even stranger to see horses and carriages come out of the houses.

No plazas or fountains or the other ornaments familiar in Italy are to be seen in American cities. Water is abundant. There are frequently pumps in the street for public use, and there are underground pipes that carry water to the various houses. In the interest of quiet and cleanliness, the slaughterhouses are on the outskirts of the city and only the meat ready for sale may be brought to shops and markets.

Civil order and public tranquillity are generally well-maintained. The abundance of bread makes certain that those who are not lazy will not be poor and will not beg in public. However, many artisans spend as much as they earn, and whenever they are ill find themselves reduced to the most deplorable misery.

English is the language universally spoken, and it is not corrupted here as in England by a variety of dialects. Weights and measures follow the English manner, but there is a decimal money and the dollar is worth one Spanish piece. To avoid the inconvenience of carrying around coins, they use a great deal of bank notes.

Among the inhabitants of the United States, those from New England, called the Yankees, are regarded as the most knavish and capable of the most ingenious impositions. The large volume of business that they carry on in all the other states, and the tricks they resort to for profits have fixed this conception on them. It is certain that to deal with such people one needs much sagacity and an exact knowledge of their laws of trade. But it seems to me unfair to extend this reputation, which may fit some individuals or even a whole class of people, to all the inhabitants of those states.

The limitless liberty that reigns here, the frequent drunkenness, the intermixture of so many adventurers, the number of Negroes held in slavery, the variety of sects that take hold everywhere, the slight knowledge of the true religion, the incredible quantities of novels read, and the eager pursuit of profits, are, in truth, elements that stand in the way of a proper view of American customs. At first view, it is hard to realize the waste that is common in this country, since it is often covered over by a veil of superficial well-being. But that waste is not difficult to discover when one becomes a little familiar with these people, especially in the cities.

The sight of gambling and of drunkenness is more frequent here than in Italy, if that may be believed, and the consequences are fatal to individuals and to entire families. Behavior is generally civil, but one will find many deficiencies in the niceties. It is, for example, not regarded as uncivil to cut the fingernails and comb the hair in the presence of others, or to remain seated, feet on the next chair or propped up high against the wall. When a stranger is introduced to a group by an acquaintance, the latter will point out and name each person individually. Friends who meet again after many years will not embrace each other; they are content to shake hands. Mothers have the praiseworthy custom of suckling their offspring themselves; they would be even more worthy of praise if they were to do it more modestly.

The custom of binding babies has altogether been given up in the United States. The complexion of the natives is rather pale, although few lamed and deformed people are seen here. Even a wealthy man will not be above handling the plough and the pick in the fields, or eating there with the day laborers. Luxury in clothing has reached a degree unknown even in Europe; in the country they dress as well as in the city, and the cost of a holiday garment is no index of the condition of the persons who wear them. Balls are the most common entertainment of Americans; the mania for jumping about in this manner is not less powerful here than in France itself.

Points of honor occasion frequent duels. To evade the laws, the combatants go to the borders of some neighboring state to settle their quarrels in this barbarous, foolish, and superstitious manner, in which the aggressor always wins, and in which the innocent bear the heaviest burden of injuries. To reprimand such madness, and to excite the public authorities to more zeal in suppressing it, one need only think of the tragic accidents which were fatal both to individuals and to the public, such, for instance, as the killing of Hamilton by Burr. On the site of this death a monument was erected as a constant warning to the duelists of New York. Two years ago, two young officials in Virginia lost their lives in a duel with pistols, the method ordinarily used here. These are the advantages which result from such affairs of honor.

The observers of American customs have always deplored the fact that the fathers, especially in the South, yield sadly and foolishly to their children whom they seem unable to contradict and whose capricious wishes they do not restrain. Education is, however, far from neglected, especially insofar as it helps to maintain status or to earn a fortune. To facilitate that training, even for the poor, parents and guardians are, by law, authorized to put young people under some artisan who binds himself to hold them as apprentices until the age of twenty-one, and to teach them a trade, reading, writing, and reckoning. The laws insist very strongly on the last points, so important for the public good. Such education is so highly esteemed that a father will use almost all the capital which will be the portion of his son to give him a literary education. A rich farmer will often send one of his sons to the university and keep another with him at the plough. Finally, some young men of narrow fortunes will spend a winter teaching in rural elementary schools in order to earn enough to maintain themselves at some college.

There are two sorts of literary education, one classical, the other simple English. The first includes belles-lettres, Greek and Latin, rhetoric, mathematics, and the various branches of philosophy, and is designed for those who intend to practice law or medicine. The second, for those destined for agriculture or trade, consists of the study of good reading and correct writing in their own language, arithmetic, a little geography, and similar subjects. In New England the laws compel every town of fifty families to maintain a public school. The Lancastrian system is common in America. When it was first introduced even the genteel parents of good position sent their children there, but these were compelled to withdraw very soon because of the rusticity of the customs and the corruption of manners that came from contact with the dregs of the low common people. The education of girls rarely permits them to handle well the needle and the spindle, but never lacks instruction in the dance. Sometimes a few lessons in music, in drawing, and perhaps even in French top off their education. It is a matter of prestige for the ladies to be able to say they have studied music, drawing, and French.

The European instructors brought to teach in America have always admired the docility and modesty with which girls behave whenever they find themselves in a school with a regular discipline, at least if they are not spoiled to begin with. These qualities are united to a certain freeness and maturity of judgment, rarely found elsewhere. But, especially among those born and raised among Negroes, there are rarely found noble and disinterested thoughts and sentiments, generosity, honor, or gratitude.

Instability of fortunes seems more common to Americans than to the youth of other countries; they frequently have the misfortune to see the finest hopes betrayed by tragic changes. When they reach a certain age they become impatient with suggestions, at least with those that do not coincide with their own. The liberty that they assume often descends to insubordination and to violent revolts against superiors. Such uprisings are not unusual in American colleges, and have lately occurred in Princeton in New Jersey and in William and Mary in Virginia; the students broke windows, chairs, furniture, and everything that came to their hands, and were at the point of destroying the very buildings. Since the people who preside over such places are concerned only with the injection of a little knowledge into the students, it is not surprising that the latter bring themselves to certain excesses of misbehavior which are condemned by honest Americans.

In the United States, where the spirit of trade and avidity for profits distinguishes all classes, it is not surprising that the flowers of poetic genius fail to flourish. There are no lack there of gifted men; but a wide acquaintance with many subjects is more characteristic than a profound knowledge of any single field. A kind of superficial tincture of learning is perhaps more widespread and more common in America than elsewhere. The well-educated man is continually surprised to hear the decisive and certain tone with which all manner of subjects are discussed. There is probably not a house in which will not be seen instructive books, stories, and novels; even if there is no Bible or catechism, there will infallibly be a newspaper. These are in America the most common fonts of erudition, the universal encyclopedias that speak on every subject, the tribunals in which literary controversies are brought to the judgment of the public, the heralds that announce everything that happens in the four corners of the world—declarations of war and treaties of peace and commerce, the expenses of government, the decisions of the courts, the prices of all sorts of merchandise, accidents, deaths, marriages, and new inventions.

A European can sometimes hardly restrain his scorn and laughter when he reads in the same issue an enthusiastic eulogy of liberty and the advertisement of the sale of a number of slaves, or a notice that a certain Negro is in prison for having attempted to become, through flight, one of those heroes of liberty. An incredible number of these newspapers are published, and, to encourage circulation, the government charges only one cent for carrying a large issue a hundred miles. To the continual and universal reading of newspapers must be attributed the purity of the English language, even among the vulgar people. Another consequence is that politics is one of the most frequent subjects of conversation and every man thinks and talks as does the paper he reads.

There are also some scientific and general journals, but these rarely continue for many years. The one that has best survived is the edition of the *Edinburgh Review* reprinted in New York. Greek and Latin literature are commonly cultivated, but, with few exceptions, not well enough to bring a true knowledge of the beauties of the original masterpieces. Otherwise, could their public prints hail Barlow's *Columbiad* as a poem equal or even superior to those of Homer and Virgil? Would they speak of their public oratory as superior to that of Demosthenes and Cicero?

I will not deny that Americans express themselves with much facility and elegance and now and then produce pieces of fine eloquence. Eloquence is, in fact, after gold, their highest ideal. But of all the parts which, according to the great masters, make up the art of speaking well, they cultivate elocution with most zeal. A speech with elegant expressions, ornate phrases, and harmonious periods will be considered a great oration although undistinguished in originality of invention, beauty of thought, weights of ideas, force of argument, regularity of development, or movement of the emotions. In view of the encomiums of American eloquence, I wished to procure at least a single example worthy of presentation in Europe and to posterity as equal to that developed among us across the Atlantic; but no one could give me one, and frequently those which were cited as masterpieces by some were rejected by others as of slight worth.

There are many students of medicine in all parts of the United States, but from the point of view of the quality of studies there is an important distinction between the northern and the southern states. In the former there are wise regulations for the study and the practice of this noble art, in the latter it is often only necessary that a young man assist a licensed doctor for some time, to qualify himself for a license. The use of mercury is common enough, and what in Italy would seem even stranger, the doctors themselves also act as apothecaries, so that it may well be imagined how much must be paid for medicines. The United States, already, glory in having produced Doctor Rush, whose works are highly esteemed in Europe.

What might be called the material parts of literature are more advanced than is thought in Italy. The printing establishments are numerous and turn out books of remarkable elegance, embellished with fine engravings. The series of Latin authors published in Boston, the American ornithology with fine colored plates in Philadelphia, and an edition of Barlow's *Columbiad* are fine examples and will always be monuments of the excellence of American typography.

Trade in books is brisk. There are also many circulating libraries from which each one may borrow for a given time by paying a certain sum. But unhappily the most popular reading is in novels which serve to deprave hearts and minds. As far as the various public libraries are concerned, that at Philadelphia is the largest, and that of the college in Cambridge reputed to have the best collection. On hearing that the government library in Washington cost $24,000 an Italian would be well impressed, but he would be quite disillusioned if he actually saw and examined it.

Painting, sculpture, and the arts of ornamentation are on the whole in their infancy in the United States. They are not regarded with respect or esteem. In Philadelphia and in New York there are academies of fine arts, and the success in painting of two Americans, West and Trumbull, is proof sufficient that the natives of the United States are not lacking in the genius needed to succeed in the arts, if they wished to cultivate them. The philosophical society established in Philadelphia in 1769 is already well recognized in Europe for the transactions it publishes from time to time.

The sciences more immediately useful are well- and much-cultivated in America; mathematics, even in the more abstract branches, physics, mineralogy, and chemistry are taught by professors of high ability. Until now they have not yet made of astronomy as a science as much as might be expected of a people concerned with navigation; they are content simply to reprint the *Nautical Almanack* for the use of their seamen. Yet there is no lack of individuals very proficient in both the theory and the practice of that science whose efforts have thrown new light on the field. The work of Nathaniel Bowditch on practical navigation and the various articles and treatises by Father Wallace of the Society of Jesus prove that assertion. I may add that the government has already acquired astronomical instruments of the best construction, for lack of which it has not been possible to determine the exact longitude of Washington. The investigations that many other people carry on into perpetual motion, if they do no honor to a knowledge of mechanics, nevertheless illustrate a certain spirit of inquiry that is prevalent in the United States. In surveying they make use of the magnetized needle, but the slight heed they pay to the variations of the pole will some day be the source of innumerable law suits, to which they are in any case inclined.

The ingenious Americans make up for the lack of hands to do their work by the invention of mechanical tools. To encourage this branch of industry a patent office is established in Washington, through which the government gives inventors the exclusive privilege of using or selling their machines, of which they must present models preserved to satisfy the curiosity of the public. It cannot be denied that among the great abundance of these models (many are considered new which in reality are old) there are some of very great ingenuity. Particularly worthy of attention is a water saw that cuts the trunk of a tree, sets it in position, and saws the boards. There is also a machine which cuts an iron wire into pieces, bends it as desired, inserts it into leather, and in a short time forms a very exact card. The construction of mills is also very ingenious, and proper tools almost always conserve labor.

Nothing is more striking to the Italian at his arrival in America than the state of religion. By virtue of an article in the federal constitution every religion and every sect is fully tolerated, is equally protected, and equally treated in the United States, at least if its principles or practices do not disturb the civil order and established law. Or, to put it more precisely, the government will not interfere in purely religious matters.

The number of those who openly deny the revelations is not as large as might be supposed, considering that this country is the refuge of all sorts of European wretches. The bulk of atheists is restricted to the French, who abandon the religion of their ancestors but rarely assume a non-Catholic belief.

Indifference, which is so common in the Europe of our times, takes on a special character in America. It does not consist of despising and giving up all practice of religion; many people continue to speak of religion and, generally, with respect. What then? They act as if God had never manifested His will to men, never pointed out the narrow path to salvation that is followed by a few, had never warned that there are other, broader, easier ones traveled by many whose principles seem correct but which ultimately lead to inevitable perdition—in a word, as if the Bible, so highly esteemed, so often read, and seized by all as rule of their religion, does not speak of an infallible God. Every sect there is held as good, every road as correct, and every error as the insignificant weakness of poor mortals.

In accordance with such principles, it is not surprising if America gives birth to innumerable sects which daily subdivide and multiply. Although how can one speak of sects? Those who describe themselves as members of one or another of the sects do not thereby profess an abiding adherence to the doctrines of the founders of the sect; they simply call themselves by the name of the sect to express the fact that they are not without any religion and that they frequent assemblies of a certain kind, or that they are brought up within a certain persuasion, whatever may be the actual state of their thoughts. Thus the Anglicans of today no longer take much account of their thirty-nine articles, nor the Lutherans of the Confession of Augsburg, nor the Presbyterians of the teachings of Calvin or of Knox. On the contrary, imitating the example of their masters, they examine, change, and decide as seems best at the time.

The very word *sect* does not have in America the derogatory meaning that etymology and usage have given it among us, so that a man there does not have the slightest hesitation in saying, "I belong to such a sect." Among the peculiarities of America, not the most extreme is that of finding persons who live together for several years without knowing each other's religion. And many, when asked, do not answer, "I believe," but simply, "I was brought up in such a persuasion."

Better to explain how religion is regarded here, I will give a few examples. In Georgetown, a suburb of Washington, there was a militia regiment which was, in accordance with its regulations, obliged to go to church each Sunday. But since the members belonged to various sects it was not easy to decide to which church or meeting to go. The matter was diplomatically adjusted as follows: they would go one Sunday to the Catholic church, another to the Methodist, a third to the Anglican, then to the Calvinist, and so on until they completed the circle, when they would start over again.

The impartiality of the government in religious matters is observed in practice, as was solemnly promised. This was never more clearly illustrated than in the following incident which occurred in 1813. At that time a considerable theft was brought to the notice of the police, who searched for the criminal; but the latter, penitent for his misdeed, went to confess to the Jesuit Father, Anthony Kohlmann, and in the act of confession gave to his confessor that which he had stolen to be restored to its owner, whom he named. The priest quickly acted and returned the property. The owner informed the police. A non-Catholic magistrate, having learned that the restitution took place through Father Kohlmann, hurriedly demanded the name of the thief. The priest answered that, having learned that through the sacred confession, he could not in any way violate a confidence that natural law and the Catholic religion impose on confessors as most sacred and inviolable. The magistrate answered that the civil law made no exceptions, but ordered under heavy penalties that anyone who knew the perpetrator of a crime must make him known. To this the priest replied that he had every respect for the civil laws but that those same laws guaranteed the free exercise of the Catholic religion which obliged a confessor never to reveal the secrets of his confessional.

Not being able to agree, a solemn trial was held on the matter. On the appointed day, Father Kohlmann, accompanied by non-Catholic lawyers, appeared before the supreme court of the city. The tribunal opened with a demand on the priest for the reasons why he did not believe himself obliged to reveal the name of the thief, and these were briefly set forth. Then the lawyers began to speak, and in excellent orations answered the objection of the prosecutor and demonstrated that such a revelation could not be demanded of Father Kohlmann without an open violation of the laws which guaranteed freedom to every sect and did not restrain in any respect the Catholic religion, so old, so much the same throughout the world, so well known in its principles, so useful in the public welfare, as the facts of the case well proved.

When it came to the verdict, Judge Clinton, according to English practice, delivered a summation in which he concluded, after emphasizing the spirit of the country's laws and its well-known principles of liberality, that it would not be just to oblige a Catholic priest to reveal a criminal made known through the medium of the confession, and that therefore Father Kohlmann was free of any crime. This decision was everywhere applauded, and was recorded so that it may in the future serve to determine similar cases. The speeches of the attorney and of Clinton, together with the facts of the case, were printed in a volume entitled, *The Catholick Question in America.* At the end of this book, in the form of an appendix, was added a little tract on the sacred confession, which helped much to confirm Catholics on this article of faith and to diminish the prejudices and make known the errors of the non-Catholics.

Despite the indifference as to sect, there is, especially in the North, much show of piety. Everyone reads the Bible, and in New England they will not permit a traveler or allow a messenger to continue his journey on a Sunday. Also, almost every year petitions are presented to Congress to prohibit by law journeys on the Lord's Day. The captain of the ship on which I sailed from America to Europe would not allow the passengers to play dominoes or to sing on Sunday. Yet when we arrived in port on a Sunday morning he made the sailors work the whole day without the slightest reason. The observation of holidays in the North was formerly carried to truly extravagant rigor. In certain states religious laws still remain on the statute book, particularly those which insist on the observation of the third commandment. These laws, although not repealed, are no longer rigorously enforced, and are called the Blue Laws.

From the arbitrary interpretation of the holy scriptures come results often truly lamentable. People with the best of wills are agitated by all the winds of doctrine. In Southington, Connecticut, there are some who read in the Bible that God commands the sanctification of the Sabbath; they observe precisely the Sabbath and not Sunday. There is a sect in Pennsylvania called the Harmony Society, which is directed by a chief who explains the Bible to them. Several years ago, having found in Saint Paul that virginity is better than matrimony, he promulgated an ordinance that all should observe chastity. There were sharp remonstrances that *melius est nubere quam uri,* but all was in vain; the leader was inflexible. In Virginia, in the spring of 1812, a preacher announced from his pulpit the fatal prediction that on the fourth of July of that year would come the end of the world. The people believed it true, and let the season go by without planting or cultivating their fields, saying, why should they trouble to work since the end of the world would surely come before the harvest.

Part Two

THE CONSEQUENCES OF EXPANSION

The Consequences of Expansion

THE HALF CENTURY AFTER 1820 WITNESSED THE UNLOOSING OF REMARK-
able expansive energies that transformed the face of the United States
and remade the character of its people. In that period the territorial
frontier reached the Pacific, the Rio Grande, and Oregon. The line of
settlement moved from the Ohio Valley well into the trans-Mississippi
West, with substantial outposts in California and Utah. Meanwhile a
mounting population, fed by immigration, peopled these vast expanses;
the number of inhabitants grew more than four-fold between 1820 and
1870.

These were the outward manifestations of expansion. Internally,
analogous forces were at work modifying more subtly the basic conditions of life and the critical institutions of the people. In the South
and in the North ancient labor systems felt the strain of new and unexpected burdens. The plantation economy, swelling to the demands
of cotton production, confronted the nation with the prospect that a
large segment of the population would remain permanently enslaved.
The development of transportation by road, canal, and rail helped to
integrate a great American internal market. But the same development
dislocated the handicraft artisans who were ultimately displaced by the
relentless spread of the factory. In their stead arose a proletariat new
to American life. Everywhere growing cities faced enormous physical
and social problems, and everywhere their residents wrestled with the
tasks of supplying housing and public services to thousands of newcomers, of erecting a line of social defenses against the maladjustments
of metropolitan life.

Men's ideas could not escape the consequences of these changes.
The sense of power that came from great and visible achievements
found expression in an overwhelming confidence in the capacity of human beings to mold their own destiny. The difficulties attendant upon
expansion, the very disasters that fell upon individuals and large groups
in the process, seemed only challenges to further efforts. The displaced
and the uprooted, no less than the thriving, maintained an imperturb-
able optimism. The revivals of religion, the eternally sprouting reform
movements, and even the southern aspiration, perverted by defense of

its peculiar institution, to reëstablish a Greek democracy south of the Mason-Dixon line, all were rooted in this confidence. All sought to turn the achievements of expansion into contributions to the dignity of man.

What was accomplished in the realms other than the purely material gave point and substance to the confidence that infinitely more could be achieved.

The extension of democratic control over politics, the creation of numerous educational, humanitarian, and social institutions, the conquest of yellow fever and smallpox, and the gradual lengthening of the life-span seemed to this generation impressive evidence of progress. Until the tragic blow of fratricidal war, and its aftermath, there seemed no limits to the hopes of this society nor any basis for questioning the assumptions on which it rested.

The travelers who came to the United States in these decades were still impressed with the old stereotype of America as Liberty. That impression was the more vital to the extent that Europeans were at home preoccupied by questions of liberalism, nationalism, and democracy, the varied strands interwoven in the mid-century revolutions. Yet the maturity of the United States altered the nature of the judgments passed on it. Strangers were no longer ready to concede it the tolerance due to youth. Often they were shocked by the realities they discovered, for expansion was neither neat nor orderly in its manners and in its effects upon the human beings involved. Some observers never got over the initial effects of contact with the ugly surface. Others learned that disorder and instability were themselves aspects of the great unloosing of constructive energies in the process of conquering a continent and creating a society.

11.

A GRAND DUKE IN SEARCH OF A COUNTRY

Bernhard Karl, Duke of Saxe-Weimar-Eisenach, was born in 1792 just as revolution and two decades of war were about to blow apart the little world of petty principalities in which his family played a modest part. There was not much else a noble young man could do then; Bernhard fought as an officer through the war years, serving in turn Napoleon and the kings of the Netherlands and Saxony. Waterloo and the peace that followed left him without prospect of a career. Liberal by disposition and by education, he thought for a while of settling in the United States; and the tour described in his volume, Reise . . . durch Nord-Amerika in den Jahren 1825 und 1826 *(1827), was made to survey the prospects. He liked what he saw but still went back to the Old World, where he became commander of the Dutch army. At one point, the great powers thought of him when they cast about for a Greek king. They passed him by, however. For a while he lived a retired life in Mannheim; but he returned to the service of Holland and died in 1862 while on a mission to Java.*

On August 14, 1825, we took passage on the *Albany*, a ship especially built for canal traffic, on our way from Albany to Lake Erie. This canal has already cost 2,500,000 piastres and will be finished in four weeks. Last year the sections open for business alone took in $300,000, and this year an income of $500,000 is expected. The total cost will therefore shortly be repaid, and unless many repairs absorb a substantial part of the income the state ultimately will earn an unbelievable profit.

Extensive canal systems were hitherto unknown in the United States, and the idea was not very popular. It was therefore important to flabbergast the public, so to speak, through a great, rapidly earned profit. As a result, this canal was completed as quickly as possible without drawing upon the experience of other nations in similar construction. Indeed, the scale of this canal will earn the respect of the traveler —362 miles long, it has 83 locks, which take the ships from the Hudson to Lake Erie with a rise of 688 feet. But those who have freshly in mind

French, Dutch, and English projects will conclude that there is still room for progress here in the art of building canals.

The canal is no more than four-feet deep, so that only ships and barges expressly built for it can navigate it. The vessel that brought us to Schenectady today was 70 feet long, 14 wide, and drew 2 feet of water. It was covered, included a roomy salon and a kitchen, and was very neatly maintained. On account of the numerous locks on the way, progress was very slow; our ship did only three miles an hour, since passage through each lock took four minutes. The craft was drawn by a three-horse team which plodded along a narrow path parallel to the canal, even under the frequent bridges. These bridges, about 300 between Albany and Utica, are made of wood and very coarsely built; generally they belong to farmers, and serve to connect the fields on either side. From Albany to Schenectady by land is only 15 miles, and the journey can swiftly be made by coach. But to see the canal we took the longer route by water, 28 miles.

Five and a half miles from Albany, near Troy, is a government arsenal which seems to be a very considerable establishment. Until that point the canal runs parallel to the Hudson. A branch canal with two locks gives access to Troy via the Hudson and with another canal to Lake Champlain. At this point the canal veers away from the Hudson and begins to run parallel to the Mohawk River. There was great difficulty in continuing the canal along the right bank of the river and it was necessary to build an aqueduct more than 1,000 feet long to the left bank. This aqueduct forms a kind of wooden canal resting on 26 stone piers, but will certainly soon call for repairs and will eventually have to be replaced by iron. Along the left bank the canal is cut out of rock and holds up very well. Twelve miles further it returns to the right bank along another aqueduct, 748 feet long on 16 piers. Above this aqueduct is a handsome wooden bridge large enough for wagons. From Albany to Schenectady we passed through 27 locks. These are built of hard limestone and will soon need repairs. They already leak in many places and the gates do not close very well, so that the water filters through in cascades.

Utica, through which the canal passes 80 miles beyond Schenectady, is a flourishing town of some 4,000 inhabitants. In 1794 a tiny tavern was the only occupied building in this neighborhood; now Utica is one of the most thriving cities in the state of New York, and new houses are constantly being put up. In truth, one begins here to wonder at the gigantic strides this young country is making in the development of culture, and one gets an altogether new idea of the spirit of human creativity and enterprise. This place now has two banks, four churches, an academy, large, well-stocked shops, a bookstore, and a printing office.

Aside from ordinary saloons, there are three large inns, at the largest of which, Shepherds Hotel, we received a very pleasant reception. In this establishment more than seventy beds are constantly prepared for the accommodation of travelers, and these are sometimes hardly enough. In such American houses everything is extremely tidy, and relatively cheap. One can get room and board for one dollar a person. The bedrooms are very roomy, the beds wide and good, and the baths very clean. Above all, every bedroom is furnished with the necessary washing utensils.

You are generally called to get up at seven. After dressing, you descend to the ground floor to the barroom where are found all manner of refreshing and heartwarming drinks; this is also the headquarters of the headwaiter, who keeps the accounts. The host is naturally a gentleman who eats with the guests and dominates the conversation. Apart from the halls, where boots and shoes are put out in the evening to be found polished in the morning, there are several public rooms, for lounging, reading, and writing. Those who wish to have a private sitting room may have one at additional cost, a great convenience especially when traveling with ladies.

Breakfast is announced a half hour after rising time. The table is set in the dining room and laden with beefsteak, mutton, a chicken or other roasted fowl, fish, and boiled potatoes, generally of good quality. The waiters, or, in some places, the waitresses, pass around tea or coffee. Since the Americans are usually reticent people, such a meal passes very quickly and silently. Dinner is normally served at two in the afternoon and tea at seven. The table is then set as at breakfast, with the addition of stews and pastry. Wine is never drunk at meals. On the table are water and whiskey which mixed are considered the healthiest drink in the summer. Everyone must reach for what he likes, since the food is never passed around. There are no napkins; the tablecloths must fill their place. Apart from the spoons, there is no silverware on the tables. The two-pronged forks and the knives are made of steel with handles of staghorn. A praiseworthy usage absolves the traveler of the necessity of tipping at his departure.

Coming down the romantic valley of the Lehigh River, we arrived at the village of Lehighton at the junction with Mahoning Creek. This place has very few houses and maintains a narrow existence, since the region is too rugged and too hilly for agriculture and since three miles away the busy town of Mauch-Chunk takes away all its trade. Mauch-Chunk itself is only four years old and owes its existence to the opening of the nearby coal mines which, with all the neighboring subsoil, belong to the Lehigh Coal Company. That corporation is well supplied with capital, has existed longer than its competitor in Pottsville, and has its operations more systematically organized. One of the most important stockholders, a Quaker named White, lives here. He was instrumental in founding the company and directs everything on the spot.

On the next morning, Mr. White led me to the mine. The site was a very narrow valley surrounded by high hills which rise up from the Lehigh and are covered with woods. To carry the mined coal easily and cheaply to Philadelphia, the corporation is making the Lehigh navigable through a series of dams, locks, and canals, already partly completed. I saw the locks invented by Mr. White in operation here and wondered at their excellent and easy performance. The canal, in which there are two locks 130 feet apart, is 30 feet wide and lined with wood.

The coal is loaded into flatboats six-feet wide and ten-feet long and the boats are then coupled two abreast and five in line to make a chain of ten or more links. When they reach the Delaware at Philadelphia and the coal is unloaded, the boats are dismantled and the wood is sold as timber, while all the iron that is found in them is brought back to Mauch-Chunk in carts. Two sawmills are in constant operation producing the materials for these boats. The boards are thus prepared in advance and skilled workers can nail together one of these craft in an hour. When the canal and the locks are really finished, this cheap and wood-sparing means of transportation will come to an end, and the coal will be carried on steamers, able to go up and down the canal and river. So that the action of the paddlewheels should not damage the sides, they are lining the canal with stones or even plastering it over.

The coal is brought out of the ground in four-horse carts, taken to the loading point and weighed on a weighing machine. From there the carts are driven onto a turntable where the horses are quickly unharnessed. Then the carts are lifted up by a machine powered by a horse treadmill. At a certain height they are tipped so that the coal falls out into a sort of donjon where it remains until it is loaded on the boats. The loading is done through a movable broad iron pipe which can be adjusted for height according to the level of the water. In it are grills through which the dust and the coal that is too small fall, so that only the marketable coal gets onto the ship.

Near Mauch-Chunk there is also considerable iron ore, in sandy ground and near the surface. A pair of furnaces have been erected to smelt this ore. They have not yet succeeded, however, in bringing the coal to the smelters, and charcoal is even more necessary. This iron is needed to build railroads to the most important coal fields nine miles away. A railroad would greatly facilitate the carriage of coal to the water, make it at least 75 per cent cheaper. Iron carts will be used on this railway. The grade to the mine has a rise of one foot every hundred. On the way up the empty carts will be drawn, four by a horse, at a rate of three miles an hour. Loaded, they will roll down to the river under their own power and make the trip in an hour. When they come to a certain point not far from the stream, they will roll onto an inclined surface at an angle of forty-five degrees and through an appropriate device will by their own weight draw up the emptied carts.

The coal is not deposited here in veins; rather the whole mountain is a solid mass of coal, covered with no more than a foot of earth. They have bored to a depth of sixty feet and found nothing but coal. They have, however, only dug some forty feet and prefer to mine broadly rather than deeply. At present, the coal works, which is really a quarry, for they operate in the open air, covers a surface of about four acres. To loosen the coal they use an iron wedge which they drive with a hammer. The workers are paid by the day and earn as much as eighteen dollars a month. They live in nearby houses.

The company employs almost 1,800 laborers, some of whom live near the coal fields but most of whom occupy little houses belonging to the company along a mile and a half of Mauch-Chunk Creek. Many are married and have their families with them. The company has given them a preacher and a school with a good teacher for their children. Near the creek is a great grist mill which turns out all the flour needed in the district. But the region is too hilly for agriculture. In the valley, however, they have planted some wheat to supply the hay needed for the 120 horses that labor here daily.

The company also owns a store well supplied with all necessities. Here the employees may buy all they require on credit against their wages. Each worker has his own page in a great book where his credits and debits are reckoned, and he also is given a pass book in which the same are inscribed. Every month, or more often if the laborer desires it, there is a reckoning and he may have a note to the cashier for his balance if he likes. The company profits greatly by this arrangement; most of the money it pays out flows back into its own coffers. The land of the company stretches for three miles up and down the Lehigh so that no one can invade its store's monopoly. Even if other companies should attempt to dig coal out of the other hills around Mauch-Chunk, they would not be likely to profit very much by it, since this corporation dominates the only outlet, the Lehigh River, and by control of the locks could put many difficulties in the way of the carriage of strange coal.

At several places through the South we could observe various kinds of plantations. Not far from Columbia, South Carolina, are some great cotton fields that belong to the wealthy Taylor family. On one of these fields fifty-eight Negroes of both sexes were toiling on the soil. With their fingers they took the cotton from its casing, watching that no hard leaves were attached, gathered it in sacks which hung before them, and then poured it into large baskets. These blacks made a very unpleasant impression upon me, especially since a few women begged for chews of tobacco from my companion.

On the way from Charleston to Savannah we often passed through country wooded, but thickly settled with plantations. Some of these plantations were very large; usually the way to the main house was lined with old and well-cared for live oaks with a gate at the entrance. Cotton and corn is raised here, and also some rice, which is the chief product of the southern part of South Carolina. The rice fields must remain under water for several months a year and are therefore located in swampy sections, surrounded by ditches. For that reason, too, these districts are very unhealthy, and hardly a white planter will risk staying on his plantation in the summer. That season is usually spent in Charleston or in traveling in the North. The Negroes are the only human beings upon whom this wicked climate has no ill effects, and they are therefore essential for the cultivation of this soil.

In the Georgia Indian territory we came upon an isolated plantation surrounded by woods, generally long-needled pine. The soil is mostly hard sand; here and there, especially in the hollows, it is mixed with argillaceous earth of a quite yellowish color. The Indians have thrown bridges over a pair of brooks, at each of which we paid a half-dollar toll with great pleasure. These structures are not very elegant, but still are better than those in the Christian parts of Georgia and better even than some in the northern states. We passed very few Indians; these were all wrapped in woolen blankets. We saw only three wigwams, and those were toll houses at the bridges. These redskins seem to prefer the log houses.

Mr. Currel, the owner of the plantation with whom we spent the night, is a Virginian who settled among the Indians, from whom he bought the land on speculation. To judge from his drunkenness, he has also taken on their manners. His plantation, like all others, is made up of log houses. Through our quarters the wind blew to its hearts content; no light could keep burning, so that we had to see by the flames of the great fireplace. There was no ceiling, only the shingle roof directly above us through which the light penetrated. I was surprised to find the works of Shakespeare here. In one of the outhouses we were served a very fine supper, which included some very superior venison.

The layout of the plantations follows a general pattern. The main building is built either of logs or of clapboards, with a piazza and with an open hall between the rooms. The outbuildings, again of logs or boards, include a kitchen, quarters for guests, and huts for the Negroes. Beyond are the barns, stables, and sheds. The whole is surrounded by a worm fence, with a gate in front and in the rear an inclined stack of logs over which one may climb.

Upon crossing the Alabama line, one notices an immediate improvement in the quality of the soil. It seems darker; most of the wood is cleared; everywhere are signs of culture. On most of the plantations the cotton fields are in good order. Log houses are here used only as slave quarters; the masters' homes are often two-stories high, painted white, and ornamented with balconies and piazzas. In most of these estates cotton gins and presses were in operation. Because of the unusual dryness, the planters have not yet shipped out all their cotton. The Alabama River was so low that the steamship from Mobile was not able to reach Montgomery for several weeks. The latter place consequently suffered from a shortage of the most necessary provisions, normally supplied from Mobile; a bushel of salt cost fifteen dollars.

We met several parties of emigrants from the eastern sections of Georgia on their way to Butler County in Alabama. They proposed to settle on lands that they had acquired very cheaply from the federal government. The number of their Negroes, horses, wagons, and cattle showed that these wanderers were well off.

In New Orleans we were invited to a subscription ball. These affairs are held twice a week, on Tuesdays and Fridays, in the same hall, the French theater. Only good society is invited to these balls. The first to which we came was not very well attended; but most of the ladies were very nice looking and well turned out in the French manner. Their clothing was elegant after the latest Paris fashions. They danced very well and did credit to their French dancing masters. Dancing and some music are the main branches of the education of a Creole woman. Be that as it may, a stranger who comes here with no intention of finding a wife, will find the lively girls who make up this company much more pleasant than the rigid prudes who consider the waltz indecent but find nothing objectionable in walking for hours tête-à-tête with a young man.

The native men are far from matching the women in elegance. And they stayed only a short time, preferring to escape to a so-called "Quarterons Ball" which they find more amusing and where they do not have to stand on ceremony. There were, as a result, soon many more women than men.

A "quarteron" (octoroon) is the offspring of a mestizo mother and a white father, just as the mestizo is the child of a mulatto and a white man. The "quaterons" are almost completely white. There would be no way of recognizing them by their complexion, for they are often fairer than the Creoles. Black hair and eyes are generally the signs of their status, although some are quite blond. The ball is attended by the free "quarterons." Yet the deepest prejudice reigns against them on account of their colored origin; the white women particularly feel or affect to feel a strong repugnance to them.

Marriage between colored and white people is forbidden by the laws of the state. Yet the "quarterons," for their part, look upon the Negroes and mulattoes as inferiors and are unwilling to mix with them. The girls therefore have no other recourse than to become the mistresses of white men. The "quarterons" regard such attachment as the equivalent of marriage. They would not think of entering upon it other than with a formal contract in which the man engages to pay a stipulated sum to the mother or father of the girl. The latter even assumes the name of her lover and regards the affair with more faithfulness than many a woman whose marriage was sealed in a church.

Some of these women have inherited from their fathers and lovers, and possess considerable fortunes. Their status is nevertheless always very depressed. They must not ride in the street in coaches, and their lovers can bring them to the balls in their own conveyances only after nightfall. They must never sit opposite a white lady, nor may they enter a room without express permission. The whites have the right to have these unfortunates whipped like slaves for infractions to which there are two witnesses. But many of these girls are much more carefully educated than the whites, behave with more polish and more politeness, and make their lovers happier than white wives their husbands. And yet the white ladies speak of these unfortunate depressed creatures with great disdain, even bitterness. Because of the depth of these prejudices, many fathers send their daughters, conceived after this manner, to France where good education and wealth are no impediments to the attainment of a respectable place.

Only the colored women are admitted to the "Quarteron Ball"; the men of that caste are excluded by the whites. To endow these dances with the qualities of good society, a high admission fee, two dollars, is fixed, so that only the upper class of men can attend. I found this ball much more decent than the white masquerade. The colored ladies were under the oversight of their mothers; they were elegantly dressed; and they behaved themselves with decorum and modesty. Both counterdances and waltzes were performed, and most of the girls danced very well. I could not remain very long for fear of spoiling my reputation in New Orleans, and returned to the masquerade. I had also to be careful lest I mention to any white woman where I had been. Were it known that a foreigner who has entree to good society resorted to such a ball, he would receive a very cold treatment from the white ladies.

Traveling by land through Ohio we came to Union Village, a Shaker settlement. There was no inn, but we were received in one of the dwelling houses with great hospitality, and given roomy and clean quarters.

As soon as our arrival became known we were visited by a crowd of Brothers, who began questioning us with great curiosity. The curiosity of these people was very like that of monks, with whom they have many other similarities. Among the group I particularly noticed two old men who had formerly been Presbyterian ministers and who were now leaders here. The community consists of more than six hundred members and was recently formed out of older groups in the state of New York. Made up of unpropertied people and impecunious to begin with, it had to struggle against difficulties and make great sacrifices. They have not yet reached the enviable position of their coreligionists at New Lebanon. The products of their labor barely suffice to cover their own needs, so they have not yet been able to open the stores that are so profitable at New Lebanon.

The houses are well built and neatly maintained. Almost all are made of bricks, and there is adequate space in between. Each has a stone staircase which leads to two entrances, separated from each other only by a window. The door to the right is for the men, that to the left for the women or Sisters. Behind the dwelling houses, each of which holds a family of almost sixty members, are separate buildings for the kitchen, for the dining room, and for workshops. The houses are surrounded by lawns over which are placed boards leading to the pumps, the stables, and the washhouses. Through the village boards are also placed along the streets for the benefit of pedestrians.

At six in the evening I was invited to dine with the members in the dining room near the kitchen. Two large tables were set along each of the long sides of the hall. Behind them were benches, and in the middle a serving table. At a signal blown on a horn, the Brothers marched out in pairs from the door at the right, the Sisters from the left and all took their places near the tables. Six Sisters appointed to serve came out of the kitchen at the same time and arranged themselves in a line before the Sisters' table. All together fell to their knees and offered up a silent prayer, rose together, seated themselves, and started their meal in the greatest stillness. That procedure, I was assured, was followed at each of the three meals of the day. They ate bread and butter and cake, and drank tea. Each member found placed before him a full glass which was refilled when necessary by the serving Sisters. The meal was quickly over. Then the whole assembly rose together, pushed back the benches, offered another prayer on bended knees, rose, made a right and left turn, and marched in files, in quick time out of the room.

Through the evening I had a succession of visits from Brothers who cross-examined me. Among them were two Frenchmen, a father and son. The latter had taken on a thoroughly monkish demeanor, did not raise his eyes, affirmed that the principles of his sect were in accordance with the Bible, and that they were the only true Christians living in the true spirit of the scriptures. Their political beliefs rest upon community of property, security to each member in the satisfaction of his needs, and full equality of conditions.

A part of the worship of God according to the believers of Mother Ann Lee, as the Shakers call themselves, consists in dancing. Mother Ann Lee, the founder of this sect, taught that one must pray to God not with the tongue and mouth alone, but with the whole body. On Sunday they dance publicly in the church to the accompaniment of hymns composed for that purpose. Strangers are admitted as spectators. During the week they have morning and evening dances in the living quarters. The walls of the dwellings, which are made of great sliding doors, are moved apart and, with the corridor, form a great hall in which they can dance and jump. Because of our presence they seemed timid and omitted the evening session, which was a great disappointment to us. At our departure they refused, to my astonishment, to take either money or gifts in payment. We could only express our gratitude for this hospitality in words.

We visited a Rappist settlement near Pittsburgh. Rapp's principles rest upon community of goods and the coöperation of all members for the common good to insure the welfare of each individual. But Mr. Rapp holds his band together not only by this hope, but also by bonds of religion. It is wonderful that such a simple man should manage to keep together a community of seven-hundred people and influence them to the point that they consider him a prophet. It was, for instance, as a result of his opinion that celibacy was imposed. They found that the community was growing too numerous and agreed to live with their wives in a sisterly relationship. Any more intimate association is forbidden, as is marriage. There were nevertheless a few earlier marriages, and each year a few children are born for whom there is a school and a teacher. All the members feel the greatest respect for Rapp, call him Father, and treat him as one.

They have found that agriculture and cattle raising were not productive enough and have joined to those pursuits a number of industrial enterprises, a cotton and wool factory, a brewery, a distillery, and a grist mill. At a good German lunch we drank a very respectable wine they had made in their old settlement in Ohio.

After our meal we walked about the place, which is laid out in a very orderly fashion. The streets are wide and joined at right angles. It was just two years ago that they began to clear the forest where the settlement now stands; as reminders, the stumps still jut out into the streets. Yet it is astounding how much united and directed human power can accomplish in so short a time.

Some families still live in log houses; but many streets are already occupied with frame houses well set apart from each other, so that each has space for a garden. Only the four-story textile factory, Mr. Rapp's still unfinished home, and a warehouse in process of construction, are made of brick. The log houses are raised in back of the space that will ultimately be taken by the new dwellings. They will in time, then, be able to build new brick structures without disturbing the families that occupy the old ones.

Mr. Rapp's residence seems to testify against that equality of which he preaches, but this seems to arouse no jealousy or hostility. It consists of a two-story main building with two lower wings, and is hung with wallpaper from Philadelphia. Behind the house is a piazza and a balcony which opens out on a garden of several acres, planted with flowers, vegetables, and vines. In the middle is a round basin with a fine fountain. Mr. Rapp wishes to build a little temple there in which to place a statue of Harmony. The statue is already finished, made by a sculptor in Philadelphia out of wood, like the figurehead of a ship.

All the machines in the factory are run by a steam engine of 75 horsepower, made in Pittsburgh; this engine pumps its own water out of a 50-foot well. The factory makes wool and cotton cloth. The community has its own sheep, including some Merinos and some Saxony; but it also buys wool in the neighborhood from farmers who now begin to concern themselves with sheep-raising. After the wool is washed it is picked by the oldest women in the community, who work on the fourth floor, and then it is sent down to the lower floors through a kind of funnel. The wool is sorted into four groups according to quality, and dyed in their own dye-house near the factory. It is then brought back to the factory where it is combed and spun thinner and thinner into fine threads on machines like the Jenny. Once spun, it is woven and then fulled on a machine operated by steam. This machine is so adjusted that it needs no soap or fuller's earth, but rather uses the steam it produces itself, a very great economy. The cloth is cut on a cylinder through which a strong piece of steel winds. The woolens for which there is the best market in this country include a kind of blue middling cloth, a grey pepper and salt that is especially used for trousers, and red and white flannels.

This factory does only spinning and weaving. They have not yet undertaken to print cottons because the preparation of the cards is so expensive and so difficult and because the fashions in print are so changeable.

In the winter, heat is supplied through pipes that lead off the steam engine and extend to every story of the building. All the workers, and especially the women, had very healthy complexions, and the sincere friendship with which they greeted Rapp moved me deeply. I was also pleased to find vases of fresh flowers near all the machines, and everywhere was a praiseworthy cleanliness.

After visiting this interesting factory we went for tea to Mr. Rapp's temporary dwelling, a good frame house. Here I met his daughter, a pale spinster, and a blooming granddaughter, Gertraud, child of an only son whose death made a deep impression on the old man. The table was set with fine silver, and Rapp seemed pleased to be able to show me the degree of his prosperity. He started out, as he himself told me, with very slight means; in the beginning he had to struggle with the bitterest want and not seldom had to seek bread for his community.

We also spent the evening with Mr. Rapp. He had the musical members of the community come together to entertain us. Miss Gertraud played the piano, and three girls sang. There were also a violin, cello, and two flutes. The music was in fact not so good as that we heard last year in Bethlehem, but it was very pleasant.

The next morning we continued our tour of the settlement. We inspected the distillery which turns out fine whiskey well esteemed in the neighborhood, although there was no need for it in the community itself for the members had convenanted with each other to make no use of spirituous liquors. The distillery is very useful for fattening the hogs and the cattle, and earns a neat profit. For lack of barley the brewery, which is still not finished, uses wheat in making its beer. The grist mill, which is also not entirely completed, is operated by steam. There will shortly be four sets of millstones in operation and also an oilwork connected to it.

On every floor of the mill and of the other factory buildings are great iron tanks filled with water so that there will always be at hand the means of extinguishing fires. The community also has its own fire engine and a company to man it.

Farther along were the workshops of the smith, the locksmith, the cabinet maker, and the cooper, and everywhere we saw signs of the respect and affection in which the old Rapp was held. We also visited the storehouse where all sorts of finished articles lie ready to be sold and sent out. I was surprised at the excellence of all the arrangements.

The articles for the use of the members are kept separately. There is no private property and everything belongs to the community, which must provide the individuals with all the things they need. The cloth for clothing is of the best quality, as are the provisions. Flour, salt fish, and other goods that keep for a long time are distributed to the families monthly; fresh meat and other articles that spoil easily are distributed, according to the size of the family, more frequently. Since every house has a garden, each family may raise its own vegetables and fowl, and each bakes its own bread. For articles which are not made in the community itself, there is a store from which members may draw on an order by the directors, and in which outsiders from the neighborhood may buy.

Finally we returned with Mr. Rapp to the factory. He told us that the girls had asked me to come back to hear them sing. Some sixty or seventy of them gather to sing spirituals and other songs while they rest from their work. They have their own song book, in which they have collected some pieces from the Württemberg Songbook together with a few composed by Rapp. The latter were in prose but the girls had adapted them to well-known melodies. In this songbook I find a number of songs the words of which might be considered scandalous, were not the pure, childish sentiments of these girls so obvious.

12.

PHILOSOPHER OF POLITICS

Alexis de Tocqueville was a liberal aristocrat, dissatisfied with the reactionary regime of Charles X but unwilling to accept the demagogic regime of Louis-Philippe that came to power in 1830. In the crisis, the United States offered an opportunity for escape and for contemplation. In 1831, when de Tocqueville was twenty-six, he left, with his friend Beaumont, for a nine-month tour, ostensibly to inspect the American prison system.

De Tocqueville, however, had another purpose in mind. His view of society was essentially pessimistic; the influence of equality (which was the meaning he gave to démocratie*), he thought, steadily leveled downward the condition of all civilized people. His description of the United States, published as* De la Démocratie en l'Amérique *(1835– 1840), where that influence had played itself out to the full, was intended as a warning to France. Since the forces of* démocratie *could not be stayed, he hoped it would be possible to adopt enough safeguards to prevent the worst of all evils, tyranny. To that end, he attempted to set forth, in the extract which follows, the advantageous features of democratic government in the United States, and the manner in which they contributed to the functioning of an orderly state.*

The defects and weaknesses of a democratic government may readily be discovered, whereas its healthy influence becomes evident in ways which are not obvious and are, so to speak, hidden. A glance suffices to detect the faults, but the good qualities can be discerned only by long observation. The laws of the American democracy are frequently defective or incomplete; they sometimes attack vested rights or sanction others dangerous to the community; and even if they were all good, their frequency would still be a great evil. How is it, then, that the United States still prospers?

A distinction must carefully be observed between the end at which laws aim and the means by which they pursue that end, between their absolute and relative excellence. If it be the intention of the legislator to favor the minority at the expense of the majority, and if his measures accomplish the object he has in view with the least possible expense of time and exertion, his law may be well drawn up, although its purpose is bad; and, the more efficacious it is, the more dangerous will it be.

Democratic laws generally tend to promote the welfare of the greatest possible number, for they emanate from the majority of the citizens, who are subject to error, but who cannot have interests opposed to their own advantage. The laws of an aristocracy tend, on the contrary, to concentrate wealth and power in the hands of the minority, because an aristocracy, by its very nature, is a minority. It may therefore be asserted that the purpose of legislation in a democracy is more useful to humanity than that in an aristocracy.

This, however, is the sum total of the advantages of a democracy. Aristocracies are infinitely more expert in the science of legislation than a democracy ever can be. They have a self control that protects them from the errors of temporary excitement, and they form far-reaching designs, which they allow to mature until a favorable opportunity. They operate with the dexterity of art, understand how to make the collective forces of all the laws converge at the same time on a given point. Such is not the case with democracies, which often unwittingly adopt unfavorable measures.

Let us now imagine a community so organized that it can endure the transitory effect of bad laws, can await, without destruction, the effect of the general tendency of its legislation. Under such conditions a democratic government, notwithstanding its faults, may be best fitted to produce the prosperity of this community. This is precisely what has occurred in the United States; the great advantage of the Americans consists in their ability to commit faults which they may afterwards repair.

An analogous observation may be made respecting public officers. American democracy frequently errs in the choice of the individuals to whom it entrusts the power of the administration; but the state prospers under their rule. If, in a democratic state, the governors have less honesty and less capacity than elsewhere, the governed are more enlightened and more attentive to their own interests. More vigilant in their affairs and more jealous of their rights, the people prevent their representatives from abandoning the general line of conduct which their interest prescribes. Furthermore, if the democratic magistrate is more apt to misuse his power, he possesses it for a shorter time.

There is yet another, a more general and more conclusive reason for the merits of democracy. It is no doubt important to the welfare of nations that they be governed by men of virtue and talent, if those men are not swayed by interests different from those of the community at large. But I am not aware that there ever existed a state of things in which the rulers had the same interests as the whole population. No political form is equally favorable to the prosperity and the development of all the classes into which society is divided. It is no less dangerous to place the fate of these classes exclusively in the hands of any one of these than it is to make one people the arbiter of the destiny of another. When the rich alone govern, the interest of the poor is always endangered; and when the poor make the laws, that of the rich incurs very serious risks. The advantage of democracy does not consist, therefore, in favoring the prosperity of all, but simply in contributing to the well-being of the greatest number.

The men who are entrusted with the direction of public affairs in the United States are frequently inferior, in both capacity and morality, to those whom an aristocracy would raise to power. But their interest is identified with that of the majority of their fellow citizens. They may frequently be faithless and frequently err, but they will never systematically adopt a line of conduct hostile to the majority.

The maladministration of a democratic magistrate, moreover, is an isolated fact which has influence only during the short period for which he is elected. Corruption and incapacity do not act as common interests permanently to unite men.

A corrupt and incapable magistrate will not combine with another simply because the latter is as corrupt and as incapable as himself; and these two office holders will never join to promote the corruption and ineptitude of their remote posterity. The ambition and the maneuvers of one will serve, on the contrary, to unmask the other.

In the United States, where public officials have no class interests to promote, the general and constant influence of the government is beneficial, although the individuals who conduct it are frequently unskilled and sometimes contemptible. There is, indeed, a secret tendency in democratic institutions that makes the exertions of the citizens subservient to the prosperity of the community in spite of their vices and mistakes; while in aristocratic institutions there is a secret bias which leads those who conduct the government, despite their talents and virtues, to contribute to the evils that oppress their fellow creatures. In aristocracies, public men frequently do harm without intending it; in democratic states they bring about good results which they could never have conceived.

One form of patriotic attachment arises principally from an instinctive, disinterested, and indefinable feeling connecting the affections of man with his birthplace. This natural fondness is united with a taste for ancient customs and a reverence for traditions; those who cherish it love their country as they love the mansions of their fathers. This patriotism is sometimes stimulated by religious enthusiasm, and then is capable of making prodigious efforts. It is in itself a kind of religion; it does not reason, but acts from faith and sentiment.

But like all instinctive passions, this kind of patriotism incites great transient exertions rather than continuity of effort. It may save the state in critical circumstances, but often allows it to decline in times of peace. As long as the manners of a people are simple and its faith unshaken, as long as society rests upon traditional institutions the legitimacy of which is never questioned, this instinctive patriotism may endure.

But there is another species of attachment to country which is perhaps less generous and less ardent but is more fruitful and more permanent. It springs from knowledge, is nurtured by laws, grows by the exercise of civil rights; and, in the end, it is identified with the personal interests of the citizen. A man comprehends the influence of the well-being of his country upon his own; he is aware that the laws permit him to contribute to that prosperity; and he labors to promote it, both because it benefits him and because it is in part his own work.

There are sometimes periods in the life of a nation when the old customs change, when public morality is destroyed, religious belief shaken, and the spell of tradition broken. At the same time the diffusion of knowledge may yet be imperfect and civil rights ill-secured or confined within narrow limits. Nationality then assumes a dim and dubious shape in the eyes of the citizens. They no longer see it in the soil which they inhabit, for that soil is to them an inanimate clod; nor in the usages of their forefathers, which they regard as debasing; nor in religion, of which they are skeptical; nor in the laws, which do not originate in their own authority; nor in the legislator, whom they fear and despise. The country is lost to their senses and they retire into a narrow selfishness. They are emancipated from prejudice without having acknowledged the empire of reason; they have neither the instinctive patriotism of a monarchy nor the reflective patriotism of a republic.

In this predicament retreat is impossible. The period of disinterested patriotism is gone forever; the people must go forward and accelerate the union of private with public interests.

The most powerful and perhaps the only means that we possess of interesting men in the welfare of their country is to make them participants in the government. Now civic zeal seems inseparable from the exercise of political rights, and the number of citizens will augment or decrease in Europe in proportion as those rights are extended.

In the United States the inhabitants have only recently immigrated to the land they now occupy. They brought with them neither customs nor traditions. Here they met one another for the first time. The instinctive love of country can scarcely even exist, yet everyone takes as zealous an interest in the affairs of his town, his county, and his state as if they were his own because everyone, in his sphere, takes an active part in the government of society.

The lower orders understand the influence of the general prosperity upon their own welfare. Besides, they are accustomed to regard this prosperity as the fruit of their own exertions. The citizen looks upon the fortune of the public as his own, and he labors for the good of the state, not merely from a sense of pride or duty, but from what I venture to term cupidity.

The manners of the Americans illustrate the truth of this remark. As the American participates in all that is done in his country, he thinks himself obliged to defend whatever may be censured in it, for it is not only his country that is then attacked, it is himself. The consequence is that his national pride resorts to a thousand artifices and descends to all the petty tricks of personal vanity.

Nothing is more embarrassing in ordinary social intercourse than the irritable patriotism of the Americans. A stranger may be well inclined to praise many of their institutions, but he begs the indulgence to blame some, an indulgence that is inexorably refused. America is therefore a free country in which, lest anybody be hurt by your remarks, you are not allowed to speak freely of private individuals or of the state, of the citizens, the authorities, public individuals, private undertakings—in short, of anything at all except, perhaps, the climate and the soil, and even then Americans will be ready to defend both as if they had coöperated in producing them.

After the general idea of virtue, I know no higher principle than that of right; or rather, these two ideas are united in one. The idea of right is simply that of virtue projected into the political world. The idea of right enabled men to define anarchy and tyranny, taught them how to be independent without arrogance, to obey without servility. The man who submits to violence is debased by his compliance; but when he submits to a right of authority which he recognizes, he rises in some measure above the person who gives the command. There are no great men without virtue; and there are no great nations without respect for right. For what is a union of rational and intelligent beings who are held together only by the bond of force?

The only means at the present time of inculcating the idea of right and of rendering it, as it were, palpable to the senses, is to endow all men with the peaceful exercise of certain rights. When a child begins to move in the midst of the objects that surround him, he instinctively appropriates everything he can lay hands upon; he has no notion of the property of others. But as he gradually learns the value of things and begins to perceive that he may in turn be robbed, he becomes more circumspect, and ends by respecting those rights in others which he wishes to have respected in himself. The principle which the child derives from the possession of his toys is taught to the man by the objects he may call his own. The complaints against property, which are so frequent in Europe, are never heard in the most democratic of nations because in America there are no proletarians. Everyone has property to defend, and everyone recognizes the principle upon which he holds it.

The same thing occurs in the political world. In America, the lowest classes have a very high respect for political rights, because they exercise those rights; and they refrain from attacking the rights of others in order that their own may not be violated. While in Europe the same classes sometimes resist even the supreme power, the American submits without a murmur to the authority of the political magistrate.

Democracy brings the notion of political rights to the level of the humblest citizen, just as the dissemination of wealth brings the notion of property within the reach of all. This is one of the greatest advantages of this form of government. In our times, religious belief is shaken, and the divine notion of right is declining. Morality is debased and the notion of moral right is therefore fading away. Argument takes the place of faith, and calculation that of sentiment. If, in the midst of this general disruption, the notion of right is not linked with that of private interest, the only immutable point in the human heart, what means will there be of governing the world, except by fear? When the laws are weak and the people turbulent, when passions are excited and the authority of virtue paralyzed, some measures of the kind must be taken. And governments should be more interested in taking them than society at large, for governments may perish, but society cannot die.

But I do not wish to exaggerate the example that America furnishes. There the people were invested with political rights at a time when they could not be abused, for the inhabitants were few in number and simple in their manners. As they have increased, the Americans have not augmented the power of the democracy; rather, they have extended its domain. The moment at which political rights are granted to a people that had before been without them is very critical. The measure, though often necessary, is always dangerous. This truth may be perceived even in America. The states in which the citizens have enjoyed their rights longest are those in which they make the best use of them. Nothing is more arduous than the apprenticeship of liberty. Liberty is generally established with difficulty in the midst of storms; it is perfected by civil discord, and its benefits cannot be appreciated until it is already old.

Popular origin impairs the excellence and the wisdom of legislation in America, but contributes much to increase its power. There is an amazing strength in the expression of the will of a whole people; and when it declares itself, even the imagination of those who wish to contest it is overawed. This fact is well known by the political parties, which consequently strive to achieve a majority whenever they can. If they have not the greater number of voters on their side, they are foiled. They have no recourse to persons who lack the right to vote, for in the United States, apart from slaves, servants, and paupers supported by the public, there is no class which does not exercise the elective franchise and which does not indirectly contribute to law-making. Those who wish to attack the laws must consequently either change the opinion of the nation or trample upon its decision.

In the United States, furthermore, everyone is personally concerned in enforcing the obedience of the whole community to the law. Since the minority may shortly rally the majority to its principles, it is interested in professing a respect for the decrees of the legislator which it may soon have occasion to claim for itself. However irksome an enactment may be, the citizen of the United States complies with it, not only because it is the work of a majority, but because it is his own, and he regards it as a contract to which he is himself a party. In the United States a numerous and turbulent multitude which regards the law as its natural enemy does not exist. On the contrary, all classes display the utmost reliance upon the legislation of their country and are attached to it by a kind of parental affection.

I am wrong, however, in saying all classes, for in America the European scale of authority is reversed. There the wealthy occupy a position analogous to that of the poor in the Old World, and it is the opulent classes that frequently look upon law with suspicion. In the United States, where the poor rule, the rich have always something to fear from the abuse of power. The natural anxiety of the rich may produce secret dissatisfaction; but society is not disturbed by it, for the same reason that induces the wealthy to withhold their confidence from the legislative authority makes them obey its mandates. Their wealth, which prevents them from making the law, prevents them from opposing it. In civilized nations only those who have nothing to lose ever revolt. If the laws of a democracy are not always worthy of respect, they are always respected, for those who elsewhere infringe the laws cannot here fail to obey what they have themselves enacted; while the citizens who might be interested in their infraction are induced by their character and station to submit to the decision of the legislature. Besides, the people in America obey the law not only because it is their work, but because it may be changed if it is harmful. Even an evil law is observed because it is well-imposed and because it is of transient duration.

On passing from a free country into one which is not free, the traveler is struck by the change; in the former all is bustle and activity; in the latter everything seems calm and motionless. In the one, amelioration and progress are the topics of inquiry, in the other the community wishes only to repose in the enjoyment of advantages already acquired.

Nevertheless, the country which exerts itself so strenuously is generally more wealthy and more prosperous than that which appears so contented with its lot. When we compare them, we can scarcely conceive how so many new wants are daily felt in the former, while so few seem to exist in the latter.

If this observation applies to free countries which have preserved monarchical forms and aristocratic institutions, it applies even more to democratic republics. There, not a portion only of the community is engaged in the task, and provision has to be made for the exigencies and convenience not of a single class, but of all classes at once.

It is possible to conceive the surprising liberty that the Americans enjoy; some idea likewise may be formed of their extreme equality; but the political activity that pervades the United States must be seen to be understood. No sooner do you set foot upon the American ground than you are stunned by a kind of tumult. A confused clamor is heard on every side, and a thousand simultaneous voices demand the satisfaction of their social wants. Everything is in motion. Here the people of one quarter meet to decide upon the building of a church. There a representative is being elected. A little farther, the delegates of a county are hastening to consult upon some local improvements. Elsewhere the laborers of a village quit their plows to deliberate upon a projected road or public school. Meetings are called for the sole purpose of declaring their disapprobation of the conduct of the government; while other assemblies salute the authorities of the day as the fathers of their country. Societies are formed which regard drunkenness as the principal cause of the evils of the state, and solemnly bind themselves to set an example of temperance.

The great political agitation of American legislative bodies which alone attracts the attention of foreigners, is a mere episode, or a sort of continuation, of a universal movement that originates in the lowest classes and extends successively to all the ranks of society. It is impossible to spend more effort in the pursuit of happiness.

It is difficult to describe the place of the concern for politics in the life of an inhabitant of the United States. To take a hand in the regulation of society and to discuss it is the major interest and often the only pleasure an American knows. This feeling pervades the most trifling habits of life; even the women frequently attend public meetings and listen to political harangues by way of respite from their household labors. Debating clubs are, to a certain extent, a substitute for theatrical entertainments. An American cannot converse; but he can discuss, and his talk falls naturally into a dissertation. He speaks to you as if he were addressing a meeting; when he becomes warm in the discussion, he will say "Gentlemen" to the person with whom he is talking.

In some countries the inhabitants seem unwilling to avail themselves of the political privileges the law gives them; perhaps they set too high a value upon their time to spend it on the interests of the community. But if an American were condemned to confine his activity to his own affairs, he would be robbed of one half of his existence. He would feel an immense void in the life he is accustomed to lead and his wretchedness would be unbearable. If ever a despotism should be established in America, it will be more difficult to overcome the habits that freedom has formed than to conquer the love of freedom itself.

This ceaseless agitation which democratic government has introduced into the political world influences all social intercourse. This may, on the whole, be the greatest advantage of democracy; and I am less inclined to applaud it for what it does than for what it causes to be done.

It is incontestable that the people frequently conduct public business very badly, but it is impossible that the lower orders should take a part in public business without extending the circle of their ideas and breaking the ordinary routine of their thoughts. The humblest individual who coöperates in the government of society acquires a certain degree of self-respect; and as he possesses authority, he can command the services of minds more enlightened than his own. He is canvassed by a multitude of applicants, who seek to deceive him in a thousand ways, but who really enlighten him. He takes a part in political undertakings which he did not originate, but which give him a taste for ventures of the kind. New improvements are daily pointed out to him in the common property, and this gives him the desire of improving that property which is his own. He is perhaps neither happier nor better than those who came before him, but he is better informed and more active. The democratic institutions of the United States, joined to the physical constitution of the country, are the cause of the prodigious commercial activity of the inhabitants. It is not created by the laws, but the people learn how to promote it by the experience derived from legislation.

The opponents of democracy are right when they assert that a single man performs what he undertakes better than a government by all. The rule of an individual, supposing an equality of knowledge on either side, is more consistent, more persevering, more uniform, and more accurate in details than that of a multitude, and it selects with more discrimination the men whom it employs. Even when local circumstances and the dispositions of the people allow them to exist, democratic institutions do not display a regular and methodical system of government. Democratic liberty rarely completes its projects with the skill of an adroit despotism. But in the end it produces more than any absolutism; if it does fewer things well, it does a greater number of things. Under its sway the grandeur is not in what the government does, but in what is done without it or outside it. Democracy does not give the people the most skillful administration, but it produces what the ablest governments are frequently unable to create, an all-pervading and restless activity, a superabundant force, an energy which will produce wonders however unfavorable circumstances may be. These are the true advantages of democracy.

13.

A SAVANT FROM AUSTRIA

Isidore Löwenstern was born in Vienna in 1807. He attended German universities and, having some means, devoted himself to the study of ancient civilizations. He was particularly concerned with deciphering Assyrian writing and made an analysis of the cuneiform inscriptions in Persopolis. In Constantinople, on the way to the Near East, he died suddenly in 1856.

*Löwenstern had made a tour of North America in 1837 which furnished the material for two books, one on the United States (*Les États-Unis et la Havane souvenirs d'un voyage, 1842), *from which this account was taken, and another on Mexico.*

In Philadelphia I was impressed by the Wistar Association, an organization formed by several members of the Philosophical Society as a means of spending a pleasant evening together once a week. The members met in rotation at each other's homes between October and April. They gathered at about eight o'clock in the evening and separated at about eleven. At ten there was a bountiful supper which, according to the rules of the group, could consist only of cold dishes and wine; tea, coffee, pastry, and ices were prohibited. It was also forbidden to serve any refreshments before supper. The member at whose house they gathered had the right to invite twenty citizens of the city. The others could bring strangers, not residents of Philadelphia.

I found the tone of these gatherings very pleasant, the conversation lively, informed, and free of the air of stiffness and restraint that generally reigns in American society. I attributed that cordial spirit to several likeable and distinguished men who guided the affairs of the group—Ponceau, Vaughan, Dr. Patterson, Moncuré Robinson, Cane, Tyson, and Chapman, among others.

I suspect that the social atmosphere of Philadelphia has not its equal anywhere in the United States. Few travelers have noticed that in the past because they neglected to provide themselves with the recommendations necessary for admission into good society. The facility of making acquaintances elsewhere in the United States led many to regard such precautions as useless. But precisely that abuse made entree difficult into the circles of what I call the aristocracy of Philadelphia.

The Philadelphians usually do not entertain during the day; all gatherings take place in the evening whether they be small teas or large parties which, according to usage, end in a supper. The society of which I speak is principally made up of attorneys, of government officials, merchants, and the higher officers of the navy; that is, people who do not simply live off income but who are all busy during the day. There is really no time for entertainment other than in the evening, Sunday being given over entirely to piety as in all Protestant countries.

I pause to describe the customs of Philadelphia partly because they give the most exact view of the upper class in the United States, and partly because I believe those customs are already on the decline. The desire to ape European habits, and particularly European luxury, shows itself everywhere and is introducing significant changes. It will not be long before the meal hours change too. The present usage is already regarded as too bourgeois; there is some desire to follow European practice and thus establish a harmless differentiation between the rich and the lower classes. Distinctions of rank have their defenders in America, as zealous as in the Old World. The only difference is the necessity here of concealing the tendency. As in England, for instance, the Americans, and especially the merchants, take great care to separate their homes and their offices. The countinghouses and stores have their fixed place near the river, while the residences of their owners are as far away as possible.

This tendency is most openly manifest among the women, who express anti-republican sentiments with as much frankness as their husbands take care to hide identical opinions. The ladies of Philadelphia cannot bear the thought that fortune and social position give them no special prerogatives. They therefore take infinite pains and use all their cleverness to differentiate themselves, and as much as possible to avoid contact with inferior classes. On the other hand, the husband, no matter how elevated his position, if he be in politics, finds himself obliged to shake hands with every cobbler, every farmer who has a vote to cast.

By consequence of this exclusiveness, I found the parties I went to in this city attended by and large by persons who were well brought up, and I must ascribe the difference between their manners and ours simply to local causes, to the diversity of customs in each country, and not to a lack of tact or of good behavior.

The stranger will always be surprised by the place occupied by women in American society, by the respect and the deference of which they are the objects. The English also lavish a kind of consideration on the ladies, but that is only superficial and has rather the objective of concealing a real indifference for the charm of their society. Englishmen gladly renounce the pleasure of female company in favor of the more boisterous enjoyments with which the presence of the fair sex might interfere.

The marks of deference which are only formal among the Britons are taken seriously by Americans. Those tokens turn into a sort of limitless respect and a boundless submission, so that the ladies in America can always enjoy the pleasure of having if not chivalrous admirers, at least most humble servants. *The Ladies!* At these magic words which announce their approach, like that of a sovereign, every man must rise, whether it be at table, or at the theater, and display the signs of most profound respect. Everywhere women receive the foremost and best places, a burdensome but imperative duty for the poor American who is so happy when he once succeeds in adjusting his body and legs in a restful position.

The prerogatives of the ladies extend to all manner of civil transactions as well as to social relations. But to enjoy all these rights the American women are subjected to other restraints, pushed farther here than anywhere else. They must be careful of their conduct, in appearance at least, since every person is guardian of the virtue of his neighbors.

In Philadelphia, ladies are unusually beautiful. I have never seen so many fine figures. And physical charm is not their only jewel; they are also likeable and intelligent. Yet all these qualities are lost for society by the restraint which compels them to seem cold and stiff in public, to conceal the grace which is the greatest attraction of the sex. Unhappy is she too well endowed with these qualities by nature. Amiability and enjoyment of company expose her to loss of reputation under the Puritan regime, and free and easy manners do not comport with American conceptions of aristocratic conduct. People here know no other way to oppose the pretensions of inferior classes than by stiffness and icy tone.

One evening in a circle of friends I spoke with a lady. Her conversation was free, comfortable, engaging, with neither prudery nor affectation. She acted with the carefree but reserved manner characteristic of the good society of Europe, where she had spent several years. "A fine woman!" I said to my neighbor after having left her—"Yes," was his response; "but . . . you see . . . they say . . . it seems . . . well . . ." Who then, after that, would wish to be amiable in such a country? The custom known in England, but even more prevalent here, of not being able to address a word in company to a lady or to a girl to whom one has not formally been introduced, is most annoying. And even after having been introduced according to the rules, the stranger hardly dares the first time to speak with a woman for more than a few moments. He is always watched; an extended conversation would certainly lead to whispering. The more beautiful and more graceful the ladies, the more they are the butts of gossip, a circumstance which deprives them of charm in mixed company, makes them cold, or at least embarrassed.

In Europe, if one is presented to a lady or placed near her in a gathering in which the tone of the house is guarantee enough that one will meet only proper persons, it is she who takes the initiative in conversation and puts the stranger at his ease. She asks a whole series of general questions about his arrival, about the length of his stay, and about other matters equally inconsequential, while the stranger can limit himself to answering. A traveler does not, however, find things so easy here; the lady remains as stiff as she can and as dumb as a statue. She expects the stranger to begin matters, perhaps to throw her a compliment *à l'américaine*. And it's too bad for him if he fails to do so. The conversation languishes, and by the time it begins to acquire a degree of animation, it is time to break it up.

The Philadelphia ladies are always luxuriously dressed, whether it be to go out to parties in the evening, or just to stay at home. The everyday garments, even of the middle classes, are made of silks and of the richest cloths. As for the wealthy, they shine in the most elegant dresses, particularly their evening gowns. They make it a point of honor to follow the Paris fashions exactly. They rarely wear jewels, but use flowers in profusion.

In public the men maintain a republican simplicity. They have the habit of taking off their hats before entering a room. That performance would make it difficult even for men more agile than the Americans not to be embarrassed with their arms. That remark should suffice for their grace in society. As for the rest, I prefer them as they are, that is, full of stiffness, rather than when they are foolish enough to ape the Europeans and play the dandies. They then attain a complete ridiculousness, and I would rather see them play the windmill with their arms than with a hat.

A very remarkable custom in the United States gives girls the freedom to choose a husband according to their fancy; practice does not permit either the mother or the father to interfere in this important matter. It is enough that the prospective groom should please the young lady, and she will bring him her dowry, large as it may be. As a result of this independence and of the immoderate fondness of the maidens for titles and for ranks which exist only among foreigners, some of the richest and most likeable girls in the first families of the United States have recently given themselves to nameless adventurers who were, often, already married on the other side of the Atlantic. Stripped of their dowry and abandoned, these unfortunate victims of a foolish ambition can only bitterly bewail the irreparable disasters into which they were led as much by their own vanity as by the indifference of their parents.

Indeed, no matter how just it may be to allow a girl freedom in the choice of a husband, a wise mother knows by guidance how to make her understand the depths to which passions and inexperience may betray a woman. But vanity, which in the United States acts as powerfully on the mothers as on their daughters, often renders the former even more imprudent and more culpable than the latter.

The penitentiary, one of the most important institutions in Philadelphia, is distinguished by a special character derived from the healthy and unprejudiced conceptions of a new people. Here they have rejected the idea, relic of a barbarous past, that punishment is the only reward for crime. They have replaced it with the civilized objective of reforming the guilty, of making them safe for society, without the permanent loss involved in being branded as a criminal. I did not fail to visit an establishment which has given rise to so many controversies. The justification of the system lies in the fact that the criminal is actually reformed. There is not a single example of a discharged convict who was ever brought back for a new crime.

The basic principle of this prison is solitary confinement. Each prisoner is separated from all the others, and is alone in a cell, which he never leaves until the day his sentence expires, a period which may last from one to twelve years. Until his release he is strictly forbidden to communicate with anyone, even with strangers who visit the place, unless the latter secure from the director a special permit, very difficult to obtain. The prisoner is thus entirely isolated; he has no distraction but his work, which alone can relieve his terrible solitude. He becomes industrious by despair, by necessity to forget the torments of his isolation. From that necessity comes a habit, a need for work, which is so powerful that there is no punishment in the prison more severe than depriving the criminal of the consolation of his labor for a few days.

The prison building lies in a court surrounded by a very high wall. From a central rotunda seven long corridors stretch out like the spokes of a wheel. The cells open onto each of the corridors in such a manner that a guard in the hall can survey all the corridors in a few seconds. Each cell is about eight feel long and twelve high, and receives the light of day only through a very narrow and high window.

An enclosure twice as long as the cell leads off each cell so that the prisoner may get some fresh air for an hour every day. He enters and leaves directly from his cubicle through a little trap door raised and lowered by a mechanism from outside. Each enclosure is surrounded by a high wall, so that the prisoners can no more be seen there than inside, except by the guard on top of the rotunda. The latter watches all the inmates who go in and out at the same time, but all remain isolated.

The convicts are fed three times a day through a locked opening in the door of their cells. In this manner 12 unarmed guards can take care of 586 criminals. The prisoners work at weaving and cobbling. They are taught at the beginning by the guards, who thereafter are chiefly concerned with preventing conversation. The revenue from this work is enough to pay the expenses of the prison, for the inmates themselves receive absolutely nothing, even when they are dismissed.

On Sundays and holidays the doors of the cells are opened for morning and afternoon prayers. The prisoners remain behind their open doors so that they can hear the minister at the end of the corridor, but cannot see or be seen by him. Everything is thus arranged so that the convict cannot be recognized by anyone. As soon as he is sentenced he is taken to the penitentiary in a completely closed carriage. Before getting out he is blindfolded with a black handkerchief and two men, holding him under the arms, lead him to his cell, so that no one can know him and he himself has no idea of the place in which he is. When he is released he is taken out in the same way, and leaves prison confident that no one but the director is aware of his name, for he himself knows the name of no one else.

14.

OBBLIGATO BY HERZ

Henri Herz was born in Vienna in 1806. As a child, he was taught the piano by his father and by the organist Hünten, and, at the age of eleven, came to Paris to study at the conservatory. Thereafter he was a Parisian. He had a successful concert career and also acquired a reputation as composer in the semiserious style of the boulevards. His

tour of the United States, in 1846, was immensely profitable, for he
never permitted artistic scruples to constrict his own or his manager's
sense of what would appeal at the box office. Twenty years later he
wrote down a witty description of his adventures in the New World,
and it was published as Mes Voyages en Amérique *(1866). As befitted*
a man who consistently made a good thing of life, he lived until the
ripe age of eighty-two.

The hotel at which I stopped in Boston, like almost all those in the
United States, was comfortable to a degree which astonishes and delights the European traveler. There are vast tables d'hôte admirably
served, if not well cooked (there are no good cooks outside France);
elegant washrooms in each chamber, with hot and cold running water;
gas lights, carpets everywhere, a large drawing room in which I saw for
the first time an American piano, so heavy and square it might have
been some antediluvian animal. Right in the building, on the ground
floor, a barroom or tavern offered voyagers excellent American drinks
with a large number of newspapers stretched out everywhere, even
under one's feet.

In France the whole world of servants follows the custom, less dignified than irritating, of *pourboire*. This habit of tipping does not exist
in the United States, and I congratulate that country for it. To say to a
man, "Here my friend is something for a drink!" is implicitly to say, "I
consider you a drunkard, and wish to encourage you in this vice, by
giving you the means of satisfying it." Unhappily, this evil seems unlikely to die out, for it is based on the vanity of those who give and on
the servility of those who receive; and neither vanity nor submissive-
ness are prone to give way to modesty and dignity. In fact, the disease
has a faculty for spreading, even to America. I have heard it said that
the practice is already common in the summer resorts of the United
States, where tipping has become a sort of ransom from famine.

There are few countries where wine is not a luxury drink; France
in this, as in many other respects, is the happy exception. Here people
usually drink only water at their meals. When they celebrate some
special occasion they call for champagne, a wine of which America
consumes more than any other country in the world.

In the barroom I saw a score of Americans smoking away in a very
original and comic position, which has furnished the material for so

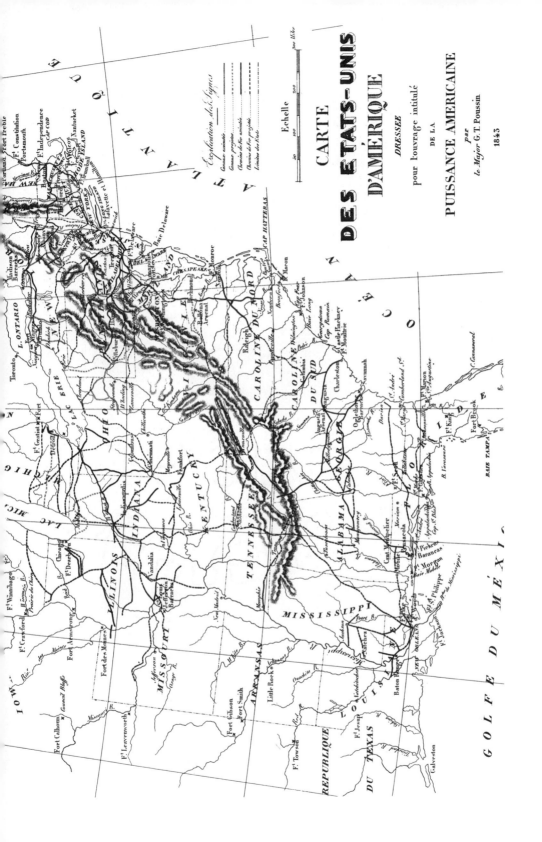

CARTE
DES ÉTATS-UNIS
D'AMÉRIQUE
DRESSÉE
pour l'ouvrage intitulé
DE LA
PUISSANCE AMÉRICAINE
par
le Major G. T. Poussin
1843

Échelle

Explication des Signes
Grandes routes
Grandes projetées
Chemins de fer exécutés
Chemins de fer projetés
Limites des États

Nach der Natur gez. v. C. Köhler.

Stahlst. v. F. Foltz.

Ein Bethaus methodistischer Farmer

IN ILLINOIS

many joyous criticisms. They were seated with their legs elevated above their heads and exposed a view of the soles of their boots to the passers-by outside. These soles were so evenly aligned, they might have been suspended for inspection.

For that matter, everything in Boston is well aligned, buildings as well as streets, most of which are bordered with trees in a manner charming to the vision, and useful in purifying the air. Walking about, I lit a cigar. I had not proceeded ten feet when a constable stopped me, shocked:

"Sir, smoking is forbidden."

"You are joking, constable."

"Not at all. Smoking in the streets is forbidden. If you cannot contain yourself, go home to smoke."

"But yesterday I saw twenty people smoking with their legs in the air. Is that the only position in which smoking is permitted?"

"You may smoke in any position you like, but only in your own home. The law forbids any smoking in the streets, and your infraction is all the more shocking and blameworthy on Sunday, the day consecrated to the glory of God."

I could not help but consider this taboo, in the land of all the liberties, tyrannical. But I had to obey.

In New York, before thinking of giving my first concert in the New World, I wished to see the city and learn something of the strange civilization of this hardy and laborious people. The prodigious number of cases of merchandise which I saw in the port and the commercial movement which reigned everywhere gave me the impression of an enormous fairground. A feverish activity seems to obsess these inhabitants of North America. I felt myself the only idler in this nest of human ants.

The churches of New York seem quite ordinary from the outside. Made of brick for the most part, they are topped by a steeple, ending in a point of painted wood. But their interior offers the philosopher a broad field for curious observations. All religions, all sects are represented in free America which has placed at the head of all human liberties the liberty of conscience.

We entered the places of worship of several sects and for the first time I saw a Quaker specimen. There was a couple, very respectable in morals, I am sure, but in physical appearance quite ridiculous. In

America, where everyone dresses alike, where even the Catholic priests wear nothing or almost nothing to distinguish them from other men, the Quakers have adopted the ugliest of uniforms. The men wear coats of somber colors, large trousers, wide and heavy shoes, a low-crowned hat with a broad brim and a cane. The women wear heavy shoes and blue wool stockings, a sort of bonnet on their heads, and a pointed shawl across their shoulders. They fit into their narrow and plain gowns like an umbrella in its sheath, and their stiff and formal bearing confirms that comparison. Add thereto a green pinafore, and see whether the graces of Venus could survive such an adaptation.

These people must especially be seen in their places of worship. They tremble in calling to themselves the favor of the Holy Spirit, and preach without distinctions of age or of sex when they feel themselves inspired by the divinity. God knows what extravagant conversations these Quakers must hold with that unhappy divinity!

After some hesitation, I decided to offer my first concert in Tabernacle Hall. Although it was neither elegant nor well constructed from the point of view of acoustics, I preferred it to any other for its size, and because it was well known to the public.

The concert was announced in the newspapers and immense advertisements were posted up on all the walls, so that almost all the 3,000 seats were taken in advance. Despite my familiarity with public performances, I was somewhat nervous in my initial appearance before an American audience. An overture by the orchestra preceded my first piece, my C-minor concerto. The overture was performed in the midst of a tumult of late-comers who found difficulty in getting to their places, to the distraction of the general public. I will pass over the details of this evening, much too flattering to be repeated by myself, and will only halt at one incident characteristic of American habits.

Just as I was about to retire, having finished my concerto, I saw one member of my audience leap onto a chair, wave his arms, and deliver a speech in a vibrant voice in my honor. When he had finished I thought I had no further business on the stage. But the French consul seated near me said:

"Well, answer."

"Answer what?"

"The flattering words just addressed to you. Good usage requires that you do so."

"Impossible; I am not familiar enough with the language of Lord Byron to answer such a speech with another."

"Ah, the devil! . . . Well, someone will have to answer for you."

The consul whispered to a gentleman, who began to orate for me, turning to me from time to time to be certain he said nothing to displease me, and pointing me out with his gestures to give added force to his words. I was certainly uncomfortable in this singular position, but the enthusiastic hurras which greeted the last phrases of my eloquent spokesman put a very happy end to my torture.

I must now speak of my first interview with Mr. Ulmann, then an unknown, but since become a most celebrated impressario. He was at the time a young man, chasing his fortune, like everyone else in America.

"What can you do?" I asked him.

"Nothing," he answered frankly, "but by that token alone, I am capable of doing anything. Try me. I will advertise your concerts, print your programs, see that everything is in order at the auditorium. I will make sure the newspaper editors know all about you; the press is the source of the artistic, just as gold is the source of military good fortune. And, if you wish, I will advise you as to certain critical tactics, for success does not always come with talent. Finally, I will act in your interests, which will be also mine, and will do many things that have to be done, but which you cannot do yourself."

I tried him, and the apprentice quickly became master. A few days were enough to establish the most intimate contacts with the principal newspaper editors. Ulmann knew how to capitalize the slightest incidents to fix public attention on the artist, whom he compared poetically to a brilliant meteor which the whole world had to admire during a too brief passage.

At that time, Barnum, the most famous entrepreneur of public entertainment, who had already made his fortune by exhibiting a deranged old Negress as the nurse of Washington, was concerned with other means of improving the condition of his purse. He came to see me at my hotel.

"Do you know Jenny Lind?" he asked.

"By reputation, yes," I answered, "although I have never heard her sing."

"I intend to bring her to America," said Barnum, "where she will create a sensation."

"I should think so, for she has both a fine voice and artistic talent."

"There is something else. I intend to present her as an angel descended from heaven, a pure and radiant symbol of Young America."

"Do you really believe you will get people to believe that this fine singer studied in a celestial conservatory?"

"Well, they won't believe it at first. But I will have it said, and repeated everywhere, with so much confidence and so well, that they will end by believing it."

One day Ulmann walks in and announces that we are leaving for Philadelphia, where we give a concert the next day. The hall is rented, advertisements set, all the tickets sold, our trunks are packed, our railroad passage arranged, and there is a carriage at the door to take us to the station. By this time I had an inflexible rule: always to obey. Without a word I followed, and in an hour we were on our way.

In Philadelphia and in the state of Maine the temperance societies have their greatest influence. In this city there were a great many water drinkers who deliberately condemned themselves to imbibe only this very primitive liquid under the pretext that some people abused the use of distilled liquors. If it were necessary to deprive oneself of everything that was abused by someone we should soon renounce almost everything. But in America temperance is a passion, like any other, and there is no reasoning with a passion.

Naturally, the members of temperance societies maintain the greatest austerity of manners, and I have even known some serious Puritans whose modesty was comprehensive enough to stretch from the human species to the least flighty type of furniture, the American piano. One day I saw one of these instruments, the legs of which, thick as the trunk of trees, were covered with bags in the form of bathing drawers.

"They are there," said the Puritan owner, modestly lowering her eyes, "because it is not proper even for a piano to display naked legs."

Everything in this world wears away in time, and the pleasure of listening to music is no exception to this rule. Despite the interest which the American public continued to display, Ulmann thought it necessary to add a new attraction, something powerful, irresistible, to attract new audiences to the music. He thought it over, then was inspired: "Eureka!"

"What a concert, what an idea!"

"What's on your mind?" I asked. "Do you plan to hire an orchestra, two, three?"

"My idea is worth all the orchestras in the world."

"Well, tell me!"

"You are really the last one in the world to be told, for you are always difficult about the means for attracting attention; but, since you want to know, it's a matter of a thousand candles."

"I don't understand; are these musical candles?"

Ulmann laughed and left me understanding his plans less than before. I had forgotten this conversation when I noticed, in a walk about the city, placards announcing my next concert at the head of which was printed:

A THOUSAND CANDLES

I read this sign and finally understood that the plan was to light the auditorium with a thousand candles, a means of attracting a crowd that seemed to me not only ridiculous, but likely to be ineffective.

I was certainly mistaken. These thousand candles aroused such curiosity among the American people, so virile by nature but so naïve and childish in impressions, that all the seats were sold in less than a day. Ulmann's candles, I must confess, had a greater success than my "Rondo Russe," which I played in the midst of the general disorder. I was disgruntled, but Ulmann was triumphant as he counted the receipts which justified all in his eyes.

The appetite grows as it is fed, and confidence comes with success. The thousand candles with which Ulmann had enlightened the audience at my last concert, to the profit of our accounts and the glory of the impressario, gave him many sleepless nights. The bizarre ideas he dreamed up to stimulate the flagging interests of the piano lovers would make a fantastic story. He would tell them to me, and despite my efforts to preserve a serious demeanor, I was often forced to receive his confidences with a burst of laughter.

One day, after a proposal more extravagant than usual, I let him know that I wished as far as possible to have recourse to no methods for drawing crowds to my concerts other than my art.

"Art, art, always art," answered Ulmann skeptically. "And what do you think music is?"

"Music is the art of moving the emotions by a combination of sounds."

"That's all?"

"I think so."

"Not at all. Music is the art of drawing into a given hall, by means of accessories which often become principals, as great a number of curious people as possible and in such a way that the receipts will exceed the expenses. And," he added, "I have thought of a new program for your final concert in Philadelphia. You will give a political concert."

Without saying another word, my ingenious secretary drew from his pocket a long paper from which I read the following:

ADIEUX

TO THE CITY OF PHILADELPHIA

A great festival in honor of the Declaration of Independence published in this city before the assembled people, in the midst of indescribable enthusiasm on July 4 of the immortal year 1776.

PROGRAM

1. HOMAGE TO WASHINGTON, cantata in eight parts, with solos and choruses, performed by five orchestras and eighteen hundred singers. NOTE. The bust of the father of his country will be crowned at the last chords of the cantata.
2. CONSTITUTION CONCERTO, expressly composed for this solemn occasion by Henri Herz and performed by the author.
3. LECTURE on the genius of the American people and on the rights of women, by Miss ——.
4. GRAND TRIUMPHAL MARCH dedicated to Young America and arranged for forty pianists by Henri Herz.
5. THE CAPITOL, a chorus of apotheosis to the spirits of the presidents of the United States.
6. "HAIL COLUMBIA," national air performed by all the military bands of Philadelphia and vicinity, especially united for this occasion.

N.B. Illumination in the interior of the hall will form allegorical figures of the great deeds of the republic.

Admission: SIX DOLLARS.

I looked at Ulmann with astonishment. I could not tell whether he was serious or joking.

"I've got it all figured out," he said confidently. "We will have eight thousand dollars in expenses and will take in sixteen, balance eight thousand profit. Is that all right?" He was exceedingly disappointed when I resisted his cajolery and withheld my consent.

Ulmann, who never abandoned one of his ideas, repeatedly came back to the notion of a political concert, insisting especially upon the effect that would be created by a triumphal march for forty pianists. I finally consented to write a piece, not for forty indeed, but for eight, which seemed enough to me. A concert was announced—eight pianists playing together on four instruments. And the public justified my secretary's reasoning by its eagerness to witness this new type of exhibition. They would certainly have been impressed had there been forty.

I took some charming walks in the neighborhood of Philadelphia and did not fail, like the other sight-seers, to admire the hydraulic machines on the Schuylkill which supply all the inhabitants of the city of brotherly love with fresh water. Here, as elsewhere in the United States, man had fought against great obstacles raised by nature, and had triumphed. The task was to raise the water from the river to a reservoir large enough to supply Philadelphia abundantly. And God knows the terrific consumption of water in America, where every house has a bath, where many housewives do their own laundry, where many rooms are furnished with hot and cold running water, and where the servants wash the fronts of the houses every Saturday with pumps.

I visited the reservoir with a family at whose home I spent one of my pleasantest evenings in Philadelphia. A description of each member of this family, and of course of their working day, will give a picture of the life of an honest household in Pennsylvania.

The head of the family, a merchant, is about fifty years old; his wife, about thirty-five and in the full bloom of a rather chaste and severe beauty. They have one son of seventeen, and twin daughters aged fourteen. The girls are identical and dress alike so that their father often takes one for the other.

Mr. G. is a native of New York and the son of English parents. He began his business career as clerk in a draper's shop. At the age of twelve he was charged with the task of collecting debts and was often obliged to travel about with six-thousand dollars in his pocket. At the age of sixteen he had the run of the firm, and at twenty-four had set up in trade on his own account. His early life thus passed without the opportunity of enjoying any of the pleasures of youth. His energies were directed toward one single end, to make himself rich through his labors. And there are thousands of similar experiences in the United States. As for France, was there ever a child who was anything but a child?

I draw this contrast not in criticism or in praise but simply to reveal a characteristic trait. Mr. G. now has a fortune of three or four million francs, but continues his business and has not modified his mode of life in any respect. At the height of winter he gets up before sunrise, has a cup of tea, and leaves his sumptuous residence to go to the dingy little rooms in a sort of immense barracks which he calls his office. In this miserable retreat, badly furnished, badly ventilated, and always littered with cases of merchandise, Mr. G. daily carries on his affairs, large and petty, with that calm and righteous spirit characteristic of the Anglo-Saxons. Neither rain, nor snow, nor ice will keep him from his task. When the streets are glassed over to an extent that imperils his limbs, he attaches a little spiked apparatus to the soles of his shoes and somehow gets to his office, as the soldier to his post, the priest to his church. Apparently trade is more than a source of livelihood, it is a veritable ministry.

After getting to his desk he puts his books in order. About an hour later his clerks arrive. At nine o'clock he leaves his chair to breakfast at a restaurant frequented by merchants. In five minutes he has his snack, a meal that invariably consists of a bit of beef and a dish of raw cress seasoned with vinegar and mustard. He then goes back to his office, receives his clients, reads the newspapers, tours the exchange and the customshouse, then returns to the office again to give his final orders, and at last comes back to his home. He dines silently with his family in a quarter of an hour and spends the evening in a little room reserved for his own use, or else goes to a club of which he has long been a member.

Mrs. G., as is the custom in Pennsylvania, gets up very early through the year, and does not leave her bedroom unless fully dressed, as if for the street. Her daughters, well brought up and elegant without affectation, come down a little later. Promptly at eight, whether in January or July, breakfast is on the table. Eight times in ten they will have ham fried with eggs, and drink coffee in large cups.

After breakfast the girls take their books and go by themselves to school. Mrs. G. then fixes an apron, white as snow, around her waist, and gives her orders to the servants, setting an example by her own hard work. Every day the house is cleaned and set in order from cellar to attic. When everything is arranged, formally, and a little coldly, it is true, but irreproachably, Mrs. G. retires to her room and makes a second toilette.

She then invariably goes out, either in a carriage or on foot, for two to five hours, touring the stores. Generally without any intention of making a purchase, she has a score of bolts of cloth pulled down, looks through box after box of ribbons and tries on a dozen shawls. This manner of passing time, to the despair of the salespeople, is usual among American women who have given it a special name, "shopping."

Mr. G.'s son works in his father's business without any respite from morning to night. After dinner he goes to the theater or retires to his own place in the basement where he studies German and the piano. Such is the life of the G. family, and such is the life of almost all the families of American merchants, whatever their status or fortune.

Before leaving the city of brotherly love for Baltimore, I suffered quite a characteristic experience. I was dining with a Frenchman of my acquaintance. Dessert having arrived, there remained on the dish a single cake. The Frenchman offered it to me; I refused and begged him to take it. He insisted courteously; I must certainly have it. The cake looked tempting and I repeated my denials.

"It's really for you," I said to my obliging neighbor.

"I've no desire for it."

"Please do have it."

"You are offending me."

"Well, then, since you absolutely do not want it, I will take it."

I was about to reach out, when an American sitting near us and witness to the scene, took up his fork, leaned halfway across the table, and to our stupefaction adroitly speared the cake which he consumed with a great deal of pleasure. There seemed to be nothing in the world unusual about this procedure.

On the way to Baltimore I was asked by Ulmann to improvise. "Improvise in public!" I said. "That is most ticklish. I might be ill-disposed and it would be cruel publicly to expose a pretentious lack of skill, unless one follows the practice of some improvisers who learn their improvisations by heart."

"That is certainly a wise precaution," said Ulmann, "but it would not go over in America where each man insists on the right to offer his own themes. In any case, it will not be necessary. If you run out of ideas, simply play the theme with one hand and some chromatic scales with the other. The audience will be delighted."

At his insistence I resigned myself to that rule. Thereafter I was condemned by Ulmann to improvising, a task which was boring at first but ended by diverting me. The announcement was made that any themes on which I was desired to improvise be submitted on the way in. Fifty or sixty themes were thus handed to the ticket taker. Among these were some well-known melodies; others must have come from the repertoire of the redskins.

When the time for improvising came, I appeared before the public with all the manuscripts, which were subjected to a majority vote. This occasioned a great uproar, for an air which pleased some, offended others, and I often had difficulty in discovering what was the will of the majority. When five or six themes were thus chosen, I arranged them into a fantasy, as inspiration dictated.

This musical trickery was very successful and proved quite popular with the American public. But the most striking cases were those in which my auditors could not write out their music, yet would not forego the opportunity to make themselves heard. They would whistle and ask me to write down the notes myself. Music lovers of this species would silence the rest of the audience, climb onto a chair and gravely whistle away while I tried to make out their baroque and vague tunes. The public waited patiently while they tried, often four or five times, and applauded both the whistler and me when I finally got the motif.

I never allowed myself to laugh while participating in these innocent musical games, although I often had a mind to. Everyone was serious; most serious of all, Ulmann, counting away at the box-office receipts.

Musical taste in the United States at this time left much to be desired, despite the efforts of a number of worthy philharmonic societies and of a few good musicians to popularize the works of the masters. For example, I once noticed in a music shop a piece of music on the cover of which I read "Sontag Waltz" by Henri Herz. I turned the pages; I certainly had never composed any such music.

"What is this?" I said, much disturbed, to the music dealer.

"You ask me! Why this is the composition that made your reputation in America; your other works are more or less esteemed, but this is universally regarded the best of all."

I wished to disclaim the honor, but Ulmann perceived my intention and drew me aside.

"Don't say anything," he told me, "you will offend him, and no one will believe you anyway."

I followed my secretary's advice, and probably I am still remembered in America today, if at all, as the author of "Sontag Waltz."

This is perhaps the place to speak in detail of the music trade and of the manufacture of pianos in America. The business is everywhere extensive but the American instruments leave much to be desired, except those of Chickering, whose reputation has even crossed the ocean. Without having the same excellence of tone, timbre, and power that distinguish French pianos, the Chickering has some merit and the concert models hold their own when compared with the English pianos to which they are similar.

Music sales are large everywhere in the United States. There are some publishers who have as many as 200,000 plates. This music, adequately engraved and well printed, keeps the country well supplied. Not having as yet made any international treaties for protecting literary and musical copyrights, the Americans, without paying anyone, can publish with impunity all the works which appear in Europe. This unjust privilege gives them a most important advantage in competing for this business, not balanced by their higher labor costs.

At this period there were some fifteen daily newspapers in New York City, two-thirds of which appeared in the morning, the rest in the afternoon. In addition, there were published in the same city, three or four weeklies on Saturday, and as many more on Sunday. Finally, there were two monthly reviews, a quarterly, a newspaper by and for the English, two or three German sheets, and the French *Courrier des États-Unis*. Except for the German and French papers, all the journals were in size, make-up, and content modeled after those in England.

Everything which might conceivably be of interest is gathered into these publications. They do not yet publish novels but they make up for that by detailed correspondence from all parts of the world, and by official reports reprinted *in extenso*. Many people carry on private cor-

respondence through the medium of the press, and it is often curious
and amusing to read the columns given over to personals. The following
give a general idea of the nature of these advertisements:

"Tomorrow Wednesday. Prudence and Secrecy. N.O.A."

"If S . . . keeps his price up, let it go. Z."

"You are an old fool, Miss R. If you return to my home, I'll strangle
you."

The American press has often been accused of practicing blackmail.
Even if this accusation is not altogether false, and there may be venal
pens in the New, as in the Old World, this charge has been much exaggerated. I have never encountered any evidence of it. Everywhere, on
the contrary, I saw American journalists very independent, yet respectful of the talents and personalities of the artists whom they judged.

The *New York Herald* has been most bitterly accused of blackmail,
for its rapidly gained prosperity inevitably inspires the jealousy and
the hate of the powerless proud who try many things and succeed in
none. To have succeeded is, in the eyes of some people, the unforgivable sin of which James Gordon Bennett, the owner and editor of the
Herald, is guilty. But Mr. Bennett is a philosopher, American style. He
knows that perfect happiness is not for this world; and the dollars he
has earned easily console him for the enemies he has gained precisely
because he earned those dollars.

The daily editions of the *New York Herald* have a circulation of
some 40,000 or 50,000, the weekly, even more. Together they form an
enormously valuable property. Since its establishment, the *Herald* has
made a point of printing European news as soon as possible. Two hours
after the arrival of the transatlantic steamers, the *Herald* sells in the
streets thousands of supplements with the latest European information.
This incredible speed is due, in large part, to the most efficient printing machines in the world. These cylindrical presses are capable of
turning out 300 copies in a minute, or 18,000 papers in an hour.

Of all the New York papers, the *Herald* is most concerned with art
and the artists. Mrs. Bennett, the wife of the owner, is herself in charge
of the accounts of the theaters and the concerts. She puts a great deal
of spirit into this work, and brings to it a sentiment which almost
amounts to a passion. Her reviews are sometimes ingenious and always
lively. For her you are either a God or nothing. She recognizes no degrees between good and bad. For, like all women, this young and pretty

critic judges more with her sympathies and antipathies than with her reason.

After the *Herald,* the most popular journals are the *Tribune,* the *Daily Times,* the *Courier and Enquirer,* the *Sun,* the *Journal of Commerce,* the *Express,* the *Evening Post,* the *Commercial Advertiser,* the *Home Journal,* and the *Mirror.* The *Tribune* has for editor-in-chief Mr. Horace Greeley, a man of strong originality, at the same time Utopian and practical, partisan of the Fourierites, of Bloomerism, of the knocking spirits, and a Whig.

The *Daily Times* is abolitionist, more puritanical than any other paper, and temperate. Speak to it of wine or liquor, and water rushes to its head. The *Sun* takes for its field the enlightenment of the intelligence of the masses by vulgarizing all the fields of human knowledge. In the United States, more than almost anywhere, the *Sun* has a reason for being. For everyone must know a little bit of everything in a country where professions are changed with astounding facility. There, doctors sometimes become building contractors, colonels are innkeepers, and the pianists, grocers. The *Sun* is printed on a colossal sheet in tiny type and costs only one cent. Its editors are the Beaches, father and son.

The *Courier and Enquirer* has a relatively restricted circulation but considerable influence. The *Journal of Commerce* is concerned exclusively with trade and with certain religious doctrines.

In America trade and religion often give each other mutual support, for the churches belong to private societies which often rent them out, without scruples, for concerts and conferences. Tabernacle Hall, for instance, where I gave my concerts, was a sort of temple in which the profane succeeded the sacred without inconvenience, provided always that the profane had the necessary funds. It belonged to the owners of the *Journal of Commerce.*

In New York I had the pleasure of attending a lecture by a liberated woman, one of those who later founded in that city the Free Love Club. Liberty is a beautiful thing, but too much is not. The free woman to whom I listened spoke at length, demanding for her sex certain rights which up to now have remained the exclusive privilege of the other sex. She was arguing what seemed to me an untenable thesis. Are there not already enough politicians, soldiers, firemen, ministers of all sorts of churches, and policemen in the United States, as everywhere else, without mixing in the women?

Women have a providential mission in this world, which is enough for their existence, for their glory indeed, and which guarantees them our recognition and admiration. What else do they want? Do they seek the means of domination? And what male orator has the powers of persuasion of a blue eye in which trembles a tear, or the terrible authority of dark eyes flashing with anger? With such weapons feminine victory will never be in doubt, but there are no limits to the ambitions of the free woman in the United States. She has pleaded her case so well that almost all careers are open to her.

As in so many other American cities, the cemetery is the favorite place for a promenade in Charleston. The living there are refreshed by the shade, and the dead, before resting for eternity, pause in an establishment, original enough, known as the Winding Sheet.

The Americans who decorate their omnibuses with paintings, by the leading artists of the moment, of beautiful women, of Washington, and of landscapes, have also ornamented this antechamber with funerary emblems. It is so hot in Charleston during the summer that it is impossible to conserve the dead in their own homes more than three or four hours. When someone dies, his relatives must inform the authorities who carry the corpse to the Winding Sheet.

I had never seen any slaves before coming to Charleston, and the sight of these unfortunates aroused in me the most painful impressions. Not that they seemed oppressed or were generally badly treated; their features, on the contrary, reflected rather gaiety, or at least indifference, and materially they might be thought better off than a good many Europeans. But they were slaves, and that thought, despite myself, overshadowed all other considerations. A man placed outside the pale of humanity, and owned by another man by the same title as a beast, seemed to me monstrous, especially in the land of all the liberties.

I attended one of the auction sales of Negroes opposite the customshouse of Charleston. Ten unfortunates were up for sale. I noticed one mother with her child, a pretty young mulatto, and a Negro of twenty-five to twenty-eight years, whose intelligent features and proud appearance drew my attention. First to mount the platform was an elderly Negro who was promptly sold to a wealthy rice planter who also bought the mother and child.

Then came the turn of the pretty mulatto girl about whom pressed a crowd of men of dubious morality, and who, by their embarrassing questions and cynical attitude, brought a blush to the yellow skin of the slave. This poor girl, object of a criminal lust, was long bid on, and finally sold for twice her worth to a professional gambler who intended to put her up in a lottery for a profit.

I gave several concerts in Charleston and it seemed to me that there was a more cultivated taste for music in the South than in the North. I played two or three of my concertos and was happy to find that they did not displease my audience, which appreciated compositions somewhat more elevated than the simple airs and variations. As for Ulmann, he told me that he held the Carolinians in high esteem, that is to say, that the receipts measured up to his expectations. Making several stopovers for concerts in intermediate cities, we then proceeded to New Orleans.

I could almost think myself back home in the French quarter of New Orleans, and in truth, this quarter is a bit of old France that has resisted the torrential sweep of American civilization. The English or American quarter and the French quarter are, properly speaking, two cities in one, two cities perfectly distinct from each other in the aspect of their buildings and in the nature of their inhabitants.

English alone is spoken in the American quarter and all the manners are English. The houses are built of brick several stories high, and business is king. The French quarter has old creole houses, French is spoken exclusively, and there is a certain ease in habits which has nothing in common with the rigidity and seriousness of the businessmen in the other quarter.

Were it not for yellow fever, New Orleans would probably be the largest and most flourishing city in the union. But the terrifying epidemic has always clogged up the flow of immigration, which is the principal source of the rapid growth of population in the United States. It may be said that most immigrants only pass through New Orleans in transit. They no more disembark than they hurry on to the rich farming regions of the West, where the Germans particularly have made fortunes.

But New Orleans, despite the yellow fever, has shared the good fortune that spreads over all the United States. Figures here speak more eloquently than words. A city which in 1785 had less than 5,000 inhabitants, by 1840 had more than 100,000. The cause of this remark-

able growth in places like New Orleans which do not profit from immigration, must be more frequent and more fertile marriages than in
any other part of the world.

We lodged at the Hotel Saint Charles, a monumental building
topped by a dome modeled after our Pantheon in Paris, although in
more modest proportions. I was told there were no less than two-
thousand separate rooms in this caravansary where one could hear
spoken all the languages of all the men of all countries. Alas, the Hotel
Saint Charles went the way of so many other grand establishments and
so many modest homes in the United States: fire, that national disease,
struck it down one day and I am not sure this phoenix of a hotel will
ever rise from its ashes.

I had hardly been installed when a deputation of free Negroes came
to see me. I had no conception of their purpose but I hastened to see
them. The Negroes, well dressed, and perfect gentlemen, told me the
object of their visit. One, speaking for the rest, said:

"Sir, we come to ask you to give a concert for the colored people.
You no doubt know that we are forbidden to mix with the whites in any
public assembly, and yet we would very much like to hear you. If you
think an audience of colored people not unworthy of your talents, and
if you feel that the men of our race ought not to be deprived of the
sweet emotions of art, we ask you not to reject our petition and to set
aside a day for us. You may fix your own terms and we will guarantee
payment before the concert."

"Gentlemen," I answered, "your invitation is very flattering and I
would accept on the spot were it not a rule with me to consult my
secretary, Mr. Ulmann, on all the details of the concerts. I will send
you my answer tomorrow."

The Negroes having left, I called Ulmann.

"If you commit the inexcusable fault of playing for the Negroes," he
said, "be assured that you will never have a white audience in New
Orleans."

I therefore had to inform the poor Ethiopians that I could not accept their offer. It pained me, I must confess; but Ulmann was right; I
would have lost face with all the whites if I had been weak enough to
play even once for the blacks.

As Ulmann and I were boarding a ship for Mobile, a dispute arose
between two Creoles over what I later learned was a very petty matter.

The adversaries, without any regard for the crowd in which they found themselves, and at the risk of wounding innocents, reached into their pockets and each drew out a revolver. They exchanged a dozen shots in the open street and the fight did not end until one of them fell with a shattered shoulder. No one was astonished at this impromptu duel; it was hardly questioned. New Orleans has always been sadly notorious for such savage combats, which are elsewhere almost unknown.

Until 1813, when Spain ceded it to the United States, Mobile was a sink of infection. The yellow fever decimated its population, which had fallen to four thousand, and commerce had come to a halt. Today the marshes and swampy grounds have been almost entirely redeemed and covered with shops and warehouses for the cotton of Alabama. The yellow fever has been conquered by the courage and the industrial genius of the American people, who are never halted by difficulties and who seem to grow in stature as the obstacles they face become larger.

Several steamship lines connect Mobile with the interior, with Tuscaloosa and Montgomery. Steamers also run regularly between Mobile and New York while others coast along the Gulf of Mexico.

By land Mobile is connected with the central part of the United States by the Mobile and Ohio Railway, some 450 miles long, which, by links to the railways of Illinois, furnishes a direct route from the Great Lakes to the Gulf of Mexico. This gigantic network is tied toward the east with the Girard and Mobile Railway in Georgia and in the west toward New Orleans with the Mobile and Madison. What achievements are accomplished everywhere on this virgin earth of the United States, what wealth accumulated, what resources created by labor and by genius! Without doubt, the young American peoples had the example of Europe to guide them, but in such matters they have undeniably surpassed their master.

15.

CORRESPONDENT FROM THE HOMELAND

In 1847 the Norwegian government sent a prominent lawyer and jurist to the United States to study the operations of the American jury system. It selected for the task Ole Munch Ræder, a young man of thirty-two who had received an excellent legal education in Norway, Denmark, France, and Germany. Ræder agreed to send home, in the course of his travels, regular dispatches for newspaper publication (these have since been published, in translation, under the title, America in the Forties, *1929). An avid demand for information on conditions in the New World by Norwegians who contemplated emigration assured him an eager audience. After his return to Norway, Ræder had a long, successful career as a jurist, and died in 1895.*

The trip on the Erie Canal, from Albany to Buffalo, costs only $7.50, including meals, and lasts a day longer than the journey by rail. This price, however, is only for ordinary travelers. The spirit of speculation has led to a rather material reduction in the price for immigrants. Some canal boats, I believe, transport them and their belongings for $2.00, but they have to provide their own food.

The railroads, too, in their case have made an exception to the general rule of having only one class. Sometimes a large boxcar labeled in huge letters "IMMIGRANT CAR," is added to the train, and here the immigrants are piled together in grand confusion, with all their trunks and other belongings. In New York there are companies which arrange the entire journey for immigrants, making their profits through the large masses they transport, as well as whatever they can make through cheating—by dropping them off half way, and so on.

The consul general at New York has made a splendid arrangement for the immigrants whereby they deposit a sum of $6.00 and are then transported to Wisconsin by one of the most dependable companies, which is paid by the consulate upon notification from the immigrant that the company has faithfully discharged its obligation. This plan is announced to the immigrants upon their arrival in New York, but they are so suspicious—or perhaps so unsuspecting when it comes to the

Yankees and their agents—that they seldom make use of this splendid means of securing a journey that is both safe and cheap. They cannot resist the temptation of an offer to transport them for a few cents less. The immigrant companies have in their service Norwegians and Swedes who carry on a very profitable business.

On the Great Lakes there is only one means of travel, for immigrants as well as for others, and that is the steamship. The elegance of such a ship is quite remarkable. The vessel is equipped in every possible way for the convenience of the passengers; there is, for example, a barber shop. There is also a band. Its performance on brass instruments we found none too good, but in the evenings it won general approval by presenting comical Negro songs, accompanied by the guitar, and by playing dance music, to which the youthful Yankees executed their favorite cotillion, a sort of quadrille, with many dainty skips and steps. There was also a good piano on board, on which those passengers who thought they knew anything about music frequently tried their skill, more to the horror and dismay than to the enjoyment of their fellow passengers. It was strange to see how easy it was to induce these American ladies, noted in Europe for their prudery and finicality, to play or sing for this audience of absolute strangers from every corner of the earth.

And now, finally, to get at a very important item; both the food and the service, provided by Negro servants, were as good as can be found in the best hotels; and the cost was remarkably small, only $10 for the whole voyage from Buffalo to Milwaukee, which took four days. Such a voyage on the Great Lakes, accordingly, does not cost much more than a stay of the same duration at one of the best hotels. The price is, by the way, the same to Milwaukee as to Chicago.

At last we arrived in Milwaukee, the flourishing emporium of a large part of the West, so richly blessed by nature. It is said to rank first among American cities for the energy and the rapidity with which it has grown; a few years ago it was merely a nameless spot in the wilderness.

In 1838 the population of Wisconsin was 18,000; in 1842 it was 42,000; in 1845 it was as high as 117,000, according to the estimate by counties made by members of the legislature; and, in 1846, it was over 150,000. I have heard that this year the population will increase by about 50,000, and this does not seem at all improbable, when we con-

sider the steady stream from the East, not only of immigrants but of
Americans as well. Under such circumstances one can easily imagine
what a spirited sale there must be of government land priced at $1.25
per acre. I recently saw an account of the receipts at the Milwaukee
land office for one week. They amounted to $175,000! Just now the fall
immigration by way of Milwaukee is beginning, and a recent issue of a
newspaper of that city reports that every steamship brings so many
newcomers that they could make quite a respectable little town of their
own. The newspaper says it is amusing to watch them go up through
the streets in great throngs and it compares them to the tribes of Israel
on their entry into the Promised Land. I, too, saw a group of them moving along, in grand confusion, with their heavily loaded wagons, and I
think the comparison is very apt.

Milwaukee has a population of 11,000 or 12,000 and, about a dozen
churches, a beautiful courthouse, a land office, a bank, and so on. The
price of lots is said to have increased fivefold or more during the past
five years. One of the results of this rapid growth is that the city has
"sights" of a quite peculiar nature—for example, a sixteen or seventeen
year old boy is the oldest person native to the place.

One of the first things we did in Milwaukee was, naturally, to look
for fellow-countrymen. It was easy to find them, and in large numbers
too. Just a few steps from the hotel we found a group of people whose
language and appearance revealed their nationality. We soon heard, as
we have since become so accustomed to do, complaints of sickness,
hard work, and homesickness, alongside of expressions of satisfaction
with the good wages and the low cost of provisions, as well as the hope
that their condition on the whole would become better.

The next day, which was Sunday, a driver called for us in the morning with a coach drawn by two horses, and after a drive of a couple of
hours towards the southwest we arrived at the Norwegian settlement at
Muskego Lake. The first people whom we met were a couple from
Tinn, both of whom seemed greatly pleased with the visit. True-
hearted and simple, just as we find our countrymen here and there up
among the mountains in Norway, they had preserved their customs,
dress, and general arrangement of the house unchanged, as well as their
language. They served us with excellent milk and whatever else they
had; and, when they had become confident that we were altogether
Norwegian, they also brought some excellent *flatbrod*, made of wheat,

which they had at first held back because "these Yankees" are so ready to make fun of it. The Yankee who was with us, however, seemed very well pleased when we let him try it. On a later occasion we induced him to try another dish, just as Norwegian and just as unfamiliar to him, namely *fløtegrøt* which he declared first-rate as he licked his lips. Our friends from Tinn were well satisfied with their condition; they had managed so well during the first four years that they had paid off the debt they had incurred and now they already had a little surplus.

We next visited, among others, Even Heg, who seems to be one of the leaders among the Norwegians in these parts. He has earned the gratitude of the Norwegians in Wisconsin by starting a printing establishment on his own farm, with the assistance of Mr. Bache, a financier from Drammen. Here they publish the Norwegian-Wisconsin newspaper, *Nordlyset,* edited by Mr. Reymert. It is without doubt a very good idea through such a medium to maintain a cultural link between the Norwegians here and the mother country, as well as among themselves. Everyone, indeed, who would like to see them preserve their national characteristics and their memories of their native land as long as possible must, first and foremost, turn his attention to the problem of preserving their language by keeping it constantly before their eyes and ears.

I have been greatly interested in finding out how far the Norwegians have progressed in their understanding of American affairs; for example, as to the differences between the political parties. I must say I believe they have not reached beyond the first rudiments of a republican education. To be sure, I shall not lay too much stress on the fact that a couple of them called the government price on land "the king's price," because it would be stretching the point a bit to charge a mere thoughtless expression to their political ignorance.

On the other hand, there are undoubtedly not a few to whom can be applied what an American told me of one whom he had asked if he were a Whig or a Democrat. The American had soon discovered after questioning the Norwegian about the meaning of the terms, and particularly about what he had against the Whig doctrine concerning banks and the protection of industry, that the man did not have the least idea that these matters were the main issues involved in the political struggle. If he had been asked not if he were a Democrat, with which expression he is well acquainted from his home country, but if he were a Locofoco, he would presumably at once have admitted his inability to answer.

It is the common accusation of the Whigs against the Locofocos that they decoy the immigrants to their side at the elections and on other public occasions where voting is done through the use they make of the name Democrat, which the Whigs claim rightfully belongs to themselves. The Irish and the Germans are especially deceived in this manner, while, on the other hand, the English, who have a constitutional education and have learned to think for themselves, or, as the Locofocos would say, have been corrupted by the aristocracy which infests Great Britain, willingly take sides with the Whigs. The Norwegians often understand the true state of affairs just as little as do the Irish and the Germans, and most of them if asked will affirm that they are Democrats; but most of them, on the other hand, seem to be sensible enough not to be enticed into voting either for the one party or the other until they have learned a little more about what they stand for. Furthermore, most of them have as yet had no opportunity to vote, because it is necessary to have lived five years in the country and to have renounced all allegiance to the mother country in order to obtain American citizenship.

Thus almost the only opportunity to vote that the great mass of the Norwegians have had was on the question of the proposed constitution on which the Wisconsin legislature declared that every man over twenty-one years who had been six months in the territory and had declared his intention of becoming a citizen should be entitled to vote. When the constitution was framed and came up for a referendum of all the voting citizens, the great majority of the Norwegians in the territory voted against it. Their votes were not without influence, because the Norwegian population must be at the very least 6,000, and presumably 7,000 or 8,000.

The outcome of the whole affair was that the constitution was rejected, and as a result Wisconsin must still be content to be classed as a territory without the privileges of a state. The truth of the matter is that the Locofocos, who made up the majority of the assembly, were a little too ambitious and passed regulations which offended both the common sense and the prejudices of the people, so that many allowed themselves to thrust aside party considerations and vote quite independently. Thus it happened, in spite of the fact that the Locofocos have the majority in this territory, that their constitution was rejected because of its rather farfetched provisions, much to the joy of the Whigs.

This was, as already stated, almost the first political affair in which the Norwegians took any real part. The objections which seem to have borne the most weight with the Norwegians were concerned with what a couple of them spoke of as the "women's law" and the "money-law"; married women were to be given the right to separate property, and paper bank money was outlawed. Furthermore, twenty-four acres or property to the value of a thousand dollars was made exempt from distraint for debts. I should most certainly not have voted for the absolute prohibition of banks, although it is easy to understand that people in the West have become alarmed as the result of the bitter experiences they have had with the disastrous effects of giving the banks a free hand.

The chief objection raised by the Locofocos against banks is the same in Illinois as here and everywhere in America, namely, that they will encourage the growth of an aristocracy, and it is, for that matter, the same question which at an earlier period split the people in the whole Union when the national bank was being discussed.

I have already suggested how desirable it would be for the Norwegians to see their language frequently in a purer form, not only in their religious literature, but otherwise as well. I had in mind particularly the great ease with which they learn the English language and, unfortunately, the equal facility they have in forgetting their own as soon as they cease to use it every day.

They do not bother about keeping the two languages separate, so that they may speak Norwegian to their own countrymen and English to others; instead they eliminate one word after the other from their Norwegian and substitute English words in such a way that the Norwegian will soon be completely forgotten.

Such a practice, to be sure, is rather common among uneducated people who emigrate to a foreign country, but the Norwegians seem to have a special knack at it. The first words they forget are "ja" and "nei," and, even if everything else about them, from top to toe, is Norwegian, you may be sure they will answer "yes" or "no" if you ask them any questions. Gradually other English words, pertaining to their daily environment, are added. They have a "faens" about their farm and have probably "digget" a well near the house so that they need not go so far to get water to use on their "stoven." Such a well is generally necessary, even if there is a "laek" or a "river" in the vicinity, because such water is generally too warm. Near the houses there is frequently a little garden, where they grow "pompuser" (pumpkins) among other things, and a little beyond is "fila" (the English word "field" with the genuine Norwegian feminine article "a").

The ease with which the Norwegians learn the English language has attracted the attention of the Americans, all the more because they are altogether too ready to consider them entirely raw when they come here. "Never," one of them told me a few days ago, "have I known people to become civilized so rapidly as your countrymen; they come here in motley crowds, dressed up with all kinds of dingle-dangle just like the Indians. But just look at them a year later: they speak English perfectly, and, as far as dress, manners, and ability are concerned, they are quite above reproach."

On the other hand, he did not seem to know a great deal about the Norwegians in this country. My impression, after many visits extending over a number of settlements, is that the great mass of the families have essentially changed very little. I shall not deny, however, that they have been able to meet the severe strain of the work with an iron will, and thus have had ample opportunity to strengthen their moral courage. It also seems a fact that there is less drinking here than in Norway, although there are enough drunkards here, too, and among them some who have acquired the habit since they came. Cleanliness is, here as in Norway, for many almost an unheard of thing. The entrance to one of the houses I visited was guarded by a formidable cesspool. If a place looks really filthy and disreputable, you must expect to meet either Norwegians or Swiss or Irish.

Of course there are some notable exceptions, but, on the whole, one must admit that it is among young people who have gone into the service of Americans that one finds that real desire for improvement which makes the Norwegian name respected and almost loved here. This has given our people such a general reputation for respectability, morality, sobriety, and natural ability that I frequently hear expressions to the effect that the whole of Norway might well come here and be received with open arms.

About three thousand Norwegians as yet do not belong to any religious organization. Such a situation is rather serious, and yet no worse than among the Americans themselves. The complaint is frequently heard here in the West that religion has few adherents and few ministers, but progress is being made in this respect almost everywhere. Even if the situation is by no means what it was among the Puritan settlers in New England two hundred years ago, when a church was the first thing provided for, nevertheless spiritual needs do assert themselves even out here in the West, as soon as the first severe struggle with nature is over. Many a person who never has experienced the influence of religion in a thickly populated civilized country, learns to appreciate in his loneliness, how deep an influence religion exerts upon the soul of man.

Besides, a man is not of necessity an absolute heathen merely because he has not joined a congregation. As a result of the great variety of sects, some denomination or other frequently is, even in the most populous districts, not well enough represented to form a congregation and there is none in the vicinity which the people may join. Here in Madison, for example, there are only Presbyterian services. Under such conditions the external confession of a man's religion is temporarily suspended; but, as soon as a house of worship is established in the vicinity, he is likely to go there, even if it does not altogether conform to the creed of his own denomination.

Americans who live near the Norwegian churches attend services at times despite the fact that they are not Lutherans and do not understand the language. They say, however, that since they know that an act of worship is taking place, it does them good to be present. This is not at all surprising, as Pastor Dietrichson conducts the services in such a beautiful and dignified manner that it will naturally make an impression even on a person who is not able to derive benefit from the actual meaning of the words. Pastor Dietrichson has been requested to preach occasionally in English. I do not believe he will venture to do so; and, although it might be desirable insofar as it would enable him to do more good, and, through establishing an American congregation alongside of the Norwegian, he would gain prestige both for his church and for himself, nevertheless, for my part, I hope it will not be done. It would tend to Americanize our countrymen too soon. Let us rather keep the church, as well as the language, to ourselves at first; through them alone can we hope to preserve our nationality.

I hope you are not looking to me for any account of the economic conditions among our good countrymen in Wisconsin—this vale of tears—this Land of Canaan. You will have to be content with quite general remarks that Wisconsin is a fertile territory, the land is cheap, and farm products also are cheap. The last item is almost self-evident when one considers the fact that grain, in order to reach New York, has 1500 miles to travel, and that on this journey it has to pay high enough freight rates to make a paying business of the navigation on the Lakes, the Erie Canal, and the Hudson River, and then the canal tolls as well as the merchant's profits, commissions, and the like. From New York it still has 3000 miles to travel before it reaches the European market, where it has to compete with English, Russian, Danish, and Austrian products. It is true that a great deal is consumed in the United States. But as it is a fact that huge portions go to Europe, it is obvious that the prices even in New York and Boston must be somewhat lower than in the European markets. Recent events have proved conclusively that they are quite dependent on the prices in England.

It is quite obvious, then, that the profits of the farmer cannot be very great after he has paid high wages to his workers and with difficulty has managed to have his produce hauled to town over wretched roads. Here in Madison people do not raise more wheat than they need for local consumption, as it really does not pay to haul it to the lake shore, and the six-hundred citizens of the town, most of whom are farmers themselves, do not buy much. They find it more profitable, therefore, to cultivate Indian corn, root-crops, and the like for their cattle. The farmers did not make any considerable profits as a result of the hard times in Europe. Since the Lakes and the canals are frozen during the winter, the farmer must hasten to sell his produce immediately after the harvest. Thus it happened that it was already in the hands of the merchants before the people had any idea how bad conditions were in Europe. And, as navigation could not set in until late in the spring, you will readily see that what was shipped from here would not arrive in England until shortly before the harvest season. The circumstance that navigation must ordinarily cease until late in April, and that most of the shipping must therefore occur in the fall, naturally tends to increase the freight rates; and, if one gets his crops to town too late, he naturally gets a still lower price because they will have to lie over during the winter and bear the storehouse expenses and all kinds of risk.

Finally, we must bear in mind that interest on money is as high as 7 per cent or more, and the taxes, although they are not yet heavy, must also be taken into account. They vary according to time and place, as to whether much or little is needed to keep the affairs of the community going, and the amount of land owned is not the only basis for taxation; in other words, taxes vary here just as among us in Norway, and there is no definite ratio. To judge by such tax lists as I have seen, however, the tax is seldom less than $1 or $2 to 40 acres. A Norwegian farmer not far from Madison, who has 160 acres of good land, of which about 50 are cultivated, paid $8 in taxes last year.

If we are to estimate the scarcity of money by the amount of real estate which is sold in payment of taxes, it must be rather considerable. Thus I recently saw not less than six long columns in the *Wisconsin* [*Argus*] filled with lists of farms and city lots, one to each line, which were sold in December 1844 for delinquency in payment of taxes, and which cannot be reclaimed unless the obligations are met before December 10 of this year. This list applied only to Dane County, in which Madison is located; the entire population of the county in 1844 was only about 4,000; since then it has risen to 10,000 or 12,000. But the amount of the taxes is more dependent on the number of acres of land involved than on the population, as a large part of the land belongs to non-resident speculators. The very insignificance of the amount involved is probably just as much the reason for negligence in the payment of taxes as actual financial distress. Furthermore, the speculators grow weary of paying taxes for property that is bringing them no income. In the above discussion of the taxes no account is taken of church expenses, of course, nor of certain other obligations, such as work on the roads.

The economic situation, accordingly, is by no means ideal, as indeed the legislature itself admits through its frequent petitions to Congress for help in carrying its heavy financial burdens. Nevertheless, there can be no doubt of the fact that a territory so richly blessed with natural resources is certain to acquire a high degree of prosperity as soon as it has had time to develop them. The rich soil amply rewards one's efforts;

and the raising of sheep and cattle, bee-farming, the maple sugar industry all thrive in this favored clime.

Even if his produce does not command a high price, it means much to a farmer to be able to provide with ease practically everything he needs in the way of food and clothing. Hunger is an enemy from which many of our highlanders in Norway never feel safe. Just think what an impression it would make on a poor highlander's imagination to be told that some day he might eat wheat bread every day and pork at least three times a week! The fact that wages are not dropping in this country in spite of the increasing stream of immigration seems to be a clear indication that the country is rising in prosperity and that agriculture does pay.

I must add, that among all the people I have talked with I have found very few who said they were dissatisfied and wanted to return to Norway, and with some of these it was more a matter of talk than a real desire to go. And it is not strange if there are some who have been ruined through their emigration. The emigration fever spread through our country districts like a disease, paying no heed to age or sex, rich or poor, the diligent worker or the lazy good-for-nothing. Naturally, many have emigrated who are totally unfit for the strenuous life here, which calls for so much energy, common sense, and endurance if one is to succeed. It is equally true that many have made a mistake in buying or claiming land before they had either the necessary understanding or means to proceed with its cultivation. The fact that there have not been more wrecks than there have, in view of all the mistakes made, gives evidence both of the inherent strength of character of our people and of the excellence of the country itself.

I do not mean to imply that few complaints are heard. Quite the contrary. In addition to the fact that many, indeed most, admit that they had expected the land to be far better than it actually proved to be and that they had been fooled, to some extent, by the false reports contained in letters, there are many other complaints; but all of them are of such a nature that time and habit will presumably remedy the situation. Some complain that the work is too strenuous, others that there is so much ungodliness, others that there is too much sickness.

Practically all the Norwegians have been sick, some of them as much as a year at a time, and this misfortune has hampered many. The daily newspapers are half filled with all kinds of quack advertisements of pills and marvelous medicines against fever and ague and bilious fever; and a certain Dr. Champion drove by here most ostentatiously the other day with two huge boxes of pills. I do not believe there is any other country on earth where sound, healthy people use as much medicine as here, for the prevention of disease. The worst complaint of all is homesickness; everyone experiences that, of course. But time can heal even deeper wounds than that of having been severed from one's native land. Furthermore, most of the immigrants seem to cherish more or less consciously a hope of returning some day to their native land, having realized only after they had broken away how strong were the ties that held them there.

In addition to all these troubles and complaints, I found, particularly among those who had owned considerable property in Norway, a quite general feeling of satisfaction that they had come, built rather on their hopes for the future, to be sure, than on what they had already achieved. Among those who have worked their way up from poverty this feeling of satisfaction is so great that they are likely to overestimate their present prosperity. A certain Lars Hedemarken is now a well-to-do man and is highly esteemed for his uprightness. I mentioned one of the largest farms in Ringsaker and asked him how he would like to trade his present farm for that one. He said he would not do so under any circumstances, chiefly because the farm in Ringsaker would prove far too small for all his sons, while here the whole prairie was theirs. His house was one of the better kind. Very few Norwegians have yet built comfortable houses. The great majority live in log cabins of the sort that can be erected in a day.

It is my opinion that if it is impossible to get a combination of woods and prairie or glade, it is advisable to take prairie land. It appeared to me that those who lived out on the prairie as a rule were more successful than those who had cut their way into the woods. All the prairie farmers I spoke with said they were well pleased with their choice, a thing which I cannot say of the settlers in the woods. Many of the latter have already toiled for three or four years without being able to raise enough food for their own use, whereas one or two years will generally suffice to fill the barns out on the prairies. The reason is, quite obviously, that it takes many times as much work to clear and cultivate wooded land. A poor man, who finds it difficult to hire help, is at a great disadvantage if he settles on woodland, while out on the prairie, for the same work or at the same expense, he can obtain a far richer harvest. For well-to-do people this does not mean so much, and yet even such people do not seem to have succeeded so well on woodland as one might expect. I think capital can be invested more profitably than in felling trees.

A very profitable business consists in buying up large stretches of prairie land, taking part of it into use for oneself and then parceling the rest out into farms for sale, building a log cabin on each and plowing up an acre or so; immigrants are glad to pay a fairly good price for such a farm, as they like to have a house ready to receive them when they arrive and to find the work of cultivation already begun. I know many Norwegians who have made good profits in this way, and I have met no one who denied that it was a paying business.

It is probably true that it is harder to find water on the prairie than in the woods, and yet it is only necessary not to lose patience if water is not struck at a depth of thirty or forty feet. It is in any case necessary to drill, and that is not very expensive in most places.

Out on the prairie, of course, there is no timber for buildings, fences, kindling, and the like. But there is nothing to prevent a man from buying a small strip of woods also, as near his farm as possible; nowhere is woodland very far away. To have his woods one or two miles away may be somewhat inconvenient, and yet in Norway we are certainly accustomed to greater distances than that. To be sure, most of the woodland in the vicinity of the prairies is in the hands of speculators, but their price is not as a rule more than two or three dollars per acre, or about twice the government price.

As there are everywhere people living on land which they have not paid for, it is necessary for the immigrant to be careful to avoid getting into trouble. Even if the map at the land office designates a piece of land as unoccupied, there may be someone living there and one will either simply have to leave well enough alone or else pay him whatever people decide is fair. This is in accordance with the famous "Club Law" which the people have established as a protection against a clause in the act of Congress by which it is specified that if a person is not able to pay for a piece of claimed land after a year he loses all rights to it. The people have organized themselves to oppose this clause and they arrange things as they please between the buyer and the holder of such a piece of land. The buyer runs the risk of being seized and forced to waive his right to the property and to write out a deed on whatever conditions they dictate.

Many Norwegians are members of such organizations, but they often get into trouble because they are not so clever at it as the Yankees, who know how to introduce a certain appearance of law and order even into a practice which in the nature of the case is the direct opposite of law and order.

To put an end to such abuses the legislature has petitioned Congress to prolong the period for the payment of land held on claim to five years. It is plain that a respite of only one year is worse than useless, because a man who has no money at the beginning of the year is practically sure to be just as badly off at the end of the year, as the first year always brings heavy expenses and little or no income.

The maps of the land office, in addition to the fact that they do not indicate what land is really unoccupied, soon become quite unreliable in respect to what is actually sold, because of the heavy stream of immigration. The best procedure is to ask at the office itself. Presumably new stretches of land will soon be for sale, because the district between the Wisconsin and Mississippi rivers is being surveyed now. Most of the Indians have already been driven out of this territory.

I cannot refrain from saying a few kind words on behalf of the favored pet of the Americans, the swine. I have not yet found any city, county, or town where I have not seen these lovable animals wandering about peacefully in huge herds. Everywhere their domestic tendencies are much in evidence; no respectable sow appears in public unless she is surrounded by a countless number of beloved offspring. These family groups are a pleasing sight to the Americans, not only because they mean increasing prosperity but also because a young porker is a particularly delicious morsel. Besides, the swine have shown certain good traits which are of real practical value; in the country they greedily devour all kinds of snakes and the like, and in the towns they are very helpful in keeping the streets "cleaner than man can do" by eating up all kinds of refuse. And then, when these walking sewers are properly filled up they are butchered and provide a real treat for the dinner-table.

As with everything else that is typically American, this fondness for pork is most noticeable in the West. In New York war has even been declared against these animals; it was decreed that any pig found walking the streets of New York after the first of July of this year should be outlawed and become the property of anyone who could catch it. I do not know if the law was dropped or if a common feeling of sympathy prevented its execution, but at any rate I have seen pigs wandering about just as freely as ever, even after that ominous day, on Broadway itself, and evidently with perfect peace of mind, just as though no one had ever thought of depriving them of life, liberty, and the pursuit of happiness.

That which has annoyed me most in my associations with the Americans is their prejudice against Europe, which they regard as hopelessly lost in slavery and wretchedness. Three-fourths of the people in the East and ninety-nine hundredths of the people in the West are fully convinced that the other side of the Atlantic is nothing but a heap of medieval feudal states, which, indeed, show some slight indication of reform here and there, but have not made much political progress and have not enough vitality to rise from the abyss of misery and corruption into which they have fallen as the result of centuries of ignorance and despotism; their doom is inevitable. If one tries to dispute any portion of this creed of theirs, they simply point to the foreigners: "What further evidence is needed than these immigrants who swarm into our country by the hundreds of thousands every year with the traces of suffering unmistakably written on their faces and curses in their mouths at the tyranny they are escaping?"

If the Americans hear of any scandal about some European government, and such have been rather plentiful this last year, they at once use it as a weapon against the monarchical system itself. It is rather a big job to defend all Europe; and I have on various occasions declined to do so, no matter how agreeable it might be once in a while to lay aside my little Norwegian, or even Scandinavian, patriotism and to pose as the champion of a whole continent. It does not help much to reject this constituency of 200,000,000 people, because people here do not recognize many differences among the various nations; every European is responsible for the whole thing. They have a special grudge against England, to be sure, in return for the English prejudice against them. Even the strong resemblance between these two nations and the common origin of their institutions only tend to irritate them the more. The Englishmen, who regard their own laws and institutions as quite ideal, naturally consider the development which has taken place in

MISSISSIPPI STOOMBOOT.

STOOMBRANDSPUIT TE CINCINNATI.

"Hair Fixing"

America a degeneration and perversion. The Yankees, on the other hand, if possible even more proud of their own, consider the English institutions to be antiquated and impracticable because they have not kept pace with the improvements and progress made in America.

16.

THE HOMES OF THE NEW WORLD

Fredrika Bremer was already well known in the New World when she came to the United States in 1849. Born in 1801 near Abö, the daughter of an iron master, she had received an excellent upper-middle-class education and had then retired to a life of good works as a nurse among the peasants on her father's estate. There she turned to writing, and produced a succession of novels that were sentimental, naïve, and moralistic, but also fresh in approach to the everyday life of the common people among whom she lived. These books were enormously popular and, translated from Swedish into English, earned her a devoted following in England and in the United States.

Miss Bremer therefore had an entree to the most significant intellectual circles in the United States. Her attention was naturally drawn to the reform and transcendentalist groups; until her death in 1865 she was to remain interested in German romantic philosophy and in philanthropy. But she also found time to note and to comment on the common affairs of the American people, and on the American home in Hemmen i den nya Verlden (1853), *from which this excerpt is drawn.*

The moral idea of man and of society seems clearly understood in the United States, particularly in those northern sections that have derived their population from the original colonies. I have acquainted myself with the demands made by man and society, demands for which young America fights as for its true purpose and mission. They appear to be as follows:

Every human being must be strictly true to his own individuality —must stand alone with God, and from this innermost point of view must act alone according to his own conscientious convictions.

There is no virtue peculiar to one sex which is not also a virtue in the other. Man must in morals and conduct come up to the purity of woman. Woman must possess the means of the highest development of which her nature is capable. She must, equally with man, have the opportunity of cultivating and developing her intellect. In her labors for freedom and happiness, she must possess the same rights as man.

The honor of labor and the rewards of labor ought to be equal to all. All labor is in itself honorable and must be regarded as such.

The principle of equality must govern society.

Man must become just and good through a just and good mode of treatment. Good must call forth good.

The community must give to every one of its members the best possible chance of developing his human abilities, so that he may come into possession of his human rights. This must be done both by legislation, which removes all hindrances and impediments, and by educational institutions, which give to all the opportunity for the full development of the human faculties, until they reach the age when they are capable of caring for and determining for themselves.

The ideal of society is attained in part by the individual rising up to his own ideals, in part by mutual responsibility and by those free institutions and associations which bring men into a brotherly relation with each other.

Everything for all is the true object of society. Everyone must be able to enjoy all the good things of earth, temporal as well as spiritual, according to his own capacity for enjoyment. No one must be excluded who does not exclude himself. Everyone must receive a chance of regaining his place in society. For this reason the prison must be a second school, an institution for improving those who need it. Society must, in its many sided development, so organize itself that all may be able to attain everything.

The ideal of the man of America is purity in intention, decision in will, energy in action, simplicity and gentleness in manner and demeanor. Hence there is something tender and chivalrous in his behavior to woman which is infinitely becoming to him. In every woman he respects his own mother. In the same way the woman's ideal is independence of character, gentleness of demeanor and manner.

The American's ideal of happiness is marriage and home combined with public activity. To have a wife, his own house and home, his own little piece of land, to take care of these and to beautify them, while at the same time doing some good to the state or to the city—this seems to me to be the object of human life with most men.

In the American home the women have, in general, all the power they wish. Woman is the center and the lawgiver, and the American man loves it so. He likes his wife to have her own will at home, and loves to obey it. In the happy homes in which I lived, however, I saw the wife equally careful to guide herself by the wishes of her husband.

The educational institutions for women are much superior to those of Europe, and perhaps the most important work which America is doing for the future of humanity consists in her treatment and education of woman. Woman's increasing value as a teacher, and her employment as such in public schools, even in those for boys, is, in these states, a public fact which delights me. It even seems as if the daughters of New England have a peculiar faculty and love for this occupation. Whole crowds go hence to the western and southern states where schools are daily established and placed under their direction.

That which is most admirable in New England is the number of great schools and asylums for the education of youth, and in aid of the unfortunate. These are the offspring of a large heart, and they have a broad basis. It is a joy to see and hear children taught in these free public schools in large and airy halls. One can see that the pupils are all awake and full of life; one can hear that they understand what they read and learn. The great reformation in the conduct of schools, and the impulse toward universal popular education are the result, in great measure, of the enthusiasm, perseverance, and determined resolution of a single individual, Horace Mann. This reformation is, without question, one of the most beautiful and significant phenomena of this national culture, especially since it embraces woman as well as man, and places her side by side with him as teacher of the rising generation.

I have traced this from the East to the West, from magnificent academies where five-hundred students, boys and girls, study and take degrees preparatory to public life as teachers, to the log huts of the western wilderness where school books open the minds of ragged children to the whole world and reveal the noblest pearls of American and English literature. I have talked with Horace Mann and have derived great hope for the intellectual and moral perfection of the human race, and for its future in this part of the world. That which already *is* in the Northeast, sooner or later *will be* in the South and the West. A great and living popular intelligence mixes itself up more and more in the question of popular education, and goes onward like a subtle power of nature, a stream of spiritual life forcing a way for itself through all impediments.

At a socialist meeting this evening I saw a great number of respectable-looking people and heard theories for the future as to how human beings—instead of going to heaven, as now, by the thorny path—will wander thither on roses. I heard also various beautiful plans for accomplishing this, all remarkable for their want of basis in possibility and in human nature as it is. In general, it seems to me that the socialists fail by not taking into consideration the dualism of human nature. They do not see the evil, and they believe that everything can become right in this world by outward institutions. I have during their discussions a feeling of wandering among the clouds, or of being lost in a great wood. The humane side of their theories, of their endeavors for the best interests of humanity, cannot be doubted.

Near Redbank, New Jersey, we saw some of these theories put to the test of practice. In the town we were met by a wagon from the Phalanstery which had been sent for the guests, as well as for potatoes, and in it we stowed ourselves. A handsome young man from the Phalanstery drove the pair of fat horses which drew us; and after we had plowed the sand for a couple of hours we arrived at a group of large houses, with several lesser ones standing around them, without anything remarkable in their style of architecture. We were conducted into a hall and regaled with a dinner which could not have been better if it had been in Arcadia; it would have been impossible to have produced better milk, bread, or cheese. They also had meat here.

This association, which calls itself "the North American Phalanstery" was established eight years ago by a few married couples. Each member advanced the sum of one thousand dollars; land was purchased, and they began to labor together, according to laws which the society had laid down beforehand. Great difficulties met them in the commencement, in particular from their want of means to build, for the purchase of implements, and so on. It was beautiful and affecting to hear to what fatigue and labor the women had subjected themselves, women who had been but little accustomed to anything of this kind; and how the men, in the spirit of brotherhood, did their part in any kind of work as well as the women, merely looking at the honor and the necessity of the work, and never asking whether it was the fit employment for man or for woman. They suffered much from calumny, but through it all became a stronger and more numerous body.

They had survived the worst, and the institution was then evidently improving. They contemplated building a new house, in particular a large eating hall and place for social meetings, together with a cooking and washing house, provided with machinery to dispense with the most onerous hand labor. There were somewhat more than seventy members. They had an income from mills and tillage as well as from orchards.

One evening many members assembled in one of the sitting rooms. The men wore coarse clothes; but all were neat, and had a kind of great earnestness and kindness in their whole demeanor. Needlework was brought in and laid upon a table. They made small linen bags for the hominy they prepared in their mills and which they sold in New York.

I had a little room to myself for the night, vacated by some of the young girls. It was as small as a prison cell; had four bare white walls, but was neat and clean, and had a large window with a fine view. I was wakened in the morning by the sound of labor throughout the house; people were going and coming, all full of business; it sounded earnest and industrious. I entered as a worker into one of the bands of workers. I selected that engaged in cooking because I consider that my genius has a bent in that direction. I was soon standing therefore by the fire and baked a whole pile of buckwheat cakes. In my fervor of association I labored also with my hands and arms up to my very elbows in a great kneading-trough, but very nearly stuck fast in the dough. It was far too heavy for me, though I would not confess it; but they were kind enough to release me from the operation, in the politest manner, and to place it in abler hands.

I went through the mills where everything seemed excellent and well-arranged, and where the little millers were already at their work. Thence we went across the meadows to the potato fields, where I shook hands with the chief who, in his shirt-sleeves, was digging up potatoes among his senators. All seemed clever and excellent people; and the potato crop promised this year to be remarkably rich.

I learned various particulars regarding the laws and life of the Phalanstery; among others, that they are wise enough not to allow the public to absorb private property. Each individual may invest as much as he likes in the association, and retain as much of his own property as he wishes. For that which he invests he receives interest. The time required for labor is ten hours a day. All who work more are paid overtime. The women participate in all rights equally with the men; vote, and share in the administration of law and justice.

Anyone who applies may be received as a member after a probation of one year, during which time he must show himself unwearied in labor and steadfast in brotherly love and good will. No questions are asked as regard religion, rank, or former mode of life. The association makes a new experiment in social and economic life; it regards the active principle of love as the ruling power of life, and wishes to place everything within the sphere of its influence.

Being asked in the evening my opinion of this community, I candidly confessed that it appeared to be deficient in the profession of religion and public divine service, being based merely upon a moral principle, the validity of which might easily be called into question as they did not recognize a connection with a life existing eternally beyond earth. "The serpent may one day enter your paradise, and then —how can you expel it?" An elderly gentleman who sat near me, with a very good and honest countenance but who had a horrible trick of incessant spitting, replied to my objections. But his reply and that of the others merely served to strengthen my impression of the cloudy state in which the intellect here is at present.

Friday morning we drove to Hopedale Community, a little socialist settlement a few miles from Uxbridge, Massachusetts. This small society is altogether founded upon Christian principles and rests upon a patriarchal basis. The head of the establishment, Adin Ballou, a handsome old gentleman, received us, surrounded by a numerous family. Each family here has its separate house and garden. The greater number of the people in the community are handicraftsmen and farmers.

We were received with songs of welcome and flowers. I noticed in the young people a singularly joyous and fresh life, and it was delightful to see the happy groups passing to and fro in the sunshine. The church of the little community struck me as remarkably unchurch-like. Various moral aphorisms, such as "Hope on, hope forever," and "Try again," might be read upon the naked walls. For the rest, it was evident that the poetic element had much more vitality here than in the community in New Jersey. The moral element constituted, nevertheless, the kernel even here; the poetic was merely an addition—the sugar in the moral cake.

We dined in an excellent little home. They asked no questions of the guests, merely entertained them well and kindly. A Negro and his wife came hither wishing to be received as members of the community —which is now seven years old and consists of about thirty families, one hundred and seventy souls in all. Every member pledges himself to the Christian faith, nonresistance, and temperance. Adin Ballou has published a work on the right understanding of these subjects.

Taking one thing with another, it seemed to me that life in this community was deficient in gaiety, had few enjoyments for the intellect or for the sense of the beautiful. But it was at the same time most truly estimable, earnest, God-fearing, industrious, and upon the whole an excellent foundation for a strong popular life. From these small homes must proceed earnest men and women, people who take life seriously, and have early learned to labor and to pray.

We drove to Concord in the midst of a regular snowstorm. Emerson came to meet us, walking down the little avenue of spruce firs which leads from his house, bareheaded amid the falling snow. He is a quiet, nobly grave figure, his complexion pale, with strongly marked features, and dark hair. He seemed to me a younger man, but not so handsome as I had imagined. He occupied himself with us, however, and with me in particular as a lady and a foreigner, kindly and agreeably.

He is a very peculiar character, but too cold and hypercritical to please me entirely; a strong clear eye, always looking out for an ideal which he never finds realized on earth; discovering wants, shortcomings, imperfections; and too strong and healthy himself to understand other people's weaknesses and sufferings, for he even despises suffering as a weakness unworthy of higher natures. This singularity of character leads one to suppose that he has never been ill; sorrows, however, he has had, and has felt them deeply, as some of his most beautiful poems prove. Nevertheless, he has only allowed himself to be bowed for a short time by these griefs. He interested me without warming me. That critical, crystalline, and cold nature may be very estimable, quite healthy, and, in its way, beneficial for those who possess it, and also for others who allow themselves to be measured and criticized by it; but— for me—David's heart with David's songs!

I am not sure that I have judged Emerson rightly. I confess that I was a little staggered by the deprecating way in which he expressed himself about things and persons whom I admired. I am not certain whether his steadfastness and pride so little akin to my own did not lead me to act the fox with the grapes. Emerson may be unjust or unreasonable, but it certainly is not from selfish motives; there is a higher nature in this man, and I must see more of him, and understand him better.

It is very difficult to give, by extracts, any correct idea of Emerson's mode of thought. His essays are chains of brilliant aphorisms which often contradict one another. But that which permeates them—the marrow of all, the metallic vein which runs through them all—is the cry, "Be genuine—be thyself!! then wilt thou become original, and create that which is new and perfect!" Thus he addresses the individual; thus, the public. And the force and beauty which he gives to this watchword is indeed his peculiar power over the American mind; his peculiarly beneficial work on the people of the New World, only too much disposed to bow themselves to mere imitation and walk in the footsteps of the Old World.

Emerson is at this moment regarded as the head of the transcendentalists in this portion of America. These are a kind of people found principally in the New England states, who seem to me like its White Mountains, or rather, they aim at being so. But so far as I have yet seen and heard, I recognize only one actual mountain, and that is Emerson. The others seem to stretch themselves out, and to powder themselves merely to look lofty and snow-crowned; but that does not help them. They have more pretension than power. Their brows are in the clouds instead of towering above them. One has lived for fifteen years on bread and fruit and has worn linen clothes because he would not appropriate wool, the property of sheep, and has suffered very much in acting up to his faith and love. Another built himself a hut in the western prairies, and lived there as a hermit for two years; he has, however, returned to everyday life and everyday people. Still another went out into the wild woods and built himself a hut and lived there—I know not on what. He has also returned to common life, is employed in a handicraft trade, and writes books which have in them something of the freshness and life of the woods—but which are sold for money. Ah! I do not wonder at these attempts by unusual ways to escape from the torment of common life. But they, and Emerson himself, make too much of these attempts, which are, in themselves not uncommon. Nor have they produced results which are so. The aim, the intention, is the best part of them.

I must also say a few words about that young disciple of Calvin, Henry Beecher, who has left far behind him whatever is hard and petrified in the orthodoxy of Calvin, and, breaking away from that, has attached himself to the true Christian doctrine of mercy to all. He was with us last evening, and told us how as a missionary he had preached in the West beneath the open sky to the people of the wilderness, and how he had, during his solitary journeys amid those grand primeval scenes, by degrees introduced order into his own inward world, had solved hitherto difficult religious questions, and had come forth from the old dead Church into one more comprehensive and more full of light. He described also, in the most picturesque manner, the nocturnal camp-meeting of the West; the scenes of baptism there on the banks of rivers and streams, both in their poetical and their frequently comical aspects. There is something of the power of growth peculiar to the great western wilds in this young man, but also something of its rudeness. He is a bold, ardent, young champion of that young America, too richly endowed, and too much acknowledged as such, not to be quite conscious of his own *I*. And even in his sermon this *I* was somewhat too prominent.

Theodore Parker, on the other hand, belongs to that section of the Unitarian body which denies miracles and everything that requires supernatural agency in sacred history. He regards Christ as standing in no other relationship to God than did all mankind. When we met I told him frankly my objections to his Christology, and we had a good deal of quiet controversy. I found Parker extremely agreeable to talk with, willing to listen, gentle, earnest, and cordial. He heard me with much kindness and seriousness, and conceded various things; among others, the reasonableness of miracles, when regarded as produced by a power in nature but not out of it—the law of nature on a larger scale.

Parker has a pure and strongly moral mind; he is, like Emerson, captivated by the moral ideal; and he places this before his hearers in words full of a strong vitality, through which he produces a higher love for truth and justice in the human breast. Parker, however, as a theologist, is not powerful; nor can he talk well upon the most sublime and most holy doctrines of revelation, because he does not understand them. In his outbursts against the petrified orthodoxy and the petrified church, he is often happy and true. But I think that people may say of him as somebody said of Luther, "Il a bien critiqué mais pauvrement doctriné." Parker, however, investigates earnestly and speaks out his thoughts honestly, and that is always a great merit. More we can hardly desire of a man. Beyond this he teaches to be very good, to do much good; and I believe that from his kind and beautiful eyes. In short, I like the man.

I was present at one of the "Conversations" of Alcott, the transcendentalist, and even took part in it. There were present from forty to fifty people, all seated on benches. Alcott sat in a pulpit with his face toward the people and began by reading aloud something from the writings of Pythagoras. The transcendentalist is a handsome man, of gentle manners, but a dreamer whose Pythagorean wisdom will hardly make people wiser nowadays. He himself has lived for many years only on bread, fruits, vegetables, and water; and this is what he wishes everyone to do. Thus fed, they would become beautiful, good, and happy beings. Sin will be driven out by diet. Both the proposition and the conversation were in the clouds, although I made a few attempts to draw them forth. Alcott drank water, and we drank—fog.

He has paid me a few visits and interests me as a study. Every blond and blue-eyed person, according to him, belongs to the nation of light, to the realm of light and goodness. All persons with dark eyes and hair are of the night and evil. I mentioned Wilberforce and other champions of the light with dark hair. But the good Alcott hears an objection as if he heard it not, and his conversations consist in his talking to and teaching himself. He drank tea, and I endeavored to persuade him to drink at least a glass of milk. But that was too much akin to animal food. He would not take anything but a glass of water and a piece of bread. He is, at all events, a transcendentalist who lives as he teaches.

On a second visit Alcott explained himself better, and I came to believe that there was really a true and excellent thought at the bottom of his reform movement. This thought is the importance of an earnest and holy disposition of mind in those who enter into the bonds of wedlock, so that the union may be noble and its offspring good and beautiful. His plans for bringing about these beautiful and holy marriages between good and beautiful people (for none other are to enter into matrimony—oh! oh! for the many) may be right for all I know. They are better, and more in accord with human nature than those of Plato. But who will deny that it would be better for the world if those who bring human beings into the world did it with a higher consciousness, with a deeper sentiment of responsibility?

"But why do you not enunciate these views fully?" I inquired. "They are more important than any I heard during your conversations, and are really of the highest importance to society."

Alcott excused himself by the difficulty of treating such a subject in public and spoke of the intention he had of realizing his views in a little society, in which, I presume, he would act as high priest. Again a dream. But the dreamer has risen considerably in my estimation by the reality and the nobility of his views on this subject. I will even excuse his whim about diet.

Another forenoon I saw the distinguished lawyer, Wendell Phillips; Charles Sumner, a young giant in person; and Garrison, one of the principal champions of the abolitionist cause, who, at a time of excitement was dragged through the streets of Boston by a mob. One sees in his beautiful countenance and clear eagle-eye that resolute spirit which makes the martyr. Speaking with him, I told him candidly that I thought the extravagance in the proceedings of the abolitionists, their want of moderation, and the violent tone of their attacks could not benefit, but rather must damage their cause. He replied with good temper, "We must demand the whole loaf, if we hope to get half of it!"

He expressed himself mildly regarding the southern slaveholders, said that he valued many of them personally but that he hated slavery and would continue to combat it as the greatest enemy of America. This gentleman brought us William and Ellen Craft, two recently escaped slaves. The woman was almost white; her countenance, which was rather sallow, had the features of the white, and though not handsome, a very intelligent expression. They had escaped by means of her being dressed as a man; he acting as her servant. In order to avoid the necessity of signing her name in the travelers' books, for she could not write, she carried her right arm in a sling under the plea of having injured it. Thus they had succeeded in traveling by railway from the South to the free states. They appeared to be sincerely happy.

"Why did you escape from your masters?" I asked; "did they treat you with severity?"

"No," she replied; "they always treated me well; but I fled from them because they would not give me my rights as a human being. I could never learn anything, neither to read nor to write."

"How is it," said someone in the company to the Negro, "that the assertions of the antislavery party regarding the treatment of slaves, that they are often flogged and severely beaten, are declared to be false? Travelers come to the North who have long resided among the plantations and have never seen anything of the kind."

William smiled, and said, with a keen expression, "Nor are children whipped in the presence of strangers; this is done when they do not see."

There is one principle of movement in the United States which seems to me creative, or, at all events, a power of organization. This is the movement of association. The association, founded already in the federal government—an association of states, governed by a general law or constitution—exists as a fundamental feature of popular life. These people associate as easily as they breathe.

Whenever any subject or question of interest arises in society which demands public sympathy or coöperation, a "convention" is immediately called to take it into consideration; and immediately, from all ends of the city or the state, or from every state in the Union, all who feel an interest in the subject fly upon wings of steam to the appointed place of meeting. The hotels and boardinghouses of the city are rapidly filled; people come together in the great hall of assembly, they shake hands, they become acquainted with one another, they make speeches, they vote, they carry their resolutions. And forth upon the wings of a thousand daily papers flies that which the meeting or convention has resolved. These resolutions may sometimes be merely the expression of opinion; they hold, for example, "indignation meetings" when they wish to express disapprobation either of public men or of measures. The *savoir-faire* with which these people act in self-government, the rapidity with which they proceed from "proposed" to "resolved" is always admirable.

In the populous free states meetings of the members of different trades and professions, as well as of agriculture, are ordinary occurrences. Thus one hears now of industrial congresses in New York, where the trades-brethren of certain kindred occupations meet every month;

and agricultural fairs are already held in the young states of Michigan and Illinois.

The great trading towns have mechanical and mercantile associations, meetinghouses, libraries, assembly rooms, and guilds on a large scale. And these related associations are all connected with each other. An artisan who cannot get work in the eastern states is, for instance, passed on by means of these associations to the West where there is abundance of work for all hands.

Life in this country need never stand still or stagnate. The dangers lie in another direction. But this free association is evidently an organizing and conservative principle of life, called forth to give law and centralization to the floating atoms, to the disintegrated elements. The United States thus provides at the same time for the highest development of the individual and of the community at large.

This internal, social movement of humanity is assisted from without by the free circulation and communication which is afforded by the numerous navigable rivers of North America, upon which thousands of steamboats go and come; and in still later years by the railroads and telegraphic lines which extend over all parts of America. The great diffusion of newspapers within the country, of every book which wins the love of the popular heart, of that religious popular literature which in millions of small tracts is poured forth over the nation, these all belong essentially to this life-giving circulation.

Wherever the sons and daughters of the Pilgrims find their way there are established homes, schools, and churches, shops, and legislative assemblies, the free press, hotels for strangers, and asylums for the unfortunate or the orphaned. There the prison is converted into the reformatory, a new school for the ignorant and depraved children of the earth. Wherever the Anglo-American advances, the same cultivation, the same vitality arises. He accomplishes with astonishing certainty his mission as cultivator of the New World and framer of free, self-governing communities. Not even the institution of slavery is able to withstand the power of cultivation which advances with him over the earth.

17.

THE FRIENDS OF KOSSUTH

Ferenc Aurelius Pulszky, member of a prominent Hungarian family, was born at Eperies in 1814. Interested in archaeology, he showed a precocious talent for the subject, but became involved in the liberal movement that eventually produced Kossuth's revolution in 1848. With Kossuth, Pulszky and his wife, Theresa, fled into exile after the failure of their uprising, and they were condemned to death in absentia. In 1852, the Pulszkys accompanied Kossuth in a tour of the United States. In 1853 the Pulszkys published White Red Black, *an account, in English, of their travels in America, and then went to Italy where they collaborated in Garibaldi's struggle for Italian independence. At last, in 1866, a pardon from Vienna made possible a return to Hungary. In 1872, Pulszky became director of state museums and libraries, and lived uneventfully in Budapest until his death in 1897.*

Washington is like the eastern metropolis of a half-nomad nation, where the palaces of the king are surrounded by the temporary buildings of a people, held together only by the presence of the court. Society is formed here by two distinct classes of inhabitants, one temporary, the other permanent. For the President, the heads of departments, the senators, and members of the House, it is but a temporary abode; almost all live in hotels and lodgings, not in their own houses. They remain strangers in Washington. Even those who live here for ten years and longer do not feel at home. Henry Clay lived and died in a hotel, and during his long career in the city Mrs. Clay never visited him, though their marriage was always a happy one.

The permanent population in the city are the clerks in the departments, the judges of the Supreme Court, the editors of the papers, a few merchants and bankers, and the foreign ambassadors who keep house here and in social respect have an importance far superior to any that they could occupy in Philadelphia or New York. They are the hosts who give elegant dinners and balls and evening parties. The members of Congress and their wives and daughters are the guests, unable to return at Washington the hospitality they receive—a position which, for a clever diplomat, is of no small avail. To the floating population belong also the agents for elections, for private claims, and for government grants—"the lobby members," as they are called—who, like the sharks around the vessels, ply around the senators, rushing at every job and government contract. For political intriguers, there is no richer gold field in the United States than Washington—an arena, not only of political contests, but also of "log-rolling," "pipe-laying," and "wire-pulling."

As to the wire-pullers, they are known all over the political world; and the philosopher, studying history, is astonished how men often act the part of puppets, without their own knowledge. In America, the magic word is called "peculiar institution," and "abolitionism." Whenever an opportunity is wanted to disturb men's minds, to raise politicians to greatness, or to bury others, the stage is always ready and the play always successful. The plot is "secession from the Union," and the finale, "the country saved," with triumphal arches and nosegays and garlands for the saviors of the country. Minor plays are daily enacted by the wire-pullers, who have a continual practice in the elections; where it is not only important to canvass for the friend, but also to weaken the enemy by drawing off his votes for a third person.

"Log-rolling" is a simpler affair. It is the combination of different interests on the principle, "daub me and I daub thee." Whoever is too feeble to carry his own project combines with others in the same position, in order to get influence. Local affairs and grants are often brought to notice and pass in this way.

Of "pipe-laying" I got two different definitions. According to one, the origin of this expression is traced to an election job, where an undertaker sold some Irish and German votes by a written agreement in which, of course, the ware could not be named; it was therefore styled *pipes;* "pipe-laying" would therefore mean corruption. But it is also applied to political maneuvers for an aim entirely different from what it seems to be. For instance, wishing to defeat the grant of land for a special railway or canal which has every chance to pass, you vote for it, but in your speech you describe, in glowing colors, the advantages of railroads in general, and wind up by presenting an amendment for the extension of the grant to all the other railroads in construction

—on the principle of equality—and thus you make the grant impossible.

In a democratic country, where freedom of speech is not limited and the press is unfettered even by fiscal laws, every movement of government is exposed, judged, and condemned in the most unmeasured words. One party denounces the other, and corruption is mentioned so often that it would be very easy for a malicious tourist to write a book on the decline of the United States composed exclusively of extracts from public speeches and party papers. But every impartial observer will find that government is carried on in America with remarkable integrity and economy. Large as the Union is, the expenditure of the federal government, including the interest of the United States debt and the annual payment toward its extinction, is met by the income from the duties on imports and the sales of land. No direct taxes are levied for federal purposes. If we compare the estimates of the United States with the European budgets we find that the sums expended without necessity are much smaller than anywhere else, though the party criminations and recriminations are so loud that a foreigner is tempted to believe the government to be a compound of corruption and dishonesty.

The Senate of the United States, as a body, contains more practical statesmanship and administrative experience than any other legislative assembly. All its members have been trained in the legislative assemblies and senates of the individual states. Many of them have passed several years in the House at Washington, have been at the head of their state as governors, or have transacted the business of the Union as heads of the executive departments. But southern rashness sometimes deprives the Senate of the gravity and dignity which befits the fathers of the great republic.

The House of Representatives, renewed every two years by general election, has here a more subordinate position than in any other constitutional realm. The great parliamentary battles are all fought in the Senate. The speeches of the great American orators, Clay, Webster, Calhoun, and Cass have resounded within its walls, and the eloquence of Soule, Seward, and Sumner is equal to that of their illustrious predecessors. Personal collisions, rare in the Senate, are frequent in the House. During the last session Messrs. Wilcox and Brown, both from Mississippi, boxed one another's ears in open session. The Tennessean representative gave the lie to his colleague from Kentucky, and abusive language was often heard, though it was not a time of great political excitement and no important question stirred up the passions.

The powers of Congress are very different from those of the legislative assemblies in other countries. Congress does not govern or control the government of the states. Nor has it anything to do with the church, with education, prisons, the civil or criminal law, or with private bills. The chief objects of the English parliament are, therefore, removed from its sphere. Congress has only the power to decide upon the commercial policy of the United States, and to provide for defense and for certain matters of general interest. The ministers, or, as they are called, the heads of the executive departments, are not members of Congress; they are only the advisers of the President, and it is not necessary that they should have a parliamentary majority. The chief function of European parliaments, the defeat or support of the ministry, is therefore not to be found at the capitol. A Frenchman would find the Congress very dull, but as a president is elected every fourth year by universal suffrage, the American can easily spare the excitement of a ministerial crisis, though this is the necessary safety valve to constitutional Europe.

With such restricted powers—all those not mentioned in the Constitution as belonging to Congress being reserved to the individual states—the members of Congress and the senators are not overwhelmed by business. Unless, therefore, the Union needs again to be saved from secession, or the tariff is discussed, or the admission of a new state connected with the question of slavery to be decided—the spare time of Congress is employed for personal explanations and political speeches as they are called, or "speeches for Buncombe" as they are nicknamed. In fact, they are lectures on every topic which has political interest, on slavery or abolition, on the land system, the Maine liquor law, on the merits or demerits of the parties, or on any other abstract political principle intended for the constituents of the representative or senator, not for the House or the Senate. This is so well understood that members often are considerate enough to announce that they will send their speeches straight to the congressional newspaper without robbing the House or Senate of its time by delivering them.

But the great object of Congress, every fourth year, is the making of a president. The election belongs, of course, to the people, but the

masses are influenced from Washington and therefore speeches on the
merits of the party nominees, and the defense of them against party
attacks, are great themes in the halls of the capitol. The session preceding the presidential election always lasts long, from the first Monday
of December often till the end of July. Then follows a short one, closed
after the inauguration of the new president, which takes place on the
fourth of March. The ensuing session is again long and important, succeeded by a short one; thus their duration alternates from four to seven
months.

In New York we enjoyed a quiet Sabbath in the amiable family
circle of Mayor Kingsland. It was numerous; as families generally are
in America where people marry young and where society is in the
happy state that many children are considered great blessings and not
great cares, as is generally the case on the continent of Europe. And
this, as I often had opportunity to remark in America, is not owing only
to the greater facility of getting employment, but more especially to the
rational view that young men have to push their own way, and that
after they have got the benefit of a good education they are not to depend on their parents for support—therefore, it is not only the son of
the poor and of the little-educated families who must look forward *to
make himself a man.* In all classes we meet *self-made men* who, in consequence, are independent not only in position and fortunes but likewise by their practical experience, and who, for this very reason,
become fit to be self-governed citizens.

Mrs. Kingsland, a mother of nine children, is one of those who, by
youthful appearance, denies the prejudice that the bloom of American
ladies is but short; and I have since found so frequently mothers of
large families whom I mistook for the sisters of their daughters, that I
may affirm that their household cares do not wear them out.

And yet I have heard with them so frequent complaints of the difficulty in managing servants, that the task of a housewife might seem
Herculean indeed. I know one instance where the lady with whom we
dined excused herself for the imperfections of the meal she offered us
by the circumstance that her cook had left her just as the dinner was
going to be prepared. "Without any previous notice?" inquired I, astonished. "Oh, she did it on purpose to annoy me," was the answer, "because I had repeatedly found fault with her management. It is a sad

thing with us, seriously interfering with our domestic comfort, that we cannot get an attendant to remain any length of time; they think nothing of changing places ever so often."

"But do not the masters think it very unsafe," I remarked, "to take people who have not the recommendation of steady characters? If those who leave service for any petty reason could not find employment again without considerable difficulty they would take good care not to run away."

"No doubt that this would be a check," answered the lady, "but then there is the difficulty of getting servants—the demand is larger than the supply."

"Is this the case likewise here in New York?" asked I, "where emigrants abound, and would be glad to earn something before they proceed farther into the country?"

"The emigrants who come here willing to serve," continued the lady, "are either ragged Irish, filthy and negligent, and therefore little desirable as servants, or Germans, generally small farmers or poor mechanics, whose daughters at home had been accustomed only to the meanest housework, and are but little adapted to attend to a larger and more refined establishment. Worst of all, they are impertinent, because they know that we cannot do without them."

"Excuse me," said I, interrupting my amiable friend, "this is the point —*that they know you cannot do without them.* If cooking, sewing, and washing were elements of the practical education of an American lady, she would seldom be called upon to leave her piano for the kitchen fire, and she would have good servants. The uneducated are like children, who instinctively feel with whom they have to deal, and who obey only those who are consistent and just in their orders; and it is obviously impossible to be either consistent or just in the direction of work we do not understand."

The lady acknowledged the truth of this assertion, but objected that her daughters were initiated in the domestic arts, but that the servants were so accustomed, by the general habit, not to be told anything, that they would not submit to the slightest reproof, and that, in consequence, she had to change her cooks from six to ten times in a year.

Of course, it is difficult for individuals to counteract an evil which is rooted, as it seems to me, partly in the accidental circumstances of the country, but much more still in certain habitual prejudices and customs. That employment is more accessible, and that thrifty people can more easily keep up their hearth in the United States than in Europe, are facts which necessarily diminish the competition of servants; but the prejudice which I have found very much spread in America, that the female sex is honored by being expected *not to work;* and the custom to attach a selfish meaning to "independence," that is, "every one for himself," certainly acts much more to demoralize the servants and to discomfort the masters than any other influence.

It is a common boast with American gentlemen that their ladies rule, and are more respected than anywhere else in the world. I heard this often repeated in the society of New York, and I inquired of a gentleman, who was repeating this pet phrase, in what way they ruled. "Why, they have all they like," was the reply: "They dress and go shopping and have not to care about anything; we even live in hotels to save them the trouble of housekeeping."

"I see," observed I, "you are almost as courteous as the Turks, who allow their wives every amusement in their harems. The elegantly gilded parlors of your hotels, where the ladies meet to rock away time in the easy rocking chairs, are admirable harems; but what has all this to do with *the rule* of your ladies? Even granted that you accepted their wishes as commands, still you are no pashas whose whims claim obedience from the community. You, yourselves, rule only by the active part you take in public affairs, and do you mean to say you consult your ladies about these matters?"

"Well, not exactly," answered the gentleman; "but, a lady can travel alone without danger of an insult, or unbecoming behavior; our daughters go out often and are in society without their mothers—every man is their natural protector."

"Quite as in Turkey," replied I; "no man, not even the husband, would ever dare to follow his veiled lady in the streets. All the difference, perhaps, is that the morality in the United States is more sterling than in France and Italy or in the capitals of Austria and Russia, and therefore flirtations with married ladies are unheard of."

"But in Europe," he said, "women even work in the fields and they must assist the husbands to earn a subsistence; with us, even in the factories, the girls work until they marry, but once married, the maintenance of the family is the care of the husband, and an American farmer would feel degraded if his wife or daughter should hoe the corn or break the flax."

Of course, I readily acknowledged that owing to the greater facilities of earning a livelihood, the women of the lower classes were much better off than in Europe, but I did not understand in what way the respect for the fair sex is connected with this fact. The gentleman turned to other topics; I sought information on the other side, and understood from some very intellectual ladies that their lords, *in general,* little consult the opinions of their female rulers, even as concerns their own private affairs. I learned that it occurs but too often that a lady who believes herself to be in affluent circumstances is suddenly informed by her husband that they must give up housekeeping because they cannot afford it. It appears as if the gentlemen would atone for their all-absorbing passion for business by the privilege they give to the ladies of idling time away. And as business is a passion with the Americans, not the means, but the very life of existence, they are most anxious to keep this department exclusively to themselves; and, well aware that there is no more infallible way to secure noninterference, than by giving the general impression that they never act for themselves, *the lady's rule* has become a current phrase, but by no means a fact in the United States.

The nurseries are by no means the only realm of the children. They roam about the house, upstairs and down, circulating freely like little birds not confined to cages, but fluttering about the whole precinct of an ample hothouse. And thus the little ones are not abandoned to the nurses, but the mother has them constantly under her eye, though I cannot say under her control, for they have their own way. They run in and out and play, tumbling and dragging about books and cushions and chairs and climbing up and down just as they please. In consequence they never are embarrassed, and meet everyone who chances to come with the most perfect ease. Unconstrained and not preoccupied by any conventional rule, they grow strikingly sharp and answer every inquiry with a self-dependence and self-observation which never can be obtained by a training to accepted notions and habitual manners. But on the other side, such children, unaccustomed to check and to control their impulses easily become spoiled to all discipline, and this explains in a great measure the habit prevalent in America of placing even the girls at school, thus depriving the mother of her most precious privilege, the education of her own daughter.

Another phase of female life struck me very much. In Columbus, a very sensible gentleman mentioned to me that there are persons in the United States, and especially in the West, who have communications with the spirit of deceased persons. I was much amused and began to speak jestingly about the matter. To my great astonishment, however, I found that the gentleman was in good earnest. He told me that some years back, in a certain house in Rochester, New York, rappings were heard which could not be accounted for in any natural way, and tables and chairs were moved without any visible agency.

"It was," he said, "soon found out that three rappings meant 'Yes' and two 'No.' Questions were put, and the replies proved almost always correct. The communications became more frequent, and several ingenious inventions were made to get longer answers from the spirits. For instance, an alphabet was taken; the letters were numbered, and the spirits marked by rapping the number of the letter which they wished to be reported. For A they rap once, for D four times, and so on. But later, the spirits prepared for themselves *writing* and *speaking* mediums who write and speak without any volition. They don't know what they are writing; their hand is moved by the spirits. Most of them do it with closed eyes and often about matters and in languages they do not understand. Several books have been written in this way."

"I can assure you," he concluded, "that sincere men of sound judgment and of good education have had visions—Judge Edmonds, for example, of the New York Supreme Court. And is not the last communication from Benjamin Franklin, by rappings through a young girl of twelve years, entirely in his style and his turn of mind? 'To use time well, does not mean to do the most in an hour, but in a lifetime.' "

"Then you believe in all those manifestations, sir?" asked I, astonished.

"There are," said he, "I must confess, statements which are not to be relied upon. In one of those chronicles of spiritual manifestations which abounds in poetical beauties, we find that the spirits are taught French and Italian in the other world, that they may understand Racine and Dante, which is rather strange, so much the more as the German language is not mentioned. Besides, the spelling of the spirits is sometimes wrong. Nevertheless, the rappings I myself have heard repeatedly, and

I cannot find any physical explanation for them. Like many other people in the United States, I do not believe, but I do not disbelieve. I register the facts and wait either for a natural explanation or for an evident proof of supernatural communications." I dropped the conversation. I remembered that in Germany such alleged manifestations had also been fashionable for some time, but that they soon disappeared in this crude form and merged into the phenomenon of mesmerism.

Soon after, I was in the midst of Rappers, and Mediums, and Believers. In the first week of our stay in Cincinnati, Captain Kalapsza told me that the Misses Fox, with whom the rappings had originated at Rochester, were staying at the Burnet House, close to our rooms. He had already paid them a visit and was astounded by the rappings themselves and by the answers conveyed in this manner. Yielding to his entreaties, I went with Mr. Pulszky into the room, where we found the two very handsome Misses Fox, their mother, several of the Hungarian gentlemen, and two reporters.

The manifestations immediately began. The young ladies requested us to put questions. I naturally asked: "Shall we return to Hungary?" Three distinct raps were heard on the table from below; the table was uncovered, Miss Fox stood near it, keeping her hand on the edge of the table. I closely watched her movements, the rap did not proceed from her. I asked several other questions of a similar kind, and got just as favorable replies as I could wish.

Doctor Spaczek, our clever physician, also could not tell in what way the rappings were produced, but he rejoiced at least to get an evident proof that they came not from the spirits of the deceased persons. He asked whether his father was in heaven. Three raps answered "yes," whilst the father of our friend lives in good health in Poland. The spirits likewise were at a loss to guess how old Mrs. Spaczek was—they added ten years to her actual age. When the doctor began to protest against these manifest falsehoods, Miss Fox coolly replied that she and her sister were not responsible for anything the spirits said, as they, in fact, could not tell whether the spirits who manifested themselves were veracious or lying spirits. That there were lying ones amongst them, they had found out by experience.

On the next day, our visit to the rapping spirits was duly trumpeted and commented upon in the papers. As the exhibitions of the Misses Fox are for an entrance fee, I was not surprised at this progress of "the

philosophy of advertising." But the newspaper report became an introduction to us for the spiritual circles of the city. We were mistaken
for Believers, and got invitations to several such gatherings.

I understood that a spiritual circle is formed in the following way:
A number of persons who are not skeptical, and amongst whom one at
least must be a medium, sit silently around the table, holding one another's hand, and concentrate. If they meet in such manner at least
once a week, the spirit manifestations begin. Rappings are heard, writing mediums are formed, others become clairvoyants. There are several
such circles in Cincinnati, and the spirits who manifest themselves
through the mediums are generally George Washington, Andrew Jackson, Benjamin Franklin, Zachary Taylor, and Emanuel Swedenborg.
There are, besides, two spirit messengers amongst them, and the spirits
of the nearest relatives of those who form the circle. Even Sir Robert
Peel has made his appearance, and, strange to say, he has become a
thorough republican in the other world, predicting the approach of
republican governments all over Europe, and even in England.

We visited one of the spiritual parties on the anniversary of the
birthday of Washington. We entered the room, followed by a young
lady and her husband; she was introduced to us as a medium. In the
second room sat an elderly lady, clad in bright green, with a smile on
her radiant face. As she beheld Mr. Pulszky, she stretched her arms out
over his head and advanced toward him. He retreated to the wall.
"What is she doing?" I inquired. "She is blessing him, in Washington's
name," replied our host. "We do not know her; she was sent to us by
the spirits, who told her that you would visit us today. She came at
their bidding. There is also an old gentleman whom we do not know,
and who likewise was sent by the spirits."

We sat down at the table, and scarcely was the circle formed when
the elderly green lady began to shake her grizzly curls, whilst an old
periwigged gentleman, on the opposite side of the table, uplifted his
tearful eyes. The green lady stretched out her hands, and spoke with a
solemn tone, word after word, as if it were dictated to her:

"Let the Lord have all the praise! To me this is the happiest anniversary, and there will be lasting good come of it, to all who will receive me and all I may say. I am rejoiced to meet all who are here.
And the Lord will be with his vicegerent [sic], who has been kept
away by physical infirmation [sic]. I bless you all in the name of the

Lord, who rules over heaven and earth.   George Washington."

I thought the communication was not less strange than the style of George Washington, and glanced at our host. He seemed to understand me, and asked the green lady whether they had ever before had communications of George Washington in this circle.

"You shall have them in the future," said she.

"Where is my uncle?" asked I, in Hungarian.

"All shall be done in the right time," was the answer.

This was conclusive enough; yet the gentlemen in the circle seemed not to feel how ludicrous they appeared. One of the ladies wept, another laughed; a medium handed a line to Mr. Pulszky, containing the words, "You had better go!" and so we did. I was no longer astonished at the great number of insane persons in this country—above 15,000 in 23,000,000, 150 per cent more, in proportion, than in Hungary.

The Americans, especially in the West, have little leisure to enjoy nature, no art to refine their feelings; their manners proscribe the amusements of Europe. The soul must grow weary of the tinkling of dollars, of the purely material aim of their life. They long for excitement; the ladies grow nervous, and work themselves into trances and visions, and cheat themselves and others. Spiritual circles are formed in lieu of balls, and concerts, and theaters. The gentlemen attend these representations, and are too much worn out by business to look deeply into the matter. Besides, such fancies become epidemical. After all, it is here in the West that people get spasmodic contortions and begin to roll, to jerk, to dance, and to bark in the camp meetings and the forest gatherings of the Methodists. They have visions and trances, and are thrown into a state of ecstasy similar to a protracted catalepsy. I fear that the great progress of which our age boasts is only progress in the instruction of the understanding, not in the education of feelings. The believers of spiritual manifestations are on a level with the early believers in witchcraft in New England.

Boston and its society has a peculiar character, different from all other cities of the world. It is the only one where knowledge and scholarship have the lead of society. A distinguished author, an eminent professor, an eloquent preacher, are socially equals of the monied aristocracy, which maintains its position only by its liberality toward literary institutions. The bankers and money-kings pride themselves in being connected, by family ties, with the aristocracy of intellect. Boston is, therefore, for America, what the court of Weimar once was for Germany—the center of literature and science. But there it was only the generous liberality of one prince which drew together the sages and poets of Germany into one brilliant constellation, which sank with his life. Here it is the spirit of the people—public opinion, the manners and customs of the city—which encourage the development of talent by assigning to it the most honored position, without fettering it by gratitude to one individual and transforming the scientific men into flattering courtiers. They need not here cook their meal at the fire of their own genius.

As to the charitable institutions, again no city in the world can boast of so many. The words of Increase Mather, "For charity this town has not many equals on the face of the earth," are still as true as they were in the beginning of the eighteenth century.

Yet all this liberality does not exclude the worship of the "almighty dollar." Boston is a great commercial city; less enterprising perhaps than New York, but also less exposed to sudden reverses. Nature has denied to Massachusetts the great advantage of a water communication with the western lakes, by which New York has secured for itself the lion's share of American commerce. But as canals were unsuitable for New England, Massachusetts has availed herself of the great invention of Stephenson, and has covered her territory with a net of railroads, radiating from Boston, and surpassing in extent every similar system in any state of the Union. Boston capital has also given a stimulus to the manufacturing industry, and has established mills and factories in the state, competing with those of England.

The great money interest is, here as everywhere in the United States, predominantly Whiggish and conservative. The rich capitalists of Boston look besides with a kind of piety on Old England. They are proud of their English descent; they are in continual intercourse with the merchants of England. English opinions are more authoritatively received by them than in any other part of America; and an English title is a better introduction in those circles than any American merit or American reputation. Though the United States have asserted their political independence of the mother country, they yet remain dependent upon the "old country" in matters of taste and literary judgment. America has not yet the moral courage to establish the reputation

of an author or an artist without the sanction of England. English re-
prints are the principal literary food of the people. But nowhere is this
moral dependence on England more prominent than with the Boston
conservative Whigs.

In one respect Boston is deficient, as is America in general—I mean
in respect to art. The feeling for the beautiful is not yet developed so
far as to bring collections of objects of art into the number of the neces-
saries of life for the wealthy. Like the great bulk of the manufacturers
of England, the Bostonians admire only skill and costliness, and do
not yet appreciate taste and beauty. But this is natural. If we watch
the development of human faculties in children, we find that their attention is first directed to the strange, curious, and interesting. Collections of foreign animals and plants captivate them above all. In the next
phase of their intellectual progress they admire difficulties surmounted
by human skill; the artificial attracts their attention even in works of
art. They have no eye for the beautiful, but only for the process by
which it has been produced; if they had to choose between an original
of Raphael and a copy in mosaic, which has cost five years of labor,
they would take the latter. In the next phase they appreciate nicety and
elegance; and only the full systematic development of their faculties
awakens in them the feeling for the grand and the beautiful.

Nations pursue the same course. Collections of stuffed and living
animals, equestrian feats, rope dancing, and jugglers, living monsters
of every kind, still amuse Indian princes and are as highly estimated by
their courts as they were prized in the Middle Ages in Europe, and as
they are still sure to attract the crowds of European capitals. Almost all
the museums of Europe grew up from collections of natural history;
artificial curiosities were next added to them. Then, only, galleries of
painting and sculpture were formed—by-and-by their connection with
the curiosities was severed, and monuments became appreciated not by
the material labor which they cost, not by their rarity, the costliness of
material, or their remote age, but by the spirit which pervades them
and which they transmit to the soul of those who behold them. The
Americans, in general, have not yet reached this phase of development,
but there is no reason to think that they never will attain it. When I
was speaking about this matter with Mr. Ticknor, this eminent scholar
mentioned that, at the time when he began to apply himself to the
study of the Greek in 1812, it was with great difficulty that he got a

copy of Aeschylus and Thucydides in Boston. "But *now,*" he said, "we have at least twenty private libraries here which contain all the Greek classics. We had first to turn our attention to the necessary and to the useful, but now we care also for the embellishments of life."

We had scarcely arrived at the elegant Revere House, where the Massachusetts legislature had provided us with sumptuous apartments, when Dr. and Mrs. Howe, our excellent friends whom we had known for many years, came to greet us. The doctor had in his younger years taken part in the Greek struggle of independence as a zealous phil-hellene. He afterwards became renowned as the philanthropic teacher of the blind; and has founded, by his exertion, the magnificent institution for them which still occupies his time. His education of Laura Bridgeman, who is deaf, dumb, and blind, is a proof of how genius can invent not only machines for saving labor, but also means of in-struction even for those hapless beings to whom nature has blocked up nearly all the ways of external impressions. Laura Bridgeman could neither hear, nor see, nor speak; it was only by the sense of touch that she was put into communication with the external world, that she learned to think, to understand, to read, and to write.

Doctor Howe now bestows his care on idiots likewise, to rouse in them the divine spark, buried in their defective physical constitution; and his efforts are in this instance, too, attended with success. Though he is a man of eminent talent and keen observation, it is yet not to his abilities alone that we can trace the blessed results of his labors. Skill, experience, knowledge suffice for brilliant success; but the earnest faith in the divine origin of human nature and the deepest sympathy with human misery alone can impart that devotedness to the exhausting task which characterizes Doctor Howe, and truly makes him the regenerator of many a child who, without him, would not only be lost to the world without, but would likewise remain blind to the light within.

Not far from here lives Mr. Agassiz, the celebrated geologist of world-wide reputation who left Europe, with all the attractions which the Old World offers to a renowned scholar, in order to carry to the New World the love of natural history, and to transplant the science which he illustrates to a virgin soil.

Professor Felton, who brings the sublime beauties of Greek and Roman poetry, by his popular lectures, within the reach of the public at large; Doctor Grey, the botanist; and Jared Sparks, the learned biographer of Franklin and Washington and president of Harvard College, through the close vicinity of Cambridge to Boston, belong to that rare circle of intellectual notabilities in which we meet Mr. Ticknor, the accomplished historian of Spanish literature; Prescott, of the conquest of Mexico and Peru; Everett, the well-known ambassador at London, who has lately become Secretary of State; Doctor Warren, the celebrated physician and proprietor of a remarkable collection of fossils; and others whose personal acquaintance we have not made.

In London or in Paris many more celebrated men of science may be found; but these capitals are of such immense extent, and so many different interests divide and split people into sets and coteries, that the literary and scientific element is entirely diluted, whilst in Boston it forms one of the principal features of society. Love of science is inherent in New England; the Whig principle that knowledge is the best safeguard of freedom, more so than armies, and that therefore every citizen, whether childless or blessed with many children, must contribute to public education; that the common schools must be free to every child, and that the state must afford the greatest facility for higher education, prevails here generally, even amongst the Democrats. It is through schools and instruction that Massachusetts strives against crime and oppression, and in the regular expenditure of this state public education has the prominent place which in Europe is given to the army and navy estimates.

Governor Boutwell, Amasa Walker, the secretary of state, and Nathaniel Bishop, the inspector of the schools, with the most amiable complacency afforded us all the means of getting insight into the working of the school system, and of the moral condition of the working people. The state is most anxious to provide for the wants of them all, yet the great tide of immigration in the last years has raised many difficulties. According to statistical accounts, there were, in 1849, almost 25,000 paupers in Massachusetts, 91 per cent of them foreigners. In the city of Boston, there are about 1,500 vagabond children between the ages of six and sixteen years, who from neglect and bad habits were unfit to enter the public schools, 90 per cent of them foreigners. The Boston Society for the Prevention of Pauperism has received during the last five years application for employment from more than 15,000 females, of whom 90 per cent were foreigners, and from more than 8,000 male applicants, of whom 58 per cent belong to this class. More than three-fourths of all the arrests by the night watch and the police at Boston, and nearly three-fourths of all commitments to the county jail, and of the cases before the police and municipal courts, were foreigners. In the Boston dispensary, 88 per cent of the cases are those of foreigners; in the almshouse, 97 per cent.

Yet the legislative committee in their able report of a general plan for the promotion of public and personal health does not suggest political measures to discourage immigration, but recommends that efforts be made to elevate the sanitary and social condition of foreigners, and to promote amongst them habits of cleanliness and better modes of living. It is really strange that many of the immigrants cluster in the seaport cities where they rarely can better their fortunes, instead of proceeding westward, where their labor is required and remunerated. In Indiana, the legislature gives them the citizenship of the state after a residence of one year; they have every inducement to settle in Minnesota; yet many of them have lost their energies under European oppression, and remain a burden to society even in America where labor is well paid and talent is appreciated.

The laws of Massachusetts give perfect equality to the colored people. They are here full citizens; nevertheless, socially even here they cannot become equals of the whites. In some respect they themselves are the cause of it. We were told that one of them was returned to the House of Representatives in the state, but when elected by his fellow-citizens he had not the moral courage to accept the trust. There is now a colored lawyer in Boston, whose talent has overcome the prejudice against his race to a certain degree; yet when he came to a public concert in the Melodeon he was refused admittance to the hall.

The feeling against the Roman Catholics has much subsided here in recent times. A convent would not now be burned down by the mob as it was twenty years ago. An intelligent gentleman with whom I spoke on this subject, told me that this turn in public opinion was entirely due to toleration, and not to an approach to the Roman Catholic dogmas; conversions were rare, and could almost always be traced to disappointment in love or ambition. Old maids sometimes make themselves nuns, and unsuccessful literary men turn disciples of the Jesuits.

Upon my request to see a plantation, Mr. H***, a rich merchant, obligingly invited us to his country seat on the Mississippi. On board ship a planter accosted our host, telling him what an excellent bargain he had made. He had brought three girls from Virginia, field hands, strong enough, said he, to split rails for fences; none of them twenty years old; they had cost only $800 apiece. They were called up; they looked passively content, pleased, as it seemed, with their new and clean apparel.

I got into conversation with a young lady, whose parents had a large plantation near Baton Rouge. I began to speak about slavery, and expressed my sorrow that the child can be sold from the mother, and the husband from the wife.—"A good master never sells the husband from the wife," was the answer; "those who do it are despised by public opinion. The law here does not allow the separation of the child from the mother until it is ten years old; after that time they have to submit to it."—I asked whether the feelings of the blacks were perhaps stunned, so that they were less aggrieved by the separation? "No," the young lady answered, "they always are very sad when such things occur."

Mr. H*** possesses nine different plantations. He had lately bought the estate which we were going to visit from a Frenchman, and keeps there 180 slaves; 20 are old, 50 children, and 100 are working [*sic*]. It was stormy, and night had set in when the boat stopped; we went through the garden to the house. It is not large, built merely of wood. Its most attractive feature is an open gallery, supported by columns running all around the building. Mrs. H*** received us here, seated on the veranda, where we spent the evening in conversation.

Mr. H*** told us that twenty years ago he thought slavery wrong and sinful; he therefore freed about twenty families, but until now they have not got on well. They toil in vain and cannot compete with the whites. They have already offered Mr. H*** to work for him again in the plantation, merely for food, lodging, and clothing, but retaining their freedom. Our host did not accept the proposal. He said: "Mixed labor won't do on the plantation; there must be equality amongst the laborers. Light colored people likewise won't do among black; they are bad workers, and spoil the Negroes." He has given up the idea of freeing all his slaves, but he tries to make them comfortable. "My slaves," said he, "are treated better than some and worse than others."

"How so?" I inquired.

"I do not live amongst them; they are managed by overseers, and therefore cannot be treated as well as if I heard all their complaints and always saw after their wants."

The slaves on this plantation speak only French, and are Roman Catholics, as the late proprietor was a French Creole. It is remarkable how the habits of the masters act on the slaves. Those on the plantations who speak English and are Protestants all work harder and are less idle than the Frenchified Negroes. On the whole, the Creoles proper treat their house-slaves better than the English; but the field hands have more to suffer from the outburst of the passions of their masters, which are stronger than their love of money.

The Negroes here have their own little gardens; they keep their poultry and sell it to their master. "This is the general custom," said Mrs. H***; "the planters think it mean to rear their own poultry, and not to leave the profits to the slaves, who are likewise allowed to sell the produce of their garden to the steamboats, or to the New Orleans market, but never without the written permit of the master or of the overseer." (Most of them spend their money on finery; a few husband it well and buy their liberty. Some of Mr. H***'s slaves keep fifty and more dollars in cash. In the household of the New Orleans ladies there is a slave for every occupation; one cooks, the other washes, the third sews, and the fourth dresses her mistress. Scrubbing and all hard work about the house is done by the male slaves. The little colored girls are treated like dolls; the young ladies in the house amuse themselves by dressing and adorning them.)

"Our children," continued Mrs. H***, "are spoiled by our institution. It is very difficult to educate them; they never exert themselves in any way; they always depend on the slaves. A boy of twelve years is hardly able to wash his own neck. The tutor of my son, wished him to be more independent, and told the slave who was the playfellow of my boy not to attend on him for every trifle; but then the slave refused even to bring him a glass of water from the cistern. If the slaves are treated very kindly, they easily get overbearing."

Yesterday morning we went first over the house, at the back of which is an orange grove which last year yielded 300,000 oranges—this season it was frostbitten. As the colored children have the free use of the fruit, no other fruit trees than oranges are planted here, for fear the "pickaninnies" should catch fever by eating unripe pears and peaches. We proceeded to the sugar-house, and on our way visited the cabins. They are very poor, but Mr. H*** is erecting better ones; some of them are already put up, and when I expressed my opinion that he certainly was one of the good masters, as he seemed anxious for the comfort of his people, he answered that it was a good investment to have the slaves well lodged, as their health was then generally better. The cabins were now almost all empty; in some of them we found women suckling their babies. In one there was an aged man, nearly a hundred-years old, surrounded by chickens, which he rears. We were told that he sometimes walks to the garden of the master and there digs the ground. When Mr. H*** told him that he should leave work to younger hands, he replied, "I must work, that, when I am dead, you may say, 'I have lost a good old nigger.'"

A larger building in the village is the kitchen. Here the food is cooked in great kettles, for all the "hands," three-quarters of a pound of pork a head, boiled with peas, sometimes with rice or other vegetables. Close to it is an oven, where the corn bread is baked every day. At noon the meal is sent to the field, where an hour is allowed to the slaves for dinner and one hour more for rest. The Negroes prefer pork and bacon to all other food; of any other meat and fish they soon grow sick. Here they get as much corn bread as they please. I tasted it and found it similar to the *polenta* of the Italians. A host of little black imps hovered around the kitchen, eating their hot corn bread. They were very dirty, and appeared to delight in mud as much as any gipsy.

We took a ride in an open carriage to the sugar fields, the gentlemen preceding us on horseback. A light-colored hunchback with the classical name of Homer, who was overseer and son of the housekeeper, went with them, armed with a whip—the symbol of southern authority, as the stick is in the Austrian and Russian army. In the fields the people were ploughing. It was a rich, black, alluvial soil, covered along the paths with white clover. The plough was very primitive; four mules dragged it, and by the manner in which work was performed we saw that great economy of labor can yet be introduced here. A surveyor, now the manager of the estate, showed us how much land had been recovered by drainage in the last year. But much more is yet covered by a large swamp studded with large oaks, and home of alligators and rattlesnakes. The estate contains 1,600 acres of cultivated land, and yields $20,000 a year. The rotation of crops is winter cane, summer cane, and Indian corn.

18.

A HISTORIAN'S FOREBODINGS

Karl Theodor Griesinger (1809–1884) was a member of the German liberal generation of the 1840's. Editor of a radical newspaper in Baden, he offended the Catholic government of that state and was jailed for two years. After his release he spent five years in the United States, but found the American type of democracy in action not to his liking. He wandered about and wrote a succession of books on his travels and upon historical subjects, all distinguished by a kind of mordant humor and by a sharp sense of frustration. This selection comes from a volume entitled Lebende Bilder aus Amerika *(1858).*

A man who marries in Germany knows not his bride alone; he knows also her brothers and sisters, her parents and grandparents, her uncles and aunts, and her whole line of descent unto the third or fourth generation. He knows how the girl was brought up, the nature of her environment and relations, and the circumstances under which she lives. He knows the condition of her father; all the intricacies of inheritance and reversion are arranged in advance. The young pair can set forth on their life's journey with everything adjusted beforehand, children and deaths excepted.

How far different in America! The American is abrupt; he has no time to beat around the bush. He meets a girl in a shop, in the theater, at a ball, or in her parents' home. He needs a wife, thinks this one will do. He asks the question, she answers. The next day they are married and then proceed to inform the parents. The couple do not need to learn to know each other; that comes later.

The German in America is even worse off. Where in the world can he find a wife? He has little opportunity for family life. He generally lives in quarters that are too constricted to leave much room for the old amenities. And then, not a single day can be spared from his work without losing a critical day's wages. On Sundays though—well on Sunday, one must booze. So the young people get acquainted only in public places, in restaurants, concerts, the theater, balls. But what can they learn of each other there?—Everything, except that which relates to a wife and her duties.

And then, how many maidens are there in the United States born in the homeland or brought up after the German manner? Aren't they all long since Americanized, disdainful of newly arrived Germans, especially of the laborers?—But are there not enough newly immigrated girls? No question, but what kind of girls? Take a single trip on an immigrant ship, notice life as it's lived there, go below decks, where the travelers sleep in tiers by hundreds, think of the condition of the girls, how modestly and bashfully they behave themselves within a single week, and how reserved they are after the second when they get to know the sailors! How could you think of marrying an imported bride! And even if she is "upright," do you know anything else about her or her family? How she looks, you see at once; how she views things only the future will tell.

In the last resort, you will be satisfied to drift into a marriage bureau and pay your half-dollar for a glimpse of the feminine daguerreotypes on display there. Or better still, you advertise in the papers. A hundred to one, you get a dozen answers. If you are willing to take one without a fortune, and don't demand a miracle of beauty, you will get at least two-dozen letters. Well now, read out the replies. There are people who claim to discern character from handwriting; but if you lack that ability, what do you do? You simply buy a pig in a poke; but remember, you can still take a look, and if she doesn't meet your requirements— the whole thing's off.

Or if you don't like this method, write to Germany, import a fresh blossom, and put your trust in the circumstance that she will come across with an "honest" family.

The main thing is, naturally, finding the bride; getting married is simplicity itself. There is no need for going to a minister unless you want to; civil officials will do as well. Any magistrate has power to perform the ceremony either in his office or in a restaurant. Every alderman can arrange a wedding. In a few minutes the whole thing is over. You pay your dollar and walk out with your wife. A wedding feast is also not necessary unless perchance the minister who marries you is also an innkeeper (which often is the case) and sees to it that he gets the price of a few bottles of wine in addition to his fee.

There are no formalities, no hindrances, no questions as to age or status, no need of certificates of citizenship or residence. Your wife may be a Catholic, you a Jew, that is no obstacle. The permission of the church is as little necessary as that of the parents. As long as you are twenty-one and your bride at least fourteen then no one, nothing, can stand in your way, even were you her uncle, or she your aunt. It would be a fine thing if such "trifles" were questioned! Not more than a promise is necessary in America to marry. Many reckon it superfluous even to go through the procedure of a ceremony, and simply live together. Their children are legitimate, for open cohabitation between man and wife in the eyes of the law is worth as much as a knot tied in a church. The rights of women are well protected in the United States!

And so you are married. The whole thing is over in a quarter-hour. Now get settled. You have an apartment, now only the equipment is lacking. But that is no embarrassment. You go to a furniture store; the broad double bed, the bureau, the easy chair, mirror, and, above all, the rocking chair are soon purchased. And now to the tinsmith; you may choose from among a hundred cook stoves, all equipped with a complete set of vessels necessary for cooking. In an hour you are installed—everything in the house. Meet your girl in the morning, marry in the afternoon, and by six in the evening you are settled in your home, man and wife.

Marriages come easy in America; whether happiness comes in the same way is another question. It happens hundreds of times, the thing simply will not click. The individuals are not compatible with one another, and each finds himself drawn into a hell instead of a heaven. A tragic prospect stretches out before their long lives! Brawls for breakfast, scuffles at lunch, and blows for supper! And so for twelve or more years! A fine outlook that!

By no means. Why does man have feet, but to run? The husband rarely does so voluntarily. He must take care of his business and cannot easily change his residence, like a pair of gloves. But his wife has time and leisure, and generally also the will. She packs and leaves. One evening you come home from the shop to find empty rooms. Your wife has disappeared, and to keep her company all the furniture has run along with her. This night you will sleep on the naked boards; tomorrow morning though, you will move to a boardinghouse and act as if you had lived in single blessedness all the days of your life. Feel fortunate if you never hear from her again!

Divorce is not easy to come by; judicial divorce is more difficult in the United States than anywhere in the world. Only adultery before witnesses, or death, can end a marriage. The German immigrant finds it hard to believe. He thinks that where marriage is so free, divorce must also be. He runs off to a notary and demands a decree of divorce. If both parties agree, he can indeed arrange a separation, but only from "bed and board," a division of property and mutual settlement of accounts. But this decree is of no use when it comes to remarriage. Many Germans also insert notices in the newspapers, "This day, my wife, Mrs. — — abandoned me. Unless she return in three days, I will consider myself separated." Those who insert such public announcements, which can daily be read by the dozens in the papers, take them as the equivalents of a divorce. They are not, however, worth a straw. He who marries again under such circumstances and is prosecuted by his first wife will be mercilessly punished for bigamy, and the punishment for bigamy is the penitentiary.

But be consoled; your old wife will no more sue you than you her when you hear of her second marriage. How many thousands of men and women are there in the United States who have married for a second and a third time, while their earlier spouses were still alive! Both parties are free by this mutual tolerance and no one loses a wink's sleep over such a trifle as a second marriage. If, however, you wish to be entirely secure then move to another state and take another name. Who will trouble himself about that? And even if a charge is made, why there are lawyers, and much can be done with money.

Sometimes it may even please you to maintain both wives, and live with both, a proceeding which, one may well believe, happens often enough. To be sure, the wives married in the old country do not let themselves be so easily put off, and if you have one of those and are apprehensive that she will come after you, then better leave marrying in America to others.

Above all, however, beware of promises of marriage, for these are even more treacherous than marriage itself. A promise of marriage must be kept in America. In Germany it is not taken so seriously. What's a simple promise? But in America breach of promise is something else again. Go out once with a female, take her to a ball, to a dining place, be pleasant and tell her she pleases you, then stay away the next day and pay attention to another; well, see how quickly a suit is clapped on you. You are dragged before the judge and there she stands, the beautiful plaintiff, and swears that you promised her your hand—with heart or without. Well, what will you do then? A few years in jail, or marriage? You naturally chose the latter and the judge promptly joins you before the assembled crowd; the trial becomes a marriage.

Irish girls are especially dexterous in this proceeding. They know the law and are anxious to be married, particularly to Germans. They give you every opportunity to put your trust in them. Do so, and you are caught. No God can save you unless you prove that you already have a wife. Then you must pay.

No matter how unfortunate may be the marriage of Germans in America, it shines by comparison with the marriage of a German and an Irishwoman. Language, in truth, is a barrier easily overcome—but, Irish and German habits . . . Ten times out of eleven she is drunk when you come home, and if you deprive her of money and warn the grocer to give her no credit, she will simply pawn one piece of furniture, one garment after another, to be able to buy whiskey. And what will she cook for you! Sauerkraut and Bratwurst? Your very obedient servant—tough beefsteak or stewed fish. The food is ready in five minutes, and you cannot persuade her to work for you for more than five minutes. Say something to her, and she scolds back; notice how quick she is with her tongue and how prompt in reference to the damned Dutchmen. In dealing with an Irishwoman only blows are understood.

And in the final extremity marry an American girl, then, poor German, you are really lost; in her eyes you always remain a despised German. So it goes for the Germans who marry in America. Nothing but ease!

The grocer is always a German countryman. Before these people came to New York the Americans must have run these businesses themselves. But for a long time it has been quite different; these Germans have a monopoly of groceries. And there are few such Germans who in their lifetime have not been grocers, or, at least, expected to be.

Who has not seen a grocery cannot possibly imagine what is contained therein. The grocer carries everything except *krametsvögel* and church steeples. There will be found: sugar and coffee, tea and chocolate, cheese and eggs, milk and bread, hams and sausages, brushes and brooms, snuff and cigars, kindling wood and soap, cords and firewood, charcoal and coal, radishes and sauerkraut, beets and cucumbers, beans and lentils, whiskey and wine, beer and cider, oil and vinegar, pepper and salt, shoe polish and onions, starch and toothpowder, butter and washtubs, fats and smoked bloaters, dried apples and turnips, rice and sliced pears, plums and juniper berries, herrings and salted meats, onion cookies and leeks, potatoes and horseradish, honey and Cologne pipes, polishing powder and bricks for the cook stove, mustard and writing paper, candles and thread, needles and dyes, and hundreds of other articles. On his platform are brought together stockings, shoes, cloths, linens—in short anything that a man, who does not wish to live like a Hottentot, might need in his household.

A grocery is, wherever possible, located on a corner, and, in the more thickly settled districts of the cities, there are always four groceries on the corners where two streets cross. A corner shop is visible from all sides and he is no fool who chooses such a place.

The grocer is no fool. True, he was only a poor bumpkin at home, watching the swine, chasing the geese. He lived off rye bread and smoked bacon, dressed in ragged castoffs and in a twenty-year-old leather jacket. He went to school as little as possible, having no time for it, and learned enough reading and writing to be able to scrawl his signature and to spell out the words in the Bible. He grew up wild, without culture, knowledge, or understanding, not even by hearsay. But one thing he did learn, an essential for America, how to reckon. And even that he learned not in school, but at home. His mother was accustomed during her pregnancy to repeat a long multiplication table instead of paternosters, and so stamped it into him from the start. He had only to fall back on this memory to master the whole art of counting without teachers of method.

He understood also one thing more, worth as much as his facility in reckoning—to do without.

When the high German comes to New York, his first call is for good food and drink. He must make up for the long sea voyage. The south German soaks himself in wine and lager, the north German in whiskey and beer. But the low German drinks nothing. He drags the last morsel of bacon rind from his pocket and gnaws upon it until the pangs of hunger pass. Then he is on his way to seek out his uncle, cousin, godfather, whomever he knows who has written him to come and sent the passage money, that is, just enough to get him across the cheapest class of the cheapest boat, on the cheapest Liverpool route. Naturally, this relative has a grocery, and the newcomer is well received, gets a tumbler-full of whiskey and a great slab of bacon. After a half-hour he is at home and is shown what he has to do.

Naturally, the uncle, cousin, or godfather has not sent the money out of pure love of kin. He has his own ends in mind, and the newcomer, now obligated, must work off the loan like Jacob who served his seven hard years for Leah. The relative is busy, his shop prospers and he himself must frequently be out in the markets. He must hire a clerk, that is, a person who unites in himself the functions of bookkeeper, salesman, and apprentice. But if he hires one who is already broken in, then he must pay at least twelve dollars a month, together with warm clothes, a room in which to sleep, and meals. That is too high. So he writes to this dear relative at home, that is, to the swineherd, and makes a virtue of the necessity. He will educate the lad, sends him passage money, and thereby he helps himself. Two birds with one stone!

In four weeks the young man is trained and must then serve a year for four dollars a month. There alone is a net saving of ninety-six dollars a year. And not only that. Don't believe that the foreigner will demand his own room. God forbid! Every evening when the store closes he takes out his sack of straw, throws it in a corner, and is off to sleep as well as anyone in his bed. And don't think that the grocer's wife will take the trouble to cook a warm meal every afternoon. She also serves in the store and has no maid, that costs too much, so half the week they are satisfied with smoked fish, and half with bacon and ham, and when that is too high, with eggs. The clerk is, however, satisfied with everything, for he is learning the business and saving.

The low German strips off the marks of foreignness in a short time. After a single year he is no longer green, and no one can discern how short a time he has been in the country. In that respect he profits from his occupation and his language. To the shop of his cousin or uncle come all sorts of people, men of all nations, south Germans, north Germans, Jews, Irish, Americans, English. The grocer serves all alike, that is, he takes from all their money, and that the young newcomer learns right quickly. Presbyterian or Methodist, Catholic or Protestant, Unitarian or Mormon, Atheist or Jew, it is all one to him. Their money is the thing. And then, he learns the language so quickly. Not that he has any particular linguistic talents, not that any scraps of Latin or French he may have picked up earlier are of any use, but low German is already half English, they sound alike and many words are identical. A good percentage of English words are derived from the low German. And then, there is the daily contact with English-speaking people, which serves the young German even better than the young Jew.

After two years the young peasant lad has become a proper clerk; that is, he speaks English well and understands the business from top to bottom. His pay has climbed from four to eight dollars a month, and it is now time to look for a better position. His relative actually helps him look about and he ends up in the place of another German where things operate on a larger scale. The cousin, uncle, or godfather does not lose thereby, for he simply imports another lad who starts at four dollars a month.

After four years it occurs to the clerk to set up in business for himself. He has saved up a hundred or two hundred dollars and found a friend who has as much again. One fine Sunday, the two are off to see the grocer with whom they served their apprenticeship. The grocer notices what is up at once. The back room, behind the shop, is opened and a flask of good old brandy loosens tongues. The two have learned that the grocer has opened a new enterprise or that he contemplates investing in a wholesale house, and they have come to purchase his store. Naturally the few hundred dollars are not enough; but the relative will give them credit for the rest, and with the last glass the bargain is sealed. On Monday the new bosses move in, the old moves out. After a few years they have paid off their debts, and in a few more each partner owns his own store.

Such is the way of the world, at least for the low Germans.

The German's greatest vexation is the Sunday law. He must keep his shop closed on that day, but likes to earn his money every day. Nevertheless, he knows how to help himself; every store has its back door, well known to the customers when the front door is closed.

The grocer's greatest joy comes from the sale of liquor. He buys by the gallon at thirty or thirty-six cents and sells by the glass for three, by the half-pint for six cents, a mere matter of 150 to 300 per cent profit. Whether the whiskey is whiskey, or well cut, is still another matter.

A few people are unkind enough to charge that there is something peculiar about his weight and that his gallon measure is a half-pint too short. It may be that here and there a few minor errors creep in. Who is to blame if the scale, with the passage of time, gets off balance, or if the tinsmith puts too little tin into the measures?

Three peculiar characteristics mark off the low German grocer from all other Germans: he cannot tolerate lager, he does not sport a mustache, and he cannot believe that people will not lie when they have the opportunity.

So much for the grocer!

God's sun shines brightly over the whole globe on which we live; men, however, are jealous of the rays which fail to warm their hearts. Would God have created the hills and the trees, the streams and the fields, the light and the flowers, the evening and the morning, the vines and the barley, if he simply wanted to turn the earth into a vale of tears? But those who lead men to God, who impart an understanding of the great all-good Creator and Master, teach that the earth is only a prison and life on it a prison term to which man is sentenced before he attains heavenly bliss! The birds in the air, the beasts in the forest, the fish in the rivers sing and play and sun themselves; they all enjoy their being. Man alone does penance in ashes and sackcloth because God allowed him to be born. That is not the teaching of the Bible, or of nature; it is the lesson of those who propagate the love of God. They are the ones who invented the American Sunday. A fine invention indeed!

If churches were the expression of the piety of a people then the Americans would be the most pious in the world. Here there is no established religion. Every creed is tolerated; the Jew, the heathen, the Moslem, the Catholic, Reformed, Protestant, Unitarian, Episcopalian, Methodist, Presbyterian, Mennonite, Mormon, Quaker, all enjoy the same rights and are free to worship in their own way. Nowhere in the wide world, however, are you more likely to be asked whether you belong to a congregation, and to which. Nowhere in the whole world is more done for the conversion of the heathen, nowhere more Bibles distributed, more money collected for missions. Churches and chapels are legion, and nowhere are they more heavily frequented than in this land of tolerance and freedom.

When the American gets up on Sunday, his first concern is the weather; he must see whether he may go dry-footed to church. But rain or shine, nothing will keep him away from his house of prayer. All week he may think of nothing but defrauding his neighbors, he may do things from which the worst infidel would shrink with disgust, but on Sundays he takes his prayerbook under his arm and is off to church —and with him, his wife and children. Where else on the face of the earth do you find such piety?

But just wander into the church and consider the nature of this piety. Notice the girls dressed in their finery, how they glance sideward at the young men, see the intimate nods, the winks, the signals. Observe the women pompously decked out in crinoline, how they whisper with their neighbors, how they pout, turn up their noses because another woman is even more richly turned out than they. Look at the men, how stiffly they sit, working out the strategy of a coup set for Monday. And listen to the preacher. What does he talk about? Is it of the sweetness of the heavenly manna? No, rather of the earthly manna, of the stinginess and stubbornness of his honorable audience, of the church members who live in abundance, while he, the guardian of their souls, if not left to starve still is not as well-paid as he deserves. Nine times out of ten this is the theme of the sermon. And from what does this condition derive? In the United States the government builds not a single church, pays the salary of not a single minister. The congregation itself does both. And how would it be if the congregation were sluggish in attendance? The preacher is dealing not only with listeners but with customers, for a visit to church costs an admission fee, just as in the theater, unless you have at considerable cost purchased your own pew, money for which also goes to the minister.

Clergymen in America must then defend themselves to the last, like other businessmen; they must meet competition and build up a trade, and it's their own fault if their income is not large enough. Now is it clear why heaven and hell are moved to drive the people to the churches, and why attendance is more common here than anywhere else in the world? It is an element of high fashion and good manners, and woe unto him who takes a stand against manners and fashion. Better to commit a slight forgery than to miss a Sunday in church.

But then, what else could the Americans do on the sacred Sunday? Boredom alone would bring them there! "Six days shalt thou labor and on the seventh shalt thou rest." Reasonable men have understood this to mean that Sunday should be a day for the relaxation of body and soul. The Americans have arranged matters, however, so that the rest of Sunday is the rest of the tomb. And they have enacted laws that make this arrangement compulsory for all.

On Sunday no train moves, except for the most essential official business; no omnibus is in service, no steamer when it possibly can help it. All business places are closed, and restaurants may not open under threat of severe penalties. A gravelike quiet must prevail, says the law, and you may buy neither bread, nor milk, nor cigars, without violating the law. Theaters, bowling alleys, pleasant excursions—God keep you from even dreaming of such things! Be grateful that you are allowed in winter to build a fire and cook a warm supper.

People who make such laws must be half crazy; these Sunday laws are mad enough! Travel in any New England city, in Rhode Island, Massachusetts or Connecticut, in Pennsylvania and New Jersey, indeed anywhere except in New York, Cincinnati, and Saint Louis, everywhere you will find pleasure places closed, restaurants, theaters, shops shut tight, all means of communication halted, all the streets empty, the whole city a cemetery. And what about the country? The farmer rides ten miles to his church, then ten miles home, and sleeps. That is his recreation. A wonderful discovery, the Sunday law! A very peculiar way indeed to serve the Lord! It certainly must amuse the angels above to observe the self-scourging down below.

The pious American sits in his parlor, rocks in his easy chair, his feet spread out before him, and smokes cigar after cigar. Now and then he summons up energy to get to the cabinet and take a good swig out of the brandy bottle; by evening he has put away enough to forget the passage of time. And his wife? She sits across from her husband and also rocks, holding her prayer book upside down, nods her head as if in sleep, and in the evening is overjoyed when a friend of the family appears. And the daughter? These rush also to church in the morning, but particularly are fond of the evening prayer meetings and of walking home with an escort.

This is an American Sunday. On no other day, at no other hour, does the German feel more deeply that he is a stranger in a strange land, and always will remain a foreigner.

The Irishman—well, he is satisfied with his whiskey bottle. He gets it filled on Saturday and, if necessary, can replenish his stock at the apothecary who is, naturally, not closed on Sunday, and who carries rum and brandy, only at a slightly higher price.

But the German, with his love of music and song, with his joy in God's free nature, with his inclination toward companionship and *Gemütlichkeit,* with all his recollections of a Sunday in the old home-land, what has he got? Dear reader, I'll tell you what he has—lonely homesickness. Only one recourse is open to him. He tiptoes across, taps on the back door of a familiar saloon and, if he is known as loyal, not an informer, then the tightly shut door opens to reveal his friends sitting in the gaslight, with the windows tightly sealed so that no ray of light can reach the street, making a good night of it in the middle of the day, and drinking beer besides. "Six days shalt thou labor in the sweat of thy brow, and on the seventh shalt thou drink lager to thine heart's content, but secretly and by theft, like a thief in the night." Thus do the Germans interpret the Sunday law. They've no alternative.

Of course, nothing of this appears in the letters home that persuade other people to come across. There is not a hint that your Sunday's recreation is "stealthily and secretly, mutely, deep in silence, without songs or the clink of glasses, without sunshine or promenade, to drink your high-priced beer."

The Germans have actually often tried to transfer their Sundays to Mondays, but to do so they would have to work on Sunday, and that is not allowed by their masters. It sometimes reaches a point where one goes on a spree Monday morning to get in what is out of reach on Sunday.

But New York is quite different. If the Americans have discovered the Sunday law, the New York Germans have discovered the "Sacred Concert"; God bless the discovery. At the "Sacred Concert" pure church music is performed. The Sunday papers carry long announcements of such concerts in German restaurants. Even the German theater presents a sacred concert. If you go to the theater you will find that the sacred music never gets to be presented. In fact it will seem to you that a comedy is being offered, with perhaps some pleasant music between the acts. And in the restaurants it will sound as if there were Strauss waltzes issuing forth from the trumpets. It may be a little difficult to recognize the church music in the billiard games, the target practice with air guns, the amusing performance of the yodelers, the gymnastic leaps of an acrobat, even the tinkling sounds of the beer glasses. The whole place is thick with people, men and women all sit with full glasses before them, munch on bread and cheese, and do their souls good. This sacred music is certainly worth its twelve-cent admission fee.

Let the American saints grumble over this German Sunday; let them send for the police because the place is open. New York is a cosmopolitan city and will not fall into the hands of the preachers. In any case, the words "Sacred Concert" are enough; church music is allowed on Sundays.

The young Americans increasingly find this kind of church music pleasant, particularly when it flows with beer; and many come around to spend an evening in this manner instead of in the rocking chair with the brandy bottle. They discover that music harmonizes well with lager, and in a decade beer will have effected a revolution against which all the doctrines of the world will not stand. Americans have already discovered that lager, as they call it, not only quenches the thirst without extinguishing understanding, but is actually good for them. They have begun to compare the merits of a German and American Sunday.

"Last Chance! A homestead for a few dollars!"

A homestead! What a beloved word in the ears of an immigrant! The German has left a homestead such as has few equals in the world, cut through by brooks and streams, covered with hills and gently rising elevations, planted with everything necessary for man's needs and pleasures, inhabited by people whose honesty and integrity has become a byword throughout the world. He left this homestead to seek his fortune elsewhere. Whether he went off willingly or unwillingly he cannot get it out of his mind, and the mere mention of the word makes his heart skip a beat.

A homestead! Here is the German, in a far-off land, in the midst of people whose language he understands hardly or not at all, people whose customs and manners are quite different! He is fortunate to find work, shelter, bread, and food, but he now discovers that happiness is

not a matter of food and drink alone, nor even of the amount of money
earned. He understands that there is really only one good fortune in
the world, to feel secure in the midst of one's own kind.

Ah well, now the newspapers call:

> Eigner Herd
> Ist Goldes werth.
> Nur im Kreise deutscher Brüder
> Findest du die Heimath wieder.*

This is the true pith of the matter. The Germans must come together,
even in a distant land. They should build villages together, plant their
own colonies. Then they might enjoy their own language, customs,
manners, together with the material advantages of the new fatherland.
A welcome thought indeed! Call it out again, "Last Chance, a homestead for a few dollars." You will find takers in plenty.

How wonderful it seems to the German to live in his own house on
his own land. How wonderful seems the prospect to plant corn and
potatoes on one's own land among one's own German brothers. How
tempting the whole idea seems. But just nibble at the bait and see how
completely the roof falls in on the cottage dreams have just completed.

Let us examine the farm, land, and lot association a little more
closely. In America many fortunes have been made through land speculation. A man gets hold of a large tract in a region still unsettled and
still uncultivated. The land belongs to the government and its cost is
low. Its value is, however, also low; it will be quite a few years before
the flow of population reaches it. A few will come first, then more will
follow, and at the end cities and villages and prosperous farms will
stand where a decade earlier the Indians wandered and the deer grazed
undisturbed. The German who has been here some time makes a note
of this and reckons he might speculate in a little way as the American
does on a large scale. Soon there gather a small group of like-minded
men who decide to buy a parcel and resell it in smaller lots. The tract,
of course, is not so large as a principality, but is often a good-sized
duchy. They buy everything at second hand, but no matter, they can
resell at a profit so long as there are enough German "brothers" passionately eager to take advantage of the opportunity to establish a home.

* "One's own hearth/Is worth a fortune./Only midst your German brothers/Can
you find a home again."

These philanthropic organizations are either land or building organizations, and some unite the two functions. But the objective, the means, and the results are always the same.

The building association does not need much land; an area of a hundred acres or less is enough. But the land must be near some large city and is therefore rather expensive. Yet one must help himself. The suburbs of American cities will not be so intensively cultivated as those in Europe for a hundred years yet to come. There are stretches full of rocks and sand, property that lies in wet and swampy regions that remains uninhabited and unbuilt upon. Such empty and uncultivated tracts can be had in plenty. No reasonable man thinks of relieving its original owners of such land, which either is inherited from ancestors or thrown in with more valuable property for a blanket price. But the building association thinks of it. It buys the tract, generally for a trifle, or sometimes takes the owner in for a share in the enterprise. Then they proceed to subdivide; that is, to lay the land out in urban building lots, usually 25 by 100 feet. In the city these would cost anywhere from $1,000 to $20,000, here, $20 to $50. Blueprints for the new city are drawn, streets are laid out on paper, sections set aside for schools, churches, restaurants. Now for the sale.

On the whole, the land association operates in the same manner. It buys a large piece of land, 10,000 to 50,000 acres. The tract lies either in the Far West, in a region where no man's foot has yet trod, or better still, in a well-cultivated state, New York, New Jersey, Pennsylvania, Illinois, or Missouri. In the latter places, of course, it is not the best of land, good land calls for a pile of gold. Also no timber stands upon it, for forests fail to grow in sand, on rocks, in swamps. But—is there any higher service to the state and to humanity than to bring under cultivation land that the more knowing American farmer has stubbornly passed by, land that would not have known the plow for another hundred years, had not the association put its hand to it? The land is bought, a small deposit paid, and the rest promised for the time when settlement should develop. Now to lay it out. In the middle a section is reserved for a new city, which is always given a properly German name like Hermann or Germania. The balance is cut up into small parcels of 25 to 40 acres, which receive the respectable title of farms. Soon the plan of the whole colony is ready on paper, and it too is ready to be sold.

Selling is the main thing. What will the association do with its land. Its members will not settle it themselves, they are well off enough in the city where they live. It will build no houses which may never be sold. It will operate no farms from which after many years of effort a straw will come forth. The association can do only one thing: sell. And it will sell, it will even sell were the commodity offered worth less, which in many cases would be impossible.

The first step is to put some well-known names at the head of the association. These must be good German-sounding names, names of men with some weight among their countrymen, names to which perhaps some title carried away from the homeland is attached. If such men are involved in the matter, surely there can be no nigger in the woodpile.

The second step is to appoint as agents people who have a wide acquaintanceship among their fellow countrymen, people who are trusted and have property of their own, who set a good example for others by taking one or two shares of which, according to secret agreements, the association will later relieve them. These agents do not work for nothing, and we must not begrudge them what they get, for they must circulate in all the restaurants and saloons, to put the matter before customers in a good mood. Besides, what harm is there in letting the agent have 25 per cent? Is there not enough left?

The third step, and the most critical, is advertising—and what advertising! Advertisements are very expensive in America, so expensive that six small lines cost a half-dollar. But what has the association to lose if it spends fifty dollars for the insertion of a long article, as long as it draws? And day by day you read such pieces, not simply in one, but in a half-dozen newspapers. These advertisements are enticing. Whoever composes them is no fool, and no doubt allows himself to be well-paid for his work, since the masters of the association are not so familiar with the pen as to venture into print themselves. In the advertisement the location is set forth, the land described, and the subsoil minerals referred to. True, no railroad yet passes through the tract, but one shortly will, and then the produce will be disposed of at high prices. Wood, springs, and rivers stocked with fish are not lacking. As a matter of fact, a few houses are already up, a few farms are being worked, and the school and inn already exist. "There is still time for a few hundred dollars to get possession of a parcel the like of which no farmer in Germany has bigger or better; take advantage, countrymen, before it is too late."

Even more impressive are the descriptions of the building lots near the cities. "Oh, how expensive it is to live in the city! How constricting it is to live in the midst of mad crowds! And what fine homes you can buy for payments of seven or eight dollars a month. Then buy a building site in this newly established suburb, so near that you can reach the heart of town for a few cents daily. The site costs practically nothing, a cottage on it only a few hundred dollars. Then you have a home all for yourselves, with a garden in back, that will supply you with your own food. Then you will live like human beings; and not simply among any men, but among your own German brothers."

It is a real pleasure to read these announcements. There is no choice but to agree! And how easily the payments are arranged. Five or six dollars down, and the balance in monthly installments. The very poorest can manage it, and in a few years become debt-free freeholders. Yes, the association knows its business. Everyone has the same opportunity because it wishes to make everyone happy. Of course, if one skips a single monthly payment, or is unable to pay, then everything paid in is lost. The association takes back the share and sells it to someone else. There must be a system to everything.

As soon as a certain number of lots or farms are sold, then the lottery proceeds; that is, the sites are distributed by drawing lots. Naturally, a corner is worth more than a site in the middle of the block and a dry plot is preferred to one in a swamp. But what's the difference! Let those who draw lucky lots rejoice; in a few years they too will sing another tune.

And often it doesn't even take that long.

The workingman has, with his hard-earned savings, bought a building lot or farm. He has scraped along, plagued himself until the monthly installments are paid off. Now he owns his place free and clear. But what will he do in his cottage. He must journey to the city to work or to deliver work made up at home, and the passage back and forth costs him more in a year than would a residence in the city. And what can he do with a farm? The plot is too small, the soil too poor, the sediment too heavy to make a living from it. And where will he find the cash to buy cattle and tools? The farmer's life is the most wonderful life in the world when he starts with a substantial piece of land, with cattle enough, and roads good enough to bring his products to market. But this way . . .

A few years ago, the good man was impatient to get into the association; now he is impatient to sell. And sell he must, unless he has other resources or is willing to operate at a loss each year. But who will buy from him? Around New York are hundreds, thousands of lots and houses in German settlements available at one-half or one-third their original price. No one buys since they are not worth more than an eighth. And it is everywhere the same. The poor man will be wisest to abandon his few acres; then he will simply lose his investment. In a hundred years when speculation drives prices higher and higher, it will be necessary to use even those places which are now too sterile to be farmed without great expense. When the cities spread out a few dozen miles more even those building lots will have some value which are now bought only by fools or innocents.

In America people know how to console themselves. Once having sunk his own money into the venture, each man schemes to trap others; but once gone, the money is gone for good, for the members of the association have it deep in their pockets. True, the agents got some, and the "President" for the use of his good name. Also advertising costs run heavy, and the plans, well-drawn on fine paper, were also a source of expense. But the 100 acres of stone and swamp from which the building lots sprang, 16 to an acre, cost only $1,000 in all. And the 16,000 lots at $50 brought in a total of $80,000. Out of a profit of $79,000 there is room for expenses. Those 50,000 acres of sand, and swamp, and woodland set aside for the farms, cost $100,000, that is, twice its true worth, since it was bought not for cash, but on credit. But the 50,000 acres yielded 2,000 farms at $200 each, or $400,000 in all. And a profit of $300,000 leaves plenty of margin for maneuver.

Dear reader, you now know what to expect when you meet the announcement, "Last chance, a homestead for a few dollars." Americans generally now know too, and only the "green"—that is, the newly arrived, those who remain eternally green—let themselves be lured.

A farm and lot association finds itself in an unpleasant predicament when a newspaper exposes its swindle. But the advertisements of the association bring in a great deal of money and the papers keep quiet. One hand washes the other.

Sapienti sat, says the Roman.

19.

BENJAMIN II

Israel Joseph Benjamin, born in Falticeni, Rumania, in 1818, spent the early part of his life as a timber merchant. In 1845 he conceived the notion of traveling through the world to visit the scattered Jewish communities, after the model of the medieval Spanish wanderer, Benjamin of Tudela. Benjamin the Second, as he called himself, journeyed through North Africa, the Near East, and China, and composed a widely read account of his peregrinations. A decade later, he decided to visit the New World; and described his travels in a two-volume work called Drei Jahre in Amerika 1859–1862 (1862). *Two years after its publication, Benjamin died in London.*

The first and highest of the peremptory demands that religion and duty make upon every man of Israel is to give his children a good education, to prepare them for life, and to put into their hands the means for making their own way. The American schools furnish a guarantee of one aspect of this duty. But there is cause for concern that the provision, wisely made, to exclude therefrom all religion and the study of the Holy Scriptures, leaves the daughters of Israel much neglected.

Jewish boys are, in the course of events, taken care of in religion, as are the sons and daughters of the Christians; they either attend a Jewish school or receive private instruction. But the case of the girls is quite different. In what a sad condition is the religious preparation of the future Jewish wives and mothers! How little they learn of their duties toward God and men! What do they know of the commandments which bind them as daughters of Israel? Should not those who are bound by the holiest religious duties be soundly prepared to fulfill them? These duties are numerous and heavy and one is astonished that not half the American Jewesses of the future are ready to take worthily and to fill properly the places in life appointed to them. Yet that is far too true.

The causes lie in neglect of their education. To illustrate this contention and to corroborate its truth it will be worth while to sketch the kind of schooling that American Jewish ladies now receive.

The mother of a daughter, any good-hearted, passably wealthy woman, seeks to impress upon the immature minds of her children as much good as she can. This private influence lasts until about the age of five. Then the child, it is clear, must go to a public school, or what seems more respectable, to a so-called "Institute." In the latter establishment the child begins a normal course of study, makes the acquaintance of friends of other religious persuasions, and may without shock and without meaning kneel down in the mornings at the opening of the school during the prayers offered by scholars of other religions.

After school, she prepares her lessons for the next day or plays as all children do. On going to bed or on getting up she may say a Hebrew or English prayer with her mother, but she learns little and knows nothing of what Judaism means. So the education of the girl continues until she is fifteen, except for the slight difference that in time she leaves the institute and goes to a high school or "college." At fifteen begins a new period in her life. At her birthday her mother and father have promised she will be free, she leaves school, graduates to her great joy.

What useful knowledge has she acquired in all this time? All in all, very little! She has passed ten precious years of her life in contact with all sorts of books, but has made little progress; the time is wasted, and generally forever. What she has acquired is of no use to her. She does not understand the use of the needle, has no knowledge of housework, and even less of higher things. Ask who created her, who clothes her, who gives her daily bread; she may give the proper answer, but more likely will say, "I did not learn that in my books."

During the ten years her good parents have increased their wealth and form the praiseworthy resolution that their daughter should not forget everything she learned. To complete her education they engage a music teacher, a singing teacher, a drawing teacher, a governess who will provide instruction in French, and also in sewing and weaving. To cap it all, they add a teacher who will furnish a Hebrew education and who will introduce her to the alphabet of a language in which she should, even as a child, have been lisping the name of God. The maiden, as might be expected, finds this last in the line of instructors irksome. The language seems silly, and also too difficult. She cries at her lessons, so that her indulgent parents, who suffer at her tears, give notice to the teacher who should have been the first engaged and the last dismissed. They have, however, out of a deficiency of true religious feeling, blundered onto the opposite path; they hire him last and let him go first.

Having in this manner completed her religious education, the young woman goes on much as before, saying the few prayers she learned as a child from her mother in English. If she occasionally visits the synagogue, she uses a prayer book in the same language. The remaining teachers soon earn the same dismissal as the Hebrew teacher. The maiden becomes capricious through the parties, balls, and soirees which now absorb her attention; her mind is distracted, she is hungry for the praise of the young men, and has no thoughts for learning. The young lady—she no longer lets herself be called a girl—believes that her education is complete in all branches and considers herself prepared to take her place in the world, prepared to make a man happy and to become a Jewish mother. I must also note that this is but one instance among a thousand that occur in this country with only slight variations.

Who is to blame for this altogether neglected education, the heedless girl or the overindulgent parents? I believe neither the maiden nor the parents are responsible. The former is like any other child; the latter do everything in their power to give their daughter the best possible education. They spend their wealth, their energy, their time, even their lives to make possible the highest attainable training, and they convince themselves without a doubt that they are successful. To their great distress they soon, but too late, become aware of their errors.

I blame neither the young woman, nor her parents. Rather the responsibility rests upon all the members of the whole Jewish community which as a body should, as is the case in England, France, and Germany, meet a general need and establish a Jewish school for boys and girls.

Having spoken about the education of Jewish women I would like to make a few comments on the training of Jewish young men, which is, alas, scarcely any better. The Jewish boy is sent to school from the age of six to sixteen, and learns to read, to write, and to reckon. No father has, however, spirit enough to indulge in a measure of scientific education or to allow his son to attain a higher education. As soon as the boy has a minimum of learning he is taken into the business, naturally without having attended a commercial school, since that is not necessary; the techniques of trade consist entirely of practical, mechanical exercises for making money. With facility in that line he soon earns the title of an educated man.

Only in the larger places has there recently been any concern with religious education and with knowledge of the Hebrew language. From all this it is sufficiently clear that no great learned men will spring up from among the American Jews. It is particularly notable that Jewish children very quickly find themselves at home in the American element. It is significant that they speak with their parents neither in German nor in Hebrew, but only in English and will answer only in that tongue, no matter in what language they are addressed. And so they adhere entirely to the American ways.

America worships two idols. First is that deaf, dumb, blind Mammon before whom the masses humbly bow in this land. They kneel before him, setting their honor aside, day and night thinking only of amassing wealth, of building palaces. The second idol, on the contrary, sees, hears, walks, and talks, and is above all full of life; it is the female sex. Both idols live together in constant warfare. What one builds, the other tears down; what one accumulates, the other scatters; what one makes good, the other spoils.

The reign of the women is here complete. Unbelievable as it may sound, even in the courts the word of a woman of the lowest classes is given more credence than that of the most respectable man. I was told in New York that this legal situation was a few years ago carried so far that girls who took a fancy to a man they saw in the street would learn his name, address, and condition and go to court with the complaint that he had made a promise of marriage and failed to keep it. The men were then compelled to be married, against their wills, without the slightest consideration of the consequences of such a forced union. When married women no longer enjoy their passions, their love of dress, their idleness, and the other conditions under which they live, they leave their husbands and take no notice even of their children. Such incidents are almost a matter of course. They make daily reading matter in the American newspapers.

Let us examine more closely these women who are capable of perpetrating such evils. The American women have fine and gentle features, are very delicately built, and know better than any others in the world the art of adorning themselves. They are very bright in conversation, always vivacious, and passionately love music, singing, and dancing. Their education is poor and they have little understanding of how to raise children. Many, in fact, do not wish to have any children at all, out of fear of losing their beauty, and not infrequently resort to any remedy. A New York physician asked me whether the wicked custom still existed in the Orient by which women take a certain medicine to prevent pregnancy. There is also a reference in the Talmud to women who take a preparation in order to remain childless. An American doctor could surely earn a million dollars in a single year dispensing this concoction. I informed my questioner that I had made no observations on this subject but would not fail to note it on my next trip.

The women have a characteristic, innate, and ineradicable aversion to any work and to household affairs. They love sweets and delicacies to a degree that there are nowhere in the world so many dentists as here, and all make a good living. They are indispensable because the unbounded taste for sweets rots the teeth, so that artificial ones must take the place of the natural. What is more, many ladies allow whole rows of teeth to be extracted, as I myself saw, in order to replace them with prettier ones. And though this is known and should frighten the other sex away, yet their beauty and enticements still allure men with irresistible force.

Of love, the salt of the earth, these females know nothing. Let the man only have money enough to indulge them in luxuries, then he is good enough for a husband, be he old or young, handsome or plain, religious or atheist. Let the money vanish, and with it will go faith and love. I might mention here an interpretation of a passage in the Talmud. We know that Eve, who ate and got her husband to eat the apple that brought mortality with it, was created from Adam's rib while he was asleep. Now the Talmud tells us that "when God decided to create man, he took a bit of earth from every part of the world and thereof fashioned man." Surely the rib, from which woman was created, must have originated in American soil and therefore had sensuality inherent in it. While Adam was poor and unable to satisfy her taste for luxuries, life was a burden to her and she sought to do away with herself, and with him; or, alternatively, she gave him the apple out of jealousy so that he should not take up with another woman. Such instances are not rare, in America at least.

I sought the source of woman's position here, and believe that it lies in the circumstance that, at the first peopling of America, there were so few females that a man counted it a great fortune to find a woman. He had little choice and was compelled to overlook her weaknesses and deficiencies, married her more often than not like an idol. Though there is now by no means a shortage of women, this attitude is well established.

Before us lies a little pamphlet, a speech made in New York by a lady on America and the destiny which, she says, "the Spirits" have prepared for it. The idea finds credence, and people stream from all quarters to listen to the inspirations of the Spirits commanded by the lady. This single incident characterizes the American spirit; it is deplorable that such a gross swindle should find admirers and adherents amongst a people whom Morse and Mitchell in their geography call most enlightened. How can one be angry with the witchcraft, the manias, and the other superstitious incidents pursued by humanity from time immemorial when the most enlightened people raises up in its midst Mormons, Millerites, and similar abnormalities! Why speak of the delusions of the Middle Ages when we saw with our own eyes the most enlightened nation flock to the prophetess of this superstition. And one may be sure that a fraud will find more believers, supporters, and participants, the bigger, the sillier, and the more absurd it is.

The calm and dispassionate observer might, in the face of such manifestations, have doubts as to the soundness of human understanding and come close to thinking that the world will easily be inherited by villains and swindlers. It is hard to say this, but it must be said. He is no true friend who only smiles at his neighbor and gilds the flaws in his character. And he is no true friend of the American people who enhances and supports the self-complacency and the self-deception from which the Americans suffer. The author of these lines loves this land and its people as his own and chooses it by a free choice. He may be allowed to speak freely, for what he says comes not from a passion for finding fault.

First of all, the claim to be the most enlightened of peoples is a kind of self-deception. In this land there is not a single seat of learning that could be compared with such minor universities as those of Padua, Jena, Göttingen, or Halle, to say nothing of the great institutions in England, France, in Berlin, St. Petersburg, and Vienna. This is one of the most certain criteria of learning. Enlightenment is not a plant that grows of itself, that springs spontaneously from the soil without care and attention; it is rather a blossom that never unfolds without the supporting hands of man.

From what sources could exceptionally enlightened principles, practices, or doctrines have been fashioned here? Like electricity, enlightenment must have conductors to spread broadly through the community; the best conductors are the schools and the press. The American public schools are scarcely two decades old and still suffer from the deficiencies which normally retard new institutions. The shallowness of the colleges, academies, and seminaries is commonly known. Young ladies study astronomy before they know how to spell properly; young men attain the doctorate after they rush through a mixed-up mass of Greek, Latin, mathematics, French, German, natural philosophy, chemistry, history, geography, logic, mental and moral philosophy, and still other subjects, in two or three years without ever having mastered one of them. Tailors, shoemakers, farmers, shop assistants become physicians in thirty-two weeks; policemen, watchmen, constables all of a sudden become attorneys. Any man who feels in himself the capacity for becoming a preacher, teacher, politician, statesman, or diplomat soon finds himself a sphere of activity. The whole ridiculous superficiality is yet not by far so clumsy and disgusting as the pedantry of the half-educated teachers and pedagogues who kill the spirit with words and formulae. Can we then see here a soil to nurture the most enlightened of people? The schools are still too young and the colleges too immature.

The press is likewise not strong enough. This field is dominated by the absence of principles, by the concern with making money only, and by a superficiality that makes pictures and other devices conceal its shortcomings. Here, too, other nations have a great advantage. There is no journal in the United States that is worthy of being placed beside the press of London, or the French and German periodicals. Here every kind of trash finds in the press some defender and patron, if only it will pay well enough. The result is that the newspaper is not always a beacon of light for the community, not always the honest and true chronicler of daily history, not the torch of progress and learning, but often simply a speculative enterprise in the hands of profit-seeking parties who only publish that which will do them the most good. One will seek in vain for earnestness or love of the truth, and more easily come upon articles that simply excite sensations, upon bombastic words and immoral announcements. The press is not here the mistress but too often only the pitiful servant of the people, gathering up the crumbs of news that fall from the richly laden table of humanity. Such a press could not and can not lift a people to the highest levels of enlightenment.

Nor will contemporary literature do so. With the exception of a few old names there are no sparkling intellects or radiating geniuses in the arts. But we will be countered in defense of the country with the assertion, "It is the freedom for which our fathers bled and died, it is the constitution and the laws which our wise ancestors left us which make us the most enlightened people." More properly they should say, "which should have made us." Truly, such examples should have inspired a quite different spirit. The constitution and institutions only show that the fathers of the republic were very enlightened. But what is the status now of the constitution, in theory and practice? We must remain silent. Where is the constitution? Where is our liberty? We ask often but get no answers.

The firmest and most imposing structure of state that yet was erected by human hands on the solid basis of political and religious liberty, personal and civic freedom, is now threatened by a crash brought about by its own sons.

Its present shortcomings arise from no organic defects in the government of the United States, but rather from a rotting element of demagoguery which is found in many lands. The current position of the United States and the misfortunes that befell it, blow by blow, at the beginning of this war, encouraged its enemies to slander its constitution and derogate its institutions.

This war began through the abuse of freedom and wealth, just as a man may kill himself through overindulgence and immoderation. This abuse of the unlimited wealth of the land and of freedom took two forms, materialism and the neglect of learning. As quickly as our steamboats cut through the sea and as quickly as our locomotives fly across the western plains, even more quickly do we rush into materialism and ignorance. To make money now has a magnetic, a magic attraction. Public officials accept offices, and others long for them, simply to enrich themselves. They set themselves no more honorable objective; no purer motive moves them. The good of the commonwealth concerns them not at all. There are, of course, exceptions; honor and the public good are the stars that guide a few, but for the overwhelming mass it is money that serves that function. Have ever so many traitors among officials been discovered as here in the past few months of political squabbling? The reason is clear. Treachery is more profitable than loyalty; and he who is faithful only for the sake of gold is easily drawn into a betrayal when the tempter has a longer purse. Wealth is the key to respect, honor, and esteem.

Almost every man is therefore constrained to become a merchant, a banker, a speculator, or a manufacturer, to secure a position that will bring a sizable income. The child learns from his father, the pupil from his teacher, the scholar from his professor, that gold commands a mighty power in every circle of society. Cupidity enters the bloodstream at the expense of every gentler, better, and higher feeling, and is nourished with sacrifices of spiritual capacities and happiness. Thousands give up their health and their lives in the service of Mammon.

In consequence of this general overwhelming passion, the human spirit is altogether repressed; the determination, from childhood on, to make money, deforms the beauty of nature, the pleasantness of humane education, the truth of science, the loftiness of art, the holiness of religion, of morality, of truth, of honor, of duty. Everything is pushed to the background, takes a subordinate role. This is the center from which our demoralization proceeds. Why should the number of dishonest officials and of traitors seem remarkable? They travel the same road as all the others; they also make gold like the others and do not differentiate themselves from the crowd.

Here lies the source of the disease; this is truly the cancerous growth. The spirit of the American people is troubled by an illness that must arouse the liveliest apprehensions, an illness that ought not to be found in a constitutional state. The result is that now, after fifty years as a going concern, often brilliantly, the United States stands at the brink of the precipice and runs the risk of a fall unless a man appears who will help with advice and deeds.

We come now to the second point mentioned above, the place of learning. This too, like all else, is only the slavish handmaid of passions which are only worked up by the pursuit of wealth. Learning is not loved for its own sake; it is not resorted to as a sun to light up the way; it is rather another article of commerce. There are shops where professional politicians make up politics, and priest factories which deal in religion. The position of a professor, of a scholar, a thinker, a rabbi, or a preacher is thought of as his business. We have no time to do anything for ourselves and demand that our fellow men should earn money just as we do. We rejoice, when for our comfort they manufacture in advance shoes, boots, clothing, hats, also medicine, magnetic pills, galvanic circuits, health, morals, religion, truth, or any other commodity. For that reason, produce any absurdity whatsoever, if it is ridiculous enough to create a stir in this country it will be believed. Delusions, quackery, shams, ridiculous and childish superstitions each makes a profit and, as a matter of course, lasts a certain time, until it must make room for some other, from Barnum on down to the fortunetellers, from Dr. Townsend's Sarsaparilla to the various stomach bitters, from John Smith and Miller down to Mr. Lederer of New York. We are so often deceived because we wish to be deceived.

Under such conditions science cannot thrive. Where these are the prevailing conditions, they lead to the following conclusion: Everyman knows everything and is capable of doing anything. Circumstances teach here any man knows everything and can set himself to any job without studying it and without previous experience. In this country we come across a professor who allowed himself to become a bookbinder and bookdealer, that is to say a good husband. His life's task was unsuccessful. Instead of applying himself to science to develop and further to educate himself, he was compelled, like all those around him, to make money after his fashion. We meet a professional astronomer, distinguished in his subject, but who must occupy himself with civil engineering. Most fortunate are many doctors who never learned very much but give themselves over to boasting and swaggering and who do not miscalculate in doing so. Quacks and frauds have the greatest influence and are almost every place the arbiters of the spirit. Everyone must concede that learning still stands here at a very low point.

The students have no time to concern themselves for long with serious studies, they must hurry right through. But in the rush there can be no thorough mastery of any subject.

There is no trick to being a captain, so long as the sea is quiet, but when a storm blows up the experienced seaman begins to take precautions. As long as freedom and unity reigned undisturbed over the American ship of state, every man was good enough and competent to hold office; but now, at the first serious storm, the consequences emerge of the simple-minded system by which every man knows and is capable of everything. Yet the trial through which we must now pass will show us how small we are in our overblown pride, will teach us that there are higher and more important interests than gold and luxury. So long as it is the highest aim of each individual to amass goods and possessions, so long will that also be the highest aim of a nation which, after all, is made up of individuals.

Some of the general causes having been sketched above, it is now time to say something of the more particular elements. The weaknesses of a community must in large measure be reflected in the school, the church, and the state, the institutions with the greatest influence upon the members of the community.

The press has more than once revealed the fact that the public schools are only hothouses for memory, calculation, craftiness, and indifferent minds, and leave untouched and altogether uncultivated the higher capacities of youth, the noble impulses and lofty ideals of young hearts.

After a child's love of learning, his aptitude for reflection, and his independent thinking have been thoroughly stifled by several years of eternally deadening spelling, he is crammed full of a mass of names, from geography, history, and grammar. These remain only words, are never understood, never take on flesh and blood meanings. The child absorbs nothing but words. For assistance he has the textbook, which the poor student must learn without comprehending. The mind is in this manner exercised and overtaxed for six or eight years at the expense of the higher intellectual capacities, and nine times out of ten the scholar forgets, since it is all absorbed without reflection, in one year what he has learned in six.

Arithmetic also belongs in the class of studies of dead words. Here, too, in most cases there is only an exercise of the capacity to remember.

Even in the most fortunate cases when it is properly learned with a plan and system to develop ideas, it then develops simply the capacity for cold, earnest, and sly calculation that is by no means natural or educational for the young spirit.

What is left now for the moral aptitudes of youth which also should be fostered, and what is done for that? Nothing. They earn not even a glance in education. In this case, externals reflect the internal conditions; and the site and structure of the schoolhouse characterize the spirit of the school. We see schoolhouses on a plot of land on which no blade of grass, no tree sprouts, while in Europe on most of the land around the building luxuriant flowers and plants flourish, and in the larger cities exceptional sums are spent on gardens, to aid in learning botany, more particularly pomiculture and gardening, and to awaken a feeling for nature. In American schools there is not the least idea taught about living nature; everything presented to the student is dead and deadening. He is offered only words and more words, and gloomy calculations which are alien to nature, which do not suit the moral feelings, and which have no regard for the thousand beauties of God's creation, or for the honorable impulses which rest in the breasts of men and live in the figures of history. Under such conditions does the student leave the public schools and enter into the general stream of life.

Let us now glance at the few exceptional cases—very few, in comparison with the number who attend the elementary schools—who go on to the academies, the seminaries, high schools, colleges, or however else the facilities for higher education may be entitled.

We begin with the young ladies who are expected to learn Latin, Greek, and mathematics, subjects which are not included in our first part. No greater perversion of nature is conceivable! The young woman whose every nerve is sensitive, whose heart is full of gentle emotions, in whom the admiration of the good and the beautiful is innate, must fix in her memory mathematical formulae and the paradigms of Latin and Greek which she will forget within a year after having graduated with honors. Similarly with history; here there is no effort by the instructor to demonstrate the connections of cause and effect, to demonstrate the wisdom of Providence or cautiously to use it as a model for life. The teacher simply says, "You must learn ten pages for the next assignment," and so the poor creatures overload their minds without deriving the least profit from their torments.

A few mechanically learn music (piano), drawing, and painting, but the principles of aesthetics with their very intimate consequences for feminine feelings are altogether neglected. Others get to the study of natural philosophy and chemistry, but without instruments or laboratory. They investigate astronomy without observatories, learn botany in the winter in their rooms, and study the crystallization of snow and ice in the summer; the conception of uniting studies with nature itself and with its manifestations seems to occur to no one.

Let us now turn to the institutions for young men, in which we discover precisely the same deficiencies, joined to a superficiality that comes from the neglect of the older and newer classics. Of all the branches of knowledge, only mathematics is truly studied.

No one learns in the schools how to study by himself; the great goal toward which all the reading is aimed is to pass examinations. The human is thus alienated both from art and nature; all is judged by its immediate utility.

The consequence is that we meet among educated men so much egotism, so little interest in the public welfare and concern for private good. A gentleman, to whom I once expressed my astonishment at the number of perjuries and public frauds, remarked to me, "Not all are infected, not all are corrupt, only those, unbelievable as it may sound, who are well educated; we get fresh men from the common mass." There is a creeping disease here which must be healed from the roots unless this republic be brought ever nearer decay.

Religion has always shown itself the forerunner of civilization and humanism. The blessings of religion which render each individual perfectly happy and give the community a secure existence are so numerous that even the worst of religions is better than none.

The practical result of religion must be good morality, the elevation of the whole man. The sacred revelations teach man what is good, right, just, and what is not; and the main objective of the synagogue, church, or mosque is encompassed in these revelations. To awaken in the soul the germs of good, to repress the lower passions and make of man a useful link in the human community, that is their goal.

Is that goal being reached in the United States?

One goes to whatever church one wishes, when, and as often as one wishes. You will find many denominations, but little religion; much dogma, and little belief. The attempt is rarely made to preach and develop the principles of the right and the good; everyone is as active as possible peddling separate dogmas. Seldom do they choose as text for their sermons, honesty, righteousness, uprightness, truth, the sacredness of promises and of oaths, chastity, obedience to parents and teachers, or thankfulness. Nothing of all that is heard. They preach as the spirit moves them, what one should or should not believe to reach salvation according to their own pattern. The child learns from the start, from his mother, from the minister, from the Sunday school, a religious lesson that cannot excite or enthuse him: "Pray and read the Bible," or, "Learn a catechism by heart." Religious education consists of such lessons. He comes to church and listens to singing which he cannot understand, then he hears from the pulpit how bad and corrupt man is. He is not strengthened or stimulated. He does not gain confidence in himself and in his Creator, but instead is depressed and loses even the last remnant of self-assurance.

That the constitution of the United States is one of the best instruments yet devised by man to govern a nation is testified to by the rise and happy position of the people governed by it during the past seventy years, especially since the expressed will of the majority was realized through it. The conclusive evidence is supplied in the proceedings of the seceding states. Their representatives found no basis for altering any important provision of the constitution, but had only the intention of improving that instrument so that it would better meet the needs and conditions of the times, at least according to their ideas. This constitution was put to a rigid test, and to the satisfaction of all parties came out of the assaying pot, pure gold. The basis of public life is then healthy and the source of the disorders of which the community complains does not lie in the forms of the structure. This community which scarcely has a history of its own, which is compounded of people of diverse nationalities in diverse phases of development, must not be compared with European communities. Its unlimited freedom encourages desires which leave no room for the ideal life, and the drive for self-improvement and for material profits must, for the time being, be the only goal of its striving. Before any improvement there will first have to come the slow formation of a class, secure in position and interested in public life, an aristocratic core, ultimately able to lead the masses.

In practice we now meet in government the following influences: the officeholders in the various branches, the seekers after office, the professional politicians, the influential gentry who buy votes, the demagogues with or without principles, the press, and the orators. Up to now the most reprehensible corruption has been uncovered among the officials of government. The reason is that before a man secures a public office he must pass through all the shades of corruption. Using even the most ignoble means, he must make himself popular through intrigue, through deals with ward politicians and with the influential men, and so show that he is fitted for the post. When the time comes to vote he must understand, under every condition, how to turn truth into falsehood and give falsehood every appearance of truthfulness. These are facts; what is most to be wondered at is that the government officials are not even worse than they are.

A poor man can, furthermore, be elected to no office, and the wealthy must spend freely before they can hope to be nominated or elected. It follows naturally that once a candidate has attained his office he must act to reimburse himself. The people cannot complain thereof, after having stripped him to his shirt; it itself teaches him, forces him to put his power to good account.

To these evils are added the fact that no official of the government is responsible to the people; most are rather under the control of one of the executive departments, which in turn are responsible to the party which put them in office, and not to the people that it must serve. "What will the party say? What impression will this make on the party?"—these are generally the ruling questions. Since the officials are not responsible to the people they are not concerned with the opinions of those who do not belong to their party. When they are accused of an irregularity they receive the support of the party members, while the press serves anyone who hires it.

There is no question of capability. Second- and third-rate attorneys and merchants who have failed are good and capable enough to govern a country, although they cannot keep their own affairs in order.

A fundamental deficiency of America is the lack of influence of any public opinion. There is really nothing but party spirit. Almost every man is harnessed to some party wagon, and although he may not be aware of it, he must draw along the place seekers who ride in it. Moral sentiments are not strong enough to condemn men who are guilty of crimes against the republic. Let a man steal thousands or millions, rob widows and orphans of their all, yet if he becomes wealthy he will everywhere be accepted as a respectable personage.

When corruption spreads for several years down to the people from above, there can no longer be any morality in politics. When the moral powers are again strengthened in the nation, and Mammon lays down his scepter, everything will return to good order.

20.

GEOLOGY BRINGS AN ITALIAN

Giovanni Capellini (born 1833) was professor of geology at the universities of Bologna and Genoa. He was an early exponent of Darwinian ideas, did significant work as a paleontologist, and was instrumental in establishing the discipline of prehistoric archaeology. His journal, Ricordi di un viaggio scientifico nell' America *(1867) was the product of a scientific exploration in the western United States in 1863.*

I must take this occasion to say a word of the commodiousness and other advantages of the railroads in America, which I could well observe on my trip from Chicago westward. The possibility of covering long distances by rail in the United States under unfavorable climatic conditions depends on the use of materials and devices much superior to those that serve in Italy. The front of the locomotive is furnished with an apparatus capable of removing not only the little stones, but any objects that may obstruct the roadbed, especially animals and plants torn away from the sides. At the rear is a little glassed-in compartment designed to protect the engineer against the elements.

The cars are about fifteen meters long, and very large. They are supported on eight wheels combined into two units on which the cars may easily negotiate the sharpest curves. At each end, at the level of the floor of the car, is a vestibule, and before it is a little platform by which one may pass from wagon to wagon or descend to the level of the station by means of two or three steps. Every car is divided by an aisle in the middle. The seats, no more than thirty in number, are arranged transversely and accommodate two each, so that the car can hold sixty people. There are, moreover, two lavatories, served with cold water and in the winter sufficient heat. Illumination is by gas.

In all trains there is no lack of vendors of papers and books for the journey, as well as of fruits and tobacco. There is a special coach for smoking, and others are set aside as restaurant and sleeping cars. The brakes are on the platform and not inconveniently hidden. Consequently, the guards can attend to their duties and still, in case of need, be prepared to give help to the travelers in the various cars. A little cable runs along the side of the train and puts the guards in direct communication with the engineer. Meanwhile, a conductor passes from one end to the other to make sure everything is in good order.

From Burlington we went back as far as Galesburg to catch the railroad which leads to Quincy and ultimately to St. Joseph on the Missouri River. We were compelled to wait several hours for a train at the junction before we could be on our way. Galesburg is 42 miles from Burlington and 100 from Quincy. From the latter point to St. Joseph is another 205 miles. This route ran through a stretch of land that for some time had been disputed by Federal and Confederate troops, and that was often infested with guerrillas, as the presence of numerous military posts along the railroad gave notice. The soldiers were there to defend and protect the bridges, since it was principally by destroying those that the guerrillas disrupted the flow of trains and then, at their ease, robbed and murdered the passengers.

The small number of passengers on the train from Quincy to St. Joseph, and the fact that almost all were armed with revolvers, excited my curiosity. Tactfully making some inquiries, I learned that the guerrillas had several days earlier committed a series of raids and robberies along this stretch of track. The place where the train had been halted was pointed out to me and several of the scenes described, although I like to suppose the stories erred on the side of exaggeration.

Pursuing my investigations in St. Joseph, I decided to make a tour through some of the hills near the city, which are in large part covered with flowery vegetation. Needing a guide, I thought it advisable to engage the services of a wagon, for in that manner it would be possible to save much time. But to our great surprise, after having traveled a few kilometers, the coachman stopped and refused to go on for fear that his courage might cost him his horses if not more. There would be no resisting the guerrillas, if they found us. Our protests did not change his mind, and we had to agree to return. We then passed through a stretch of land dotted with well-kept brick houses in the midst of cultivated fields. We gathered that the farmers here were well-to-do and no longer concerned with further emigration in quest of still greater riches.

With these sections of land where agriculture already is mastered, there alternate others, covered with woods, across which the axe has never yet blazed a trail. Thousands of bushes and low herbacious plants reach well until the ends of the forest. There follow a quick succession of nut and plane trees, of oaks of various kinds, of poplars, of maples, and some lindens. The areas that were clear of high-trunked trees were filled with filberts, delight of the squirrels, and with diverse liana and vines, interwoven in a thousand forms not permitting even the most daring to penetrate.

The railroad lines end at St. Joseph, and those who wish to go on to the northwest must change over to the steamboats which go up the river, some to the very foot of the Rockies, most to Omaha or Sioux City. In the absence of the railroad, the personal security of the traveler shrinks, the more so since the region through which we were about to journey is infested not only with guerrillas, but also with Indians, especially the Sioux who, for several months, have been at war against the United States.

Being destitute of arms, I was advised to add a revolver to my equipment, since no citizen, no matter how alien to his mind aggressive acts may be, goes about unarmed, not only in traveling, but even in moving about in the city.

St. Joseph was then almost under a state of siege, martial law having been proclaimed in all Missouri and in Nebraska. Contrary to the custom of the other countries, men were permitted to carry arms, but not to sell or buy them. I therefore had to present myself to the military authorities and secure a permit to acquire a revolver and the ammunition for it. The commandant to whom I applied was a certain Bassett. Two mounted guards, ragged and unarmed, were at the foot of the staircase that led up to the military headquarters. In the middle of the office was Mr. Bassett, stretched out on a stool with his feet extending onto the desk on which a bottle of whiskey kept company with an inkstand and a human skull. The last-named object was shaped like a well and designed to serve as a glass, not for drinking purposes, at least not at the moment, but to hold sand.

To finish this description of the commandant of St. Joseph in September 1863, I must add that in the end he proved to be a very fine man. Having lost the first permit for ammunition, I convinced him that I had no hostile intentions and merely wished to replenish my supplies; he granted me a new permit without the slightest comment.

Going through St. Joseph I noticed several streets that were almost deserted; the houses fallen into ruin, not through time but defaced and dilapidated through vindictive hands, were like an eloquent page in the sad story of civil discord. St. Joseph for some time found itself on the boundary of the two parts of the United States. It was not therefore surprising if the city was divided into different parties and if those who at first suffered the insults of the initial victors, when favored by turn of fortunes, made the weight of their vengeance felt on the property of their adversaries. The latter, forewarned of the danger, succeeded in large part in flying for salvation. The most prosperous left the city, which saw a goodly quantity of its riches transported elsewhere to build up new centers which soon will end by surpassing it.

While we stayed at the Patee House waiting for the time of our departure for Omaha, we had the opportunity to become acquainted with some officials and to discuss with them the unusual conditions in which their country found itself. One of them, a pleasant and likeable person, seemed to me very preoccupied, and since I knew that he had traveled in Europe, curiosity led me to pay particular notice to his story.

The brave young man then told me how he was at first unable to come out in favor either of the Union or the Confederacy. When the war first broke out he went to Europe. His family, stricken in their most vital interests, decided to support the southern states to which they belonged, and his father and brothers enlisted under the rebel banner. Meanwhile, my acquaintance, visiting Europe, became persuaded that no humane person could avoid being an abolitionist. His mind full of these ideas, he returned to his country resolved to fight for the Union. Perhaps he hoped to convert his family. But everyone else had already chosen the other side; none was disposed to change his mind. He joined the ranks of the volunteers, and he assured me that twice already a malignant fate had thrust him into combat with certain enemy columns among which he knew were found those he held dearest on earth. Understanding then completely his gloom, and not finding words to comfort him, I shook his hand and he left me with a sigh without desiring as much as to learn my name. Scarcely thirty years old, he had already reached the rank of colonel. But what honors can possibly bring him joy?

In the neighborhood of St. Joseph, the Missouri takes a very tortuous course which together with the sand banks and the snags makes navigation very difficult at the end of the summer. Snags are branches of great trees torn out along the banks and carried along by the floods until they get covered with sand and remain fixed with their heads extended at an acute angle in the direction of the current. These branches are generally either oak or cottonwood trees, which abound along the shores of the river. Such difficulties are characteristic of the Missouri. The maneuvers they make necessary, and the savage and deserted aspect of the place, together made a setting so strange and new for me that I almost found this kind of travel funny. But I was surprised at night to see the fires in the engines extinguished while the boat was brought close to shore and secured to the trunk of a poplar. I then fell into a more somber frame of mind, since I realized we would not travel in the night, and with the delays imposed while evading the snags, it would probably take twice the three days in which we were assured we would reach Omaha City, which was to be our first halting place.

The quantity of wood, which can be had at a very good price along the banks of the Missouri, makes that the desirable fuel for the steamboats that move from St. Joseph to Sioux City. But that fact was increasingly wearisome for the travelers, since at least twice every day a brief stop was made to secure the logs, generally cottonwood.

On the twenty-seventh of September we arrived at Council Bluffs on the left bank of the river, almost opposite Omaha City. We had by now been seven days on board ship, and since much remained to be done to complete our project it is not surprising that we were exceedingly impatient to get swiftly to our destination. The sun was close to setting, the ship had much cargo to discharge in Council Bluffs, and it was obvious that we would not leave for Omaha, which was scarcely a few short miles away, until late at night or perhaps not until the next day. While we waited uncertainly, a coachman persuaded my companion that we could reach Omaha in a couple of hours by passing through Council Bluffs; and although I had little faith in so roseate a promise, I resolved to follow my friend who resolutely wished to abandon the boat.

In the twinkling of an eye we were on shore with our baggage. But we had scarcely gone a few kilometers when the driver tried to persuade us that it would be desirable to pass the night in Council Bluffs, assuring us that we would arrive too late for the ferryboat. Here it is necessary to note that the coachman was right, but he had been wrong in the importunate argument that led us to follow him. Now we did not wish to be the butt of the sarcasm of the other passengers who would be sure to taunt us when we arrived much later than the boat.

Night fell shortly, as we followed, across the forest, the trail of a road that was to lead to the shore of the river near the ferryboat. Alas, by the time we arrived, that had made its last crossing for the day. Our complaints were futile, and we were compelled to resign ourselves to an effort to cross the river higher up, where the coachman assured us we would easily find a boat. While my friend and the driver advanced to explore the ground, I remained to guard the baggage. Apart from all other inconveniences, we also lacked torches. Unexpectedly, an individual drew near, out of the forest, and advanced to ask me where we were going at so late an hour. I confess that before learning his intentions I had put my hand to my revolver; but this gracious gentleman was lost like us, and wishing to find some means of getting to Council Bluffs simply wanted to inquire if we were on our way back there.

The explorers returned with the pleasant news that they perceived a little light on the opposite shore, where they thought the cottage of the boatman must be. Taking with us the lost wayfarer, we advanced in that direction. What a consolation to discern a glimmer when all about us was deep darkness! We yelled, shouted, swore, until a human voice reëchoed from the other shore and we saw the light move in assurance that we had been heard. A few minutes later something seemed to advance out of the shadows in the river, then we heard the beat of the oars, and finally we made out a boat, at least half of which was occupied by the man who rowed it.

This means of crossing appeared at first sight useless, and it did not seem the less so when the boatman told us that his craft could only carry one person and one trunk at a time. As a result, the operation was long drawn-out and dangerous. My companion passed first, then the bags, and finally I went across in the little wooden bark which in its last trip seemed nearer to sinking than previously.

The coachman settled our accounts and turned back to Council Bluffs. But once carried to the other side of the river near the cottage of our boatman, who was also a trader in boards, we were still some miles from Omaha, and had no means of going on without some sort of wagon.

Our rescuer offered to go himself to the village and bring back what was needed, and in the meantime we were invited to enter his humble home where we found his wife preparing supper for four lively children, pretty as four roses. The accent with which she spoke revealed that she was not American, and not even of English origin; indeed, she told us a little later how she had emigrated from Germany with her whole family, and after having been married had already several times changed her residence. The little wooden house had one story divided into two compartments, one of which served as kitchen, dining-room, drawing-room, pantry, and study. Nearby was the woodworking store in which was contained the whole fortune of her husband. She assured us that they were doing marvelously well, that in a short time they had been able to save a considerable sum, and that before long they hoped to be able to give up these temporary quarters.

In order not to annoy us, she presented us with a newspaper in which the little shop of her husband was spoken of. When we seemed very surprised to find a newspaper in such a cottage, the lady assured us that they would rather deny themselves many other things than newspapers. That fact explains why there is not a village in America, no matter how small, in which there is not a printing press and a newspaperman, who ordinarily thrives and often is the most secure and authoritative person to whom all others turn for information. Finally a wagon came; we paid several dollars to compensate the good boatman, and toward eleven at night finally reached the hotel in Omaha. There, with great hardship, we were able to secure a room, which, to tell the truth, was more than modest.

Part Three

URBAN AMERICA

Urban America

THE YEARS OF PEACE WERE AT FIRST PREOCCUPIED WITH THE RESIDUAL problems of the years of war. Yet it soon became clear that while the nation's attention was fixed elsewhere, newer issues were rendering anachronistic the old questions of reconstruction and slavery, of political unification and states' rights.

In the last three decades of the nineteenth century factory production came to dominate the American economy. Industrialism had a long history in the United States, but now it came of age and took on a distinctive form. Factories moved by power, particularly by the power of steam, stimulated the exploitation of enormous new reserves of coal. At the same time new sources of energy, petroleum and electricity, only tapped for the present, revealed their limitless potentialities for the future. Industry became increasingly mechanized. Steel played a part in production far more prominent than earlier; the output rose from 68,000 long tons in 1870 to 26,000,000 in 1910.

The new scale of industry called for heavier outlays and greater investments of fixed funds, management of which involved a new role for the corporation, the concentration of industrial controls, and the development of the banker as manipulator of capital. Manufacturing and its attendant processes also depended upon a large proletariat, upon a fluid labor force fed by the ever-mounting tides of immigration. Meanwhile, the integration of the internal markets matched the pace of industrial progress. The construction of improved roads, of trolley and rapid-transit lines knit together the local units, while the completion of the great railway systems (the 52,000 miles of 1870 had become 240,000 in 1910) bound the nation together as an economic entity.

All these changes were linked to the phenomenal development of the city. Steadily and rapidly the American economy fell into a new configuration, at the center of which lay the new metropolis. The cities grew in size and in number, and their influence permeated the rest of the nation. The agricultural regions, under the attraction of urban markets, felt a far closer tie to the fluctuations of the industrial economy. The fields became tributary extensions of the factories, and cultural forces from the city began to reshape farming as a way of life.

These tumultuous changes left behind them a host of problems that perplexed the citizens who lived through the last years of the nineteenth century. The purely physical difficulties of housing a population that rose in forty years from 38,000,000 to 91,000,000, of bringing into being the bare facilities for decent existence, were alone staggering. But there were other complexities, more subtle, but not less troubling consequences of the transformation of American society.

For a vast working force threatened with unemployment and successive depressions, and for farmers and small proprietors menaced by incalculable changes, insecurity generated a questioning spirit that attacked the presumptions of politics which now seemed unrelated to realities. The accumulation of monstrous fortunes created a society of the new rich, uncertain of itself, blindly seeking a way to justify its own position, sometimes even simply a way to spend its time. The injection into American life of immigrants of many origins raised questions as to the meaning of Americanization and led some to seek artificial security in isolation. Meanwhile, the end of the old frontiers, real or apparent, induced a few people to look for new areas into which to expand beyond the borders of the North American continent.

The gravity of these inescapable problems intensified the earnestness of those who wrestled with them, who hoped through reforms, great and small, to rectify the weaknesses of society in the United States. There was serious thought over how to shift the emphasis in religion away from narrow doctrinal matters to broader social concerns; the temperance movement touched on a wide range of human questions; and the organizations of working people focused their efforts on the general well-being of the whole society. The men of the time were not always aware of the true nature of the difficulties involved in the transition to the new society; nor did they achieve unanimity as to the means for resolving them. But no one could escape the consciousness of the enormous strain upon the human beings whose lives were now moving to the rhythm of the inhuman machine.

Yet over this whole period loomed the unparalleled abundance of goods. From the workshops of the New World and from its virgin farms came a surging flow of products that daily became available to more and more people. In this material abundance was the justification of the human difficulties that were the cost of creating the new industrial society. In the mountains of commodities never before accessible to the great masses of humanity were the rewards for the trials of creation, the promise of American life. All that was needed was knowledge of how to use the goods, of how to bring the promise to realization.

21.

A HAPSBURG DIPLOMAT

The Baron von Hübner (1811–1892), Austrian career diplomat, served as ambassador in Paris and in Rome between 1849 and 1868. He then took a leisurely trip around the world, which he wrote up in a charming two-volume work, Promenade autour du monde, *1871 (1873). After his return he settled in Vienna, and, in 1879, became a prominent conservative member of the Reichsrat. After the manner of his class, he used French as his literary vehicle.*

New York in its outward aspect reflects in a very remarkable manner the characteristics of the whole Union. One might say that the intellectual, moral, and commercial life of the American people is here condensed, to spread its rays afterwards across the immense tracts which are called the United States.

Broadway is the representative and the model of those great arteries which bind together the different portions of this great continent from ocean to ocean. The great thoroughfares of London, the boulevards of Paris, the Ringstrasse and other great streets of Vienna, are as busy and as animated perhaps as Broadway; but their animation springs from the needs and the commerce of their respective cities. But this great artery of the American metropolis is more than a street; it is a royal road leading everywhere. Certainly New York is a great capital in the European sense of the word. But it is also more than that; it is at the same time an enormous railway station, a depot, to use an American term, both of travelers and goods, where one meets a floating population large enough to give the impression of that agitation and preoccupation and that provisional state of things which is the characteristic of all the great American cities. To sum up, Broadway represents the principle of mobility.

Let us pass on to Wall Street, the center of all great financial operations. Here the resemblance with the city of London is incontestable; the buildings are nearly all banks; and the jostling crowds, the very air one breathes smell of millions! Yet even here the analogy with Europe is not complete. I will quote but one of a thousand little indications of difference. A banker will not pay you even the smallest sum at once. He sets the telegraph to work, and after a few minutes the money is brought to you from the public bank where the funds of his particular house are deposited. Nothing can be more praiseworthy than this practice, for these banks are real fortresses, to break into which would be impossible.

Now we are on Fifth Avenue, and consequently far from the industrial quarter. Here the eye rejoices in the contemplation of all the luxury that money can bring. Do not let us be hypercritical or examine too closely the artistic taste of these pretentious buildings, which seem to parade their magnificence in pompous architecture. After all, the identical meretricious taste has spread to Europe. The Belgravia of London, the Ringstrasse of Vienna are both examples of the same style.

But what struck me most in New York is the enormous number of public buildings consecrated to divine worship. I speak not of the great Gothic cathedral which the Irish are now building, and which belongs to another date and another order of ideas, but of the innumerable little churches belonging to the different sects, built very often at great cost and with a profusion of ornament in every possible and impossible style, which attracts the attention and piques the curiosity. In Europe, the massive pile of the cathedral, and the belfries, spires, towers, and high roofs of the other churches, stand out against the sky, tower above the houses of the faithful and, seen from a distance, give to each town a particular character. In New York it is quite the reverse. Seen from the river or from Jersey City this huge metropolis is a great mass of red, grey, or yellowish brick. At most, one or two steeples rise above the roofs, which from far seem all of the same height, one long horizontal line stretching toward the plain beyond. Europeans landing for the first time cannot help wondering how two or three churches can possibly suffice for upwards of a million Christians! They learn their mistake when they walk through the town, especially along Fifth Avenue where the commercial fever is at rest, or, at any rate, gives way to a little quiet, to study, and perhaps to meditation and prayer.

Not that all those little chapels impress one with a feeling of sanctity or fill the mind with that grave spirit of recollection which comes over one in the aisles of our great cathedrals. Far from it! The *sanctitas loci* is entirely wanting in this worldly quarter. These little buildings, each consecrated to a different form of worship, are only accessories to the whole. They are only open during their respective services on Sundays. But there they are, and however poor they may be they prove that religion persists in the hearts of these rich people, who had perhaps little or no time to think of the soul when they were making their fortunes, but now that they are millionaires begin to remember that they have one.

In a society of which the most energetic, the most important, and the youngest portion lives in a perpetual millrace, it is evident that spiritual or inner life must be stifled. Indeed, it seems dead; but it is not. From time to time there is an extraordinary awakening. Enormous sums are then given for the construction of new churches; and in revivals, great meetings in the forests and prairies of the Far West, a sudden thirst for spiritual consolation bursts out among the masses like an epidemic of extraordinary violence, producing the most fantastic scenes, now tragic, now comic. These are only different manifestations of the same spirit—the spirit of faith, kept down, but not exterminated by the worship of the Golden Calf, which is the religion of the state, the only apparent religion, of the merchant, the miner, the carrier, the porter—in a word, of the fortune hunters of young America.

When we turn our steps to the West the look of our fellow travelers gradually changes. Bankers with their clerks, elegantly dressed ladies from Boston, Philadelphia, or Baltimore, officials from Washington, all those people in fact, whose cosmopolitan aspects remind one of their like in Europe, disappear from the scene. They are replaced by a lot of men, mostly young, bearded, ill-dressed, not overclean, armed with one or sometimes two revolvers and wearing round their waists great coarse woolen bags, generally empty when they start for the Far West and as commonly full of gold on their return. There are also a number of farmers of a less equivocal appearance and draymen who go to the banks of the Missouri, at Leavenworth and Kansas City, to rejoin the caravans confided to their care. These men are important personages in their way. The intrepidity, the perseverance, the habit of command (if it were only of bullock-drivers conducting their teams) and exuberance of health, a certain brutal strength, and a strong sense of their own value, are all marked on faces reddened with whiskey and with exposure to the burning winds of New Mexico and Arizona. The merchandise they convey to Santa Fe, Prescott, San Diego, Lower California, or by the Paso-del-norte to Chihuahua, is worth many millions. They take three, four, or five months to reach their destination and brave every hardship and danger, from Indians and desert monsters to the dreary snowdrifts of the higher levels and the terrible passage of the canyons.

I was advised at New York to provide myself with letters of introduction to the landlords of the different hotels and to the station masters of the places where I meant to stop. In a previous journey I had already discovered the advantage of such a precaution. The train arrives at a little town where you mean to sleep. At the inn, behind a long bench, stands a gentleman of grave and majestic air. The travelers are all arranged in a single file before him. Ladies are served first and taken to fine apartments on the first and second stories; under their wings pass, likewise, their husbands, or brothers, or anyone who has the privilege of being their masculine escorts. But single men are ruthlessly sent up to the garrets. My turn comes at last, and I present myself with my letter of introduction, given to me by the master of the hotel where I had slept the night before. The Minos of the place reads it rapidly, looks at me for a moment with a cold but keen glance, then passes me over and sends my fellow travelers to the aerial regions. When everyone has been provided for, I find myself alone, face to face with this important personage, who turns toward me, his countenance visibly brightening. He presses my hand warmly and smiling graciously says, "Now for us two, Baron. You wish a good room, Baron. Very well, Baron, you shall have one." And he gives me the best room he has.

Here I cannot help making an observation which has been made hundreds of times before. The American has a thirst for equality, but a mania for titles. Those who can lay claim to the dignity of governor, senator, colonel, general—and their name is legion—are always accosted by their title, and never by their name. As to titles of nobility, the forbidden fruit of republican America, those are pronounced with a sort of voluptuous pleasure. By analogy, I might cite also the naïve pride of those old families which descend from the first Dutch emigrants, the English Puritans, or the French Huguenots. I never made the acquaintance of any one of these men or women who did not say to me, immediately after my introduction: "I am of a very old family. My ancestors arrived in this country two hundred years ago. My cousins have a seat in the House of Lords"; or else, "We descend from Hugue-nots—men well known in the court of France before the revocation of the Edict of Nantes." And these very persons, who begin by proclaiming their genealogy, are generally the most distinguished by their polished manners and first-rate education. These anomalies, however strange they may seem to us, are to be explained, I think, less by motives of vanity than by the essence of human nature, which cannot exist without variety and repudiates the notion of equality.

On the railroads, too, I found my letters of introduction invaluable, especially when traveling alone. The stationmaster begins the acquaintance by shaking my hand, calling me "Baron" half a dozen times, and introduces me to the conductor of the train. Then comes a fresh exchange of civilities. The conductor gives me my title, and I call him "Mister." In the Far West, they call one another, not "sir" but "Mister," without adding the name; for no one has the time to inquire, or it is forgotten as soon as told. If you are a white man and an American that is enough; that constitutes your superiority over the wild man of the desert, over the red man of the prairie, over all the other nations of the earth. It is the species to which you belong which they consider, not the individual. You are then "Mister," which means "Master"— master of creation. After being duly presented to the guard there is one more formality, equally important: to be introduced to the colored porter. In this case, with a due consideration for the shade of skin, there is no shaking of hands. In spite of emancipation we have not yet arrived at that!

When night comes on the passengers prepare to try to get some sleep. In the sleeping cars the armchairs are rapidly transformed into beds, separated from one another by boards. Each window allows for two beds, one on top of the other, unless the traveler has taken a section; that is, the whole space of one window. Under the shelter of the heavy curtain men and women put on their night things, in the interests of cleanliness pin a handkerchief over the pillow provided by the authorities, lie down on or scramble up to their beds, and strive to sleep, in spite of the noise, the shaking, the dust, the stifling atmosphere, and the nauseous smell of this most infernal dormitory.

In Chicago I alight at the Sherman House, one of the great American hotels. Thanks to my letter of introduction, the gentleman at the office is most courteous and gives me a charming room on the first floor, with a bathroom alongside. The water cocks are as usual stopped up; but the Negro servant promises to have them fixed for me. In the meantime I stroll about the streets. The heat is intolerable and the first sight of Chicago is not encouraging to an idle man. It is closing time in the shops and factories. Streams of workmen—men, women, shop boys, merchants of all kinds—pass me on foot, in omnibuses, in trams, all going in the same direction, that is, all making their way to their little homes outside the town proper. All look sad, preoccupied, and worn out with fatigue.

The streets are like all others in America. The houses are built of wood, but in imitation of brick and stone. Clouds of coal smoke issue from innumerable factory chimneys, accumulate in the streets, throw dark shadows on the brilliant shop fronts and on the gorgeous gold letters of the advertisements which cover the façades up to the garrets. The soot seems to stifle the crowds, who, with bent heads, measured steps, and arms swinging like the pendulum of a clock, fly in silence from the spots in which they have labored all day long in the sweat of their brows. In all the great thoroughfares, as far as one can see, rise the gigantic telegraph poles, placed quite close to one another, and topped by a double bishop's cross—the only kind of cross seen in this city of which the God is money.

I mix with the crowd, which drags me on with it. I strive to read the faces I pass, and everywhere meet the same expression. Every man is in a hurry, if only to get a few minutes sooner to his home to make the most of the few hours of rest, after having expended the largest possible amount of work in the long hours of labor. Everyone seems to dread a rival in his neighbor. The crowd is the embodiment of isolation. The moral atmosphere is not charity but rivalry.

In my room I light the gas with some difficulty and prepare my bath. Unfortunately, no sooner do I plunge into the tepid water than the gas goes out; it escapes through the jet, which had unfortunately been left open and fills my whole room with a horribly mephitic smell. I rush out of my bath to stop the mischief, and in so doing displace the cock. My matches are useless, for my hands are wet. I turn off the gas and try to find my way back to the bath in the dark. But alas, in the meantime the water has all run out. And there I am, without a light, without a bath, without my clothes, and with no possibility of finding the bell. Besides, was an American servant ever known to answer one!

The moral of this little misadventure is, that one must learn everything, even how to use those thousand practical, ingenious inventions which constitute "comfort" in American hotels, and which have for their object to reduce the number of servants to a minimum, and to make the traveler independent by placing within his reach mechanical processes which enable him to shift for himself. He is waited upon at dinner, and they will clean his room and his boots; but they "calculate" that he will brush his own clothes and "guess" he will understand the gas cocks and the hot and cold water apparatus.

Into the pavement, all along the principal streets of Chicago and of other towns of the West, are sunk strong iron rings for fastening the horses. It is a way of doing without grooms or coachmen. To spare a man's strength and time, and to get out of both as much as can be—this is essentially the American maxim. Before this inexorable theory, all false shame, human respect, and the prejudices which in the Old World exclude the higher and middle classes from manual labor entirely disappear.

The lower classes gain the most by this system, for at a low cost it places at everyone's disposal the material and intellectual enjoyments which raise the moral tone, and which in Europe are the privilege only of the upper strata of society. So, when the European immigrant, sprung from the dregs of the people and arrived at a state of ease and prosperity here, returns to his native country, he is miserable and comes back to America as soon as he can. I met some Italian peddlers once in the Pacific States. They had just returned from Turin. One of them said to me: "There are upwards of four hundred of us in Nevada and California, all more or less doing well. Twenty-four, with their boxes full of gold, returned a short time ago to their native village. But only three could stand the life there; the others came back to California. This is easily explained. You see, in Europe we can't associate with the gentry and we can't live with our equals above whom we have unconsciously raised ourselves. We feel therefore like fish out of water, and so we give up the dream of living in our native land and return to America."

Chicago, which only dates from 1855, now contains 300,000 inhab-

itants. Built on a marsh, it was at first horribly unhealthy, an evil reme-
died by raising the houses on piles without moving the inhabitants.
Some houses were transported bodily from one end of the town to the
other. Two branches of commerce contribute to the riches of this town.
It has become the great emporium of the grain of Minnesota and Wisconsin, and the market where all the population of the western states
come to supply themselves with dry goods of all sorts. By water and
rail, wheat arrives in incredible quantities. Here the inexhaustible
granaries of the neighboring states become objects of speculation, are
bought and sold, stored up in warehouses, and shipped at the favorable
moment, either on the lake boats or on the railroad. The mechanical
appliances which facilitate these operations, and the lifts and winches
whereby these huge stores are conveyed are the pride, and contribute
to the riches of the inhabitants.

Retail trade with innumerable peddlers who come here to buy the
contents of their packs, is another source of prosperity, and one for
which Cincinnati and St. Louis were long rivals. Today, however, the
superiority of Chicago is assured and firmly established from the
geographical position of the town.

In the West the towns are quickly seen, and are all alike. One may
say the same of the hotels which play so great a part here, not only
in the life of travelers, but in those of the residents. A great number of
families, especially newly married couples, live in hotels. This method
saves expenses and the bother of housekeeping; it also makes easy the
frequent moves from one town to another. But it has the inconvenience
of condemning the young wife to a life of idleness and solitude. All day
long the husband is at his office. He comes in only at mealtimes, and
then devours his food with the silence and dispatch of a starving man.
Then he rushes back to his treadmill.

The children are sent to school when they are five or six years old.
They go by themselves, and pass the rest of their day exactly as they
please, no one thinking it right to interfere with their liberty. Paternal
authority is nil, or at any rate is never exercised. There is no education
in our sense of the word; but there is instruction, public, good, and
accessible to all. The little gentlemen talk loudly, and are as proud and
sharp as the full-grown men of their nation. The young girls at eight
and nine years old excel in the arts of coquetry and flirtation, and
promise to become "fast" young ladies; but nevertheless they make

good and faithful wives. If their husband should be rich, they will help him ruin himself by extravagance in dress; yet they will accept misery calmly, and the moment there is a change in the wheel of fortune fly into the same follies as of old.

The home of the English, so dear to their hearts, is only a secondary consideration in the lives of their cousins beyond the seas. This is easily explained. In the New World man is born to conquer. Life is a perpetual struggle, a rivalry from which no one can exempt himself, a race in the open field across terrible obstacles, with the prospect of enormous rewards for reaching the goal. The American cannot keep his arms folded. He must embark on something, and once embarked he must go on and on forever; for if he stops, those who follow him would crush him under their feet. His life is one long campaign, a succession of never-ending fights, marches, and countermarches. In such a militant existence, what place is left for the sweetness, the repose, the intimacy of home or its joys? Is he happy? Judging by his tired, sad, exhausted, anxious, and often delicate and unhealthy appearance, one would be inclined to doubt it. Such an excess of uninterrupted labor cannot be good for any man.

The woman suffers most from this regime. She sees her husband at most for half an hour once in the day, and then in the evening, when, worn out with fatigue, he comes home to sleep. She cannot lighten his burden or share his anxiety and cares, for she knows nothing of his business; for want of time, there is little or no interchange of thought between them. As a mother, her share in the education of her children is of the smallest. As soon as her little ones can run alone they pass their lives away from her, out of the house. They are entirely ignorant of the obedience or respect due their parents but, on the other hand, learn early to do without care or protection, to be self-sufficient. They ripen quickly, and prepare themselves from their tenderest years for the fatigues and struggles of the overexciting, harsh, adventurous life which awaits them.

Besides all this, a woman boarding at one of these huge caravanseries has not even the resource and occupation which ordinary domestic details involve. Is it as a compensation for these privations that American society surrounds her with privileges and attentions unknown in the Old World? Everywhere she is the object of a respectful gallantry, which might be called chivalric were it less frivolous, and sometimes even grotesque and ridiculous. For example, I am sitting in one of these tram cars which cross all the principal streets of the great towns. A tap of a parasol or a fan rouses me from my meditations. I see standing right in front of me a young woman, who looks at me from head to foot with an imperious, haughty, even angry expression. I wake up to the situation and hasten to give her my seat, which she takes at once, without deigning to thank me, even by a look or a smile. The consequence is that I am obliged to perform the rest of my journey standing in a most uncomfortable position, and to hold on by a leather strap which is fastened for that purpose along the roof of the carriage.

On the other hand, it is the fashion to disparage American women. People call them frivolous, flirtatious, extravagant, and say that they are always running after pleasure. These accusations seem to me unjust. The American woman bears the stamp of her position and of the atmosphere around her. As a young girl she naturally follows the inclinations of her sex which are not, as with us, regulated and controlled by the teaching and example of a mother. She wishes to please, and if she is naturally lively she will become "fast"; that is, she will laugh loudly and by smart repartee and piquant looks will endeavor to attract the greatest possible number of young men. But this vulgar coquetry, however jarring to good taste, rarely goes beyond a certain point. There is always a father, a brother, or an uncle near by, armed with revolver or bowie knife, who is quite ready to ask you, with every imaginable politeness, if your intentions be fair and honorable.

Married women in America are, as a rule, unexceptionable. If they are too fond of dress, it is generally their husbands who wish it. If they are often seen abroad, it is because they have nothing to do at home. If they are rather free and easy, such manners are allowed in society; it is, after all, bad taste—not sin. Their minds are generally well cultivated, for they read a great deal, mostly novels, but also English classic authors and encyclopedias. And they attend the public lectures and literary conversations held in all the great towns of the Union.

In Salt Lake City, I turn my steps toward Main Street, and find myself in a regular city of the Far West. Here there are no trees. Houses line each side of the street, the greater portion built of brick, or rather of adobe. The more modern buildings have some pretension to architecture. In all, the first floor consists of open shops. The walls are, without exception, covered from top to bottom with gaudy advertisements. The streets are thronged with bullock wagons and carriages of every description. A stagecoach drawn by ten horses, belonging to Wells Fargo and Company, draws a crowd and increases the confusion. Formerly these coaches were the only resource of the impatient traveler; but they have nearly disappeared since the railroad opened. Porters, miners on foot or on donkeys—in a word, a whole body of strong, intelligent-looking men, with tanned weather-beaten faces and brawny arms, whose life is one continual fight with savage nature, and who are justly termed the pioneers of civilization—jostle one another in the crowded thoroughfares.

In the forenoon, "old" Townsend, the innkeeper, took me to see the Tabernacle. This is a long low hall, entirely bare and destitute of religious emblems, with a raised dais at one end, on which are the armchairs of the prophet and bishops, the whole being covered by a heavy oval cupola. Alongside they are building a new temple, which is to be an immense edifice of cut stone in the Roman style. But only the foundations are as yet laid; and no one hopes or seems to wish for its completion. There are scarcely any men at work on it, for both money and fervor are wanting.

The theater is far more popular. This is one of Brigham Young's thousand schemes, and the great resource of the inhabitants of Salt Lake City. It is open almost every night. The house is badly decorated, and still worse lit. In the pit I saw groups of children, who had evidently come all alone. On benches and in the galleries sat a number of men in blouses, each with two or three wives dressed with a certain amount of care. The offering, a sensational drama which had a great run in England some years ago and is full of English habits and institutions, contrasted singularly with the public of the New Jerusalem. Nevertheless, the play was listened to with great attention, although there was neither laughter nor clapping. Brigham Young, who is himself the censor and excludes all indecent pieces, is very anxious to encourage people to go to his theater. It is in his hands a kind of school of art, whereby he strives to refine the habits of a society which has been reduced by circumstances to a condition of perpetual forced labor.

Brigham Young is the keystone of the Mormon enterprise. To have conceived the migration, to have carried it out, with the loss of a great number of men, it is true, but without shaking the faith or confidence of a single one of the survivors, is a historical fact which would suffice to immortalize the name of any man, whether he be king, captain, or prophet.

Brigham Young unites in himself these three qualities. As prophet, though taking good care not to utter any prophecies, he rules over men's consciences; as sovereign, he exercises his power without the slightest check; as general, he has organized so large and respectable a militia that the central government hesitates to force this potentate to respect the law of the land.

The first three years after the exodus were very trying ones. George Smith, the historian, told me that he and his wife, as in fact everybody else, were reduced to half the food necessary for the support of animal life. For many weeks they lived entirely upon roots.

The work of preaching among the gentiles was then taken up with renewed fervor. But they did not make any proselytes except in England and Wales, in Australia, and, in a lesser degree, in Scandinavia. Brigham Young always chose his emissaries by inspiration. He has often accosted perfect strangers in the street, and by a sudden inspiration given them apostolic missions to Europe, Australia, or to the islands of the South Seas. The men thus summoned leave wife, children, and business, and start out.

The Mormon missionaries never attempt to preach to the rich, or even to those who are tolerably well off. Nor will they go near an educated man. Their proselytes are always the poorest and the most ignorant. The recruits spring either from those who have been born in misery or who have fallen into it from their own faults or the fault of circumstances, men who have nothing to lose, and who can only gain by being dragged out of the moral and physical degradation in which they exist.

It is quite impossible that *doctrine alone* should touch people's hearts, strike their imaginations, and attract from the worst quarters of London, from the dockyards of Liverpool, from the agricultural population of Wales, the three- or four-thousand converts who arrive every year. The converts are simply men who find themselves in a state of utter destitution and want to get out of it. If Brigham Young's missioners had nothing more to offer than a continuation in another world (with a God who is like themselves) of an existence as miserable as that which has fallen to their lot here, the proselytes would not accept the Mormon teaching with such eagerness. They would at once turn their backs on the missioners.

But the envoys tell them more than that. After having promised, as all religions do, eternal felicity in a future state, they offer what no other religion does, a most brilliant prospect even in this lower world. On the single condition of moderate work they guarantee the converts the enjoyment of all the good things to which the heart of man can aspire.

How are such poor fellows to resist these brilliant promises without the restraining force of strong Christian convictions which they have not got? Besides, no sooner have they indicated their adhesion than Brigham Young's bankers at once advance to them the money necessary for the voyage. At New York they receive a pass and letters for the whole of their journey, and, unlike the majority of other immigrants, they are sure to find help and protection at the different stations of their itinerary.

Once arrived, the bishops and elders procure work for the strong, help for the sick, food for all. In fact, the church provides for the wants of the newcomers until lands are assigned them for cultivation. Young then advances money to them to build their houses—brick or adobe, boards, and tools. The value of the land and the objects furnished to the immigrants is calculated in dollars and inscribed in the creditor's books. Payment is made in installments, to which is added the tithe, a tenth of the gross rental of the farm, levied for the wants of the church.

Young thus becomes the creditor of the whole community. Few, if any, Mormons can ever clear off their debts. They gain a livelihood by dint of work; they may even become tolerably well off, but it is extremely difficult to save, and next to impossible to become rich. The rarity of specie and the difficulty of procuring ready money adds to the financial embarrassment which is the normal condition of this society.

To leave Utah the saints must pay their debts; to pay they must sell their farms; to sell they must find buyers with ready United States money. Now, there is only one man in Utah in that position, and that is Brigham Young. But Brigham Young is precisely the man least interested in facilitating the sales. The great secret of his political and religious power consists, in a large measure, although not entirely, in the nature of his financial relations with the majority of the Mormons who are all, more or less, his debtors.

But, strange to say, the immigrant, instead of independence, has found the one thing which he lacked in Europe when he embraced the religion of the saints, and that is Faith! Yes, this unbeliever of yesterday, not only in the old religions but in the new, has become today the staunchest of disciples. He believes firmly, blindly, in the Prophet Brigham Young. How account for this strange yet incontestable fact which everybody confirms, and which besides bears the evidence of truth on the very face of things?

Until 1869 Brigham Young was in the zenith of his power. One may affirm without exaggeration that in the normal condition of affairs the prophet is literally the absolute master of the bodies and souls of his believers. He disposes of their wills and consciences, and even of their thoughts; for he gives them a certain direction and takes care it shall be maintained. Besides, who dares to think for himself in Utah? They believe, they work, but they do not think. The Tabernacle on Sundays, the shop or the farm during the week, the theater and the harem every night—that is enough. There is no time left for reflection, everything is done by inspiration. God inspires and the person who is inspired is Brigham Young. In every kind of business, trouble, difficulty, or doubt, Brigham Young is the referee. Young is not an incarnate God, but he acts as such. That is why I say that he disposes of the souls of men.

Now for their bodies. He concentrates in his own hands the strings of all their material interests. He exploits the whole territory. He likewise exploits the physical powers and the mental faculties of 200,000 people. He has, in consequence, the reputation of being one of the richest men in the United States. People say he has a fortune of more than $12,000,000. He rules the markets; he fixes the price of food; he makes the roads, and exacts enormous tolls. After having created all these different industries he works them all for his own benefit. With his armed force, his militia, perfectly well-exercised and equipped, his telegraph which he has carried to every point of the territory, he is master of the situation. In addition, till two years ago he had the advantage of being geographically inaccessible. Add to this a prompt and summary execution of justice, in part occult, and you have a very fair picture of the unheard-of powers of this one man.

But there is still another element which grows out of the imposition, under cover of a pretended revelation in 1852, of the doctrine and practice of polygamy. Under the influence of Young, an assembly of delegates adopted the principle, which was declared a duty and a privilege; but it could not, however, be exercised without a special command of God, through the medium of his prophet, Brigham Young, who, before giving his decision, examines the merits of the case, or has it examined by his bishops.

The higher a man advances in the ranks of the hierarchy, the more his duty compels him to use the privilege of plurality. Brigham Young at this moment possesses sixteen wives, without counting sixteen others who are what is called "sealed." Some of these latter live with him in a conjugal fashion, but the greater part are widows or old maids, who by this means hope to become, in a future state, what they are not here below—the real wives of the prophet. George Smith, the historian, has five wives; the other apostles content themselves with four. None has less than three.

Look at it which way you will, polygamy bears within it the seeds of destruction; for the family first of all, and for society afterwards. But its first victims are the women. All those I have seen have a sad, timid look. In their homes they have not the place due a wife. The men avoid speaking of them, and never allow them to appear before strangers; one would fancy they were ashamed of them, or rather of themselves. These poor women have fallen from the place they once held; they feel themselves degraded, and degradation is read on all these melancholy and faded countenances.

Labor and faith, two words forever in Brigham Young's mouth, explain these strange phenomena. But what secret motives caused the birth of this faith in the hearts of those who never possessed anything of the sort when they embraced the new doctrines? How was this transformation effected? How did men who left their native land believing in nothing, soon after reaching the Valley of the Saints, begin to believe in everything—that is, in everything which it pleased Brigham Young to make them believe? The following are the conclusions at which I arrived.

The beginnings of Mormonism are like those of any other sect. With some people, spiritual needs, the thirst for more supernatural help, the wish to draw nearer to God, from time to time arise in a sudden and unexpected manner. The rarer these revivals, the more violent they seem; like mill dams long closed and suddenly opened. The waters at first rush out furiously, but when they have had their flow, they resume

their usual calm course. This is the history of the famous religious revivals. This is also the origin of the greater part of the sects, especially
in America where everyone is so occupied with material interests that
there is no time for meditation or prayer. Moral wants long neglected,
the voice of conscience long stifled, repentance, even despair, suddenly
take possession of souls. People ask for reassurances and accept them
from the first comer. At such moments men always turn up ready to
put themselves at the head of the movement, to direct, master, and, if
possible, work it for their own ends. These are sometimes hypocrites,
often fanatics, or a mixture of the two. But the hypocrite lacks the light
of faith; the fanatic, the light of reason. Bad passions, cupidity, and
sensuality mingle in the business. What wonder then that they merge
into the absurd and monstrous? Under these conditions Mormonism,
like the other sects, was born.

The first founders, those influenced by Joseph Smith, were certainly
in earnest; they were genuine fanatics. They were Americans and
formed the moral center which afterwards received the European immigrants.

The great migration to Salt Lake marked a turning point in the history of the sect, by consolidating the prestige and authority of the
modern Moses. Amidst a thousand dangers and fearful privation, but
under the guidance of this wonderful man, the Mormons found the
spot exactly as God in His vision had revealed it to His elect. Certainly
Brigham Young must be a supernatural being; if not a god, very near
one. And after all, what is God? The Mormons do not trouble their
heads with such inquiries; and besides, their prophet has told them
that man is the equal of God. Certainly no one is so more than Young.
It is evident—it is clear—everyone thinks, repeats, and believes it.

Thus public opinion formed itself in the Valley of the Saints and
was quickly imparted to the newcomers. The European immigrant had
no means of defense. He was poor, ignorant, and debased; and in declaring himself a Mormon he had already renounced the religion in
which he was born. He could not find arguments against the errors of
the sect he had just embraced in the dogmas of the old faith he had
denied. Moreover, he had burned his ships; he belonged body and soul
to the president. He behaved, then, like everyone else, shut his eyes
and became a believer, that is, a believer in Brigham Young.

Two years ago defections were very rare. Since the opening of the railroad, Anglican and Presbyterian ministers have devoted themselves to their apostolic labors in Salt Lake City without serious risk. But it has been so much lost time in the sense that the few men willing to leave the sect have been incapable of receiving any religious impressions or any moral sense. From believing Mormons and good workmen, they became, when emancipated, frank atheists and incorrigible scamps.

The influence of the railroad, of the discovery of the silver mines, and of the influx of miners in the last few months has already been felt in various ways. In the first place, the Reign of Terror, under which the few gentiles groaned, has entirely disappeared. Once Helots, the Christians are now independent. Soon they will become a power. Even in the heart of the community the situation is much modified. Immigrants who are not Mormons have arrived, brought in capital, opened stores, and extend their operations every day. Everything, in fact, is changing. There is no longer talk of sudden sentences and secret executions; no more bodies of apostate Mormons; no more avenging angels! The young girls themselves are in rebellion. They openly proclaim against plurality, and swear never to accept polygamist husbands. Even the Beehive has been invaded by insubordination; the eldest son has told his father that he does not consider the children by later marriages legitimate.

I stop under a shed which serves also as a stable. Men who trade between Corinne and Montana are dining at long rough tables. These cavaliers have just arrived from Virginia City. They have traversed thousand of miles, followed the Missouri up to its source, crossed and recrossed the mountain chains which are the backbone of this great continent, avoided, or if necessary fought, the Indians who harassed their path, and served as escort in certain dangerous passes to the stagecoach which runs twice a month through these desert regions. That conveyance leaves Corinne full of passengers of both sexes, but does not always arrive with all its human cargo. Cold and fatigue, or in summer excessive heat, and privations of all sorts, to say nothing of the Indians, thin their numbers. The dead are interred in haste along the roadside, or rather in the deep ruts left by the wheels, and then the rest pass on.

Corinne has only existed for four years. Sprung out of the earth as if by enchantment, this town now contains upwards of 2000 inhabitants, and every day increases in importance. It is a victualing center for the advanced posts of the colonists in Idaho and Montana. A coach runs twice a week to Virginia City and to Helena, 350 and 500 miles to the north. Despite the serious dangers and the terrible fatigue of the journeys, these diligences are always full of passengers. Various articles of consumption and dry goods of all sorts are sent in wagons. The "high road" is but a rough track in the soil left by the wheels of previous vehicles.

The streets of Corinne are full of white men armed to the teeth, miserable looking Indians dressed in the ragged shirts and trousers furnished by the federal government, and yellow Chinese with a businesslike air and hard, intelligent faces. No town in the Far West gave me so good an idea as this little place of what is meant by *border life,* the struggle between civilization and savage men and things. Nowhere is the contrast more striking between the marvelous, restless, abrupt energy of the whites, the methodical, quiet, businesslike habits of the Chinese, and the incorrigible idleness and indifference of the Redskins. In his exterior manners and dress the American of the frontiers is unbuttoned, coarse, and rough to the last degree; the Chinese, careful, polished, and respectable in appearance; the Indian, the very type of misery and degradation.

All commercial business centers in Main Street. The houses on both sides are nothing but boarded huts. I have seen some with only canvas partitions. The smartest are distinguished by a wooden façade much higher than the roof, which gives them the appearance of awkwardly made drop scenes in a theater. The pavement is made of wood and varies in height according to the taste of each proprietor. As it is, however, full of holes, I cannot say that it helps traffic very much. The lanes alongside of the huts, which are generally the resort of Chinese women of bad character, lead into the desert, which begins at the doors of the last houses. South of the town I saw some slight attempt at cultivation and the feeble beginnings of gardens. As for the rest, there is not a tree. It is desert and nothing but desert, saving a few oases, some Mormon establishments at the foot of the rocks or perched midway.

To have on your conscience a number of manslaughters committed in full day, under the eyes of your fellow citizens; to have escaped the reach of justice by craft, audacity, or bribery; to have earned a reputation for being "sharp," that is, for knowing how to cheat all the world without being caught—those are the attributes of a true rowdy in the Far West. The terror of parents, but the model of young men, universally popular among the fair sex, the rowdy is not necessarily a rogue and a villain. Sometimes he reforms to some extent and, as he possesses in a supreme degree the art of making himself feared, he often becomes the head man of a village. Then he grows old amidst the respect and consideration of a large number of his fellow countrymen, over whom he has made himself absolute tyrant.

Such is the career of a good many rowdies; others, less fortunate or less clever, close their short and stormy lives hanging from the branch of a tree. These are the martyrs, the others the heroes of this civilization. Endowed as they often are with really fine qualities—courage, energy, and intellectual and physical strength—they might, in another sphere and with the moral sense which they now lack, have become valuable members of society. But such as they are, these adventurers have a reason for being, a providential mission to fulfill. The qualities needed to struggle with and conquer savage nature have naturally their corresponding defects. Look back, and you will see the cradles of all civilization surrounded with giants of Herculean strength ready to run every risk and to shrink from neither danger nor crime to attain their ends. It is only by the peculiar temper of the time and place that we can distinguish them from the backwoodsman and rowdy of the United States.

The miners who came to California with the discovery of gold were followed by an entirely new class of men. New immigrants brought with them both experience and capital, and a few old pioneers having made their fortunes at the diggings, returned to the pale of civilization. These first-rate men of business installed themselves quietly in Montgomery Street, put the miners at once into a secondary rank, and embarked in their speculations with sagacity, boldness, and resolution. These men were above all distinguished by intuition and courage. They seemed to divine their business, saw profits as in a vision, and pursued their ideal with a vigor which converted it into a reality.

These merchants started a number of companies and private banks, which operate with English and American capital. Their ramifications extend to London, Shanghai, Hong Kong, Calcutta, and Bombay. One of the most remarkable is the Wells Fargo Company—an enormous concern embracing in its operations the whole western side of the great American continent, from the Rocky Mountains to the Pacific, from the confines of British Columbia in the north to the frontiers of Mexico in the south. Its agents are scattered over all this immense surface. In the most remote corners of the mining districts and the primeval forests, wherever there is a white settlement there is sure to be a neat, clean little house, bearing in colossal letters the inscription, "Wells, Fargo, and Co." This company acts as bankers to the settlers, the backwoodsmen, the miners, and to the little towns which spring up one day and the next either disappear or become important centers of new districts. The transport of both letters and parcels forms one of the most important branches of the operations of this great company. They buy stamped envelopes from the post office, add their own stamp, and charge a small percentage on each. The regularity and safety of their postal service amply repay the public for the small extra charge. These dealings have fallen off since the opening of the great railroad. The coaches and cars of Fargo and Wells no longer convey travelers to Fort Laramie or Salt Lake City. The railroad has taken away all this work; but they continue to supply all the carriage roads leading to the railroads, and unite the important points of Idaho, Montana, Nevada, and the Pacific States, from Olympia to Los Angeles and San Diego. The capital of this company is not derived from the gold fields; almost all the shares are in the hands of New York bankers. The amount of English capital embarked in the great banks of San Francisco also grows larger every day. California gold does not, therefore, feed the commercial activity of San Francisco, but on the contrary finds its way abroad, and especially to England.

Industry is continually on the increase. Wool manufactures hold the first rank. The numberless flocks of the country supply the raw material. Californians boast also of the perfection and strength of the machinery manufactured in San Francisco; workshops here furnish the miners with all their tools, and importation of such articles has entirely ceased. Formerly skins were sent East to be tanned, and then came back in the shape of boots and shoes; now they are made as well here as anywhere else. To sum up, we may rest assured that what is already done is only the beginning of what will be done. Natural riches abound, and form elements for a healthy and flourishing trade independent of the gold fields. Neither capital nor hands are wanting; for the Chinese who swarm here are excellent workmen.

The real riches do not consist in gold, but in the fertility of the soil. Only a sixth of the available land is as yet under cultivation. California's principal products will always be cereals, although the agricultural pursuit most suitable here is gardening. The quantity of vegetables and fruit produced from this soil is fabulous. Vineyards are also thriving, and I have heard that the wine made in San Francisco is excellent, although as yet little is drunk. I do not fancy, however, that the vintage of the country can ever compete with that of France. One thing to be set against this extraordinary produce is the ever-increasing price of land, especially on the borders of the railway. Speculation of course has something to do with that, but nevertheless it must be remembered that the value of land always corresponds with the value and amount of production; and no one can deny the present brilliant results of cultivation, or think that future hopes of still more surprising returns are altogther chimerical.

The more commerce, trade, and agriculture prosper, the stronger is the reaction against gold digging. I have even heard men, authorities in such matters, declare that the cost absorbs the profits, and that you bury in the earth as much gold as you get out of it.

Whatever the causes may be, the feeling against mining gains ground every day. The grievances are endless, and each man will give you a fresh one of his own. To begin with, the gold diggers generally belong to the least respectable class of immigrants; they arrive alone, without capital and without any guarantee of character or morality. When they set to work at the mines they naturally fall into the ways and habits of those around them. As the rights of property are badly defined, constant quarrels arise among the miners and between the miners and the farmers whose land runs nearest the mines. The whole existence of these men is, in fact, a constant protest against the fundamental conditions of civilized life. Finally, only in very rare instances can individuals compete with companies. Sooner or later the miners are ruined, give up the diggings, and become the terror of the settlers— real bandits and a running sore in California society.

On the other hand, the companies both large and small, and there are upwards of three thousand of them, run fearful risks. Their transactions are nothing but a huge game of chance; enormous gains are frequently followed by tremendous losses. It is, therefore, a reasonable conclusion that gold digging in all its branches is a permanent source of demoralization. Looking at it from an agricultural point of view, it involves, of course, the utter destruction of arable land that would indeed be precious were it simply cultivated instead of being burrowed into and destroyed. To have the least idea of the extent of the devastation you must visit the mining district. Wherever the hydraulic process has been in operation the most fertile land has been converted into a chaos of rock, gravel, and mud.

Most of San Francisco is perched on the flank of a mountain, that is, on the steep incline of a granite rock covered with a thick bed of gravel and sand. If the pioneers had marked out the plan of the streets in conformity with the lay of the ground, it would have been easy, by taking advantage of its very irregularities, to make good carriage roads and picturesque terraces. But the first founders were either Yankees or Missouri men who would not hear of anything but straight lines and right angles. Thanks to this bold determination the result is marvelous, but I cannot call it successful. In the streets circulation is impeded at every turn and the houses are not only ugly but positive caricatures. After having laid out some straight streets with houses on either side it was found that owing to the shape of the ground they were not accessible to carriages. The level of the streets was then lowered till they became like deep ditches; while flying staircases were added to give access to the houses.

Very soon it was discovered that from the nature of the gravelly soil the action of the wind very seriously endangered the foundations of these aerial habitations, perched on the ledge of a precipice. Serious accidents were the result. More than once the northwest breeze undermined the foundations, which the excavations in the carriage road had laid bare, and simply threw the houses down into the trench below. The expense of all these repairs was so great that this absurd system was at last given up. They now use steps to rise to the different levels, as the houses are built on the sides of the mountain. But the result is that if you go in a carriage you have to make tremendous detours. When you look up from the lower town the eye is shocked by the optical effect of these straight lines broken by the level of the ground. Everywhere else, looking at a long line of avenues, the houses and trees on each side seem to descend toward the horizon. Here, owing to the extraordinary way the ground has been dealt with, they ascend.

Do not fancy, however, that these men are too busy about making money to care for the comforts of life, or that they disdain the fine arts. In the designs of the new homes of the rich bankers and merchants I saw several attempts at real beauty of form and proportion. I do not say that these attempts were always successful. I complain chiefly of the material of which they are built. To cover a lot of beams and planks with plaster colored like marble or cut stone is to commit a sin against good taste which any eye accustomed to architecture would at once detect. But the interior of these houses is very fine, spacious, and comfortable; they are handsomely furnished without being overdone. Very few knickknacks are about; California taste disdains them. But on the other hand, they possess some very fine works of art.

I like the modest houses of smaller men. Hardly ever is a little garden missing. The mildness of the climate in winter permits a constant change of flowers, and the lawns are well watered and carefully mowed.

The great hotels and the public buildings are alike everywhere in America. There are also some really fine churches. The most sumptuous ecclesiastical edifice, however, is undoubtedly the synagogue. I put it first, because from its position on one of the highest points of the city it attracts the eye before all the Christian churches. It testifies likewise to the local importance of the Jewish element. St. Mary's, the Catholic cathedral, is a fine and noble Gothic structure. The Protestants likewise have churches for each of their particular sects. Nor must we forget the two *joss houses* or pagodas of the Chinese worshipers.

Until now the Chinese have been nothing but birds of passage. Not one of them ever dreamed of settling himself in America for life. All leave their native land with the hope and intention of returning there. They make provision that their remains, in case of death, may be transported to the village where they were born. To have their bodies sent home is one of the first conditions of their contracts with the governors of their companies, or with the individuals who wish to employ them.

All these Chinese come from the south of the Celestial Empire, and are as a class superior to the coolies exported from Maçao to Chili and Havana. They are for the most part peasants in easy circumstances.

Some have a certain amount of education; others are artisans. A great many bring with them some capital; all, vigorous arms and willing hands, minds ready to embrace every chance of success, and a firm determination to make a little fortune.

These immigrants are divided into companies, the presidents of which reside in San Francisco, and these men have great influence over their fellow countrymen. The leaders receive the newcomers on their arrival, provide for their wants, settle any little disputes or quarrels among themselves so as to prevent resort to the American courts, and exercise, with the consent of the contending parties, a certain judicial power, even in criminal cases. The companies give relief to the sick, facilitate the emigration of the living and the return of the dead, try, in a word, to soften the hard lives of their countrymen. Without their constant paternal intervention the well-justified animosity of the Chinese against the whites would break out in acts of open violence, and would probably endanger the very existence of the colony.

I cannot find terms severe enough with which to censure the conduct of the Californians toward the Chinese. These last are virtually put out of the pale of the law. Their evidence is refused before the courts. Those who work at the mines are taxed to the extent of $4.00 a month a head. Bloody scenes periodically recur at the gold diggings. The white miners chase away the Chinese, expel them from legally acquired claims, and kill them if they attempt to resist or to defend their just rights. Without the least provocation, the Chinese are constantly beaten and robbed. But this is not the worst; there is not an instance of a verdict by a jury in their favor or of any punishment ever inflicted on the guilty.

This extraordinary hatred originates in a question of dollars and cents. The white miner receives, besides his food, $3.00, $3.50, or $4.00 a day. The Chinese is not fed and is content with $.75 or $1.00 or at most $1.50. It is the same with every other branch of industry. In the towns the Chinese act as domestic servants, and are excellent cooks and laundry men; in the country they excel as gardeners. The beautiful terraces and earth works are all the results of Chinese labor. As these workers are very numerous, and as immigration increases, their competition in the labor market lowers the wages of the white workmen. This is the only crime of the Chinese. They are forced to expiate it as victims of brutality, even of murder, of legal enactments which are the shame and disgrace of American legislators, and of decisions which are as contrary to justice as to common sense.

And yet they hold on, nothing seems to discourage them. Each of the great steamers which plies monthly between San Francisco and Hong Kong brings between 800 and 1200 Chinese passengers. A far smaller number, emigrants who have served their time, return home in the same ships. They carry away in their trunks the fruit of their long and patient toil; in their minds, a sovereign contempt for our civilization; and in their hearts the bitterest hatred of the Christian.

If we, children of old Europe, who cling to the present as the logical natural continuation of the past, who cherish old recollections, traditions, and habits, if we do homage to your success, obtained under institutions which, on all essential points, are contrary to ours, this is a proof of our impartiality. For let us not deceive ourselves, America is the born antagonist of Europe. The first arrivals, the precursors of your actual greatness, those who sowed the seed, were discontented men. Intestine divisions and religious persecutions tore them from their homes and threw them on America's shores. They brought with them and planted in the soil of their new country the principle for which they had suffered and fought—the authority of the individual. He who possesses it is free in the fullest sense of the term. And, as in that sense you are all free, each of you is the equal of every other. Your country then is the classic soil of liberty and equality and it has become so from the fact that it was peopled by the men whom Europe expelled from its bosom. That is why you, in conformity with your origin, and we by a totally different genesis are antagonistic.

You offer liberty and equality to everyone. It is to the magic charm of these two words, more than to your gold fields, that you owe the influx of your immigrants, and the enormous and ever-growing increase of your population. Russia and Hungary still have miles of uncultivated lands; Algeria needs and clamors for hands. But no one goes there. The great mass of emigrants turn their steps to North America. Why? First, to find bread, an article which in our overpopulated Europe it is no longer easy to procure; next, to obtain liberty and equality. The emigrants go to you for bread, individual liberty, and social equality, and they find space; that is, liberty to work and equality of success if they bring with them the necessary qualifications.

All the world admires you. But all the world does not love you. Those among us who judge you from an exclusively European point of view see in you nothing but enemies of the fundamental principles of society. The more they appreciate your work, the more, in fact, they admire, the less they like you. I should add that they fear you. They dread your success as a dangerous example to Europe, and as far as they can they try to stop the spread of your ideas. But they are a minority.

Your friends are more numerous. They see in you the prototype and the last fruits of civilization, and they desire to transform themselves after your example. There is a third class, those who are resigned; their opinion is the widest spread. Although they do not like you, they are willing to submit to you; to submit to your principles, your habits, your institutions. They believe that Europe will become Americanized, fatally, but inevitably.

As for me, I share neither these hopes nor these fears. I maintain that these fears, these hopes, this blind faith in imaginary decrees of Providence are founded on an imperfect knowledge of America, and of the fundamental differences between the Old World and the New.

Compared to Europe, your country is as a sheet of white paper. Everything has to be begun; everything is new. In Europe one rebuilds or restores or modifies or adds (if one has space, which is more and more rare) a wing to one's house. But unless you demolish what exists, you don't rebuild the foundations; for what abounds in America is what we lack most—space. To become American would be to presuppose the entire destruction of Europe.

There is another reason why you cannot serve as a model in spite of the admiration you excite. How choose as a model a thing which is incomplete? You are at the growing age; you are not yet fully formed.

What will you be when you have come to maturity? You do not know and no one can predict, for history offers no example of such a genesis. What new race will spring from this mixture of Celts, Germans, and Mongols? We cannot tell, no one can, we only know that a great change will result.

There remains also the unsolved problem as to liberty of conscience, the right of each one to worship the Supreme Being according to his own fashion. Until now, this system has worked well. Life is easy here for everybody, for everyone has space. To prevent a disagreeable meeting, one has only to cross to the other side of the street; it is wide enough for all. But the day will come, although it is now far-off, when this illimitable space will be narrowed, and when it will be difficult by flight to escape those who do not share your religious convictions. Even in your country the question of liberty of conscience has not yet been definitively settled.

To sum up: you have the great advantage of space, which is wanting in Europe; and you are at the growing age. North America offers an unlimited field of liberty to the individual. It does not simply give him the opportunity; it forces him to employ all the faculties with which nature has endowed him. The arena is open. As soon as he enters it he must fight, and fight to the death. In Europe it is just the contrary. Everyone finds himself hemmed in by the narrow sphere in which he is born. To get out of his groove a man must be able to rise above his equals, to make extraordinary efforts, and he must have abilities and qualities above the average. What with you is the rule, with us is the exception. In Europe a man works to live, or, at most, to arrive at comparative ease; here he works to become rich. Everyone does not attain this goal, but everyone tries for it. Such supreme efforts on all sides lead to extraordinary success.

This miraculous difference is due in large measure to the political institutions which govern your nation. To convince yourself of that fact you need only look at Canada. Perhaps its inhabitants are all the happier for it; but taking things altogether, in a material point of view, the British colony is incontestably inferior.

So much that is brilliant must have its dark shadow. Every mortal man is afflicted with the faults inseparable from his good qualities. And you are not exempt from this infirmity. One cause of your greatness is the unlimited expansion of individual liberty. But the liberty of the individual must necessarily be limited by the liberty of all, represented by the state. The balance of the two is the guarantee of each. In the Old World the state claims too much and the individual obtains too little. With you, the fault is just the contrary. It is the conviction of most of your eminent men that you grant too much to the individual and too little to the state. Most of the scandals and abuses in your country arise from that source. The control of the organs of public opinion is insufficient. There is no subjection to an admitted authority recognized by everyone.

You have obtained, and are obtaining every day, enormous results; but at the cost of excessive labor, of a permanent tension of mind, and a permanent drain of physical strength. This excess of toil seems to me the source of serious evils. It produces exhaustion, lassitude, and premature old age; it deprives those who give themselves up to it first of time, and then of the power of enjoying the results of their labors. It makes money the principal object in life, excludes gaiety, entails a sadness which is the natural consequence of overfatigue, and destroys the family ties and home joys.

22.

CHANCE IN AMERICA

*Ernst Otto Hopp (1841–1910) was a German journalist and historian who spent a good deal of time in the United States. In addition to the account from which this selection is taken (*Federzeichungen aus dem amerikanischen Leben, *1876), he wrote a study of the American Civil War and also the volume on the history of the United States in Oncken's* Allgemeine Geschichte *(vol. XLIII).*

"Everything has already happened," says Akiba; "everything in life repeats itself," sings Schiller. In Berlin the old-time loafers have now more or less disappeared, and in Naples the *lazzaroni* seem about to die out. A mixture of both, or, if you like, of many other kinds of humanity, characteristic of the great cities—the Paris gamin, the English boxer, the Berlin bully, the Italian lounger in the sun, and the universal confidence man—this is the distinguished pedigree of the American street-corner loafer. The rowdies not only blemish the city of New York by their existence, but they may be found as well in the other cities of the United States, large or small.

On the street, corner buildings are their inevitable meeting places, especially when a saloon, a grocery, a post office, or any other public place is located there. At any hour of the day, and through many hours of the night in snow and rain, the gang may be seen there, inspecting the passers-by, spitting and smoking, not quite drunk but not quite sober. They are a part of the American city, and their characteristic physiognomy is almost as necessary for completeness as a shoe to the foot or a hat to the head.

Vain to ask who they are! People know their names, and yet again, know them not. On the corner first names are enough: Jimmy, Freddy, Johnny, Charlie, Henry; nothing more is needed. One might well ask how they manage to live. But these existences are like those of Solomon's lilies of the field, although perhaps not so pure and innocent. They sow not, neither do they reap; yet our heavenly Father provides for them. Yes indeed, they seem well-fed, stout, and bold, and their clothing is by no means ragged, in fact, often faultless. As for what they do, they drink, curse, spit, pick fights, chew, smoke, play billiards or cards, and at any hour are prepared for any infamy. Their busiest season is around election day; then they are constantly occupied. Almost always a candidate finds them a necessary evil.

A sort of secret brotherhood, a private code of behavior, and mysterious signs of recognition bind these men together. They sometimes include unemployed workers who join them temporarily. They are not always a danger to the stray individual; they do no damage to the casual passer-by other than perhaps to soil his shoes. But woe to the stranger they trap! Too bad for the poor devil who earns their hostility! And you may well pity any pretentious man dressed to attract attention, who feels insulted when jostled in walking by. Fear, caution, and respect are words that do not appear in their dictionary; they are on good terms with the police, and it is ten to one that unless you are a person of consequence, or politically important, the constable will arrest you instead of them for disturbing the peace. They are always ready for perjury, since their religion is only skin deep and honor means nothing at all to them.

Swaggering as they may seem, they have little enough courage when considered by light of day. Unexpectedly and without warning they will fall upon you from ambush, and not always for a specific reason; you may be a "damned Dutchman" and that is enough. A physician and pharmacist, well known to me, was attacked by such a rowdy in a small town near New York. The assault came by surprise and simply out of hatred for Germans. Without any special reason the tough, at his pleasure, broke several ribs by kicks, and made my friend sick for life. There are dozens of similar examples. The rowdy willingly works with a revolver; he is a skilled pugilist, but does not despise the lowest weapons. Among some nations there is a certain kind of honor among thieves who will not unnecessarily harm a weaponless opponent unable to retaliate. The rowdy, however, who very often is of Irish descent or has some Irish blood in his veins, reaches the height of his bestiality only when his victim lies on the ground beaten and powerless. Then he will kick your body to a pulp and gouge your eyes out. Some Germans also belong to the gangs of loafers and rowdies. The Irish-American members treat them badly, call them "Dutchie"; but the sort of Germans who join have long since shed every national sentiment or feeling of pride.

There are several different classes among the rowdies. The smallest groups are thieves, since this is not elegant enough; at least there are few petty thieves or common pickpockets. Large-scale robbery is however nothing to be ashamed of, since the miserable oaf who steals a bit of bread out of hunger and bitter poverty will be severely punished, while the great knave who absconds with millions is admired for his smartness and becomes the ideal of the growing youth.

All the loafers suffer from the so-called noble passions, such as dog fighting, hunting, fishing, ratting, pigeon shooting, horse racing, voting, boxing, and prize fighting. They follow every kind of sport with pleasure, and are always ready to wager on the results. The phrase "I bet you" slips like a magic formula from their lips. Were it not for the rowdies, horse racing in America would have a very sparse audience, since gentlemen who would patronize the sport are as scarce as noble dispositions in a cross section of the population. The loafers give the lie to the saying that everyone must work in America, that a restless life of labor is lived there, and that a convulsive striving for money reigns there. These men work only very sporadically and make their living from votes, bets, and games.

The gambling rowdy and loafer is most easily recognized. A thick gold chain (imitation), a mustache dyed black which often contrasts wondrously with blond hair, and a velvet coat distinguish him from all other members of the human race. While the last-named piece of clothing in Europe is the trade-mark of the artist and inextricably associated with long hair, it is in America the sign of the professional gambler, who wears it with special love, in summer as in winter.

In New York City some 30,000 people earn a living from gambling and from similar branches of industry. It is clear, then, that no recent events have been able to stifle the love of gaming in the hearts of people across the Atlantic. The gamblers' bread may be poor and bitter, but it is also easy and pleasant. Beside the Americans' lust for work stands the fear of work in some circles. Morally neglected natures which cannot lift themselves out of the low sphere of their common thoughts love to be drawn away from the sordidness of everyday life. America's lack of ideals takes its revenge here. Lock a plant in a cellar and give it rich humus; it will shoot up, long and discolored. Thousands of lives in American cities conform to this botanical analogy. These above all turn to gambling. The driving, fertilizing power is abundant, the shrubs grow rank and fast; but the growths lack the light, the light of true religion as well as of education and learning.

There are a great variety of games; roulette, faro, poker, and keno are most popular. There are extravagantly decorated salons furnished with every luxury, and low filthy dives. The former make a pleasant impression—nothing unsavory on the surface that might frighten away the high-strung pleasure seekers. There are rooms furnished with every comfort; thick carpets, marble tables, alabaster figurines, gilded mirrors, soft chairs, and velvet drapes, and curtains embellish the first-class playing rooms. The buffet is amply equipped; a drink of brandy or claret costs as little as the food—at most, a tip to the Negro waiters on leaving. Not in all these places is the player cheated from the outset; in many, only gentlemen may play, respectable people. But the host and his partners hold the bank and even if they lose for one or two days, make up for their losses in the others. An individual may sometimes take away substantial sums, but in the long run the banker must win.

Some of these places are not public, but charge an admission fee for which food and liquors are supplied. In most of the better-class establishments there is a secret device for opening the door; but it is not too difficult to gain an entree. In these gambling dens everything is well arranged, tidy, and polished. The company is well clothed; were you to learn their names you would find many well known in public life. But study the facial expressions. Note the changes in complexion as they win and lose, the intent look with which they follow the play. See their sleepy, dull, dissolute appearance when the morning light shines through the windows; and then follow them to their homes and observe their disrupted family life. Vice follows vice, since, even in the best of cases, deceit is linked to gambling. They play at first secretly, then openly, when a certain deep moral degradation and moral dullness is reached; and finally drunkenness, deception, and lust become the inseparable accompaniments of the desire for betting.

From the outwardly fine gambling houses we step down to the more vulgar and coarser places, where you are relieved of your money without so much finesse, and where, should you protest, you would not fail to be ejected with a black eye. Watch our country cousin. He is a stranger in the big city; the monotony of rural life induces him to take a fling here. A fine gentleman has somehow attached himself to him and becomes his cicerone. They go to a house on the Bowery, a very lively street, climb one flight up. There is a table. The rustic sits down. He plays and wins. But to continue the game he must change a twenty-dollar bill. He wins again, and soon has forty dollars. But he is careful; not for nothing has he been warned of the pitfalls of the metropolis; when the opportunity presents itself, he leaves with the forty dollars. The gamblers notice his exit with satisfied smiles. The twenty-dollar bill he changed was genuine and good; the forty dollars he takes away are counterfeits, only good for lighting cigars.

Like faro, poker is a game particularly popular in America. It depends primarily upon lucky betting; skillful, clever playing is not really necessary in this as in most American games, only luck or blind accident which favors one man rather than another. But the most widespread game, the one with the greatest popular appeal, is keno.

Keno playing has a demoralizing and corrupting influence upon the people. Faro and poker are more often played by the upper classes, but keno is the game of the great mass of the middle classes, laborers, shop assistants, factory workers, the unemployed, and unoccupied. For a single individual the losses through keno are of small consequence, but more generally the evil influence is deep, since some 50 per cent of the players are young men who are drawn close to being good-for-nothing through such gambling. In the busiest districts of New York, in the vicinity of the theaters and other pleasure spots, are scores of keno houses, open and accessible to all, often separated from a bar only by a swinging door.

Entering one of the large establishments of this kind you see a brilliantly lighted hall, in which there are a great number of little round tables on which lie keno cards and buttons. Around each table are five or six chairs, and by eight in the evening all will generally be occupied. Between 200 and 300 people gather here. The leaders of it all, the masters of the game, stand on an elevated platform. One of them sells the tickets, little ivory chips about as big as a silver dollar with a black half-moon in the middle; the other watches the urn. The keno urn is naturally ornate and elegant, the cover comes off so that the ivory keno balls, each with a number on it, can be put in; a revolving mechanism makes it possible to shake up the balls; and at the very bottom is a little opening through which a single ball is released when a spring is pressed. On the wall behind the man who manipulates the balls in the urn is a large board with countless holes under each of which is a number.

To play, you must first of all select one or more of the cards, which lie on the tables. Keno is a game of pure chance yet there are frequently exciting scenes in the choice of a card, since many people through superstition attach a particular significance to certain numbers, just as in the case of the lotteries in Europe. One chooses a number he saw in a dream; another a lucky one on which he already has won; a third one that which corresponds to the date of his birth.

A keno card looks something like this:

8	12	26	30	**19**		51		79	
			36		44		62		83
	18	22				58	68	76	

The big number 19 is the number of the card, which costs twenty-five cents. Before the game begins boys pass about gathering the money or tokens, each of which stands for twenty-five cents. The boy calls out the number of the card and the man at the urn puts a little peg into the hole on the big board corresponding to that number. As soon as all the numbers are entered on the board and all the cards are paid for a Negro puts the keno balls into the urn. On the balls are numbers which correspond to the little figures on the cards. The pegs on the board are counted, and since each stands for twenty-five cents everyone knows how much is in the purse. The balls in the urn are then set in motion, and can be heard clicking against each other. Then comes the sound of the spring being pressed; a ball appears; its number is read aloud; and every fortunate one who finds that number on his card puts on it one of the pile of black buttons lying on the table. The first to fill a row of five numbers is the winner and receives the purse after a deduction of 10 per cent as the fee of the house.

In addition, there are all manner of other temptations. Whoever gets five numbers in a line before the tenth ball leaves the urn receives a prize of $500 in addition to the purse. Success by the fifteenth ball brings a premium of $250. And there are a whole series of other awards ranging from $25 to $200. It is, however, very rare to find these actually paid out.

When a player successfully fills his row, he calls out, "Keno!"— "What number?" asks the man at the urn. The number is reported and checked against the pegs in the board on the wall. If it agrees, the winner must call out his five small numbers which must correspond with those on the balls already drawn. "Everything is in order," acknowledges the director. "Number 19 wins the purse." And so it goes. This is keno, to which thousands devote themselves nightly.

Politicians and pickpockets, bank clerks and robbers, white-haired elderly men and speculative factory boys participate with equal zeal in the play. The whole thing is considered an honorable business, since the purses and prizes are always properly and openly distributed, at least, that is what seems to happen. I racked my brains for a long time in the effort to figure out how the house cheated in the game, for I was morally certain that there was some deception; all the operators of keno games became wealthy in a short time. Evening after evening I watched the play and occasionally participated, trying to discover the catch to the game. Everything, however, seemed to be in order and to follow the rules. I could discover absolutely nothing improper.

At last fortune brought me the answer. Close to my table sat a man with a fur hat, a gray coat, and light trousers. He wore small whiskers, with only a thin light mustache. He called out keno twice in a remarkably short interval, and was paid his money. For that reason I noticed him carefully before he got up; on his finger was a very striking ring, embellished with a Masonic emblem, and he also had matching studs. He left the establishment with his winnings. After a half hour or so appeared another man with a black coat and dark gray trousers, silk hat

and black whiskers. He too soon called out, "Keno!" Now I kept my
eyes fixed on this person; the matter seemed to me noteworthy. I
strolled past his table and took a good look—he wore the same noticeable ring, and unmistakably the same studs. There was no doubt it was
the same winner as before, only with other whiskers and other clothing.
The secret was now revealed; the operator of the game hired these
people who worked for him. They frequently called keno and took the
prizes without long or careful examination of their cards; they were
paid agents.

This particular man noticed that I was watching him and therefore
changed his place to another table and again called out keno. This time
I surreptitiously inscribed the numbers of his keno on my cuff. He left
the hall, and I took his card which still lay on the table to compare it
with the numbers I had marked down; there was no comparison. The
deception is entirely simple and therefore rarely discovered. The owner
of the keno den who maintains a half-dozen such paid agents, is able
to divert to his own pockets hundreds of dollars every night, while the
true players are shamefully bamboozled. Now and then the genuine
players are allowed to take a purse, perhaps even a prize, to encourage
them and to entice others. But the great mass of winnings in this manner flows back to the owner of the gambling house through the channel
of his agents.

The great popularity of keno with all classes of the population
seemed to decline a bit when the above revelations were made in the
widely read newspapers. But the game has by no means come to an
end. There are many people who seem to want to be deceived. There is
no help for them. And apart from keno there are many other lottery
games which are conducted secretly and yet openly enough in every
large American city, without any exceptions.

Young as American history may be, there is great zeal in fostering
it. National pride demands that. Everywhere in the larger cities are historical societies, in the meetings of which the members may compliment
each other on their learning and read each other "papers" on historical
subjects, often the products of bitter sweat and compiled by the light
of the midnight oil. American history is short. Yet the Americans have a
decided aptitude for history. Great men are only the expression of what
lies in the people, and that accounts for the large number of great his-

torians, of whom one need only to mention Irving, Prescott, Bancroft, and Motley. The taste for history also led Americans to celebrate the great centennial of the declaration of American independence on July 4, 1876, not in New York which is now the largest city in the United States, but in Philadelphia, the place where the declaration was signed and the seat of the congresses of the revolting states.

The site on which the Worlds Fair will be conducted was exceptionally well chosen and should satisfy even the most exacting requirements. True, many say that there have been so many expositions in the last decade that they have become outmoded and their power of attraction has long since faded. "From where," ask the skeptics, "can come a great mass of people to see what is still new and what has not formerly been shown?" It may be said in reply, however, that an American exposition is quite different, and capable of demonstrating altogether fresh phases of human achievement and human understanding, apart from the fact that it is joined to the centennial celebration of the creation of the republic.

They will surely celebrate the union of these two occasions in Philadelphia in the same manner as at the great musical festival in Boston several years ago, only on a far larger scale. They will hammer out the rhythm of the national anthem on a hundred genuine anvils, artillery salutes and steam organs will intone the hymn, and fifty-thousand school children, clad in red, white, and blue will raise their voices in "Hail Columbia" or "Yankee Doodle."

It is fortunate that the Worlds Fair is not directed by the government, since in America whatever is paid for out of the public purse, which indeed is deep enough, often leaves troubles afterwards. Americans guard against their own corruption, because they know each other; private enterprise has more chance of success than public. Quick building is characteristic in America where nothing is impossible. The promised structures will certainly be ready at the appointed time and will not be too small.

The outside world, however, has thus far had no proper conception of the young giant that has grown to gigantic proportions in the far lands of the west, since the United States was poorly represented in Paris and Vienna. Foreigners will be astounded at the vision of America's production, which will certainly impress in mass and size if not in taste and beauty. The pits of Nevada will display their enormous stores of silver, Michigan its copper, California its gold and quicksilver, Missouri its lead and tin, Pennsylvania its coal and iron. Fruit from the shores of the Pacific, gigantic pears and heavy lemons, will give Europeans an inkling of the unparalleled abundance of nature. The surprised guests will be shown Indians and buffaloes, turkeys, cotton, and rattlesnakes, which they never saw before. And from a thousand factories will come the evidences of the wonders of American mechanical skill.

23.

AN AMSTERDAM JOURNALIST

Charles Boissevain (1842–1927) came to the United States as correspondent of the Amsterdam Algemeen Handelsblad *in 1880, his purpose, to make a survey of economic and social conditions throughout the Union. After his return, he continued his career in journalism and ultimately became editor of the* Handelsblad, *which he made one of the most distinguished liberal newspapers on the continent. In addition to the articles assembled and published as* Van 't Noorden naar 't Zuiden *(1881) he wrote a book on his travels in the Near East and a series of influential pamphlets on the Boer War.*

The Negro regime in the South which now frightens away immigrants and drives the whites out of Louisiana to Texas, will not, I think, last long. Every new white immigrant tips the balance in favor of the dominant race. Every year more cotton is produced and brought from the upcountry to Galveston in Texas or to New Orleans. On the broad, high levees, which form a kind of platform for miles and miles along the Mississippi, bales of cotton are piled up, waiting for the various sail and steamboats. These almost endless quays present a merry sunny scene in the morning.

The singing of the blacks and the constantly repeated thunderous hiss of escaped steam let you know from afar that a cotton press is in operation. I went into a high wooden shed, on two sides of which the great doors were open. A gang of roustabouts, broad-shouldered Negroes, wild and savage in appearance like their forefathers on the shores of the Congo, their arms and shoulders bronze models of muscularity, dragged in the gigantic bales with iron hooks. Tied about with iron bands and already somewhat compressed, the cotton is brought from the plantations either on creaking carts drawn by plodding oxen or on steamboats on the decks of which they lie piled up fourteen high. The bales are rolled in, one by one, on iron trucks and lifted up from two sides by iron hooks. In the twinkling of an eye the iron bands are removed; a cloth on which a trade-mark is printed is laid upon one end of the bale and another on the iron plate on which it rests. With a shriek of the steam engine, the two iron plates are forced together; the bale is reduced to a fourth or a fifth of its initial size. It is then rebound and ready for shipment.

After the cotton is packed and compressed in this manner, in bales as hard as stone, it becomes very difficult to clean. It must, therefore, be freed of all impurities beforehand. The cotton is treated as soon as it comes out of the gin, and in that manner is improved with half the labor that would be necessary in the factory.

There is a bustling lively scene to be witnessed on the levees of New Orleans, and the cotton presses interested me enough to induce me to make another visit and watch hydraulic as well as steam machines in operation. The latter seemed to me, in general, preferable.

Going by the levees I saw in many places that shiny, feathery cottonseed which has nowadays become so valuable. Freedom and the fruitful competition of free laborers have already done a great deal for the development of the South and of its industry. Much that formerly was discarded as useless or made to serve only as fertilizer now is reckoned among the most valuable products of the land. With few exceptions the old-time plantations have disappeared; and small white or colored farmers have taken the place of the great planters. In the South more than 300,000 persons now share the income of cotton culture. The largest share goes to those who plant and pick the plant, a smaller portion to those who transport the crop to its destination. Each farmer must strive and do his utmost to get as much as he can for his work; and that has led many people to devote their attention to the utilization of parts of the plant other than its silky, feathery down. If the cotton crop brought to New Orleans is reckoned at 5,000,000 bales, weighing 1,200,000 tons, then it is clear there were left over, after the feathery down was removed, some 3,000,000 tons of cottonseed, which formerly seemed to be only a worthless part of the plant and was thrown away.

Yet cottonseed is a mine which now yields 100,000 tons of phosphates, of lime, and of potash yearly. Cottonseed contains 4 per cent of those minerals concentrated chiefly in the husk. At present, 1,500,000 tons of the seed are yearly gathered, from which is made oil and oil-cakes, a matchless food for sheep and cattle. The yield is about 375,000 tons of the former, about 225,000 of the latter. If they wished to treat the seed so as to distill from it only the chemical components, they could get fibers, from which a beautiful white paper might be made; and in France they already know how to derive first-rate dyes from cottonseed oil. Free labor has thus opened up a valuable gold mine which was formerly passed by as valueless.

A visit to one of the many oil mills will show how this cottonseed, once treated as trash, is converted into a profitable product. These establishments are not so fit as a ballroom for exquisitely dressed ladies, but they nevertheless present a cheerful and exciting spectacle. Everything shines and sparkles. The operatives chew the sweet oilcakes while they work, and look healthy and well-fed. Such are the results already achieved with this oil that the cottonseed has become the most valuable part of the plant.

"This is the new South!" said a manufacturer to me as he courteously showed me through his factory. Up to now, farming, and especially cotton culture, was almost the only source of income in the land. But the "new South"—made wise by adversity—is more diversified, esteems skilled labor, intellectual effort, artistic feeling, and scientific research. A new current has entered men's thoughts and desires. An enterprising spirit attracts capital from the North and even from England —factories are erected, mines opened up.

I traveled for two days with an old officer of General McClellan, who had been here some ten years ago; his continuous expressions of surprise, his exclamations of wonder at the changes which have come about since then were more instructive than statistical tables or labored arguments. The present leaders and pioneers of the South are responsible neither for slavery nor rebellion. They were boys or unknowing young men when the terrible contest began and they have turned the bitter experience to good account.

There is so much iron ore throughout the South that it seems amaz-

ing that all the tools were once imported from the North. As soon as
hard times compelled people here to get to work, they built factories,
forged the iron, and beat the anvil with rhythmic blows. They manufacture their own agricultural tools now and turn out, as well, steam
engines, cotton presses, and sugar vats. Wagons, carts, and beautiful
carriages are also produced by the hundreds. Iron foundries spout their
flames and tongues of black smoke out of great chimneys in Alabama,
Mississippi, and Texas, and in most of these factories Negroes work
next to white laborers. The preparation of tobacco and the making of
cigars is almost exclusively entrusted to former slaves, although the
blacks do not yet work in the cotton spinning and weaving factories.

Anyone who wishes to have the pleasure of meeting industrialists
who do not complain, who praise the times and acknowledge that they
make good products, should visit the cotton factories of the South.
These manufacturers think it is a waste of time and money to send raw
cotton to Massachusetts, have it spun and woven there, and then have
it come all the way back to the great region from Virginia to Texas and
Florida where it was raised in the first place. The improvement of the
mouth of the Mississippi through the genius of the American government engineers makes it possible for the southern producers to ship
their cotton goods by sea, and they thus send their calicoes as far as
Shanghai. They have the best machines, comparable even to those I
saw in the Pacific Mills in Lawrence and Lowell, and although the
finer goods are not yet made, they expect that in a few years the South
will compete with New England even in those branches.

To be sure, I speak now of discoveries, inventions, and industry in
which free competition and the incentive to labor were the goads that
produced progress. It is perhaps of equal interest that I touch at the
same time on what is now done in Louisiana and elsewhere in the
South to make use of the fibers which grow with such abundance in
this tropical climate. Bamboos, plane trees, bananas, aloes, and man-
goes are rich in fibers that could be worked up in many useful ways.
In New Orleans, for instance, I lived at 17 Orleans Street, a gathering-
place of industrious merchants who took an interest in this subject.
There Mr. Thomas Spear and his son-in-law, Paul Surgi, showed me,
with machines of their own contrivance, what use could be made of
the stems of the cotton plant.

The woody parts of bananas, cotton stems, bagasse, and jute are passed between two rollers, a smooth and a coarse cylinder, as in the sugar mills. The smooth cylinder makes a soft material of the banana stalks and jute, the rough one bends, breaks, and shatters the woody fibers of the cotton stems. Mr. Spear assured me that there are in Louisiana alone 139 plants whose fibers are valuable. The cotton stems are already worth ten cents a pound on the markets of New Orleans. From jute they make cord, twine, sacks, carpets, and a substitute for silk. Because they can raise two jute crops a year in Louisiana (the first in June), its manufacture will probably soon increase.

To conclude, I can report that American newspapers are now being printed on paper made of wood and straw. In Chicago the editor-in-chief of one of the journals told me that the cost of newsprint is one of the heaviest expenses of publication. The first task of anyone who begins to publish a newspaper is to buy or rent a stream, the water power of which can be used to make paper of the nearby forest.

I visited an old-fashioned plantation and spoke with some intelligent whites, and with some free Negroes who had once been slaves. Walking through the cotton fields in the thick red clay mud, a great deal out of the past and present became clearer than before.

Among other things, I discovered that I always too readily identified the champions of the South with the defenders of states' rights and that I was partially blind to the double principle for which both the North and South fought.

Mr. Cabot Lodge of Boston, one of the most talented men in the Union, still young but very learned, made this clear to me. The true contest between the North and the South was the same as that which once was joined between the Puritans and the Cavaliers. This was the battle between democracy and aristocracy, between the rights of all and the rights of a few. Two social systems were established in the United States, and even in that gigantic land there was no room for both. This South could not be exploited by free labor, and free labor was stifled in an atmosphere in which slaves drew breath.

It was the heroic age of America, when the battle between these two systems was joined, when the young Jasons and Hercules left countinghouses and shops in their young manhood to fight against the many-headed monster that threatened the Republic. American nationality had to be rescued from the menace of separatism; American democracy had to defend itself against the hereditary aristocracy of

Virginia. New England, with Boston as its center, represented democracy; for its system and its principles were based on the church government of the illustrious old Puritanism. Virginia, with its aristocracy of slaveholders, with its great landowners and gentry of English descent, who were raised with the inherited, deep-rooted prejudices of the ancient regime, was the torchbearer of those who wished to preserve an oligarchy, of those who wished in theory and in practice to maintain a dominant class of slave owners, of those in whose eyes democracy and anarchy were equivalent. These men used as weapons, as means for reaching their goal, the sovereignty of the individual state which fortunately both now and earlier was always respected and supported by all American parties alike.

The aristocracy of Virginia, which once gave America a Washington, was more and more degraded and weakened through the accursed system of slavery. The gentlemen became no more than overseers and slave drivers. It was a masterful, luxurious, merry life that they lived; and walking about here I wished, despite myself, that I might once have been the guest of one of the old masters of the land on his plantation. Yet the system was accursed and inherently rotten, just like the regimes of Louis XIV and Louis XV that prepared France for revolution. Men, out of pride, were forced to defend a system that, in their hearts, they despised as degrading and demoralizing for both masters and slaves. The unlimited power over their fellow men, who were treated like beasts in the forest, bought and sold, led the masters to lose both their good manners and their good principles. The Cavaliers had identified themselves with an evil, immoral system and principle. But, thank God, in the New World too, the Puritans won out. Government by one class, by one social group, by an aristocracy with boundless rights over its slaves, was beaten, killed, exterminated.

Democracy now reigns in this great, rich land and our children will become aware of this great, powerful attempt by all to govern a state for the good of all.

I have spoken with several old slaveholders who acknowledge that slavery was properly abolished and that free labor is more profitable than they had ever thought. But they complain bitterly because the government went too far in giving the right to vote to the emancipated Negroes, and thereby ruined both the land and the people.

The South always lagged a hundred years behind the North in development and energy, and this was a result of slavery. Now the institution has disappeared; but its consequences still remain. It could not be otherwise. The usual creative influences of our times—freedom, education, business enterprise, industry, the exploitation of fresh resources—will slowly bring steady improvement, but patience is necessary. The wounds of the war are slowly being bound up, although it is undeniable that the reconstruction policy, the government's attitude after the war, at first kept the sores irritated by giving power over the conquered people to republican adventurers from the North.

It was unavoidable that a revolution so radical should at first cause much misery. The uprooting of a massive old tree like slavery would not occur without a great shock to the whole surrounding terrain. But nevertheless, a great deal of the desperate misery was the consequence of the folly of suddenly giving the full powers of citizenship to the slaves scarcely freed, not yet capable of thinking for themselves, who inevitably became the simple tools of clever place seekers and professional politicians.

The worst disservice that could have been done for the freedmen was to throw them, unprepared, into the American political battle, an enticing prey for the hungry adventurers from the North who received the picturesque name of carpetbaggers from the suitcase which was their only luggage when they came down the Mississippi. The state can easily give infants the right, but never the ability to cast a vote.

Now the carpetbagger instead of the slave owner is master of the Negro, for the idea that the blacks in the South or elsewhere are able to govern whites is laughable. The white must remain the older brother, the leader; this can no more be resisted than can a law of nature.

The Negro has been pressed into the service of a party just as he was formerly compelled to serve in the house or fields. The Republican Party has harnessed him so that it could, in accordance with its own conceptions, organize the South in such a manner as to retain office and keep control of the rich posts and patronage. When the Civil War ended, the government had to decide how to develop the liberated areas and feed the citizens, since the South had fallen into anarchy and all public institutions were overthrown. The central government had complete power. The Confederacy was conquered, unarmed. Its means of existence, as well as its government, had for the time being come to an end. The slaves were freed, but not through their own power or through their own heroic struggles; they were emancipated by Lincoln as a measure for the general welfare. Freedom, bestowed and not earned, must be guaranteed for the future. It was, moreover, hoped that the colored people would furnish the basis for reconstruction of the seceded states; they were therefore immediately given the same privilege as the white citizens of the northern states, while the former masters were stripped of all civic rights.

A new political system was thus artificially planted and cultivated, in flat contradiction to the convictions, habits, character, and traditions of the two races. The public funds, the income, and the power of the various southern states were actually placed in the hands of Negroes who formerly were not trusted with a dollar for domestic purposes. It is no wonder that in some states a reign of terror followed as a matter of course, that elections and appointments were horribly botched, that bribery and crude deceptions gained the ascendency in the courts, and that taxes were imposed with absolute arbitrariness. Adventurers from the North who, with the support of the Negroes, did as they saw fit in the conquered land, drove up the debts of such states as Mississippi, Texas, Alabama, and Georgia. All that made no difference to the Negro electorate; and the southern white, the natural sufferers, had nothing to say in the matter, but were forced to stand by while the carpetbaggers had a free hand. To comprehend fully the nature of the reign of terror, of the anarchy to which the South was prey, it must be understood that ignorant Negro jurors handed down the law to the whites.

The same Negroes, whose great loyalty and faith was so wonderful while they watched over the women and children of their absent masters, became drunk with sudden freedom, mad with sudden power. At first they roamed through the land in bands, waiting for something unforeseen, miraculous, melodramatic to happen. Egged on by mean whites they began here and there to commit horrible crimes, to treat women in a low manner. Property was in danger, there was no law, no justice, and when the threatened whites themselves united to resist they resorted to the tragic, cowardly means of a secret society of masked men, which simply interfered with and obstructed the administration of justice. The Ku-Klux Klan probably had good intentions to begin with, when it attempted to judge and punish violent misdeeds. But a secret society works in the dark; masked executioners put into effect the death sentences passed by an unknown power; and that power began to serve as an easy means for satisfying personal hatreds, greed, and low passions. The Negroes were followed, hunted down, and murdered. Those who wish to know how the Klan went to work should read the exciting, masterly book by Judge Tourgée, *A Fool's Errand*. This impartial work, full of humor and feeling, describes in an impressive style what honest courageous northern men, who tried to reorganize the South after the war, had to suffer. This book is truly a sequel to *Uncle Tom's Cabin*. It is an account that is lived rather than written, and whoever desires to learn to know the South should study the spirit of restrained tragedy embodied in Judge Tourgée's volume.

The Ku-Klux Klan is at present as good as suppressed, but the Negroes are in no better position to make free use of the right to vote. In addition to the fact that many masters make renunciation of the privilege a condition of employment, the colored people are directly prevented from voting for whomever they wish through trickery and through open frauds at the ballot box. The two races stand hostile to each other, almost armed, in Louisiana and Arkansas. They have reached a sort of truce in Texas and Mississippi; in Alabama and Georgia there is a compromise, but they lay traps and countertraps to outflank each other. There is still no thought of coöperation. In Mississippi, southern Alabama, and Louisiana the Negroes cannot vote without illegal interference by the whites, who either use force or else take no notice of the votes of the colored people—not even taking the trouble to count them.

Every year less raw violence is needed and less blood is shed. Instead, the whites now use innocent words to conceal guilty practices. They have contrived ingenious, neatly arranged magic boxes and mysterious receptacles, like magicians, to neutralize Negro influence. In the black districts there are separate ballot boxes for white and colored voters. The voters must pass through a narrow space between two fences which scarcely lets through one man at a time. If the white group is in danger from a great attendance of black Republicans, they then challenge the vote of some single ignorant Negro, preferably one from a distant district or neighborhood. While the other colored people, who wish to vote, press together behind him in the narrow passageway, they send for witnesses who can testify that the voter is known to them and qualified to vote. When the proof is presented, the Negro is permitted to cast his ballot. The comedy is played out with politeness and dignity and follows the best forms. The other Negroes cannot vote until this difficult case is decided. In a little while a similar difficulty rises. Meanwhile, the time for closing the polls approaches, and before long it is evident that a Democratic majority will be preserved.

In other parts of the country not even that much attention is paid to the forms; the votes of the Negroes are simply not counted. It is openly known that this is done, but such acts are justified as measures of self-defence, protecting society. The most vital interests, it is claimed, force the use of these illegal measures, so long as the place-seeking leaders of the freedmen are robbers and brigands.

A new party alignment, desirable everywhere in America, is essential if the South would oppose the greedy Republican Negro-drivers. The line between the two parties should no longer be that of skin color. The entire white South should cease to be solidly Democratic, if not from conviction, then simply from self-interest. But before this can happen, all honest and thoughtful citizens, all those who recognize the sovereignty of the law and approve no low deception, must together protest against the frauds at the ballot box. Recently the federal government failed to secure the conviction, in the courts of South Carolina, of several Democrats who had openly and without denying it falsified the ballot. The press rejoiced over "the fortunate and heroic frustration of the plot to Africanize the state." This Africanizing plot consisted in the indictment of those who had dishonestly turned a minority into a majority. Double bottoms and the substitution of spurious for genuine boxes cannot be the appropriate means of giving the southern states honorable, respectable governments. The Negro's lack of fitness for the exercise of the ballot can be the basis for a movement for amending the constitution, but the defenders of a regime who know no better means than deceit at the polls will earn the confidence of no one. To rule by falsified rolls and by ballot boxes with double bottoms is worse than a military dictatorship.

The knowledge, the healthy understanding, the calm judgment which are essential to a citizen before he gets the right to exercise the high privilege of voting, are entirely absent in the great majority of colored voters. With respect to that, there is no real difference of opinion between the parties. Sheep, driven to the pen by their shepherds, can as well decide as to whether they should remain out in the open field. The sheep would at least exercise a preference between sleep and food, but the Negroes have no understanding of the problems before them and therefore no real vote. The former slaves simply act as the Republican party leaders tell them to, since they know that the Republicans put an end to slavery. Content with so little, they are taken in by the greatest rascal and put the revenue and treasury in the hands of the unworthy. A new party alignment is therefore necessary. The South must no longer remain solid against the party dominant in the North.

The bitterness of the whites toward the black race happily diminishes year by year. Many Negroes are gradually moving toward the alluvial soil, the climate of which they can alone resist, and toward tropical Mexico. And as more European immigrants establish themselves in the South, the relations between the two races will grow better and better. Precisely for that reason, the civilized whites should offer a good example and cease to drive the Negroes from the polls by deceit and by violations of the law.

24.

AMERICAN SOCIETY—A NEAPOLITAN VERSION

Carlo Gardini, author of this account (which is taken from his popular book, Gli Stati Uniti, *1891), had many official contacts with the United States prior to his visit. For a time he actually served as American consular agent in Bologna. In the 1880's he had occasion to come to the United States several times and became well acquainted with some parts of the country. His work was well received in Italy and was also translated into German.*

The Americans say that London is the city of business and that Paris is the capital of pleasures, but that New York unites the attractions of both. That there is some basis of truth in that judgment seems to me not unlikely, since the metropolis of the New World has innumerable places for every kind of entertainment. The theaters are indeed very much frequented, and theatrical investments in New York and in the other American cities are, I think, more secure and more lucrative than in Europe. It is particularly worth noting that absolute freedom reigns in American theaters and that therefore government taxes, authors' royalties, and publishers' fees are almost unknown there.

There is no characteristic national musical theater in the United States, at least not unless you would assign that appellation—which I think would be absurd—to the jolly performances of the minstrels. But these are no more than popular spectacles, buffoonery of a special kind. The minstrels are comics, endowed with some talent, who appear on the stage in frock coats and made up as Negroes to amuse and entertain their audience. They sing; they play; they recite; they offer farces, pantomimes, and parodies; and, as in the Athens of Aristophanes, they make allusions full of spirit and of sarcasm to the personalities in vogue and to the most pressing questions of the day.

During these presentations I was interested to hear the minstrels play masterfully on the banjo, a stringed instrument new to me. This instrument is somewhat similar to the Italian guitar, but the sound box is instead round and made of skins like the Neapolitan tambourine.

Italian opera is the musical spectacle that is generally most attractive to the upper class of the population. The art of *bel canto,* of harmoniously singing the melodies of Bellini, Donizetti, Rossini, and Verdi, interpreted in the most rhythmic and most musical language in the world, even today draws spontaneous enthusiasm from the Americans. And often I had occasion to hear from opera-goers of mature age recollections of the times, the best in the history of the musical theater in New York, when Lind, Sontag, Parodi, Grisi, and Mario enchanted the audiences of the old Castle Garden theater.

In more recent years, however, the works of the great German and French masters have also succeeded in winning the favor of the public, especially in New York where they are performed fully as well as among us. The operas of Wagner have thus become very popular and attract great crowds.

During my first stay in New York, Italian opera was presented only in the Academy of Music, which was then considered the really aristocratic theater of the city. This building is worth describing in brief, since most of the other theaters in America were modeled after it.

The hall was in the French style; that is, with galleries outside the proscenium and all around on the first floor. In these galleries are built boxes which belong to those who hold stock in the theater. Each box, to distinguish it, carries, instead of an ordinary number, the name of a celebrated composer of the operas presented on that stage, or sometimes the name of a singer who had there been received with much applause. The boxes are thus called Rossini, Bellini, Mozart, Donizetti, Verdi, Gounod, Lind, Patti, Mario, Geisler, and so on. At the performances of the Italian opera the women wear elegant gowns, and the men evening clothes.

Some years ago the so-called young aristocracy, that is, the families of those who accumulated their millions in recent times, were not able at any price to get to own a box in the Academy of Music. They resolved to build a new theater for opera (the Metropolitan Opera House), larger than the Academy of Music. As may happen in America, scarcely twelve months went by from the day when the project was planned to the celebration of the opening.

Following that, in the autumn of 1883, the Metropolitan presented Italian opera, and precisely at the same time when Italian opera was also being offered in the Academy of Music. That season was really a golden age for the theater in New York; the artists, because of the war between the young and the old aristocracy, pocketed veritable treasures, and the public had the luck to hear in a single winter all the living celebrities of the world, a luxury certainly not afforded by any capital in Europe.

As in England and in Germany, the taste for classical, choral, and instrumental music has already struck root among the Americans, and I had occasion several times to hear the best musical productions in the Steinway Piano Company's beautiful hall.

In May of 1881 and 1882 there were two festivals in New York dedicated to classical music, sacred and profane. The most renowned compositions of Bach, Beethoven, Cherubini, Spontini, Gluck, Mozart, Wagner, and the best oratorios of Händel and Mendelssohn were performed. In the rendition of these masterpieces, aside from the celebrated artists who took the solo parts, and aside from the 320 piece orchestra, there participated a chorus of 3500 voices, men and women of the choral societies of New York and vicinity. The locale chosen for this solemn occasion held 12,000 commodious seats, without counting the space for listeners willing to stand. Including the performers, this place, or rather plaza, was capable of holding 18,000 people at once, and I was assured that there was not a vacant space during the performance.

If Newport occupies first place for ocean bathing in the United States, Saratoga must take the palm for its mineral waters. Two powerful attractions draw the Americans, particularly those in high life, to the latter town. On the one hand there is the therapeutic value of its springs, which were secretly used even by the Indians, who venerated them as gifts of the Great Spirit; on the other there is the splendor and richness of its hotels and the irresistible fascination of the enchantress we call fashion.

There may be mineral baths in Europe pitched by nature in sites more pleasant and more beautiful than those in Saratoga, but there is no place on earth that can equal the New York resort in the splendor of its establishments and in the overwhelming luxury that surrounds the families of the millionaires who frequent it, especially at the height of the season. There are about 11,000 permanent inhabitants in the town; but the number triples from the first of June to the middle of September, a period in which lodgings are most difficult to secure.

Saratoga boasts the finest hotels in the United States, and that means in the world. The best known are the United States Hotel, the Grand Union Hotel, and the Congress Hotel, which like most of the others are located on Broadway, the main street. There they profit by day from the shade of fine maple trees, and by night are illuminated by electricity.

The Congress and the Columbia are the most popular springs. These may be found in Congress Park where they flow in the shade of two magnificent wooden pavilions, connected with each other by a kind of colonnaded gallery. There is also a kiosk for the orchestra, which is made up entirely of more or less skillful Germans who, paradoxically, seem to play only Italian tunes. I tried the waters of the Congress Spring and found them slightly sour but not unpleasant.

The Saratoga hotels are open only during the summer. To avoid the inconveniences of the season they are almost all situated in the midst of large splendid gardens, and built with thick walls to keep the excessive heat out of the living quarters. As in the houses of the southern cities, they have files of spacious and elegant columns built into both the exterior walls and the walls surrounding the inside courts and gardens. These colonnades are topped with parapets in the form of a gallery. These piazzas, as the Americans call them, supply a place

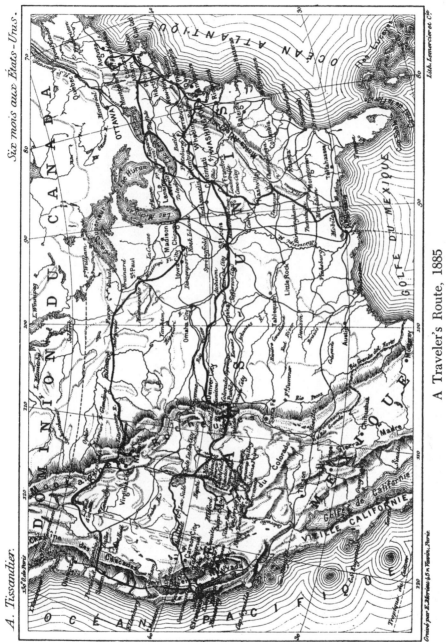

A. Tissandier.

Six mois aux États-Unis.

A Traveler's Route, 1885

Reno Station, Nevada, 1875

where the travelers may enjoy the open air while they remain protected from the rain and from the heat of the sun.

Every night the United States Hotel, like the other two mentioned above, presents an impressive spectacle. The spacious interior garden, adorned with trees and fountains and lighted by electricity, is crammed with the flower of aristocratic society—three-fourths, women elegantly dressed—who listen to the music played in the center. Part of the crowd stroll in the aisles among the blossoms; part is seated on chairs around the numerous tables scattered here and there, and engages in lively and jolly conversation. In the piazzas is the same luxury, the same happiness, the same movement. From the open doors of the parlors, and from the other regally furnished rooms, pour streams of light. There is dancing in the ballroom. There I tried the "Boston," which seemed to be a kind of waltz embellished with a graceful circular motion. Apparently, however, the American aristocracy do not consider it altogether dignified to indulge in this diversion; I was told that even at the evening garden parties, in which they dance on a platform built over the garden, only a very few men participate.

Walking through the halls, the garden, the piazzas, I had the opportunity to study high society, more so than in New York, in Boston, or even in Newport. And I could particularly note the difference in character between the two sexes, a difference so great that one might suppose them members of two different races.

The men have a rigid temperament; they speak little; and all, whatever their title—senator, governor, general, colonel—dress always in morning clothes, except for a white cravat which they wear everywhere. In the salon the American male is a fish out of water; not one of them will deny that his true place is the office, the countinghouse, or the political meeting.

The women, on the other hand, are full of spirit, chatter freely and coquettishly, yet do not go too far. They seem in their natural element. The alpha and omega of their daily routine is to rise, to eat, to talk, to change their costumes three or four times, and to sleep. When they come back in the morning from the mineral waters they have a substantial breakfast at about ten; then sit on the rocking chairs on the piazzas until it begins to be warm; then go to their rooms to change for lunch, which is at two. At the end of that meal they again retire to their chambers, and steal a nap on the sofa. At about six they reappear in traveling clothes, and ride in a carriage to Lake Saratoga, some seven kilometers away by a beautiful road lined with trees. There they may have an ice before they come back in time for supper. At nine they dress for the evening, almost always in gowns, half-décolleté and not seldom edged with lace, the value of which might easily come to 100,-000 lire. After an hour they descend to the piazza by the steps, a journey which reveals to best advantage their elegant shoes, on which there are often buttons or buckles made of diamonds.

It is then that the life of the hotels really begins. The elegant people who live in the United States Hotel go to the gardens, the parlors, and the piazzas of the Grand Union and the Congress hotels, while in return those who live in the latter two come to the United States Hotel. Thus the women give each other an opportunity to observe and criticize the clothes and the jewels of their rivals and to make full show of their own.

In the United States Hotel, as in most of the best American establishments, the waiters are Negroes. A European entering the dining hall is to some degree always surprised to see the long line of Africans in gala dress, their shining white linen strangely in contrast with the color of their skin, a color which varies in all the gradations from ebony black to the lightest shade of coffee.

The menu boasts a long list of foods in all languages, including the Indian. It is not only startling by comparison with the strict diets which are generally imposed in health resorts in Europe, but indeed demands that you be endowed with the stomach of an ostrich to eat, without indigestion, even half of what is put before you.

My Negro waiter quickly won my sympathy. I asked his name and was told it was Tom, a name very common among his race. He spoke with such assurance, moved with such swiftness, that he seemed to act as if propelled mechanically. He was almost always smiling so that his very white teeth showed, and on his breast shone a gigantic diamond that could not possibly have been genuine.

The conversation at our table was concerned first of all with the fair sex in Saratoga, and then with the names of the people who had become the season's rage through charm, eccentricity, or luxury. Then it turned to the great doings of the aristocracy of the hour and to politics, and finally it moved on to our hotel. One of my table mates, a pure American and therefore endowed with a special sense for figures, knew exactly the area of the plot on which the building stood, the number of halls, rooms, corridors, piazzas, doors, and windows, how many kilometers the carpets, telephone, telegraph, and electric wires would measure if laid end to end, how many tons of food were consumed in a day, the horsepower of the elevators, of the laundry, pumping, and other machines, the candlepower of the gas and electric lights, and the size of the great, complex army of administrative and service personnel. And to make all this interesting to me, he added that the many millions invested in the construction and equipment of the United States Hotel brought its stockholders a return of more than 5 per cent a year, despite the fact that it was open only during the summer months.

That which, however, made me open my eyes wide with surprise was the assertion of my companion about the Jews. These people, he said, would not be admitted to the best Saratoga hotels, not even were they the Rothschilds in person. In the land of democracy, where freedom of laws and of religion reach their apogee, I would have thought such restrictions fantastic. However, these were the facts, and one must come to believe that anti-Semitism has roots so deep and so strong in America that it will be impossible to extirpate them.

25.

A RUSSIAN MAN OF BUSINESS

Tverskoy was the pen name of Peter A. Demens (born in 1849). He became a member of the Imperial Guard. At the age of twenty-nine he quarreled with a member of the royal family, and found it expedient to go into exile. In America he turned his hand, with some success, to a variety of businesses, and wrote a book which in translation is titled "Sketches of the North American United States" (1895). Later he was a sympathizer with the Russian radical movements and wrote a revolutionary novel. In addition, he composed an account of the Dukhobers. In 1916 he aided in reorganizing the Russian Purchasing Bureau in New York City and he died, in the United States, in 1919.

In 1883 my lumber business grew to the extent that I was obliged to add a wood-processing factory to my sawmill. The number of workers in our hamlet then increased greatly, and since the local stores could not satisfy their wants, I opened a general store in order to keep the laborers on the spot.

Obviously I had no understanding of commercial affairs, and this business demanded specialized knowledge; you had to know all the prices as well as where and how to buy. I therefore secured a partner, a man completely unknown to me but one who had a good acquaintance with general merchandise. I must note here that companies and partnerships are formed amazingly swiftly in America. People who meet in the morning for the first time, by the afternoon are joined in some enterprise. No one bothers about your past, who you are, whence you come, why you need help. In the North, recommendations or references are sometimes demanded, but in the West and South you are taken at your word. A stranger is considered an honest citizen until he proves himself the opposite.

My new partner was a man without any means, having just lost his entire substance in an unfortunate venture in Virginia. We came to an agreement within a quarter of an hour, and agreed to bring in about $1500 each. By this time I possessed unlimited credit. Thanks to my lumber and contracting business, I had already entered into direct relations with the North, buying all that I needed in New York, Philadelphia, and Boston. My name meant something in all the commercial credit agencies which take account not only of the financial but also of the moral character of every independent merchant or factory owner throughout the whole Union. Thanks to these facilities, we bought goods at 10 per cent discount and began to work. We maintained this store until 1888.

Nine-tenths of all American commerce is in the hands of various commission men and brokers. It is almost impossible to buy anything directly from the producer; every factory sells off its entire production to some sort of broker, who then resells it to retail merchants throughout the entire Union. Furthermore, as soon as the broker has some degree of monopoly over a given branch of production, he designates local wholesalers for a given territory—sometimes a state, sometimes several counties, sometimes one large city. It is then completely useless to try to deal directly with the producer. The purchaser must buy third-hand and pay two commissions. Among the goods thus distributed are

Minneapolis flour, California canned fruits, the better kinds of soap, the best candies, agricultural and other machinery, glass, pianos and organs, cheeses, good boots and galoshes, and the best hats. On all these one is forced to pay excess charges, sometimes twice the original value, for the maintenance of the middlemen. The commission men even control the commerce in such merchandise as cotton and woolen fabrics, although these are made in factories dispersed throughout the country.

Such an abnormal position is easily explained. In America a mass of free capital constantly seeks investment, and therefore competition is great in all manufactured articles. Overproduction appears now in one, now in another branch of industry, and then goods cannot find a market, since demand does not correspond to supply. The chief anxiety of every factory owner is, then, how and where to sell his product. Labor is dear and to pay his labor he must have ready cash, for there is hardly a state without a law obliging the employer to pay all his workers in full at least twice a month. If there is not a rapid turnover, the entrepreneur must have two or three times the normal capital to be in a position to conduct his business.

Under these circumstances, the middleman steps in as the savior of the manufacturer. The middleman has abundant capital and can help out the factory owner in a difficult moment. Such agreements are usually completed in a period of stagnation when money is dear and industry is especially in need of it. The broker generally buys up the entire product of a factory, often at his own price, and then can hold the manufacturer in his grasp for a long time, dictating when to increase, when to decrease, and even when to stop production entirely for a while. The Minneapolis miller, the Ohio wool manufacturer, and the Alabama industrialist depend completely and unconditionally upon agreements with their commission agents in England, or Australia, or South America, and become the slaves of the business fluctuations.

From their own point of view, the agents naturally try in every way to expand their business. They usually have extensive resources and use all sorts of cunning devices, the more quickly and the more profitably to sell the goods. Huge sums are spent in advertising of every kind. Nowhere in the world is there such a mass of newspapers; in the majority of cases these hold almost nothing but advertisements. There are also many other methods. All the fences, the sides of buildings, and often the roofs are inscribed with signs. Many commercial houses have specially organized publicity departments which spend tens of thousands of dollars annually; the mails are choked with the circulars, throw-aways, and brochures of these enterprising men of letters. Frequently visited public places are equipped with billboards which command a high price. In omnibuses, trolleys, and at railroad stations, the ceilings and walls are written over with these advertisements, frequently in rich frames and adorned with luxurious pictures and huge letters. About two months ago an enterprising soap dealer paid $17,000 at an auction sale for the right to advertise one year on the wall of the main entrance of the suspension bridge across the East River. The New York elevated trains annually receive more than $100,000 for the rights to their stations. And, most recently, shrewd speculators have reached the point where they hire special railroad cars, cover the outside walls with praises of their goods, and send them traveling over the whole Union.

But the most expensive, the most widespread, and the most unpleasant means of advertising is the dispatch of special people, called "drummers." These are clever, brash, nimble-tongued young gentlemen, usually foppishly dressed, uninhibited in manners, and supplied with an inexhaustible fund of shrewdness and impudence. The drummer is provided with great trunks of samples of the goods he sells. Sometimes he works for a commission, but more often for a fixed salary, and his boss pays all expenses. Such a migratory young man costs a commercial house no less than $3,000 a year; the smart ones may even cost $5,000, and especially good ones get up to $15,000. I myself know many firms which support as many as ten or fifteen such traveling salesmen, and know dozens of companies the advertising costs of which exceed $100,000 a year.

Obviously, all these expenses are ultimately paid by the consumers. These unhappy people do not even suspect that they support such a dreadful army, two or three times the size of any European force; they do not even realize that they frequently pay ten or fifteen times more than they ought to.

In the course of the last ten years many branches of industry and commerce have labored to create a common organization to pool their specialized interest and to form great monopolies. The well-known Standard Oil Company, which at present controls not only the trade but also the production of every kind of oil through such a combination by its amazing success has given an impetus to similar attempts by others. The process leads to even more dangerous measures, against which almost all the state legislatures have fought in vain, at least until now.

These so-called trusts arise from agreements among all the factories in a given branch of industry, flour mills, oatmeal-processing plants, and sugar refineries, for example. Each establishment is capitalized according to a valuation made by a special committee chosen from the ranks of all the owners; then each issues trust certificates in return for shares in the common central company. The shareholders then elect a central administration which manages all of the external affairs of the "trust," directs all the measures of production, buys the raw materials, fixes selling prices, and manages the joint merchandise warehouses. The internal affairs of each separate factory and the details of production remain in the hands of the actual owner. But, as a shareholder in the common enterprise, his profits depend upon the success of the trust, since all gains and losses are distributed through the trust, and not through the separate producing companies.

The Standard Oil Company achieved amazing results through the resolution and initiative of Rockefeller and Flagler, its entrepreneurs. All competition has been crushed in the most pitiless manner; about two years ago, for example, the retail price of paraffin oil, normally ten or eleven cents, was lowered to two cents a pound in order to kill off a newly rising competitor to the trust in Ohio. The founders of the new company lost millions in the unequal struggle and were annihilated in about two weeks.

In the course of the last two years trusts have been formed in sugar, pork, oatmeal, glass, and wheat flour. At this very moment a great struggle is going on between the sugar trust and the legislature and courts of New York State. Up to now the trust has been the victor on all points, although the courts have succeeded in making public many facts about the internal workings, and, more important, about the profits of this trust, facts hitherto carefully concealed from the people. It emerged, for instance, that there is a rigid discipline in all the details of the business, and that the ringleader, Havemeyer, made more than $12,000,000 in one year.

The legislatures and the courts find it very hard to battle these monopolies which, thanks to their fabulous profits, successfully circumvent the letter and the spirit of the law. So, for example, as soon as New York State declared the sugar trust illegal, that trust seemed to fall into ruins. But at the very same time a new organization with the identical members and operating in an identical manner appeared in the state of New Jersey, which by geographical location is nothing but a suburb of New York City. New Jersey now pays the major part of all of its expenses from taxes on this company, which finds it uncomfortable to lead an official life within the boundaries of the state of New York. Since the jurisdiction of the latter state does not extend beyond its own lines, the sugar trust continues to flourish; it conducts all its business in New York City, and across the Hudson maintains only a small office with one secretary. Years will pass before public opinion in New Jersey triumphs over the greed of her legislators; it is hard voluntarily to renounce millions in income from the taxes of these companies, which pay without any complaints and are never in arrears.

These trusts spread ever more rapidly; almost every day the newspapers announce the formation of new combinations in all parts of the Union and in all branches of industry and commerce. They have declared a most pitiless and cruel war against firms which, for some reason, remain independent. Thus, several weeks ago the Illinois whiskey trust by hired agents dynamited a distillery in Chicago that refused to enter the combine. The secretary, the real boss, is accused of being the chief ringleader of the plot, although the courts will scarcely succeed in proving anything against him personally or against the trust as a whole.

Closely related to the question of trade in America is that of credit. Both in wholesale and in retail business agreements in terms of cash are exceedingly rare; everything is sold over a period—thirty days, sixty days, three, four, six, and even twelve months. Every branch of commerce has its own customs, its own rules. Foodstuffs are usually bought by retailers from wholesale dealers on a thirty or sixty-day basis; furnishings, boots, hats and ready-made clothing for four and six months; machines and agricultural implements for twelve months. In retail trade these terms are observed quite strictly; but in the South the majority of dealers still are unable to accustom themselves to obligatory periods for settlement of accounts, and the credit system is quite disorderly.

Of course, nowhere in the world has personal credit developed to such a degree as it has in America. Once a man, who stands at the head of any sort of manufacturing or commercial enterprise, has been able to earn public confidence, he can buy on credit, according to the customary conditions, whenever and wherever he may be. It is consequently possible to have both extensive businesses and extensive reverses in America with comparatively insignificant personal means. Thanks also to this system great fortunes frequently and rapidly accumulate from nothing. With the exception of the Vanderbilts and Astors, none of the richest people of this generation inherited wealth —they made it themselves, through credit and successful speculation. Jay Gould, Andrew Carnegie, Rockefeller, Flagler, Armour, Stanford, and Pullman—all began with a few coppers and now reckon their annual income in tens of millions.

Americans, in general, are therefore deeply infected with the speculative spirit. And, unfortunately, speculation is not confined to Wall Street, to shares, stocks, and to land. All branches of commerce and industry suffer from it periodically. Agricultural and industrial prices constantly fluctuate, and change more often because of unexpected and, for the masses, unexplained manipulations of speculators than because of the natural laws of political economy. Prices are usually raised or lowered in quite an artificial way; huge funds, often tens of millions of dollars, are concentrated at certain points, and one fine morning a well-known product unexpectedly and completely disappears from the market or sometimes suddenly gluts it. Prices therefore momentarily go up or down and great sums are made and lost. These perturbations reverberate in all the far-flung corners of the Union. Wheat, flour, nails, iron, glass, pork, coffee, sugar, in a word, every possible kind of merchandise in turn serves as the object of these manipulations. Some dealers grow rich in these operations, some poor; but all must give them careful attention and use constant caution in the choice of commodities since, thanks to local newspapers, the telegraph, and the railroads, the retail market is exceedingly sensitive to the condition of prices in the chief centers. I myself more than once gained and lost considerable sums, thanks to unexpected and unexplained fluctuations.

I cannot resist giving a short sketch of those peculiarities and distinguishing characteristics of the American people which seem an immediate result of its institutions, laws, and mores. Having lived in various sections for ten years, not as a tourist on holiday, but earning my bread by work, I am not in danger of falling into the gross errors of the casual traveler. At the same time, many features of American life are so strange and incomprehensible to a Russian that to this very day I have been unable fully to become reconciled and acclimated to them.

The great mass of people in the United States, despite differences in material conditions, is relatively on the same level of mental development. The sons of the poor, unlucky, day laborer and of the wealthy banker or merchant go to the same school for five or sometimes ten years. They grow and develop mentally under the same influences, in the same atmosphere, as if there were no difference in conditions in their home life and background. One, perhaps, will finish in a six grade public school, another will go to a university, perhaps will even travel for two or three years in Europe. But in the great majority of cases, their moral and mental life will be formed under the influence of the public school; and the spirit of equality and mutual respect which they there assimilate will remain inviolable to death. One will become a merchant or a manufacturer or enter a profession and earn a large income, another will remain a hired craftsman. But they will constantly meet each other; they will read the same newspapers and magazines; they will attend and take part in the same public meeting; they will belong to the same Masonic lodge; they will go to the same church; in a word, they will live an identical mental life.

The press of the country plays a great role in this regard; the newspapers and magazines are so cheap and so widely diffused that I do not think there is one family that does not get at least one, and more often two or three publications.

The report of the D. P. Royal Company, an advertising agency, revealed that there were in 1891 almost 20,000 periodicals in the country, weeklies, monthlies, and dailies. The diffusion of some publications is simply amazing: the monthly *Century* is published in 550,000 copies, the daily *World* is published in 300,000, the weekly *World* in more than 2,000,000. All of these periodicals are comparatively very cheap; the monthly magazines, magnificent in format and luxuriously illustrated, cost three or four dollars a year; the biggest daily newspaper, eight or ten; the daily in the small towns, from four to six; and the weeklies from a half to two. Furthermore, the publishers send copies to every end of the Union to be sold at retail at every stationer's. In every tobacco shop, at every station—everywhere you can buy a copy of any newspaper or magazine without subscribing. I regularly read more than ten different journals, but subscribe only to one big New York political paper and to the local daily; all the others I buy as they come out, at little more than the cost of subscription.

In New York City there are twenty-five dailies, in other big cities three or four, and in middle-size towns, usually two—one Republican, the other Democratic. It would not be far from the truth to suppose that 500 daily newspapers are published in towns of less than 8,000 inhabitants. Every one gives all the European and international telegrams of the international press association and prints American news in its entirety. The most insignificant little hamlet with a few hundred residents unfailingly has its own weekly in which, along with world news, are communicated all the local events of the week—marriages, baptisms, arrivals, and departures. It is obvious that these papers are supported not by subscriptions but by advertisements, and sometimes by the subsidies of local bosses and the gifts of land agents. In every issue such a newspaper extols some local specialty and attempts to entice new settlers. Yet at the same time, not one important political or commercial occurrence will escape its attention, and the poorest local day laborer is therefore invariably acquainted with these affairs and in a position to be quite clear as to their meaning.

In addition, all American newspapers and particularly the big dailies reckon it their duty to interfere in every kind of current event. Nothing is hidden from them. Reporters often dig up all the details of criminal offenses, and they air, unbelievably, not only the public but also the family life, the religious belief, and the habits of the candidates for every public position. Many papers support whole armies of detectives, and every blemish, every questionable step of a man in public life will certainly be uncovered and investigated to the tiniest detail.

The church serves as another powerful instrument of union and social intercourse among the American people. According to the last census, there were almost a hundred different sects in the United States. As is well known, religious teaching, as it is usually understood, is completely excluded from the elementary and higher schools which are supported by public funds; every church, therefore, has its own Sunday schools, and some have universities maintained by church funds and entirely separate from public education in the strict sense of the term. The Constitution of the United States, which is repeated with only insignificant changes in the constitutions of the separate states, guarantees forever the complete freedom of religious belief. A citizen of the Union has the right to believe anyone or anything he pleases, unless his faith cuts across the fundamental laws of the Union, as for example, in the case of the polygamous teachings of Mormonism. Thirty-one of the above-mentioned sects hold communistic ideas, in which number are the Shakers, the Harmonists, the Separatists, and the Altruists. Every year many new religions are introduced; others die out. Some assume a practical form; they found settlements and communal houses. Yet up to this time only the Shakers have persisted with some durability, and even their communities seem to decline every year; at present there are fifteen at most, although in 1880 there were over forty.

The Catholics compose no less than one-quarter of both the church organizations and the church members of the Union. The remainder are scattered among different kinds of Protestant churches with Baptists and Methodists in the lead. The Catholics have the very same organization as elsewhere in the world. The United States already has two cardinals and will apparently soon receive a third.

The organization of the Protestant churches is quite varied. Only the so-called missionary parishes have clergymen who are nominated by their regional synods and are on a fixed salary. In all the remaining cases, the parishes conclude private agreements with the clergymen, who in big cities and wealthy parishes are often paid large salaries, $5,000, $6,000, $10,000, even $25,000 a year, according to the extent of their popularity and of their ability to make themselves indispensable to their flocks.

Since the American people in general and the Protestant sects in particular are distinguished by an extreme of toleration, parishioners are not particularly constrained with regard to which church they attend. The churches, therefore, devote all their powers to attracting as many visitors as possible; in the cities there is quite a sharp competition in this respect. The churches buy expensive organs, and support excellent choirs, often with large salaries to professional singers. Recently boy choirs have been introduced, often of sixty voices. The churches, so to say, follow the fashions; revenues rise and fall with the volume of visitors; with every influx one or another sect gains the upper hand in a given locality.

I must, nevertheless, render justice to the American clergy. I have come in contact with many clergymen of different sects. The vast majority are people of deep faith and conviction, with good education and understanding. They not only interest their audience by a capable and shrewd approach to religious matters, but also give effective aid to the poor and unfortunate of their districts.

Parish charity in the most varied forms is a widespread and an extremely useful activity in America; it may take the shape of a society for the spread of useful knowledge or a society for the distribution of help to the poor. In connection with the first, I must not fail to mention the young men's and women's Christian associations which do a great deal of good by their lectures, reading rooms, gymnasiums, and, most important, by leadership and moral supervision over their members. In many counties there are independent societies which choose as the focus of their activity the poorest part of a town. They rent quarters, furnish them, and either teach the local girls the cutting-out and sewing of clothes, or explain various practical arts to the boys, or simply make the cold warm and feed the hungry. The effective work of aid is usually carried out by women under the direction of the clergymen; the male members of the church collect the money. Hypocrisy and the vain desire to shine by one's charitable works are often the most powerful attractions to the work. Men of affairs who figure diligently in church matters frequently enjoy an ugly business reputation, although, of course, this in no way diminishes the importance and usefulness of their assistance. We must be just both to the clergymen and to the ladies of the societies; their help is usually extremely effective.

Masonic lodges of various names also play no small role in the social life of America. The Masons have preserved all the old external forms and the ceremonies of the past century. But their chief task has become mutual aid for their members—insurance of their lives and earnings. The group commands huge amounts of property and capital; the most expensive and highest building in the world, an edifice finished not long ago in Chicago, belongs to the Order of Odd Fellows, an order which had more than 650,000 members and expended almost $3,000,000 in aid in 1890. The Order of Freemasons is about the same size, has direct ties with orders of the same name in England and Germany, and recognizes Prince Vallissky as its grand master. The total membership of American lodges approaches 3,000,000. There are twenty-eight orders, of which the two mentioned above are the most important.

Literary, music, singing, reading, and debating clubs are quite numerous. Every little hamlet inevitably has some such societies; in thickly populated agricultural areas every inhabitant also inevitably belongs to two or three of them. The most significant one, the Chautauqua Literary and Scientific Circle, founded in 1878, now has some 50 separate chapters and more than 500,000 active members throughout the country. Its goals are the diffusion of the habit of reading, and the study of nature, science, and art in connection with the routine of daily work. It hopes to give those who have finished their education the opportunity to repeat courses they have once taken and to give to those of limited education the opportunity to broaden their horizons and to assimilate the breath of outlook on life of people who have enjoyed higher education. All these goals they try to reach by local circles and by correspondence between the members and the central administration, which includes in its ranks many scientific luminaries. Chautauqua uses the mails to supply its students with books, examinations, themes, and exercises. Ten years ago this idea was seized upon as a novelty; the society grew exceedingly rapidly until it had several million active members. But later on those who had no serious intentions fell behind little by little and dropped out. The society at present, although considerably smaller, is genuinely alive and undoubtedly achieves its goals; last year the annual meeting attracted over 4,000 visitors from all parts of the Union. The debates were printed everywhere in the press and were read with genuine interest.

Literary and so-called reading clubs usually select some classical writer and study him from all sides and in great detail. They inevitably begin from the beginning, go forward slowly and solidly, and conscientiously analyze each chapter, sometimes each phrase. Then when the work is finished every member undoubtedly not only fully understands all of the subtleties but can even successfully explain every obscurity, every puzzling phrase. Debating societies usually select some theme for a future session, sometimes purely in the abstract, sometimes linked to some outstanding local event or question. They name a leading speaker and after he finishes give every member the right to retort to him and to examine the question from every view. Sometimes two speakers are named to debate, and then only they have the right to speak. The statutes and rules of all these societies are clear and definite; all the conditions of parliamentary procedure are strictly and undeviatingly observed.

I consider this talent of the American—exactly, consequentially, and cleverly to judge the most burning questions—one of his most noteworthy traits, one to be envied by a Russian. This is even more striking when it is noted that in all these societies workers and artisans take an active and significant role; as, for example, in the North Carolina society of which I was a member for more than two years. One of the most active members and speakers was a worker in my own factory, a good master of his craft, who had received a meager education and who wrote with noticeable spelling errors. He read a great deal and was able to deal cleverly and shrewdly with every question and also to speak on it in public clearly and convincingly.

So-called sports and athletic associations of all kinds play no small role in American social life. There are horse races, yacht clubs, hunting and fishing societies, shooting clubs, lawn-tennis clubs, cricket clubs, and billiard and chess societies—and that still doesn't complete the list. Every town inevitably has some of these societies, corresponding to local conditions and to the character of the population.

Baseball, something like the Russian game of *lapta*, is the national sport and annually costs the American people many millions of dollars. This game has long since become an art; whole books have been written on its subtleties, and committees meet constantly, now in one place, now in another, to adjust the details of the rules. All the larger cities support professional clubs, and good players receive large salaries—$5,000, $6,000, or even $8,000 for a season of five months. Since you must have two sides of nine men to play, some cities unite in a league of eight, twelve, or fourteen teams. The clubs travel from one city to another through the course of the season and fight for the reward of being named winners of the "pennant."

The unusual mobility of the American people and their passion for change of residence also foster in strong measure both the diffusion of knowledge and the spirit of general equality. Tens of thousands of people, artisans for the most part, constantly move around over the whole Union. On the road and in the new places, as a result of the national quality of quickness in acquaintanceship, they constantly come in contact with new people, new ideas, and new impressions, which they assimilate very rapidly. I have often been amazed at the many-sidedness and knowledge of my own workers. Where have they not been, what have they not done, in what positions have they not found themselves? It would seem that there is nothing in the world of which they have not heard, nothing they have not seen. Several Germans and Englishmen always worked for me. Although they were excellent workmen and perhaps in cleanliness and fineness of work surpassed the Americans, they were inferior to the latter in every other way—difficult at making a beginning, extremely conservative in their mode of work, and always exceedingly specialized. The Europeans knew a certain part of the job; nothing else interested them. In the great majority of cases they learned nothing else; as they left their training, so will they die. They never took a direct part in public affairs, they lived apart, and in them was hidden the secret of the Democratic Party in all the large cities of the Union.

The trade unions are also a powerful channel in the diffusion of knowledge and the raising of the level of the intellectual development of the American workers. In the beginning the different societies of workers acted independently, but by 1866 there was a national congress of the representatives of the various organizations of labor in Baltimore. Thereafter, these groups came ever closer together. In 1869 was organized the society of the Knights of Labor; and in 1886 was formed the American Federation of Labor, a combination of many separate unions. These two national organizations represent at present the organized labor of the United States. Their influence is said to grow ever greater in the internal life of the country.

Up to now they have stayed away from politics, but the time is near when they will inevitably be drawn in; even now both political parties flirt with them. The politicians express themselves very cautiously in their public "platforms," but at the same time conduct secret conversations with the leaders of the labor movement. Powderley, "the grandmaster workman" of the Knights of Labor, and Gompers, the president of the Federation, already hold the balance of power in some states.

Many individual unions are also very powerful, rich, and influential in their sphere of activity. For toughness of organization and power of discipline the Brotherhood of Locomotive Engineers stands foremost. The Brotherhood of Carpenters and Joiners is outstanding in membership and wealth. The bricklayers' union and the stonecutters' union also stand out from the general mass, and have attained excellent results. Generally, questions of hours and of wages are the main issues in the struggle of labor and capital.

This struggle, in the 1870's and even more so in the 1880's, assumed such dimensions, the conflicts became so frequent and so serious, that the federal government was obliged to give it its attention. By 1884 Congress had established a National Bureau of Labor, which became in 1886 an independent department of the federal government. Many separate states also appointed commissioners of labor, whose responsibility it is to keep an eye on these conflicts, to try to prevent them, to offer to conciliate, and in general to keep busy with the labor question, both theoretically and practically.

I do not think I err in asserting positively that the most frequent conflicts and the most stubborn struggles occur over the question of the number of working hours. This problem is assuming an ever sharper character. The workers affirm that long hours are turning them into cattle, and that they therefore will no longer be reasoning human beings fit to take part in the management of a huge and rich country. They say that a man who works conscientiously for ten hours is then in no position to occupy himself with anything but eating and sleeping. They want every man to have some free time every day for self-development and for the preservation of his store of strength, since otherwise his spirit will succumb to physical exhaustion. I shall not repeat the replies of their adversaries; I suppose those are the same wherever capital and labor meet as foes. But in any case, both Congress and the legislatures of many states have already passed special laws making eight hours the maximum working day for all public works. In many large cities also all the building trades work only eight or nine hours. The ten-hour day, which up to the beginning of the last decade was found all over the Union, slowly but steadily is giving way to a shorter day.

With the greatest pleasure I can verify the fact that in recent times arbitration by means of the above-mentioned commissioners of labor is practiced ever more in all these conflicts. Many boycotts and strikes were not only put off but entirely averted by it. Where the personal passions of the leaders are not involved and the position of affairs can be judged coolly and calmly arbitration is always crowned with success.

Certain industries, such for example as the glass, steel, and to a significant degree coal industries, have in the course of the last ten years reached the point where representatives of the two sides, capital and labor, come together a few weeks before the new year and consider both the position of production on the market and the corresponding scales of workers' hours and wage rates, sometimes for the entire year following, sometimes for six months. When the market is glutted, as happens with coal after the exceptionally warm winter of 1889, it becomes necessary to guard against overproduction. The representatives then decide that the men will work only three-quarters, sometimes even only one-half of full time. Thus all have work, even though not full work, and they prevent the relative prosperity of some and the complete starvation of the others. Sometimes wages are lowered or raised by mutual agreement. Some manufacturing districts have never known strikes or hostile conflicts, since all misunderstandings were settled by means of mutual concessions and understandings.

At the same time, the most stubborn, unyielding strikes, accompanied by street riots, incendiarism, and the destruction of valuable property, as for instance in the time of the well-known Pittsburgh workers' rising of 1877, have quite often shaken whole regions and sometimes completely undermined their welfare. Americans in general are obstinate. In some parts of New England one comes across evidence of that national trait in abandoned factory buildings and deserted towns. The bosses and the workers had a quarrel, were unable to come to an agreement, and the factory moved to another city, often to another state. The owners refused to yield and the workers were forced to leave their homes and scatter in many directions. During a strike the laborers not only refuse to work themselves, but they also refuse to allow other workers to take their places. When a particularly persistent manufacturer tries to bring in his own new people under the protection of the police and even of the state militia, then there begins a battle between the old and new workers, a battle sometimes with guns. There were cases in which the new employees had to live for three months in the factory buildings under the constant protection of the police, and when that protection was removed found themselves under a regular siege by the former workers.

In the majority of crafts all the skilled workmen belong to trade unions, and it is then impossible to get new hands since no member of the union will work for an employer against whom a strike has been called. Several years ago many factory owners who saw their employees begin to get agitated quickly sent their agents to the industrial centers of Europe and at their own expense imported whole complements of new workers. Many strikes were broken in that way. Then there began a campaign against the immigration of contract labor; this campaign quickly assumed such dimensions that Congress was forced to pass a law which forbade the importation of contract labor of any sort, under penalty of long jail terms and heavy fines. This law is at present applied quite strictly. In all the ports where immigrants arrive special federal commissions investigate each newcomer in the most detailed way—and very rarely can the contract laborer succeed in slipping through unnoticed.

In the course of the struggle of capitalists and laborers, the former often resorted to blacklisting, the latter to boycotting. These methods were and are used with great persistence. In the one case they drive an individual to the point where he is completely unable to earn his bread; in the other, they completely disorganize whole enterprises. Matters went so far in some states that their legislatures had to interfere; thus Illinois and Wisconsin have decisively forbidden both methods under pain of heavy punishments; many others, such as Indiana, New York, and Michigan, have prohibited them under pain of fines. The southern states, however, are far behind their northern and western sisters, since the organization of labor is still rudimentary there. Some, like Georgia, spoke up against the boycott quickly enough, but did not seem to keep the blacklists in mind. The former slave owners now guard their prerogatives as carefully as in the days of slavery!

Attempting as far as possible to clarify that high level of equality of the masses which one notes in America, I cannot fail to mention the occasional attempts to form an hereditary and moneyed aristocracy. Of course, anyone in the slightest degree acquainted with the history of the country of the common man could recognize these efforts as the stillborn children of outlived aspirations and tendencies. The constitutions of the Union and of all the several states unconditionally and forever prohibit all titles and distinctions; and the laws of property of all the states stand in the way of any entails or consolidation of property for private persons. The attempts to get around these laws by means of cleverly concocted wills have always been frustrated soon after the death of the testator. American jurors have always considered even the slightest hint of anything in the nature of an entail sufficient to destroy the will and to divide the estate according to the laws.

In general, the wealthy people in America do not really strive for exclusiveness. The millionaires of California, for example, without exception have remained loyal to the habits of their youth. Many of them have erected luxurious residences, have introduced expensive furnishings, have transported their families to all the capitals of Europe, and brought back with them a mass of expensive pictures, statuary, and all that money could buy—yet they still remain the same democratic, informal miners and gamblers that they were in their youth. I personally have met and done business with many rich Americans, such as Drexel, Armour, and Flagler. Armour, who now is one of the wealthiest people in America, began his life fifty years ago as a village butcher in Wisconsin and many times has publicly spoken in my presence of his early experiences and austere life, not only not being ashamed but evidently proud of his beginnings and his success. Neither in him nor in other millionaires have I ever noticed even the slightest attempt to separate themselves from others, to draw apart. They are as polite with simple day laborers as they are with their fellow tycoons. I shall never forget the time when traveling once with Armour in a sleeping car in the North we went out to have breakfast at a station. The Negro porter of the sleeper, who had just finished cleaning our shoes, sat down at a table with us. I was very astonished—but Armour chatted with this colored man very calmly, and very obligingly passed the salt or whatever else the porter needed.

Just as an upper class and aristocracy of whatever name or kind are insignificant and unnoticeable, so are pauperism and beggary. While in Great Britain in 1890 out of every thirty-nine inhabitants one was a beggar, in America there was only one out of every eight hundred and fifty-seven in this category. Pauperism then was twenty-two times as widespread in Great Britain as it was in the United States. It seems superfluous to add anything to these revealing figures; they speak for themselves.

During the decade 1871–1880 the Union received almost 3,000,000 immigrants in all; in the last decade, 1881–1890, more than 5,000,000.

It might seem that such a constant and huge influx of worker-immigrants would lower wages. But the development of the country and the increase of its wealth has been so swift that, on the average, wages have not declined. On the contrary, slowly but surely they rise in all branches of human work, with very slight temporary exceptions, caused either by overproduction or by some sort of temporary, local condition. The reduction in the number of working hours, of which I have spoken above in detail, in itself represents an increase in remuneration. But even apart from that, wages in dollars and cents are constantly rising.

This rise would have no meaning for or influence upon the general well-being of the masses if costs of living increased too. But this latter phenomenon has not occurred; on the contrary, the prices of the objects of primary necessity are declining absolutely, and the expenses for living are lessening. Flour, sugar, salt, meat, petroleum, coal, iron of all kinds, cotton stuffs, all these have declined from 15 to 40 per cent in price. This fall in the prices of manufactures of all kinds, completely unnatural in view of a rise in wages, I explain by the specialization of all types of production, that is, by the application of machine work to its maximum possibility and by the concentration of industry in those places where the product can be produced most cheaply.

The result is reflected in the savings banks, which are developing with astonishing rapidty over the entire country. The whole Union contains 4,250,000 depositors with deposits equal to the fabulous sum of $1,500,000,000, an average of $358 each. By themselves these figures offer such an understanding of the general welfare of the country that I am unable to expand upon them. No description could be more eloquent than these figures, and if the reader would compare them with those presented by the states of Europe, then the difference in the position of the worker would be evident.

As far as wages are concerned, too, it is necessary to observe that a difference exists in the pay for physical and mental labor in the United States, but that it is less significant there than anywhere else on the globe. I personally think that this difference, with few exceptions, amounts to nothing. An especially prolific writer or lawyer, an especially clever businessman, a well-known speaker or doctor, of course, earns big money sometimes, and such labor is very highly valued. But these are really exceptional cases which are encountered even within the spheres of physical labor: an especially skilled engraver, jeweler, or machinist also sometimes earns substantial sums of money. Speaking of the nation in general, of its masses who live over the entire expanse of the Union, a good joiner receives the very same pay as a good teacher; a good locomotive engineer, the same as a good doctor or judge; a skilled house painter, no less than a county sheriff or treasurer; and a bank cashier, no more than a good cutter.

One must not forget, too, that the so-called heavy work of day laborers is incomparably lighter in America than in Russia or in other European states. Machines have taken the place of this hand labor to a significant degree. A few machinists, classified and paid as skilled labor, can then do the work of a mass of unskilled hands. Only very rarely does one meet a native white American in the ranks of heavy toilers. Such a man will be a chronic failure, or an artisan who has temporarily fallen in status as a consequence of a confluence of unfortunate circumstances and who is unable to find work in his trade in a given locality. The Negroes, Italians, Hungarians, Poles, Irish, Chinese, sometimes the Germans and Scandinavians, and, in the Southwest, the Mexicans make up the bulk of the raw-labor supply.

In general, wages in the South are lower than in the North and particularly lower than in the West. On the average, any unskilled worker receives for a ten-hour working day $1.25 in the South, and for a nine-hour day $1.50 in the North, and $2.00 in the West. On the Pacific coast the rate has never dropped below $2.00, and fluctuations are comparatively unimportant. In the black districts of the South, where there are endless numbers of Negroes, wages are as low as $.75 a day; in the West, especially in mining regions, as high as $5.00. The legislature of the state of New York established as the minimum rate for every state, county, and municipal employee in no matter what type of work, $2.00 for eight hours; but this wage is higher than the market rate and the law was pushed through by the Democratic Party to gain votes in the elections.

The wages of artisans on the average are more than twice that of unskilled laborers. Carpenters and joiners in the South receive from $2.00 to $3.50 a day; in the North, from $3.00 to $4.50, in the West, from $3.00 to $6.00. Masons, stonecutters, and stucco-workers get one or two dollars a day more than carpenters, house painters approximately the same as carpenters, and blacksmiths and machinists of all kinds as much as $8.00 a day. These rates sometimes fall or sometimes go higher; but chronic shortages of labor so usual in various industries in Europe, especially in England, are unknown in America. At least, during the ten years of my residence here, I have never heard or read about them.

The salary of elected officials, with the exception of a few in the federal government and in the very largest states and cities, is usually the same as the artisan's wages—from $50.00 to $125.00 a month. Clerks, bookkeepers, and all sorts of assistants in private enterprises receive about the same remuneration. And the identical circumstance will be noted in all the remaining fields of labor; the locomotive engineer earns no less than the railroad passenger agent; a stoker no less than the station official; and a good machinist in the roundhouse no less than an auditor or bookkeeper in the main office.

Besides fostering this comparative equality in the material relations of the bulk of the population, the absence of a sharp difference between physical and mental labor also encourages that ease with which Americans generally change their occupations. I personally know hundreds of people who in the course of their lives have shifted through tens of different occupations. You constantly meet men with specialized education or with specialized practical skills who are busy with commerce, farming, and contracting; artisans who study law or who prepare for the priesthood work at their crafts at the same time; merchants who give up their shops to toil at a craft or in farming. Thanks to this tendency, even class prejudices do not exist; every occupation is noble and honorable.

All American history is full of examples of this exceedingly important condition. Lincoln, one of the greatest people of the nineteenth century, was a lumberman, a ferryman, a teacher, a lawyer, and a legislator of his state. When, thanks to an unexpected event, he became president of the Union, he won the absolute faith and respect of his contemporaries and wrote his name in letters of fire on the tables of universal history for the wonder of generations. President Johnson was a country tailor and learned to read and write at the age of twenty-one. Sherman, next to Grant the most important general of the Civil War, was a teacher, a land agent, a lawyer, and a banker. Blaine, who is regarded with respect by the whole country, began his career as a public-school teacher in a remote mountain hamlet in Kentucky. The biographies of almost all the foremost people in America in every field, political, commercial, and industrial, usually begin either with labor on an isolated farm in some lonely spot, with the sale of newspapers or matches on the streets of a large city, or with the earnest struggle for existence in the family of a simple worker. Thus, of the eighty-four senators and four-hundred and twenty-two members of the lower house of the American Congress, only eleven received an education higher than the public school and only two attended private schools. All the rest are of the flesh and blood of the mass of the people; all began their careers at the very lowest grades of social position, as that would be understood in Europe.

26.

POET BEYOND THE SEA

Charles Joseph Paul Bourget (1852–1935) early became known as a poet, novelist, and critic. When he came for a year's visit to the United States in 1893 he was already acquainted with James Gordon Bennett of the New York Herald *and was asked to write a series of articles for that paper. His impressions were later embodied in* Outre-Mer *(notes sur l'Amérique), published in 1895, a book that provoked a great deal of controversy. Although he was attacked by critics like Mark Twain for excessively harsh generalizations, the observations in this volume on manners and customs showed considerable insight.*

The pleasures of Americans, like their ideas and their labors, are unrestrained and immoderate; they involve vigorous excitement bordering on violence, or rather, on roughness and restlessness. Even in his diversions the American is too active and too self-willed. Unlike the Latin, who amuses himself by relaxation, the Yankee amuses himself by tenseness; and that is the case whatever the nature of his amusements, for he has both coarse and refined ones. But a few illustrations will explain better than any theories his kind of nervousness, and his fitful sharpness in amusement—if we can use in this context a word which is ordinarily synonymous with the least American things in the world, relaxation and repose.

The most vehement and the most deeply national of pleasures are those of sport. To that word are attached none of the connotations with which we French have endowed it. We have softened the term in adopting it, and make it imply elegance and dexterity. But for the American sport must involve some danger, for it does not exist apart from competition and daring. Thus yachting, which to us means pleasant cruises along the coasts, to them means either voyages around the world or trips through the storms and the vast solitudes of the Atlantic, or rivalries of speed which take into consideration everything except human life. When I visited one of the private yachts at anchor in Newport harbor, I noticed an arsenal of guns and pikes hanging in one of the staterooms. "That's in case we go into the Chinese seas and meet pirates," said the proprietor of this dainty traveling toy. There was no vain boasting in that statement. It was the natural expression of an energy that instinctively likes to associate the idea of play with that of peril, and to which a little tragic risk is the necessary condiment to its most innocent festivities.

No sport has been more fashionable for the past few years than football. Last autumn, in the peaceful city of Cambridge, I was present at a game between the Harvard team and that of the University of Pennsylvania. I must go back in thought to my journey in Spain to recall a popular fever equal to that which throbbed along the road between Boston and the arena where the match took place. The electric cars, following one another at intervals of a minute, were filled with passengers, seated, standing, or hanging on the steps crowding, pushing, crushing one another. Although November is cruelly cold under a Massachusetts sky, the contest was held as were Roman gladiatorial combats, in a sort of open-air enclosure. A stone's throw away from Memorial Hall wooden stands were erected, on which were perhaps fifteen-thousand spectators. In the immense quadrilateral hemmed in by the stands the two teams of eleven youths each waited for the signal to begin.

What a tremor in that crowd, composed not of the lower classes but of well-to-do people, and how the excitement increased as time went on! Although a feverish thrill ran through this crowd, it was of itself not enough for the enthusiasts of the game. Propagators of enthusiasm, students with unbearded, deeply lined faces, passed between the benches and still further increased the ardor of the public by uttering the war-cry of the University, the "rah! rah! rah!" thrice repeated, which terminates in the frenzied call, "Haaar-vard." The partisans of the "Pennsy" replied with a similar cry, and in the distance, above the fence of the enclosure, we could see clusters of other spectators, too poor to pay the entrance fee, who had climbed into the branches of the leafless trees, their faces outlined against the autumn sky with the daintiness of the pale heads in Japanese painted fans.

The signal is given and the play begins. It is a fearful game, which in itself points to the differences between the Anglo-Saxon and the Latin world—a game of young bulldogs trained to bite, to rush upon the quarry, the game of a race made for wild attack, for violent defense, for implacable conquests, and desperate struggles. With their leather vests and sleeves of cloth, so soon to be torn, with leather gaiters to protect their shins, with their great shoes, and with long hair floating around their pale and flushed faces, these schoolboy athletes are admirable and frightful to the sight when once the demon of the contest enters into them. The entire object of the game is to throw an enormous leather ball, which each side holds in turn. All the excitement of this ferocious amusement is concentrated in waiting for this throw. He who holds the ball is there, bent forward. His companions and his adversaries likewise bend down around him in the attitude of beasts of prey about to spring. All of a sudden he runs to throw the ball or else with a wildly rapid movement hands it to another, who rushes off with it. All depends on stopping him.

The roughness with which the opposing players seize the bearer of the ball is impossible to imagine. He is grasped by the middle of the body, by the head, by the legs, by the feet. He rolls over and his assailants roll with him. As they fight for the ball, the two sides come to the rescue, and fall into a heap of twenty-two bodies tumbling on top of one another, like an inextricable knot of serpents with human heads. This heap writhes on the ground and tugs at itself. One sees faces, hair, backs, or legs appearing in a monstrous and agitated melee. Then this murderous knot unravels itself and the ball, thrown by the most agile, bounds away and is again followed with the same fury.

Often, after one of those frenzied entanglements, one of the combatants remains on the field motionless, incapable of rising, so hard has he been hit, pressed, crushed, thumped.

A doctor whose duty it is to look after the wounded arrives and examines him. You see those skilled hands shaking a foot, a leg, rubbing the sides, washing the face, sponging the blood which streams from the forehead, the eyes, the nose, the mouth. A compassionate comrade assists in the business, holding the head of the fainting champion on his knee. Sometimes the unlucky player must be carried away. More frequently, however, he recovers his senses, stretches himself, and ends by scrambling to his feet. He takes a few steps, leaning on a friendly shoulder, and no sooner is he able to walk than the game begins afresh, and he joins in with a rage doubled by pain and humiliation.

If the roughness of this terrible sport was for the spectators only the occasion of a few hours of nervous excitement, the young athletes would not indulge in it with the enthusiasm that makes them accept the most painful, sometimes the most dangerous, training. "The feats of the champions keep the game fashionable," explained one of the Harvard professors; "hence all the small boys in the remotest parts of America take up this exercise, and thus athletes are formed." He was putting into abstract form the instinct of the American crowd, an instinct which does not reason and which shows itself in very strange ways. During the contest, which I have attempted to describe, I heard a distinguished and refined woman, next to whom I was seated, crying out, "Beauty!" at the sight of rushes that sent five or six boys sprawling on the ground.

No sooner are such matches announced than the portraits of the various players are in all the papers. The incidents of the game are described in detail, with graphic pictures, so that the movements of the ball may better be followed. Conquerors and conquered are alike interviewed. From a celebrated periodical the other day I cut out an article signed "A Football Scientist," wherein the author sought to show that the tactics of this game were the same as those used by Napoleon. What can be added to this eulogy, when we know the peculiar position occupied by Napoleon in the imagination of the Yankees?

Matching the passion for football is the passion for boxing. When Corbett and Mitchell met last winter at Jacksonville, it was necessary to run special trains to carry their partisans to that fortunate city in Florida. There was not a newspaper in which the physical condition of the two rivals was not mentioned morning after morning. The names of the relatives and friends who assisted them, the furniture of their

hotel rooms, the menu of their meals, their reading and their thoughts
—what details did one not find in the columns of the newspapers!
When I went to Jacksonville a few weeks later the fight was still the
subject of every conversation, and people only stopped talking of it
to discuss the next fight, between the California champion and Jackson
of Australia. Even the election of the future President will not excite
more popular feeling.

A "prize fight" is an encounter which ends when it becomes impossible for one of the boxers to continue. But I witnessed a contest
regulated by an athletic club, that is, one in which the rounds were
counted and the blows limited. This particular affair took place in
Washington. On the third floor of the club, in the gymnasium, a platform was built at the height of a man's head, closed in with ropes. All
around a thousand spectators were waiting, some seated on chairs,
others standing in the gallery. Along the walls were hung gymnastic
implements framing the scene most appropriately. The electricity—it
was nine o'clock in the evening—lighted and chiseled the outlines of
the impatient faces of the votaries, and on the square platform the
"referee," the arbiter of the fight, was nervously pacing up and down.
This man wore one of those jackets that exaggerate the fashion and
have a cut so ample, so round, that it makes the wearer resemble the
shell of some vast coleoptera.

At last a murmur of satisfaction rises. The first two boxers arrive
with their trainers. The gladiators are covered with big bathrobes,
which they cast aside as soon as they get upon the platform; their
bodies appear quite naked, thin, knobbed with muscles. They seat
themselves upon chairs and give themselves over with a singular passivity to the care of their trainers, who wash them, comb them, rub
them like animals. Meanwhile, the personage in the ample jacket announces the order of the fight, its duration, the number of rounds, and
the names and weights and places of origin of the fighters.

One is from Philadelphia, the other from Wilmington. The first has
a dark face, almost that of a mulatto, in the center of which is flat-
tened out a broken and crooked nose. The other is fair with a square
face, the nose also broken in two places. His arms are extended along
two cords crossed behind him at an acute angle. His marble muscles
gleam under the massage, which does not even seem to move them.
At last the toilette is finished. Both men draw on their gloves. A gong

sounds. They rise, walk toward one another, shake hands, and the contest commences. A gurgle of pleasure escapes from the audience, an interrupted gurgle which will change by and by from a sigh to a howl as the fight becomes brisk. The Philadephian attacks with more vigor than his opponent, but he is too nervous. His legs do not balance. He dances and hops, his arms moving in a mechanical and irresolute manner, like a pair of hesitating pincers, advancing, retiring, then advancing again. His adversary has a better guard. He advances, he retires without moving his body, and his cruel face, in which the eyes gleam as from two blue hollows, is really like that of death. The blows fall more heavily as the fight progresses. The bodies bend to avoid them. The two men are furious. One hears their breathing and the dull thud of the fists as they fall on the naked flesh. Soon the "claret" is drawn, the blood flows from the eyes, the nose, the ears; it smears the cheeks and the mouth, it stains the fists, while the public expresses its delight by howls, which the striking of the gong alone stops.

It is the pause between two rounds. The boxers, again seated, give themselves up, as before, to the care of their trainers, who rub them like hostlers grooming a horse. The seconds spring upon the platform, taking off their coats, and once in their shirt sleeves, begin to fan the unfortunate pugilists, who are half faint from loss of blood, from blows received and given, and from the intense nervous effort of the fight. Another sound of the gong, and the next round begins.

There were four such fights that evening, one of six rounds, the second of eight, the third of five, the last of eleven, and during the two hours and a half that this terrible scene continued not a spectator left his place. Not for a second did the passionate interest, which fixed every face on the ring, seem to be suspended.

The pleasures of sport are not so far from those of the theater as might at first sight appear. Passion for the play results in the respect for actors so common among Americans; we know what receptions they gave Sarah Bernhardt, Eleonora Duse, Coquelin, and Irving—to mention only four famous artists, and not to speak of singers. It was not alone the performances of these great actors that interested the public, but also their personalities and their ideas about art.

In every town in the United States there is a group of amateurs who delight in discussing and studying more or less intelligently plays and musical works. I have said study, for even here the evidence of purpose is visible. At Boston, for instance, the program of each concert is accompanied by a technical commentary, so accurate, so lucid, and at the same time so erudite, that the pamphlet is really a chapter in the study of musical history. At Chicago when Coquelin gave *Tartufe* the newspapers of the following day contained dissertations on Molière's comedy which were as scholarly, as analytic, and as critical as would have been the *feuilleton* of the *Temps* or the *Journal des Débats*. And yet, despite these evidences of fastidious taste, this same public accepts the most astonishing oddities.

I remember a gala night at the opera in New York when the music was sung by one actor in German and by another in French while the chorus replied in Italian, and no English was heard. But there is a secret harmony between such apparently contradictory manifestations. Such things shock and annoy the dilettantes of music, the epicures of harmony. Their enthusiasm cools and they have an uncontrollable desire to take up their hats and walk out. But those who are conscious that they are studying the genius of a master or the talent of an artist, accept the performance, though mutilated. They accept it, above all, if they are consumed with that need of European assimilation which takes possession of intellectual, no less than of fashionable America. Unable to have the whole opera and the whole *Comédie Française* from the other side of the ocean, these people take what they can—the very best, it must be acknowledged—and they enjoy it, as the English enjoy the frieze of the Parthenon, which is broken into fragments and lacks cohesion. Their double passion is satisfied—in the first place, they cultivate themselves, and in the second, they have all the best actors of London and Paris in New York.

We must seek the genuine American genius and the true dramatic pleasures of the people in performances of quite a different kind. The drama in which the authors and actors of this country excel is a kind of comedy, almost without affectation and intrigue, entirely composed of local scenes and customs, and mixed with pantomime. If the hackneyed expression "a cross-section of life" can ever be applied to plays, it is to these. Here emerge all the peculiarities of the different states— the singular customs of the South, as in *The New South;* those of the West, as in *In Mizzoura;* and those of the North, as in *A Temperance Town*, which I saw in New York. In the subtitle of this last play— the most typical, perhaps, of all—we are told that it "is intended as a more or less truthful presentation of certain incidents of life relating to the sale and use of liquor in a small village in a prohibition state." The great curiosity aroused by this comedy lies in the fact that the sympathetic character is a drunkard.

"Is it worth while to destroy the abuse of drink in order to install the triumph of hypocrisy?" asks one of the heroes in the last act. Therein lies the whole moral of this singular work, in which the most pathetic scenes are followed by buffooneries such as this: It is Christmas Eve. The daughter of the minister, expelled by her father, is dragging herself along the walls of the church in which her father is preaching. Meanwhile a facetious drunkard places on the steps of the church a large plank covered with snow, over which, one after another, all the members of the congregation fall as they come out. The public seems to take a wild delight in such extraordinary contrasts. Laughter is not, as with us, excited by the witty and somewhat free joke with the double meaning. Rather, it is cold-blooded and totally unexpected drollery that seems funny. All of a sudden, at a tragic moment, one of the actors executes a clown's trick; he kicks the hat from the head of his interlocutor as he performs a dangerous jump over a table. Then the scene continues, these extravagances having done nothing more than raise the wild laughter of the audience. To the eyes of the stranger, unaccustomed to this mosaic out of real life, to scenes of local customs and of extravagant gambols, this epileptic gaiety savors of the bar, of the intoxication of alcohol, and of incipient madness.

Oddly enough, these players, who are in a way gymnasts and clowns, are also extraordinarily simply and realistic in the serious portions of their roles. In one of these comedies, called I think *The Country Circus,* I witnessed a theft scene acted with incomparable perfection by three chance performers. One represented the manager of the circus at his ticket office, the second was a Negro asking for a ticket, and the third was a policeman guarding the entrance. The Negro gave a ten-dollar bill to the manager, who only returned change for five. The Negro complained. The manager bent over toward the opening, cried, "Officer!" and accused his victim of theft, whereupon the policeman collared the poor black, and pushed him by force into the circus. Then, returning to the ticket office, he received two dollars from the manager. The startled passivity of the Negro, the cutting banter of the Barnum who was "taking him in," the brutal and sordid duplicity of the policeman—all these features were marked as in an etching. The pantomime was almost intolerable in its truthfulness.

The Negro and the policeman are, moreover, two of the favorite characters of the really popular farces; another is the chivalrous black-guard. But the unrivaled protagonist is the "tramp," the professional vagabond, in the toils of his two enemies, the policeman and the brake-man. The struggle around a freight car, in which the tramp wishes to ride and from which the brakeman expels him, is an unfailing theme which lends itself to all sorts of tricks and jokes. The tramp is, in fact, the great popular humorist. It is he who gives their nicknames to the railroad companies; who, for instance, baptizes the Baltimore and Ohio, the "B. and O.," "Beefsteak and Onions." In a Washington theater I have seen an audience rise in wild laughter at that joke.

The large box in front of the stage, one of four in the hall, was occupied the night I attended by a spectator who had placed his feet on the velvet balustrade. He manifested his delight by knocking his heels against the red velvet, which served as a support in his comfort-able position. Probably this man, who must have paid fifteen dollars for his box, was one of those newly enriched westerners who have tried twenty vocations, have made a fortune several times, and have kept company during their adventurous existence with people of all classes and of all descriptions. Such individuals, and they constitute the foun-dation of the American public, have too complete an experience with human life not to expect exact observation and real pictures of manners in a comedy. On the other hand, though often unscrupulous, they have retained, through their Odyssey in business, a certain youthful, almost infantile naïvete which is traceable everywhere here. They are, besides, honest enough, even strict, in questions of love.

Such local studies, interlarded with buffooneries, from which all obscenity is eliminated, correspond to these American characteristics. And the managers understand it well. Read this puff which I copy from a program:

The actors of this troupe propose to act only native plays by native authors. This drama is essentially American in scenery, in action, and in aim. It breathes everywhere an American freshness which is in keeping with the greatness of America. There is not a single bad character, man or woman. Not a syllable is uttered which could bring a blush to the most modest cheek. This piece attacks the vices of dissipated society and the miseries which are

HET OUDE POSTKANTOOR (VROEGER HOLLANDSCHE KERK.)

HET NIEUWE POSTKANTOOR.

Improvements in Architecture, the Gilded Age

Ragpickers Court, Mulberry Street, New York

the outgrowth of the concentration of civilization in the great towns. No soiled dove beats its soiled wings here; no brigands in dress clothes fly round in search of prey . . .

This announcement was entirely accurate; it was incomplete on one point only. The piece ended without any reason ever given for the appearance of a family of acrobats.

I have turned over the leaves of a great number of illustrated comic newspapers, those which friends in New York have pointed out to me as the best. The Americans dote on these publications, which are found in all the halls of the hotels, in all the railway carriages, and on all the club tables. Without exaggerating the importance of these pamphlets, we must recognize in them a certain documentary value. They characterize the humor of the race and its delight in mockery. Besides, they contain a thousand details of habits, described casually and with such exaggeration that they are perceptible to the traveler.

Running through a collection of several numbers of these papers, I was immediately struck by the entire absence of those nude drawings which constitute the perverse attractiveness of similar periodicals in Paris, and also by the no less remarkable absence of allusions to marital misadventures. One might believe, in noting these lacunae, that neither gallantry nor adultery existed in the United States, or that, if they exist, it is in such a shadow of secrecy that they escape even satire. The caricaturists, however, do not profess to be particularly prejudiced in favor of marriage. But they see its defects from the point of view of the budget, as is fitting in the country of the almighty dollar.

Family life is too costly and the men must work too hard. This is their principal grievance. Here, for example, is a wedding reception. The drawing-room is full of people congratulating the newly married couple, and the parents. "Congratulations on the marriage of your daughter," says one of the visitors. "I see you are gradually getting all the girls off your hands." And the father answers, "The misfortune is that it costs so much to keep their husbands."

When it is not the father who works himself to death, it is the husband. Here on a Christmas eve appears a certain Popleigh, prematurely aged, thin and bent, his arms full of presents, which bespeak a numerous family. A gentleman wrapped up in a comfortable fur coat, cigar in his mouth, gazes at him sarcastically. "It is Mr. Singleton," says the legend simply, "a rejected suitor for the hand of the present Mrs. Popleigh." Even aside from the question of money, this nation does not seem to believe that marriage is a very fortunate affair. Listen to this dialogue between a husband and wife. *She:* "After all, what have you men got at the club to make it so attractive, that you don't have at home?" *He:* "My dear, we have not at the club what we have at home; that is the attraction." This is the bankruptcy of the happiness of the man. As for the happiness of the woman, she herself does not expect it.

If a thousand little signs do not reveal to the traveler the social sovereignty of the young girl in the United States, he would find proof of it in the caricatures. The young girl appears as often in these papers as Lorette in the albums of Gavarni, as the fast woman in those of Grévin, and as the *marcheuse* of the opera or the sidewalk in those of Forain. As those three great masters have felt the gracefulness of the Parisian woman at three different epochs, so the American artist feels with incomparable delicacy the beauty of the young girl of this country.

There she is, smiling, dreaming, talking, alive, with her fine figure, her well-developed shoulders, her daring elegance, her white teeth, her eyes wide open on the world—too wide open, for they see too clearly. Listen to the conversation which the artist attributes to these admirable persons, and you will be edified by their intelligence. Here is one taking a country walk with an admirer, who bitterly says, "If I were rich you would marry me at once."—"Ah, George! George!" she replies, "your devotion breaks my heart."—"What do you mean?"—"Well, you have often praised my beauty, but until now I did not know how much you valued my good sense."

These realistic girls, just as the most realistic men, know that marriage is an association to which their partner will ask them to bring money—a great deal of money. Furthermore, the handsome young men do not conceal their interested motives. "Would you have loved me had I been poor?" asks a maiden of a fine young fellow of twenty-two, who replies, clasping her to his heart: "Ah, darling! I should not then have known you."

And you do not feel overindignant at seeing money constantly mixed up in affairs of the heart. The heart is so little in question. The caricaturist takes care to let you know it. Engagements which are tied and untied so easily do not shake the hearts of such elegant dolls. "Ah, dear," murmurs a Perdita, raising her beautiful, half-veiled eyes, with their long lashes, to the lips of a dashing cavalier, "tell me truly how much you love me."—"You are my favorite fiancée," he replies, seriously, "the only one that I love."

And the chances are that she will see a delicate flattery in this singular declaration, for she herself does not attach a very deep significance to the word "betrothal," at least if we are to believe this other dialogue between two young girls who are exchanging confidences. "They told me that you were in love with him," says one.—"No, no," replies the other, "it was not so serious as that. We were only engaged."

"Lots of fun." There is the best summing up, not only of the situation, but of all these caricatures. There is nothing less like the sharp and grim acerbity of our own humorists. There is jovial good-humor in this chaffing of young girls, which might so easily be cruel. The same may be said in regard to the caricatures of the lower classes—notably the tramps, the Negroes, and the Irish. Indeed, poverty is less tolerable in the United States than elsewhere, in a climate so severe in winter, so scorching in summer, and amid crushing competition. Listen, however, to this vagabond, whom a piece of money given by a generous passer-by has enabled to enter a bar, where he stands in front of a free lunch table: "Haven't you eaten enough?" cries the proprietor, overcome by the sight of the ham, fish, bread, butter, and fried oysters disappearing in the abysses of that rag-bedecked stomach.—"Do I look like a man who has eaten enough?" replies the vagabond, sneeringly. This impertinent joke shows the tone of the replies ascribed by the caricaturist to these tramps. Their idleness amuses him without making him indignant.

Nor does the humorist develop the worst and most atrocious features of the Negro. The artist joyously makes merry over the colored man's vanity and familiarity. He has drawn Tom, for instance, entering his master's room wearing a pair of checked trousers of the same material as the coat of his master. The latter says, "Look here, Tom, I have told you already not to wear those trousers I gave you when I wear the rest of the suit." And Tom replies: "Why, boss, are you afraid they will take us for twins?"

So, in regard to those terrible Irishmen, so astonishing with their poetry and their cruelty, their patriotic flame and vindictive rage, their eloquence and drunkenness, their spirit of enterprise and disorder, it is noteworthy that the caricaturists only show the drunkenness and disorder. One time it is an Irish servant girl, saying in her brogue to the inspector of immigration: "Oi'm a Frinch nurse." Again, it is an Irishman coming home intoxicated, whose state the sketcher represents by multiplying the head of his wife seven times, as she looks at her husband and, out of her seven mouths, says: "If you saw yourself as I see you, you would be disgusted."—"And if you saw yourself as I see you," replies the drunkard, "you would also be astonished." Sometimes it is a domestic quarrel, in which everything gives way, the man assaulting his wife with a chair and she retorting with a flatiron. And policemen, themselves Celtic, preside at this carnival of tramps, Negroes, and Irishmen, drinking hard and hitting like the others, and shouting, "Take that!" as they progress in their game of head-breaking.

No bitterness spoils the joviality. One would imagine that for these observers life in the streets and in the drawing-room is really a clownish pantomime. Yet they are very exact—their drawings, without imagination, come very close to reality. One guesses that they are goodhumored people, very lucid, very positive, writing and sketching for lucid, positive, and good-tempered readers. The dark misanthropy of a Gavarni or a Forain makes you suffer as you laugh. It entails long reflection and nerves worn with thought and powerless for action. The American belongs to a world which is too active, too hasty, and, in certain respects, too healthy for such poisoned irony.

It is curious to compare the sarcasm of political caricatures with the indulgent gaiety of the caricature of manners. The same sketchers, simple and light in dealing with the ridiculous characteristics and vices of everyday life, develop, when it becomes a matter of politics, a kind of frenzy and hatred which can hardly be surpassed. The nomination of an ambassador who does not suit them, the adoption of a bill against which they are campaigning or the rejection of a bill which they uphold, a hostile candidacy, a stirring speech—these are occasions for severe blows, the hardness of which contrasts in the most unexpected manner with the good temper of the sketches of manners. You suddenly feel calumny and its bitterness, anger and its insults. From amusing and easy fantasy you fall into the depths of the harshest polemic.

It seems to me that both phenomena are logical and well in keeping with what may be seen everywhere among Americans. So far as regards the affairs of everyday life they are good fellows—amiable, open, easy;

but as soon as it comes to business, they are as keen and energetic in defense of their interests and in the conquest of yours as they were easy and generous before. The reason is that they are no longer amusing themselves; now they are fighting.

Politics is one of the most important businesses of a country where each triumph places all public offices at the disposal of the party. It interests not merely a small number of ambitious people, but an enormous number of citizens enrolled under the Republican and Democratic banners. Their antipathies must be gratified, their enthusiasm stirred, their passions served.

In all countries where universal suffrage is the rule, it becomes necessary to speak to the people by means of pictures. They see everything as a whole, and naturally like coarse and striking things. The colored caricatures which are set forth on the first pages of the illustrated newspapers satisfy their taste. As the editor of a Chicago newspaper said to me, they always like a fight. The fight here takes the form of a pictured burlesque, but the burlesque is ordinarily so exaggerated and so plainly unjust and prejudiced that it becomes offensive.

Such means of combatting an adversary may succeed with voters of the lowest class. They are far from clever; for, according to Talleyrand's profound remark, "Everything exaggerated is insignificant." For this reason, the Americans do well in caricaturing social customs, treating them lightly and inoffensively, but their political caricatures, with few exceptions, are commonplace.

27.

OPERATIONS OF POLITICS

Ernst Below (1845–1910) was a German who traveled through the United States and was particularly interested in the position of the German communities in this country. In addition to his volume on the United States, Bilder aus dem Westen (1894), *he wrote an account of his travels in Mexico.*

In Kansas City we sat on the veranda, taking coffee with Mr. Held, the attorney. The women turned the pages of a picture album; they

were busy arranging an excursion to the pretty Missouri Valley. The
men spoke of the chances of our host's election to Congress. Our friend,
Karl, had the latest precise news from the battlefront and told of the
little tricks and stratagems used by one party or another in the attempt
to make sure of victory. I showed my surprise that an educated, honest, thoughtful man, under such conditions, could bring himself to be
concerned with politics.

"Therein lies the difficulty," answered Held. "It is hard to take an
interest in the public affairs of so polymorphous, so immature, and
often so corrupt a land. But do we have a right to give up the fight
because the highly idealistic objectives set forth in the constitution
of the country and in many of its laws are not now understood by the
majority or are even subjected by the people to their own petty purposes?"

"Right now there is a question prominent in discussion that should
compel every thinking man to exert his energies to the utmost. This
question is concerned not with empty phrases or with political slogans,
but rather with a principle of the widest significance. Under the cloak
of the words, 'America for the Americans,' a small group of bankers
is trying to curtail European immigration in order to get a freer hand
in their efforts to monopolize everything. Naturally, they cannot openly
come out for such a program; therefore they push forward the sancti-
monious temperance crowd to fight the battle for them. So it happens
that the people themselves know absolutely nothing of what is going
on. The two major parties build their platforms, but as is their custom,
they do so behind a great façade which, in the end, so conceals the
fundamentals as to make them unrecognizable. The people are thereby
deceived. They think they are supporting or opposing principles of a
purely local character, and they actually are deciding by their votes
things altogether different. Do you understand now why we are so
interested in the little tricks and intrigues, the moves and countermoves,
seemingly strange to the ends we really have in view?"

"In itself, it makes no great difference whether the next mayor of
our city is a Republican or a Democrat, whether the police magistrate
is a free-trader or a protectionist, whether the next alderman believes
in the gold or silver standard. But we must never once forget that the
party which carries off the victory in the coming municipal election
will appoint all the city officers and dispose of all municipal jobs. If

my party, the Republican, wins, then every clerk, every porter, every messenger will be a Republican for the next year. For their own self-protection, in order not to be dismissed by the Democrats at the election following, they will become our staunchest supporters in the battle for votes. And they also make useful allies in their circles of friends and acquaintances. When the day of decision finally arrives, all these people vote for us, not because they have the same objectives as we, but because they hope thus to satisfy their own limited ends. On this basis, we have done so well that we will probably win in the next municipal election, although that has absolutely no relationship to the decision as to whether the obstacles to immigration be raised or lowered."

"We must not be surprised," he went on, after a short pause, "if our own good, narrow countrymen upset all these plans and shortly allow themselves to be taken in by the other party which, to win their votes, has promised to be less strict in closing the bars on Sundays. I am afraid the Germans will swallow the bait. When they become involved in the question of beer, everything else recedes into the background. So do not fail, Doctor, to come to the turnhall tomorrow. The *Verein* celebrates then its anniversary, and the politicians will not fail to use the opportunity to take voice. You will then be able to see, with your own eyes, how great problems of national significance are determined in this country."

The next night the great turner hall was brightly lighted. The stately redstone building with its impressive gabled façade at the corner of Oak and Twelfth Streets shone from the sparkle of electric lamps. On the colored transparency over the main entrance, visible from a good distance, sparkled the motto of the German-American turners, "Vigor, Freedom, Strength, and Faith."

When I entered the hall the turning exercises had already begun. Now and then these were interrupted by a song from the choir or by little declamations by individual members. On the stage between green leafy plants was a bust of Jahn, the father of the turners, behind which were draped the black, white, and red, and the star-spangled banners. On the walls hung decorations, among which were pictures of Washington, Lincoln, and Grant; side by side with William I, Bismarck, and Moltke, they looked down on the crowds of earlier arrivals. Below, the parents and members of the society intently watched the performances. Girls in becoming short-skirted turner uniforms rivaled the lively boys in agility and in perseverance. Their rhythmic marching, their exercises with the staff, and their performance on the swings gave evidence of the earnestness with which they had practiced these drills. The performances of the older ones on the bars and the rack were superior in skill and assurance to anything I ever saw in a *Turnverein.*

At one end of the hall sat old Kumpf, the former mayor. Speaking to him from either side with great seriousness were two German Democrats, city officials. Kumpf was, like most of the old German turners, once a solid Republican and still lives in the tradition that has united the turners and the G.O.P. since the Civil War. Yet even he was displeased by the flirtation of his party with the temperance and prohibition forces in recent times. Nevertheless, he could not bring himself publicly to go over to the Democrats, and he laughingly parried the attacks of the two city officials who hoped to win him over to their side.

A little later one of them tried another assault. "Now Herr Kumpf," he said, "just look at that shameless man. How he puffs himself up in there, and how the stupid herd let themselves be fooled by him!" With that he pointed to the adjoining room in which a great many men surrounded the refreshment table. In their midst stood Joe Davenport, the Republican candidate for mayor, who was ordering a round of beers and cigars for everyone.

"Listen to what he says," went on the Democrat. "He claims to be the best and worthiest follower of 'Old Kumpf.' He will trod the path you marked out! As far as the Sunday question is concerned, everything will remain as it was. He is a bold, faithless fellow. I know for a fact that he wrote yesterday to the Young Men's Christian Association promising in return for their votes a complete closing of all saloons on Sundays. Either here or there he must break his word. I fail to understand how you can remain loyal to a party which tolerates breach of promises in this shameless fashion and how you can come out in support of a candidate like Davenport who runs from pothouse to pothouse, telling the Swedes that Swedish blood runs in his veins, boasting to the Irish that he is by birth a son of the Emerald Isle, and letting the Germans know that his mother is of German descent. Go up to the scamp and expose his game! You will certainly win the thanks of every German and you will yourself gain in influence, for you will thus demonstrate that you are capable of freeing yourself from the ties of party and standing on your own feet when it is necessary."

"I guarantee you," he added in a whisper, "the nomination of the comptroller, and you know yourself that the position of municipal minister of finance is important and influential. But you must act before it is too late. Look now how the waves of enthusiasm next door mount higher and higher."

Meanwhile, at the refreshment table, Davenport treated the by-standers once more to beer and cigars; at most he was relieved now and then by one or another of the candidates for the other offices. Soon the talk became louder; greetings and wishes of good luck for the complete success of the Republicans were shouted around. Suddenly fat Buschmann, the saloon keeper with the flushed complexion, climbed onto an empty beer barrel. Wildly gesticulating and waving high a great roll of paper, he yelled to the crowd, "Gentlemen! We are all agreed that we must have as mayor of our city only the very best man. There are many good men, and I don't want to hurt anyone's feelings. But he is unrivaled who has, like our friend Davenport, today been elevated, by the document I hold in my hands, to the highest honor that can, after all, come to a man in return for services to the community. This is the very best, and we must elect him mayor."

In response to loud cries of, "Read it out, read it out," he went on: "I can bring you the most joyous news that our friend, the defender of German habits and customs, the enemy of the temperance fanatics and prohibitionists, at a public meeting of the Order of the Knights of Pythias, was elected Honorary Grand Master. Long live our dear comrade Joe Davenport, our next mayor! *Hip, Hip, Hurrah!*"

"Long live Davenport—and at his side, Buschmann who always knows what's new," yelled the majority of the spectators. Only in the corner where a few Democrats stood did this speech bring no applause; and the group of which Kumpf was center also remained dumb.

Now the mayoralty candidate climbed onto the barrel and praised Germany and the Germans, the Rhine and the "Fatherland." He used the identical words that have already often enough been heard from American and Irish candidates who set out to snare some German votes, empty words, delivered in rhetorical periods which nevertheless seemed to make a great impression on the emotions of the listeners well worked up by free beer. After Davenport finished there was no end of *hochs* and *hurrahs*. Only with difficulty did Old Kumpf succeed in getting the floor and drawing the attention of the crowd. He pointed to the older division, the so-called Bear Group, which was preparing to go into its exercises in the hall above.

"Surely," he began, "we have had enough of talking, of listening, of drinking, and of shouting. Now it is a question of whether, apart from all the fine words we have heard, we really are also men of action, capable of acting properly. Now the question is, 'Will every man be at his post?' The post of the true German is, moreover, not where speeches are being delivered, but where the occasion calls for power and energy. As president of the Bear Group, I command you to your posts. Form your ranks! Forward march!"

Thereupon he went to the head of the line and led all the men into the middle of the hall. After a number of exercises were there performed, he again began to speak: "I ask you now to keep in mind our motto. We must establish a solid front against the temperance fanatics, against the apostles of water who wish to circumscribe our personal liberty and to dictate to us where and what to drink. We must also fight those who flirt with them." At these words his eye fell on the mayoralty candidate who had followed along, apparently in the hope that Kumpf, his fellow-Republican, would enjoin the audience to remain true to the party banner and to give its votes to him. Before Davenport could fully grasp the situation, Kumpf went on, pointing to Mr. Holmes the rival Democratic candidate who had, unnoticed, come into the hall during the concluding exercises: "Although I do not fight for exactly the same principles as this man, still I must acknowledge that he offers a true guarantee against the hypocritical attempts of the prohibitionists. We Germans, in this land, allow ourselves easily to be pleased, and always compromise. But we will not let them take our beer away. Whoever infringes upon our rights in that respect must be fought; whoever offers us a pledge for their maintenance is our man. With this in mind, I say, 'long live our next mayor, Mister Holmes!'"

Loud applause arose from all sides; men, women, and children jostled about trying to shake the hand of the future mayor. The band struck up the "Star-Spangled Banner" while the whole assemblage rose to its feet and loudly sang the words.

Holmes gave his thanks with a speech, and then by an unmistakable gesture invited everyone to follow him into the next room, where there could already be heard the blows of a hammer opening a new cask. Now two groups formed; at the center of one were Davenport and Buschmann, at the other, Holmes and his new ally. Soon a loud uproar reigned in the refreshment room. One group yelled against another, as the satellites of Davenport sought to ridicule the sudden change in sentiment. After the beer had been poured out in streams on both sides for some time no one really knew what was going on; not a man could tell exactly who belonged to which party. But still it was a nice, pleasant evening, or so it seemed, as they slowly prepared to disband.

As I left the hall I was greeted by Rothmann, the director of the German school. He was indignant at the scenes which had so unworthily closed a meeting that had begun so well. "This time at least," he said, "the Germans should have held together to show that they could unitedly support Held, our candidate for Congress. But when it comes to the most vital interests of the Germans in America, they are only concerned with their own little appetites, and let shortsighted politicians turn their festivals into carnivals, in which a glass of beer can purchase the allegiance of a man. This is indeed corruption of the worst kind."

As we talked, we descended the steps. Rothmann invited me to take a look with him into the clubroom on the ground floor, and went on to say, "We must not now be surprised if we find here at the card or reading tables, those who should have been upstairs helping to decide matters of concern to the Germans, the Irish, and the Know Knothings."

"And, indeed, there they are," he called out, as we opened the door. "Now, dear sirs," he asked, "why was not a single one of you up above?"

"Because, generally, no decent man will mix into politics," answered the rich Tiemann, who sat at the card table with Muller the teacher and with a third man. "After all, what is politics? It is simply the attempt of those in office to stay there and of others to replace them. Your turn, Muller."

"Naturally," continued Rothmann, "since all think so, then it is clear why the Germans have so little influence in politics and remain only the drudges; they are overloaded with the burden of obligations, and are rewarded with none of the nourishment of rights."

28.

THE NATURES OF WASTE

Giuseppe Giacosa was an Italian dramatist born in Piedmont in 1847, the son of a distinguished magistrate. The success of a first play, written at the age of twenty-four, induced him to give up the study of law and devote his full time to the theater. His dramas were popular in Europe and in America. But he was best known as co-author of the librettos for Puccini's operas. In 1898 he made a visit to the United States which he described in a volume, Impressioni d'America *(1908). He was also editor of the journal* La Lettura, *from 1901 until his death in 1906.*

When it comes to making judgments about the characteristic qualities of a whole people, and especially of a people as varied and as kaleidoscopic as the Americans, one must necessarily speak in generalities. The great cities of the Union, and particularly those of the Atlantic coast, now shelter a cosmopolitan society in which ethnic traits are in appearance at least being remodeled and reformed by the process of contact with European peoples, by culture, by travel, by new kinships, by vanity, and by fashion.

The cultured European who finds a place in this society on arrival in the United States will discover the most exquisite fastidiousness of taste and, especially among the women, a great concern to exaggerate the affinities and to minimize the differences of nationality. The elegant circles of New York keep informed as to what goes on daily in the great capitals of Europe in the fields of art and of the theater; they keep abreast of the holidays, of world events, and of the *Almanach de Gotha,* and speak of all those as things near and familiar to them. American ladies, who often display a contemptuous ignorance of the politics of their own country, would be humiliated if they did not know the name of the maid-of-honor of the Queen of England, or if they could not distinguish the degrees of relationship between the Houses of Assia and Mecklenburg, or if they were ignorant of the proper titles of the papal chamberlain. It is curious to observe the intimate knowledge these beautiful Protestants have of the ceremonies and of the intrigues of the Vatican, and still more curious, the unctuous respect with which they discuss those matters. The papal court exercises upon them a kind of seductive power not in origin altogether unlike that which comes from the beauty parlors of Worth and from the erotic compendia of Paul Bourget.

But the importation of the refined tastes of European high society and the polish that comes simply from the possession of wealth alter the native characteristics only superficially. True, the Delmonico dandies display a kind of delicacy that must come at the expense of continuous self-vigilance, but this tenuity of thoughts and of actions clashes with their vigorous physiques which call for action.

Of course, there exists in America a plutocratic aristocracy with titles of nobility that are derived from millionaire ancestors. But whatever subtle influence comes from millions long in possession has not yet begun to polish off the surface roughness that reaches from the roots to the ultimate branches. Certainly wealth in America has not yet produced what we consider the supreme expression of secure objective elegance, a love of simplicity. Will it ever? The very question is vain. Less vain is the query whether it would be well to produce it. And I hold to the negative.

In Italy we have crystallized our tastes. A sense of proportion is both the shield of quality and the source of timidity. Whoever visits the United States, once having recovered from his initial amazement, will begin to doubt the legitimacy of our aesthetics. To tell the truth, since people capable of genuine judgments are extremely rare, the general acceptance of sound aesthetic principles proceeds among us from a traditional reverence, not far removed from laziness. We do not welcome innovations unless they are rather decrepit, and we conceive that the primary and principal reason of being is to be the same. Thus we are ever more likely to confuse the lazy man with the man who thinks with his own brain.

The American, on the contrary, has more taste for the present than for the past. The lack of centuries of tradition which seems to us Europeans a deficiency and which produces a sense of incompleteness in our habit-bound minds, actually frees him of timidity and helps him develop his own personality. I do not reprove, like so many others, the want of American originality, and I do not at all wish to say that all, or most, of the aesthetic products of the New World seem to me endowed

with genius. An Italian, I react like an Italian, and am only less prejudiced than most of my countrymen in that I do not mock the Americans for feeling differently from myself. In noting down these traits,
therefore, I took care lest I describe as faults what were only differences
between us. I noticed and was pleased at the thought that cosmopolitan
contacts have not yet led to and will not ever harden into a troublesome
uniformity of all peoples.

In withholding our derision from the Americans we are not being
simply lukewarm. We will treat alike the caricature we have made of
Uncle Sam or Jonathan and that exotic vanity which induces them to
adopt European manners. I will not deny that there was sometimes an
element of sour grapes involved, but it was certain that the sourness
of the grapes was not very tempting. And I firmly believe that among
all the citizens of the United States there is none who so regularly and
constantly apes foreign mannerisms as does the Anglomaniac in our
own high society.

It is another matter to see if the wealthy are more discreet on one
side of the Atlantic than on the other. In matters of taste—that is to
say, of artistic sense applied to common things—the luxurious and
wealthy society of the two continents on the whole balance each other.
The newest houses of the very wealthy and even of many noblemen of
ancient lines are not less luxurious and stupefying in Europe than in
America. The only difference is that in the Old World there is the
attempt to make much of little, and in the New questions of cost are
of no concern. Given the choice between an authentic tapestry and its
clever imitation, the European would be satisfied with the latter, while
the American would take the former.

But in any case, there has been a notable revolution in the origin
and application of taste in Europe in the last few years. The refined
taste that in past centuries was the exclusive privilege of the highest
and richest has now descended into the hands of the middle classes.
The greatest benefits of this evolution may be seen in England, where
greater emphasis in artistic industries is placed on pure line and proper
proportions than on richness of ornamentation. Nowadays the common
utilitarian objects have more elegance than the pretentious and luxurious ones. We have lost the secret of that broad, confident pomp that
was familiar to the substantial aristocracy of earlier centuries. Our
hodgepodge ostentation expresses the slight faith of the rich in their

own stability and their desire to enjoy pleasures before the final deluge. And of all the pleasures of luxury, none is sweeter than to exaggerate their cost.

It is said that the Americans, in the act of showing some valuable object, always take care to mention price. That is sometimes true. But the difference between them and us may be reduced simply to this, that they speak out openly while we ingeniously let the same information slip out by a play on words. For their single act of vanity we substitute two; we wish to make a good thing of the cost and an even better thing of the appearance of negligence. I will not deny that the primitive measurement of works of art in terms of dollars and cents in the United States leaves me with a sense of disgust. I remember a visit to the home of a very rich collector of pictures in New York. He accompanied me himself, set me at the best point of view before each item, and declaimed in Ciceronian accents: "Corot, ten thousand dollars; Millet, fifteen thousand," and so on. He spoke to me as if reciting in an accent memorized by rote, and made such a play of the proper attitudes of the possessor that I could perceive that the notion of price had become, by his standards, an integral part of the work and inseparable from the name of the artist. But everyone of us at home can recall in his own experience some amusing scene in which a Maecenian millionaire, in the act of displaying a recent acquisition, will not deign to mention the price, but who with lordly nonchalance will let an intimation of its value slip through the involutions of his discourse.

As a matter of fact, it is not in the greater or lesser degree of refined taste that I note the chief difference between us and the Americans, but rather in their mania for heaping up the elements of pleasure in excessive quantities under the erroneous impression that they thereby multiply happiness. They act like the man, delighted with a whiff of a fragrant perfume, who empties the flask on his handkerchief. There are examples in every land of such intemperance in enjoyment and particularly in the more refined delights for which more than anything else a sense of proportion is necessary.

A millionaire in New York wished to build himself a home worthy of his purse. A cultivated man, long resident in Europe and a connoisseur of artistic things, he at first succeeded in an admirable manner; but he then proceeded to overload it by continually adding new marvels to the old. By their very abundance, the good things almost drove their master from his house. If he wished to go up the staircase to his quarters he had to light the lamps in full daylight. This palatial staircase took up a good third of his house, yet was not harmonious or fitting. Fusing together the German and Italian styles of the sixteenth century, this was, from top to bottom, a miracle of imitative art, carried out so carefully that the new parts did not clash with the many precious authentic objects there collected. It was covered with an entablature of dark cabinet wood, and the largest landing places were antique, of wood dark as night, worked out, and carved. In every corner were arms and armor with a dark patina. Along the wall, on the landings, in the openings of the balustrades, carved furniture, wooden statues, a profusion of all sorts of knickknacks, gave the impression of a museum. In a little obscure niche a stupendous Luca della Robbia made a background for a little fountain. Why a fountain? In all American houses, and especially in this one, water runs through pipes in the walls to every room on every floor, and in any case this water spout is incongruous, jutting out of the marble in the midst of so much carved wood and oriental tapestries. But wealth will not be denied, and so a fountain it is. And to the fifteenth century, to the Italian and German renaissance pieces, to the lavish furnishings, to the painting of Luca, and to that burbling water, we must surely add the impressive light of stained-glass windows! As for colors, let them be striking—blue, green, violet, purple. But the windows are not wide enough, the house next door cuts you off from the sun, the heavy tints only admit a thread of light, the dark wood fails to reflect even that thread, and that is why this marvelous, expensive home sleeps in darkness through which the visitors must move about one by one, by artificial light.

In another house I saw a stupendous Japanese salon, which cost a quarter of a million dollars. This is a room of bronze, literally of bronze from the top to the bottom, where the metal meets a beautiful red wooden flooring, imprinted with fantastic figures upon which it is a crime to walk. Every part of this monstrous whole is a masterwork of art and the indiscriminate assemblage of so many masterworks produces a vivid sensation—not unlike a punch in the eye. Compared to this room, which was meant to be lived in, a museum would seem as intimate and as homelike as the kitchen of a cottage.

Another example: In America, as in London, and as now in all large European cities, the clubs, once intended only for evening entertainment, have gradually become private hotels where the members can spend whole days, attend to business, dine, and on occasion find lodgings. In New York the most fashionable are the Union Club, the Manhattan Club, the Athletic Club, and in a special category, that is to say, more meticulous than any other in the admission of new members, the Knickerbocker Club. But all these are not essentially unlike the European. It was necessary that the Americans invent a new type, and that is the Club of Tuxedo Park, New York, open only to the most refined few.

The club is on a large tract of considerable and varied natural beauty. Run through by little brooks, beautified by a lake and by amply wooded hills, these lands belonged thirty or forty years ago to a rich New Yorker who conceived the idea of founding a new city there. That was not unusual in the United States, but the plan fell through, the town never came into being, and the natural beauties were not marred. Failing in this effort, the man did not wish to break up the holding and sell in small fragments what he had bought as a whole; furthermore, a single house in the vast tract would be desolate. After several years of fruitless possession some friends came to his assistance.

They acquired the land and erected a building in which people could come together to spend a vacation. Thus was born a rural club, the *ne plus ultra* of the species. Each member had his own spacious lodge for himself and his family, his own stables and coach house, and also had access to the quarters for the collective use of the community; common halls for dining and for games, sitting rooms, party rooms, a library, pharmacy, medical service, post and telegraph offices, and everything that luxury and ease could demand, was supplied in the new club with the lavish quality worthy of a sultan or nabob. As was to be expected, this Eldorado tempted many who clamored for admission, the more so when a railroad line brought the place much nearer to New York. Direct trains reached Tuxedo Park in an hour and a half, as much as it takes to go from one end to another of the city. The number of members grew rapidly and buildings were put up as permanent residences. The sociologists and moralists will some day be able to examine whether such an extension of collective life, aimed at multiplying pleasures and excluding all domestic intimacy, will not in the long run dry up the spirits and spoil the most delicate sentiments. But now a great part of high society, in Europe as well, lives ten months of the year in hotels and counts the home a place of passage. In any case, from the point of view of immediate pleasures, Tuxedo Park leaves nothing to be desired.

On the last Thursday in November the United States celebrates Thanksgiving Day, a holiday proclaimed annually by the President to give thanks to God for the favors of the year. On this day New York was full of students from Yale and Princeton, the two most celebrated universities in America, assembled for a football match which divided the whole city into two factions. Today New York did not show the sad brightness which is the mark of a holiday in all American cities. Early in the morning the midtown district, instead of being deserted of inhabitants, was more than usually full of uproarious people. All the faces were marked with a pleasant aspect and with that disposition to familiar communication which children carry as of right and which shines even on adults. The immense metropolis seemed transformed into a little college town altogether wrapped up in the life of its students. All the New Yorkers, of whatever state or condition, men and women alike, carried on their hair, arms, cravats, or elsewhere, the colors of one of the two universities as a sign of sympathy and support. Before the houses, the hotels, and the clubs, immense open carriages, their four horses bedecked with garlands, waited to take the spectators directly to the playing field. Troops of students marched like conquerors through the crowds which burst into cheers to wish them success. This was a pleasant occasion dedicated to the flower of American youth.

The game follows, a stupendous and elaborate exercise of strength and skill. In the evening the streets and the theaters are jammed with students, but the flower of American youth has begun to fade and gives forth the odor of alcohol. The young men break into the theaters by force and are thrown out by violence. They do not indulge in those exhibitions of salacious gaiety by which our students on a spree compensate for distracting the peaceful spectators. Instead, the American boys emit an annoying, deafening yell on a single continuous note that expresses the immobility of their sluggish minds. No smiling, no laughing! Their supreme power, unmitigated by any grace, seems like that of a conquering soldiery. They stagger tipsily through the streets, sunk in a dark drunkenness without a ray of merriment. The less funereal beat time out loud, trying to march in step, but voices and step are independent of each other and agree only in wandering off on their own accounts. Their voices give off noises like the sound of drums muffled for a funeral, sounds so strained that they seem to express the delirium of the paralytic. What a difference from our lively and sparkling drinking songs and from the subtle exaltation that mounts to the brain from our wines! And their walk! A three-year-old could fell the most vigorous of these athletes like a log. Late at night many lie down like corpses in the gutter.

This brutal viciousness is equally characteristic of the rich and poor, even making allowance for differences in the quality of their drinking and of its inebriating capacity, for the latter rises in inverse proportion to the former. It is well known that in the very exclusive clubs the most fastidious members come in on foot, but go out, in the small hours, on the backs of their servants who bundle them into carriages, take them home, and put them to bed before they recover consciousness.

I judge that the American is more interested in getting drunk than in drinking. That statement may seem paradoxical, but is not. I have rarely seen an American, accustomed to drinking, sip a glass of liquor and show signs of savoring the aroma. They all act as if the bitter alcohol is unpleasant to the palate, and hurry the act of imbibing as if eager to get rid of the disagreeable substance. They do not drink, they guzzle. When they bring the glass to their lips and empty it at a gulp it is clear that the column of liquor must sink like lead through the throat without affecting the taste. The act of imbibing generally is not accompanied by any sign of pleasure. Deep and habitual drinkers reach the state of drunkenness without passing through the process of getting drunk. For them inebriety is not a height to be climbed, but a well into which to sink, and that, not little by little, gradually, but purposely and deliberately. True, this process involves a conservation of energy; it imposes a rest and suspends the intellectual activity of minds, so heavily taxed and so thoroughly fatigued by business. Americans feel a violent need to paralyze cerebral activity with external aids. Or perhaps the source of the invincible seductiveness of alcohol that steadily leads them to the ultimate stupor lies in their impatience for extreme sensations; they love to save time, to get there all at once. That is the same gross sensuality that reveals itself in a thousand ways, disdainful of delicacy, loving enormities, giganticism, excess.

The first product of the prodigies of mechanization that impressed me in the United States was the appearance of universal prosperity, and consequently the visible equality of social conditions. There was equality of dress, of fashions, of habits, of manners, and, above all, a kind of physiological equality; I don't venture to say equality of health, but the kind of healthy well-being that comes from sufficient, nutritious food.

In New York, toward evening, when the working day ends, miles of carriages scatter the innumerable crowds, which all day long conduct their affairs downtown, to all parts of the upper city. The six parallel elevated railway lines each run trains of five or six enormous coaches every five minutes, all jammed to overflowing with people. There the millionaire sits beside the porter, and may well be asked by the conductor to get up and give his place to an old serving woman. Some elegant Wall Street bankers are marked by special clothes of English cut. But with that exception, no European would be able to pick out by eye who there represents the infinite variety of professions, trades, states, fortune, culture, education, that may be encountered among the whole people. The gentleman who sits at your side and can scarcely edge himself into the tiny space available while he nonchalantly reads his immense newspaper might with equal likelihood be the attorney of the richest railroad in the world, a shoe clerk, or a cab driver from City Hall Park just finishing his tour of duty. At most, some hands might betray the exercise of the more menial trades, and some odors, peculiar industries. But the shape and texture of the clothing in all shows the same care, the same cut, and almost the same easy circumstances; and in manners and speech all display the same vigorous sentiments of an egalitarian society and of personal dignity.

The stranger who wishes summarily to learn the home manners of the Americans will spend a Sunday in New York riding the length of an elevated line. For that purpose, the Ninth Avenue Line is best. It reaches from the edge of the harbor to the Harlem River, a distance of some twenty kilometers, and the entire journey costs five American cents. The structure of the railroad, following the gradual rises of the ground, generally runs at a height parallel to the first story of the houses, except when it comes to certain dips that furrow the city. There the line runs along the second, third, or fourth floors, and now and then even above the ridges of the roofs.

Leaving the Battery, at the edge of the harbor, the train passes first through the oldest part of New York, the *city* of business, of very old buildings, given over in their ground floors to stores, to offices, banks, and establishments of all kinds. Every evening, as I have already said, this city of wealth which finances the agricultural and industrial activity of the United States entirely empties itself. No one sleeps there. The press of business forestalls the introduction of improvements; the streets remain narrow and tortuous, the houses dark and inconvenient; the pavement is broken and buried under a layer of thick black mud, the air stagnant and fetid.

So the dollars are accumulated in ugliness, only to be spent in elegance. That accounts for the deathly silence that falls upon this deserted quarter of the town on holidays. The train moves up the avenue, cutting across the numbered streets which open in places on gardens and plazas or offer glimpses in the distance of the great North River, the Hudson, which is dotted with masts and sails, and animated by the aerial seesaw of the ferryboats. Higher up, above Central Park, are the working-class quarters, monotonous, but spacious, convenient, well furnished.

On Sunday, whoever watches these homes from an elevated train and knows something of the social condition of their inhabitants will believe himself witness of an Anglo-Saxon form of the dream that earned Faust his easy pardon. Every family passes the entire day in serene rest before the spacious windows. The father sits in his rocking chair, pipe in mouth; he reads and reads, from first to last line, the thirty-two large pages of his Sunday paper. Another illustrated paper of equal length busies the mother, seated in another rocking chair near another window. If there is a son in the family, and the house has a third window, there will without fail be a third paper and the same sight without variation, as in a figured tapestry. Only the girls modify the monotony of this silent and instructive felicity. Rich-blooded, blooming in blond or rosy beauty, they do not sit still but lean against the sills, looking curiously into the street, smiling at the passengers who fly by in the elevated, chatting with neighbors, making eyes at whoever notices them, nibbling almonds, and laughing continually with sincere freshness. It may be said, parenthetically, that nothing is more graceful than the bold, saucy, gay nimbleness of all these American girls; nothing is more refreshing than the open pleasure with which they encourage and receive the admiration, express or tacit, of passers-by.

When the train runs at its highest along the level of the top floors where more light enters, the whole interior equipment and furniture of the house becomes visible. There are pleasant draperies, cloths on the tables, nice curtains, copious and commodious furniture, in general an air of solidity and comfort which in Italy we do not see in our provincial cities, except perhaps for such exceptions as the homes of lawyers, doctors, judges, merchants. These people, be it understood, live by their own day's labor, with salaries of four or even three dollars a day, the ordinary pay of a worker. These are settled people; they neither owe nor are owed; they are not in danger of ruin; and their needs are not limited to that which barely keeps them from dying but also include what is desirable for living.

Let us see them from another perspective.

The slaughterhouses of Chicago are famous even among us. They are famous and fabulous because everyone thinks them more organized, polished, and mechanically perfect than in reality they are. To me they seemed the nastiest pits the human mind could imagine. It is enough to say that these immense places are entirely made of wood— floors, columns, stairs, and all—although in certain months of the year close to 60,000 head of cattle are slaughtered, bled, skinned, quartered, and packed there daily. The vapors of blood impregnate the pores of the walls, dribble down from the ceiling in rivulets of blood, soaking into the vats, the benches, the pillars, and the tables. On the floor the blood forms into a dark, pestiferous, glutinous, slippery mud; frequent washings cannot mop it out, only cause it to penetrate more deeply into the fibers of the wood. In addition, these places are low and crowded; the workers trample upon each other; and the visitors suffer loathsome contacts. The vapors that escape from the boiling water and from the palpitating meat render still more uncertain the uncertain light that penetrates from the little windows into those dark walls.

Hundreds of laborers move about in such quarters, each one fixed to a special job and constrained to furious and uninterrupted labor by a mechanical routine of a succession of operations. These unfortunate men have neither the face nor the body of humans. Their features are contracted by an overwhelming disgust and by an irritating intoxication from the blood around them. Their eyes are constantly strained by the necessity for distinguishing through the penumbra the precise point at which to strike. The greasy matter, reddish and shiny, that stains their foreheads and cheeks, the encrusted blood hardened on beards and hair, the abrupt and rapid movements by which they throw severed pieces to neighboring workers—all that amidst the smoke, the moldy smell, and the moans and gurgling cries—gives them an appearance altogether inhuman, and rather like the savage animals they destroy with so much dispatch. And the clothing! The shirts and trousers are so hard with dried blood that the men are forced to walk with long stiff strides. Stained from tip to toe, lined with blood and flowing with blood, the bottoms of their trousers drag in the bloody mud, so that every step makes a splash, and the feet, detached from the soles by force give forth a sucking sound and leave a bubble that seems like a live tumor.

Flee from this pit of horrors and the nausea will pursue you for a long time, will follow you through the streets and into the gardens; the sounds will continue to disturb you; and for several days any non-vegetable food will be disgusting. But should your mind allow you to spy at the exit of this intricate parcel of streets, alleys, buildings, huts, and viaducts that covers a space larger than Milan, the sight that would greet you at the end of the working day would give you a more just conception of the complexity of American life.

A half hour after the end of work there come forth from the enclosure a lordly collection of gentlemen whom one of our courtly ladies would take as models of sporty elegance. They are often young, tall and blond, with well-trimmed mustaches and polished shoes. They wear handsome ties, plaid jackets in the English style, and little hard hats. The more mature men are clad in dignified black and in derbys. All are solemn and sober; you would think they were leaving an aristocratic club or a classical concert at twenty lire a ticket.

Who would recognize amidst such refinement the butchers and slaughterers of a while ago? Having taken off their filthy clothes, scrubbed their hands, arms, and faces, they are now disposed to enjoy politely the money they earned in the blood and mud. These men undertake the most loathsome and most fatiguing work, but they do not thereby renounce the good things of life, food in plenty, and curtained homes. Machine-like during their hard work, they wish to retake at its end a humanity superior to that of the Negroes and the redskins. Do we not know the progress of a people by the multiplication of its wants? Born of a nation which knows no ease, the Americans accept the inequality of labor in order to attain a relative equality of goods. Members of a society which knows how to utilize all human activity, they are not obsessed with the future of their own families; as the father worked and works, so will his children; today does not have fewer rights than tomorrow.

We value and practice the saving of surpluses, but their surplus comes out of easy circumstances, not out of poverty. The privations that degrade a man, that leave him no solid food, that expose him to the hardship of the seasons, that disarm him against the harshness of life, that humiliate him in the sight of his peers, are, in their judgment, true human wrongs. And they recognize in them signs of an inferior and decadent race.

Let us now glance briefly at the Italian quarters in New York and the life, the vile life, of too many Italians in Chicago. I have already said that downtown New York is given over to business, that no one lives there, and that it is deserted at night. That is in general true of the native Americans, not of the Chinese or of the Italians. The narrow quarters of those immigrants are right in the middle of the lower city, near the Five Points, where are the narrowest and darkest alleys and the most horrible decrepit buildings.

It is impossible to describe the mud, the dirt, the filth, the stinking humidity, the nuisances, the disorder of these streets. People live there out of doors, in view of the inclement climate, a sign of how much worse must be the inside of their homes. Indeed, I saw little of the interiors except some obscure shops that so disgusted me as to kill any further curiosity. There, as in Naples, the sky is spiderwebbed with hanging clothes spread from one house to another. But what clothes and coming forth from what a washing—as if extended in the sun to dry the dirt! Ragged, thin men wander about laboriously from one shop to another or gather around the entrance of a saloon from which they are served the bitter dregs of the beer bottles retailed in healthy places to healthy people.

On the steps of the exits, on the steps of the staircases, on wooden or straw stools, almost out to the middle of the street, the women carry on in full view all the pitiful tasks of their domestic life. They suckle their children, sew, clean the faded greens which are the only substance of their soup, wash their clothes in greasy buckets, untangle and arrange their hair. They prattle, only not in the lively and witty chatter of the Neapolitan lands, but rather in a sort of painful chirp that strikes the heart.

At the corner an overturned cart (in this street carriages never pass) induces them to get up and frenziedly to gather the few goods; then savage and bestial sounds, shrill and reproachful cries are exchanged by the carter and the whole swarm of women. Some old cripples pass, laboriously carrying some dirty junk in hampers. Vain toil! Everything will go the same way. The clothes on people's backs, the merchandise exposed for sale, the fruit, the herbs, the moldy yellow meat that hangs on hooks in the butcher shop, the furnishings displayed in the open stalls, even the sordid Italian and American notes arranged in lines in the windows of the numerous banks, yes even the gigantic portraits of King Victor, of Garibaldi, and of Umberto, and the tricolored flags which hang at almost every window and are quartered before every shop—everything, absolutely everything will be thrown on the dunghill. Those flags arouse both a sense of tenderness and a sense of shame. These people, so harshly tried, still have a thought for the far-off homeland, and may yet find in this imaginary symbolism a little compensation for the urgent and sad reality about them. But, at the same time, is it not humiliating for the fatherland which reduces its children to such squalid misery?

But the saddest sight of all is that of the children, thrown half-naked into the open streets. Who does not know at first hand the climate of New York cannot conceive the sadness of this spectacle. I visited those streets in the middle of November and the little creatures had nothing but shirts to their backs. On the last Sunday of November we had a fall in temperature of thirty degrees. At noon it was eighteen degrees above, by evening twelve below zero (centigrade). A layer of ice quickly covered the streets. Always, when the tremendous storms that are felt even across the Atlantic to the west coast of Europe break through from Canada and Alaska, New York moves in a single step from stifling heat to wintry blasts. The change comes unannounced. The whirlwind descends unexpectedly upon the placid gaiety of sunny skies. Think of those babies! Who succeeds in surviving this mortal test, will, as an adult, be able to defy all the seas and all the deserts. But many fall at the first shock, or grow suddenly, prematurely old, as if a breath of wind had transformed them.

Such miserable sights, of course, are only encountered in the streets where are gathered the dregs of Italian emigration, although these are still a hundred times preferable to the dregs of the Irish, whose degradation proceeds from debauchery rather than, as among our countrymen, from exhausted powers, from economic prejudice, and from ignorance.

But it must not be thought that the greater part of the Italians remain there. Not by far! Italians in New York and in Brooklyn supply a large part of the labor in the building trades; they are masons and stucco workers. Many are also barbers and waiters, and some are fruit dealers, established in fine shops to which they have worked up after going around for years with baskets and little carts. These people are more dispersed, as their business requires, in various parts of the city. But they do not know how, or do not care to assume a bourgeois air, and continue to live below the American level. There is a certain petty concern with saving, a frugality which verges upon stinginess, a meticulous counting of pennies that causes them to wear hand-me-downs and to crowd many heads into narrow and incommodious spaces. The lowest Americans recognize in these people, already improved over their first condition, the same race that infects Baxter and Mulberry Streets, and finds in that tattered multitude the sign of their true nationality.

As far as I know, Chicago does not have districts particularly given over to Italians, where the spectacle of our misery can be discovered by all. There, the distinguishing feature of our co-nationals is more the exercise of certain undesirable occupations. The most common consists of grubbing in the stinking junk piles near the great warehouses, the grain elevators, the piers, and the railroad stations. This is an industry of old women from our southern provinces who have come across with their husbands and children. The men attend to their trades or business, while the women, rain or snow, pass the whole day before the sweepings, to bring back in the evening a few cents worth to make them rich. Papers, scraps of leather, rags, nails, tickets, pieces of wire, everything that is discarded by a great industrial and mechanical life is collected and packed away by them. A pair of sandals, a torn blouse, a vial with the remnants of some unknown medicine, are in their eyes veritable treasures. Who can fix the ultimate limits of that which may some day be useful! They put on the sandals, wear the blouse, the eternal woman in them makes no concession for the needs of dressing up. At the first sign of illness they swallow the medicine, thinking thus to save the expenses of a doctor. Can they not nourish themselves as well off garbage? I have seen them bite greedily into some remnants of sweet potatoes recovered from the refuse. God knows those potatoes, several days old, were spoiled and sour! Celery, carrots, withered and wrinkled cabbage, soggy apples, such as the poorest kitchen would throw into the garbage heap, make up their daily meals.

They have their own fixed places, on which they maintain a kind of right of possession and which they take up each day in groups of five or six or even more. Going down from the hotel I was accustomed to pass a stretch of track near which a triangular opening gave a glimpse of piles always replenished with dirt and refuse. Sometimes I passed there early in the morning, the old women were already at work; returning at noon, I found them there again; again at two, still again at six. The old women were always there, bent over or seated or kneeling in the mud and dust, scraping and scratching like hens. Some went about with naked feet in order to call upon the sense of touch while their eyes ranged the farther distances. Soon after I arrived in Chicago one of them died of tetanus after having cut her foot on a piece of sheet iron. I wanted to talk with them. The long slow cadenzas of the Neapolitan speech sounded sad, in this place, under such skies, coming out of such pitiful lips. I asked them if they would not earn more staying at home, knitting stockings, sewing clothes, or doing some other work.

"And this, who would look after this?" answered one pointing to the pile.

Here is the secret of so much agony: the fear that some minute particle of wealth might be wasted. They might gain more by healthier and cleaner labor but this tiny bit of value attracts them. It is a blind adoration of goods as such, abstracted from any practical application.

I could say more on this point, but wish to pass from one grief to another, from the elderly to the very young. There is always the same misery; misery, not poverty, since the miserable condition of these people does not proceed simply from a lack of means. Here in Chicago, as in New York, the willing worker can earn at least three dollars a day, many make four, and some even five. The dollar is worth five lire and twenty-five centesimi. And it must not be thought that the price of necessities increases in the same proportion as the monetary unit, for the buying power of the dollar is relatively equal to that of the lira in Italy. Many deny that, but it is true. Certain rare luxury goods—gloves, English hats, carriages, for instance—are twice or three times as expensive as at home. But the rates of the first-class hotels, by far more commodious than the best European ones, more plentiful in their food and more liberal in their dining hours, are not dearer than in Europe. In Europe the price varies from twelve to fifteen lire a day, in New York it is three dollars at the Fifth Avenue Hotel, reputed to be the most splendid in the United States. And if we descend from the elegancies of high life to the level of the common man, the difference of costs would be even less noticeable. As far as basic necessities are concerned there is no difference, or only a very slight one.

If the over-all cost of living is higher, that is because it brings a larger sum of goods. If our countrymen were willing to live in America as poorly as in Italy they could get by for twenty-five or thirty Italian pennies a day. But it is precisely the inclination to get by with little that the Americans deride and despise in the Italians. When Italian immigrants begin to live with more human liberality then they will begin to cancel out the sad impression left by those who denied themselves the good things of life.

Men commonly think of the characteristics of each race only in terms of its extremes; those alone are essentially differentiated, and those alone form the conception that gets fixed in the popular mind. People who are born and who grow up in America amidst so many different races cannot fail to be aware of profound ethnic differences. The Americans are the most indomitable, the most ambitious, the most audacious, the most eager for pleasure and for a full life, of any nation that has ever existed. In the eyes of the Americans, the Italian who dresses, lodges, eats, and sleeps like themselves is simply a citizen of the Union who happens to speak a language different from their own. But one who is resigned, humble, willing to be abstinent, inured to labor without pause, who in such a storehouse of good things, and owning the means to enjoy his share, voluntarily renounces it, who lives in filth instead of in cleanliness, who degrades the beauty of the human form with outlandish garments, who, in sum, reduces the needs of life to the bare minimum compatible with existence, such is not a man of their race, is not even a man. From whence does he come? From Italy. Are such then the Italians? So is formed a reputation.

29.

A CHURCHMAN FROM HUNGARY

Count Vay de Vaya und Luskod was born in 1865, scion of an ancient noble family. He entered the Catholic Church and advanced rapidly in its service, becoming privy chamberlain to Pope Leo XVIII in 1895. Four years later the Count was sent as Prothonotary Apostolic to Asia. In the course of his travels he passed through the United States several times between 1903 and 1906, and in 1908 appeared his book, Nach Amerika in einem Auswandererschiffe. When he returned to Hungary, in 1908, he became Lord Abbot of the Monastery of St. Martins.

The bells are tolling for a funeral. The modest train of mourners is just setting out for the little churchyard on the hill. Everything is shrouded in gloom, even the coffin lying upon the bier and the people who stand on each side in threadbare clothes and with heads bent. Such is my sad reception at the Hungarian workingmen's colony at McKeesport. Everyone who has been in the United States has heard of this famous town, and of Pittsburgh, its close neighbor. This is the great center of the iron and steel industry of America. Here are the innumerable foundries of the famous, or infamous, Steel Trust, that monstrous industrial excrescence.

Fourteen-thousand tall chimneys are silhouetted against the sky, along the valley that extends from McKeesport to Pittsburgh; and these 14,000 chimneys discharge their burning sparks and smoke incessantly. The realms of Vulcan could not be more somber or filthy than this valley of the Monongahela. On every hand are burning fires and spurting flames. Nothing is visible save the forging of iron and the smelting of metal. From thousands upon thousands of these plants the thud of the steam hammers and the hissing of escaping steam smite aggressively on the ears. One can hardly imagine this to be the conscious labor of human beings; the thundering tumult, blinding flame, and choking steam which surround us suggest rather a horrible calamity fallen upon the land. From above, soot, ashes, and glowing embers rain in a steady shower, as though from some volcanic crater; indeed it is difficult to believe all this chaos to be wrought by human hands. It is like the nether world of Pluto, the valley of Hades—of eternal night. Only the imagination of a Dante could depict the horrors of a hell so dreadful, and well might every newcomer to the Monongahela Valley be addressed in the words of the *Divine Comedy:* "All hope abandon ye who enter here!"

In this mephitic atmosphere, mist-laden, the tolling bell performs its solemn function in a manner suggestive of some tired and struggling creature, while the funeral cortege wends its sorrowful way slowly toward the distant churchyard.

Along the valley below, clumps of workmen's homes and the mighty conglomeration of forges and factories unfold themselves to our view. Pittsburgh, Homestead, Braddock, Duquesne, McKeesport, follow each other like links in an interminable chain. The impression made by this series of gigantic industrial hives is horrible. It may best be characterized in the language of the Americans themselves: "Pittsburgh is Hell with the lid off." And this fearful place affects us very closely, for thousands of immigrants wander here from year to year. Here they fondly seek the realization of their cherished hopes, and here they suffer till they are swallowed up in the inferno. He whom we are now burying is the latest victim. Yesterday he was in full vigor and at work in the foundry, toiling, struggling, hoping—a chain broke, and he was killed. Today he is a new addition to the row of silent sleepers in the churchyard; tomorrow, who knows how many may be added?

Like the terrible idols of the past, the implacable iron and steel works must have their daily human sacrifice. Scarce an hour passes without an accident, and no day without a fatal disaster. But what if *one* man be crippled, if *one* life be extinguished among so many! Each place can be filled from *ten* men, all eager for it. Newcomers camp out in sight of the foundry gates, while a little farther away others arrive with almost daily regularity—thousands of immigrants to don the fetters of slavery.

Humble wooden dwellings, smoke-begrimed, dirty, miserable, barn-like structures line both sides of the road leading to the barren and dreary churchyard. It may be that there was no longer room for dead Magyars in the other burial-grounds; a separate place has been allotted to them. The ditch dug a few hours ago awaits its occupant, who is now being escorted to his last resting place by a few comrades. His family is back in the old home; they expected to join him in America later. His wife is not yet aware that she is a widow, and his children do not know they are fatherless.

The sad dirge of the Psalms is rendered still more pathetic by the confused and angry murmur arising from the forges and foundries. The hissing of the boilers, the roar of the blast furnaces, and the whir of the wheels accompany the last "farewell" of the old *cantor,* in cruel and menacing disharmony.

The sun goes down. But it will not become dark. The tranquillity of evening is unknown here, and twilight brings no peace. The fires burn on, the steam hammers clang, the rain of sparks continues with even greater fury. Labor continues without intermission. There is no Sunday on the Monongahela; no holidays are observed. There is no day and no night; for God's day is darkened by steam, and smoke, and clouds of soot, while the dark pall of night is snatched away by a conflagration worthy of Satan himself.

Everything and everybody is black and gloomy, the place, the air, the sky itself. Day and night, these 14,000 chimneys pour forth their noisome vomit, killing everything that grows, trees, grass, flowers, and shrubs. In the works, around the furnaces, the atmosphere is poisonous, the heat infernal. In some places the human organism cannot endure the temperature for more than a few minutes. The workmen are relieved every quarter-hour, but even in this brief period the perspiration rolls down their naked bodies, and their constitutions are fatally infected by the poisonous gases thrown off by the filthy materials in use.

This is scarcely work for *mankind.* Americans will hardly undertake anything of the sort; only immigrants, rendered desperate by circumstances, take up this degrading means of earning their daily bread. When a foreigner arrives, he is quite alone. No one takes an interest in him or guides him with friendly advice. He comes from the shores of the blue Adriatic or from the sunny valleys of the Carpathians without means, and must perforce obtain work. He knows neither the language nor the customs of the strange land and thus he is at the mercy of the tyrannous Trust, which gathers him into its clutches and transforms him from a free being into a regular slave.

This is one of the saddest features of the Hungarian emigration. In making a tour of these industrial prisons, wherever the heat is most insupportable, the flames most scorching, the smoke and soot most choking, there we are certain to find compatriots bent and wasted with toil. Their thin, wrinkled, wan faces seem to show that in America the newcomers are of no use except to help fill the moneybags of the insatiable millionaires, by the sweat of their brows, by their blood and flesh, by their very lives. After all these depressing experiences comes the saddest of all—absolute unappreciation, callous ingratitude; they are despised for the very pains with which they have filled their taskmasters' coffers.

In this realm of Mammon and Moloch everything has a value—except human life. Scientific brains cogitate how to turn the filthiest dross to account, but no one concerns himself about the sanguinary destruction in the ranks of mankind. Why? Because human life is a commodity the supply of which exceeds the demand. There are always fresh recruits to supply the place of those who fall in the battle; and steamships are constantly arriving at the neighboring ports, discharging their living human cargo still further to swell the phalanx of the instruments of cupidity.

It is true that the factory laborers of Pittsburgh get more money than farm hands; but they have also to sacrifice much more. Day after day, week after week, year in, year out, their tired eyes rest upon nothing but glowing iron and molten steel. But yet, there is some change—a constant recurrence of disasters, the bloody tax exacted by the Moloch of the furnaces, who claims his victim every day. If one could compute the fatal accidents that take place in a year at the Pittsburgh plants, the number would be incredibly large. And if one ascertained the extent to which preventive measures are taken to minimize this waste of life, one would find practically nothing done. Accidents are steadily on the increase.

How can the inhuman callousness with which the owners of the works regard the annihilation of their employees be accounted for? The only plausible answer is: the indifference of the employers is confirmed and rendered chronic by the ghastly calculation that there are more men outside the works than are required inside. Obsolete machinery and appliances are very often used instead of the expensive improvements, for the simple reason that alterations would cost much more than the "death-money" which the firms have to pay to the families of their victims. The new Compensation Act, recently passed, actually protects the employer instead of the employee, for it not only lowers the rate but also provides that the injured workman who has no family in America is not entitled to compensation at all. Half the workmen leave their wives and families in their native land, and arrive alone to commence their new existence; when such men happen to be injured or killed, their wives and children become paupers. This Act is one of the most unjust, pernicious, and heartless ever passed by any nation, and it is doubly unjust, pernicious, and heartless, in view of the superabundance of capital, which is being further piled up hour by hour.

The most astonishing feature of this land of dollars is the absolute indifference and contempt of the rich toward the poor. One might well suppose that, in a democratic country, such as have risen from the lowest strata of society would entertain more liberal and humane sentiments toward the less fortunate. But in the struggle for gold there is no room for sentiment. One might perhaps suppose that a sense of duty at least would prompt them to kindly actions. Sad experience, however, teaches otherwise. Strange as it may seem, often the most unsympathetic and the most callous are those who have themselves graduated from the hard school of adversity.

In this eternal turmoil the worker's lot is hard in an especial degree. But most difficult is that of the Hungarian and the Slav, who, while getting the least pay, do the most degrading and dangerous work. Usually these people are appointed as engine-men or as stokers in the foundries and blast furnaces, always where the heat is most intense and the danger most imminent. And the daily remuneration for such strenuous labor and appalling risk is only about one dollar and seventy-five cents.

It is hardly credible that men risk their lives for such a paltry pittance, yet so it is. When we consider that in Pittsburgh, lodgings, clothing, and all the necessities of life are very dear, the sum mentioned brings only half or a third of its value elsewhere in the country. How a man can live upon it, and even save from it, seems past comprehension. Yet while the immigrant cannot be said to live, he exists, and actually manages to put a little aside. Most of the alien workmen have no families, and having no homes their wants are few and simple. They are not regular members of the social order; they are, as it were, outlaws. As many of them are herded together in rooms as can well be packed therein, without regard to the requirements of decency or hygiene; others do not occupy rooms at all, but find shelter from the elements in outhouses. There is no proper furniture in these hovels, simply rude wooden benches on which the occupants may lie down and sleep, closely crowded together. No comfort, no cleanliness, no light, the atmosphere is sickening.

To sustain life under such conditions is hardly conceivable. Is it surprising that various diseases decimate the denizens of these foul quarters? Often the most terrible epidemics rage. The food is even worse than the lodging. The people, it is true, eat meat three times a day, but the meat is in nine cases out of ten unwholesome, as the recent Meat Trust scandals have sufficiently proved. The noxious effects of this tainted diet are aggravated by the fact that the workmen take very little farinaceous and vegetable food with it. Their employment is dangerous; they have no homes; their work days are gloomy and cheerless —what can their Sundays, their holidays be like? The program of their recreations is very brief. Ignorant of the language, they can enjoy no society, they are debarred from all pleasures except the questionable ones of drinking and gambling. And so the most sober-minded of them are induced to indulge in these vices.

Is there no one to rescue, to ameliorate, to help? Are there no millionaire employers with the enthusiasm to build cottages, plant gardens, and establish decent homes for their employees? Not seeing anything of these, I timidly asked various people to show me some of their benevolent schemes, and at once, with an air of pride, they pointed to certain marble halls, lofty edifices, and gilded cupolas, "In memory of Mr. X.," "To the honor of Mr. Y.," and "For the glory of Mr. Z." I failed to understand, and said so; and then they explained that one of these palaces contained a famous collection of antediluvian skeletons, another some marvelous ancient parchments, while a third sheltered thousands of volumes. Yet I could not quite see the connection between these magnificent specimens of architectural art and the practical well-being of the toilers. It seemed to me that they served much less for the benefit of the poor than for the glorification of the rich. And I thought how laudable it would be if Messrs. X., Y., and Z., instead of advertising their own wealth and greatness in this fashion, would erect humble, yet clean and comfortable dwellings for their laborers.

Is it to be wondered at if these poor, neglected, good-natured creatures—having no wholesome counterattractions, no friends, no benevolent patrons—cannot resist the temptations lying in their path? Their environment and lusterless existence drive them into the abyss.

Alas! that men should be driven to earn their daily bread by such inhuman labor, such bloody sweat! How heart-rendering that man should sacrifice all his noblest aspirations and every lofty ideal, and, blindfolded by primitive instincts, should see nothing but the alluring, chimerical gold! In the effort and struggle to obtain it he sacrifices peace, happiness, even God's precious gift of life, and risks what is more precious still—his immortal soul.

Yet materialism is an evil which, alas, is permeating the whole world, and it would be highly erroneous to endeavor to make any one nation responsible for this dangerous scourge, for it is universal. If it finds a more congenial soil in America, and there develops more formidable proportions, we must remember that in the New World everything is on a larger scale, everything is exaggerated. Each process is more intense and magnified. Life is something infinitely larger.

These rudimentary conditions in the United States are perfectly natural and the outcome of the general situation. Although one cannot help noticing these conditions, and though Americans themselves are the first to deplore them, it would not be just to look entirely on the black side, and to criticize in a pessimistic spirit.

Labor, as such, in the New World is what strikes each new arrival most forcibly—labor which provides daily bread and occupation to rich and poor, labor which has become identical with the thought of terrestrial life, labor which is the chief object of existence and its highest ideal.

Work in the United States is everything, and everything has become work. Toil and relaxation, hours passed at the office or at home, only give pleasure when there is something to do. The old idea of *dolce far niente* is incomprehensible; fatigue, whether as a means of providing subsistence, or whether for distraction, or as a habit, becomes a necessity of life.

One must keep moving; rest is not understood, and is avoided whenever possible unless rendered compulsory by a general breakdown. The impulses toward motion govern every one; so much so that if they sit down their chairs must have rockers, so that they may continue an action of some sort even when resting.

The day begins very early, about two hours earlier than in England, with a hurried toilet, a hasty breakfast, and the rush to the factories and offices. Time is far too valuable to permit a midday meal at home. There is not even time for proper food; the restaurants would find their efforts wasted if they advertised a good cuisine and well-appointed table. Instead, to attract the passers-by they put up notices with such inscriptions as "Quick Lunch," "Hasty Meals," "Chops in a minute." And on office doors at about midday we often see a card with the words, "Away for lunch; back in five minutes." The rest of the day, of the week, and of the year, passes in the same way. This encumbered existence, as intense for the capitalist as for the laborer, gives American life its high pressure.

However disconcerted the stranger may be on arrival by this incoherent and whirling bustle, it will carry him away mechanically; he will become, in spite of himself, an atom in the general turmoil. One gets accustomed to it; then it becomes a necessity, and one adapts oneself to the novel life.

People come from many parts of the world—astute and stubborn Teutons, lazy and casual Latins, Orientals of vague dispositions—all amalgamating in a seething caldron, everything boiling and effervescing, everything glowing.

Work here is divided up, distributed, and multiplied among many elements, great or small. It is, in fact, a huge, unseen machine in which each individual, high or low, plays the part of one of the wheels. Each revolves, each whirls, each is in ceaseless activity.

Everything is done with great facility. Enterprises, manual or spiritual, simple or complicated, small or great, of little or much importance, are all initiated with the same simplicity. From the modest clerk, whose only apparatus is a fountain pen, to officials who carry portfolios under their arms, equipment is reduced to a minimum. Everything that is superfluous or an encumbrance is dispensed with. There is no room for the useless.

The same tendency shows itself in all fields of labor, in every kind of negotiation. Simplicity reigns supreme. The formality and ceremonies of the Old World are dispensed with. In the largest companies, two or three directors meet in a casual way to decide in a few minutes on the disposition of millions. And if there is no time to lose when it comes to investing millions, that is even more the case among those who handle tools. The main feature of American work is the absence of waste, either of time or labor. The way in which the workman suits his work to the time and space at his command gives American labor its character. He spends less time at work than in other countries, yet has more to show. It is, of course, to his interest to produce as much as possible, since he is generally on piecework. When he works by time he is under a strict supervision and under high pressure; if he is not up to the standard he will be dismissed immediately.

Thus the workman does his utmost, in his own interest, to keep up to the mark. The simplest laborer, even the newly arrived immigrant, does not have the long hours he was accustomed to; but he must adapt himself to the tension expected here. This relationship of toil to time is one of the main factors of the marvelous rate of production in this country.

Another is the division of labor. Where wages are high, hours short, and competition extreme, only a precise division of labor can assure the success of a factory. Only thus have Americans been able to secure their own markets against foreign competition, and, in certain branches, to dominate European commerce as well.

The apparent confusion of machinery and humanity in the factory at work is at first sight quite bewildering. Everything is moving, revolving, hammering, or whirring. Looking more closely, one begins to perceive that the chaotic movement, the cacophony of sound, follows hard and fast rules. As each revolution of a wheel is ordered and each hammer only strikes to command, so each human limb moves only in coördination. As each wheel or lever of the vast machinery accomplishes only a certain action, and produces only a part of an article, so each human hand is engaged only in one detail, performing and reperforming the same action, doing the same work to perpetuity. Whether or not it is desirable for the individual to become a piece of machinery is another question. But the division of labor is simply wonderful, and so complex as to be almost incomprehensible to the uninitiated.

Like everything else in this country, this is the result of organic and natural development. The history of one of the great commercial enterprises sounds as incredible as a fairy tale, although in a novel edition appropriate to an age of smoke and invention. We hear descriptions that can hardly be believed of the time when formidable towns were wildernesses with only a few wooden huts, visited from time to time by peddlers who eventually erected booths, out of which grew many of the commercial undertakings that we admire at the present day.

This natural development explains the growth of these establishments and their complicated system of organization. The personnel adapted itself to conditions in the same way, and increased until it attained its present size. Walking around the workshops and departments of Marshall Field and Company, the pride of Chicago, founded when the sixth city in the world had only just been begun, we are surprised to hear that the present owners themselves laid its foundation as a small shop.

If the relation of toil to time and the minute division of labor are the most prominent traits of the factories, in the shops it is the organization that impresses us most. These huge buildings, where dozens of elevators constantly shoot up and down, swarm with hundreds of employees and thousands of customers, elbowing their way hither and thither. The ability to organize and manage such a place is amazing.

It would, of course, be impossible to start such an establishment all at once; it could only develop and grow naturally to its present proportions. By this organic growth the largest commercial enterprises preserve the unity and intensity that they had when first established. Thus the manager, who is often the proprietor himself or the largest shareholder, continues to hold the threads of each department in his own hands, paying attention to the pettiest details, and giving his employees the widest opportunities to show their worth.

Men, therefore, have a chance to improve themselves and to rise. Sometimes they are their own masters from the very beginning, and sell matches in the street; sometimes they are hired by others as errand boys and the like. Their sphere of activity increases with their age, according to their gifts. The whole procedure maintains an organic relation between the development of the individual and his business. The magnate and his enterprise grow together by a continuity of work; at the same time, the business acquires its manifold character and the proprietor increases his business capacity. Only thus can we explain the great American businessman, who has every branch of his undertaking under his own control, just as in the old days when his whole stock in trade could be held in a box.

Everybody works in this country, out of respect for work, and each individual tries to make his work as lucrative as possible. Labor that is not well paid is not understood. Rich and poor must be equally well remunerated. The richer and more comfortable a man is, the higher will be his prices or his fees. The idea in old countries that people of independent means should not earn money, that the rich who work should do so gratuitously, or at least preserve the appearance of doing so, is inconceivable here.

The false shame of work, which is one of the drawbacks of our social life and national activity, is unknown in America. In fact, there no one starts working without first fixing his price. There is no mystery or embarrassment. People talk as openly about it as about stocks and bonds, and the higher his price the more candidly will a man advertise the fact. Individual worth has its rise and fall as shares do, and clients take pride in making it known that they can afford the services of such and such a lawyer, doctor, speaker, and so on.

This is why America is the paradise of all artists, lecturers, and writers; in a word, of all mental work. For intellectual effort is not less respected, and certainly is not less lavishly paid, than any other kind of work. The fabulous salaries of celebrated singers and actors are proverbial, and every rising star regards an American tour as an El Dorado.

An El Dorado it is indeed, for while they sweep in the dollars, they also enjoy every social advantage, are received everywhere cordially, are feted in the most exclusive circles, and become leaders of society. For America is not only a state based on democratic principles, its inhabitants are out-and-out democrats, and its conceptions of work and the workman are essentially democratic.

The practical cast of American intelligence is its most prominent trait. From infancy, mental faculties are directed to the purely utilitarian point of view. No one has either leisure or taste for other questions. Their most distinguished thinkers have produced hardly any influential books. In the literature of this nation much talent of a remarkable order is displayed, but it expresses itself in wit and cleverness rather than in original thought.

It must be remembered, however, that the past of this people as an independent country reaches back little more than one century. The

United States is still in the midst of a period of active struggle and toil, and has not yet reached the era of leisure for higher thought and intellectual perception. It is, so to speak, still in its heroic age; the epic of its national evolution remains to be written and sung by future generations.

American literature is commonly reproached with seeking inspiration from other countries and with being more interested in the traditions of Europe than in its own history. These undeniable facts can scarcely be considered faults. American literature is the descendant of European, and especially of English literature, and possesses more of a present than a past. It is only natural that the memory of the country in which it was cradled is continually reflected in its pages, and that its poetry turns longingly to the shores on which it first drew breath.

Moreover, every young nation shows an interest in the intellectual life of the nation from which it sprang. Did not Rome for many centuries remain the docile pupil of Athens, and for how long a time did not Europe consider it more important to study the classics than to interest herself in her own conditions?

The lack of aesthetic sense and the uncouthness of form with which American literature has been reproached are defects, but they are frequently intentional. The sentiment of the Puritans was hostile to all expression of feeling; modern thought, on the contrary, demands it. Meaning is everything: *what* is expressed is primary; *how* it is expressed, quite secondary. Such a style is often unrefined, but is undoubtedly powerful. It is in any case clear and intelligible; it loves strong phrases and startling contrasts; it surprises with unexpected turns. When employed in the field of belles-lettres it is almost offensive, but in technical and scientific works it is very helpful, for it seizes the attention and impresses the memory with almost mechanical effect.

Through the influence of the press, the short story reigns supreme. The majority of readers want brief tales, as different and as exciting as possible. These may be comic or tragic, but the great thing is that they should be concentrated, that the movement should be rapid, and that the development and ending should be as unexpected as possible. The readers must above all be thrilled, the more exciting the narrative and the more surprising the denouement the more widely popular will the work be. This accounts for the demand for tales dealing with detective and criminal adventures. These stories hold the imagination, they give an interest to the odd moments that must be spent in train or streetcar, and most people do not ask for more than this. Scarcely less in demand are simple romances unaffected in construction and above all furnished with happy endings.

The immense circulation of monthlies, reviews, and magazines depends largely on the popularity of the stories they contain. Editors pay well, and, in addition, give prizes for the best contributions. In this manner the leading periodicals have been successful in discovering for their readers various talented writers. The most famous and best known of recent years, Mark Twain, Bret Harte, Winston Churchill, Marion Crawford, Gertrude Atherton, Mrs. Hodgson Burnett, Edith Wharton, and others, have won popularity by their contributions to periodicals.

It is debatable, however, whether this general prostitution of literature to the transient requirements of journalism has aided the higher development of the art. It has encouraged rapid writing and, still more, rapid reading, so that neither writer nor reader are sufficiently inspired to concern themselves with form and style. They have simply no leisure for serious matters. Conditions allow no deeper critical sense, and the public is indifferent. Novelty and originality are the essential ingredients of success; and at present the tendency of American literature seems to consist in the selection of unusual themes, in the use of startling phrases, and in the portrayal of effective situations.

Yet any progressive tendencies should not be lost sight of. Although the thought of the New World has been imbued with sensationalism during the last decades it is now rising to an ever-higher plane. That is particularly true of imaginative literature, of the novel and of poetry. After a long period of the monumental style, during which the historians, essayists, and poets simply followed in the steps of the greater European masters, a characteristic American style came into existence. This occurred in the latter half of the nineteenth century, and the exponents of this style developed precisely in the same way as artists and men of letters amongst us. In art, as in literature, there is a new style. The popularity of some writers, especially of novelists, depends entirely on this originality, which is sometimes uncouth and lacking in refinement, but, being generally vigorous, derives much of its effect from its unconventionality.

Sensitivity to form, in literature as in external life, develops with time. America is still striving and struggling, axe in hand, to clear the way. If she seizes the pen and pours forth the thoughts and feelings of her sons in their own language and their own manner, it is both just and of supreme interest to listen to what she has to say, however unformed these utterances may be.

The most important point to notice in all this seems to be the upward trend. The characters and descriptions are becoming finer, more delicately chiseled, more appealing to nobler natures. Even the novelettes sometimes reflect elevated sentiments, and instead of being therefore voted tiresome and left on the booksellers' shelves, are becoming more and more popular. American literature, although still in its cradle, is often judged too severely. It is not only very prolific, but it endeavors, I think with some success, to become purer; it seeks no longer merely to awaken curiosity and to excite the reader, but rather to acquire a truer value and more elevated character.

The same criticism applies to American art. A very interesting movement is now passing through the country, and especially through Boston. The exponents of this movement are artists of no mean order, the real excellence of whose pictures and sculpture lies in their force, their vigor, and their boldness more than in the originality of their conceptions.

The technique of such great painters as Whistler and Sargent, or sculptors such as St. Gaudens and Flanagan, is admirable; particularly in the case of young artists on the highroad to fame, we are constrained to extol the daring of their composition and the way they treat their subject, and we are astonished by the hardihood of their brush and the fearlessness of their chisel.

In architecture alone, of all the fine arts, do we discover innovation. American thought expressed in literature has followed well-worn tracks, though it has certain specialities, such as short magazine stories and the yellow press sensations; and in the fine arts, in spite of the freshness and vigor of works of undoubted talent, there has not been a new departure of any kind. In architecture, on the contrary, there are not merely new tendencies, but new ideas.

America introduced the extensive use of steel and iron in building through the system of constructing regular metal skeletons. The structure of thirty or forty stories—the famous skyscraper—is a purely American invention. Whether one likes or dislikes it, one must admire the victory of technical skill, as well as the spirit of invention of which it gives evidence.

The development of the technical sciences offers the best field to those who desire to study American thought and its results. A visit to one of the great industrial centers, a walk around a large factory, or merely an hour passed at a railroad station, will give an idea of the complexity of all mechanical matters. One can hardly believe that the innumerable, seemingly incongruous parts, the thousands of wheels and miles of belting, form part of an organic whole; that the most minute screw has its special work, and is indispensable to the correct adjustment of the gigantic monster.

Another point even more impressive is the intricacy—I am almost tempted to say mystery—of the mechanism. The ingenuity, for instance, displayed in a printing machine capable of performing singlehanded the smallest details of the work of fifteen men, is astounding and perplexing. Fuller comprehension brings some ability to grasp the magnitude of the genius that created these marvelous devices and lifts for us a corner of the veil that shrouds the mind of the nation. All these remarkable engines, this complex mechanism, are so many documents bearing testimony to the intelligence of man. As we trace the record of the mental development of the Ancients from their monuments, as the mind and the genius of the Greeks and Romans are revealed by their great works of art, so, also, the mental force of America is most easily discerned in her inventions and innovations. After all, the most noble works of art, whatever their intrinsic value, are really important only insofar as they are so many brilliant representations of thought—so many instructive pages in the universal history of human culture.

In the United States, man's intelligence has branched out in a different direction, or, let us say, has found "fresh woods and pastures new." This is the country of practical invention. It is exceedingly interesting to observe how this practical tendency, this aptitude for technical science, manifests itself at the tenderest age. The schools are often supplied with machinery, in order that the children may have an opportunity of learning to understand simple mechanics. There are also courses of instruction not only in the technical institutions, but also in the high schools. The latter are the most popular, and consequently have the largest classes. There the talents of the children, doubtless inherited to a certain extent, are awakened and fostered, and there, probably, new ideas will come to the little ones.

This is the country of invention. Gigantic innovations have gradually changed the conditions of everyday life, made realities of hopes that once seemed only suited to fairy tales. But more important, everyone is in some degree an inventor. Apart from men of recognized genius, such as Edison and Westinghouse, there are thousands who have contributed to technical perfection. Great inventors, like the thinkers and philosophers of old, inspire new conceptions, which their disciples popularize and render practicable, interpreting to the rest of the world the master's idea. A slight improvement in a part of any machine produces a very great effect, not merely in the machine itself, but in the relations existing between the mechanism and the workman who manipulates it. Each step leads to the application of the device to fresh purposes, and therefore to a readjustment of the conditions of labor. In short, every invention, great or small, has social significance. Before a machine can be turned to account it must be perfect and complete, and the practical utility of its application must be understood. For nothing is left to chance. There must be no "almost"; everything depends on method and calculation.

Precision and rapidity of comprehension take the first place. The manner in which the children of the New World grasp an idea is remarkable. *Quick* and *cunning* are the two most coveted adjectives applied to a child. Later on in life these two adjectives are still the most often employed to convey a compliment, whether its subject be a businessman or a politician, a man of letters or an artist.

In short, Americans are quick and cunning to a degree probably unequaled by any other people, and in their boldness and assurance are more than a match even for the Oriental races. American thought is especially remarkable by reason of its precision; however quick, it is always clear, orderly, and businesslike. Their intelligence is practical; it must lead to something definite.

30.

THE ABBÉ AND THE STRENUOUS LIFE

The Abbé Félix Klein was born at Château-Chinon in 1862. Educated at the seminary in Meaux and at Saint Sulpice, he became professor at the Institut Catholique in Paris. His preface to a French translation of Elliott's Life of Father Hecker *unwittingly started a long controversy in which Abbé Klein espoused a more liberal, less traditional view of Catholicism than was common in France, a view which he identified with the Church in America. Papal intervention in 1899 led to a retraction of these ideas. Nevertheless, Abbé Klein remained sympathetic to the United States and became a great admirer of Theodore Roosevelt. The volume from which this selection was taken,* Au Pays de "la vie intense" *(1905), was the product of a tour in the New World in 1904, one of several trips by the abbé, who later became chaplain of the American War Hospital in Paris.*

I traveled from St. Louis to Pittsburgh by train. I do not think I missed much in rushing through the countryside of Missouri, Illinois, and Indiana in the dark. Ohio, which I saw by daylight, revealed simply a well-cultivated and monotonous plain. But the landscape changed as we approached Pennsylvania. Agriculture seemed to lose its importance, gradually diminished, and soon disappeared. We were penetrating a great industrial area. Contrary to my preconceptions, the scenery was not ugly. Away from the immediate sites of the factories, the country was covered with green, split up by valleys and rivers, and sprinkled with little cottages where, it might seem, each man could live according to his own fancy. There was nothing reminiscent of the environs of Creusot or of Montchanin; nothing of the desolate and naked countryside, where identical workingmen's houses stretch in long, monotonous rows. As far as one could judge from the railroad, the urban areas proper included only the shops and factories; no one lived where he worked.

Nevertheless, we passed immense coal trains more and more frequently. The air grew dense, smoky, almost black. We were now enter-

ing the city of Carnegie, of Edison, of Westinghouse, the city of iron
and steel, the most active industrial furnace of the world.

Pittsburgh offers the most convincing example to support the theory
that the geography of a site determines the work done on it, the nature
of the property, and the organization of life. The regional resources
could not fail to produce an industrial city here. Pitched between two
navigable rivers which together form a natural channel to the ocean,
hemmed in on the right and on the left by mountains of metal, it is
blessed on the east and southeast with an enormous bed of coal, a bed
from which it ships coke as far west as Colorado and as far east as the
factories of the Atlantic coast, and yet has surplus enough to manufacture gas for the whole Mississippi Valley. On the north there are bot-
tomless resources of petroleum, and on the northeast marvelous reserves
of natural gas. These are the subsurface riches of this favored section.
The Americans had only to touch them to bring forth an industrial
growth such as never has been seen before.

In a chapter of his *Empire of Business,* Mr. Carnegie extols the
treasures of the gas and oil wells of western Pennsylvania with a lyrical
tone which does not seem altogether out of place when one is aware of
the astounding forces that human genius has been able to extract from
them. The author, however, is not too far carried away by his poetry to
recall with satisfaction the success of his first venture into petroleum;
an investment of 200,000 francs in a single year brought 5,000,000 in
dividends—rather a good return. His good humor roused by memory
of this profitable investment, Mr. Carnegie is amused, not without
cause, at the human gullibility which was willing to endow this oil with
powerful medicinal virtues when it cost ten francs a bottle but lost faith
when the price fell to one sou.

Mr. Carnegie also speaks with high spirits of the discovery and exploitation of natural gas. He played a prominent part in utilizing this
product as a source of light for cities and as a source of power for
motors. This new force has become familiar now, but it was certainly a
strange sight when this emanation from the earth by accident began
to burn for the first time. Perhaps nothing more would have come of it
had not chance led some workingmen, digging a well for petroleum, to
penetrate a pocket of this gas and to set off a frightful explosion. It
was then only necessary to harness the monster, regulate its flow
through impermeable pipes, and use it like manufactured gas. And

that, like so many other achievements, could safely be left to the Pittsburgh people.

To spend time speaking of Carnegie in a discussion of Pittsburgh is not irrelevant. There are two heights from which Pittsburgh may be surveyed: one is Mount Washington above the Monongahela; the other is Andrew Carnegie who towers above all the other businessmen of that bustling city. I say that not only because he gave the town a library that bears his name, the building of which alone cost more than four million francs, not even because his furnaces are there, but for the more decisive reason that he was formed in Pittsburgh and there became the kind of great man he is. The introduction to his *Gospel of Wealth,* "How I Was an Apprentice," gives an exact idea of the most successful type of American businessman.

There is nothing more instructive than to watch this little Scotsman of twelve, brought to Pittsburgh by his parents, go to work in a cotton factory and proudly earn his six francs a week by hard labor. At the age of thirteen he is in charge of firing the boiler in a spool factory. At fourteen he is a telegraph boy, and by coming early to the office manages to pick up the code. One morning when no one else is there he takes a telegram alone, and soon is earning a hundred and twenty-five francs a month, a salary which had obsessed his youthful dreams; because that figure was enough, he thought, to satisfy all the necessities of life. By extra work for the reporters who came to the office he earned five francs a week more; this, he notes, was his first business venture.

The true foundation of his fortune was laid, however, when, realizing that the railroads could not go on indefinitely using wooden bridges, he organized a company in Pittsburgh to build iron bridges. He then attained his greatest desire, for he had always wished to be his own master, to manufacture something, and to employ many people. But he could not stand still once that goal was attained. To stand still is to move backward; no matter what is already accomplished, more remains to be done. Now, he and his associates, the old Pittsburgh factory boys, still continue to extend their enterprises, year after year, to satisfy the ever-growing and ever-changing needs of their progressive country.

To make money, according to Andrew Carnegie, is only half the task; the other half is to use it well. Whether or not one shares the ideas expressed on this subject in his *Gospel of Wealth,* these ideas undeniably possess a kind of nobility. They are worth noting since they are not his alone, but those of a very powerful aristocratic group.

His philosophy, like that of all Americans, is fundamentally optimistic. The good old times were not good old times. The present organization is such that each man must grab and use what he can. Communism is absurd; there is no alternative but ruin to the acquisition of immense riches by the leaders of industry. But these people are only the temporary administrators of their fortunes for the good of all. When they have spent that which is necessary for the maintenance and the comfortable education of their families, the surplus must be consecrated to the public welfare.

There are three modes of disposing of such a surplus: by bequests to one's descendants, by bequests to public institutions, and by administering it during one's own lifetime. The first is the worst. Parents owe their offspring an education; children should, through every possible means, be put in a position to earn their own livelihood and (an important concession), it is proper that they be assured a comfortable income should they devote their lives to useful but unremunerative public services. Beyond that, to leave wealth to children will do them great harm. On the other hand, the man who leaves his fortune to benevolent purposes in his will proves by that that he is capable of acting well only after death and would not give away his wealth if he could take it with him. The logical conclusion of that position, according to Carnegie, would be that nothing is more just than a progressive inheritance tax.

The third method of using the surplus alone is worthy of a man, of a Christian, of a citizen of the modern world. It can counteract class hatred and the temporary inequality of conditions. It is conducive to harmony, and leads to an ideal which, unlike socialism, requires not the destruction of civilization and of the existing order, but only their regular and peaceful evolution. The duty of the rich man, after he has established a moderate pattern of living, without ostentation and without extravagance, and after he has reasonably provided for his dependents, is to consider his surplus income as trust funds to be administered for the common good. He is thus the guardian of his less fortunate brothers, putting at their service his superior prudence, his experience, his administrative talents, working in their interests better than they could for themselves.

Such general principles are of course subject to differences of interpretation. The American millionaire, like the Fathers of the Church, exalts the ideal of improving the lot of his brothers and bases his ideas on the teaching of Jesus Christ. But he wishes to follow the spirit rather than the letter of the Scriptures, and to adapt the manner of expressing that spirit to the changed conditions under which we live. Nine-tenths of the money spent on charity today, he feels, is simply wasted, if not, indeed, used harmfully. Every man undoubtedly comes across some cases in which temporary help is useful and praiseworthy; in general, however, society, not the rich, casual benefactor but society as a whole, has the duty of taking care of the poor, of clothing, feeding, sheltering them, and of isolating them from those who can work and who might be demoralized by the sight of people supported by charity. The individual administrator of a fortune should take as his province those who are capable or wish to become so. His role is to sustain the courageous, to help those who help themselves, to hold out a hand to those who are climbing; he should multiply, for the benefit of anyone who wishes to use them, the means of physical and moral perfection, everything which is conducive to popular education in the largest sense of the word, from parks, public baths, and medical schools, to monuments of art, libraries, museums, meeting halls, universities, and religious structures.

The philanthropist will still not have done his duty if he simply leaves his money for the common welfare, even perfectly interpreted. He must distribute his gifts in such a manner and under such conditions that they should never stifle initiative, or restrain the self-development of those who receive them. The donation should be administered so as to yield a maximum of advantage to the greatest possible number for the longest possible time. That proposition assumes that the donor will demand some sacrifice from those who will be his beneficiaries; the municipalities must supply the funds, for instance, to maintain the park he buys or the library he builds. That also assumes that he will personally take a part in managing his handiwork, that he will continue to be interested, to devote time, experience, and attention to it. That is why there is a tendency for millionaires to specialize in the certain fields they know best, one in universities, another in parks, and Carnegie in libraries.

This is the mission in this world of those who, by the regular play

of social laws, receive more than their share of the profits of the common labor. And this makes comprehensible Carnegie's statement that
he who dies rich dies dishonest.

It will be objected, it has been objected, that Mr. Carnegie's gospel
is hardly practiced. He may answer with reason that the other Gospel
is not always literally followed, yet that does not diminish its validity.
Enough examples, known even in Europe, show that a certain number
of millionaires believe in this ideal; in the field of education especially,
private liberality furnishes larger funds than do the compulsory budgets
of governments in our old countries. Has not Senator Stanford given
away, at a single stroke, $100,000,000 to found a university on the
Pacific coast?

An old French acquaintance now employed there conducted me
through the Westinghouse plant in East Pittsburgh. This really includes
about ten factories—the Westinghouse Manufacturing Company, making all sorts of machines and electrical equipment; the Westinghouse
Brake Company; the Westinghouse Machine Company, making turbines and gas and steam engines; and most important of all, the Westinghouse Electric Company. We entered the last-named group, the
buildings of which cover no less than twenty acres. Eighty-two hundred
men and 1,200 women work there, apart from 2,500 engineers and office employees. The women earn 7½ francs a day, the men start at 12½,
although some earn as high as 20 or 25. We visited the section which
manufactured alternating-current generators capable of yielding 5,500
kilowatts, or 7,500 horsepower. The central power stations of the New
York elevated and subway railroads, probably the most powerful in
the world, were equipped here. What pleasure would not this sight
have given some of my engineer friends? Ignorant as I was, I had to
admire the beautiful simplicity of the distributors which conducted
such frightful amounts of energy, and the ease with which a score of
traveling cranes above our heads carried 30 to 50 ton loads, moving at
need the machine tools from one end of the factory to another when
the pieces being fabricated were too heavy. I say I admired all this,
but without understanding very much. Yet I felt that my admiration
would only be the more profound if I really did understand.

The Carnegie battery of blast furnaces impressed me even more,
although no more within the range of my comprehension. A special

ticket is needed for admission; but that is the only precaution taken with regard to visitors, and I certainly think it insufficient. There is no tour more dangerous than that which I made without a guide through this hell; Dante, at least, had his Virgil. We had scarcely entered when we saw a long serpent of fire unwind right near us, a fine bar of red iron, ten to twelve meters long, which was coming out of a rolling mill. We found ourselves in its way. But no one bothered about us; *help yourself*. Then we saw advancing majestically toward us some blocks of hot castings which seemed to wander about on rails, as if by chance, while cooling off. Their very proximity cast upon us waves of stifling heat that forced us back, but we had to beware of other blocks of the same kind, of unattended trucks, and of all sorts of machines which did their jobs with great stateliness and without the least respect for spectators. All this went on automatically, with the assistance of an extremely small number of laborers; here it is workmanship that counts. Each machine has its own task and performs it easily without oversight. But we risked at one time or another being burned, smashed, or thrown a good distance. However, once having become accustomed to the noise and discovering a safe vantage point, we could enjoy the extraordinary spectacle of the order and peace in the play of these colossal forces. Becoming familiar with the monsters we even began to find a kind of beauty in them, to enjoy the clashing of the forges, the transparency of the refined bars, the rapid changes of color through which the castings pass when they emerge from the crucibles, white, red, rose, and incredible shades of violet.

In the preparation of technical personnel there is an interesting relationship between the factories and the colleges and universities. The profession of electrical engineer is not absolutely closed to apprentices without technical training, and a few such master it. But, in general, an engineer in a factory must have finished a college course, and the instructors in the college actively engage in the profession that they teach. There was the time when a college education was a liability in industry. But now two personnel managers at Westinghouse annually visit the leading colleges and technical schools in the United States to recruit the students who seem to them most qualified to enter the service of the company. These young men are taken on trial as student engineers, are paid 8 centimes an hour, and the best ones get to earn 20 or 30 francs a day in less than a year. But although they are paid, the company is above all interested in training them and to that end moves them about from shop to shop every three months.

Although the great factories become more and more accustomed to giving the direction of their works to college men who have had this type of practical experience as well, it does not follow that the ordinary apprentice must renounce the hope of a rise in position. Every little American can plan to become a millionaire or president of the Republic. The obstacles between the dream and the reality are by no means slight, considering the number and the energy of the competitors. But no difficulties are placed in his way by the institutions or the habits of the country. If a college education is now more often necessary than formerly, still such an education is accessible to all, and a considerable number of those who penetrate to the halls of the university are those who have themselves earned the means of opening its doors.

It is almost midnight when I return to my hotel. The clerk says that a reporter waited for me until almost eleven and would like an appointment. On the telephone I name an hour so early in the morning that he requests an interview on the spot, and before I know it I am on the carpet. Not hearing very well, I call in the clerk as intermediary and he passes questions and answers back and forth over the telephone. The next morning I awaken to learn some surprising things about my travel plans, and also that I am called "one of the foremost savants in the world."

With a friend who joined me, I laughed at my new-found glory and led it out into the streets where it got lost in an impenetrable incognito. We wandered through the crowded streets of the center of town and went to see the little blockhouse, the remains of Fort Duquesne, which became Fort Pitt or Pittsburgh when the English finally seized it in 1758. Neither they, nor the Frenchmen, were concerned with the mineral wealth of the country, but they appreciated the strategic importance of the junction of the great rivers. The idea of any foreign domination is today far from the minds of the Americans, and even the memory is effaced. There is nothing less colonial, more independent, more American in the fullest sense of the word than Pittsburgh.

Two or three times in my last day here I was impressed by the powerful originality of the Americans. At about one in the afternoon we went to have lunch with a millionaire in the Frick Building. This man works on the fifteenth story. One of ten elevators, which operate without pause or rest, took us to him directly. The Paris notary is no better established, no more comfortable in his ground floor on the Place Vendôme or Place de la Concorde than this Pennsylvania lawyer in his aerial roost. He took us to the Union Club, the best in the city, in the same building, seven stories up. The club occupies the whole top floor of this rich and colossal structure. After the meal we sat on the terrace, or rather, on the roof which, like the rest of the building, is made of white marble and which might be reminiscent of the Cathedral of Milan were there not around us and around our feet, the least Italian of scenes, buildings of all sizes, the black hills that hold the city in a vise, the noise and smoke, and rattle of the trolleys, the boats, the factories, the railroads.

But the spectacle seemed to us even stranger when we looked down upon it from the heights of Mount Washington, to which we were taken, or rather flung, in a funicular railway more distinguished for speed than for elegance. All along the Ohio, and along the two rivers which give birth to it, and as far in the distance as the eye can reach through the black smoke, one sees, one hears, one feels, with all the organs and all the faculties, one is aware of a superhuman life, a gigantic life, in all its confusion and all its power. It is a life that thinks and works, that calculates, that agitates and creates, that raises and brews with the freedom of a god, all the combined forces of spirit and matter. There is nothing more terrifyingly beautiful. And I was so struck by the scene that I returned to the mountain in the evening to contemplate the constellation again by the electric lights of the city twinkling at my feet, and a little farther by the furnaces, under the low sky and in the black night, infernally lit up by the red hearths.

Philadelphia has changed a great deal since William Penn planted the first Quaker settlement there two centuries ago. That sober and simple sect still flourishes, and many other Protestant churches have taken a place beside it; but none has developed as much as Catholicism, the communicants of which include three-fourths of the city's population. There are now 475,000 adherents of the faith in the diocese, with 374 secular, and 103 regular clergy, 106 seminarians, 98 Christian Brothers, and more than 2,000 nuns in 19 convents. Apart from the 7 colleges and 2 industrial schools, they educate 45,000 children in their parochial schools and about 3,000 in orphanages. There are 84 parishes, 14 more than in Paris.

And these parishes are full of an active life. I visited the presbytery of the Church of Our Lady of Mercy in North Broad Street. The parish is less than fifteen years old, yet has built a church as fine as could be desired, a large and comfortable presbytery, a school for 500 pupils, all of which cost about 3,000,000 francs. In America, when a new city is built, or even when an existing parish becomes too large, the bishop calls in a young priest and marks out a territory for him. "You are assigned the area between such and such streets; go do your best." There is no question of building or money; he must shift for himself. In a few years everything is created, organized, and almost paid for. The bishop may come to consecrate the church, bless the school and congratulate the priest and his parishioners. It is understood that the priest, to do his job, must be active and must keep on good terms with his parish.

Certainly my host, Father Coghlan, was remiss in neither respect. I visited him on the eve of the installation of a new organ. I never saw a hive so active. The sacred concert the next night had to be a success for the honor of the parish and the school—also to pay the debt incurred in the purchase of the instrument. The tickets were priced at a dollar; but even those who could not come sent in their contributions, and some paid two, three, ten times the marked price. With all expenses met, the evening will bring in a thousand dollars, and the society founded to acquire the organ will have no cause for complaint. From noon on Saturday to midnight Sunday there was no rest for the priest, his assistants, his recently ordained nephew, and his niece who kept the accounts. And these material labors did not absolve the poor clergyman from calls to confessional four times an hour.

I am ashamed to admit that I was more interested in the dinner with my confreres that preceded the concert than in the concert itself. A dozen of the leading priests in Philadelphia were there. Almost all had traveled in France several times, a fact which testifies both to liberality of the mind and money in the pocket. They receive from the church a salary of $800 a year, and all their expenses are paid except for food and clothing. In addition, they make $400 or $500 in fees. The same rate prevails in New York, while in Baltimore they may receive as much as $1,000. These are certainly high wages, but the priests are not miserly and do not cavil at very generous expenses. As in Ireland, the faithful take care that their clergy should not want for anything, knowing that they can turn to them in the time of need.

The church funds come mostly from the annual sale of seats and from collections on Sunday. The property is administered by the parish considered as a civil person and represented by the vestry of which the priest is the principal member. The other members of the vestry are chosen by the bishop. In some dioceses the bishop is the civil personality and delegates his rights in each parish to the priest and two parishioners. The two systems are essentially the same and leave the spiritual power completely master over the management of property.

In speaking of the sentiments of Catholics toward their priests, we have already alluded to the similarity to Ireland. The extent to which that *rapprochement* touches on all the affairs of life is perhaps the secret of the prosperity of the American church, of its generosity, its piety, and of the mutual devotion of clergy and faithful. Without belittling the valuable services of the French priests, it is proper to say that the American church is essentially an Irish church. Many of the priests were born in Ireland; almost all are the sons of Irishmen. Most of its communicants come from Ireland; and if other countries, Germany, Italy, Austria, today add more immigrants, it must be remembered that these are received and must settle in communities that are already completely formed. The character of these communities is without doubt based on Irish zeal and American patriotism; they have preserved the emotional enthusiasm of the country of their origin and join to it, if not the independence, at least the practical sense of the country of their adoption. My dozen Philadelphia priests spoke always of Ireland as of their fatherland. In the toasts at the end of the meal, I was, as a Frenchman, greeted as a Celtic brother. At our separation Father Coghlan, who is propriety and goodness itself, could not forbear from saying to me that he liked me as I was, but that he would like me even more had he not noticed, in a few words I had spoken, traces of some sympathy for England.

Part Four

THE BURDENS OF MATURITY

The Burdens of Maturity

～～～～～～～～～～～～～～～～～～～～～～～～～～～

AMERICANS WERE ACCUSTOMED TO REGARD THEMSELVES AS OTHERS SAW them—as youthful. In this perspective the objective fact of a short experience as a nation was less important than the illusion of youth created by constant expansion. The uninterrupted accretions in national strength in all the recognized forms—wealth, size of population, extent of territory—gave the impression of limitless growth to come; the boundless confidence that such growth would continue, the length of the future before it rather than the brevity of its past, was the true sign of youth in the community.

Americans flaunted their tender age as a people, for it made the magnitude of their achievements all the more imposing. But they also used their youthfulness as a source of justification for the aesthetic, intellectual, and social failures of their society. Whatever admitted wrongs and deficiencies existed about them could be explained, if not mitigated, by reference to the lack of time, to turbulent adolescence.

But what if the fundamental assumption of endless youth were no longer valid! Would that not necessitate significant alterations in the total American scheme of things? As the new century unfolded, the idea gained strength in ever-widening circles that the United States had entered upon a new stage in its development. Surrendering the old optimistic faith, many groups began to call for radical alterations in the American way of life.

It was true that the time-tried indices showed the same, sometimes indeed an accelerated, upward trend. But measurements in terms of tons of steel and bushels of wheat, of the number of car-loadings or bales of cotton, no longer seemed adequate, no longer seemed valid. Such expansion now appeared not to bring the society any closer to the realization of its ends. The significant question had ceased to be how to extend resources; it had rather become how to apply what was available. The old optimism had counted time an ally; sooner or later all would be well. Now time was a foe; with no certainty in the future, men strove to outwit the present before it was too late. Whatever the reasons for it, that transformation was itself a mark of maturity and an omen of the burdens of maturity.

The relationship of the United States with the rest of the world offered a spectacular illustration of the nature of that transformation. Foreign affairs had always concerned the American people, both on the level of commercial intercourse and on that of humanitarian sympathy for the efforts of other people to attain liberty. Significant changes came on both levels. American businessmen continued to hold interests in widely scattered portions of the globe; but they were no longer content to rely upon profits through free competition, and more frequently called upon the imperialistic intercession of their government. Americans in general remained attentive to the spread of democracy and republicanism through the world; they were, however, now less inclined to wait upon the slow workings of historical forces. Yet the intensified compulsion to positive action produced only stumbling and ineffective steps, revealed in practice unsuspected contradictions, unexpected consequences.

Even more important were the underlying domestic trends. In the face of expansion there was a growing fear that there would be an end to expansion. The threatened curtailment of opportunities seemed to empty freedom of much of its value. The quest for security, which began among the groups that lacked it most, spread upward through every stratum of society. What was of concern primarily to social workers and to the handicapped before 1920 became important to the farmers in the twenties and to the broad masses at every economic level who supported the New Deal in the thirties. However, the successive efforts to legislate security into being frightened some people; dread of hidden repercussions developed a conservative unwillingness to venture into the most innocent innovations, a hardening of spirit that resisted any change.

By 1939 a prolonged depression and the imminent threat of another world war accentuated those fears. If the pessimistic forebodings as to the capacity of the old forms of American life to survive were not necessarily destined for fulfillment, they seemed at least justified as a cause for concern. The ending of immigration, itself a product of fear and of the failure of confidence, reduced the rate of population growth, and contributed to the creation of rigid barriers of class. Everywhere social mobility slackened and left the society in a state of perpetual strain, of ever-impending crisis.

Moreover, for some Americans there were times when the whole question of whether the familiar forms were equal to achieving their ends receded before the deeper question of whether the ends were themselves valid. The sanctity and perfectibility of the common man in the 1920's were significantly called into doubt. Millions of Babbitts jeered at Main Street. Temperance, the goal of three generations of earnest American reformers, turned into a mockery, so that the very words "noble experiment" somehow acquired a ludicrous connotation, which extended also to "uplift" and "improvement." In the popular arts, in jazz, and in the movies, there was not only a vulgarization of ideas and sentiments, but also an inclination to turn away from the idealistic rationalism of earlier days. Few had yet heard of Freud, but many felt the desire to shed their inhibitions, to relieve themselves of restraints, to disregard, in a civilization of material things, whatever was not material in man himself.

In the 1930's the dignity of the common man was somewhat refurbished. But on the horizon were still ominous threats to the whole order of American democratic assumptions. Under the impetus of racial thinking some people denied the equality of man; under the sway of native and foreign totalitarianism others denied the principles of freedom. Could a mature nation accept the burdens of maturity and apply under such pressures the ideals and aspirations of its youth? That was the evidence Europeans still sought in the fall of 1939 as the crisis burst that was to make America and American ideals the dominant factors in the fate of the western world.

31.

AMERICAN SOCIALISMS—A GERMAN VERSION

Arthur Holitscher (1869–1941) was born in Budapest but early moved, first to Fiume, and then to Vienna where he embarked upon a literary career. He was successful as a novelist and playwright. He was also associated with a distinguished group of German and Austrian intellectuals on the fringe of the socialist movement. He traveled a great deal. This account came out of a voyage to the United States in 1911, being published in 1912 under the title Amerika Heute und Morgen Reiseerlebnisse.

"Now what shall I do with you, Paul? I think it would be best for you if I send you to Golden."

"I won't go to Golden. I don't want to go to Golden; I want to go home; that's where I belong."

"But Paul, when you are home not a week goes by but that you take up the same course again. You drift about for days on end, play the truant, stay out nights. You are not a bad boy, Paul; I know that. But you are weak, and it seems to me it would be best for you to go for a while to Golden."

"Don't send me to Golden. I couldn't go to Golden."

"Now Paul, wipe your eyes and give me your hand. So. Now tell me: didn't I give you a fair deal that other time when you stole the overalls with that other fellow? You promised me that you would be a good boy from then on, and now you are here again. After all, what can I do with you?"

"Give me another chance! I can't go to Golden!"

A cold, hard woman sits in the first row, and her gray eyes are pointed at the youth like two sharp knives. He is her child. She nods sarcastically at his every word. That does not escape the attention of the man near me. He surreptitiously strokes the hand of the weeping youngster: "You are a weak fellow, Paul; it will be better for you in Golden."

"I don't want to. I want to go home."

The woman on the bench laughs ironically. The man near me says: "Paul, look at me. Didn't I play fair with you the other time? How did you repay me?"

"Try me again. I just won't go to Golden!"

The man near me sighs, folds his hands, looks at the disdainfully gloating woman in the audience, thinks it over, looks from the woman to the boy, looks down at his folded hands. . . .

This scene takes place in an American court of justice, in the children's court of Denver, Colorado, and the man near me, the man who invited me to visit a session of his court is Judge Ben Lindsey, "Honest Ben," the idol of American children and one of the finest and most popular men in this great land.

This is a public session; some sixty people are present. Assisting Mr. Lindsey is a probation officer, an official whose task it is to supervise the children who have already once appeared before the court and were sent back to their parents with a warning and handshake through the mild and just decision of the judge. Among those on trial are ten children, all between the ages of ten and fourteen. The probation officer stands up and calls out a name.

Three little souls rise together and come up before the judge's table. Two are little children, a boy of fourteen and a girl of ten; and between them hobbles an old, sad, mother, clad in a black shawl, and not taller than her children.

Lindsey beckons to the little girl and has her open her mouth. The room bursts into laughter.

"Fine," says Lindsey. "I see you've used the toothbrush since last time. But Filistes, your face is dirty. I am sorry you didn't wash it this morning. Show me your hands. Oh dear!"

"Judge, you bet I washed my face this morning; only it got dirty again."

The child is the sister of the fourteen-year-old youth who was the evil spirit of the boy, Paul, and who led the latter into all manner of little thefts, nightly tippling, visits to the movies, and even worse. Filistes is appearing only as interpreter. The mother, a shriveled little Viennese Jewess, has not learned the language of the country in the seventeen years since the family came over and is therefore completely dumb. The youth is typical of the degenerated Jew, a great jeweled stickpin in his tie represents his standard of values.

The Judge tells Filistes what he thinks of her brother. Filistes yells into her mother's ears: "He says that Gary must go to bed at nine o'clock, and if he's caught playing cards once more, will be sent to Golden for a year!"

The mother mumbles something in Yiddish. Filistes translates it into fluent English, naturally in slang, the jargon of the poor. But Judge Lindsey understands that vernacular. In his court he speaks with the street boys in their own language as a friend and defender who wishes to understand them.

"He's not a bad kid, mama says; she will go around an' look for a job for Gary, so don't you send him to Golden." Then Filistes again translates for her mother: "He says, he knows we are poor people and Gary must try to make good so he will give Gary a chance to the first of December. If he is not better then, there will be no alternative; he will have to go to Golden."

The mother vouches for Gary, who has already earned ten dollars a week as a messenger for Western Union.

Lindsey: "The trouble is, Filistes, you know Gary, he can't stick to a job when he's got one."

Filistes to the mother: "He says Gary can't stick to a job; that's the matter with him!"

These are poor people. The probation officer found hardly a crust of bread to eat in their house. The youth must support the whole family since the eldest daughter who can shift for herself has deserted them. What is to be done? The American judge near me, Honest Ben, the friend of the children, experiences more tragedies than his meager body and his great soul can bear.

When he stands up, Lindsey seems no taller than a fourteen-year-old boy. Perhaps this circumstance helps give him such power, such inner power, over youngsters. He can look them in the eye without stooping. When he takes a child by the shoulders, his arm lies horizontally between the two of them. On his fine face is always a youthful expression, and the Colorado children call him, "our little Ben."

Often they forget where they are and a babble and tittering breaks out, as in a schoolroom when the teacher goes out. Then the judge bangs on the table with the palm of his hand. The children laugh and make signs that they will be quiet; the proceedings go on.

Lindsey speaks with the young people like one man to another. This is a further reason why they love him. In America, where the child is treated as a man, not as a doll or as a little animal, they have learned to laugh at the bugbears which are productive of so much evil in Germany. What is due a child, and basically what does he want? Simply, that he be recognized as a rational human being. He mistrusts those who tell him fairy tales and take mysterious attitudes in order to impose on him; he feels insulted and responds by becoming a liar. The American teacher, judge, is a friend and comrade of the child. It often happens that the mother or father of the child, angered, springs up in court and calls out, "That's a lie! No, he is lying!" and yet, you may rely on it, the child is then speaking the truth. Not because he is in a court of law and intimidated, but, on the contrary, because the human sense of justice, planted by God in his child's heart, draws him to the man before whom he stands.

Heaven alone knows how many children were ruined in body and

soul through the fact that, as little criminals, they were locked up together with old and hardened convicts in miserable, crowded, and un-
sanitary prisons. Lindsey has performed an immortal service by wiping
out this barbarism, and almost all the states have by now imitated Colorado in this respect. In Golden there is an industrial school to which
the children are sent, generally for eight to twelve months, and where
they are far better off than in the usual reformatory. Their education
begins in fact on the way, for they are sent alone without any escort.
Whoever wishes may escape. But of the hundreds of children Lindsey
has sent to Golden, only six have fled.

Benjamin Lindsey has occupied his difficult post for ten years, and
those years have left their trace on this tender, overburdened man. He
specified that he was to be able to use his power as his reason dictated.
But things were certainly not made easy for him. A man who refuses
to think of lawbreaking simply as crime and who traces it back to its
roots will soon gain the insight that these are nurtured in the genteel
quarters of finance and politics. In his office, Lindsey showed me a map
of the slums of Denver. He pointed out the extent to which tuberculosis, vice, and crime were at home in this district. However, the true
haunts from which the people are corrupted must be sought in the
dives which operate in the services of the politicians. In the back rooms
of these places alcohol and syphilis do their best to poison the souls and
hearts of the children. Here in the wild and woolly west, if anywhere,
the saloonkeeper is the influential ally of the politicians and grafters.
The alcohol fumes give forth an evil smell to accompany the solemn
tones with which the ideals of American politics are proclaimed, especially before elections. The cozy brothel there in the back room is only
one of the little privileges that the influential men in the government
extend to their faithful henchmen for services rendered. The policeman
on the beat keeps a sharp eye on the place—so that business be not
interfered with.

Only this single man, Ben Lindsey, more interesting than all the
mountains and mines of Colorado, broke a lance against the greater
and lesser evils of the slums. His enemies, the mighty of the land, naturally did everything they could to force him to give up his work or
to remove him. Now, however, the women have the vote in Colorado.
And besides, in the United States, the children are real Americans! I
heard talk in Denver of great battles, battles which were waged when

no party, neither the Democratic nor the Republican, would place on their ballot this improper man who is a true socialist if there is one in the world.

But Lindsey's name stood high on the ballot of the women and children, and so he was put in the place to which he was elected in the name of the great party of humanity. When the situation was critical, I have heard it said in Denver, the children poured into the streets of the city. From every section of the town, rich and poor, the elegant and the overpopulated, the little children, boys and girls, came in troops to the playgrounds, ran about and prepared to take action. Then they formed themselves into squads, into an army, and marched through the streets of the dumbfounded and bewildered town. The army halted before the windows of the political clubs, and shrilly yelled to demonstrate their opinions to those who sat behind the walls. Inside, however, all became quiet and not one of the men who controlled the fate of the government dared to come to the windows out of fear lest he see down below in the street the angry visage of his own child. A woman whom I came to know in the court told me of this Colorado children's crusade. The youngsters had contrived a little marching song, which rang out from thousands of clear voices:

> Who? Where? When?
> We wish we were men!
> So we could vote for our Little Ben!

The men behind the windows had no alternative but to capitulate.

A youth goes to Golden only when nothing more can be done with him at home, when he has no parents or such as do not deserve the name. The great majority are let out on probation and their behavior in their homes is checked by men and women officers specially appointed for the task. Many single or widowed women undertake these jobs voluntarily, and in this manner create a fine career for themselves. In New York I heard of an institution that operates in conjunction with the children's court, the Big Brothers. This is the result of a voluntary effort by young people, often students, each of whom assumes the oversight of a single child, acts as his friend and counselor, and remains for years his daily comrade and protector.

In Lindsey's court every Saturday is report day. The children released on probation assemble before the judge to show him a report from their teachers on their work during the week. Then Lindsey makes a speech, in which Christ and the evils which He helps men resist appear. Then follows a little secular question and answer game:

"I need strong young men. Who is a strong young man?"

"One who can ride a bike for ten hours"—"One who earns twelve dollars a week"—"One who resists . . ."

"Right," interrupts the judge. "Resists what?"

From one end of the room comes: "Stealing"; from another end: "Smoking." One boy calls out: "Temptation!" and he has guessed it.

One by one the children come up to Lindsey's table. The judge knows each one; remembers the weekly report of each. Those who have improved are praised. They turn, facing the audience, as Lindsey says, "This is Mike or Jack so-and-so, a model and example for all of you, do you hear?"

One brings up an unfavorable report. "What's the matter with us, Johnny? Do you want to make a liar of me? What will your teacher think, that I am a man who can swallow anything? After all, you have already spent a term in Golden." The child lowers his head to the table. Soon two great wet flecks appear on an official blotter. "Well, be a square kid. Cheer up. Don't make a liar of me again." And it is ten to one the next report will show an improvement.

So they file by, the little and the littlest, thieves, cutthroats, terrible criminals; each is rewarded with a good look, reproved and corrected with a troubled and sad one. Now and then one or another of the youths disappears into the office behind and then a whisper goes through the crowd, "Golden! Golden!" But that really is not so certain. A word, a glance, from the child can revise the opinion of this humane judge. And this is certain, that whoever once goes through the ordeal of the private office comes tingling out into the open court where the other children wait for him deep in conversation about their little Ben.

The crimes committed by children are related to the crimes committed upon them. The socialists are the only ones who demand an end to child labor in America. The two major political parties only play around with the question. After all, children are not voters, while the parents of the children whose earnings help to support the family are. The party that robs parents of the toil of their children will therefore lose votes. The children belong to no political organization, have no corruption funds, no lobbyists. Their situation is consequently not enviable.

In the anthracite mines of Pennsylvania 12,000 boys between the ages of seven and fourteen work as breakers nine hours a day with a lunch period of twenty minutes. A breaker sits astride an inclined chute through which the coal comes down from above and with a hammer breaks up the big pieces. After one hour of this labor, his pores, and after one day, his lungs, are full of coal dust.

In the cotton-spinning factories of South Carolina, in the silk mills of Georgia and Louisiana, little nine-year-old girls stand at the machines from seven in the morning to seven at night. The electric lights blind their eyes. They must watch the speedy shuttles which dart back and forth through the thread. For twelve hours on end they cannot sit down. In the southern cities you see eleven-year-old blind children begging through the streets with tin cups.

What else must I describe? Shall I write about the bleacheries in New York where boys stand up to their hips in blue dye baths; about the factory in Connecticut, in the phosphorous plant of which, the notorious white match heads are made; about the shoe plant where youngsters color tennis shoes a pretty white with ether? How many other examples are necessary?

The work of the children is poorly paid. It represents the lowest order of labor, labor for which no previous skill is necessary. The child snatches the bread out of the mouths of grown men, away from the illiterates, the immigrants, ignorant of the country's language. There are many branches of production in which the manufacturers could not get along without these cheap hands. The industrialist who was today to dismiss the children from his plant and replace them with better-paid workers, tomorrow would not be able to meet competition, and the day after tomorrow would be ruined.

Six states, mostly western, have laws relating to child labor that are worthy of imitation; not one, however, forbids it entirely. Naturally, those states, the industries of which depend most heavily upon this form of exploitation, have the laxest regulations with regard to it. Now and then some state will forbid it in certain trades; Tennessee, for instance, once tried to do so. What happened? The children were sent away in wagonloads to the neighboring state of South Carolina. The

Tennessee factories closed down while those in South Carolina paid fat dividends.

Five years ago there was a proposal before Congress that would finally have dealt with this national crime, a proposal that would have excluded the products of child labor from the country's markets. An investigation was undertaken which put off indefinitely the prospect for action, and the victorious lobbyist stood as always between the will of the people and its execution.

In the halls of Congress in the wonderful marble Capitol in Washington sits a jovial elderly man with observant eyes shaded by scholarly eyeglasses. This is Victor Berger, the only socialist in the United States sent as a member to Congress. Hungarian by origin, he is a teacher by profession, and Milwaukee, the German socialist city in Wisconsin, has put him where he now is.

From time to time, this jolly individual rises in his place and speaks on the point under discussion. He points out how the socialists of France or Germany would act in this or that situation; what Marx, were he living, or Kautsky, or Bernstein, Jaurès, Guesde, or Keir Hardie would say on the proposed legislation. The Democrats and Republicans listen carefully to his speech. Victor Berger is a conciliatory, universally loved colleague; and the Democrats and Republicans always learn something, since he is an educated man who achieved excellent results back in Wisconsin. He sits down in his place again and everything goes on quietly as before; he has the effect of a cricket chirping in a cage.

Indeed, it hardly matters whether one or twelve-dozen socialists sit in Congress. A legislature is essentially an agreement-machine and a compromise-mill. The parties seemingly work by rubbing against each other; but in truth they grind a common grain. The absurd notion of the representation of the interests of all by some has long been seen through and rejected by those who grind the grain of the future. Yet deep human stupidity lets itself be taken in by the farce. From every fall to every summer the people's servants become its commanders and dictators. And always the mass forget the comedy by which they are led along by the nose when they are called on by great harangues and by advertisements again to vote so that those who guided them for so and so many years should guide them again for so and so many years more. Many a man here has torn the word progress out of his dictionary and has pasted in instead a new page with its own paragraphs and laws, valid for himself alone.

Here in the tempo of life in America the difference between evolution and revolution is felt more meaningfully than anywhere else. The official socialist under the dome of the Capitol has forgotten that. Other worthy souls, like him, do not wish to understand it. Instead they look from the New World, full of wonder, over across to the France of Jaurès and Millerand and to a Germany that is on the road from a Bebel to a Millerand. But the difference to which those people are blind can be seen very precisely by anyone who has an eye to the swiftness with which the capitalist system in American society is developing to its ultimate consequences. It is snowballing into trusts, concentrated into ten, into six, into three hands, until, in the foreseeable future, the great god Mammon, endowed with a Scottish- or Irish-sounding name, in unlimited majesty will rule the world from Wall Street.

Occasionally the academic socialists, Berger, Hillquit, and Gompers, must become alarmed and anxious when they contemplate the results recently achieved and still being achieved by the I.W.W., the Industrial Workers of the World. At the head of this movement is the powerful and bitter personality of William Haywood, a former miner, whose story is epochal in the history of the American labor struggle. The I.W.W. has in its underlying principles as well as in its tactical methods great similarities to the radical syndicalists of France. In the great strikes of the past year it rendered the working class far more positive services than did the leaders of the American Federation of Labor who were constantly engaged in mediating between employers and employees.

Expropriation of the trusts by the state and creation of an industrial democracy are pious wishes at which the Money-Kings of the land can smile indulgently and securely. But they see something more serious in the matter when suddenly, out of the harmless ranks of the workers, leap men of direct action like the McNamara brothers whom Haywood defended and justified in a historic speech to listening America in the New York Cooper Union.

The wonderful basic democratic consciousness of the United States is responsible for the fact that in that country the socialists and anarchists do not fight each other as bitter foes; rather, the boundaries between them are here and there altogether wiped out. The end of the revolt seems more important to them than the roads by which it will be reached. While, like everywhere else, the American socialist begins as a Utopian for whom the idea is not a matter of ambition but of conscience, he has in his country fewer opportunities to develop into a political opportunist than in the countries with traditional oppositions. Politics and politicians in America have become altogether professionalized; the old puritan divines and the gentlemen-farmers of Virginia, to the anarchist Emma Goldman, seem more likeable, and seem to express a wider point of view than the interested and disreputable lobbyists who fill the Senate and House in Washington's Capitol.

In this land of free economic competition, they distinguish more carefully than in Europe between occupation and opinions. Even if the great principle of democracy is only regarded as a first step, the road to the free society of the future seems shorter in the American than in the European tempo; the backing and filling of the Old World seems exceedingly dilatory from the perspective of the New. The man whose goal is in the day after tomorrow does not here suffer the disdain that would be his portion across the Atlantic. I am sure that the congressmen have more respect for a man like Haywood than for those like Berger perfectly able to work as hacks in the congressional mill.

Relatively, the most sympathetic characters in Washington are the insurgents, who still believe in the machine, but are dissatisfied with its operations and hope to reform it. The Middle West is their home. The states of Wisconsin, the Dakotas, Minnesota, and Iowa, thickly settled with German elements, are represented by men like Berger and the popular senator, Robert La Follette. Here may be noticed attempts to reform the democratic principles on an economic basis. Here the prophetic words of Bismarck to Karl Schurz hang as mottoes over the beds of progressive German-Americans: "The test of American democratic principles will come when, inevitably, the great battle is joined between rich and poor in the United States." I readily believe what Berger told me, that the German socialists of the American Middle West have drawn forth insurgency from the progressive opinion of the still irresolute. But I must repeat over again that in a frantically rapid country like America, less than nothing will ever be achieved with all these basically conservative and vacillating types. They act as ballast on the journey to progress rather than as obstacles to capitalist development. One extreme must give birth to its opposite: the ceaseless taper-

ing of a system must inevitably come to the ultimate point at which all
will end in a crash.

Good friends in New York, such as the worthy Moses Oppenheimer,
told me that ten years ago socialism was held in suspicion by the natives as an alien phenomenon imported by foreigners and Jews. But its
great practical progress in the organization of the fight for wages, in
the fight "to make good," has altogether altered its position in the last
ten years.

But is this really high praise for a revolutionary movement? Everyone knows what success means in the United States. And one can quite
readily realize that under present circumstances the American will only
strive for the success of that from which he will personally profit, directly or indirectly, for that which will help him make good and come
closer to his goal. In this sense, the I.W.W. has had no success in
America. Its abrupt rejection of any deals closes the door to the possibility that it might be drawn into the drive for "making good." The
aspiration of the Federation of Labor, rich in success, is: "A good wage
for good work." That could just as well be the motto of any middle-
class employment agency. The Wobblies, however, have thus formu-
lated their point of view: "Away with wages! Give us the means of
production and the fruits of our work!"

The period in which fundamental gains could be attained by free
and easy agreements between trade unions and employers is already
far behind us. Those poor old pants can take no more patches; to the
rubbish heap with them! Only when the methods of the I.W.W. make
good in America will America attain the objectives of the I.W.W. But
by then the whole conception of "making good" will be quite different.

Even on board ship I became aware of the word "muckraker." In
speaking with an American, a sportsman and New England aristocrat,
I mentioned a few names that I respect, Robert Hunter, John Spargo,
Charles Edward Russell. My American blew that word into the air after
each of these names, like a smoke ring out of his cigar. I had never
heard the word before and had him write it for me on the border of
the ship's newspaper.

Now I find it in a few letters of introduction that my Canadian
friends gave me to people in the United States. In these notes it is

bestowed as a mark of honor, of which one must be proud: "He is a good muckraker!" they say of me in these letters.

For four months now I have conscientiously read the newspapers and periodicals of the country and am astounded at the mass of social services performed by the muckrakers. Open any number of the great journals that appear in editions of a hundred to five-hundred thousand, of a million to a million and three-quarters copies, monthlies or weeklies, *Everybody's, Munsey's, Collier's, The Saturday Evening Post,* and you will surely find a muckraker at work. You will be able to read an article written in the strongest, boldest, and frankest words, in which one of the great social evils of modern America is laid bare. Revolt is preached, and the impulse toward goodness, toward the ideal of Lincoln, and the American principle of care for the individual is strengthened and supported.

Two great Augean stables are cleansed over and over again, the trusts and political corruption in Washington and in the individual states. The trust king and the grafter are the targets against which the muckraker breaks his lance; and since the grafter is the creature of the king, his skin receives as a matter of course the first feel of the prongs. But the filth that splatters out of his punctured organism sullies the earthly little gods behind, to such a degree that already everyone of these Rockefellers, Goulds, Carnegies, and Morgans stand before the indignant American feeling for justice clad from head to toe in a garment of blood and filth.

Everyone of the millions who here read the newspapers now knows all about the great robber trusts, the milk, wool, ice, steel, oil, railroad, and meat combines. Everyone knows the operations of the lobby in which the politician deals with the briber; any child between the Atlantic and Pacific can point to the Boss, who gives out municipal franchises to his favorites in return for money. Before the eyes of the Americans the newspapers which all read reveal in rotation the shame of the land, the corruption of the great cities and of their local rulers.

Beside the protest literature of the newspapers there has also developed a protest literature in the American novel and drama. It must be boldly said that every significant author in the United States today is a socialist. He fights with the weapons of enlightenment or with mechanics' tools for the liberation of his country from enslavement to a system that mechanically and automatically impoverishes the masses and lifts a few to the dizziest heights of prosperity.

There are among these authors an enviable few who have exercised direct influence on the reorganization of worth-while institutions, or who have at least gotten a reorganization under way. Every right-minded person between the two oceans hears their names with sympathy. There was Frank Norris, who died young but who had time, in his masterpiece *The Octopus,* to expose the Southern Pacific, the very road on which I now ride from North to South. There is also Upton Sinclair, the author of *The Jungle.* There is the genial Jack London, prophet and revolutionary in the guise of an adventurer.

It happened that on my arrival in California significant events were taking place in the political life of the state. The women had won the right to vote. In Los Angeles the McNamara dynamite case was under way. In a few days the accused brothers, the secretaries of the steel and bridge workers' union, would openly confess their resort to the propaganda of direct action. Meanwhile, the forces of reaction, with the rotten old "General" Harrison Otis at their head, were fighting the rising young governor, Hiram Johnson, of whom the world will yet hear.

It is not hard to foretell who will win, the decadent capitalist who vents his rage against the ever-onsurging mob, or that sympathetic idealist who spoke the following words:

> When you create a class to govern in this country, just that instant you violate a fundamental principle, on which we founded this government, and you strike a blow at liberty itself. It's a survival of the old worship of power. The rabble and the mob! We're all the rabble and the mob in this Country, and the present design of the government of this State is, that you shall all participate in it.
>
> (From a speech to lawyers and judges by Governor Johnson.)

Out here, these words are not arrogant and pompous; on the contrary, they inspire with enthusiasm. Farther east they would smile at them and say you could only expect high-flown phrases from the first citizen of any western state. In the East, westerners seem showy people, people who express their opinions loudly, forcefully, and in a shrill manner. The West, in retaliation, calls the easterners Jingoes and cold-blooded

Hyperboreans with locked-up purses and hearts. In truth, one seems
to draw nearer Europe as one travels from West to East. In Chicago
it is already cool, and the atmosphere of New York is as chilly as that
of Europe.

Let the westerner be as shrill and as loud as he likes; he is also
naïve and good-natured, quick to enthusiasms and hospitable, easy-
going and swiftly moved. He builds rapidly and sits not long weeping
on the ruins around him. He is longer in the year under the sun, and
the sun over him is hotter than that over his brother on the Atlantic;
and when a phrase is toasted long enough in the sun, a living truth may
grow out of it.

32.

IBERIAN SKETCHES

*Julio Camba, born 1882, is a well-known literary figure in
Spain and Portugal. He has written several novels and dramas. A long
trip through the United States in 1916 furnished material for a volume
of travel notes, called* Un Año en el otro mondo *(1927).*

A Frenchman may be defined as a man who is very much decorated
and who eats a great deal of bread. The American, for his part, may
be defined as a man without much decoration who chews a great deal
of gum.

Gum chewing is the great national vice of the United States of
North America. The Americans chew their gum as readily as the Chinese smoke opium. Chewing gum is the artificial paradise of this nation.
In a trolley or railway car I have seen, seated opposite me, fifteen to
twenty people in a row opening and closing their mouths as if they
were fish, all with a beatific expression on their faces. This expression
corresponds with the sensation they experience in chewing gum.

In the past year, the Americans chewed away gum to the value of
$30,000,000. That is to say, they spent in this manner almost as much
as a country like Spain spends on its food. The figure is really astonishing since, while there are some people who use a fresh stick for each

short interval of mastication, there are others who preserve their wads to be chewed on over and over for weeks on end. After all, when there is too little money, it is necessary to stretch out the gum and make it last.

The chewing gum is perfumed and exceedingly mild, and it is sold in the form of a pastille. Poor families, however, must, I think, buy old tires and chew them in common; that is, father and mother, sons and daughters, probably sit all around the tire and chew on it simultaneously. An automobile tire used in this manner I suppose could last a family for a whole year.

Everyone chews in America, rich and poor, black, white, and yellow, the citizens of English origin and those of French or German origin. And precisely there, it appears, is the utility and the social and political significance of gum chewing. It is not so much that the habit constitutes a common element among the different races that inhabit the United States, something that levels out all the Americans of most diverse origins and at the same time differentiates them from the citizens of other countries. More important, little by little, chewing will create a typical American physiognomy, in which the jaw will predominate. If in the future there ever exists a typical American, with clearly marked characteristics, as there is today a typical Englishman, a typical Frenchman, or a typical Spaniard, the Americans will be able to say that they formed him by chewing away millions of dollars in gum. This country will acquire cohesion by gum-power.

There is nothing so American as an American barbershop. No, nothing! Not the American skyscrapers, nor the American saloons, nor American journalism . . . An American barber shop is much more energetic, much more complicated, much more mechanized, much more rapid, much more expensive, and much more American than anything else.

One enters and immediately finds himself attacked by two or three prize fighters, who relieve him of his hat, his coat, vest, collar, and tie. The proceeding is effective enough, if perhaps too violent.

"Why do you manhandle me in this manner?" a stranger is once said to have asked. "It is not necessary. I've no intention of resisting."

The disrobing completed, one is led to a chair that, in a fraction of a second, is converted into a field of operations. Then a man with enormous hands takes the head with one hand, as if he were grasping a peach, and, waving a razor with the other hand, asks:

"What will you have, haircut, facial, massage, manicure, shoeshine, shampoo, quinine . . . ?"

One is completely at his mercy and can deny him nothing. "Yes," you say, "whatever you wish."

The man gives certain orders, which you cannot hear since with a single stroke of the brush he has just covered your eyes and ears with a layer of lather. You feel that someone is working on your hands, and guess it is the manicurist. At the same time a Negro appears to be polishing your boots. Meanwhile, the barber subjects you to a scientific course of torture . . . You are shaved and the coat of lather gives way to a coat of pomade. The enormous hands massage you. Then your face is covered with a hot towel which scorches the skin. Soon the hot towel is replaced with one soaked in ice-cold water. You cannot see, speak, or breathe. What can be the intention of this man in subjecting you to these alternations of temperature? Is this not a procedure used to kill certain kinds of microbes?

Freed at last of all the towels, you can see the manicurist working on your fingers, you can see the barber and the Negroes. All your extremities are in strange hands. Numerous persons work for your comfort, and give you the satisfaction of thinking that you supply a livelihood to so many people. In reality, I have not even enumerated all the persons who serve you. In the corner of the shop there is, for instance, a man whose job it is to brush, polish, and crease your hat. The hat thus receives its own massage; it is, so to speak, your sixth extremity.

And your torture continues. Now you are introduced to a running current of electricity. The barber passes over your face a vibrating device which has the effect of a patting machine. Finally the shoes are polished. The manicurist releases your right hand and takes possession of the left, while the barber begins to cut the hair. And in the midst of all these agonies there is really a kind of voluptuousness. Thus when the barber passes alternating currents of hot and cold air across the neck it adds to the pleasure of the feeling of your hands between those of the manicurist.

At last the torture ends. That is to say, it ends after the bill is paid. You pull out a bundle of bills and distribute them to the crowd. And all that, including the payment, which seems to take the longest, only lasts a quarter of an hour. Everything is effected rapidly and mechanically. Did I not say that the American barbershop is the most American thing in the world!

With all due respect to everyone's sensibilities, I may truthfully say that the American citizen is being developed by a procedure very much like that of breeding horses. "We are getting too many blond brachycephalics," says a doctor of the Immigration Commission unexpectedly. "Don't you think we should get a few hundred dark dolicocephalics?"

One race tends increasingly to mingle with another. Yet a limit has been imposed on the entrance of certain races. In some states the marriage of whites and Negroes is forbidden. In others, where a single element has acquired too much preponderance, the statesmen are in favor of the immigration of an opposing element which might fight with and counterbalance it . . . The ideal will be to obtain, even if it cost a fortune, several examples of a first-class race and fully to entrust to them the task of peopling the country. "It will always be easier for us to breed eaglets, by placing the eggs of an eagle in the coop of a hen," said Lowell, "than by arranging the eggs of a hen in the nest of an eagle." Unfortunately, whether the United States be a hen or an eagle, it is certain that it does not always secure the eggs that it wishes. Immigration is almost entirely monopolized by labor contractors and by the big agriculturalists, and these people are not concerned in the slightest degree whether their employees are Aryans or not as long as they work a great deal and take low wages. The stimulators of immigration have successively tapped the most backward countries in the world, those which have remained on the lowest plane of civilization. And in the nest of America, the proportion of hens' eggs grows daily larger than the proportion of those of the eagle.

In any case, there is the question of assimilation. The war has shown that a large part of the inhabitants of the United States are not Americans but only partial citizens; that is, the country has not really absorbed them, has not fully assimilated them. The higher the quality of the immigrants, it seems, the more difficult their assimilation. A hen can hatch the eggs of an eagle; but in the process it will always run a great danger.

And since the degree of assimilation is of concern to the United States, the Americans give it particular attention. Professor Franz Boas has presented the Immigration Commission with a most interesting memorandum on the types of immigrants. The Hebrews of eastern Europe and the Sicilians seem to divide themselves into two groups distinguished by the form of the head, which is round in one of the two types and oval in the other. Well then, this difference tends to disappear in the United States. "Now," says Professor Franz Boas, "more similarity exists between the children of the two groups than exists between the children and the parents in any given group."

At first sight, the reader will not be able to comprehend the significance of this transformation. To give a round form to oval heads, and an oval form to round heads, in effect seems less a political and social ideal than a hatter's.

"And is it at that," some one may ask, "at that which people in the United States aim? To disfigure their heads?"

We who live here cannot avoid a certain preoccupation when faced with memoranda like that of Professor Boas. For better or worse, one is accustomed to one's skull and dislikes changes in it. What will the Board of Pensions say after having sent here six or seven dolicocephalics, if as the total result of their vacation in the United States these gentlemen return to Spain with deformed heads?

Yet it is clear that the United States will not haphazardly transform anyone's head. Here, where a political formula superior to that which is based on race and nationality might be thought to exist, experience has shown that it is very difficult to bring into agreement men with oval heads and men with round heads, people with white skins and those with black or yellow skins. The lesson is somewhat discouraging for those who believe in a federation of nations as the final outcome of the European war. And above all it is sad for the United States. Today the United States proposes candidly to breed a race and it goes about it, as I have said, just as one breeds horses. Why not, after all? Why not develop a race of men as one develops a breed of horses? What is strange, is that with such a procedure even they have not obtained better results.

For the first time in our lives, explained *Current Opinion*, we will see a political campaign in which not a single internal question plays the principal role. What greater proof can there be of the transformation through which the United States has passed? Formerly the American elector acted without attention to the opinion of the parties on international affairs. Now the United States has decided to emerge from its isolation, and it is international politics that will prevail in the coming presidential election. More than of the banks, of the tariffs, of the trusts, of the Negroes, they will speak in this election of England, of Germany, of Mexico, and of Japan. The partisans of an alliance with England, for instance, will not vote for anyone who has shown sentiments sympathetic to Germany, and the Germanophiles will fight with all their power those candidates sympathetic to the allies.

And the allies as well as their enemies will put themselves out to intervene, directly or indirectly, in this election. Both sides possess considerable power here. Of course, both by reasons of origin, by language, and by the spirit of its political institutions, this country tends to incline toward England. France, which has done so much for the liberty of the United States, can also count on a great many supporters here. Still, it must not be forgotten that of the 100,000,000 inhabitants of this country, some 15,000,000 or 20,000,000 are Germans or of German descent. Here there are published almost 1,200 German language periodicals, and of the 18,000 which appear in English, about a third are entirely in the hands of Germans, while in 6,000 or 7,000 others Germans have a half or a quarter of the shares. And German influence, so strong in the press, is no less powerful on the bench, in industry, and in trade.

The battle has already been joined. The Republican and Progressive parties have assembled in Chicago—the most important German city in the world after Berlin and Hamburg—in a convention to nominate candidates. Soon the Democratic Party will meet, and afterwards, in the month of November, will come the elections, first for the electoral college, then for the president himself. The names which are most often heard now are Wilson, the present incumbent, Roosevelt, and Hughes.

The first period in the election campaign in America may be considered over with the nomination of Wilson as Democratic candidate, decided upon at the convention in St. Louis. The German element will naturally fight Wilson with all its power, and Wilson has already spoken of the hyphenated Americans as a great national danger. By the hyphenated he means the German-Americans. The hyphen of German-Americanism is an object which terribly angers President Wilson and all the partisans of Americanism. They think that no American citizen should retain his hyphen, whether he be German-American, Anglo-

American, Franco-American. Each man must be simply pure American. "What are they?" they ask of the German-Americans, "Are these men more German than American, or more American than German?"

The hyphen in question has thus sprouted from the roots of war. Previously it was believed that all American citizens were true Americans. "It must not be thought," said Roosevelt, "that immigration changes the sentiments of our country. In one or two generations our immigrants are assimilated, and think like us. We have an excellent digestion." Then came the war, and the Americans of German descent declared themselves German-Americans. This declaration was so much more grave since there existed a German law, the Delbrück law, by virtue of which Germans could keep their German citizenship even if they had, for reasons of expediency, adopted some other nationality. This indicated that the Americans of German origin were not assimilated, and that there thus existed a powerful nucleus of refractory population. The stomach of the United States had not digested the German hyphen.

"Down with the hyphen!" shouts all America today. And if God does not intervene this hyphen will cost rivers of blood, since its possessors defend it with a heroism worthy of the trenches.

The hyphenated, as I said, will fight with all their power the candidacy of Wilson. And apart from this, Wilson and Hughes will fight with equal arms. The Republican and Democratic platforms are more or less the same and the struggle will be one over personalities rather than over program.

We must prepare to see one of the most picturesque spectacles in the world; that is, a presidential election in the United States. To give you an idea of the sporting spirit with which the people regard such equal contestants it is necessary to quote the following paragraph from the *Evening Post:* "It is a pity that two men as eminent as Wilson and Hughes could not appear together on the same platform! That would be a sensational match, and spectators would pay a fabulous price for admission."

Hughes holds over Wilson the enormous advantage of the offensive. The ex-justice can attack all the presidential labors of Wilson, who will have to take enormous pains to defend them. In his turn, Hughes will have to reveal how he would have acted had he been president, what he would have done with the question of Mexico, of the *Lusitania,* and so on. On the other hand, Hughes can rely on a greater number of personal sympathizers than Wilson, who seems to antagonize his friends. Wilson, in return, enjoys great intellectual prestige. He writes very well, speaks well, and is considered, moreover, a most honorable and well-intentioned man.

The candidates are ready. The boxers have put on their gloves. The first round is about to begin.

There are two fundamental tendencies in the life of this country: an idealistic and humanitarian tendency with a great moral content, which reaches from William James, the philosopher, to Henry Ford, the manufacturer of automobiles; and a materialistic tendency without any content of idealism, a tendency of capitalism and of capitalist imperialism. The two tendencies, as may be seen in this election, are now in a state of equilibrium.

For it is incontestable that Hughes and Roosevelt, as against Wilson, represent the second of those tendencies in opposition to the first. Hughes stands for the Wall Street capitalists, who gained him the nomination. He speaks for the trusts. He represents the *big stick* against the backs of the Mexicans. He represents the scorn of money for moral values. His friends have plastered New York with signs which read: "We don't want professors meddling in our affairs," and "What's the use of democracy in business?" Hughes, in short, represents the materialism of a quantitative civilization in which quality counts for nothing. Dollars, many dollars, business, bridges, telephones, cranes, skyscrapers, noise, speed . . .

If matters continue as they have until now, and if Hughes does not triumph this time, he, or another who represents the same things, will triumph in four years. The second tendency is steadily winning out over the first. To the degree that this people covers itself with gold, it denudes itself of spiritual content. The nineteenth century, which was the century of quantitative civilization, is dying in the trenches of Europe, but will be reborn here with a vitality it never had in the Old World. France and Germany, England and Italy, will face, at the end of the war, in the United States, a people whose ideals are those of the corporation—to do business. And *what is the use of democracy in business!* What help is democracy in making money? And indeed, democracy hardly yields a return of 2 per cent. Much better, the railroads, cotton, the potash mines, or bananas.

This moral difference between that which Hughes represents and that which Wilson represents is, without doubt, much more important for the relations of North America with the rest of the world than the possible difference of opinion between those two men on the European war. One must, moreover, be aware of the position of the President of the United States to understand the importance of the election. The President of the United States is a kaiser elected by a democratic process, a kaiser for four years; yet a kaiser who gets what he wishes.

Yesterday, the seventh of November, all the inhabitants of New York believed that Hughes had been elected President of the Republic. The newspapers gave us the news, and corroborated it in extras.

All New York passed last night in the streets, talking, discussing, drinking, betting, and fighting. Tables in the restaurants were reserved two and three weeks in advance. This was election day, the day on which democratic America chose the man who would guide its destiny for the next four years. Beyond the political interest there was in the public a purely sporting passion. In the Waldorf-Astoria Hotel alone, thirty-thousand dollars were bet in the last few hours of the day. Generally the party of a candidate wagers for him; yet not a few sincere Democrats who thought Hughes more likely to win than Wilson, bet against their own candidate. Interest in the money at stake thus mingled with the political interest in the election, and it would not be unlikely if some Democrats voted for the Republican candidate and if some sincere Republicans supported the Democratic candidate with their ballots.

Hughes? Wilson? All New York had those two questions on its lips last night. The newspapers said that when the result of the election would be known they would announce it by reflectors, with a white light if Wilson should win and a red if the election went to Hughes, or with a straight beam in one case and a zigzag in the other. The expectation in front of the Times Building was high-pitched. To keep the crowd entertained and at the same time to profit from it, the papers issued extra editions almost every quarter hour with the results they were able to accumulate up to the moment. Some indicated a triumph for Hughes, others for Wilson.

And toward eleven o'clock the triumph of Hughes was announced in an absolute manner. There arose a shout which extended from mouth to mouth from the center of New York to its outmost limits, an enor-

mous yell which lasted more than a quarter of an hour and which said
"Huuuuughes." In this yell one could notice all the modulations of sen-
timent, from the most enthusiastic joy to the greatest despondence.
Among the former could be easily distinguished a strong German
accent, since as was well known, Hughes was the candidate of the
German-Americans.

The nervous tension was relaxed. The last glasses were drained, the
last blows struck, and soon after, American democracy went to bed,
dreaming of Hughes.

Then on the following day it appeared that Hughes had not been
elected. The American elections take place by states, and in the calculation of probabilities before the election it had been supposed that
certain states in the confederation, especially the most industrialized
ones in the East, would vote in favor of Wilson, while the western
areas would give a majority to Hughes. It was the results from the industrial states which first became known in New York, and, contrary
to all anticipations, Hughes triumphed in those places.

Doubtlessly, reasoned the journalists, if Wilson lost in the states
considered most favorable to him, he will surely lose even more in the
others. And they not only announced the triumph of Hughes, but they
also wrote long editorials in honor of the new president. On the following day, however, a great surprise appeared. Wilson had won in the
western states. And today, the ninth, at eight o'clock in the morning,
he had a slight advantage over Hughes.

"America," one of the Americans who knows best the politics of his
country said to me, "is directly interested in the subject of submarine
warfare. This is not simply a matter of so many of our compatriots dead
as victims of German terrorism; it is a matter of something basic to our
existence as a nation. The American people who protested against the
sinking of neutral ships had logical reasons for their protests, but in
reality were acting in response to their own instinct for self-preservation rather than out of any pure reasoning. The United States is a
product of the freedom of the seas. To the degree that those liberties
increased, our fathers came here. Now we depend on no road more
than on the highways of the seas through which we are linked to the
rest of the world, and both our national security and our commercial
prosperity depend on a policy which will guard those routes. It is clear

that our protest is not simply a quixotic gesture, but that we have a very real interest in the subject. Do the Germans take account of that?"

This was said to me by a very well-informed American. But there are still other elements to observe in the attitude of the United States with respect to the European war. The United States commences now to study a lesson that England has already thoroughly mastered; the lesson that the world is ever smaller, and that no people can keep itself apart from the others; that its most vital interests are mingled and inter- mingled with foreign interests; that no nation can really consider itself at peace while others are fighting; and that the only peace possible for a people is a world peace.

The United States of today, with its 100,000,000 inhabitants and its enormous commerce, with its shores only four or five days distant from Europe, is something quite distinct from the America of Washington. In the time of Washington, America lay far away from the other hem- isphere. The means of communication between the Old World and the New were limited, insecure, and slow. The commercial and financial relations did not represent a thousandth part of what they amount to today. Few persons traveled between the two continents. News was delayed and incorrect, and kept one continent in ignorance of the other. Today one does not need more time to go from New York to London than to go from New York to San Francisco. Before the war thousands of Americans bought their clothes in London, summered in Switzerland or Bohemia, gambled in Monte Carlo, studied in Germany, and entertained themselves in Paris, adding their personal relations to the commercial and financial relations of America with Europe. The world has shrunk, and the Americans are citizens of the world. That which takes place today in Europe is known here in detail within a few hours. America and Europe have come closer to each other, just as if there had been a geological cataclysm. This is the miracle of steam, of electricity, of the cable, and of the wireless telegraph.

And America will not be able to ignore events in the Old World. Any war that breaks out in Europe will immediately affect American life. The results of that war will be felt as well in the stock exchange, in trade, in the price of potatoes, and finally, in the gowns of the women. Do we not today, in the streets of New York, see all the women dressed in black and white because American industry meets such dif- ficulty in securing German dyes?

Formerly, the Americans believed that the division of the world into two hemispheres was not only geographical but also political, and that they could remain aloof from everything that happened in Europe because the splashings would never reach them. The myth of American impunity existed until the beginning of the European struggle. The war exploded, and all the Americans who happened to be in the belligerent countries began to decorate themselves with labels. They imagined, no less, that the title of American was a safe-conduct which would bring them across the lines of fire with guarantees that the bullets would not touch them. And when they found themselves obliged to abandon their homes, their interests, or their trunks; when they tried to make a train and could not catch it; when they wished to cable to America and had to prepare the message in French or German; when their letters of credit were rejected in the banking houses—then they began to think that the European was also a source of trouble to them. Then came the torpedoing of the *Lusitania*, full of American citizens. After that were other sinkings, and commercial complications followed.

Now America has learned. It knows that no isolation is possible, not for the United States or for anyone, and American politics have consequently flowed over into international politics. The actual conflict will be resolved in one way or another; but whatever the solution may be, its importance will be secondary to this inevitable circumstance: the entrance of the United States into world politics. America is already thinking of alliances and planning to reorganize its army and navy. From now on it will increasingly be true that Europe will have to deal with a new colossus.

33.

WHAT IS WORTH IMITATING IN AMERICA

Alma Hedin, born in 1876, the sister of the explorer, Sven Hedin, was a nurse and social worker in Stockholm. Her visit to the United States shortly after World War I was partly motivated by the desire to survey the new American methods of social and industrial welfare work. Her book, from which this account was taken, was published in 1920 under the title Arbetsglädje; Lärdomar från Amerika.

In New York we visited many persons to whom we had introductions because they seemed to be acquainted with the subjects we wanted to investigate. We were also shown through many large industrial and business plants. True, there were almost everywhere so-called Welfare Departments, in which there were officials particularly charged with the assistance of the workers, but that was not really what I had in mind.

Everywhere in industry there was an effort, as far as possible, to put the right person in the right place, to avoid fitting square pegs into round holes. They know how much better and faster a job can be done by one who has an inclination for it, an interest in it. To that end they have undertaken a great mass of psychological tests, which are often resorted to even when it is a matter of trifles. In the public and trade schools they also take notice of the talents of each student to develop them most properly.

Naturally, this system can be driven too far and it may give rise to mistakes. But its underlying presumption is correct, and in many cases is of great value. When once it is fully developed, society may be able to make full use of the talents of its members. There are many tasks that could well be performed by invalids or less talented persons, as well as by those with their full capacities and well educated.

Many factories support nurses, who among other things have the duty of visiting in their homes laborers absent from their work without informing the management. Since apart from their knowledge of nursing, these women often have good training in social work, they can be very useful. If the laborer is sick and neglects to secure medical attention, the nurse can give directions on how to get help; if he stays away from work through dissatisfaction or negligence, she can often bring him to his senses and induce him to return, in his own interest as well as in that of his employer. She can also discover the reason for his dissatisfaction, which is often justified and capable of easy rectification. It may happen that his family situation is at the root of his unhappiness or a cause of anxiety, and here too she can perhaps restore order.

The work of the visiting nurses is of great importance but limited in nature, partly because they come in contact with only a few workers and partly because one can only rarely hope to find a person in whom are united the technical skill of a nurse and the sharp psychological insight, the tact, and the understanding essential to the task. Otherwise their time and their thoughts are engrossed by the job, and they can only show slight interest in the complications of life. We know from our own experience how useful these women can be. But that also was not the knowledge I sought in the New World.

When one has lived for some time in the fashionable sections of New York and time after time has watched the flow of fashionable people along Fifth Avenue, one becomes deathly tired of the picture. All the women seem to have been cast in the same form, a very nice form indeed but still one and the same. All are well-dressed, all wear coats and pointed shoes, and all are rouged, which heightens the similarities but wipes out the finer shades of expression. One longs then to see another type, real people with larger points of view and free of selfish interests. And if one has the good fortune to be invited to live for a week as a guest in the Henry Street Settlement, then one feels the need to describe the sort of people one meets there.

The word settlement takes in a whole complex of things and is therefore difficult to describe. The settlement movement began in England. The basic thought was to bring as residents into the poorest quarters of the great cities educated men and women who wished to serve and to elevate the people. They invite their neighbors to the house. They form clubs for the various age groups and sexes; they offer training in many practical things; they open to the youth of the district opportunities for gentle entertainment; and they educate and occupy the children. Soon the settlement becomes the center of the district, and it develops further and further until almost everyone who lives in the neighborhood is somehow drawn into it. Then more and more people come to the house, where they are always sure of a friendly reception and where everything is done to help them enjoy themselves and to lighten their anxiety.

There are many settlements in New York, but best known is the Henry Street Settlement. Perhaps the most important branch of its work is what we would call the visiting-nurse service to the homes of the poor. The difference is that the 250 nurses attached to the settlement may be called by the poor as well as by the rich, and that their services may be paid for or not according to the circumstances of the patient. A service which is as important as the nursing proper is the education in hygiene and in other practical matter which is given the patients. Not the ill person alone is their patient; they concern themselves with the whole family and offer advice and help in every possible way. Their work is of great significance and deserves the greatest possible consideration.

Nurses receive in America a very good and thorough education. The course lasts three years, and the requirements of the profession are high as far as knowledge and character are concerned. Many nurses have an academic education. They are protected against overwork, and may serve only eight hours a day. Much attention is paid to their living quarters, their food, their entertainment, and their rest. In the United States some 50,000 nurses are trained at once in 1,600 different schools and hospitals. In this country they understand what could be the role in the whole social machine of these trained women if they are the right kind. Therefore they are cared for and receive the best training; for they come in contact with great masses of people whom they can elevate and refine, if they have the capacity for it. It is quite remarkable to hear how their supervisors are concerned that these young women should practice not only exercises and sports but also dancing; and in the planning of their recreation special care is taken to get them to the theater so that they should not miss the refining influence of that amusement.

A building in Henry Street with a great hall for dances and ball games is entirely set aside for clubs. Here the youth of the quarter gathers in the evenings and here in the mornings the little ones have a kindergarten when their elders are studying or at work. A young woman, well educated, which in America means a good deal, supervises these clubs. She is a tall brunette, who acts calmly and with dignity and makes a friendly appearance. She alone can take care of a great celebration in which about a thousand young people in great good humor dance and play. She wears a simple white dress while the others are clothed in dark colors. In the most confused shindig she moves quietly and softly like an angel of light. I christened her the "saint," a name by which she was openly called.

Another important field of endeavor is the theater. Henry Street has its own theater, with a good stage and a large space for the audience. It is the gift of a rich young girl who herself leads the work and often takes a part. There are performances every Saturday and Sunday, and almost all the roles are taken by young people from the neighborhood. The whole is of greater worth to the public than what can be seen in the professional theaters, and for the participants it is educational, cultivating, and above all amusing. At my visit two pieces were being presented. The first dealt with a young minister who believes that every joy and beauty in life is sent by the devil to lead men astray and to seduce their hearts away from God. To his alarm, he discovers that he is in love with a young, charming girl and he believes that she too is a temptation of Satan. In an excess of religious enthusiasm he seeks to throttle her, but fortunately she does not die. When she returns to consciousness she tells him that he has confused God with the devil since it is God that endows humanity with joy and beauty. The role of the minister was very well played and the others also gave a good account of themselves.

The other piece was a ballet-pantomime. The scene was a toy shop in which all the dolls step forth. The action was as follows: a couple of dolls were to their great grief sold to two different customers. In the night before they were to be sent away the two dolls with the help of their comrades escape, and the owner of the shop is amazed in the morning when he cannot find them. The dancing and the costumes were enchanting. The performers had themselves worked out the steps to the music of Rossini. It was an unusually fine ballet.

In the vicinity of the Henry Street Settlement live only Jews. Even the old Jews were familiar with and loved the stage. The theater in the settlement began with religious pieces. Little by little its character has changed, but even now purely Jewish pieces are frequently presented, and often they give well-known dramas a sort of Jewish interpretation. They offer, for instance, *The Jewish King Lear* and *The Jewish Nora.*

It was easy to see that the theater was held in high esteem by all the participants and by the whole audience. A woman who led us the next day behind the curtains and through the workshops where the sets and the costumes were prepared seemed to us to be about eighteen-years old. When she said that she had for many years gone on tour with theatrical companies in the summer as a critic, I allowed myself to laugh. But she explained that she was not nearly as young as she seemed. The secret was that in her theater one did not grow old, since one has contact only with bright and good things.

Miss Lillian Wald is the soul and the mainspring of the Henry Street Settlement. She is one of America's best-known women. Twenty-eight years ago, after she finished college and completed her education as a nurse, she began her work in Henry Street for the numerous population of the district.

Nothing in Sweden can be compared with this part of New York, especially as it was when Miss Wald first came here. Cleanliness and order were then altogether strange notions. But the abundance of children was almost as great as now. I have never seen at once so many and such sweet children as in Henry Street. The street is their health resort; there the family spends its days and a good part of its nights. Here live almost exclusively Jews who have immigrated from all the lands of the Old World. With astonishing quickness they attain good economic positions, but the ignorance of the language, the housing problem, and the lack of provisions for hygiene and order create all sorts of hardships for them.

Miss Wald began her work by visiting the sick in their homes. This task was later carried on by others; but Miss Wald organized and directed it until it came to cover the whole city. Many visits to the sick gave Miss Wald an insight into their circumstances. She prepared all the necessary courses and clubs, the entertainments and activities of all sorts that the settlement now includes. Yet even that was not enough. In her practice she often had the opportunity to notice shortcomings and mistakes in the law, especially when it came to the children. She made proposals that were always taken into consideration and often led to improvements in the legislation. In this respect America is ahead of us; there they know how to evaluate and judge practical work.

Another circumstance that made such an undertaking as Miss Wald's easier and more fruitful than it would have been among us was the fact that she never felt a lack of money. With the support of her settlement other houses were established in Henry Street, and also seven little estates for summer vacations. She made it one of the basic principles of her work never, as far as possible, to help without some *quid pro quo.* The process of paying is itself educational, and that which one must buy is cherished more than that which one gets for nothing.

One of Miss Wald's objectives is to spread beauty. She is herself well educated and appreciates everything beautiful. The houses in Henry Street that belong to her settlement are all well decorated and seem always friendly and attractive. In every club room and assembly hall there are one or more works of art, and it is her desire to equip every room with simple and tasteful furniture. For people who live in tenements in an undesirable part of the city, and who themselves lack the means to establish themselves satisfactorily in their own homes, it is relaxing and edifying to see something pleasing to the eye. She knows that beauty is also a means of educating and improving humanity.

Thanks to her wide circle of friends, Miss Wald has often been able to create suitable work for her neighbors. She now operates a real employment bureau. Apart from that, she encourages the domestic industry of the immigrants. At the time of my visit Ukrainian objects were set out for sale. There were cross-stitched pieces of the usual Russian sort. A few Ukrainian women dressed in their national costumes sat before the eyes of the public near their work. Miss Wald proceeds on the wise assumption that it is better to encourage the immigrants to retain and to exploit the skill many possess in making the beautiful domestic articles instead of forcing them into new kinds of work that they would have to learn from the beginning. Many of the products of the household industry of the Old World have infinitely greater value in beauty than the ugly and tedious products of the factory that one sees everywhere.

Miss Wald is a Jewess and a credit to her race. She has the gift of the intelligent woman of the world in an enchanting way, to attract and hold the attention and interest of other people. In the course of the years she has gathered around her a whole staff of co-workers, each appointed to his appropriate place. To increase and maintain their social interest and their information about everything that happens in this area, Miss Wald hit upon the arrangement that her co-workers should live in the Henry Street Settlement and eat at her table. From every end of the earth there also come persons who wish to get to know the work of Miss Wald, and even these strangers can live in her settlement. Consequently, people from all parts of the world meet each other in Miss Wald's house, brought together by common interests. Miss Wald is a charming hostess, pleased by all this and by the idea of maintaining a salon. With a certain childish, not to say American, pride, she will say, "Today I have guests from only six different countries." Once a week there is a special assembly with speeches in which each one may reveal his experiences and new impressions. The people of the neighborhood admire and respect her, and all know that they can rely on her intercession for help in any difficulties.

The police of the district have learned what valuable assistance Miss Wald has been to them in their difficult work. But she in turn has also been able to count upon the help of the guardians of public order. This has been a clever and practical coöperation.

Miss Wald can no longer personally take part in everything, but as soon as a complicated situation develops she puts her hands to the matter and brings it out into the clear. Perhaps her success has created what one so often sees in America, namely an almost childish satisfaction with that which one has oneself created. The organization to which one belongs is always the biggest and the best in the world. This often gives the impression of a really youthful enthusiasm. Therefore, also, they often drive themselves with youthful energy to attempt to accomplish everything that they consider good.

One must test things with a certain caution and not uncritically accept everything one sees. But it is refreshing to watch the life that goes on here in every district; it makes one realize that there is a real difference between the culture of an old people and that of a new.

Miss Wald belongs to those whose attempts reach fruition; she has had the good fortune to see her work crowned with success. By her gifts of leadership, of inspiration, and of the ability to create order, she has succeeded in raising and improving the living conditions of thousands. After her model and thanks to her example many have already spread and imitated her work. There is therefore no boundary at which one can say, "Up to here extends the territory of her labors; here it comes to an end." The greatness of every unselfish labor for others consists in this: that it has in itself an infinite quality that cannot be measured in purely material terms.

34.

THE PROBLEMS OF NORMALCY

Henri Hauser was born in 1866 and became a professor of history at the University of Paris. He wrote extensively, in particular in the fields of the history of diplomacy and of imperialism. In 1923 he came to the United States as visiting lecturer at Harvard University. A book (L'Amérique vivante) *published a year later described his observations on his visit.*

France must have learned with astonishment that the United States suffered from a scarcity of coal this winter, that the coal question was politically significant, that it might play a part in the forthcoming presidential election, and that it could influence the development of American social legislation.

America is the largest producer of coal in the world. Its fields cover an area one and a half times as large as all of France. Alone it produced in 1913 more than 500,000,000 tons, as against 730,000,000 for all of Europe. Yet there was not enough coal.

The paradoxical fact is there: New York and New England suffered a shortage of fuel during a particularly long and hard winter. How did it happen?

Last April a great strike put an end to work in every anthracite mine and in all the bituminous works subject to the miners' union. The United Mine Workers wanted the strict application of the principle of the closed shop; that is, prohibition of the employment of non-union labor. The conflict lasted almost six months and was marked by atrocities like those of a modern war. The result was that the accumulations normally set aside in the summer months did not materialize, so that when digging resumed the consuming industries and the public had to live from hand to mouth.

There followed a strike of railroad workers at the moment when coal began to pile up at the mine-heads; there therefore appeared a block similar to that which we experienced in the Ruhr. Since New York State and New England are far from the pits, the question of transportation is primary for them. Enormous snowfalls made late trains a rule on certain lines, and inadequate rolling stock aggravated the situation. Some people also charged the trainmen of the New Haven Railroad with prolonging the strike as a sort of underhanded sabotage. Others accused the management of saving money at the expense of the public.

The internal waterways were not able to compensate for the failure of the railroads. The Barge Canal, which has replaced the Erie, now too small, froze over. Significant parts of the ports were closed. A northwest wind and ice made coastal shipping very expensive. Even the cut through Cape Cod was impassable. Three barges in tow spent eighteen days in February on the way from Philadelphia to Boston instead of the usual three or four. Trucks, wagons, and sledges were pressed into service to haul the precious cargo.

Was there a real shortage of coal? Not indeed in the true sense with which we became familiar during and after the war. Nevertheless, strangely enough the Americans were obliged to restore the wartime restrictions. The United States now has a fuel commission under Mr. James Phelan, and in each Massachusetts town there is a local administrator to assure an equitable distribution.

Everyone here finds his supply of coal inadequate. I must say that the citizen of New England overheats himself excessively. A Frenchman finds it difficult to tolerate the high temperatures in these houses. The principal concern of the head of the family, after having opened a path through the mountain of snow before his door, is to refill his furnace, and there are constant complaints against the lack of nourishment for this devouring fire. It was cold this winter; the children were cold. Even today one finds meetings scheduled for one hall being held elsewhere because of the lack of heat. In the small towns, with poor communications, matters were worse. People have been disturbed by talk of deaths caused by the cold.

There were complaints to the White House asking for a system of priorities that would get coal delivered to New England. An embargo on coal to Canada was also asked when it was learned that Pennsylvania coal was being sold in Montreal more cheaply than in Boston. Montreal is already in bad repute as a "wet" city, as the city of two-thousand cabarets. Now it needed only to be known as a monopolizer of coal.

The President's response was unfortunate. He declared that there was no real scarcity of coal in New England, only a fear of scarcity, a psychological phenomenon, a sort of hysteria. These phrases unloosed a tempest. The President was vilified like the official who told the people, short of bread, to eat cake. He was asked whether the low level of the thermometer was also a psychological phenomenon that could be dispelled by auto-suggestion. This was, of course, the period of the vogue for Mr. Coué. To restore some calm the President found it necessary to disown his unfortunate words; he is now quoted as expressing his deep solicitude for the frigid population. But many electors will not forgive him.

The administration did not remain beaten. It protested that the complainants insisted on using only anthracite instead of accepting substitutes. Reputable Bostonians have told me that they were sent slate as ersatz, sometimes even under the name of anthracite. They speak jokingly of it as fireproof coal. Yesterday, the Governor of Massachusetts himself solemnly said before the legislature that no citizen could be forced to pay high prices for a fuel that did not burn.

There is no hope that the situation will improve before the middle of March, despite the improvement in transportation. Congress, before adjournment, nevertheless voted an appropriation of some $400,000 for aid, and the Secretary of War has ordered the commander of the first army corps to put all his trucks at the disposal of the fuel administrator. We will therefore have coal when the thaws begin and the streets are transformed into roaring rivers.

Meanwhile, many people seek to locate the responsibility for this shortage. Some violently accuse the United Mine Workers of grasping the people of the United States by the throat. "If New York and New England are not yet dead of cold and hunger, it is despite the miners. Legislators awake! America is not ripe for Bolshevism." In the states with no coal mines one may expect an armed uprising against the unions. The closed shop will have a bad time of it.

But the unions answer that the mine owners levy on the public an illegitimate charge of almost $4.00 a ton by the monopolistic organization of the industry. The profits of the six leading companies rose from less than $9,000,000 in 1912 to $13,000,000 in 1920. If the same proportions hold for the remaining firms, the total profits earned in coal in 1920 would come to fully $51,000,000. The prices are calculated on the basis of the least efficient mines. And was not the strike before the last precipitated by the capitalists?

Furthermore, to stimulate production the governors authorized the independent mines—that is, the groups not in any combine—to charge $.75 more for their coal during the war. Actually, this premium now comes to more than $6.00 a ton. And the fuel commission in Pennsylvania, in fixing the quota of the New England states, did not realize that the percentage of independent coal had risen from 5 to 14 per cent of the whole, a rise which undoubtedly meant an extra charge for Massachusetts alone of $800,000.

To substantiate these accusations the state commission on the necessities of life reported to the legislature, naming 126 retail dealers who sold their coal at more than the price fixed at the mines. In Washington, Congress has just decided upon a joint investigation.

Will this investigation be able to restore the equilibrium in coal? Will they be able to make up the losses of last year this summer? Or does it seem more likely, even apart from the specific factors in the recent crisis, that America is moving towards a permanent deficiency of coal? It must not be forgotten that to this very day its mines are exploited in the most wasteful and improvident manner. Before the war it was calculated that the United States had a supply of coal resources that would last a hundred and fifty years. But acceleration in the rate of industrial growth will shorten that period unless some fuel substitute is found.

Some think oil will answer the need. During the crisis one could read everywhere ingenious advertisements of machines for burning liquid fuel, but at prices so expensive as to discourage the consumers. The wastage of oil, however, has been even more thoughtless than that of coal, and the demands for it grow from day to day because of the increase in the number of automobiles. What difference does it make if the United States produces two-thirds of the world petroleum when the director of the geological survey declares that the country, once an exporter, will have to begin importing oil. He advises conservation for purposes where it cannot be replaced—lubricants, for instance—and as far as possible the substitution of other fuels.

"United States victim of oil plot. Great Britain, France, Italy, and Holland close doors on American companies." Such are the newspaper headlines. Such is the theme of a very careful article in *Foreign Affairs,* a new journal destined to play an important part in the political education of the American people. One might say, however, that this article would have seemed more authoritative were not its distinguished author, Mr. A. C. Bedford, also president of Standard Oil.

Is this affair simply another incident in the gigantic struggle between Standard and Dutch Shell, or can the United States really believe itself victim of a world plot to shut it off from petroleum supplies? Seas of ink have been spilled on this question, particularly since the intervention of Mr. Child at Lausanne again revealed the intensity of Anglo-American rivalry. It is nevertheless necessary to recall the origins of the question to understand the present situation.

The drilling of the first wells on the Ohio in 1859 raised a fever similar to that which had a decade earlier followed the discovery of gold in California. In Pennsylvania, Texas, California, Oklahoma, the pursuit of petroleum continued, madly, wildly. With the absence of foresight, the genius for waste, the disastrous habits of exploitation, characteristic of American industry, rival companies foolishly squandered the petroleum resources of the nation. Who knows how much oil was thus lost forever, that might have been saved for the future by a more rational system? Many people who now complain of the shortage of oil might well first examine their own consciences.

They drilled without reckoning. Was not the main objective to flood the markets of the world with American petroleum? Indeed, by 1902, despite Russian competition, the United States had not only outdistanced the Caucasus, but actually was supplying two-thirds of the world's supply. It is calculated that since 1859 the American companies have extracted 6,500,000,000 barrels, which now must be replaced. There is the real cause of the colossal combinations, the trusts of which Standard Oil is the most famous, the underhand dealings with the transportation companies, the construction of immense pipe lines, the fleets of tankers, and also this immense publicity and the financial maneuvers which aim to increase consumption, to discover new sources, and to assure the rapid flow of American oil. The oil question at that time was a question of outlets. The American companies had no other program than to unloose over the world an ocean of petroleum.

Already before the war there were signs of a reversal of the situation. It would have been premature to write then, as Mr. Bedford does today, that "our industrial era would come to a halt without oil"; but the industrial uses of that fuel, as a source of heat and of energy, and as a lubricant, were multiplying. And it was noticed, a little too late, that the resources were not inexhaustible. The power potential of water and of wind infinitely renew themselves. The calculations of geologists as to the moment when the last fragment of coal will disappear are of academic interest only. But the number of oil deposits is limited, and one can see the time when there will be no new ones to open. These deposits are not of equal importance, and it is hard to tell in advance when and how they will enter into production. The enormous capital invested in research, in discovery, in equipment, may never earn a profit. The industry is a gamble like roulette, and it has the attractions and dangers of the gamble.

Before the war, for instance, the first American fields in Ohio and Pennsylvania showed signs of a disturbing old age. Texas had just finished a short and tumultuous career. Only California and Oklahoma still produced. For how long? The war dramatically underlined the seriousness of the problem. First, it consumed, in sea and air transport, enormous quantities of precious oil. It pushed to perfection techniques which, after serving in war, were put to use in peace and which replaced coal by oil, while at the same time the demand for lubricants grew formidably. At precisely the time when it became evident that the resources of petroleum were limited, it began to appear that its uses were infinite.

At the same moment, two other abnormal situations developed. The two greatest producers after the United States, Russia and Mexico, ceased to furnish their usual supplies to the refineries. The Russian failure interested the United States only indirectly in increasing the demand for American oil in European markets; an increase particularly intense when the end of the blockade of the central powers augmented the number of consumers by 100,000,000. But in Mexico the Americans had invested $500,000,000 in capital. And after the revolution put a rude but effective end to the regime of Porfirio Diaz, there were no longer laws protecting foreign property. The menace of expropriation and of arbitrary taxation threatened the resources by which the American companies had hoped to extend their domains. They naturally did not regard favorably the European powers which had supported the revolution, especially when those powers began to get Mexican oil concessions.

The bare figures still seem to show the United States in a satisfactory situation. It produces 60 per cent, if not two-thirds of the world production. Why then, with this dominant position, should the United States complain, why feel itself the victim of a world plot to cut it off from petroleum? Were France to denounce a conspiracy to deprive it of iron, the world would laugh. Why should it take the Americans seriously.

America is the greatest producer of oil; it is also by far the greatest consumer. In 1922 it used 1,650,000 barrels daily of a supply, including imports, of 1,875,000. The margin is narrow. Two million motor vehicles were on the roads in 1923. Add to that an enormous number of tractors and agricultural machines, of ships, airplanes, locomotives that use oil. Think of the use of oil for light, heat, and for little installations of movable power. Compute what is needed to grease the wheels of American industrial machinery. It is expected that the daily demand this year will rise to 2,000,000 barrels!

In addition, since the almost complete failure of Russian production the Standard and its rivals are also the great suppliers of France, Italy, Germany, and in part even of Great Britain and the Far East. Tied by contracts to refineries, creators of a whole chain of affiliated companies, these corporations must deliver—that is, must find the oil.

In 1922 they were not able to satisfy the demands upon them and to maintain a slight reserve without supplementing the 470,000,000 domestic barrels by 132,000,000 imported from Mexico. But for political reasons the Mexican yield is falling off; American companies have had to abandon the exploitation of two-thirds of the area originally envisaged. Yet Mexico and the United States are their only spheres of influence, while their foreign rivals have wells scattered all over the face of the earth.

Thus the petroleum war has been transformed. A struggle for sources has replaced the struggle for markets. When the people, whether in Europe or in America, feel attacked in their vital interests, they invoke sacred principles. With its oil supply impaired, the United States has suddenly discovered the principle for which France in 1919 and Italy since have vainly fought, the principle that the indispensable raw materials, particularly when they are rare, are the common property of humanity. What a shame that this theory should not also apply to coal, to cotton, to copper, to wool, to grain, and to meat!

The United States was not particularly conscious of this principle in the period when, with the profits of its oil, it made the best part of its fortune. It is well aware of it now, and it was a former Secretary of the Interior, fifteen days after resigning his post, who denounced "a gigantic movement, essentially international, aided and assisted by certain foreign governments, to cut off the supplies of the United States by refusing to give its prospectors the right to search for oil." Invoking the authority of our compatriot Delaisi, the Americans rant against the "great oil monopoly from which the United States is excluded. It is the greatest trust the world has ever seen, a trust modeled on the original plan of the Standard but enlarged to the scale of the universe." It may be noted in passing that the Standard, which provoked the anti-trust laws, now sees American passion turn against others, strangers.

These passions naturally are directed first of all against England. The Anglo-Persian oil company already holds 2.2 per cent of world production, and its concessions cover 500,000 square miles. The deposits of Mesopotamia have an unknown value and it will be necessary to make enormous expenditures to open them up. The United States claims here an equalization of risks—and of profits. If the British maneuvers should succeed, the Americans claim the United States would have to pay in tribute more than the total amount of the English debt. Nigeria and Guiana are also closed to Yankees. The English government also defends itself for having excluded them from Burma.

But England is not the only villain. The union of Royal Dutch and Shell Transportation has created an Anglo-Dutch interest. This group has in its hands not only the wells of the Netherland East Indies, but also holdings in Borneo, Rumania, Egypt, Trinidad, and Venezuela. In Mexico it has four refineries that turn out 155,000 barrels a day. In fact, in the United States itself, it has five refineries with a capacity of 65,000 barrels! Washington already protested in 1920 against the concession by the Dutch government of wells in Sumatra to strictly Dutch companies—in fact to the Bataafsche, a subsidiary of the Royal Dutch.

Even France may be drawn into the matter because of the San Remo arrangements. We are accused of hypocrisy, because while in appearance we make concessions without distinction of nationality, actually we demand that two-thirds of the administration be in French hands. In practice, complains an American corporation, France and the French colonies are more completely closed to American companies than any other part of the world.

To sum up, the United States claims for its nationals the same rights and opportunities which are accorded to the nationals of other countries in the United States. A federal statute of 1920 prohibits the acquisition of land by the citizens of countries which withhold this reciprocity.

Well, we have pointed out that foreigners have seized a foothold not only in Mexico, which the Americans consider a private preserve,

but in the very territory of the United States itself. The Union Oil
Company of Delaware, and that of California, and the Shell Company
are accused of being subsidiaries of Royal Dutch-Shell. The accusation
might easily be proven.

Now a new case arises, that of the Roxana Petroleum Corporation
(what a beautiful Racinian name!), ostensibly an American firm, but
actually under foreign control, the majority of voting shares belonging
to Royal Dutch. Only, thanks to American complexities, there is an
American corporation in between. Straw men have given way to straw
companies, the holding companies.

The Roxana swears there is nothing in it, just as the Standard companies of Texas or Indiana affirm that they have no connection with
that of New Jersey, the group for which Mr. Bedford speaks. But the
Roxana incident has become the occasion for a demand that the Federal
Trade Commission investigate the companies suspected of having foreign capital, the extent of their concessions, their plans for expansion.
Already, it is said, the Shell Union Oil Corporation controls 3.5 per cent
of American crude oil production. The Royal Dutch-Shell groups control 11 per cent throughout the world.

This policy of reprisals is evidently a tactical procedure. But it
must be expected that the question will more and more often be raised
in international diplomacy. This propaganda has succeeded in implant-
ing two ideas in American minds: despite its enormous production, the
United States will lack oil; and the Americans are unjustly excluded
from a share of world petroleum resources.

On the day when the United States compels England to attend an
international oil conference the time will be ripe to demand that the
conference not limit itself to oil resources, but that it consider as a
whole the problem of an equitable distribution of all raw materials.
Until that question is resolved there will be no economic peace; that is,
no durable peace among men.

Accustomed as we are to thinking in terms of the English crisis, we
have a certain tendency to believe that that crisis is general in all
Anglo-Saxon countries. Since we wish to see the United States reënter
the circle of European nations, we like to think they will be forced to
come to the rescue of poorer countries to avoid the ills that trouble

England, the slackening of exports, the lowering of prices, and unemployment.

But what if our hypothesis is false? What if there is no American crisis? Since I have been in the United States I have sought this depression without success. I saw ports overflowing with goods. When, on a clear spring day, I observed them from the height of the elevated with their numberless rail lines stretching onto wooden piers to the very edge of the ship to bring or take away merchandise, with their rows of cars, their loading machinery, their naval shipyards, there was no impression of crisis. Nor was there such an impression in the railroad yards, where the shortage was not of goods for the cars but of cars for the goods.

There was an American depression after the peace, and it then seemed as if America would follow the English pattern. But that time passed, and this country is not accustomed to pause for reflections on the history of yesterday.

Now the factories grow progressively larger. I have just visited the central electric plant of the Edison Electrical Illuminating Company in South Boston. A vast open space holds its supply of coal, which is assured to it by a contract with a mine in West Virginia; it keeps always a three-months reserve on hand, and consequently has no cause for concern in the fuel shortage.

I was led first through the old factory, twenty years of age but with the machines still in use. Three years ago, however, a new plant was added to it with turbines so powerful that each produces more than all the old ones together. An immense artificial head of water moves the dynamos that serve not only the great city but all of southern Massachusetts. Yet electric traction has its own plants; this one supplies only light and power for factories through numerous substations. In the control room, black and colored lines, traced on a glazed chart, and little lights, made it possible to follow the work of the gigantic network. A few engineers were there, like the officers in the map room of a ship, commanding the lives of millions of men. With a single telephone message they send warning of a weakening of power to the man in the switching room who directs the current to the substations as surely as the dispatcher directs the trains on their way.

Every minute lights mark out in red numerals the output of the plant. Actually, the plant is approaching the limits of its capacity. Next year they will build another twice as powerful, in the outskirts of the city. The Americans have learned by experience that an establishment of this kind doubles its sales every three years. Every three years, therefore, they must double the size of the plant, if they have not in advance made provisions for expansion. Moreover, the war multiplied the number of factories powered by electricity, and the high price and difficulty of procuring coal have increased the consumption of the current. The cost of production has therefore been lowered so much that electricity, almost alone of all products, has not raised its price and is slightly lower in cost than before the war. This low price in turn attracts new consumers, which again diminishes the cost.

As the use of electrical energy grows, so does the use of electric appliances. The General Electric Company in Lynn is not really a factory. It is an industrial city the streets of which are bordered with immense plants of reinforced concrete. These are already inadequate, since there rise before our eyes structures of wood, their light walls temporarily covered with tar paper, which will soon be enormous six or eight story buildings.

Electric trains move about from one building to another or from the buildings to the nearby sea. A quarter hour of rapid travel from the office was not enough to permit us to cover the whole of this Essen of electricity. In a two-hour visit we were only able to catch a glimpse of two or three shops that produced a variety of electrical devices for automobiles, ships, and blast furnaces.

The whole is a triumph for mass production. Immense rooms are filled only with unfinished hubs. At a single blow a single tablespoon of solder attaches eight spokes to these hubs by an ingenious arrangement. Elsewhere, hundreds of women, mostly Slavic, do nothing but attach and disentangle threads. Below, a man must handle some sheet metal plates in which a channel is dug. While the press does its work on the first plate the worker prepares a second, and dips one which has just been stamped into a protective bath. When the press lifts the worker puts aside the finished piece and inserts that which is to be done, then he dips the one held aside into its bath and prepares the one to follow. Three movements, no more, rhythmic, without fatigue and without haste. The man works easily and the work goes quickly. The finished pieces pile up, all alike.

Thousands and thousands of workingmen and women—earning $35, $40 in weekly wages, more for overtime! An internal organization unites the laborers to the life of the factory: councils in each shop, and, on top, three employee delegates who meet with three management delegates in a kind of superior council where decisions are made that concern all. Restaurants, medical service, with X-ray and dental rooms, everything is conceived in the same style. Outside, hundreds of automobiles are lined up. These belong to the toilers, who soon will use them to return to their homes several miles away, consumers themselves of the electrical products they manufacture.

No sign here of a depression. And General Electric is only a part of Lynn, which is primarily a shoe city. And there are many cities like Lynn. Had I been to Schenectady I would have seen electrical factories even more powerful. Where then will one find the crisis? There is no unemployment; on the contrary, there is a dearth of manpower. The restrictive immigration laws begin to be oppressive to the industrialists. If, at times, there is an effort to arouse the sympathies of the American public for the unfortunate people harried by the agents of Ellis Island, if there are campaigns to rescue so many Greeks, or Armenians, it is in part due to the fact that American factories lack human material. This industrial philanthropy is no sign of stagnation.

A view of the statistical evidence confirms this impression. Since the month of January it is apparent that American industry has entered a period of prosperity reminiscent of the best days of 1920. All the indices agree. In the penultimate week of January the number of freight loadings reached 871,000; that is, 131,000 more than the year before, and 68,000 more than the same week in 1920. For the month of January the production of steel reached 2,230,000 tons, twice as much as in January 1922. The United States Steel Corporation worked at 90 per cent of capacity and had a backlog of 165,000 tons in orders.

This tendency continued. In February, the Labor Department announced that American industry was working at 75 per cent of capacity. And the metals were not alone; King Cotton showed the same trends. This year, for the first time in American history, more than 35,000,000 spindles were active, which resulted in an enormous consumption of cotton, 600,000 bales a month. And it was the southern factories, those closest to the source of raw materials, which were primarily responsible for this growth. The accumulated stocks of raw cotton have fallen off;

almost 7,500,000 bales a year ago, they come to no more than 3,500,000 now. By the end of July there will not be 600,000. As for cotton cloth, exports in January came to almost 39,000,000 yards, as against 31,000,-000 in 1922. We will pay more for cotton in Liverpool and in Le Havre this year.

In meat packing, the great industry of the West, Armour lets us know that the volume of business in March was unprecedented in its history. The demand is considerable, and there is full employment in the packing yards of Chicago. I know of not a single industry in which there are complaints. Optimism is thus the dominant note. The position seems even better than in 1920, because the financial situation is healthier and the banks have extended less credit. A recent report of the Federal Reserve Bank of Boston on industrial activity in New England is clearly favorable, and implies that things go as well in the rest of the country. It estimates that the country is rapidly approaching the limits of its industrial capacity and will soon have to resort to overtime.

If, therefore, the United States is passing through a crisis, it is a crisis of prosperity and one that is favorable to the working class. The year 1921 was one of sharp reductions in pay. But the tendency has now been reversed. The rise in prices inevitably led to a rise in wages, without which the purchasing power of the masses would have fallen off so that the industrialists would have been the first to complain.

Because of the shortage of manpower they are forced to pay high rates; a mason and a carpenter earn more now than a professor at Harvard. A large woolen company has just given its employees a 12.5 per cent increase, and has been widely imitated. The threat of strikes converted employers hesitant to follow this tendency. A serious textile walkout was only averted by yielding to the demands of the workers.

Will this prosperity last? People have become very cautious after the severe setback that followed the boom of 1920. They seek guarantees against the consequences of a sudden panic. The federal government in particular has wisely postponed all public works, not absolutely essential, to have them available in periods of depression. The Federal Reserve System has already proved itself, and now guards against any excessive inflation.

The only danger lies in the possibility of overproduction. Industrial activity keeping up with mounting demands resulted in a rise in prices, which in turn led to a rise in wages. The United States is now at the point where wages are pushing up against the price level. It would be well if new increases were to hold off so that the purchasing power of the masses might remain large. Otherwise, consumption would decline and slow down production, a grave affair in view of the expansion in equipment.

There is the danger. The Ford factories in Detroit actually turn out 2,000 cars a day. This output is mentioned because the price of a Ford now is just under $300, a sum many laborers can earn in a month. But when every man in America (and every woman, for these drive with astonishing skill) will have his car, what will happen to the new ones produced? Also, what would happen if the rise in the cost of steel were to prevent Ford from keeping his prices low enough to sell to his 2,000 purchasers a day?

When production slows down, then strikes become a threat. Industrial unrest is particularly ominous in a population of workers who are not exclusively American and the diverse elements of which are beyond the control of the American Federation of Labor. The old Gompers who was carried off by pneumonia last month in New York was not the leader of these men. The king of the unions could do nothing with the fresh immigrants.

Two cases excite public opinion at this moment: that of the Herrin massacre, a savage episode in the last miners' strike in which the strike breakers were assassinated, shot point-blank despite their surrender, and atrociously mutilated by a furious mob; and that of Foster, who has undertaken the job of sovietizing America, as he boasted in court. Into this fear of Bolshevism, which explains certain features of American foreign policy and the severity of the immigration laws, there also enters a large element of real fear of the internal reds, the radicals as they are called here. The members of the I.W.W. and the Moscow agents officially charged with revolutionizing the United States upset not only the federal and state authorities but also the organized labor movement which thinks of evolution within the framework of the constitution.

That is why some Americans are so frightened by the disordered tempos of American life. Even the waves of prosperity in this country have a chill in them. But, for the moment, the existence of that prosperity is undeniable. And if the United States one fine day interests itself again in the affairs of our poor Europe, it will not be to spare its population suffering similar to that which now oppresses England. The Americans can continue to believe, for a long time yet, that they have no need of Europe.

The American farmers are landowners, not tenants. Yet they are not peasants; there is nothing analogous here to our type of small proprietors, nor are there any agglomerations which resemble our villages. There are indeed many places called "villages." But, imagine a road: to the right and the left, along the road and for some distance back away from it, are little houses, generally of wood, sometimes of brick, dispersed, surrounded by lawns and trees; along a part of the road the cluster is more dense—one or more churches, for the little village may contain members of many denominations; a cemetery with simple stones; the school, and, invariably, the public library; a police and a fire station; shops; a gasoline station; almost always a movie; very often a monument to the heroes of the Revolution, of the Civil War, of the World War; statue, cannons, pile of shells or of balls. That is an American village, hardly different from a small city. I forget the inns, their façades covered with ivy, Virginia creepers, or wisteria, square, shadowy, and beflowered. These are sometimes carefully preserved in the style of the eighteenth century, with the room in which Lafayette slept, or Washington, or both. The farm buildings are out in the fields. And the village blacksmith of Longfellow is long since dead, even in the East.

The American farmer among us would be reckoned a great proprietor. There is very little morcellating of the land except in the very old sections of New England. The Puritan was a true agriculturist. The ancient books which describe primitive New England show us a rural population very like that of England at the time. But these little farms were emptied; their owners drifted in ever-greater numbers to the city, to industry. In the northeast the urban population gains increasingly upon the rural, so that many of these abandoned farms are taken up by the French-Canadians. There is, therefore, a drift across the frontier, and certain villages in Massachusetts and Vermont are now given over to the French language.

This situation is peculiar to New England. But the great agricultural lands really begin in northern New York near the Great Lakes. There also has raged the pestilent massacre of the trees. In the vicinity of Buffalo, for instance, only a few isolated clumps, or even just the stumps which no one ever took the trouble to clear, testify to the former splendor of the destroyed forests. It is even worse in the prairie West. Between Chicago and Milwaukee, west of Lake Michigan, is a true steppe, completely bare. There, there are not even villages; only the great farm buildings scattered through the empty spaces through which the electric tram hurtles at top speed. This is land that calls for cultivation on a large scale, for the machine, for uniform mass production.

The essential features of the landscape, that take the place of trees and hills, are the elevators in which the grain is stored. Our agricultural life, economically, centers about the market, the fair; here it turns about the railroad junctions where the wagons line up at the foot of those gigantic edifices, or even about the ports where the lake vessels come to take on cargoes of wheat and corn. Or even around the mill! But what is a mill? Put out of your minds all memories of Europe, of Dutch windmills or those of Sans Souci, sails flapping in the wind, bubbling streams where the wheel turns to the song of the miller, black boats moored on the Hungarian or Slovak banks of the Danube. Imagine instead the banks of the Mississippi, where the pretty queen of the northwest, the twin city of Minneapolis and Saint Paul, offers a charming sight with its parks, its brooks, its lakes, and cascades. Imagine there domesticated rapids, girdled with iron and stone put to the service of the technician. There, at the falls of Saint Anthony, the old French explorers, Father Marquette, Nicolet, and Radisson marveled before the beauties of the creation. Today the father of waters is only a factory worker; the falls have given way to dams, to inclined planes over which flow waters potent with energy. One must go downstream, descend to the beautiful avenues of which we spoke, maintained by a wise and tasteful municipality, to discover the primitive freshness of the deep gorges which Chateaubriand saw only in his dreams.

At the falls rises the mill, a fortress of eight stories. Directly over the river an enormous pneumatic tube pours the grain out of the elevators into the sides of the mill. The grain descends from top to bottom, from story to story, from mill to mill, becoming a finer and finer flour. No creaky millstones, or white powder, only closed chambers of varnished wood with glass windows in which the cylinders turn. There are in this single building 250 of these little mills, and in all 50 "millers" to take care of them. But the term *miller* can scarcely be applied to these mechanics, who follow the movement of the cylinders or of the sorting machines, who check the automatic filling of the paper or cloth sacks, the boxes and the barrels, and who may be seen in off hours playing football in front of the factory.

The elevators, the mills, the giant abattoirs, the meat factories of Chicago or Kansas City, those are the magnetic poles of the farmer, the molding forces of his economic life, at least in the regions I saw. In the South quite different social classes are categorized as farmers: the tobacco, sugar, and above all the cotton planters. But I never ventured into the realm of King Cotton. I have had in mind primarily the farmer of the Middle West in my attempts to understand the position, the mentality, and the tendencies of the agriculturists, who are undoubtedly a fundamental element in the political life of America.

The industrial wealth of the United States must not deceive us. Agriculture is still the greatest American industry. That is why the farmer is the prime element, one might say the backbone of the nation. This is still the first agricultural country of the world.

It is true that this element is on the decline. In New England, of course, one can get an abandoned farm as a country home at a slight cost; but even more generally the land is losing a part of its population. The tillers of the soil were at the last census no longer a majority of the total.

What are the complaints of the farmers who still make up 30 per cent of the active population and who produce about 18 per cent of the national income? They charge that they cannot get a sufficiently remunerative return for their products. That is difficult to believe when one sees the prodigious movements of agricultural goods, fruits, vegetables, and bacon, in the ports and markets of the great cities. The American stomach is blessed with an enormous capacity. The consumption of sugar, for instance, is amazing, and any falling off in the harvest results in a rise in price. It is useless to propose a boycott. I was in New York in front of City Hall where 3,000 mothers had announced they would come to swear to reduce their consumption of sugar; actually some 200 turned out, about as many as the police there to watch them.

But apart from sugar, the products of agriculture are more dependent than those of industry on foreign, and particularly on European markets. The United States could, if need be, absorb all the Fords, but not all the lard of Chicago, nor the wheat, the corn, the grains of the Mississippi Valley. The question of exports is central here.

If the high tariffs lead, by retaliation, to the closing of certain outlets, if the rise in the value of the dollar loses customers for American products, that does not halt a spindle in the immense cotton factories of New England or Carolina. But the farmer cannot regard these developments with the same tranquillity. The result is that, farther away from Europe, more ignorant of European affairs, he is nevertheless more sensitive to fluctuations in the European markets. Politically, he will be more moved by descriptions of the troubled state of European economy. That explains many of the characteristics of the politics of the western senators.

The country finds that it is working only for the industrialists. The latter reap the profits of the ultra-protectionist tariff, of credit facilities. The great reform which created the solid system of Federal Reserve banks is very similar to that which created our Bank of France. Negotiable paper at ninety days is commercial and manufacturing, not farming paper. Furthermore, this reform, in stabilizing the monetary situation and in making the dollar uniform in value, completely put an end to inflation, in which the farmer, here as everywhere, had an interest. The farmer asserts that his income is lower than that of the miners, of the railroad employees, of the factory workers. The only effect of the tariff on his situation has been to raise the price of articles indispensable to him.

The farmers carried on a lively agitation just before the adjournment of Congress. The administration resisted, taking the position that economic theory forbade a paper currency based on agricultural credit, necessarily long-term. But beyond the theory was that reality of politics, the farm bloc which speaks with authority in Washington and before which the administration had to capitulate.

The Federal Reserve Act of 1913 had already provided for the discount of farm paper for a period of not more than six months. But not all the banks had adhered to that system, and the result was that credit in some regions was too tight. In any case, six months are not much in terms of farm credit. A law of 1916 had also helped the producers of cotton, flax, grains, tobacco, and wool, by providing for warehouse receipts negotiable for loans as collateral. In this very year they have even set up twelve federal farm credit banks.

Finally, during the war, the War Finance Corporation aided agricultural exporters as it did others. After the suspension of its operations in May 1920 the corporation was recreated in January 1921, and authorized to make loans to farm banks and to coöperatives. But a wartime institution cannot indefinitely be extended, and a definitive end to its service was provided for by the thirtieth of June of this year. It was time to act.

It was under these conditions that the farm bloc last March pushed to a vote the law permanently creating the twelve federal farm banks. The capital of each, $5,000,000, was to be furnished by the United States Treasury, and the law authorized in addition the creation of corporations with agricultural credit, particularly elevators, with a minimum capital of $250,000. These private corporations could make loans, discount and rediscount on agricultural paper for nine months, on livestock for three years.

There will, therefore, now be a complete separation between the Federal Reserve banks which take only three-month paper and the new banks which receive nine-month or even three-year paper. The latter will play for the farmers the role of credit intermediaries that the Federal Reserve banks play for merchants and industrialists. The new banks are now being organized.

The farmer will, however, not yet be satisfied. He says that the crux of the matter for him is to be able to sell his products at a price that enables him to exist. If he can with his labor earn a profit of only 5 per cent on his capital, he would be better off to invest his money passively. Nevertheless, he has received a great satisfaction. He would get an even greater one were he furnished with manpower, which becomes more and more rare.

35.

SEA DEVIL CONQUERS AMERICA

Felix, graf von Luckner, was born in 1881 and, while still a youth, started his career by working his way around the world as an ordinary seaman. During World War I he was commander of the famous corsair, Seeadler, *which did a great deal of damage to allied shipping. In the 1920's he took to lecturing, and as a lecturer came to the United States on a good-will tour that lasted almost a year; his book,* Seeteufel erobert Amerika *(1928), was the product of this tour.*

The immense volume of traffic in America invariably strikes me with astonishment. In our large cities we have the same means of transportation, but everything here is pitched on a larger scale; matters are more simply, more practically, organized. In the subway, trains rush endlessly uptown and downtown. Expresses which only stop at a few stations swiftly hurry by the slower cars so that passengers in the latter suddenly have the optical illusion of moving backwards. There are no ticket offices in the subway; only a stand at which to change money. Without any officials about, you simply put a five-cent piece into the slot of a turnstile and then can ride anywhere you like, change at will, move from a local to an express, without any control or supervision.

For your nickel you may speed in the express like lightning for enormous distances under the earth. You could even, for the fun of it, travel back and forth if you like—but in America no one does it; after all, time is money. No official is even charged with the job of closing doors, these are operated mechanically by the conductor through compressed air. At certain hours the trains are always overcrowded. At these times I was very much impressed by the self-discipline of the Americans. Without the oversight or supervision of an official, people are altogether self-controlled; they remain patient and accommodating; there are no disorders. Under such conditions how the Berlin underground would resound with groaning and grumbling!

Most imposing of all, however, is the auto traffic. It flows along in four parallel columns, and when the traffic signal changes to a red light it promptly stops to let pass the streams of cross traffic and of pedestrians. All this takes place without blasts of whistling and without a policeman to wave his arms about like a windmill. A gesture of the hand and a tweet are enough; the whistle is reserved for a chase. A wonderful sort of discipline! Traffic really regulates itself to a large extent.

To grasp the magnitude of the automobile problem, one must real-

ize that New York alone has more cars than all of Europe. I am told that
every fourth person here owns a car. Workers and simple people have
their own machines, which they naturally drive themselves. The auto
is not a luxury here; it is in somewhat the same category as a bicycle
among us, a simple means of transportation that makes possible residence outside the city. Those for whom a new vehicle is too expensive
can cheaply buy a used car someone has traded in. Some can even
more cheaply make cars for themselves; they need only go to the great
auto junkyards on the outskirts of the city, collect usable parts from the
old machines abandoned there, and put together their own. This is not
considered illegal robbery but rather a sign of cleverness; a man makes
something useful out of worthless trash.

When I first visited New York, years ago, the skyscrapers were few
in number and were considered quite exceptional; today they determine the character of the city's physical appearance. Whether they are
beautiful or not, I don't know. But they are stupendous and it makes a
deep impression to look down from the thirtieth or fortieth story, to see
little pointed buildings and then realize that these are churches. Above
all, the skyscrapers are necessities in a city like New York in which
so much business is concentrated and which lies on a small rocky
island. Unable to expand in space, it must grow into the air.

To get a single over-all view, we visited the Woolworth Building.
This immense structure of steel and stone, the highest in New York,
was executed in pure Gothic style and dedicated as a cathedral of
commerce. It is 792 feet high, and has 56 stories, with 3 more in the
tower. It has become a sort of trade-mark for New York. In the evening, lit up, it seems fairy-like. The view from the tower is overwhelming. All around are the suburbs; in the distance, the Statue of Liberty
and the great bridges across the East River to Brooklyn. Far below is
the tiny City Hall, and before it at midday is the bustle of an ant house.
Toward Wall Street, downtown, is a little cemetery in which the tomb-
stones seem like tiny pebbles.

It must not be supposed that the skyscrapers are limited to commercial uses. That may have been true to begin with, but they are now
being put up for residential purposes as well, especially in the vicinity
of Central Park. And why not? As far as comfort is concerned it matters
not whether one lives on the second story of an old house or on the
twentieth or thirtieth of a new one; the elevators ceaselessly run up

and down. And such quarters have the advantages of height, which Americans like; they shut out the street noises, are accessible to sunlight and to good fresh air. Rents are, however, not cheap in New York. A six-room apartment in a desirable neighborhood and good house will not be found for less than $3,000 a year.

I was once introduced into a very original kind of home. Some American had the idea of building a little one-story house on the roof of one of these apartment buildings, so that he could have a little garden around it. Up there in the evening it was quite fabulous to sit in the open and to look down upon the sea of lights in the city.

The servant problem is most serious in America. Servile spirits are rare in the United States and must, therefore, be handled with kid gloves. A cook earns at least $80 a month, has her own room and bath, and condescends to do no heavy work. If one reckons in addition that a great many household tasks, such as washing windows, polishing floors, laundry, and even the washing of crockery, are done not by the house servants but by separate employees, and must be paid for, then it will be clear how expensive it is to run a home here.

The consequence is that many families arrange to live in apartment houses. These are like *pensions,* with as many as fifty flats all prepared alike and each of which often has only two rooms and a bath. This arrangement has the advantage of relieving the resident of all sorts of minor expenses, and of freeing his wife of worries about the household, since all the service is provided by the landlord; on the other hand, such dwellings sometimes lack any kind of personal note.

Through invitations, I have, however, gotten to know many such apartments which display the finest personal taste and make truly comfortable and enjoyable homes. When I sit in such a residence opposite the flaming fireplace, see on the walls genuine Titians and Murillos, am surrounded by old French furniture, dine off old Meissen porcelain, and sip a gentle wine from fine gilt glasses, then I might as well be in some ancient palace or in one of the substantial German family mansions. Even though the individual pieces may all have been imported from Europe, the ensemble does not seem ostentatious, but always reflects good taste and expresses the smooth refinement of an older culture. This grace and gentility in the homes of the wealthy we found particularly impressive. The same was true of their meals. The menus of these enormously wealthy people, who could afford twenty courses without blinking an eye, are, by contrast to the elaborateness of our prewar dinners, always simple: even on ceremonial occasions, an appetizer, two courses, and dessert. Many of these homes display a culture already distilled through several generations.

It is, however, believed that there is no aristocracy in this democratic land! In social life, the rich American merchant keeps himself as reserved as his Bremen or Hamburg counterpart. In the field of finance there are also signs of an aristocracy of birth. Already many rest their pretentions to special positions not only on the power of their wealth, but also on the genealogy of their families. Those who can display their descent from one of the immigrants who landed from the *Mayflower* in Plymouth Bay in 1620 are as proud of it as are our nobles of family trees that go back for centuries. Consciousness of heritage, pride in the traditions of a family, whether its generations number ministers, scholars, merchants, farmers, or noblemen, is a sentiment rooted in the human heart; no democratic republic can root it out.

In America, the matter has naturally also its comic aspect. Anxiety for social distinction induces many to trick themselves out in feathers that do not belong to them. In the quest for worthy ancestors there is much concern over genealogy. A New York humorous journal recently printed a picture of the *Mayflower* as it must have been to hold the ancestors of all those who claim descent from it—piled high with passengers to the top of its masts.

I must also say a few words of the great influence, even more than with us, of the cinema, or, as they call it, the movies. The external magnificence of these buildings is striking, and by far surpasses that of the theaters. The movies here, unlike ours, show not only films but also personal presentations, so they are closer to what we call "variety." We recently visited the Roxy, a palace not approached in splendor even by the New York Metropolitan Opera House. We were fortunate to have secured our tickets in advance, since there were almost 2,000 people waiting in six lines before the six box offices. Pages led us through wide corridors, up steps laid with thick carpets, and showed us to our places. The sight of the great magically lighted space is impressive. One seems to be in a palace of Louis XIV.

As we entered, an orchestra of 110 men were playing a selection from one of the Beethoven symphonies. Then the whole orchestra, the 110 men and their instruments, conductor and all, slowly and quietly sank into some underworld. To take its place, three great organs rose out of the depths. Skillfully played by three artists, their mighty tones filled the vault of the theater. Then the orchestra once more emerged from the pit to accompany a dance by a chorus dressed as soldiers and sailors and their girls. From time to time individual soloists came forth to sing and dance, among them a genuine Bavarian clog dancer.

Then followed the feature film, *What Price Glory?* This was a story of the World War. Its theme was the demonstration that this struggle, unlike earlier ones, did not involve personal bravery so much as the superiority of machines and the capacity of men to operate as masses. In the three months (August to October 1918) in which the Americans really participated in the war, they lost more than 300,000 men, whence the title. Bayonet charges and similar battle scenes were shown with shocking realism. The movie could not be considered anti-German, but rather seemed to take a neutral position. For instance, as the American company came back, its ranks thinned out, it received a contingent of replacements, very young recruits. The subtitle read, "Cannon fodder." As the captured Germans march to the rear, with tired steps, the young orderly of the American captain laughs; in a flash the captain strikes him to the earth. The whole picture was brutal but true, patriotic but not chauvinistic.

I suppose I should set forth my investigations into the subject of prohibition. Here is a new experience, at a club's celebration. Each man appears with an impressive portfolio. Each receives his glass of pure water; above the table the law reigns supreme. The brief cases rest under the chairs. Soon they are drawn out, the merry noise of popping corks is heard, and the guzzling begins.

Or, I come to a banquet in a hotel dining room. On the table are the finest wines. I ask, "how come?" Answer: "Well, two of our members lived in the hotel for eight days and every day brought in cargoes of this costly stuff in their suitcases." My informant was madly overjoyed at this cunning.

My first experience with the ways of prohibition came while we were being entertained by friends in New York. It was bitterly cold. My wife and I rode in the rumble seat of the car, while the American and his wife, bundled in furs, sat in front. Having wrapped my companion in pillows and blankets so thoroughly that only her nose showed,

I came across another cushion that seemed to hang uselessly on the side. "Well," I thought, "this is a fine pillow; since everyone else is so warm and cozy, I might as well do something for my own comfort. This certainly does no one any good hanging on the wall." Sitting on it, I gradually noticed a dampness in the neighborhood, that soon mounted to a veritable flood. The odor of fine brandy told me I had burst my host's peculiar liquor flask.

In time, I learned that not everything in America was what it seemed to be. I discovered, for instance, that a spare tire could be filled with substances other than air, that one must not look too deeply into certain binoculars, and that the Teddy Bears that suddenly acquired tremendous popularity among the ladies very often had hollow metal stomachs.

"But," it might be asked, "where do all these people get the liquor?" Very simple. Prohibition has created a new, a universally respected, a well-beloved, and a very profitable occupation, that of the bootlegger who takes care of the importation of the forbidden liquor. Everyone knows this, even the powers of government. But this profession is beloved because it is essential, and it is respected because its pursuit is clothed with an element of danger and with a sporting risk. Now and then one is caught, that must happen *pro forma* and then he must do time or, if he is wealthy enough, get someone to do time for him.

Yet it is undeniable that prohibition has in some respects been signally successful. The filthy saloons, the gin mills which formerly flourished on every corner and in which the laborer once drank off half his wages, have disappeared. Now he can instead buy his own car, and ride off for a weekend or a few days with his wife and children in the country or at the sea. But, on the other hand, a great deal of poison and methyl alcohol has taken the place of the good old pure whiskey. The number of crimes and misdemeanors that originated in drunkenness has declined. But by contrast, a large part of the population has become accustomed to disregard and to violate the law without thinking. The worst is, that precisely as a consequence of the law, the taste for alcohol has spread ever more widely among the youth. The sporting attraction of the forbidden and the dangerous leads to violations. My observations have convinced me that many fewer would drink were it not illegal.

And how, it will be asked, did this law get onto the statute books?

Through the war. In America there was long a well-developed temperance movement and many individual states already had prohibition laws. During the war it was not difficult to extend the force of those laws to the whole of the United States. Prohibition was at first introduced only for the period of the war. For the mass of the people it was very surprising when Congress in 1920 adopted the eighteenth amendment to the Constitution which made it a crime to manufacture, transport, or sell intoxicating liquor. The dry states had imposed their will on the whole Union.

On the way from Pittsburgh to Charleroi by car we passed the spot where, a little earlier, an armored car with a load of gold had been blown into the air with dynamite and robbed. That sort of thing happens here not only in the wild West but also in a highly civilized state like Pennsylvania. The criminals in America prefer to act on a large scale. They don't trouble with trifles; when they take a risk, they prefer it to pay well.

These daring adventurers do not always work with such terrible instruments as dynamite. A short time ago they played a trick on a bank that gave many Americans an understanding smile. Late one Sunday night a bank director is met in his country home by a gentleman, a revolver in hand, who says, "Follow me, and don't forget to bring the key to the bank vaults." The poor devil had no alternative but to go along and unlock the vault as directed. But his key did not open the inner door, and he told the robber so. "Thank you," says the latter, "we'll manage that too." A second director brought to the bank in the same manner by a confederate supplies the key, $800,000 are abstracted, and the two officials are locked in the safe. Later, a newspaper receives a telephone call that the two directors have absconded with a large sum. The police send out an alarm for the two embezzlers and keep up the search until Monday morning when the directors were released from their exhausting confinement. The thieves were naturally by then far away. They took with them, apart from the cash, recognition of a job well-organized and well-done.

Another problem with which America must cope is much more difficult and much more vital, that of the Negroes. Originally brought to the South from Africa to work as slaves in the cultivation of tobacco, the Negroes have, from the natural fecundity of their race, grown greatly in number and spread rapidly, even in the North. They now

make up one-sixth or one-seventh of the population of the United
States. The distribution is not even, varying from 1 per cent in Massachusetts to 60 per cent in Mississippi. They have recently begun to
move into the industrial centers of the United States, drawn there during the war by the acute need for manpower. I was constantly impressed in New York with the extent to which their number had grown
since my earlier visit. They now take up whole blocks of the city and
form a separate Negro district. Not less significant is the fact that they
are making undeniable economic progress, marked among other things
by the establishment of several banks. They have also made a considerable spiritual advance; the schools and universities for Negroes, which
open to them the riches of European culture, are good signs. Nevertheless, I have heard many Americans despair of an adequate solution to
this problem.

36.

MAN AND MASSES IN THE UNITED STATES

*Ernst Toller (1893–1939) belonged to the romantic generation of
German intellectuals who looked hopefully for the emergence of a new
society and were bitterly disappointed by what finally appeared in the
1920's and 1930's. As a young man he studied in Grenoble and wandered through southern France and Italy. When World War I broke
out he enlisted in the German army and was wounded. While conva-
lescing he resumed his studies at Munich and Heidelberg, but became
interested in socialism and participated actively in organizing the workers of Munich. He was prominent in the abortive Communist revolution
in Germany and, in 1919, was imprisoned. Thereafter his activities were
primarily literary. He became well known for dramas which attempted
to assess the effect upon human beings of mass civilization. He was not
completely satisfied with what he saw in either Russia or America,
societies which he compared in the travel notes of his volume,* Quer
Durch Reisebilder und Reden *(1930). Hitler's coming seemed to destroy
all hope. On the eve of a new war, Toller committed suicide.*

At first I thought that the position of the workers was incomparably
better in America than in Germany, and their income distinctly su-

perior. Before long I saw the reverse side of prosperity. After the war the United States was the great conqueror. It controlled the European market, and could therefore produce on an enormous scale. There was practically no unemployment; wages were high. Everybody hoped to be rich enough in a few years time to buy, on the installment system, his own house, his own car, his own piece of land. The expression "Every man has a chance," properly translated, "Every man can become rich," dominated people's minds. Everyone gambled—bootblacks, elevator boys, workmen, barbers, artists. The most important part of the newspaper was the financial section. Whether stocks went up or down was more interesting than European politics. Savings might be doubled in a day.

Nothing was impossible in a land like this, where things developed, changed, and were transformed on a gigantic scale. Nothing grew old. Houses, fifteen or twenty stories high, were torn down after ten years and skyscrapers of forty or fifty floors built in their place. A new main road for motorcars came into existence and, with it, artificial brooks, woods, and meadows.

The businessmen, wiser than their European counterparts, supported the universal mania for speculation; they offered their laborers shares at low prices, learned how to interest great masses of workers in their profit systems, and created the illusion of "work and profit-sharing." In many factories 25 per cent of the shares were in the hands of the workmen. Today things are beginning to change. The last stock exchange collapse was a symptom. Yes, in some branches of industry —automobiles, for instance—the germ of the coming crisis is observable.

In comparison with Germany, the rate of wages is extraordinarily high. There are workmen who get $.30, $.38, $.40 an hour; others $1.50. Best off are the builders, tool-makers, and printers. In the North laborers earn an average of $1,600 a year; in the South an average of $600.

Sometimes I lived with workmen. They had their own houses, which would no doubt be called small villas in Germany; well-appointed bedrooms and living rooms, kitchens with electric refrigerators, and baths. The furniture was cut to a common pattern, but, according to German notions, middle-class. Every house had large radio sets, a phonograph, and even a player-piano. The workmen ate better than their comrades in Germany; they were obviously used to comfort, they demanded comfort. They had their own cars, not only second-hand cars, not only Fords, no, expensive standard makes. In one case the auto had cost $1,000, in another $1,200.

A family in Rochester, where the daughter and father both worked, possessed two cars, one belonging to each breadwinner. The tax amounts to only a few dollars. Gasoline is half as dear as it is in Germany.

But now for the other side. If a workman gets ill or loses his job he has practically no protection. He must spend his savings and finally fall back on private charity. All toilers are not so well off as those whose guest I was. I have also been in parts of the town where there are wretched dwellings. I saw the district round Pittsburgh in which thousands of people are engaged in the great Bethlehem steel works—slums without comfort and just as filthy as many of the dwellings in the Ruhr. Characteristically, laborers in steel mills and in mines, who do the heaviest jobs, are the worst paid.

A woman in Pittsburgh, a private social worker, took me around and showed me "cases." There was a man who had worked seventeen years for the same firm and had paid the private insurance regularly. When he fell ill he received support for a short time. Then the company attorney and the company doctor made out that his illness and his work had nothing to do with each other and the support was withdrawn. Now the man is left with his wife and six small children and would literally starve if he had not the good luck to be a "case" for the charitable ladies of the town. But how many are not "cases"! Only in the light of such misery is the high rate of crime, burglary, and theft understandable.

The trade unions are tamer than in Germany. Nevertheless, many factories will not engage men who belong; Ford, for instance. The American labor movement, through the participation of the United States in the Great War, has forfeited the power it had acquired after 1900. It is no longer a political force, nor a spiritual factor in the public life of the country. The Socialist Party, a group of liberal social reformers rather than a socialist union, has not one representative in the Senate. The I.W.W., a revolutionary syndicalist organization, feared after the war, was repressed by a brutal campaign of persecution. The official unions, representatives during the war of American chauvinism, are aristocratic institutions which not every worker may join; a fee of some hundreds of dollars is required for right of entry and for a share in their benefits. Even dollars do not help the Negro; he would not, in any case, be taken on. The opposition unions, which make a point of approaching the Negroes, try to get hold of the radical elements. Splits right and left, warring factions, and exclusions condemn the numerically small Communist Party to impotence. Whereas in European countries the economic crisis that set in just after the war hastened the radicalization of the workers, the unlimited prosperity of America in the same period had the opposite effect. Only today, with the economic crisis, is a change setting in. Revolution will not flame out at the end of this crisis, but the Socialist and Communist parties will crystallize afresh and radical newspapers will be established.

The bourgeois newspapers are on their guard against socialist activities, and show not the least sign of objectivity. "Radical," "Socialist," "Bolshevist," are words which they hate like the plague, and no crime is too abominable to be linked up by them with radicalism, socialism, and bolshevism.

We travel by ferryboat across the bay from San Francisco. Then a car takes us out to San Quentin prison, through the hilly landscape of Marin County, rich in eucalyptus, laurel, and redwood trees. We pass the first lookout tower, mounted with machine guns. Later, other towers rear up. We come to the gates; we have to register our names. We cross a courtyard to another gate. We are led to an office. A quarter of an hour later we see Tom Mooney in the visiting room. The prisoners sit at a long table; opposite them, the visitors. The prisoner may not lean over a small partition made of wood rods in the middle of the table. At a raised desk sits the guard.

Tom Mooney has lived thirteen years in prison. He went in as a young man: today he is gray and his face is ridged with lines. Innocent, this man remains in prison. America—and the world knows it—keeps him still within prison walls.

Mooney was one of the most active socialist agitators of western America. He organized many workers, led strikes, was one of the best hated of men. Detectives hunted him but always lacked an excuse to arrest him.

On July 20, 1916, the nationalistic parties demonstrated on a grand scale for American entry into the war. A bomb exploded. Ten people were killed. Some days after the event a man named McDonald declared that he had seen Tom Mooney near the scene of the outrage. When Mooney learned of the accusation he went at once to the police. He was arrested, and after a grotesque trial was sentenced to life imprisonment. Protestations of innocence availed him nothing. The witnesses for the defense were suspected by the district attorney and arrested. Press photographs, which distinctly showed Tom Mooney on the balcony of a house far from the scene of the outrage attempt, did not help him. When these pictures were enlarged a short time after the verdict, a street clock revealed the time; the bomb had been thrown six minutes later. As it was impossible for anyone to run in six minutes from the house where Mooney was to the scene of the crime, Mooney's innocence was self-evident. But even this irrefutable evidence made no difference.

American public opinion began to be interested; committees were formed; liberal newspapers took Mooney's part. When documents came to light showing that McDonald, the witness for the prosecution, had been bought, the judge and the jury who condemned Mooney admitted they no longer believed in his guilt. But Tom Mooney remained in prison and with him the socialist Billings, equally innocent.

The cry for justice grew louder. His own judge, Franklin A. Griffin, spoke at large meetings and called upon the governor of California to rectify the injustice.

Three governors followed each other.

Tom Mooney remained in prison.

Six years ago a man named Smith confessed on his deathbed that he had thrown the bomb and that Mooney and Billings had nothing to do with the attempt.

Tom Mooney remained in prison.

He did not break down; through the years he fought for his rights with all his might. As he shook my hand I felt that here was a real man.

"What do they want from me?" he asks. "Shall I prove that somebody else made the attempt and not I? Is it my duty to discover the culprit? It is clear that I had nothing to do with it. The guilt is now fastened on a dead man, known to them for six years, and they wish to make an inquiry into whether his confession tallies with the truth. That may take years. I ask nothing except an inquiry into whether the pro-

ceedings which condemned me were in accordance with law and justice, and whether the documents I produced as evidence of my innocence were examined. If the governor decides in the negative, and he
must decide in the negative, it is his duty to set me free. Most of all, I
would prefer a new trial. But according to American law all doors to
new proceedings are closed. The mercy which assumes my guilt, I renounce. For thirteen years I have been in prison, and if I had to stay
here as long again, I would not cease to demand justice."

I told Mooney that his case and Billings' were known in Germany,
and that there, too, people protested against their incarceration.

"What do you do here?" I asked him.

"I have to peel potatoes."

In the visiting room, near Mooney, sits McNamara, who has already
spent nineteen years in prison. He belonged to the anarchist group
which blew up the Times Building in Los Angeles in 1911. The law
had no proof of his guilt. A bribed employee of the defendant stole
documents from his safe which demonstrated McNamara's participation. In order to save twenty-five men who had also been accused, Mc-
Namara declared that his brother, Smith, and himself were the only
perpetrators. For nineteen years these men have been in prison. In all
other cases prisoners would have been reprieved after so long a period
of punishment.

McNamara tells me that he is engaged in bringing food to men condemned to death.

"How many men condemned to death are there in the prison?"

"Sixteen. On December 9, several will be hanged."

In New York men are burned in an electric chair. In California they
are hanged.

Later on I looked over the prison. It is designed for 2,400 prisoners;
about 4,300 are now packed into it. American opinion does not inquire
into the cause of the increase in crime. It comforts itself with the belief
that only "bad people" become lawbreakers. It does not see that the
economic situation, the ever-increasing unemployment, can in any way
be blamed.

All prisoners wear uniform blue-gray suits. They work in various
workshops. Every prisoner must reach a certain daily quota before he
is allowed to leave the workshop. Work for private industry is not undertaken; only work for the state.

At first all prisoners work in the din of the dirty weaving rooms. "Here they become soft-boiled," say the convicts. In their time off they may smoke and play football and baseball. But only the favored ones enjoy these privileges; there is no room for the others in this over-crowded prison. They are herded together in yards where not a blade of grass is seen, while outside spreads the glowing landscape.

The prisoners all have their meals together. I saw a room in which 2,000 could be seated. Men of all races are there—White, Negro, Mexican, Chinese, Japanese, Indian, Greek, Italian, French, German. They are housed in pairs in narrow built-in cubicles which are separated not by doors along a corridor but by a grid, and are illuminated night and day. Illuminated night and day—never isolated; that sounds like an advantage. It is hell. The most frightful disciplinary punishment is confinement in a dark cell underground, into which fresh air is pumped through a ventilator in the corridor.

Before we leave the prison the warder leads us to the death cell and to the gallows. The day before a prisoner is hanged he is conducted to this cell, a large wooden cage in a barred room, observable from all sides. In front of the cage guards sit day and night; it is their job to see that the prisoner does himself no injury thereby to "deprive the law of its right." A year ago a prisoner attempted to commit suicide two days before his execution. He was taken to the hospital and carefully brought back to health. Then they hanged him.

In the same room there is a locker in which is kept a stock of ropes. I counted about twenty. Attached to each was a weight, the purpose of which is to reduce the possibility that the rope might stretch during the execution. The weights are of different degrees of heaviness; they are intended for bodies of different sizes. Every man gets his own rope, which is afterwards burned. In another corner of the room stands a harmonium.

In answer to my question, a warder said: "Sometimes prisoners wish to be hanged to music. Oh, they're treated well. What they want, they get. One asked for jazz, so the prison band played dances for him. They get better food than we guards—even chicken."

I enter the cages. In the drawer of the table two names have been scratched with a pencil: Johnny Malone, Frenchy Lapiere. Both had been hanged a few months earlier, one because he had killed his wife, the other because he had slain a policeman. One of the most recent of those who awaited the gallows in this cell was the nineteen-year-old Edward Hickman.

A sliding door divides this room from the execution chamber where the gallows is erected. Thirteen steps, "the last mile," lead up to it. Before the prisoner goes to the gallows his arms and hands are bound to his body with a strap, and when he stands on the deathtrap his feet are tied together with another strap. This is done so that the body shall not writhe. Should a prisoner become unconscious before the execution, a black stretcher, to which straps are attached, is buckled to his back so that the body remains upright. Right and left of the gallows are three rocking chairs for the more important officials.

Two men can be hanged at the same time. As soon as the prisoners stand on the deathtrap, black caps are put over their heads. The hangman puts the nooses round their necks and draws them tight, close to the ears. In a small space on the gallows platform are three threads fastened to a board. One of them is attached to the rope loaded with the iron ball; the trap on which the prisoners stand suddenly drops, plunging them into the depths. In front of the three threads stand three guards who, at the command, cut them. None of the warders is supposed to know which released the death trap. On the board notches made by many executions are visible.

My guide tells me that he has witnessed many hangings.

"In what condition are the men when they go to the gallows?"

"All right. I saw only a few faint. Most of them walk quite stolidly up the thirteen steps."

"Do they die at once?"

"Hanging is a splendid method, much more humane than the electric chair. With one jerk the neck is broken. Their limbs go on quivering, and that lasts fourteen to sixteen minutes, and that's why we fix their arms and feet with straps, so that they don't strike or kick out; but they don't feel any more."

We pass by the section where the candidates for death wait. In front of each cell hangs a flower pot. One of the prisoners condemned to death nodded to us; another, as I paused, laughed shrilly. Flower pots, chicken dinners, and music at the gallows—that's civilization.

In front of the prison shines, in unending blue, the Golden Gate.

How would you picture the founder of a Church? Lean, the ascetic face framed by a quivering beard, wearing a hair shirt, the loins engirdled with a cord? You must revise your picture.

In Los Angeles lives Aimee Semple McPherson, who would certainly carry off the prize in any ordinary beauty competition. Her blonde hair has the gleam which so delights the hairdressers; dark lashes shade her large blue eyes; her nose is strong but noble; her lips are finely set, her hands narrow, the fingers long. She wears a white cape, the folds of which are very decorative. On her bosom gleams a large white cross worked with silver thread; on her left shoulder a bunch of orchids. Her hair is carefully waved; well-applied make-up gives her face the sweetness necessary in America; her hands are well cared for and manicured.

She is the founder and prophetess of a large church which numbers thousands of adherents, and which is called the Church of the Smiling Light. How could a church be otherwise named in a country where the dead are made up? "Keep smiling," even in death, is the motto here.

Aimee is the daughter of a farmer. Brought up in the solitude of the Canadian prairie, at the age of sixteen she made the acquaintance of a Baptist, fell in love at first sight, married him, and went with him to China to win the heathen to the eternal bliss of the evangelical heaven. Her husband died, she returned to America, met McPherson, lived with him for a year, unhappily; separated from him and, supported by her mother, began to preach, in halls, theaters, and churches. Ultimately she gained a parish. Rich adherents gave her money to build the Angels' Church in Los Angeles, which can accommodate a congregation of some five thousand.

Behind the pulpit is the platform, fitted up with all the latest technical contrivances. Right and left rise tiers for the choir of male and female angels, hundreds strong.

Aimee heals by prayer. Aimee heals by the laying on of hands. The farmers of the West revere her as a saint. For eight years she behaves like a saint. But Aimee is too young and too beautiful to remain always a saint. One day she vanishes. She is seen one morning on the beach of Santa Monica with her lady secretary, bathing in a fashionable costume —and is never seen again. The secretary is questioned, but can give no information—Aimee has vanished.

Grain Elevator and Flour Mill: Focal Points of American Agriculture

The Old-Time Worship: Aimee McPherson Ministers to the Converted

Believers go in their thousands to the seashore, kneel down and pray for Aimee's soul. Divers seek her at the bottom of the sea; two men lose their lives in an effort to save her. Airplanes circle about the spot where she vanished; the aviators throw Aimee's favorite flowers into the sea. Aimee is reckoned as dead. The one who mourns her most is her mother. But in the end the old lady is an American—she goes to the life-insurance company and draws the not inconsiderable consolation.

Some weeks later great jubilation breaks out in the Church of the Smiling Light. Joyful messages are hurried to Aimee's mother. Aimee writes to say that she is alive; Mexican bandits had robbed her and held her prisoner in the California desert, but with the help of God she had broken free; like the children of Israel she has wandered many miles through the dusty wilderness and is now lying in a hospital in Arizona. The police try to catch the bandits. Accompanied by the district attorney, by photographers with movie cameras, Aimee travels back through the desert to the house in which she had languished. But the house is nowhere to be found. Aimee goes back to Los Angeles by a special train, and in a wonderful triumphal procession is conveyed to the church, where she joins with the true believers in thanks to God for her deliverance.

Some reporters, disbelieving heathens, cast doubts on her story, make investigations on their own, let out that her car had been seen in Carmel, that she had passed sweet days of love with her handsome young radio mechanic in a country house in that town. Only tangible evidence is lacking. Then a document in her handwriting, ordering fresh vegetables for dinner in profane words, is found in front of the house in which she had lived. This document is photographed and published.

The authorities take action. Aimee comes to judgment. She denies all. The document is a work of the devil. Smiling scornfully, the district attorney hands it over to the jury, whereupon God has mercy upon the saint; the document disappears before it has been seen by the last juryman, and Aimee is acquitted. The halo round Aimee's head grows. It is not even dimmed when her adversaries discover that she possesses a private account, with a nice fat balance. This money, so her enemies say, she appropriated from the subscriptions given by the faithful for social work. Even this charge misses fire. A dozen adherents declare that they have given her the money against a rainy day. Aimee remains unconquerable. Every day she preaches in the church.

I went twice to her services; once I heard her speak on the radio. Theatrical producers make a pilgrimage to Aimee and learn the art of production from her. I have never witnessed more impressive spectacles. One Sunday evening she presented, with her choir, an oratorio entitled "Christ the Bridge." The words were written by herself; the settings were designed by her; gestures and movements were arranged by her—but the music was borrowed from *The Merry Widow*. For her chorales she always turns to the melodies of popular songs; no operetta is safe.

In this oratorio Jesus appears—as Carpenter, as Shepherd, as Teacher, as Fisherman, as Sailor, as Doctor, as Everyman, as Servant, as the King of Kings. Across a bridge, which rises behind the altar, He steps slowly forward, always in the costume demanded by the verse, while the chorus, adorned with ever-fresh symbols and instruments, accompany Him. For example, to the tune of "Vilja, Vilja, my wood-maiden," Aimee and the chorus sing:

> *Sailor, sailor, sailor,*
> *Sailor from Galilee!*
> *Oh, oh, oh!*
> *Darkness is falling,*
> *Tempests are rising,*
> *Oh, oh, oh!*

All singers, male and female, wear sailor caps on their heads and carry oars in their hands, so that they can control the waves with vigorous movements. Aimee also wears a cap, but hers is made of silk and is richly embroidered. She wears hers at a more coquettish angle than the others; her oar is bigger and costlier and glitters with paste diamonds. Aimee's adornments are always more splendid than the adornments of the chorus girls. If they wear paper crowns, Aimee, as a sign of her chosen mission, wears a gilded crown agleam with gems.

Aimee not only sings, she conducts the choir; she "produces" the actor who plays the role of Jesus; she keeps her eye on the microphone which carries her words to hundreds of thousands; for Aimee is a modern woman who understands advertising, and has an hour on the radio.

Once a week she exhibits the sick whom she has healed. Indeed, Upton Sinclair told me that she engages lots of the healed at a good daily fee; but then, as you know, Upton Sinclair is a heathen. Women, men, children appear on the stage. Each testifies that he has been cured of a great illness by Aimee's hand alone. "Consumption of the spine," breaks in Aimee, "and now quite healthy. *Isn't that lovely?* Tumor, and cured. *Isn't it beautiful?*"

Every Thursday evening Aimee baptizes, for, says she, the baptism of children is valueless. She sprinkles grownups with water. We must step into the water; in the water one is buried with the Lord, and like Him is resurrected. Every year she baptizes three thousand persons. The floor of the stage sinks, a large swimming pool is rolled in; Aimee changes her clothes, and supported by a young man, stands in the water. The convert appears, clothed in a white garment; Aimee and the young man seize him, bend him down, duck him in the water, and lift him out again. The resurrected one flings his arms delightedly on high and cries out in an ecstatic voice: "Hallelujah! Hallelujah!" Sometimes father, mother, and child come; Aimee baptizes all at the same time, and she claps her hands with approval when the converts fall into an ecstasy. But she does not forget to remove the microphone from the pulpit and put it near the swimming pool.

The facial expressions and the gestures of this woman must be seen! She has just raised her hearers and herself to the highest pitch of ecstasy—she sees that the microphone is not fixed in the right position, and with a calculated movement she changes its position; and as she leans toward it she utters a biblical phrase in a more emphatic voice: "Ye who hear me over the radio, soon will ye see me. Shortly a talkie will be made showing our church, and I will see to it that this film is shown in your local theater."

Suddenly the telephone bells ring, for there is also a telephone near the pulpit. Aimee takes up the receiver and announces that three-hundred and sixty veterans of the Civil War are listening in. Hurriedly she turns on a wild patriotic song of prayer for the old graybeards.

Aimee takes care to provide constant entertainment. Solo singers appear, the band plays symphonies composed by Aimee herself and jazz dances. On the stage living pictures are shown amid changing scenery. These living pictures accompany her preaching. What would happen, she preached on one occasion, if Eve had not eaten the apple? The red curtain of the stage opens. In front of a flowery landscape stand Adam and Eve. Adam in a brown leather farmer's kit; Eve in a dress of gold and with a wreath on her head. Aimee turns to the picture, claps her hands. "You look delightful, quite charming!" She turns back to the congregation. "Eve gave Adam the apple." On the stage Adam takes the apple and swallows it greedily! "And naturally Eve said: 'Leave me some of it,' but Adam had devoured it, stalk and core." And even this sin had its meaning. If Eve had not sinned we should not have had the Bible and should not have got on familiar terms with God.

What would have happened if Jesus had never been born? We should not have Christmas celebrations in America! We are the grandest, cleanest, most God-beloved of nations; nobody else knows as we do how to give Christmas presents.

What would have happened if God had not come to Sister Aimee McPherson? What indeed! She tells her life story; she praises herself; she begins to sing, and she closes with the cry: "Who will pray with Sister Aimee McPherson?"

She turns to the first balcony, to the second, to the orchestra.

"Every man who is happy, say 'Amen.'"

"Amen!" rings out.

"Every man who loves Jesus, say 'Hallelujah!'"

"Hallelujah!" rings out.

"Raise your hands high, you in the second balcony."

"Now those in the first."

The hands of the faithful go quickly up.

In the spring Aimee is going to Palestine. She has chartered a ship, and intends to go with her archangels through the sacred places, singing and glorifying. Cook's, who have given her preferential terms, will conduct the tour.

The *World Almanac* notes two hundred and eleven churches in America. The number of sects is legion. Each imagines itself a manifestation of holy truth. It, and only it, leads its adherents into a paradise of human and celestial bliss. Piety and business acumen, devotion and self-advertisement, peasant shrewdness and naïvete all combine to make a most curious structure.

In the advertising columns of the *Los Angeles Times* one reads: "Miss Leila Castberg preaches in the Church of Divine Omniscience and (in parenthesis) progressive thoughts on the essential truths of Christ in dynamic and powerful form." She founded a club in Hollywood known as "The Lonely," and every now and again arranges special "Salvation services." "Even those sick unto death may be made whole."

"In the Church of the Universalists you will learn how to banish ugliness from your lives. Sheldon Shopards will show you how to make your life melodious. Make an effort to come on Sunday and you will see, at the same time, the drama of 'The Prophet of the Street.' You will be able to study twelve characters. You will also hear songs. Come! Universalism is the very thing for you."

"Hear John Wesby Lee! He preaches in the Gospel Tabernacle three times every Sunday on Carnal Abstinence."

"Would you like to learn who divided the Red Sea? Bob Schuler will give you the answer. If you are ill, tune in to KGF."

Everywhere these sects are subsidized by rich people; every church has as its patron saint, its own little Rockefeller. An excellent antidote against discontent, despair, and rebel tendencies! For the poor in spirit these hours of devotion, with music and plays, mean a change from the dreadful monotony of American workdays and Sundays. Here people, released from the fetters of mechanical habits, may let themselves go; here they may find a substitute for alcohol, morphia, cocaine, and sexual intoxication.

Douglas Fairbanks and Mary Pickford have had the courage to make a talkie out of the *Taming of the Shrew*. The attempt is a complete failure. In spite of a good deal of Shakespeare's verse, nothing of Shakespeare's spirit remains. This example demonstrates better than any theory where the limits of the talking film are fixed. A work written for the stage cannot simply be transferred to the screen. The stage has laws formed and developed over thousands of years; the talking film, which has burst through the boundaries of time and space, has yet to find its laws.

On the whole, the talkies are artistically and technically a backward step. They repeat the mistakes and stupidities which the silent film made in the first years of its development. Dozens of new talkies are

produced every month in America. The worst trash, the sickliest ro-
manticism, the stupidest make-believe tumble over one another. If only
they were amusing! But they are boring and soporific. The inevitable
naked chorus-girls' legs; always the same stupid love chatter, always
the same happy ending. In answer to my inquiry as to why the happy
ending had been raised to an absolute law, a producer in one of the
largest studios in Hollywood said: "The American public demands it.
They want to find in the movies the justification of their lives. They
want to be assured that their hard struggle for existence has some
idealistic purpose behind it."

The answer did not convince me. It is part of American "Cant."
The producers father their own wishes on the public. True, America is
a young nation, and young nations, like young men, like to foster the
illusion of eternal life, in their dreams to soften the hard lines of reality.
They lie about social disharmonies and spiritual conflicts; they shut
themselves off from the inexorableness of cosmic destiny and of death.
Is it not noteworthy that every corpse in America is embalmed, that
when a man is lying in his coffin wadding is stuck into his mouth to
puff out the sunken cheeks, and that he is then made up?

Of the dozens of American talkies which I saw, one stands out as
definitely a great performance—the Negro film, *Hallelujah*. The producer is King Vidor, whom we in Germany know as the creator of *The
Great Parade,* and who is undoubtedly the most distinguished American producer. Every one of these magnificent Negro actors is an amateur discovered by King Vidor. What faces! What gestures! What
songs! What dances! What choral singing! They are splendid in their
wildness, their naturalness, their creative grief. *Hallelujah* shows the
greatest possibilities of the talking film. If producers, actors, and authors master film technique and "the word," they will turn out talkies
to take a place as works of art beside those of the theater. I lay stress on
"the word," for the spoken word must find its own peculiar power, its
own style.

The talking film has two great possibilities: imaginative and documentary. For some weeks there has existed on Broadway a film-
theater called the Newsreel. It exhibits nothing but news from all over
the world. The newspaper has become alive. If one reads, over one's
breakfast coffee, that, in the words of Goethe, far away in Turkey people are fighting one another, one is not particularly disturbed. But when

the news comes in the form of pictures, sounds, and words, the visions compel one to share the destiny of men who work and suffer in the furthermost corners of the earth. In other words, this living newspaper, like all newspapers, has an important political function. What is shown and what is not shown, what is photographed and how it is photographed, are matters of importance. I foresee a time when these talking-screen newspapers will be on the Left or on the Right in politics. These are true documents, which might bring nations closer together, but which in unscrupulous hands might just as easily serve to alienate peoples!

Even in elections the talkies are pressed into service. In the New York mayorality election, tens of thousands of people blocked Broadway of an evening. Across a traffic island gleamed a white screen. On the screen pictures flickered; the pictures began to speak. Favorite singers sang couplets; bands played shrill jazz tunes; then the candidate, Mr. Jimmy Walker, appeared on the screen, smiled, bowed, and made his great election speech, in which—with a comical mixture of ingratiating, bigoted, philistine, boorish, and jingoistic phrases—the populace was exhorted to elect him, the faithful son of a poor Irishman, to be the Mayor of this City, chosen of God, the most beautiful and richest ever built. Pictures followed which showed with blatant bombast how many subways, skyscrapers, museums, Mr. Walker had personally built up to now. Finally, the American comedian, Eddie Cantor, appeared and in a crude but very witty song, jibed at the people who reproached "our Jimmy" with always wearing elegantly creased trousers. The effect was stupendous.

The American talkie is making rapid strides. Money in plenty is there, in such plenty as we in Germany scarcely even dream of. From the venturesomeness and the energy of the Americans we can take example, but the American talkie will not develop beyond the limits imposed by a public opinion dominated by finance. It will become brilliant on the technical side, but as a document, or as an expression of artistic truth, it will accomplish something only in exceptional cases.

A few words about the American theater. I went to New York with great expectations, but found little there. Commercialism is even stronger there than in Berlin. Every production implies the investment of capital. For, apart from a few societies which possess their own buildings and have their own companies, a theater has to be rented, and actors engaged for every new play. Therefore, managers are shy of experiments. Only the New York Theater Guild and a few amateur groups dare to put on plays which differ from the common run, either in form or matter. The theater is overrun with detective stories, drawing-room comedies, revues, and musical comedies.

Ibsen, Strindberg, Wedekind, so far as the American public is concerned, never existed. Therefore, things are regarded as audacious which we in Europe consider practically innocuous. If one attempts to treat sexual conflicts with a tenth of the frankness of Strindberg or Wedekind, that is taken as evidence of boundless courage. This estimate is not surprising in a country where actors are arrested for daring to produce a play the scene of which is a brothel. In God's own country which calls itself the land of freedom, there are few signs of spiritual freedom. You may have read that O'Neill's *Strange Interlude* was banned in Boston. When Bourdet's *La Prisonière* was produced in New York certain members of the public took offense. Whereupon the actors, the producer, and the audience were conveyed in trucks to the police station.

As in the movies, so in the theater; people here want to be sheltered from the conflicts of social life. Both the German and the Russian theaters are much more alive and much more aware of the times in which we live than is the New York theater. The American drama is an outlet for the pleasure-loving, possessing classes. Woe to the authors who show the reverse side of American prosperity. They will not be performed; this is the case with Upton Sinclair. Only small studio theaters will sponsor them.

The theater is always dependent upon the social atmosphere of a country. The unrest which throbs today through the continent of America will ere long be detected in the American theater. Pessimists, whom public opinion in America will not tolerate (a characteristic it shares with Wilhelm II!), have bitter, much needed truths to tell their country.

37.

AMERICAN PARADISES

Egon Erwin Kisch was a Czech, born in 1885. In the years be-
fore World War I, like the other young radicals of central Europe, he
looked to Germany as the source of new ideas. After the war, he be-
came a reporter and turned out a succession of popular travel accounts,
dealing with social conditions in various countries. The book from
which this selection was taken, Paradies Amerika, *was published in*
1930. He spent some time in a Nazi concentration camp. Then, re-
leased, he lived and worked successively in Prague, Paris, and Mexico
City, retreating before the relentless German advance. Peace in 1945
brought him back to Prague, where he died in 1948.

In Los Angeles, before every doorway on Main Street there stands
an elderly woman or a well-dressed man, toying with a crayon. These
people hold sheafs of paper in their hands; they have tickets to distribute, and they wink, whisper, call, shout at every passer-by that seems
tolerably solvent to take one.

These eagerly vended cards impose no obligations on the takers.
They offer instead the privilege of a full-day outing with all expenses
paid in the wonderful, wild, open spaces of California; spaces, the
names of which alone evoke thoughts of silver, gold, diamonds,
the Riviera, Venice, Paradise.

What is more, those who accept such free, romantic journeys in the
busses lined up at the curb expose themselves to no onerous duties.
They merely acquire the right to a good lunch, and a supper, and the
privilege of listening to speeches.

This is all propaganda for some subdivision, a section bought by
a promoter who now wishes to sell his lots. The speculators have already done a great deal for it; perhaps they have even incorporated
the estate, either as a town which will require sewerage, lighting, and
streets, or as a city with waterworks, or most likely as a county.

The real-estate men have chosen aldermen or set up a city council
with a mayor; they have naturally settled the ten families without
whom no charter would be forthcoming; they have divided their future

city into districts: some for busy shopping centers, some for thriving industries, some where each man will happily putter about his own home. Here is the site of the stadium for international matches, here the opera house, and here the cemetery! It is all there. The streets are paved and the street signs up. The lights are on their posts, gutters edge the lots—only the houses are missing.

A single building stands out, a chicken farm now converted into the tract office, from which issue forth prospectuses and bills of sale. This also is the terminal for the bus, the occupants of which, on arrival, can partake of a meal flavored with laudatory declamations.

This fearful gantlet set up by the dense lines of luckless pullers-in, this process of wooing through excursions, is only a mild form of the real-estate propaganda that inundates the unsuspecting visitor to Los Angeles with overwhelming vehemence. The speculators maintain substantial shops in the city; in the windows, fish swim, monkeys exercise, golden pheasants strut about, beavers chase endlessly in a revolving wheel, and anteaters nuzzle at the glass, seeking an exit—all to attract attention. Inside are maps modeled in relief of tomorrow's metropolis; on the walls are plans, blueprints, price charts, and persistent injunctions against passing by the opportunities of a paradise carved out of the naked wilderness.

The most strident propaganda comes by radio. In America, broadcasting stations belong, like the telegraph and the railroads, to private companies. The audience pays nothing for listening; but the spoken advertisement turns broadcasting into a profitable business. Everywhere merchandise is extolled; between the movements of a symphony one can hear the virtues of everything from cigarettes to vacuum cleaners.

But in California there is hardly room for miscellaneous goods. Fully 40 per cent of the advertising time is leased by the automobile industry, and another 40 per cent by land speculators. Hour after hour, Utopia after Utopia is painted in colors so lurid the ether cringes. Of course, it is criminal to lie in a private letter, since the mail is a government service, but it is no crime to lie over the air, to deceive and to mislead millions of listeners. The realty interests of the southwest made such thorough use of this American liberty that a movement started in California to jail the disseminators of false news over the radio.

All this refers to the subdividers themselves, the speculating companies, the owners of the estates. But far more numerous are the agents who establish the personal contact with the purchasers and share in the business on a commission basis. California alone enjoys the services of 62,000 licensed real-estate brokers, officially allowed to deal in land; and many of those employ large staffs.

In flimsy bungalows and in pretentious corner stores they carry on their business, letting the world know that they buy and sell, rent, lease, loan, invest, mortgage, register, give notice, inspect, administer, and collect rents. On blackboards they chalk up their offerings in stuccos, frames, and acres of open land. The city hall and the hall of records are sights; legions of real-estate men rush about the title books in indescribable chaos. To fall into a chance conversation is to risk becoming the owner of a lot. Everyone or a member of his family is in the business.

To accompany a real-estate man through his district is instructive. He is a founder of communities; beside him, Peter the Great is a small operator. The broker feels real pride and affection for his city, for its wonderful parks and skyscrapers; that they exist only on paper seems a minor detail. Self-confidently, he guides his car through the districts south of Los Angeles, Huntington Park, Bell, Maywood, and Southgate. There the streets actually hold real houses and even trolley tracks, although it was all wasteland five or six years ago when $80 could have bought an acre now worth $1500.

Then he moves on to his own domain. This is empty and desolate; but the most critical job has already been done. Yes, the Chinks who formerly cultivated truck gardens here have been dispossessed. Fortunately we have a law here to prohibit the lease of land to foreigners; and no Chinaman can become a citizen. And over there some Mexicans used to live; but luckily we got rid of them too. You know, no white man will live with the colored, and the whole district would have been worth nothing—!

Here begins the speculator's empire. Across the road hangs a banner, "Live Here." In the fields sprout many-colored flags and posters. The biggest reads, "Here is City Hall Square." And an arrow points to a newly built factory, just beyond the limits, "Three-Thousand Men will be employed there."

Yes. A Factory. This is the great moving power, and precisely because of it, a city really will spring up here, just as the little broker in his Ford expects. He tells me, "The manufacturer got his site from the land company for nothing. He needs little to build; wood is cheap, and we laid his electricity. It will all pay for itself. Workers must buy or rent, and where people live, shops, stores, and restaurants will flourish. You buy now, and I assure you, in a year your price will triple in value!"

Now the climate, with the help of efficient propaganda, draws the world to California's door, as oil once did, and earlier, gold. But will this unprecedented land business turn out like other booms, a simple speculative business with its consequent crash?

At the Holland Line pier in Hoboken, a few hundred men hang around in three groups: the deck hands form a semicircle, the gang that will work in the hold sits on the ramp, and on the slope in back are the dock workers.

The *Volendam* came in yesterday in the evening, and the laborers were already here then to hire on. Today, they wait for their work to begin. The dockmaster arrives, blows his whistle and calls out the men's numbers. Near him the union agent keeps a vigilant eye out so that only members showing the blue union button on their caps get through the gate to the steamer.

Some are not called. These turn away, silent curses on their lips, a morning's wages lost. They head for the other piers, on the chance of finding at least an afternoon's work. The pay is eighty cents an hour and a dollar twenty for overtime. The normal day lasts from eight in the morning until five in the evening with sixty minutes off for lunch.

Thirty-thousand organized dock workers are active in New York harbor. A great strike, lost in 1919, nevertheless strengthened their organization. Until that year all that was considered necessary to load and unload a ship was to keep a disorganized mob of deck and pier workers, coal heavers, warehousemen, ship cleaners, boiler polishers, lightermen, and stevedores hanging about the wharves, helplessly to be dealt with as their employers pleased. Even now these men toil under unfavorable conditions. According to official admissions, the technical arrangements for handling the ships are far behind those of European harbors. Precautionary measures against accidents, regular inspection of hoisting equipment, and careful insistence upon workingmen's protection are unknown in the New World. The regulations of the insurance companies permit the underwriting against damage, loss, or fire of freight, vessels, and harbor installations, but do not extend to human beings.

So they drive these workers, leading on more than can find room on the decks and piers and around the ports, with no thought for the heavy loads moved about over unguarded heads, with no concern for the tackle whizzing by, for the fall of crates. The accident rate among American harbor workers is higher than among miners, and insurance companies demand the very highest premiums from longshoremen.

The absence of a limit on overtime renders illusory the conventionally accepted eight-hour day and forty-four-hour week. Even when the dock worker is free, he must be in constant readiness for work. There is no pay for waiting time; he may be called to work from eight to one and then be laid off after a few hours, or else he can be kept at work till late in the evening or through the night, sometimes even for two days and two nights on end without more stops than are needed for hurried meals. Foremen are not sympathetic when a docker, wearied by a hard day's labor, holds off from the night shift—those who don't stick it out have little chance for another call.

But then, the New York longshoremen are always ready to work overtime without too much urging; first, because their pay is then 50 per cent higher than it is for straight time, and also because they cannot tell when their next streak of work will come. Drudging away to knock out one good week after another, they all age early and soon the boss stevedore is suspiciously examining them to see if they can still be of use.

On the evening of Thanksgiving Day, a national holiday, the ladies' garment workers held a mass meeting in one of the auditoriums in Webster Hall. By a coincidence, one of the brilliantly lighted entrances of Webster Hall led to another room where a group of young merchants and clerks were gathered for a Thanksgiving ball. Here I blundered in by accident, and, being a half-hour early, sat down to wait in the vestibule.

A number of other people fell into the same error and wandered in, only to be disabused by the ball committee, clustered at the door. Invariably, the information that the tailors' meeting was next door was satirically given; and when the worker withdrew, the nattily dressed young clerks nudged each other, grinned, and cracked jokes with the abysmal lack of understanding with which such people think of the labor question in this country. The American citizen finds problems of wages meaningless and strikes uninteresting. "Our laborer rides his own auto, has a radio in his house, and wants nothing more," that is the theme of the 100 per cent American, whose Americanism, of course, mounts in proportion to the percentage of European background he wishes to conceal.

A half-hour later there was no mistaking the two entrances of Webster Hall. The street was black with people moving to the union meeting. Strangely, no one came in his own car and in the course of the session it appeared that very few seemed to have a radio at home.

For a European, this was a memorable occasion. A report was made in English, but the very next speaker spoke in opposition in Italian, naturally and as if it seemed natural to his predecessor. The Italian spoke vehemently, long and loud, and expounded the anarchistic point of view of the New York paper, *Rova di Liberta*. He was followed by two orators who used Yiddish. Then came a report, in remarkable English, by a Greek from the local union of Greek fur workers. (Greek workers man fully the workshops owned by their countrymen, who are also organized in a United Manufacturers Organization.) So I heard here in New York, out of the mouths of poor needle workers, the language of the *Divine Comedy*, seconded by that of the *Odyssey*, and commented on by that of the *Nibelungenlied*—the old German that is Yiddish. This was impressive.

The exhausting garment trades are now largely in the hands of the fugitives from the Russo-Polish pogroms and their sons. They are the readers of the great popular Jewish newspapers, the Socialist *Forward*, and the Communist *Freiheit*. They also form the rank and file of the tailors' organizations, against which their employers naturally use anti-Semitic arguments, which sometimes awaken a response from Gentile workers.

Although speakers and audience were divided in language and in political point of view, they were united in their despair, the basis for which was laid open at the meeting. The International Ladies' Garment Workers' Union, which once had a membership of 125,000, has been paralyzed since a fourteen-month strike in 1926 and 1927. Its forty-hour week has been forgotten and the laborers are forced to work

fifty-four or more under the speed up, often even on Saturday afternoon and Sunday. Weekly wages have been abandoned and the piecework system everywhere reinstalled; workers' incomes have fallen by
30 per cent. The union's relief fund, which held $500,000 two years ago
is now empty, and unemployment is enormous.

Those who limit their observations of New York street life to the
elegance of Fifth Avenue, to the bustling speculation of Wall Street,
and to the garish gaiety of Broadway, miss a view of the industrial reserve army of the workless and the work seekers. Along Seventh Avenue between Thirty-sixth and Thirty-eighth Streets is the market for
dressmakers. Old tailors out of Galicia and Bucovina, out of Bessarabia
and the Ukraine, men from the sweatshops of Minsk, Kiev, Kishinev,
Vilna, and Whitechapel; forty years of hopes, of dreams, of urgent aspiration drew them across the ocean, and now they stand here, hoping,
dreaming, and aspiring. Perhaps that foreman will come by and give
them work—work for a week, even a day, at least a few dozen cloaks
to make up.

They dye their gray beards and hair to seem younger to a possible
employer, tragic versions of the joke of the old Jew at the box office in
Czernowitz who covers his flowing beard with his hands and asks for a
student's ticket.

A few blocks down between Twenty-seventh and Twenty-ninth
Streets wait the furriers—old and young, cutters and finishers, quilters
and sewers, gambling with the fortunes of the labor exchange; truly,
the most exciting and most spectacular of gambles.

The shop windows into which the unemployed furriers enviously
peep are no different from those in Leipzig; brown bearskins, gray silver fox, white-dotted antelope, brown beaver, and black caracul are
carefully cut by the light from the street, while to the rear negotiations
go forth with evident animation, in a scene from Rembrandt.

The shops and even the firm names are all alike. In the windows of
the tall buildings of the needle district you will see two, three hundred
times in identical script, "Cloak and Dress Maker" with only the name
of the owner different, even in the gloomy buildings of the gloomy
cross streets that grow ever gloomier as they stretch away, east and
west, from Seventh Avenue.

The elevators in this district show no resemblance to those of other
city buildings, to the elegant conveyances of hotels, banks, or office

buildings. These are appurtenances of the factory good enough for
freight and workers—no wainscotting, no carpets, no railings, often
without sidewalls. And the operator has no uniform.

Ten to fifteen men form the staff of the shop. Everywhere are little
iron carts loaded with dressmakers' dummies, each carrying a heap of
clothing over its waxen skin, interrupted on its way up or down. The
dummies shuttle back and forth between the workrooms of the middleman subcontractors and those of the jobber who lets out the material
and patterns, sets the price and terms; up for inspections, down for alteration, and then up for final consignment.

One workshop is like another, whether it works a hundred hands,
mostly Italians and Negroes, or only twelve in a small contracting
shop, mostly eastern European Jewish tailors; whether it turns out
dresses, or cloaks, or men's suits. Along the windows stretch the cutters'
tables crowded with rolls of fabric. In small places the cutting is done
by hand, in the large by electric shears which, under the guidance of
a master cutter, will trim thirty different cloths to an exact pattern.
Within the framework of these broad tables are more men and women,
bent over sewing machines, sewing buttonholes by hand, or moving
mechanically with the motions of their pressing irons. Over all are the
watchful eyes of the foreman.

In the shops on Third Avenue, a halt for a few minutes brings the
worker a knock on the head; a misty darkness dances in the eyes and
the brain reels. That is the effect of the "el": locals and expresses in
turn rattle the windows on their ceaseless way from north to south,
from south to north. Only a few residences lie along the line of this
elevated railroad. But in those the flimsy pottery cracks, you fail to
hear your own words, and there is a continual rumble of trains through
your sleep. You can only work here. Almost half the manufacturing
establishments lie along the tracks.

Amidst multicolored shreds of cloth and trimmings you move
through these enclaves of old Russia in new America. Work stops at
the sewing machines, the cutting, the buttonhole, the pressing tables, as
I pass. Taken for a clothing manufacturer from Berlin, I am drawn into
conversation. Some, and these seem like the speakers in Webster Hall
on Thanksgiving Day, want to know about the state of wages and
the conditions of work in Germany. Others ask how much capital is
needed to get established there, what the profits are for businessmen,

and these resemble the avaricious contractor who at that very moment begins to boil up inside because it seems as if I am about to pirate away his force.

38.

AMERICAN PEOPLES

Jan Gerard Sleeswijk was born in 1879 and studied medicine in Amsterdam. He worked in various hospitals and research institutes in Paris, Brussels, Berlin, and London, specializing in microbiology and in pathology, subjects on which he composed a large number of papers. He also taught at the University of Leyden, and now lives in The Hague. He visited the United States in 1931, writing an account of this visit under the title, Van Menschen en Dingen in Amerika (1933).

It seems now more than ever before that overpopulation is a very relative concept. Properly speaking, there is no absolute criterion for measuring it. Density as such may not be significant. In the most thickly settled area of the world the economic situation may be so favorable—wide opportunities for labor, an absence of unemployment, and good health—that no one will talk of overpopulation. On the other hand, it might be difficult even in a most thinly peopled land for people to earn for themselves the primary necessities of life—food, clothing, and shelter.

There are at work here a number of different factors, which may in this respect alter the conditions of a society. In a given country there may be, during a favorable period, a great shortage of labor power that will be called underpopulation, while in times of economic disturbance, with the same number of people, there may be considerable unemployment and that will be called overpopulation.

Since the present crisis is serious in the United States and unemployment heavy, Americans begin to talk of overpopulation even in that sparsely peopled continent. Thence comes the rising demand for the restriction of immigration. This movement, however, is not recent in origin. That tendency arose even when everything was thriving. The laborers, and especially those organized in the American Federation of Labor, were the first to wish to limit the available labor force and thus to raise the level of wages. There are those in the United States who recommend not simply the stoppage of immigration, but even want to export Americans. The proponents of emigration have not, however, troubled to ask where emigrants could go.

Since the crisis is world-wide, there is not a single country prepared to admit foreigners. Each land naturally has a right to close its borders; but to ship out laborers, the exporters must find virgin territory. In case there is no such place, or in case there is no region where the immediate opportunities for the immigrant are greater than in his fatherland, what will then become of the people? They cannot, after all, be sent to another planet. Moreover, economic conditions may, and probably will change again. Will these people then be brought back, and will they allow themselves thus to be shuttled back and forth?

The rapid increase of population through immigration and through births was until our time no burden to the United States, although it came atop an increase through the fall in the number of deaths as a result of hygienic regulations. Mortality has since 1900 declined by almost one-half; before that date there were between 20 and 30 deaths in every 1,000, now there are 12. In the last seventy-five years the average life span in this country has grown by about twenty years. Above all, the deaths from acute infections have been dealt with in a very effective manner, partly through systematic vaccination (diphtheria and typhus) and partly through care of the drinking water and milk (typhus and paratyphus).

Besides the reduction in deaths there is, however, also a declining birth rate. But on the other hand, a baby born now has a much greater chance for life and health than ever before. In the United States they still spend: for fighting tuberculosis $800,000,000, for the sufferers from heart disease, $90,000,000, and for other invalids, $37,000,000; altogether close to $1,000,000,000.

The present declining birth rate originates precisely in the tendency toward urbanization of the American people. As a result of the drift to the city, both husband and wife seek to work for wages and therefore put off childbearing, in which, from the economic point of view, there is no utility. The last word on this problem has not yet been spoken, however. There is doubtlessly a complex of causes which steadily depress the number of births per thousand.

In the United States this fact is differently evaluated by different people. Some regard it as less important than the fact that the babies born have a better chance of life. According to this point of view, the welfare of the state depends not on the number of children born, but on what happens to them after birth. On the opposite side are those who continue to regard a high birth rate as a serious national consideration.

If an average of 3.2 children a family is necessary to hold the population at the existing level, then the present figure of 2.5 betokens a retrogression in population. This trend may yet be slackened by the decline in deaths. But there comes a moment when the limit is reached after which the number of aged becomes very large; when those die out, then the supply in the younger age groups will be small. There is also a limit to the saving from the restriction in infant mortality and that saving will then no longer counterbalance the decline of the birth rate. If the decline of the population that emerges as a consequence is not counteracted through immigration then the net result in the long run will be national suicide.

And so we are still brought back again to immigration, so critical a problem in America. It is in this connection interesting to hear the opinion of a statistician very well respected in the United States, Dr. T. F. Murphy of the Department of Commerce. He has rendered the judgment that it is precisely the restriction of immigration that is responsible for the decline of the birth rate in the United States. It seems from the statistics that the birth rate of the immigrants, that is to say, of foreign-born Americans, has consistently been higher than that of the other American citizens. This opinion indicates that to maintain the population of the United States at a level, immigration must really be encouraged instead of being restricted and there must be no more talk of emigration. A temporary crisis and unemployment must thus not be the reason for putting a stop to the supply of new human materials—if Americans can still see farther than the length of their noses.

The race problem in the United States has various sides, economic, social, and humanitarian, with all of which one must reckon. The reader knows that this question is a consequence of slavery, or rather, of the emancipation of the slaves. There are many sources from which one can draw an understanding of the matter. One can read and one can talk with white Americans. One need not seek far over there for opportunities to discuss race; the subject remains there, just like prohibition, one of the orders of the day. But I also sought out contacts with the Negroes themselves. The manager of their defense organization, the N.A.A.C.P. (National Association for the Advancement of Colored People) put me in touch with educated Negroes in New York, and also in Chicago, St. Louis, Salt Lake City, San Francisco, Los Angeles, New Orleans, and Atlanta. I began my acquaintance with this subject through the very rich literature on it, and enlivened my understanding through personal contact with very many white and black Americans in every section of the country.

Black and white! This division gives the impression that there is involved only a question of the two extremes. But everyone knows that there really took place, in the course of the years, a certain intermixture of the two races, even if only to a slight degree, so that one may encounter every possible gradation in skin color and in the other signs of race.

The whites who hold fast to the principle of racial superiority keep themselves strictly away from any social contact with anyone who shows the slightest indication of having colored blood in his veins. The pure whites will thus not ask such people into their homes, nor do business with them, unless as servants. There are, however, cases in which the external indications are inadequate. When I first was introduced to Walter White, the secretary of the N.A.A.C.P.—a man who deserves well of his country both as an organizer of the Negro movement and as an author on that subject—I thought that he was completely white. It seemed strange to hear from his own mouth that he was colored. I know, of course, that skin color is only one of the signs of race; yet every summer there run around on our beaches in the sun, tanned whites who look more like Negroes than does Walter White.

Whenever one now demonstrates to an exclusive American that Negro writers like Weldon Johnson, Burghardt DuBois, White, and others, are sociable and intellectual gentlemen and may be received as such, then one gets the answer that these men are not pure Negroes, and that their higher capacities derive from a greater or lesser amount of white blood in their veins. But that argument has been adequately refuted. A rather pale Negro, a doctor in New Orleans, proved to me that the late Booker T. Washington, the father of the Negro movement in America and president of the Tuskegee Industrial Institute (an upper technical school for Negroes), just like his successor, R. A. Moton, men very highly esteemed even in white circles, were both as black as his shoes.

So one comes to all sorts of contradictions which make an absolute separation between the two races impossible in the practice of daily life. The colored people are there now, they are citizens of the same state, and one must find a *modus vivendi* for getting on with them. Indeed, the Negroes did not come to America of their own free will; the colonists imported them, and these 10,000,000 persons can hardly now be gotten rid of. Formerly the mass of illiterate and uneducated Negroes could easily be held down, but this becomes steadily more difficult as the supply of educated people among them increases. In recent years some 19,000 colored people were studying at various institutions of higher learning, of which some 2,000 graduated every year. This growing group will not wait at the door as pariahs much longer.

Furthermore, as a result, the economic position of the Negroes grows rapidly stronger, especially in the northern states where they have more room for spreading their wings. Formerly, it was quite exceptional for a Negro to live in his own home. Now many find it is possible to do so. Also, through coöperation, the Negroes have been able to accomplish a good deal in improving their economic and social position. There are in Chicago five newspapers, four hospitals, two banks, and a few hotels, which are operated only by and for Negroes. In St. Louis I visited the People's Finance Corporation which is established in a building worth $400,000 and in which are located a bank, a number of insurance companies, large shops, the offices of lawyers, and the suites of doctors and dentists. All the shareholders and all those who do business there are colored people. This building lies in the Negro district of the city and so is separated, not to say excluded, from the rest. They had to cling together, since it is made very difficult, if not impossible, for them to buy a piece of land for a house, or to rent apartments in the other parts of the city. Therefore the Negroes must live in their ghettos. I had to seek out there even the better educated among them, doctors and lawyers, for example, who were my sources of information. One must not imagine that the Negro districts are made up exclusively of collections of hovels in slums. In Harlem, the black quarter of New

York, in Chicago, and elsewhere, there are streets and boulevards that once were occupied by prosperous white people and which are now altogether in the hands of the colored people.

The economic position of the Negroes, at least of many of them, is thus somewhat stronger; but that still does not make a great difference in the race relations of whites and blacks. Conditions are naturally not the same over the whole Union; there are important local nuances. The North is somewhat more liberal; Negroes may make use of the means of transportation there, with full equality. They can even get tickets on Pullman trains and sleeping cars, although they are rarely seen there. But in the South, things are quite different. There, Negroes may only use the colored cars of the slow trains, while on the trolleys they must take special places in the rear. In the stations, separate waiting rooms are set aside for the two races. A white beggar or criminal struts with head lifted high into the waiting room for whites, while an educated, cultured, refined Negro doctor or lawyer must keep to the company of the members of his race.

The better hotels and restaurants will receive and serve no colored guests. Cultivated Negroes who come to a place where they do not by chance have family or friends, and where there is no convenient hotel for blacks, must thus satisfy themselves with the most inferior accommodations. Frequently there result quite comic consequences. Colored people from other countries are tolerated. So, for example, a man got by by brazenly saying he came from Paris, although he had never seen the capital of France and spoke not a word of French. He did not, of course, reveal that his residence was in Paris, Texas.

Colored servants are admitted in the South even to the express trains; a cultured Negress traveling from the North to the South, upon reaching the border states, tied an apron around her waist, and was permitted to go on. Also we ourselves have had to adapt ourselves to these conditions. When I sailed a few years ago on a Dutch boat from Curaçao to New York, we took on board in Haiti a fine-looking Negress with a first-class ticket. At the demand of the American passengers she was compelled to dine by herself.

In Los Angeles I heard the following story from a most reliable source. A colored woman doctor wished to send her daughter to a boarding school. She was called Turner, a "white" family name, although the slaves at emancipation assumed many such names. This mother wrote to the director of the school enclosing a letter of recommendation from the bishop and the matter was settled by mail. The daughter traveled to the school, but was promptly sent back to her mother because her skin was not white. The parents of the other girls would not wish such contacts. The white children themselves do not in the beginning feel any trace of this race feeling. Among the students in the public schools one can see white and black walk and play together in a very brotherly and sisterly fashion. But they are well impressed with the fact that that will not do later.

In the South, segregation of the races is everywhere carried through systematically: in the schools, in the trade unions, and also in the exercise of the franchise. Negroes were there not even allowed up to the ballot box. The exclusion from the unions has the consequence that the Negroes often appear as scabs during strikes, which naturally sharpens race antagonism in employment.

Where the public powers coöperate in the segregation and in the unequal treatment of citizens with equal rights, they are actually acting illegally and come into conflict with the constitution of the United States. But the South has in that respect a very wonderful mentality. "We go our own way and don't worry about Washington," they say. The hostility of North and South is still not dead.

Wherever the Negroes can vote, the great majority support the Republican candidates. That is still due to the influence of the Republicanism of Lincoln, who assured the slaves their freedom. Thus it is a question of sentiment. Among the younger Negroes, however, a real political opportunism begins to show itself. As members of an oppressed race many should feel themselves drawn toward the socialists. But that party has, until now, demonstrated no indications of influence in the United States and cannot promise immediate results. Some colored people affiliate with the Democratic Party, not at all out of sympathy, since the southern Democrats are their natural enemies, but only in order to be able to put in a word in the councils of the party in the northern states, and also there to achieve something at once for their race.

The difficulties of the situation are obvious. Friction and sometimes bitterness on the part of both groups now and then passes to extremes. One thinks of the lynchings. But this is a problem in itself.

Is indeed a solution of the American race problem possible within

the foreseeable future? One hesitates to give an affirmative answer to
this question in view of the mountains of difficulties that raise themselves on every side. Even the White House does not remain free of
trouble. A few years ago it raised a storm in the political world and in
the press. The wife of the President had invited Mrs. De Priest to tea
just as she had invited all the wives of the members of the House of
Representatives to which Mr. De Priest belonged. But he is a Negro
and his wife is also black. The result was indignation! In the North it
was at once understood that Mrs. Hoover's official invitation had nothing to do with race amalgamation. But the press in the South shrilly
proclaimed that the President could never again count on a single vote
from that region. No wonder that in colored circles one hears complaint after complaint about systematic slights.

There are almost no beds available for Negroes in the hospitals,
there are no playgrounds, and far too few theaters. In Los Angeles they
had to fight a long time to get a colored doctor admitted to the staff of
the general hospital. There was fear that he might come in contact with
white patients; apparently, however, there was no need to consult the
wishes of the colored patients. The Negroes are reproached for their
higher rates of illness and death, which are regarded as signs of their
deficiency in civilization. But can more be expected from a race which
seventy years ago was still enslaved, which was, in a manner of speaking, emancipated, but remained oppressed socially, economically, politically, and culturally? What can be expected of people who must do
the meanest and the worst-paid work and who, at a slackening in business are the first to be dismissed? And if they are reproached with the
fact that they are unfitted for higher work, then is it not proper to ask,
"Have they been given an equal chance?"

Bitterness reigns in the Negro circles. Sometimes the atmosphere is
so heavy that only a slight provocation is necessary before the storm
bursts forth. That, for example, was the situation when the riots broke
out in Chicago in 1919. A few years ago a Negro in the same city, who
opposed a white as a candidate for one of the representative bodies,
was killed by an assassin on the evening before election day. It was suspected that the white man's party, in coöperation with the police, arranged matters so that no justice was ever done. The principal of the
technical high school in Atlanta, who was my very accommodating
guide in that city, heard with astonishment that I also wished to speak

with one of the leading Negroes in the town to whom I had a letter of introduction. "But you don't intend to invite him to your hotel?" asked the professor in an anxious tone. "That would create a sensation here." I knew that and therefore always had my meeting with the Negroes in their own homes. But that necessity was characteristic.

The general opinion of the Negroes is: "How can we have feelings of national loyalty for a land that made us slaves, a land where we, despite emancipation, are still always oppressed and treated as second-class citizens?"

"But were there not always Negro regiments in the wars fought by the United States?" I asked. And the answer was, "Of course, but people joined in the hope of enhancing the prestige of their people and of securing better treatment of their race; also because they were enlisted through conscription."

"Is it not true," I once asked one of my black hosts, "that families in the South, no matter how exclusive they may be in relations with your race, generally treat their colored servants exceptionally well?" And the answer came with a bitter smile, "Sure, just as some men take care of dogs of which they are fond. But nevertheless the animal is not a human in their eyes. So, the southern whites value their colored man or maid as a good servant but not as a person. And, as soon as the Negro lifts himself out of his servitude to compete on equal terms, then there is an end to good will."

Lynching forms a black page in the American history of our times. I treat it here, partly because in most cases the Negroes are the victims, and partly to clear away a very common misunderstanding.

One must treat this phenomenon historically. Among the pioneers who went into newly opened and unsettled territories, there were naturally birds of very diverse plumage. The disorderly elements among them did not feel the restraining power of the state and of justice. When thefts, murders, and violations of morality occurred in such primitive societies, it was necessary to help oneself. Alone or with a few friends one tracked down the offender and punished him. And so it was also in the New World in the course of the westward movement. But even when a settled social order was set up, justice was often far away and slow in coming. And so the impulse to act as one's own judge, especially in the lower classes and in the rural South, has not yet been suppressed. Lynching is nothing but the yielding to that impulse, and it is a mistake to suppose that Negroes alone are its victims. The proportion fluctuates, naturally; but of the twelve lynchings in 1929 no less than four, one-third, involved whites.

Also, the conception is unjust that all the Negroes upon whom lynch justice is carried out were guilty of an assault upon a white woman. Of the eight colored men lynched in 1929, for instance, only three were so accused, properly or not.

These outrages have in recent years regularly been declining. Forty years ago, in 1889, there were as many as 175 of which 80, almost half, involved whites. The statistics of the decade 1920–1929 give an average figure of a tenth of that sum. Since then, there is, nevertheless, reason to fear an increase. This question has so incensed public opinion that a commission of inquiry has been named, and we will eagerly await the results of its labors.

It would not surprise me if economic disorganization and unemployment have some influence on this problem. Negroes are mostly unskilled laborers and as such come into competition with the so-called poor whites, the unskilled white working class. The living conditions of the blacks are the poorest, and when colored people in times like these work for lower wages, they arouse the bitterness of the white people. Besides, it is still always significant here that a depression in business works first of all to the disadvantage of the Negroes. I read a dispatch from Atlanta in an American newspaper. The correspondent had interviewed a white unemployed worker, who pointed to a passing Negro letter-carrier and said, "Why should a black man have a government position when there are still whites running around without jobs?"

The social and economic status of the colored race deserves still another comment. Last year one could read of Negro riots in Chicago, in which outrages were committed and in which the militia had to be called out. That was to be expected; what was really surprising was that an explosion had not broken out sooner. This unrest was promptly blamed on a communist plot. Let us see, however, what the gist of the matter was.

Before the war about 60,000 Negroes lived in Chicago. They formed the mass of house servants and porters and took on all sorts of unskilled labor. But things have changed. During the war years there was a great migration of Negroes out of the southern countryside into the industrial towns of the North and the West. The war industries which steadily operated in three shifts, felt a great need for manpower, above all when the government began to draw great numbers of workers into the army. Since the United States sent relatively few colored soldiers to the European front, the Negroes found, under those circumstances, opportunities opened to them to be taken on as full-fledged factory workers.

The demand continued into the years of economic expansion after the peace, and so in Chicago, for example, the number of Negroes tripled. They worked side by side with the whites, earned the same wages, at least in the great industries, and all that produced no serious difficulties. Many blacks were able to lift themselves out of the ranks of the proletariat, and, thanks to their solidarity, reached an economically sounder position. They no longer lived only in slums.

All this changed when the United States was also struck by the depression. Now race exclusiveness has regained the upper hand, and wherever there is a redundancy of labor, the Negroes must be laid off first. This process had already begun in 1930, and since then it has continued at an accelerated pace. In the American *Labor Review* of June 1931 are the results of an inquiry with interesting data on the position of the American Negro during the industrial depression.

Unemployment is greater among the Negroes than among the whites. In Baltimore, for instance, the colored people make up 17 per cent of the population but 31.5 per cent of the unemployed. This relationship is the same everywhere: in Charleston, 49 and 70 per cent; in Chicago, 4 and 16 per cent; in Memphis 38 and 75 per cent; in Philadelphia, 7 and 25 per cent; in Pittsburgh, 8 and 38 per cent. But the blacks get the short end everywhere, not only in the matter of layoffs. Whenever there are openings for labor, the employers give the preference to whites. In many cases, I have been told Negroes are dismissed to make room for the favored race.

Since unemployment is general, both the whites and the blacks are victims of the crisis, but the latter were the first to be thrown upon charity, which, moreover, in many places was inadequate to the needs of the times. No wonder that unrest reigns among the Negroes! They will take the first place in a popular agitation. Many Negroes are on the move from the small towns to the large cities in the hope that opportunities are better there. But they only add to the number of paupers and complicate the situation. The general conclusion of this study seems to be that the whole economic status of the American Negro has reached a critical point; it threatens to decline, without any prospect of improvement.

When one realizes further that the authorities in charge of public works also favor the whites, although according to the law the blacks have the same rights, then it is not surprising that unrest among Negroes is expressed in the form of disturbances and in a beginning of revolutionary agitation.

Is that communism? With that word people here seem to rid themselves of the necessity of dealing with all sorts of unpleasant social problems. It is also the peg on which many hang all their political opinions. Naturally, political factors play a part in the collisions which take place here and there, and revolutionary elements are always at work trying to fish in the troubled economic waters. Negro discontent is, however, first and foremost an economic phenomenon and an expression of protest against the prevalent distress among the members of the race, but no less against the renewed demonstration of the social segregation of their people. And, of course, I need not point out that popular agitation in times of economic disorder is a common phenomenon even in countries in which the population is purely white. In the United States, however, the situation is sharpened by race conflict.

It is just two years ago that I trod through the colored districts of Chicago with a Negro doctor as guide. I saw light; but also many shadows. And I heard my companion say: "The white American has put an end to slavery and made us formally equal. And now he fails to understand that in a land where, in practice, we are still treated as second-class citizens, we cannot feel a 100 per cent national sentiment. On the contrary, the oppressed Negro masses form the best material for revolutionary agitation." A year later, the bomb exploded.

In view of all that, it is not surprising that the colored people have sought to mobilize their strength in organizations to defend their civil rights. In 1909, a hundred years after the birth of Lincoln, their liberator, they formed the N.A.A.C.P. With main offices in New York and not less than 325 branches in 44 states, it is, everywhere and always, prepared to come to defend the rights of the race and to make propaganda for its sake.

Their greatest victory came in 1930 when President Hoover nominated Judge John J. Parker of North Carolina to the bench of the Supreme Court, a nomination which had to be ratified by the Senate. Parker had earlier behaved in an insulting manner toward the Negroes. The N.A.A.C.P. agitated against the nomination with all its power, with the consequence that the Senate rejected it. This was a defeat for the President, but was at the same time an event which was recognized as the greatest moral victory of the colored people since the abolition of slavery.

But, nonetheless, the Negro problem is still far from a solution. Some Americans think indeed that an amalgamation of the two races in the long run is the only possible outcome. Others, and those in the majority, sharply reject that idea and see in absolute segregation the only way out. They would have a sort of Negro enclave in white society; the blacks would thus have their own schools, from top to bottom, and their own churches. In part, this has already taken place, and many communities make available considerable sums of money for colored universities and churches, not out of love for the Negroes, but rather to keep them out of white colleges and churches. In a mixed society, however, where all have equal rights, such a system cannot generally be imposed. The problem thus still remains open and a definite answer still distant.

39.

A FOREIGNER LOOKS AT THE TVA

Madame Odette Keun is a French writer, born in 1890, who has written numerous accounts of her travels in many parts of the world. In 1936 she visited the United States and was so well impressed by the TVA that she devoted a study to the enterprise—A Foreigner Looks at the TVA (1937). A few years later, another visit led to a full volume on America.

The population of the Watershed, belonging as it does to seven states, consists of different strata and follows different avocations. But perhaps one citizen in six lives in a big city. Half the inhabitants dwell on farms. The predominant classes are therefore the farmers and the small-towners, and on them the TVA has concentrated—the farmer, of the two, being its chief concern.

In a great minority are the prosperous farmers on good phosphatic lands or on middling lands which they have fructified. The typical valley landowner lives on soil which was usually no great shakes from the start, which he bled in every conceivable way, and which now brings him in for himself and his large family from $100 to $150 a year. Then there are the tenant farmer and the sharecropper, white and black, in varying stages of poverty and devoid, moreover, of the independence of the poor landowner. These three categories of people, their minds, their circumstances, and their future, are at the heart of all that the TVA is planning and doing.

Among the "free" farmers, the least known and the most difficult to reach are the mountaineers, immured in the vast ranges, separated from all contact with the outer world, incredibly poor, superstitious, illiterate, talking a pidgin-Elizabethan, steeped in fierce religious convictions, following old-fashioned ways, wild, stubborn, proud. Civilization passed them by. This would have been less deplorable if they had maintained their original qualities, such as they were, but nobody and nothing can stand still; you go forward or you go backward, but go you must. They went backward. Isolation, the insensate attachment of primitive folks to their place, their home, and their relatives, which helped to immobilize them; lack of opportunity and therefore of ambition; no industries and no markets to which to sell their surplus products; no ready money; no roads, no schools, no hospitals; inbreeding, diseases and a crazy diet—add to that an influx of outlaws and desperadoes who took refuge in the mountains to escape the law, and you get communities listless and shiftless through their own anemia and infected by crime from other quarters.

All these conditions were made indescribably worse by the Civil War. Most of the mountain counties were loyal to the Union, and the highlanders sallied out of their fastnesses to fight on its behalf. While they were away bandits and bush-whackers ranged through the hills, preying on those who were left defenseless and starting a network of vendettas.

The mountaineers were not inexorably doomed to become as stupid, lazy, dirty, thriftless, treacherous, relentless, uglily cunning, brutal, and dishonorable as history reveals they were. I am completely unable to discern heroism and picturesqueness in their slovenly persons, their squalid houses, their primitive housekeeping, their repulsively cooked food, their mismanagement of the land—surely they could have applied themselves, during so many years, to learning a bit about *that,* their only means of keeping alive! Harshness, rudeness, sullenness, mutual incomprehension, and self-defensiveness, in spite of their clannishness, seem to me the note of their family relationships. I have been told by army officers who were placed at the head of a depot for mountaineers when America entered the Great War and conscription was proclaimed, that out of 20,000 highlanders assembled at that point, 5,000 had to be pronounced inapt and sent back after a few weeks. They were not ill, they were not physically unfit. They were "lost." They could not adapt themselves. They mooned about; they wandered; they fell into abstractions and silences. They forgot their names. When it came to shipping them off to their homes, they did not know in what county their homes were situated, and the authorities had the devil of a job tracing their origins. For the life of me, I cannot admire a mode of existence which leads to such deterioration of the brain that human beings no longer can do anything, not only for thought and for society, but even for themselves.

However, changes are overtaking the mountaineers. The first onrush was as usual a villainous form of commercialism and exploitation —forests destroyed, mines disemboweled, lands swindled away, pitilessly enslaving factories established, traders and profiteers pouring in —against which only the shrewdest and most capable could make a stand. But if the vanguard of this odious civilization was composed of men who were playing for their own hand—much as the forefathers of the highlanders had done in their age—in their wake followed more enlightened measures and more general benefits. Roads, schools, order; county, state, and federal institutions administering a certain amount of help; and now an organization almost mystically committed to the betterment of this people.

For the TVA is wrapped heart and soul in the evolution of the mountaineers. How to transform their thinking and their agricultural customs and adapt them to present conditions; how to develop their economic life, keeping them from the servitude of factories for which they are physically and mentally unsuited (and which in any case cannot absorb them any longer), and yet increase their cash income and

raise their material standards to the level of those obtaining in the
flourishing portions of the valley; how to preserve their independent
spirit and their culture—the TVA calls it culture, I'd call it an obsolete
form of Americanism that America needs no more than Europe needs
the ideology of the Corsican or the tribal pattern of the clans of the
Caucasus, to speak of peoples I know—and yet teach them responsibility to society and give them a significant and useful role in the community: this is the task the TVA has undertaken. It is especially for
these mountaineers and their brothers in the valley that it elaborated
its agricultural program, invented its fertilizer, created its Agricultural
Industries Division, founded its educational and training courses. It is
for them, plus the small-towner, that it is waging the fight for power
against the utilities. Its goal is to secure for them a more intelligent, dignified, and assured existence, participating in the facilities our contemporary world affords but conserving the lively characteristics of the
individual; a happy balance between the Jeffersonian dream of the self-
sufficient agricultural community and the mechanical advantages of
the power age. At least, I see the goal like that, and I do not believe I
have seen it awry.

The response, I must say, has been considerable. It is true that the
TVA came upon the scene at a moment when the farmer was up
against the wall; agriculture did not feed a man and his family, and
despair was growing. If prices had been soaring and prospects bright,
perhaps no wedge could have been driven into rural obstinacy and
traditionalism. But as it was, circumstances and the wisdom and tact
of the TVA's attitude pretty soon persuaded the farmers, highlanders
and lowlanders alike, in spite of their caution and inveterate suspi-
ciousness, that here was a friend intensely anxious to help them, not a
"passel of Yankees" come to pour scorn on their backwardness and
arrogantly to tell them how to do everything. Here was real benevolence and discretion, the first manifestation, since Reconstruction, of a
government's interest and care. The mere fact that in two and a half
years over 12,000 test-demonstration farms have been spontaneously
laid out in a region celebrated for centuries for its ignorance and stubbornness, proves the nature of the tie between the population of the
Watershed and the TVA. And if it shows the sagacity and devotion
with which the TVA has handled that prickly proposition, the farmer,
I concede willingly that it also shows more alertness and gratitude on

North as well as South, White as well as Black: San Jose, California

Erosion: People and Soil

the part of the farmer than one would have expected to find. Indeed, the tendency might almost become too much eagerness for aid and guidance, though that cannot be encouraged since it is inertia that must be extirpated from the composition of the human animal here.

The evil problems of the tenant farmer and the sharecropper, white and black, the TVA has not been able to touch. These are things that can be straightened out only by congressional legislation. You can't urge rotation of cover crops on a man who is employed by a landlord, if that landlord wants cotton on his soil; nor can you, unless you are the government, give half the rural population a house and a field to start living like free men. Nor can you find work, however hard you try, for all the laborers who have been jerked out of their farm jobs because you had to buy up the estates of their masters for flooding purposes. All that is not your fault, though it may be your sorrow. Indirectly, however, by side activities and industries, by part-time employment in its various projects, by free training, by diligent searching for new places, by all sorts of ingenious efforts, the TVA does what it can to enable the tenant and the sharecropper who drift within its orbit to obtain a little more security, a little more money, and perhaps even, in very fortunate cases, a little property of their own. But that aspect of the picture is not radiant with hope. It is the government alone that can get under the skin of these very painful matters.

Another tangle concerns the people who occupy the tracts of land the TVA is obliged to submerge for the reservoirs of its dams. Here human emotions are involved, as well as concrete questions. Families had to be removed so that engineering schemes of national importance might be realized, but you do not cheerfully acquiesce in the disruption of your manner of life, even when national issues are at stake. The monetary compensation was very fair, as public opinion recognizes, though the value of land showed a disposition to shoot up to vertiginous heights as soon as it was learned that "government" needed it, and every owner's estate was metamorphosed in a jiffy from farm land into dam land costing a hundred times more. The TVA had to bargain and bargain closely, but that over, it did a lot of humane things. It explored the valley to find farms in the vicinity of the districts to be flooded; it gave the transplanted families, whenever possible, the opportunity to choose their new homes; it worked with federal and county institutions to facilitate their installation in unfamiliar communities, providing them with social contacts, arranging, as in the case of the shifting of whole minor villages, for educational facilities in the shape of schools and communications. Entire cemeteries had been moved at the TVA's expense when the time came for flooding, so that the people should not brood upon their dead lost irretrievably in the waters. I do not say that the process of transvasement was never accompanied by suffering and loss: in such a gigantic enterprise every personal interest, every personal necessity, could not always be adequately satisfied, but what could be done to make the lot of the perforce-uprooted groups bearable or even to improve it, has been scrupulously tried. An interesting point is that better land or no-better land proposed, most of the people refused to leave their hills for the plains.

These traits of justice and kindness, this ideal of a common welfare, which characterize the relations the TVA established with the social groups existing in the valley come to a peak, I think, in the labor question and the policies the TVA adopted in this potentially stormy field. There are more than 15,000 workers, from every rank and craft of labor, on TVA projects in the watershed. You can imagine what the applications were at a time when 20,000,000 Americans were out of a job. One of the firmest rules the TVA laid down was that local labor, if it met the requirements, was to be taken on first. But it *had* to meet the requirements; patronage, favoritism and protection were out of the question, as a good many politicians and wire-pullers immediately discovered to their great disgruntlement.

The major policies were three. The first related to the right of collective bargaining; the second to wages; the third to hours and working conditions—and these applied to colored as well as white labor, for from the outset the TVA, quietly but persistently, hired Negroes in groups until their employment percentage tallied with the population percentage in the areas concerned: about 20 per cent. The Negroes received the same wages as the whites of the same category, the same housing, and the same training. Since white labor was assured that the jobs wouldn't be pulled away from under it by the ordinary trick of using cheap colored labor, there was hardly any trouble, even when leading civic lights regretted that Negroes were being educated beyond their necessities. The TVA's answer was that neither revolt nor miscegenation was being preached, and that since the Negro was a member of the community, it was better for the community that he should be a decent citizen than an indecent one. And that was that. I should like to see the TVA do something far broader and more decisive about the Negro, and this subject is the only one in which we do not see eye to eye; but I daresay it understands its business in the South better than I. I'm afraid that if I attempted to deal with the mixture of pathological impulses and racial snobbery that is at the bottom of the attitude of the white toward the black, I'd stir up a worse witch's brew.

The principle of collective bargaining, which recognizes and insists on the "right of employees to organize and bargain as a body through representatives of their own choosing, free from any and all restraint, interference or coercion in self-organization and designation of labor's own representatives elected fairly by majority rule," has been observed in every detail by the TVA. It made clear to its own supervisory executives that whatever their origins or their previous philosophy were, the Authority stood unshakably for the untrammeled right of labor to speak and act through the specific officials it voluntarily appointed. Discrimination by the supervisors because of union membership or activity resulted, in the few cases where it occurred, in changes in the staff.

As regards wages, the TVA believes in keeping them high. "It's not only good social policy, but good business as well," it says. The Act provides that the Authority, in all its operations, shall pay not less than the prevailing wage, and that due attention shall be given to wages reached through collective bargaining—so that when the prevailing wage is a very low one, the TVA worker has the chance to get a raise. In the event any question crops up as to what are the prevailing rates of wages, and the matter cannot be settled by conference between the duly chosen labor spokesmen and the Authority, it is referred to the United States Secretary of Labor, whose decision is final. Schedules of rates of pay, hourly and annual, are published and remain in force until revision, which takes place not more often than once a year so that there are no sudden shattering cuts and no mysteries.

Hours of work cannot exceed eight in the twenty-four hour period; overtime is paid for at the rate of time and one-half; during the periods of marked unemployment, hours of work are still kept consistent with a reasonable minimum income. Child labor, of course, is utterly eliminated. As regards conditions of work, the safety committees, the admirable division of hygiene (health-education program, first-aid instruction, immunization against diseases, prevention of malaria, general sanitation), the housing, catering, educational, and recreational facilities, the free training courses—I must mention some of them, they are so extraordinarily diversified, and show so much mental curiosity on the part of the workers as well as so much solicitude on the part of the TVA: woodworking, general metal, automotive, electrical, ground aviation, blacksmithing, welding, plumbing, wrought-iron work, blueprint reading, even foremanship—are evidence of the determination to supply labor with chances in the future as well as in the present. Apprenticeship, a forgotten phase everywhere in the world, has been revived. Demonstration enterprises are run for the benefit of the employees: poultry farms, communal farm gardens, dairies, stock-breeding, principles of marketing, use of farm agencies, and so forth and so on.

The TVA has further created an entirely new feature, to which no parallel can be found in any organization—a bureau for the settlement of jurisdictional disputes, and for the maintenance of proper individual and collective relations between the supervisory personnel and the supervised workers. This section investigates complaints, makes reports to the parties concerned, and adjusts differences before they reach the stage of formal grievances. It functions both for whites and blacks. (I assisted at a meeting where, among other points discussed, the Negroes, who gave me an impression of startling intelligence and moderation, objected to being invariably addressed as a "son of a bitch" by certain foremen. The white head of this "Labor Relations staff" instantly promised redress.) There is a workers' council formed by the men, who debate on problems that could not be settled within the unions and groups themselves, and which thus can champion the unorganized worker: a new departure in the history of American labor. During its three and a half years of life there has never been a strike in the TVA personnel. There has been no bluff on the part of employer or employees. The deal has been fair and square throughout on either side; the cards have been played openly and straightly; and both capital and labor reveal that they can be teammates, with good-will and coöperation in a common cause, and honesty, tolerance, and patience toward problems of industrial relations.

All this seems to me exceptionally significant. When you analyze the domestic scene of a democratic country, you find that fundamentally its normal stability depends on the relations between capital and labor. With the exception of the Scandinavian nations, where admirable adjustments have been arrived at, no democratic country in Europe is a shining example of fairness; but, by and large, capital there has been bludgeoned into a modicum of wisdom. It has been frightened into compromise. It has made concessions—and a good many concessions; sometimes, even very difficult concessions—certainly not in a spirit of magnanimity, but of self-preservation. It has perceived that the trend of the times—queerly enough, in the fascist lands, too—is going against it; public opinion is much more readily on the side of the workingman than on that of the big employer; and social legislation was, until Mr. Roosevelt appeared, incomparably more developed in Europe than in the United States. No democratic European, whatever his party, can sympathize with the earsplitting clamors of Tory Americans about measures most of us put through thirty-five or forty years ago, and which are now completely academic issues. They have become part and parcel of our social life and philosophy, and could no more be wrenched from them than the principle of religious freedom. In America the fight for the social legislation we have already achieved is continuing, and the fight for political representation is only beginning.

At first, the foreign observer, especially if he lands in New York, is tempted to think that the whole country is in violent social convulsions. That is not so at present, though it will happen in the future if the salient features of capitalism are not modified. Certain spots, notably the enormous industrial and shipping centers, are in violent social convulsions, and strikes have a tendency to become horrifyingly brutal, a tendency for which I blame almost exclusively the unimaginable methods the employers use to break them, aided arbitrarily, and much too often, by the authorities and official forces of the states. The methods with which the great corporations fight the strikers are cave-man procedures, and I can find nothing approaching their equivalent in any other democracy.

But broadly speaking, labor in America is conservative. It is one of the most flabbergasting discoveries I have made. This conservatism is partly due to the antiquated policies of the American Federation of Labor; to its egotistic and frequently unreliable leadership; to the split-

ting up of the working classes into an aristocracy of highly protected
skills and crafts and a neglected and abandoned proletariat with no
attention paid to the untrained laborer and to the Negro; and to such a
stupefying lack of organization that out of 30,000,000 American workers only 3,500,000 are unionized. Partly, however, it is due to the temper of the American workingman himself. In general, his sense of solidarity was for a very long time practically nonexistent: it is not at all
effective yet. He clung with intense persistence to the traditional hope
of escaping one day, soon, from the ranks of the employee into the
ranks of the small entrepreneur and employer, where he would be hampered by the social legislation that would have benefited him as a
simple worker. Such an ambition deprived his social outlook of all
universality. He was much more ignorant and unthinking than his
European colleague. He read much less. In the South particularly,
where unions were extremely rare, he was usually quite illiterate, and
terrified to death of a system that could retaliate with literally murderous blows if he tried single-handedly to oppose it. Don't talk to me of
the aggressiveness of the American worker, because it is a farce.

Today he is waking up. There is much less chance of passing into
the higher strata; the activities of the socialist and communist parties
are prodding him into the consciousness of the right to collective bargaining and to unionization which is his already in modern civilized
countries; John L. Lewis, a gentleman who is not what could be
termed a sentimentalist, is putting his class on a new footing, both industrially and politically. In two or three decades, perhaps sooner, labor will really be a force that may tear the American domestic scene to
pieces if capitalism is obdurate. But the point I want to make is that
at this stage, in spite of symptoms that reveal the possibility of an ultimate march instead of a stumbling about, labor is still very ready
to be conciliating. After having poked a long enquiring nose into more
unions, meetings, and demonstrations—pickets, too—than I can count,
my unalterable conviction is that, whatever the fiery extremist groups
may say or do, the working man *en bloc* is still no revolutionist at all.
He still has no fanatical hatred of the capitalist. He still has no feeling
that the system is essentially unjust, infamous, execrable, and must be
wiped off the face of the earth. He still does not hold that he is capable
of taking the lead and conducting alone his country's economics. He

still is prepared to sit at the foot of capital's table and help himself to the remains of the huge dish. The one thing he insists on with growing energy and determination is that the remains should be sufficient to satisfy his reasonable necessities.

I do not say that this attitude will be his attitude eternally. I do not say that it is the intention of labor leaders that it should be his attitude eternally. I do not say that any attitude can be eternal. What I wish to drive home is the fact that it is his actual attitude. His historical and mental make-up is such that he may continue in it until the community as a whole is attuned to a basic social change, if it is met with reason and equity on the part of the employer, with coöperation on the part of capital, and with adjustments which he himself can freely formulate and practice. If these things are denied him—well, America can count on having in time a first-class bust-up. The labor policies of the TVA and their results prove conclusively that in a capitalistic democracy capital need not be cannibalistic, labor need not be revolutionary, and that the imperishable quest of man for the millennium can be pursued by evolution and adaptation instead of by blowing himself and his fellows in mud and blood to the skies. But whether autocratic capital in this country will consent, without pressure from somebody or something more autocratic still, to take the TVA as its model, is a question on which I seem to feel a few slight doubts.

Now for a fragment of personal history.

I started my thinking life with my belief entrenched in a resplendent trinity of divinities. They were God, love, and freedom. Pretty soon God died. I took it very hard; for years I went on wondering if He were only hidden and if by a strenuous search I wouldn't find Him again in some other guise. But I didn't. Later, love died. I took it harder still, and blew and blew and blew upon the ashes for an unmeasurable time, in the hope of igniting once more the ecstatical flame. But ashes, the ashes remained. So there is only freedom left. And I am damned if, as long as my brain, my vocal cords, and my hand function, I let anybody whisk my last, my supreme idol away.

It is of no importance whatever that I am not an American citizen and that the economics of America do not affect me directly. Liberty affects me, and it transcends territories and races. If liberty is injured or extinguished in America, the only thing that makes my life worth living is injured or extinguished too. I see it in possible danger in America. That is why I have written this booklet on the TVA.

I cannot foretell the remote future of the United States. But I can examine the present, though America is in a state of flux and mutation which makes it prodigiously difficult to discern all her trends. She impresses me especially with her tragic duality: her deathless aspiration for democracy and her incessant betrayal of democracy. I believe, however, that the betrayal is inadvertent. It has not been due to a deliberate relinquishing of principles, but to external temptation—the temptation of incomparable material opportunities overpowering an immature and ununified nation, and leading to results which the people had not seen and did not desire. Hailing from Europe as I do, with the images of Russia, Italy, Germany, Poland, Yugoslavia, Turkey, Spain, in my mind, it appears obvious to me that America, in spite of grievous lapses, is fundamentally and sincerely on the side of democracy.

What alarms me is that I cannot perceive what she is doing practically to give democracy a weightier and sturdier content and stiffen its defenses against its enemies. It is not yet necessary in this country to prove that dictatorship is an insult to the human spirit and a denial of human dignity; that whatever its objectives may be, fascistic or communistic, it puts man on the level of the savage; and that life is more normal, decent, and satisfying in a liberal regime than under the rule of one autocrat's will and ideas and emotions. On all these points, there still is no dispute in America. But the disquieting thing is that while the superiority of democracy is taken for granted, no serious attempt is being generally made to organize democracy in such a way that when an assault comes from the Right or the Left, democracy will be in a position victoriously to resist the blow. The blow must come: it is quite useless to invoke isolationism. There is no such thing as mental isolationism in the world of man. The Right and the Left represent world philosophies, doctrines and activities the impact of which America cannot ultimately escape.

I assume that we all know today that certain aspects of liberty—if they ever existed in any human society, which is exceedingly contestable—have vanished. Economic freedom does not exist for the overwhelming majority of people anywhere. Not only are most of us utterly unable to choose our occupation in accordance with our tastes and our aptitudes, but we have absolutely no assurance that once we have obtained a job we will keep it. It is not only the factory hands that are turned off at a moment's notice by hundreds of thousands for reasons which are wholly beyond their volition and knowledge; not only the agricultural laborer who gets no employment on the land. Businessman, professional man, technician, teacher, writer, artist, skilled worker, all of us drop out of a livelihood without reference to our needs, our wishes, our faculties, our merits, our past services. We have no voice in our own economic destiny. Leaving aside the major cataclysm of war, an inconceivable multitude of minor things, a depression in another country, the state of a distant market, the collapse of a faroff bank, an industrial or commercial combine, a financial maneuver, a new invention, can determine—and do determine—our economic fate, and every one of them is as removed from our personal control as the rising and the setting of the sun on the horizon. To talk of individualism in the terms and conditions of life in the twentieth century is either rhetoric or wishful-thinking. It corresponds to no reality or fact or truth. It is pure gibberish.

But though economic individualism is now unattainable, though economically we have now become subjects, and though democracy can no more offer us basic economic independence than dictatorship can, under a democratic regime we are not Helots. We possess freedom of conscience, freedom of thought, and freedom of expression. Today they alone differentiate us from the regimented masses in the enslaved countries. So long as we enjoy them, we have the only liberty that remains possible in our modern world, and the only one that essentially matters, for it alone is indispensable to a full inner life and to complete self-respect. It is all we must struggle to preserve, particularly as it is all we can preserve anyhow.

The vital question before democracy is, therefore, not how to bring back an economic freedom which is irretrievably lost, but how to prevent the intellectual freedom, which is still our heritage, from being submerged. It is already threatened. It will be threatened more and more strongly in the years ahead—and the menace, of course, is dictatorship. But to fight dictatorship it is necessary first to understand in what circumstances it arises, and then to think out the counterattack which democracy can launch against its approaching force.

Dictatorship springs from two very clear causes. One is the total incapacity of parliamentary government: total, as in Germany in 1933 and in Spain in 1935. To such a breakdown neither the democratic nations of Europe nor America have yet been reduced, although everywhere there are very ominous creaks and cracks, and the authority and prestige of parliamentary institutions have greatly and perilously diminished. The other cause, infinitely closer to us and more dynamic, is the failure of the economic machine to function properly, and by functioning properly I mean ensuring a livelihood for the entire population. No system can survive if it cannot procure food and wages for the people who live under it. Man has to get subsistence from his rulers, for the most immediate and the most imperious law of our nature is that the belly must be filled. It is perfectly futile to orate on fine, high, and abstract principles to human beings who are permanently hungry, permanently harassed, permanently uncertain, who hear their wives begging for the rent and their children crying out for nourishment.

The economic mechanism in America works so inefficiently that in the past it yielded bread in an extremely unequal fashion. Furthermore, it collapsed periodically. An American workingman who is sixty years old has had to pass more than one-third of his life in conditions of economic depression. A very short time ago the mechanism stalled so completely that it yielded no bread whatsoever to 20,000,000 Americans and their families. I know it has been put, slowly, jerkily, painfully, and dangerously into motion once more—and incidentally, I am appalled that it has been patched up, for the laissez-faireists are already shouting that its inherent virtue cranked it up, and the masses of the unthinking are already sliding lazily into the age-long, the facile and pernicious dream that now all will go happily for ever and ever. But that is not really the point. The machine has had ample time to prove its quality, and it has demonstrated that its quality is unacceptable to modern civilized man. The manifest conclusion is that it must be overhauled and its parts readjusted so that the whole will function at last without interruption and for the welfare of all.

One of the main tenets of liberalism—I reiterate this like a gramophone, but I must get it to sink in—is that all necessary overhauling and adjustment ought to be done in a manner which will minimize the shock to the greatest number, and soften as much as possible the unavoidable human suffering which these changes entail. This opposition to extremes, this practice of a graduated change, we can call "the middle of the road in time and space." But it is not nearly enough to conceive it and to bestow upon it a name. We must reach it. It is unutterably foolish to look at the middle of the road, to talk of the middle of the road, to hope for the middle of the road—and never get there.

Now I have tried to show that the middle of the road is already being laid down in America. The Tennessee Valley Authority is laying it down. Handicapped and restricted though it is in all sorts of ways, it is the noblest, the most intelligent, and the best attempt made in this country or in any other democratic country to economize, marshal, and integrate the actual assets of a region, plan its development and future, ameliorate its standards of living, establish it in a more enduring security, and render available to the people the benefits of the wealth of their district, and the results of science, discovery, invention, and disinterested forethought. In its inspiration and its goal there is goodness, for goodness is that which makes for unity of purpose with love, compassion, and respect for every life and every pattern of living. The economic machine, bad though it is, has not been smashed in the Tennessee Watershed; it is being very gradually, very carefully, very equitably reviewed and amended, and the citizens are being taught and directed, but not bullied, not coerced, not regimented, not frightened, within the constitutional frame the nation itself elected to build. It is not while the Tennessee Valley Authority has the valley in its keeping that despair or disintegration can prepare the ground for a dictatorship and the loss of freedom. The immortal contribution of the TVA to liberalism, not only in America but all over the world, is the blueprint it has drawn, and that it is now transforming into a living reality, of the road which liberals believe is the only road mankind should travel.

40.

1939

Émile S. W. Herzog, who uses the pen name, André Maurois, was born in 1885 and quickly built a distinguished career for himself as novelist and critic. He was a frequent visitor to the United States and a popular lecturer. Traveling widely and frequently through the

*country, he had exceptional opportunities to become acquainted with
it. In 1939 was published his* États-Unis 39 journal d'un voyage en
Amérique, *from which this account was taken.*

"What are the French customs in 'dating'?" I reproduce this question just as it was put to me, because at the first shock I was unable to
understand it. That was unforgivable, for I have long known the meaning of the word "date" in this sense, a meeting arranged by a young
man and woman to go out together. By an extension, the "date" is also
the person with whom the meeting is arranged. For example: "My date
is late."

I asked in reply what the American customs were in this respect,
and I was given a very interesting little book, *The Etiquette of the
Co-Ed.* The coeds are the students of both sexes raised together in the
same university. That is almost everywhere the American practice, although I must admit it does not seem to me very conducive to earnest
work. The sentimental and social life of the young people becomes so
rich and so passionate that they lack time for serious studies. They pass
four years so pleasantly that everything which follows seems dull and
empty. In the older eastern institutions where the separation of the
sexes persists (Harvard, Yale, and Princeton, for boys, and Bryn Mawr,
Vassar, and Smith, for girls) studies are taken more seriously.

Leafing through this book, I came to learn how difficult it was to
define the qualities that would make a girl popular in a coeducational
university. A girl who is cold gets no dates; a girl who allows herself to
be kissed by all her dates risks the chance of repelling the serious boy
who might marry her. The solution, according to the author, is to yield
as little as possible without frightening away potential suitors by an
excess of modesty. It is a question of limits.

Conversation with a Frenchman on American women:

"They seem to me," I told him, "more aggressive than French
women, more eager to capture a husband. I know that the French girls
also are on the quest from adolescence on, but it seems to me they go
about matters more nonchalantly and more objectively. The American
girl is constantly readying her weapons for the war of the sexes. She
passes a large part of her life in beauty parlors. Salesgirls, manicurists,
and stenographers sacrifice their lunches to pay for a facial or a permanent. Every issue of the women's magazines contains the order of

the day and calls to battle the armies of the unmarried: 'Use our toothpaste or your *halitosis* (bad breath) will ruin your chances of happiness! Read our books to conquer an intellectual! Streamline your underwear. A perfect complexion will be your self-starter.' Truly, young American girls are educated in the techniques of charm!"

"Yes," I was told, "but if you reflect, you will find all that very natural and due to economic reasons. Laws make habits, and contrary to appearances, American laws offer slight protection to women. In France, a girl whose parents have some wealth is certain to receive part of it by inheritance. At marriage the family assures her a dowry by contract. Although it is perhaps less true than before the war, the normal Frenchman of the middle class still lives and works for his children. Here there is nothing of the sort. A father can simply disinherit his children; law and custom both permit it. Often he leaves them only a dollar, to forestall possible challenges to the will. Then no inheritance, no dowry. Very often a rich father does not even give an allowance to his daughter, and sits by without remorse while she struggles for a livelihood. There are exceptions, but such is the rule. Under such conditions it is inevitable that the young American girl should make a place for herself in society, and that she should be, as you say, aggressive."

"But then," I asked, "who inherits these giant fortunes?"

"In most cases," he answered, "the wife. Almost always the husband dies first; American men are exhausted by overwork. Very often they disinherit their children for the profit of their wives. I will cite you an astounding figure: 70 per cent of the wealth of the United States belongs to women. That explains, in part at least, the violence of financial crises and the power of the bankers."

"And why," I asked, "should an American prefer his wife to his children?"

"To answer," was the reply, "is to trace the pattern of the average American's love life. Suppose he is raised in a coeducational university where young men and young women live together. At twenty he goes out each evening with a resolute young girl who has cast her net for him. His ideas on marriage are shaped by the movies, by the weekly magazines, and by the radio. The microphone and the screen daily drum in on him 'Love! Love!' He foresees a long life of kisses, with a creature made of ivory, roses, and coral, against a California or Florida

background. Two such children get married. Their union is not perfect
because such is the way of things in this world. The young husband
has no experience; the child-wife manages badly; the household is poor.
The happiness promised from Hollywood vanishes. No doubt Hollywood is right, they reason, but there has been an error in the selection
of a partner. The young wife casts about, discovers a man of thirty-
five, solidly established in a good job, married but tired of his wife who
is as old as he, and tempted by youth."

"He becomes her lover?"

"Not at all. America is not a land of adultery. No, he tells her:
'I wish to take you to Reno.' Reno is a city where liberal legislation
permits a divorce after only a short period of residence. The two old
households give way to two new ones. Sometimes the second marriage
succeeds, more often not, because of the same dreadful, the same
deadly striving for perfection. Europeans, more realistic and slightly
more cynical, take their misfortunes gaily, try to establish marital com-
promises, and temper their tolerance with occasional infidelities. At
that cost, the family survives. Such men can look forward, without too
much anxiety, to the security of old age; and they rest their hopes in
their children. But Americans continue to chase their romantic Hollywood illusions, and often shatter the second marriage as they did the
first.

"Even the elderly man, whether a widower or divorced by his wife,
does not renounce his great hopes. Reluctant to surrender to loneliness
or to take a mistress, he often seeks a young wife among the friends of
his own daughters; easily finds a willing one, marries her, and becomes
altogether inflamed—after all, such is the condition of elderly men. He
finds it altogether natural to leave her his fortune because he sees nothing else in the whole world and also because, as one of them tragically
told me, after the age of sixty 'one must each day buy the woman one
loves.' Corallary effect: the stepchildren receive each stepmother with
affection and respect because their future rests in the hands of this
stranger."

"And that is why 70 per cent of American fortunes belong to
women? But after all," I asked, "the habits that you describe are those
of a rather small number of millionaires?"

"Perhaps, but don't forget that wealth in the United States is very unequally distributed and that a large part of the nation's capital is controlled by a few families."

"You say that Americans shy away from adultery and rarely take mistresses? And nevertheless, I have read numerous novels in which ravishing secretaries, unforgettable nurses . . ."

"I didn't mean to say that Americans never have mistresses. What rarely exists here is the public liaison such as is common in Paris and London, the illegitimate couple that the whole world accepts each evening with married couples. That does not exist in America because it is socially unrecognized. A banker, a university professor, a politician would be disqualified if some such scandal clung to his name. Furthermore, why trouble with adultery when divorce is so easy and when the urge in a few months can receive a social sanction that makes it inoffensive? What does exist sometimes is the *Back Street;* the mistress too timid to force a marriage, or conscious of some insurmountable barrier of conditions, accepts life in the shadows. And what also exists where heavy drinking is common, is a beastly and evanescent promiscuity that leaves not even a souvenir."

These comments are certainly true of New York and of some large cities, but we must not forget the innumerable households, excellent, faithful, and very similar to the best of the French, in which are gathered the mass of the American population. With such I was once well-acquainted in Princeton; I encountered them everywhere in my travels; there are thousands even in New York. Those marked by scandals make more noise than the others. In America, as far as direct observations, even local and superficial, could reveal, marriage and the family are still solid. And these will maintain and save this society.

A brilliant article by Roussy de Sales on love in America presents the following theses: (a) In America, love, like democracy, is a national problem. The nation wants both to function perfectly. Since neither can ever achieve more than a compromise, there is constant disappointment. (b) America refuses to accept disappointments. In everything it feels the compulsion to be "successful." The businessman must succeed, the secretary must succeed, a husband and wife must succeed. And how can one attain success? Obviously by consulting an expert. Americans believe that anything can be taught. (c) In the last twenty years America has discovered its expert for love, Freud. Until that discovery, America suffered from puritan repressions, seemingly incurable. But here at last was revealed a system which explained that all would have gone well with you if only your pregnant mother, or your father, or your nursemaid had not made some mistake and loaded you with a complex. American households have now set forth in pursuit of their complexes. Roussy de Sales notes wittily:

I know a woman whose eyes shine with virtuous contentment after every open-hearted frank conversation with her husband, that is after she has spent several hours torturing him, or rather, more accurately, boring him to death by exposing the deplorable condition of their conjugal relations. After each of these periodic exchanges, self-satisfaction induces her to recount the details to her friends and even to her hairdresser: "Dick and I passed a marvelous night. We made a real effort to discover the truth about each other, or at least, I did. And I truly believe that we established a new basis for our union. It is a terrific consolation." Meanwhile, poor Dick, if he is present, is regretfully recalling the sleepless night.

In Fort Worth, I found the hotel full to the bursting point with young women in uniform.

"What is this militia dressed in white satin, wearing violet silk cloaks, capped in high military hats lavish with lace and gold braid, and decorated with silver pasteboard medals?"

"These are the Rebeccas," I was told.

"And who are they?"

"The feminine branch of a great political organization."

"And what are those crosses and stars?"

"Those are the insignia of rank in the society which boasts a long and complicated hierarchy."

Pushed around, overwhelmed by white uniforms, I nevertheless felt admiration for these Americans. I am pleased that a democratic country could reconstitute under other titles the rungs of aristocratic society. Human nature is immutable; if the democracies refuse to indulge in its vanities, more cynical and more adroit sources will do so. We can never have too many Rebeccas, too many mutual aid societies, too many titles, too many decorations. "I am the president of presidents," said Raimu in *Carnet de Bal*.

The Daughters of the American Revolution are the women or girls whose ancestors took part a hundred and fifty years ago in the war for independence. In France we lack this type of aristocracy. The Sons of the Regicides do not hold conventions in Bourges nor the Daughters of the Victims of the Terror at Nantes. That's because our regimes followed each other so rapidly that each wiped out the loyalties of its predecessors; the conquerors of the Bastille ceased to hold reunions as soon as Bonaparte came upon the scene. In America the continuity of the regime permitted the revolution to become hereditary and conservative.

Nevertheless, the D.A.R. this year had troublous times. They refused to rent their concert hall in Washington to Marian Anderson, a colored singer universally admired. Mrs. Roosevelt, who belonged by right of birth to the D.A.R., with reason condemned the action and handed in her resignation. Marian Anderson sang in the open air and was acclaimed by an immense crowd. When the convention met in Washington, the ladies, somewhat penitent, tried to make peace; they voted a resolution condemning German racism. According to custom, they were invited to the White House, but the First Lady was not at home to receive them. Nevertheless, this morning at their final meeting they passed a vote of thanks to Mrs. Roosevelt because, their president pointed out, although Mrs. Roosevelt was absent she had ordered their sandwiches. The net effect: a large number of Negroes who have voted for the Republicans since the Civil War, will vote Democratic next time.

I think it was J. B. Priestley who last year noticed the importance of the Cinderella theme in American movies. A young girl badly dressed, badly made-up, assists in the triumph of her more fortunate sisters, not with envy, but with sorrow. Suddenly, the prince charming, a famous orchestra director, a powerful producer, an important businessman, discovers that Miss Deanna Cinderella, his typist, is the greatest singer, the greatest actress, or the greatest designer in the world, and, in a sudden reversal of roles, misery gives way to glory, just as once Scheherazade's cobbler became sultan.

Fairy tales are always true. In the Orient the cobbler could become sultan; before my very eyes Lyautey performed that miracle. In America it is literally true that magicians and fairies are ready each morning to transform a manicurist into a singer, and her bus into a limosine. Social ranks are less rigid here than elsewhere, generosity more spectacular, and success more sudden.

There are even Americans who have adopted as a vocation the search for Cinderella. Last night, for instance, friends took us to see a curious spectacle, Major Bowes' "The Amateur Hour." The scene was the broadcasting studio of a radio station. About a thousand spectators were there. Like all American programs, this was sponsored by a business firm; Major Bowes officiated for an automobile company. The salary list published by the Treasury Department, informs us that he earns $450,000 a year. Any man or woman who thinks he has a singing voice, talent for acting, ability to dance or to play an instrument, can write to him. If the letter seems interesting it will be answered with the offer of an audition. Among the thousands of candidates who thus come forward each week, twelve or fifteen are chosen to appear on the air before the American public.

You may thus see an unknown young man step before the microphone. "What is your name," asks Major Bowes.—"John Hewitt."— "And what is your occupation, John?"—"I work for a building firm, major."—"But you sing also?"—"I sing for my pleasure, but I have never taken any lessons."—"Would you like to take any?"—"There's nothing I would like better, major . . . Music means everything to me."—"Well you sing something for us and if your voice deserves it, we will find you a teacher." John then sings, and 30,000,000 Americans listen to him, for the amateur hour is very popular. John has a very pleasant natural baritone voice. He has hardly finished when telephone congratulations begin to come into the basement where more than a hundred operators are ready to receive calls from all parts of the Union. Before the end of the program, Major Bowes announces that Angelo Tirani, of the B*** Opera, offers to accept John as a pupil without charge. There, without doubt, the whole course of a life is changed.

In two minutes are laid the foundations of future glories. Four Negro children, marvelous musicians, are so good that the Cotton Club, a famous New York night club, hires them on the spot. A little girl, gracefully charming, a new Shirley Temple, goes to Hollywood for a screen test. The public, which is kept informed of the votes registered by telephone, shares in the joy of those who triumph. Several artists are engaged by Major Bowes himself who directs a number of shows.

Without doubt, such things are also possible in Europe and we have more than once seen the destiny of a young writer transformed in a few seconds by the vote of a jury. But the *coups de théâtre* in an old country are less astonishing, and one rarely sees a whole nation take part with pleasure in their preparation. Here the fairy tale is not only possible; it is of the very essence of life. Cinderella herself becomes prima donna, is transformed into the fairy godmother, and in turn gives millions of dollars to help cinderellas of the next generation emerge from their chrysalis. New York, Chicago, Boston, are cities full of sordid corners in which frightful miseries are hidden. But from every American city every evening rises the voice of Scheherazade, who tells stories consoling and true.

Some Americans deplore such sentimentality. "It is unhealthy," they say, "to give people this absurd confidence in the lucky accident. Better the sad realism of your French films, the shabby and hopeless lives of the residents of *Hôtel du Nord.* That is more accurate, more courageous, and more human." But those who speak in this fashion are the poets and critics of New York, already spoiled by European disillusionment. The rest of America holds to its fairy tales.

It is impossible not to admire the prodigious effort made by the United States in the last half century to give itself an artistic culture; it is also impossible not to recognize the remarkable results of that effort. A lover of music is today more completely happy in New York than in any other city of the world. The presentations of Wagner at the Metropolitan Opera with Flagstad and Melchior are superb, better than those at Bayreuth. We listened in the auditorium of the National Broadcasting Corporation to a sublime performance of Berlioz's Symphonie Fantastique under Bruno Walter.

The public, taught to admire perfection, acquires a taste that is ever more certain. The musical education of the American people makes rapid progress. The stranger who tends to be skeptical begins by saying, "They go to concerts or to the opera house because it is fashionable." But he is quickly convinced of his errors. The immense crowds which remain standing at the Metropolitan through a whole performance of *Tristan* or of *Siegfried,* the young enthusiasts who continue to applaud a quarter of an hour after the curtain falls and who refuse to go away are not there simply to display themselves. The radio carries these excellent presentations to millions of listeners. Each Saturday morning Schelling gives his fine concerts for children in New York, inducing them at an early age to love and understand music.

In this respect, New York is not altogether an exceptional American city. Boston, Philadelphia, and Chicago have admirable orchestras. (I add here a note written a month later: In Dallas the inhabitants informed me with pride that the Metropolitan was coming to give some performances there. The barber in my hotel commented, "Do you know sir that we're having the New York opera here? I've got some tickets. They are expensive, but after all there's no greater pleasure. But I think the Metropolitan is putting one over on us. They're not bringing Lily Pons, or Melchior, or Kirsten Flagstad." I asked, "But do you know their voices?" "Of course," he answered, "from the radio and the records.") Yes, truly, in wide circles there is an authentic love of music.

There has also been rapid progress in the development of taste and love of painting. American museums were once repressed by the capricious interests of the wealthy men who endowed them. Collections in which masterpieces were mixed with horrors had to be displayed as a whole because the owner stipulated that they were not to be divided. It was not unusual to see copies and fakes gracing the walls of millionaires' houses. It still happens, here as elsewhere, that a *nouveau riche* displays with pride a Rembrandt or a Raphael that originated in the flea market. But that becomes ever rarer. Museums and large private collections are administered by learned officials. There could be nothing more refined, for example, than the display of the Frick Collection. A few pictures, all admirable, ranging from Fragonard to the most beautiful Vermeers in the world, are housed in a quiet and well-furnished building, always full of fresh flowers. Here only order and beauty reign.

Just as the great Florentine merchants were once the first to appreciate the paintings of the fifteenth century, so the great merchants of New York, Philadelphia, and Chicago were the first to understand the painting of our times. They began to love the French painting at the time when Frenchmen hardly tolerated it. It is to America, alas, that one must go to know that dazzling period in which Renoir, Degas, Manet, Monet, Boudin, and Cézanne made France in the eyes of painters what Italy was in the Renaissance and Holland in the seventeenth century. (Here again, after my journey I added a note: The large cities which boast museums are not alone in the effort to bring the best paintings to the knowledge of their citizens. In Oklahoma, a young state, I knew a professor and art critic who had gathered a remarkable collection of reproductions in color, very faithful, of the best impressionist works and who toured from town to town presenting exhibitions with comments to shape the taste of the public.)

The Cloisters is a new museum of medieval French art in New York. Its history is interesting. Along the banks of the Hudson there was a beautiful private park. Mr. Rockefeller wished to buy and give it to the New Yorkers. A young American scholar trained in the Sorbonne and a great admirer of our Middle Ages conceived the project of carrying across certain monuments which he claimed were falling to pieces because of lack of funds to maintain them. He designed a plan, made models, sought an interview with Mr. Rockefeller, and explained the project. Mr. Rockefeller asked the cost; several million dollars was needed. "Go ahead," he said. Today the museum is complete, and dominates the Hudson Valley.

Such an enterprise seems a priori dubious. To transport stone by stone and to reconstruct the cloisters and capitulary hall for purposes of display seemed hardly possible without errors of taste. Would it not have been better to allow a monument to die a natural death in the surroundings for which it was built than to transplant it? In fact, Frenchmen, many of them specialists, who have visited the Cloisters have not been shocked. The museum contains a few well-selected statues, a single series of tapestries, and the cloisters were reconstructed with such care that the very flowers planted by the monks in their gardens were brought across. I do not believe it possible to have more adequately presented the art of the French Middle Ages in a country so far and so different.

Since I have launched upon this series of eulogies, I must add that at a time when it becomes almost impossible to publish beautiful books in Europe for the lack of subscribers, some of our illustrators have found work in America. A group of bibliophiles (Limited Editions Club) publishes collections of masterpieces printed to meet the most discriminating tastes. French works have a substantial place in this series. There will soon appear a series of the ten greatest French novels including *Princesse de Clèves* (with a preface by Jean Cocteau), *Manon Lescaut* (with a preface by Abel Hermant), *Liaisons dangereuses* (with a preface by André Gide), *Chartreuse de Parme* (with a preface by Giraudoux), *Père Goriot* (with a preface by Mauriac), *Germinal* (with a preface by Montherlant), *Candide* (with a preface by Jaloux), and *Madame Bovary* (with a preface by Lacretelle).

All this is certainly admirable. Paul Morand has already predicted that culture banished from Europe will one day find refuge in Manhattan. Some American journals proclaim that the day of American grandeur and of European decadence has already come. Despite the sympathy I bear their country and despite the undeniable progress I have already described, I cannot agree.

First of all, the creative power of Europe remains superior to that of the United States. The Americans build admirable museums, but they are filled with European works. The Metropolitan Opera has the best orchestra and the most talented singers in the whole world, but the works they present are not composed by Americans. Patriots may reply that Europe has the advantage of a longer past, and that their country was, at its start, the heir of English and French culture. That is true. Nevertheless, even as far as contemporary works are concerned, Europe still deserves its prestige. In the United States there are certainly musicians, sculptors, and painters of talent, but these artists themselves recognize the Europeans as their masters.

Furthermore, in America the longing for novelty and originality sometimes overwhelms good taste. The American public is quickly bored. Frenchmen and Englishmen, raised with a respect for the classics, immersed from infancy in the study of the human past, resemble ships of deep keel or icebergs whose submerged portion is greater than the visible; that encourages stability of spirit and a public which sins rather by an excess of conservatism. American taste is very fluid. The love of the bizarre of which Poe spoke is here all powerful. That which astonishes earns respect. The critics fear to criticize the unfamiliar beauty, a worthy scruple; but they are also reluctant to praise classic beauty, an unworthy scruple. The generosity of millionaire patrons of the arts yields fine results when a Rockefeller builds the Cloisters or a Mellon the Washington Museum, but sad ones when a manganese king, for sentimental reasons, is infatuated with foolish and insincere paintings.

The other day, my wife broke a spring on her typewriter. The firm which manufactures the machine owns a twenty-story building in New

York and my wife went there to have the repair done. She had no success.

"That is surprising," I told her, "you must have applied at the wrong department. I will go back with you."

There followed a long discussion with the employees of the store, who tried to sell me a new machine and to make me forget the one I brought. Finally, I discovered that there was a repair department on the sixteenth story. A surprised young man was suspicious and raised a thousand objections.

"We must send the machine to the factory," he said.

"But why? You can simply replace the part."

"But we don't carry replacement parts."

"All right, send the machine to the factory and return it to us at our hotel, the . . ."

"No," he said, "you must come here to get it."

"That will cost us another afternoon. Haven't you got a delivery service?"

"For new, not for repaired machines."

"And why not?"

After some hesitation, he ended by confessing that the company desired to discourage people like us who wished to bring back old machines for repair. In this country as soon as anything shows signs of wear it is discarded for something new. That is true of automobiles, of ladies' stockings, of clothing. Everything in America made by mass production is made better than anywhere else; but anything that takes individual attention interrupts the steady flow of the production lines. I had the utmost difficulty in discovering in a sixteen-hundred room hotel the person whose function it was to sew on buttons.

Another example of the inflexibility of the machines: In my fountain pen I use an American ink packed in glass cartridges. When I tried to buy a box of these cartridges in New York, I learned that they are made only for export and that Americans use ink in bottles.

"That may be," I explained, "but in my pen I can only use the cartridges. Give me a box."

"We don't carry them."

"You have them in the export department."

"Of course, but it is very difficult to make transactions between departments."

I telegraphed to France. A few days later, the *Normandie* brought me the cartridges of ink, made in New York, but forced to cross the Atlantic twice to reach me.

The District of Columbia is prosperous. The New Deal for the first time in American history made Washington not only the political but also the economic capital of the country. Everywhere monumental buildings spring up to house new federal agencies. One hundred and forty thousand civil servants live here. There are no factories; Washington industry produces only releases, formulas, and directives. Through the wide doors of the various departments, millions of them pour forth upon all forty-eight states. To influence government for their own ends, thousands of petitioners invade Washington. The lobbyist, the man who haunts the corridors of the Senate, the House, and the departments, is as characteristic of Washington as the gondolier of Venice. He comes to prove that his firm needs a tariff, that his river is drying out for want of improvements, that the New Deal must, at great expense, teach Arizona and Arkansas the love of the arts.

In the hotels the lobbyist meets congressmen and senators. A senator in Washington is like a cardinal in Rome. The French Senate is not without prestige, but the American Senate enjoys much more from the smaller number of its members, from its wider powers, and from its fantastic attitudes. Each state in the Union has only two senators, and since some of these states are veritable nations with ten- or twelve-million residents, their senators are more ambassadors than legislators and treat with the White House as with an equal power. Armed by the Constitution, with the power to oppose the wishes of the President in many cases, the Senate uses its authority with delight. Those rosy complexioned old men are as coquettish and captious as maidens. The senators revel in opposition; contrariness is a sport, and obstruction a relaxation.

The Senate ignores party lines. It is a *corps de ballet* made up entirely of stars, a troupe which leads its leaders a hard life. One-third of the Senate was able to vote down the treaty of 1919, despite Wilson, and thus keep America from entering the League of Nations.

If I had the leisure to live in this city a few months I would write *Du Coté de chez Lincoln*. Proust would certainly have found pleasure in the fine problems of etiquette that arise here. How does one place at a table, a Senator, a justice of the Supreme Court, the English ambassador, and the husband of Miss Perkins, the Secretary of Labor? Conflicts over precedence wage as fiercely between the Supreme Court, the Senate, and the diplomatic corps as in France among the nobility of the old regime and of the empire, and the republican hierarchy. The judges of the Supreme Court, being the incarnation of the law, abstract divinities in a manner of speaking, consider themselves princes of a church before whom even ambassadors should bow.

For eight days I have seen and spoken with a large number of men of all parties and all classes about the economic situation of their country. In 1933 I described the beginnings of the Roosevelt era, and now six years later would like to write of the event.

One must remember, to begin with, the circumstances under which the President took office. Conditions were tragic. I saw America at the point of crisis. The nation was in a state of panic. Fourteen-million unemployed were scarcely being kept alive. The states and the municipalities lacked funds to feed families without work. The free lodging-houses were overpacked. The ruling classes no longer ruled and no longer even proposed remedies. The country headed straight for social disaster. The elevator had reached the basement; it could go no lower. If Roosevelt had at that moment asked the citizens of the United States to save the nation by standing on their heads in the middle of a public place, they would have done so. Yes, all, at that time, from banker to laborer.

He did make that demand. I mean, he asked them to reverse a customary way of action. Indoctrinated by the young economists of the Brain Trust, the President set forth the following thesis: Until now the spirit of risk, the creation of new industries, and the development of savings brought prosperity to our land. But we have reached the end of a frontier. Territorially, the westward movement has been completed and there are no new lands to occupy. Industrially, production has grown more swiftly than consumption. The American state no longer needs to encourage savings to furnish capital to new enterprises that would be condemned before their birth; it must discourage investments and increase the purchasing power of the masses. Therefore, taxes on income, on the undivided profits of corporations, and on stock-market gains are called for, as are raises in wages, support to labor unions, and, above all, large government expenditures in the form of unemployment relief to awaken purchasing power.

Such was the program, and certainly the New Deal succeeded in discouraging investments. But did it solve the economic problem? After six years, the most sympathetic observer could not claim that. In 1937, for a few months there was the impression that a true recovery impended, but as soon as the government made a move to slacken the flow of subsidies the fall in prices was again precipitate. The patient survives and even seems cheerful, but only constant injections sustain him, and that is a treatment that no organism can long keep up. In fact, there remain 10,000,000 or 11,000,000 unemployed, 4,000,000 families to support. Wages are higher, but not the purchasing power of the masses because the cost of production has risen with wages. The American deficit has reached a stage at which the French budget, by comparison, seems a model of prudence and thrift. No one knows how or when the budget will again be balanced. Meanwhile, a bitter quarrel rages around the President between the moderates, like Secretary of the Treasury Morgenthau who wishes to throw the machine into reverse or at least to apply the brakes, and a new crowd of impenitent New Dealers who, on the contrary, wish to keep the accelerator to the floor boards.

What are the causes of the present difficulties? First, the discouragement of businessmen, who say they are and feel persecuted. To be sure, some control was necessary and many reforms urgently needed. But control did not have to be hostile. Rightly or wrongly, the industrialists have the impression that the young Washington economists govern against the capitalist. Perhaps if their coöperation had been called for in a friendly fashion, the businessmen might have coöperated, especially at the beginning, to combat abuses the dangers of which the best among them recognized. Attacked, slandered before incompetent and clumsy commissions of inquiry, they have curled up like hedgehogs. Promises of reconciliation leave them cold. Few among them dare today make long-range plans, initiate new enterprises, build, take on hands. They wait for 1940, the date of the presidential election.

Then there is the unexpected effect of certain measures. To legislate is simple, but to foresee the consequences of human laws is almost impossible. For example, the requirement that corporations distribute

their reserves prevented many from going on to make needed improvements or additions. That in turn led to a falling off in orders for machines, depreciation of equipment, and the rise of unemployment. Another example: the rule prohibiting the officers of corporations to trade
freely in their own stocks, now deprives a violently fluctuating market
of a useful counterpoise. The intentions of the legislators were good;
the effects of the legislation bad.

Again, there is the interference, always dangerous, of politics with
the means of production. The motivation of the President was admirable; the politics of his partisans much less so. Unemployment relief
became, in certain states, a subsidy to voters. The administration of
the W. P. A. (Works Progress Administration) which should, in principle, have put the unemployed to work on useful projects, fell, at least
in the beginning, into the hands of eager professional politicians. Voters
were influenced by threats of loss of wages. Thousands of persons were
placed on the W. P. A. rolls immediately before elections and stricken
off immediately after. The policy of "spend-spend, tax-tax, elect-elect"
shocked many good souls, and whether the President was personally
concerned or not, deprived the New Deal of much of its moral prestige.

Finally, there is the immaturity of labor and of employers' associations. In every country the labor unions can render great public service, if while defending, as they should, the rights of their members, they
show themselves at the same time ready to collaborate whenever the
common interests of employers and employees are at stake. That is the
practice, for example, of the English trade unions. But those organizations are rich in experience; they possess capital; they take respon-
sibilities. In America, two rival federations, William Green's A. F. of L.
and John Lewis' C.I.O. struggle for control in a battle charged with
overbidding and demagoguery. The Wagner Act, it is said, has considerably weakened the authority of management and, so long as it
remains unamended, the business world feels it is subject to an unjust
and hostile power.

I asked a Frenchman, a resident of the United States who knows its
people intimately, "What groups in this country are, by conviction,
sympathetic with Hitler?"—"Very few," he answered. "Naturally, the
Bund, and some other German-Americans, but not all, far from that;
then, some organizations like the Knights of the White Camelia; some

followers of Father Coughlin; altogether 10 to 15 per cent of the population, at a maximum."

"And the opposition of the extreme left?"

"Still less."

"And the rest is for us?"

"No," he told me, "the rest is against our opponents."

What total impression does a long voyage leave? This is an immense country made up of overpopulated islands sprinkled among the prairies, the forests, and the deserts. Among these islets of skyscrapers there is hardly any common life. The newspapers of Minneapolis are not read in Cincinnati. The great man of Tulsa is unknown in Dallas. The Negro of Georgia, the Swede of Minnesota, the Mexican of San Antonio, and the German of Chicago, Marquand's patricians, and Steinbeck's tramps are all citizens of the United States, but there is slight resemblance among them. Often in the last few months I was struck with the question of whether the unity of this country was not artificial, whether it was capable of survival.

Today, classifying, sorting out, reviewing these memories under the ocean sky, I came to an answer: This unity will come through. Despite the aspects of diversity, a common basis does exist. Let me try to enumerate the ties which strengthen American unity.

It is obviously an error to say that the interests of these regions are different, that the agricultural Middle West wants a rise in the price of wheat, that the industrial East wants wages low, that the same laws cannot satisfy both, and that they will end by separating. Diversity of production, on the contrary, renders the Union indispensable to all. The East could not get along without the Middle West, the farmer without the laborer, and economic unity prescribes political unity.

A curious unity of habits and thoughts is created by the movies, the magazines, the radio, advertising, and the newspaper chains. The daily newspaper rarely circulates beyond the limits of one state; but *Time, Life, The Saturday Evening Post, The New Yorker,* and ten others are seen everywhere; Amos and Andy are heard by more than 30,000,000 listeners; the articles of Walter Lippmann and of Dorothy Thompson are reproduced by 200 papers and read by 7,000,000 readers. Through the efforts of the Book of the Month Club the same volume is distributed in the same week from the Atlantic to the Pacific. Thus the Americans who never meet each other and who live under different skies come to have innumerable common memories and brotherly thoughts.

Little by little the American federation is transforming itself into a union, marked by the growth in importance of the role of the federal capital. In the beginning, the United States had only a small federal bureaucracy. Today the central administration is powerful and rich. Public assistance is already in large part within its province. Sooner or later that will also be true of education. Some day the railroads will be unified. One may regret that tendency, but its power cannot be denied.

Finally, most of the citizens of the United States are united by a common faith; they believe in their institutions and in the virtues of liberty. They believe in the possibility of a better future for a free people. They even hope that an understanding of free peoples everywhere will some day prevent most wars. In a word, they are optimists.

Or, more accurately, they were. The extent and persistence of unemployment, the length of the crisis, the stalemate in economic experimentation, have struck deeply at this American faith. The young men and women in the universities, the workers in the factories, the farmers on the marginal lands, begin to ask if the system is likely to live long. Foreign propaganda, communist and totalitarian alike, stirs up their resentment. Roosevelt appeases discontent somewhat by distributing acquired wealth; but when the day comes when the reserves are exhausted, it will not be easy to govern America.

Basically, the problem lies not in a choice between two opposing solutions, communism or fascism, Roosevelt or laissez-faire, but in a levy on each theory for the elements of validity it contains. Hegel's formula—thesis, antithesis, synthesis—is always true. A directed economy does not function well; total liberalism is unhappily no longer possible. Absolute laissez-faire presumed that the passions and desires of individuals, their hopes and their fears, would assure the equilibrium of the market by millions of compensations. That was once true. But in a world where propaganda and information spread in a few seconds throughout the planet, happy indifference no longer serves as counterfoil to error, ignorance is no longer the marvelous buffer that deadens the follies of the reasoning reason. The machine has lost its regulator. And, of course, how can one speak of classical liberalism in a period of cartels, of trusts, of monopolies? But to reinforce by a state economy the existing rigidity of the mechanism would be to act like a man with high blood pressure who takes adrenalin to raise it.

What must be done? I believe we must act the cautious doctor, try what we have, let that alone which works, try what remedies are at hand, increase the doses of medicines which seem to succeed, change the method if it seems to fail, and, above all, keep up the patient's morale. It seems to me that the weakest point in the recent American experiences was that they were almost all directed against someone. One class was ranged against another. No government can thus construct an enduring system. A government has the right to be firm; it has the right to be severe and to demand a respect for the laws; but it has not the right to hate. We will not emerge from our present difficulties by class war, but by love and by a mutual effort of intelligence and understanding.

Bibliographical Notes

BIBLIOGRAPHICAL NOTES

1. *Naauwkeurige Beschryving van Noord-America zynde thans het Toneel des Oorlogs, En in dat Wereldeel de Bezittingen der Spanjaarden, Franschen, Engelschen, Hollanders, En andere Europiaansche Natien, de byzondere Eilanden, Aard, Zeden, Levensmanieren der Inboorlingen, Climaat, Vruchten, Planten, Gewassen, Dieren, Vissen, en de Visvangst op de Banken van Terra Neuve.* door J.C.N. Geboortig te *Rotterdam*, dog reeds in de twintig Jaren Borger en Inwoonder in de *Engelsche Colonie.* Te Dordrecht: Adriaan Walpot en Zoon, 1780. ["An Accurate Description of North America (which is) at Present the Scene of the War, and of the Spaniards, French, English, Dutch, and other European Peoples, of the Separate Islands, of the Character, Manners, and Mode of Life of the Natives, of the Climate, Fruits, Plants, Crops, Animals, Fish, and of the Fishing off the Banks of Newfoundland. by J.C.N. born in Rotterdam but for Twenty Years Citizen and Inhabitant of the English Colonies."] The selection here presented was made up of passages translated from a chapter on the "Manners of the Savages," pp. 139–149.

2. Pehr Kalm, *En Resa til Norra America, på Kongl. Svenska Wetenskaps Academiens befallning, och publici Kostnad forrättad.* Stockholm: Lars Salvii, 1753–61. The passage here presented is based on the English translation of 1770 by John R. Forster as edited by Adolph B. Benson (New York, 1937; 2 vols.). It has, however, been revised and rearranged after a check against the definitive Swedish edition of Fredr. Elfving and George Schauman (Helsingfors, 1904–15; 3 vols.). The selections may be found in their original form in the Elfving and Schaumann edition, vol. II, pp. 121–122, 130, 132, 135–136, 153–154, 162–163, 241–243, 245–248, 251–254, 257–259, 319–327, 330, 337–344, 347, vol. III, pp. 100–103, 146–150; and in the Benson edition, vol. I, pp. 19–20, 27–28, 30, 33, 48–49, 56, 125–126, 128–131, 133–136, 138–140, 189–195, 198, 204–209, 211, 307–309, 343–346.

3. J. Hector St. John [Michel Guillaume Jean de Crèvecœur], *Letters from an American Farmer; Describing Certain Provincial Situations, Manners, and Customs, Not Generally Known; and Conveying Some Idea of the Late and Present Interior Circumstances of the British Colonies in North America Written for the Information of a Friend in England by a Farmer in Pennsylvania.* London: Thomas Davies, 1782. These

selections appear in the first edition on pp. 45–59, 62–66, 69–80, 121–125, 130–131, 146–148, 150–158, 162–167, 170–171, 176–178, 182–198, 201–203.

4. [Author Unknown], "Reise-Diarium der Geschw. Reichels und ihrer Gesellschaft von Litiz nach Salem in der Wachau von 22 May bis 15 Jun. 1780," Moravian Church of America, Southern Province Archives. These selections were edited from the translation by Miss Adelaide L. Fries in *Travels in the American Colonies.* Edited by Newton D. Mereness under the auspices of the National Society of the Colonial Dames of America. New York: The Macmillan Company, 1916. Pages 586–599.

5. Jacques Pierre Brissot de Warville, *Nouveau Voyage dans les États-Unis de l'Amérique septentrionale, fait en 1788.* Paris: Buisson, 1791. Volume I, pp. 111–146, 150–153, 157–160, 163, 167–174, 177–189, 198–199; vol. II, pp. 250–252, 257–268, 271–274, 276–289.

6. [Méderic Louis Élie] Moreau de Saint-Méry, *Voyage aux États-Unis de l'Amérique, 1793–1798.* Edited with an Introduction and Notes by Stewart L. Mims. New Haven: Yale University Press, 1913. Pages 51–55, 57–61, 160–161, 166–167, 286–293, 299–310, 312–314, 353–354. An English translation by Mr. and Mrs. Kenneth Roberts appeared after the completion of the present version.

7. *Reise von Hamburg nach Philadelphia.* Hannover: in der Ritscherschen Buchhandlung, 1800. Pages 111–115, 121–124, 136–140, 143–151, 154–158.

8. F[rançois] A[ndré] Michaux, *Voyage à l'ouest des monts alléghanys, dans les états de l'Ohio, du Kentucky, et du Tennessée, et retour à Charleston par les Hautes-Carolines; contenant des détails sur l'état actuel de l'agriculture et les productions naturelles de ces contrées, ansi que des renseignemens sur les rapports commerciaux qui existent entre ces États et ceux situés à l'est des montagnes et la Basse-Louisiane entrepris pendant l'an X—1802, sous les auspices de Son Excellence M. Chaptal, Ministre de l'Intérieur.* Paris: Levrault, Scheoll et cie., 1804. Pages 61–70, 80–86, 115–122, 203–214, 291–294, 296–299, 302–303. The English translation of 1805 is reproduced in vol. III of R. G. Thwaites, *Early Western Travels 1748–1846.* Cleveland: Arthur H. Clark Company, 1904.

9. [Louis-Elizabeth?, baron de Montlezun], *Voyage fait dans les années 1816 et 1817, de New-Yorck à la Nouvelle-Orléans et de l'Orénoque au Mississipi, par les Petites et les Grands-Antilles, contenant des détails absolument nouveaux sur ces contrées; des portraits de personnages influant dans les États-Unis, et des anecdotes sur les refugiés qui y sont établis; par l'auteur des souvenirs des Antilles.* Paris: Librairie de Gide fils, 1818. Volume I, pp. 37–42, 51–53, 66–68, 80–84, 100–102, 106–108, 123–126, 132–134, 153–156, 158–164, 166–173, 236–238, 242–246, 253, 264–267, 279–280, 305–308, 336–337.

10. Giovanni Grassi, S.J., *Notizie varie sullo stato presente della repubblica*

degli Stati Uniti dell'America settentrionale scritte al principio del 1818. Milano: Giovanni Silvestri, 1819. Pages 17–26, 29–42, 44–47, 60–73.

11. *Reise Sr. Hoheit des Herzogs Bernhard zu Sachsen-Weimar-Eisenach durch Nord-Amerika in den Jahren 1825 und 1826.* Herausgegeben von Heinrich Luden. Weimar: Wilhelm Hoffman, 1827. Volume I, pp. 115–117, 119–120, 315; vol. II, pp. 14, 15, 27–29, 37–38, 74, 78–80, 176–179, 204–212, 241–245. An English version appeared in Philadelphia in 1828.

12. Charles Alexis Henri Clérel de Tocqueville, *De la Démocratie en l'Amérique.* 12 ed.; Paris: Pagnerre, 1848. Volume II, pp. 102–125.

13. Isidore Löwenstern, *Les États-Unis et la Havane souvenirs d'un voyage.* Paris: Arthur Bertrand, 1842. Pages 151, 154–159, 167–180.

14. Henri Herz, *Mes Voyages en Amérique.* Paris: Achille Fauré, 1866. Pages 48–50, 52, 55–57, 59–62, 83–84, 89–100, 103–104, 117–118, 120–124, 126–131, 146–159, 167–171, 181–189, 194–206, 210–213, 238–239, 260–261, 273–274, 276–278, 289–292, 309, 316–318.

15. Ole Munch Ræder, *America in the Forties the Letters of Ole Munch Ræder.* Translated and edited by Gunnar J. Malmin. Minneapolis: University of Minnesota Press, 1929. Pages 1, 2, 4, 5, 10–13, 15–18, 22–26, 33, 34, 37, 38, 54, 55, 57–59, 62–68, 73–78, 83, 84, 86, 87. This volume is copyright by the University of Minnesota Press, by whose permission this selection is used.

16. Fredrika Bremer, *Hemmen i den nya Verlden en Dagbok i Bref, skrifna under tvenne års Resor i Norra Amerika och på Cuba.* Stockholm: P. A. Norstedt & Söner, 1853. Volume I, pp. 88–94, 131–133, 135–136, 138–140, 142–143, 147–149, 169–170, 195–197, 204–205, 221–225, 285; vol. II, pp. 426–427, 459–460; vol. III, pp. 264–265. An English translation by Mary Howett appeared in New York in the same year.

17. Francis and Theresa Pulszky, *White Red Black. Sketches of Society in the United States during the Visit of Their Guest.* London: Trubner and Co., 1853. Volume I, pp. 77–83, 85–86, 234–244; vol. II, pp. 120–126, 128–132, 269–275; vol. III, pp. 72–79, 81–82, 88–90.

18. Theodor Griesinger, *Lebende Bilder aus Amerika.* Stuttgart: Wilh. Nitzschke, 1858. Pages 26–35, 65–72, 113–121, 204–214.

19. I[srael] J[oseph] Benjamin II, *Drei Jahre in Amerika 1859–1862. 1. Theil. Die östlichen Staaten der Union und San Francisco.* Hannover: Selbstverlag des Verfassers, 1862. Volume I, pp. 59–66, 68–84.

20. Prof. Cav. Giovanni Capellini, *Ricordi di un viaggio scientifico nell' America settentrionale nel MDCCCLXIII.* Bologna: Giuseppe Vitali, 1867. Pages 143–151, 154–157, 240–241.

21. Joseph Alexander, graf von Hübner, *Promenade autour du monde, 1871.* Paris: Hachette et cie., 1873. Volume I, pp. 25–30, 46–51, 57, 60–62, 66–70, 80–84, 114–119, 146–156, 158–159, 161, 163–166, 168–169, 177–179, 184–186, 206–219, 230–234, 305–311, 313–319. An English translation by Lady Herbert appeared in London in 1874.

22. Ernst Otto Hopp, *Transatlantisches Skizzenbuch, Federzeichungen aus den amerikanischen Leben*. Berlin: Otto Janke, 1876. Pages 199–204, 209–212, 214, 227–228.

23. Charles Boissevain, *Van 't Noorden naar 't Zuiden. Schetsen en Indrukken van de Vereenigde Staten van Noord-Amerika*. Haarlem: H. D. Tjeenk Willink, 1881–82. Volume II, pp. 218–234.

24. Dott. Carlo Gardini, *Gli Stati Uniti ricordi con 76 illustrazioni e carte*. 2d ed.; Bologna: Nicola Zanichelli, 1891. Volume I, pp. 42–47, 223–234.

25. P. A. Tverskoy [pseud. of Peter A. Demens], *Ocherki Sievero-Amerikanskikh Soedinenykh Shtatov*. St. Petersberg: I. N. Skorokhodov, 1895 ["Sketches of the North American United States"]. Pages 30–38, 124–133, 135–140, 142–144, 150–155.

26. Paul Bourget, *Outre-Mer* (*notes sur l'Amérique*). Paris: Alphonse Lemerre, 1895. Volume II, pp. 142–153, 157–175. An English edition was published in New York at the same time.

27. Ernst Below, *Bilder aus dem Westen*. Leipzig: Fr. Wilh. Brunow, 1894. Pages 203–212.

28. Giuseppe Giacosa, *Impressioni d'America*. Milano: L. F. Cogliati, 1908. Pages 53–68, 85–89, 173–192.

29. Count Peter Vay de Vaya und zu Luskod, *Nach Amerika in einem Auswandererschiffe; das innere Leben der Vereinigten Staaten*. Berlin: Gebrüder Paetel, 1908. Pages 114–123, 133–140, 189–190, 192–194, 272–282. This selection is used by permission of E. P. Dutton & Co., Inc., New York, and John Murray, London, publishers of the authorized copyright translation, *Inner Life of the United States*. London, 1908.

30. Abbé Félix Klein, *Au Pays de "la vie intense."* Paris: Librairie Plon, 1905. Pages 191–211, 331–336. An English version by the author appeared in Chicago in the same year.

31. Arthur Holitscher, *Amerika Heute und Morgen Reiseerlebnisse*. Berlin: S. Fischer Verlag, 1912. Pages 251–255, 274–282, 287–289, 375–381.

32. Julio Camba, *Un Año en el otro mondo*. Madrid: Espasa-Calpa, s.a., n.d. [3d ed., 1927]. Pages 65–68, 113–117, 139–142, 157–159, 171–174, 179–181, 195–206.

33. Alma Isabel Sofia Hedin, *Arbetsglädje; Lärdomar från Amerika*. Stockholm: A. Bonnier, 1920. Pages 20–25, 46–58.

34. Henri Hauser, *L'Amérique vivante*. Paris: Librairie Plon, 1924. Pages 66–99.

35. Felix, graf von Luckner, *Seeteufel erobert Amerika*. Leipzig: Koehler & Ameling, 1928. Pages 97–105, 206–207, 262–264.

36. Ernst Toller, *Quer Durch Reisebilder und Reden*. Berlin: Gustav Kiepenheuer Verlag, 1930. Pages 14–19, 32–40, 44–55, 58–64. This selection was used with the permission of Sampson Low, Marston & Co., Ltd., London, publishers of the authorized, copyright English translation by Hermon Ould (*Which Way?*, London, 1931).

37. *Egon Erwin Kisch beehrt sich darzubieten: Paradies Amerika.* Berlin: Erich Reiss Verlag, 1930. Pages 42–44, 134–139, 187–191.

38. Prof. Dr. J[an] G[erard] Sleeswijk, *Van Menschen en Dingen in Amerika.* Amsterdam: Scheltens & Giltay, n.d. [1933]. Pages 204–208, 228–249.

39. Odette Keun, *A Foreigner Looks at the TVA.* New York: Longmans, Green & Co., 1937. Pages 75–89. This volume is copyright by Longmans, Green & Co., 1937, with whose permission this selection is used.

40. André Maurois, *États-Unis 39 journal d'un voyage en Amérique.* Paris: Les Éditions de France, 1939. Pages 17, 27–33, 36, 52, 60–64, 99–101, 103, 141–145, 182–185, 191–195.

ACKNOWLEDGMENTS

I am very grateful to the following authors and publishers for their kindness in granting permission to use material from works to which they have rights: Albert Bonniers Förlag (Hedin, *Arbetsglädje*); Señor Julio Camba and Espasa-Calpe, s. a. (Camba, *Un Año*); Les Éditions de France (Maurois, *États-Unis 39*); Longmans, Green & Company, Inc. (Keun, *A Foreigner Looks at the TVA*); Mr. Stewart L. Mims and the Yale University Press (Moreau, *Voyage*); the University of Minnesota Press (Raeder, *America in the Forties*); Sampson Low, Marston & Company, Ltd. (Toller, *Quer Durch*); and Prof. Dr. Jan Gerard Sleeswijk (Sleeswijk, *Van Menschen en Dingen*).

Arrangements were also made with the following publishers for the use of copyright material which they control: E. P. Dutton & Company, Inc. and John Murray, Publishers (Vay de Vaya, *Innere Leben*); and Librairie Plon (Klein, *Au Pays de la vie intense*, and Hauser, *L'Amérique vivante*).

The illustrations were drawn from the following sources: Section I. *Das Brittische Reich in America* . . . (Sorau: Gottlob Hebold, 1771), first map; [Johann Friedrich Schröter], *Algemeine Geschichte der Lander und Volker von America*, introduction by Siegmund Jacob Baumgarten (Halle: J. J. Gebauer, 1752), I, 316; Christian Schulz, Jr., *Travels on an Inland Voyage* (New York: I. Riley, 1810), vol. I; William Bingley, *Travels in North America* (London: Harvey and Darton, 1821), plate 2. Section II. Guillaume T. Poussin, *De la puissance Américaine* (Paris: W. Coquebert, 1845), vol. I, first map; Carl Köhler, *Briefe aus Amerika* (Darmstadt: G. G. Lange, 1856), p. 172; U. T. Gevers Deÿnoot, *Aanteekeningen of eene Reis door de Vereenigde Staten van Noord Amerika en Canada* ('S Gravenhage: M. Nijhoff, 1860), p. 176; *Transatlantic Sketches; or, Sixty Days in America* (London: Sampson Low, Son and Marston Co., 1865), plate 14. Section III. Albert Tissandier, *Six mois aux États-Unis* (Paris: G. Masson, [1886]), frontispiece map; Rev. Samuel Manning, *American Pictures* (London: The Religious Tract Society, [1876]), frontispiece; M. Cohen Stuart, *Zes Maanden in Amerika* (Haarlem: Kruseman and Tjeenk Willink, 1875), p. 254; G. A. Sala, *America Revisited* (London: Vizetelly and Co., 1883), p. 81. Section IV. Flour Mill (TVA photograph); Aimee Semple McPherson (International News photograph); Lynching (International News photograph); Erosion (TVA photograph).

I must also acknowledge here my gratitude to the friends who came to my assistance in the various stages of preparation of this volume. The project itself was suggested by Roger L. Scaife. It received the benefits of critical readings by Arthur Meier Schlesinger and by Samuel J. Hurwitz. From David I. Hecht, I received invaluable aid in the search of Slavic materials and in the translation from the Russian. H. W. Rosenberg and D. V. Glass were helpful in tracing some of the sources; and Miss Adelaide L. Fries kindly put at my disposal a copy of the original of the Reichel travel diary which she translated. Hilda F. Walter furnished very welcome help in readying the manuscript for the press. And to Mary Flug Handlin, of course, I owe a continuing debt for devoted collaboration.

O. H.

INDEX

Abolition, 199, 228, 229, 233
Abortions, 13
Abstinence, 168. *See also* Prohibition; Temperance
Academies, 65, 146, 221, 276, 281
Academy of Music, 344, 345
Acquia Creek, 123
Actors, 94, 127, 375, 376
Adams, John, 75
Adams, Samuel, 76
Adultery, 99, 255, 552
Advertising: agencies, 356; influence of, 566; land, 267, 269, 515, 516; medical, 214, 215; music and, 188; personal, 198, 253, 255; press and, 357; prevalence of, 242, 351, 352; religion and, 509
Aesthetics, 282. *See also* Taste
Agassiz, Louis, 246
Agricultural Associations, 231
Agricultural Industries Division, 538
Airplanes, 478, 507
Aix la Chapelle, 33
Alabama, 161, 162, 203, 336, 340, 341, 351
Alabama River, 162
Albany, 28, 33, 34, 155, 156, 204
Albany, 155
Alcott, A. B., 228, 229
Alexandria, 83, 84, 86
Algemeen Handelsblad, 333
Algeria, 94, 321
Almanach de Gotha, 390
"Altruists," 358
Amalgamation, 530, 535
Amateur Hours, 556
America: attitude of Europeans to, 1, 2, 4, 6, 7, 154, 169, 321–324, 498; English in, 35; Indians of, 9
American Association for the Advancement of Science, 72
"American Farmer," 36–59
American Federation of Labor: conservatism of, 448, 543, 544; immigration and, 523, 524; objectives of, 450; organization of, 362, 485, 565
American War Hospital, 423

Americanization, 296, 456, 458, 459, 520
Americans: character of, 38, 41–45, 93–96, 130, 131, 173, 175, 178, 258. *See also* National Character
"Amos and Andy," 566
Amsterdam, 333, 523
Anabaptists, *see* Baptists
Anarchists, 448, 503, 520
Anderson, Marian, 555
Anderson's Ferry, 59
Angels' Church, 506
Anglo-Persian Oil Company, 479
Annapolis, 109
Anti-Catholicism, 248
Anti-Semitism, 349, 520
Appomattox River, 65
Apprenticeship, 45, 50, 142, 258, 259, 429, 542
Aqueducts, 156
Arbitration, 363, 364, 541, 542
Archaeology, 232, 285
Architecture, 90, 140, 298, 319, 393, 394, 420
Argand Lamps, 136
Aristocracy: advantages of, 170, 171; European, 392; fear of, 209; institutions of, 177; opera and, 345; respect for, 300; social, 128, 129, 180, 181, 347, 365, 366, 391, 494; southern, 337
Arithmetic, 102, 280
Arizona, 300, 507
Arkansas, 341
Armenia, immigrants from, 483
Armour, P. D., 355, 366
Armour Meat Company, 484
Armory, 79, 156
Army, 65, 82, 533, 537
Arrows, 126
Art: backwardness of American, 73, 74, 145, 146, 245; development of, 420, 557–560; disdain for, 319; interest in, 390; newspapers and, 198
Artisans, 77, 153
Associations, 177, 178, 220, 230, 231, 265–269, 359. *See also* Clubs